Steps to Writing Well

With Additional Readings

First Canadian Edition

Jean Wyrick · *Professor Emerita, Colorado State University*

Sarika P. Bose · *University of British Columbia*

NELSON / EDUCATION

NELSON / EDUCATION

Steps to Writing Well with Additional Readings, First Canadian Edition
by Jean Wyrick and Sarika P. Bose

Associate Vice President, Editorial Director:
Evelyn Veitch

Editor-in-Chief, Higher Education:
Anne Williams

Executive Editor:
Laura Macleod

Marketing Manager:
Amanda Henry

Developmental Editor:
Joanne Sutherland

Photo Researcher:
Jessie Coffey

Permissions Coordinator:
Jessie Coffey

Content Production Manager:
Christine Gilbert

Production Service:
Macmillan Publishing Solutions

Copy Editor:
Elizabeth Phinney

Proofreader:
Barbara Storey

Indexer:
Bernice Eisen

Production Coordinator:
Ferial Suleman

Design Director:
Ken Phipps

Managing Designer:
Franca Amore

Interior Design:
PrePress PMG

Cover Design:
Liz Harasymczuk

Cover Image:
Adam Bortkowski/Shutterstock,
Mark Slusarczyk/Shutterstock.
Dpaint/Shutterstock,
Mathieu Viennet/Shutterstock,
Norma Cornes/Shutterstock,
Alexander Kalina/Shutterstock,
Ioana Drutu/Shutterstock,
Petro Feketa/Shutterstock

Compositor:
Macmillan Publishing Solutions

Printer:
Courier

Library and Archives Canada Cataloguing in Publication

Wyrick, Jean
    Steps to writing well : with additional readings / Jean Wyrick, Sarika P. Bose. — 1st Canadian ed.

Includes bibliographical references and index.
ISBN 978-0-17-644048-0

1. English language—Rhetoric—Problems, exercises, etc. 2. Report writing—Problems, exercises, etc. 3. College readers. I. Bose, Sarika P., 1965- II. Title.

PE1408.W94 2009   808.042
C2008-906854-8

ISBN-13: 978-0-17-644048-0
ISBN-10: 0-17-644048-8

Brief Contents

Contents

16 Writing about Literature   425

17 Writing in the World of Work   449

19 A Concise Guide to Punctuation 495

20 A Concise Guide to Mechanics 517

List of Fine Art

To the Instructor

The First Canadian Edition of *Steps to Writing Well with Additional Readings* has been written for teachers of composition who have had trouble finding a textbook that students can easily understand. Too many books on today's market, these instructors rightfully complain, are still unnecessarily complex, dry, or massive for the majority of students. Written simply, in an informal style and addressed to the student, this textbook offers a step-by-step guide to writing a variety of 500-to-1,200-word essays (the typical range of essay lengths assigned to undergraduate students). The combination of concise, practical advice, a number of student and professional samples, and a brief handbook should provide more than enough helpful information for students enrolled in a one-semester course, without intimidating them. Teachers of this new Canadian edition may appreciate the book's design and the addition of Canadian art, including a variety of paintings and photographs, many used as writing prompts for today's visually oriented students.

Although many parts of the book have been revised or expanded for this edition, its organization remains essentially the same. Part One offers advice on "The Basics of the Short Essay"; Part Two discusses "Purposes, Modes, and Strategies"; Part Three focuses on "Special Assignments"; and Part Four presents "A Concise Handbook." Part Five contains twenty-four additional readings. This textbook still begins with the essay "To the Student," which not only argues that students can learn to write better with practise and dedication but also gives them a number of practical reasons why they *should* learn to write better.

Part One, containing eight chapters, moves students through the process of writing the short essay. Chapter 1, on prewriting, stresses finding the proper attitude ("the desire to communicate") and presents helpful suggestions for selecting a subject. This chapter then offers students nine methods for finding a significant purpose and focus for their essays. In addition, a section on using the journal explains more than a dozen ways that students may improve their skills by writing a variety of non-threatening—and even playful—assignments. The section on audience should also help student writers identify their particular readers and communicate more effectively with them. As they consider their audience carefully, students will become increasingly familiar with the expectations for more academic and research-oriented, though still clear and vivid, essays at the college and university level. After finding a topic and identifying their audience, students are ready for Chapter 2, devoted almost entirely to a discussion of the thesis statement. This chapter first explains the necessity of being a critical thinker before moving to the role of the "working thesis" in early drafts. It then clearly outlines what a good thesis is and isn't by presenting a host of examples to illustrate the advice. Also included in this chapter is an explanation of the "essay map," an organizational tool that can help students structure their essays and plan their body paragraphs.

Chapter 3 discusses in detail the requirements of good body paragraphs: topic sentences, unity, order and coherence, adequate development, use of specific detail, and logical sequence. Over forty paragraphs illustrate both strengths and weaknesses of student writing. These paragraphs are not complex literary or professional excerpts but rather well-designed, precise examples of the principles under examination, written on the types of subjects students are often assigned and can understand and appreciate. This chapter twice provides the opportunity for students to see how a topic may progress from a working thesis statement to an informal essay outline, which in turn helps produce well-developed paragraphs in the body of an essay. To complete the overview of the short essay, Chapter 4 explains, through a number of samples, how to write good introductions, conclusions, and titles.

Chapter 5, "Drafting and Revising: Creative Thinking, Critical Thinking," focuses on the revision process. Because too many students still think of revision as merely proofreading their essays rather than as an essential, recursive activity, this chapter emphasizes the importance of revision in all good writing. These pages offer a system for revising drafts in stages, including a discussion of drafting and revising using word-processing programs. Students are encouraged to think critically as they analyze and evaluate their ideas and those of others. They are reminded of the important role of critical-thinking skills in the selection of evidence for all writing assignments. Chapter 5 also offers advice for participants in "peer workshops" (instructors may also find useful advice on organizing effective peer workshops in the Instructor's Manual for this edition). Also included in this chapter is a student essay, annotated to show how a writer (or a workshop partner) might use the questions suggested in the discussion of the revision process. This chapter ends with a list of suggestions for beating writer's block.

Chapter 6, on effective sentences, emphasizes the importance of clarity, conciseness, and vividness, with over 150 sample sentences illustrating the chapter's advice. Chapter 7, on word choice, presents practical suggestions for selecting accurate, appropriate words that are specific, memorable, sophisticated, and persuasive. This chapter also contains sections on avoiding sexist language and "bureaucratese." Chapter 8, "The Reading–Writing Connection," maintains that by learning to read analytically, students can improve their own writing skills. The chapter contains step-by-step directions for reading and annotating essays and suggests many ways students may profit from studying the rhetorical choices of other writers. A professional essay, annotated according to these steps, is included, as well as guidance for writing summaries of reading selections. A new section offers students suggestions for effective participation in class discussions, with advice for improving comprehension and note-taking skills. Instructors may wish to assign this chapter before asking students to read the professional essays that appear throughout this textbook.

Each chapter in Part One contains samples and exercises. As in the previous editions, the "Practising What You've Learned" exercises follow each major section in each chapter so that both instructors and students may quickly discover if particular material needs additional attention. Moreover, by conquering small steps in the writing process, one at a time, students should feel more confident and should learn more rapidly. Assignments, which also follow each major section in these chapters, suggest class activities and frequently emphasize "peer teaching," a useful method that asks students to prepare appropriate exercises for classmates and then to evaluate the results. Such assignments, operating under the premise that "you don't truly learn a subject until you teach it," provide engaging classroom activity for all the students and also remove from the instructor some of the burden of creating exercises.

Throughout the chapters in Part One, activities called "Applying What You've Learned to *Your* Writing" follow the exercises and assignments. Each of these activities encourages students to "follow through" by incorporating into a current draft the skill they have just read about and practised. By following a three-step procedure—reading the advice in the text, practising the advice through the exercises, and then applying the advice directly to their own prose—students should improve their writing processes. In addition, each of the chapters in Part One concludes with a summary, designed to help students review the important points in the material under study.

Part Two presents discussion of the kinds of essays students are most often asked to write. Chapter 9, on exposition, is divided into separate discussions of the expository strategies: example, process, comparison and contrast, definition, division and classification, and causal analysis. A new section explaining analogy expands the discussion of comparison and contrast. Discussions in Chapter 9 and the chapters on argument, description, and narration follow a similar format by offering the students (a) a clear definition of the mode (or strategy), explained with familiar examples; (b) practical advice on developing each essay; (c) warnings about common problems; (d) suggested essay topics; (e) a topic proposal sheet; (f) sample student essay(s) with marginal notes; (g) professional essay(s) followed by questions on content, structure and style, writing suggestions, and a vocabulary list; (h) a revision worksheet to guide student writers through their rough drafts; and (i) a progress report. In this edition, a new feature has been added to Part Two: in the lists of suggested essay topics, each final topic uses one or more of the artworks in this book as a writing prompt. Instructors now have the option of using paintings and photographs such as *Koskimo* and *Horse and Train* to encourage thoughtful essays organized in a variety of ways.

The sixteen student essays in this text should encourage student writers by showing them that others in their situation can indeed compose organized, well-developed essays. The student essays that appear here are not perfect; consequently, instructors may use them in class to generate suggestions for still more revision. The fifteen professional readings in Parts Two and Three were also selected to spur class discussion and to illustrate the rhetorical principles presented throughout the text. (The process analysis and comparison and contrast sections of Chapter 9 contain two professional essays so that students may see examples of two commonly used methods of organization; both division and classification are now illustrated by professional writing.) Those professional readings in Parts Two and Three most popular with the users of the U.S. sixth edition have been retained; thirteen selections are new to this first Canadian edition.

Chapter 10 discusses the argumentative essay, presenting a new pair of professional essays with opposing views and new advertisements, selected to help students analyze rhetorical appeals and supporting evidence. Chapters 11 and 12, on writing description and narration, may be assigned prior to the expository strategies or may be used as supplementary material for any kind of writing that incorporates descriptive language or extended example. Chapter 11 now includes two new professional essays, illustrating descriptions of persons, places, and experiences. Both chapters contain Canadian art designed to help students understand the importance of vivid details in support of a dominant effect.

Although this text shows students how to master individual rhetorical strategies, one essay at a time, experienced writers often choose a combination, or blending, of strategies to best accomplish their purpose. "Writing Essays Using Multiple Strategies," Chapter 13, concludes Part Two by offering advice to writers who are ready to address more complex topics and essay organization. This chapter also contains both student and professional essays to illustrate clear use of multiple strategies to accomplish the writer's purpose.

Part Three, called "Special Assignments," allows instructors to design their composition courses in a variety of ways, perhaps by adding a research paper, a literary analysis, an in-class essay, or a business writing assignment. Chapter 14, "Writing a Paper Using Research," shows students how to focus a topic, search for information in a variety of ways, choose and evaluate evidence, avoid plagiarism, and effectively incorporate and cite source material in their essays. This edition contains updated discussions of electronic sources and offers students a free, four-month subscription to *InfoTrac College Edition*, an easy-to-use online database of full-text articles from nearly 5,000 magazines, journals, newspapers, and other sources. To provide students with another avenue for collecting information, a new section on the art of interviewing has been added. This chapter also presents updated MLA and APA documentation styles and includes a student essay illustrating MLA citations.

Chapter 15, "Writing in Class: Exams and 'Response' Essays," is designed to help students respond quickly and accurately to a variety of in-class assignments by understanding their task's purpose and by recognizing key directional words. Advice for successfully organizing and completing timed writing should also help decrease students' anxiety. Because so many composition courses today include some variation of the "summary-and-response" assignment (used not only as an in- or out-of-class essay but also as a placement or exit test), this chapter also addresses this kind of writing and offers a sample student essay.

"Writing about Literature," Chapter 16, discusses multiple ways literary selections may be used in the composition class, either as prompts for personal essays or for papers of literary analysis. Students are offered a series of suggestions for close reading of both poetry and short fiction. The chapter contains an annotated poem, a new annotated short story, and two student essays analyzing those works. New selections of a poem and a story, without marginal notes, are included for classroom discussion or assignment.

Chapter 17, "Writing in the World of Work," allows students to practise composing business letters, office memos, electronic mail, and résumés. With the increasing use of technology in the workplace, students may also profit from a section discussing "netiquette" that encourages writers to cultivate a sense of civility and professionalism, as well as clarity, in their electronic communications. A sample cover letter, a second sample résumé, and a brief section on writing the post-interview letter have been added to this chapter.

Part Four presents a concise handbook with accessible explanations and examples showing how to correct the most common errors in grammar, punctuation, and mechanics. To satisfy requests from instructors, the number of grammar and punctuation exercises has been greatly expanded, and brief definitions of the basic parts of speech have been added.

Part Five gives instructors the opportunity to choose among twenty-four additional professional readings. These selections—some serious, some humourous, some familiar, with eighteen Canadian readings new to this edition—offer a variety of ideas, structures, and styles to consider. A new section, "Writing and Language," presents essays by two well-known authors writing about their craft. Studying the professional selections presented in Part Five should help novice writers as they make their own rhetorical choices.

Once again, readers of this edition may note an occasional attempt at humour. The lighthearted tone of some samples and exercises is the result of the authors' firm belief that while learning to write is serious business, solemn composition classrooms are not always the most beneficial environments for anxious beginning writers.

Finally an Instructor's Manual, updated for this edition by the author of the new Canadian edition, is available, containing suggestions for teaching and answers to exercises. Instructors interested in additional information regarding the *InfoTrac College Edition* subscription offer should contact their Nelson Education sales representative or visit www.nelson.com.

Although a new Canadian edition of this textbook has allowed for a number of changes and additions, the book's purpose remains as stated in the original preface: "While there are many methods of teaching composition, *Steps to Writing Well* tries to help inexperienced writers by offering a clearly defined sequential approach to writing the short essay. By presenting simple, practical advice directly to the students, this text is intended to make the demanding jobs of teaching and learning the basic principles of composition easier and more enjoyable for everyone."

Acknowledgments

As the author of the First Canadian Edition of this book, I'd like to express my deep appreciation to Jean Wyrick, the author of the original *Steps to Writing Well*, whose sensible, practical material as well as her lively, humourous spirit have made it a pleasure to adapt and revise this text for Canadian audiences.

I'm grateful to everyone at Nelson Education Ltd. who helped with this new edition. I thank Executive Editor Laura Macleod for her kind and generous support. My deepest gratitude goes to Developmental Editor Joanne Sutherland, without whose advice, sensible and practical suggestions, flexibility, tireless efforts, and constant encouragement, there would be no Canadian edition of *Steps*. Thank you, Joanne, for your expertise, your hard work, your patience, and your good humour throughout this revision.

Special thanks to Christine Gilbert, Content Production Manager, who helped guide this edition to print in so many ways; and to Jessie Coffey, who did such a conscientious and often challenging job of obtaining permissions for the professional writing and the new art and photography in this edition. Another big thank-you goes to Elizabeth Phinney and Barbara Storey for their professional editing and proofreading skills.

Ongoing gratitude is due the students at Colorado State University who allowed their writing to be reprinted and also to Sharon Straus, whose essay "Treeclimbing" was a prize winner at the College of Charleston.

In addition, I would like to acknowledge my colleagues who made many helpful suggestions for this edition. Special thanks go to Roberta Birks, Catherine Nelson-MacDermott, and Judy Brown at the University of British Columbia and to Moira Langley at Kwantlen Polytechnic University.

Many thanks to an outstanding set of reviewers whose diligent and thoughtful comments helped shape this first Canadian edition.

Patricia Campbell, *Red Deer College*
Cyril Dabydeen, *University of Ottawa*
Anna Ford, *Grant MacEwan College*

Georgia Irwin, *Nipissing University*
Marie Loughlin, *University of British Columbia*
Norma-Jean Nielsen, *Canadore College*
Marcel O'Gorman, *University of Waterloo*
Terri Palmer, *York University*
David Salusbury, *Algonquin College*
Erin Whitmore, *University of New Brunswick*
Helen Winton, *Yukon College*

Finally, thanks to my parents, Tirthankar and Mandakranta, and my brother, Pablo, for their help, critical insights, patience, and flexibility during the many phases of this adaptation process.

Finding the Right Attitude

If you agree with one or more of the following statements, we have some serious myth-killing to do before you begin this book:

1. I'm no good in English—never have been, never will be.
2. Only people with natural talent for writing can succeed in composition class.
3. My composition instructor is a picky, comma-hunting old fogey/radical, who only focuses on unimportant little aspects of my writing and doesn't understand my great ideas.
4. My instructor will insist I write just like him or her.
5. I write for myself, not for anyone else, so I don't need this class or this book.
6. Composition classes are designed to put my creativity in a straitjacket.
7. I don't need a composition class because I'm studying science or engineering or commerce or medicine . . .
8. I'm never going to need composition in the "real world."

The notion that good writers are born, not made, is a widespread myth that may make you feel defeated before you start. But the simple truth is that good writers *are* made—simply because *effective writing is a skill that can be learned*. Despite any feelings of insecurity you may have about composition, you should realize that you already know many of the basic rules of good writing; after all, you've been writing since you were six years old. What you need now is some practical advice on composition, some coaching to sharpen your skills, and a strong dose of determination to practise those skills until you can consistently produce the results you want. Talent, as the French writer Flaubert once said, is nothing more than long patience.

Think about learning to write well as you might consider your tennis game. No one is born a tennis star. You first learn the basic rules and movements and then go out on the court to practise. And practise. No one's tennis will improve if he or she stays off the court; similarly, you must write regularly and receive feedback to improve your composition skills. Try to see your instructor not as Dr. Evil determined to reproduce his or her style of writing in you, but rather as your coach, your loyal trainer who wants you to do the very best you can. Like any good coach, your instructor will point out your strengths and weaknesses; she or he will often send you to this text for practical suggestions for improvement. And while there are no quick, magic solutions for learning to write well, the most important point to remember is this: with this text, your own common sense, and determination, *you can improve your writing.*

Why Write?

"Okay," you say, "so I can improve if I try—but why should I bother? Why should I write well? I'm not going to be a professional writer. I'm never going to need to write in the 'real world.' Besides, I'm studying sciences, not humanities."

In the first place, writing helps us explore our own thoughts and feelings. Writing forces us to articulate our ideas, to discover what we really think about an issue. For example, let's suppose you're faced with a difficult decision and that the arguments pro and con are jumbled in your head. You begin to write down all the pertinent facts and feelings, and suddenly, you begin to see that you do, indeed, have stronger arguments for one side of the question than the other. Once you "see" what you are thinking, you may then scrutinize your opinions for any logical flaws or weaknesses and revise your argument accordingly. In other words, writing lays out our ideas for examination, analysis, and thoughtful reaction. Thus when we write, we (and the world at large) see who we are, and what we stand for, much more clearly. Moreover, writing can provide a record of our thoughts that we may study and evaluate in a way that conversation cannot. In short, writing well enables us to see and know ourselves—our feelings, ideas, opinions, and intellectual positions—better.

On a more practical level, we need to write effectively to communicate with others. While some of our writing may be done solely for ourselves, the majority of it is created for others to share. In this world, it is almost impossible to claim that we write only for ourselves. We are constantly asked to put our feelings, ideas, and knowledge in writing for others to read. During your college or university years, no matter what your major, you will be repeatedly required to write essays, tests, reports, and exercises (and possibly e-mail messages or letters home). Later, you may need to write formal letters of application for jobs or graduate training. And on a job you may have to write numerous kinds of reports, proposals, analyses, and requisitions. To be successful in any field, you must make your correspondence with business associates and coworkers clearly understood; remember that enormous amounts of time, energy, and profit have been lost because of a single unclear office memo.

There's still a third—more cynical—reason for studying writing techniques. Once you begin to improve your ability to use language, you will become more aware of the ways others write and speak. Through today's mass media and electronic highways, we are continually bombarded with words from politicians, advertisers, scientists, preachers, teachers, and self-appointed "authorities." We need to understand and evaluate what we are hearing, not only for our benefit, but also for self-protection. Language is frequently manipulated to manipulate us. For example, the American CIA has long referred to the "neutralization" of enemies, and on occasion, Pentagon officials have carefully avoided discussion of times when misdirected "physics packages" (bombs) fell on "soft targets" (civilians). (One year not so long ago, the American National Council of Teachers of English gave their Doublespeak Award to the U.S. officers who, after accidentally shooting down a plane of civilians, reported that the plane didn't crash—rather, it had "uncontrolled contact with the ground.") Some politicians have seen no recessions, just "meaningful downturns in aggregate output," so they have treated themselves to a "pay equalization concept," rather than a raise. Advertisers frequently try to disguise their pitches through "infomercials" and "advertorials"; the television networks treat us to "encore presentations" that are the same old summer reruns. And "fenestration engineers" are still window cleaners; "environmental superintendents" are still janitors; "drain surgeons" are still plumbers.

By becoming better writers ourselves, we can learn to recognize and reject the irresponsible, cloudy, or dishonest language of others before we become victims of their exploitation.

A Good Place to Start

If improving writing skills is not only possible but important, it is also something else: hard work. H. L. Mencken, critic and writer, once remarked that "for every difficult and complex problem, there is an obvious solution that is simple, easy and wrong." No composition textbook can promise easy formulas guaranteed to improve your writing overnight. Nor is writing always fun for everyone. But this text can make the learning process easier, less painful, and more enjoyable than you might anticipate. Written in plain, straightforward language addressed to you, the student, this book will suggest a variety of practical ways for you to organize and write clear, concise prose. Because each of your writing tasks will be different, this textbook cannot provide a single, simple blueprint that will apply in all instances. Later chapters, however, will discuss some of the most common methods of organizing essays, such as development by example, definition, classification, causal analysis, comparison and contrast, and argument. As you become more familiar with, and begin to master, these patterns of writing, you will find yourself increasingly able to assess, organize, and explain the thoughts you have about the people, events, and situations in your own life. And while it may be true that in learning to write well there is no free ride, this book, along with your own willingness to work and improve, can start you down the road with a good sense of direction.

Steps to Writing Well with Additional Readings, First Canadian Edition, offers a well-developed system of pedagogical features to help you learn and apply the skills you need to be a better writer. Take a few minutes to familiarize yourself with these features. Doing so will help you get more out of this book.

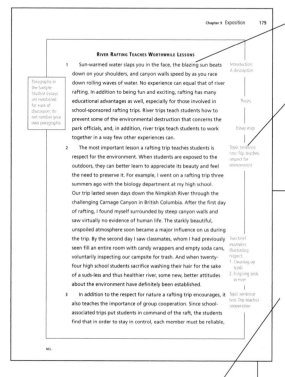

Sample **Student Essays** encourage you by showing organized, well-developed examples written by real students. The student essays employ margin notes to provide commentary on the writing samples and demonstrate common writing errors. These examples generate classroom discussion with suggestions for still more revision.

Professional Readings in the text were also selected to spur class discussion and to illustrate the rhetorical principles presented throughout the text.

Each professional reading is accompanied by Questions on Content, Structure, and Style Suggestions for Writing, and Vocabulary to help you read the essays analytically and apply what you've learned.

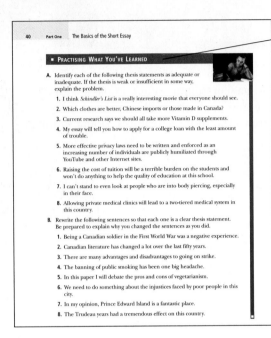

Practising What You've Learned exercises follow each major section in each chapter so that you may quickly discover if particular material needs additional attention.

Moreover, by conquering small steps in the writing process, one at a time, you will feel more confident and will learn more rapidly.

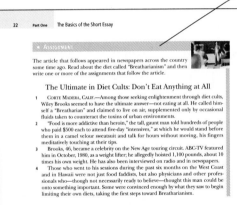

Assignments, which also follow each major section, suggest class activities and frequently emphasize "peer teaching," a useful method that asks you to prepare appropriate exercises for classmates and then to evaluate the results. Such assignments, operating under the premise that "you don't truly learn a subject until you teach it," provide engaging classroom activity.

Throughout the chapters in Part One, activities called **Applying What You've Learned to *Your* Writing** follow the exercises and assignments. Each of these activities encourages you to "follow through" by incorporating into a current draft the skill you have just read about and practised.

By following this three-step procedure—reading the advice in the text, practising the advice through the exercises, and then applying the advice directly to your own prose—you will improve your writing processes.

After learning a specific mode (or strategy), analyzing a variety of writing samples, and then practising what you've learned, you are given a list of suggested **Essay Topics** to help you get started on your own essay.

Each final topic uses one or more of the artworks in this book as a writing prompt, so that you also have some visual inspiration.

★ **ESSAY TOPICS**

Use the following broad statements to help you discover, narrow down, and focus an essay topic of your own design. What are the most effective examples you can use to develop this essay? Use the above suggestions to guide you in your choices. For additional ideas, turn to the "Suggestions for Writing" section following the professional essay (pages 184–185).

1. Heroes today are merely media creations rather than truly admirable people.
2. Francophone Canadian literature does/does not use the same themes as anglophone Canadian literature.
3. High schools do/do not adequately prepare students for college or university
4. Immigration policies should/should not give priority to refugees from countries undergoing current conflicts.
5. The willingness to undertake adventure is a necessary part of a happy existence.
6. This is the most influential Canadian of the past one hundred years.
7. Double standards still exist in society's treatment of those unable to take care of themselves.
8. Consumers are often at the mercy of unscrupulous companies.
9. Modern technology can produce more inconvenience than convenience.
10. Visits to the doctor/dentist/veterinarian can prove more traumatic than the illness.

NEL

★ **A REVISION WORKSHEET**

As you write your rough drafts, consult Chapter 5 for guidance through the revision process. In addition, here are a few questions to ask yourself as you revise your example essay:

1. Is the essay's thesis clear to the reader?
2. Do the topic sentences support the thesis?
3. Does each body paragraph contain examples that effectively illustrate the claim of the topic sentence rather than offering mere generalities?
4. Are there enough well-chosen examples to make each point clear and convincing?
5. Is each example developed in enough specific detail? Where could more details be added? Could you use more precise language?
6. If a paragraph contains multiple examples, are they arranged in the most effective order, with a smooth transition from one to another?
7. If a paragraph contains an extended example, does the discussion flow logically and with coherence?

After you've revised your essay extensively, you might exchange rough drafts with a classmate and answer these questions for each other, making specific suggestions for improvement wherever appropriate. (For advice on productive participation in classroom workshops, see pages 102–104 in Chapter 5.)

You are then provided with **A Revision Worksheet** to guide you through your rough drafts.

A list of questions and suggestions helps you to evaluate and make further revisions to your writing.

Chapter 1 Prewriting   17

☑ If at any point in this stage of the writing process you are experiencing writer's block, you might turn to the suggestions for overcoming this common affliction that appear on pages 108–110 in Chapter 5. You might also find it helpful to read the section on keeping a journal, pages 27–29, because writing in a relaxed mood on a regular basis may be the best long-term cure for your writing anxiety.

■ **After You've Found Your Focus**

Once you think you've found the focus of your essay, you may be ready to compose a *working thesis statement*, an important part of your essay discussed in great detail in the next chapter. If you've used one of the prewriting exercises outlined in this chapter, by all means, hang onto it. The details and observations you generated as you focused your topic may be useful to you as you begin to organize and develop your body paragraphs.

Throughout the book, you are offered helpful **tips** for improving your writing skills.

★ **CHAPTER 6 SUMMARY**

Here is a brief summary of what you should remember about writing effective sentences:

1. All good writers revise and polish their sentences.
2. You can help clarify your ideas for your readers by writing sentences that are informative, straightforward, and precise.
3. You can communicate your ideas more easily to your readers if you cut out deadwood, redundancies, passive verbs, and pretentious language.
4. You can maintain your readers' interest in your ideas if you cultivate an engaging style offering a variety of pleasing sentence constructions.

* Answers to sentence-combining exercise (pp. 133–134)
1. Huckleberry Finn
2. Anne of Green Gables
3. Frankenstein

NEL

Each of the chapters in Part One concludes with a **Summary,** designed to help students review the important points in the material under study.

Part 1

The Basics of the Short Essay

The first section of this text is designed to move you through the writing process as you compose a short essay, the kind you are most likely to encounter in composition class and in other college courses. Chapters 1 and 2, on prewriting and the thesis statement, will help you find a topic, purpose, and focus for your essay. Chapter 3, on paragraphs, will show you how to plan, organize, and develop your ideas; Chapter 4 will help you complete your essay. Chapter 5 offers suggestions for revising your writing, and Chapters 6 and 7 present additional advice on selecting your words and composing your sentences. Chapter 8 explains the important reading–writing connection and shows how learning to read analytically can sharpen your writing skills. ■

Chapter 1

Prewriting

■ Getting Started (or Soup-Can Labels Can Be Fascinating)

For many writers, getting started is the hardest part. You may have noticed that when it is time to begin a writing assignment, you suddenly develop an enormous desire to straighten your books, water your plants, or sharpen your pencils for the fifth time. If this situation sounds familiar, you may find it reassuring to know that many professionals undergo these same strange compulsions before they begin writing. Jean Kerr, author of *Please Don't Eat the Daisies,* admitted that she often found herself in the kitchen reading soup-can labels—or anything—in order to prolong the moments before taking pen in hand. John C. Calhoun, vice president of the United States under American President Andrew Jackson, insisted he had to plow his fields before he could write, and Joseph Conrad, author of *Lord Jim* and other novels, is said to have cried on occasion from the sheer dread of sitting down to compose his stories.

To spare you as much hand-wringing as possible, this chapter presents some practical suggestions on how to begin writing your short essay. Although all writers must find the methods that work best for them, you may find some of the following ideas helpful.

But no matter how you actually begin putting words on paper, it is absolutely essential to maintain two basic ideas concerning your writing task. Before you write a single sentence, you should always remind yourself that

1. You have some valuable ideas to tell your reader, and

2. More than anything, you want to communicate those ideas to your reader.

These reminders may seem obvious to you, but without a solid commitment to your own argument and subject as well as to your reader, your prose will be lifeless and boring. If *you* don't care about your subject, you can't very well expect anyone else to. Be confident that you will discover something important to say about your subject, and that you can make your ideas into something interesting and worthwhile. Be confident that your reader genuinely wants, or needs, to know what you think.

© Roger Allyn Lee/SuperStock

■ Thinking about Your Audience

Equally important, you must also have a strong desire to tell others what you are thinking. One of the most common mistakes inexperienced writers make is failing to move past early stages in the writing process in which they are writing for—or writing to—themselves only. In the first stages of composing an essay, writers frequently "talk" on paper to themselves, exploring thoughts, discovering new insights, making connections, selecting examples, and so on. The ultimate goal of a finished essay, however, is to communicate your opinions to *others* clearly and persuasively. Whether you wish to inform your readers, change their minds, or stir them to action, you cannot accomplish your purpose by writing so that only you understand what you mean. The burden of communicating your thoughts falls on *you,* not the reader, who is under no obligation to struggle through confused, unclear prose, paragraphs that begin and end for no apparent reason, or sentences that come one after another with no more logic than lemmings following one another to the sea.

Therefore, as you move through the drafting and revising stages of your writing process, commit yourself to becoming increasingly aware of your reader's reactions to your prose. Ask yourself as you revise your drafts, "Am I moving beyond writing just to myself? Am I making myself clear to others who may not know what I mean?" Much of your success as a writer depends on an unflagging determination to communicate clearly with your readers.

■ Selecting a Subject

Once you have decided that communicating clearly with others is your ultimate goal, you are ready to select the subject of your essay. Here are some suggestions on how to begin:

Start early. Since at least the time of Aristotle, writing teachers have been pushing this advice, and for good reason. It's not because teachers are egoists competing for the dubious honour of having the most time-consuming course; it is because few writers, even experienced ones, can do a good job when rushed. You need time to mull over ideas, organize your thoughts, revise and polish your prose. Rule of thumb: always give yourself twice as much time as you think you'll need to avoid the 2:00-a.m. "Why did I come to university (or college)?" panic.

Find your best space. Develop some successful writing habits by thinking about your very own writing process. When and where do you usually do your best composing? Some people write best early in the morning; others think better later in the day. What time of day seems to produce your best efforts? Where are you working? At a desk? In your room, or in a library?

Do you start drafting ideas on a computer or do you begin with paper? With a certain pen or sharpened pencil? Most writers avoid noise and interruptions (television, telephone, friends, etc.), although some swear by having music playing in the background. If you can identify a previously successful writing experience, try duplicating its location, time, and tools to help you calmly address your new writing task.

Or consider trying new combinations of time and place if your previous choices weren't as productive as you would have liked. Recognition and repeated use of your most comfortable writing "spot" may shorten your hesitation to begin composing; your subconscious may recognize the pattern ("Hey, it's time to write!") and help you start in a positive frame of mind. (Remember that it's not just writers who repeat such rituals—think of the athletes you've heard about who won't begin a game without wearing their lucky socks. If it works for them, it can work for you!)

Select something in which you currently have a strong interest. If the essay subject is left to you, start by thinking of something fun, fascinating, or frightening you've done or seen lately, perhaps something you've already told a friend about. If you are writing a narrative or descriptive essay, the subject might be the pleasure of a new hobby, the challenge of a recent book or movie, or even the hassle of registration for courses—anything in which you are personally involved. If you aren't enthusiastic enough about your subject to want to spread the word, pick something else. Bored writers write boring essays.

Don't feel you have nothing from which to choose your subject. Your days are full of activities, people, joys, and irritations. Essays do not always have to be written on lofty intellectual or poetic subjects—in fact, some of the world's best essays have been written on such subjects as china teacups, roast pig, and chimney sweeps. Think: what have you been talking or thinking about lately? What have you been doing that you're excited about? Or what about your past? Reflect a few moments on some of your most vivid memories—special people, vacations, holidays, childhood hideaways, your first job or first date—all are possibilities.

Still searching? Make a list of all the subjects on which you are an expert. None, you say? Think again. Most of us have an array of talents we hardly acknowledge. Perhaps you play the guitar or make a mean pot of chili or know how to repair a sports car. You've trained a dog or become a first-class house sitter or gardener. You know more about computers or old hockey cards than any of your friends. You play soccer or volleyball or Ping-Pong. In other words, take a fresh, close look at your life. You know things that others don't . . . now is your chance to enlighten them!

If a search of your immediate or past personal experience doesn't turn up anything inspiring, you might try looking in the campus newspaper for stories that arouse your strong feelings; don't skip the "Letters to the Editor" column. What are the current topics of controversy on your campus? How do you feel about tuition fee rises? A particular graduation requirement? Speakers or special interest groups on campus? Financial aid applications? Registration procedures? Parking restrictions? These types of subjects will lead you toward potentially more academic approaches to your essays. As you move toward writing university- or college-level essays, consider the material you are studying in your other classes: reading

The Handmaid's Tale in a literature class may spark an investigative essay on roles of women in society today, or studying previous immigration laws in your history class may lead you to an argument for or against current immigration practices. Similarly, your local newspaper or national magazines might suggest essay topics to you on local, national, or international affairs that affect your life. Browsing the Internet can provide you with literally thousands of diverse opinions and controversies that invite your response. One caveat about the Internet, however: do not take information and opinions found on the Internet at face value, but consider them critically. We will be discussing critical reading and thinking later.

In other words, when you're stuck for an essay topic, take a closer look at your environment: your own life—past, present, and future; your hometown; your university or college town; your province; your country; and your world. You'll probably discover more than enough subjects to satisfy the assignments in your writing class.

Narrow a large subject. Once you've selected a general subject to write on, you may find that it is too broad for effective treatment in a short essay; therefore, you may need to narrow it somewhat. Suppose, for instance, you have been thinking about the issue of responsibility in society and have decided to make this the subject of your essay. The subject of "responsibility," however, is far too large and unwieldy for a short essay, perhaps even for a short book. Consequently, you must make your subject less general. "Economic responsibility" is more specific, but, again, there's too much to say. "Governmental economic responsibility" is better, but you still need to pare this large, complex subject further so that you may treat it in depth in your short essay. After all, there are many levels of government in a country, and many categories of economic responsibility. After several more tries, you might arrive at more specific, manageable topics, such as "municipal responsibility for special-event police fee assessments" or "the responsibility of the federal government for arts funding in Ontario."

Then again, let's assume you are interested in sports. A 500-to-800-word essay on "sports" would obviously be superficial because the subject covers so much ground. Instead, you might divide the subject into categories such as "controversial training methods in gymnastics," "the dangers of over-training," "new sports equipment technology and its effect on different sports," "the place of international politics in the Olympics," and so forth. Perhaps several of your categories would make good short essays, but after looking at your list, you might decide that your real interest at this time is training methods and that it will be the topic of your essay.

■ Finding Your Essay's Purpose and Focus

Even after you've narrowed your large subject to a more manageable topic, you still must find a specific *purpose* for your essay. Why are you writing about this topic? Do your readers need to be informed, persuaded, entertained? What do you want your writing to accomplish?

In addition to knowing your purpose, you must also find a clear *focus* or direction for your essay. You cannot, for example, inform your readers about every aspect of training methods. Instead, you must decide on a particular sport, as well as on a particular part of the sport, and then determine the main point you want to make. If it helps, think of a camera: you see a sweeping landscape you'd like to photograph but you know you can't get it all into one picture, so you pick out a particularly interesting part of the scene. Focus in an essay works in the same way; you zoom in, so to speak, on a particular part of your topic and make that the focus of your paper.

Sometimes part of your problem may be solved by your assignment; your instructor may choose the focus of your essay for you by asking for certain specific information or by prescribing the method of development you should use (compare training methods in gymnastics to those in figure skating, explain the process of proper gymnastic training, analyze the effects of daily practice, and so forth). But if the purpose and focus of your essay are decisions you must make, you should always allow your interest and knowledge to guide you. Often a direction or focus for your essay will surface as you narrow your subject, but don't become frustrated if you have to discard several ideas before you hit the one that's right. For instance, you might first consider writing on how to select running shoes and then realize that you know too little about the shoe market, or you might find that there's just too little of importance to say about parallel bar technology to make an interesting 500-word essay.

Let's suppose for a moment that you have thought of a subject that interests you—but now you're stuck. Deciding on something to write about this subject suddenly looks as easy as nailing spaghetti to your kitchen wall. What should you say? What would be the purpose of your essay? What would be interesting for you to write about and for readers to hear about?

At this point, you may profit from trying more than one prewriting exercise, designed to help you generate some ideas about your topic. The exercises described next are discovery techniques that will get your creative juices flowing again. Because all writers compose differently, not all of these exercises will work for you—in fact, some of them may lead you nowhere. Nevertheless, try all of them at least once or twice; you may be surprised to discover that some discovery techniques work better with some subjects than with others.

■ Discovery Techniques

1. Listing

Try jotting down all the ideas that pop into your head about your topic. Free-associate; don't hold back anything. Try to brainstorm for at least ten minutes.

A quick list on gymnastic training techniques might look like this:

fun	training for competitions
healthy	both sexes
relieves tension	any age group
gym membership	training with friend
shoes	too much competition
shin splints	good for flexibility
rain or shine	improves circulation
good for heart	firming
muscle cramps	over-training vs. balanced training
no weight loss	hard surfaces
warm-ups before practice	pressure
getting discouraged	going too fast
hitting the wall	sense of accomplishment
teamwork	

As you read over the list, look for connections between ideas or one large idea that encompasses several small ones. In this list, you might first notice that many of the ideas focus on improving health (heart, flexibility, circulation), but you discard that subject because a "gymnastics training improves health" essay is too obvious; it's a topic that's been done too many times to say anything new. A closer look at your list, however, turns up a number of ideas that concern how *not* to train or reasons why someone might become discouraged and quit a gymnastics program. You begin to think of friends who might have stuck with gymnastics as you have if only they'd chosen the right gyms for their training or paced themselves more realistically, for example. You decide, therefore, to write an essay telling first-time amateur gymnasts how to maintain a successful program and how to avoid a number of problems, from shoes to gym equipment, that might otherwise defeat their efforts before they've given the sport a chance.

2. Freewriting

Some people simply need to start writing to find a focus. Take out several sheets of blank paper or start a new computer file. Give yourself at least ten to fifteen minutes, and begin writing whatever comes to mind on your subject. Don't worry about spelling, punctuation, or even complete sentences. Don't change, correct, or delete anything. If you run out of things to say, write "I can't think of anything to say" until you can find a new thought. At the end of this period you may discover that by continuously writing you will have written yourself into an interesting topic.

Here are examples of freewriting from students who were given ten minutes to write on the general topic of "nature."

Student 1:

I'm really not the outdoorsy type. I'd rather be inside somewhere than out in Nature tromping through the bushes. I don't like bugs and snakes and stuff like that. Lots of my friends like to go hiking around or camping but I don't. Secretly, I think maybe one of the big reasons I really don't like being out in Nature is that I'm deathly afraid of bees. When I was a kid I was out in the woods and ran into a swarm of bees and got stung about a million times, well, it felt like a million times. I had to go to the hospital for a few days. Now every time I'm outside somewhere and something, anything, flies by me I'm terrified. Totally paranoid. Everyone kids me because I immediately cover my head. I keep hearing about killer bees heading this way, my worst nightmare come true. . . .

Student 2:

We're not going to have any Nature left if people don't do something about the environment. Despite all the media attention to recycling, we're still trashing the planet left and right. People talk big about "saving the environment" but then do such stupid things all the time. Like smokers who flip their cigarette butts out their car windows. Do they think those filters are just going to disappear overnight? The parking lot by this building is full of butts this morning where someone dumped their car ashtray. This campus is full of pop cans, I can see at least three empties under desks in this classroom right now. . . .

These two students reacted quite differently to the same general subject. The first student responded personally, thinking about her own relationship to "nature" (defined as being out in the woods), whereas the second student obviously associated nature with environmental concerns. More freewriting might lead student 1 to a humorous essay on her bee phobia or even to an inquiry about those dreaded killer bees; student 2 might write an interesting paper suggesting ways university or college students could clean up their campus or easily recycle their aluminium cans.

Often freewriting will not be as coherent as these two samples; sometimes freewriting goes nowhere or in circles. But it's a technique worth trying. By allowing our minds to roam freely over a subject, without worrying about "correctness" or organization, we may remember or discover topics we want to write about or investigate, topics we feel strongly about and wish to introduce to others.

3. Looping*

Looping is a variation on freewriting that works amazingly well for many people, including those who are frustrated rather than helped by freewriting.

Let's assume you've been assigned that old standby "My Summer Vacation." Obviously you must find a focus. Again, take out several sheets of blank paper and begin to freewrite, as described previously. Write for at least ten minutes. At the end of this period read over what you've written and try to identify a central idea that has emerged. Perhaps this is the idea you like best, or that makes you think of related ideas. In other words, look for the thought that stands out, that seems to indicate the direction of your thinking. Put this thought or idea into one sentence called the "centre-of-gravity sentence." You have now completed loop 1.

To begin loop 2, use your centre-of-gravity sentence as a jumping-off point for another ten minutes of freewriting. Stop, read what you've written, and complete loop 2 by composing another centre-of-gravity sentence. Use this second sentence to start loop 3. You should write at least three loops and three centre-of-gravity sentences. At the end of three loops, you may find that you have focused on a specific topic that might lead to a good essay. If you're not satisfied with your topic at this point, by all means try two or three more loops until your subject is sufficiently narrowed and focused.

Here's an example of one student's looping exercise:

Summer Vacation

Loop 1	Summer vacations are very important aspects of living. They symbolize getting away from daily routines, discovering places and people that are different. When I think of vacations I think mostly of travelling somewhere too far to go, say, for a weekend. It is a chance to get away and relax and not think about most responsibilities. Vacations can also be a time of gathering with family and friends.
Centre-of-gravity sentence	Vacations symbolize getting away from daily routines, and making discoveries.

---

* This technique is suggested by Peter Elbow in *Writing Without Teachers* (New York: Oxford University Press, 1975).

Loop 2

Vacations help you make new discoveries. Last summer my family and I drove to the Horseshoe Falls in Niagara. I didn't want to go at first. I thought looking at a big waterfall would be dumb and boring. I was really obnoxious all the way up there and made lots of smart remarks about falling in. But Niagara Falls turned out to be wonderful. It's not just looking at the actual Falls—there's lots more to see and learn about, like these scenic tunnels that take you behind the Falls. I got interested in how people in Victorian times could only get close to the Falls by climbing dangerous rocks and cliffs and how stairs and then an elevator were built so people could get closer more safely.

Centre-of-gravity sentence

Once I got interested in Niagara's amazing tunnels, my vacation turned out great.

Loop 3

Once I got interested in the tunnels, I had a good time, mainly because I felt I was seeing something really unusual. I knew I'd never see anything like this again unless I went to Australia or New Zealand (highly unlikely!). I felt like I was learning a lot too. I liked the idea of learning a lot about the inside of the earth without having to go to class and study books. I really hated to leave—Mom and Dad kidded me on the way back about how much I'd griped about going on the trip in the first place. I felt pretty dumb. But I was really glad I'd given the Falls a closer look instead of holding on to my view of it as a boring old waterfall. I would have had a terrible time, but now I hope to go back someday. I think the experience made me more open-minded about trying new places.

Centre-of-gravity sentence

My vacation this summer was special because I was willing to put aside my expectations of boredom and learn some new ideas about the strange environment at Niagara Falls.

At the end of three loops, this student has moved from the general subject of "summer vacation" to the more focused idea that her willingness to learn about a new place played an important part in the enjoyment of her vacation. Although her last centre-of-gravity sentence still contains some vague words ("special," "new ideas," "strange environment"), the thought stated here may eventually lead to an essay that will not only say something about this student's vacation but may also persuade the readers to reconsider their attitude toward taking trips to new places.

4. Clustering

Another excellent technique is clustering (sometimes called "mapping"). Place your general subject in a circle in the middle of a blank sheet of paper and begin to draw other lines and circles that radiate from the original subject. Cluster those ideas that seem to fall together. At the end of ten minutes see if a topic emerges from any of your groups of ideas.

Ten minutes of clustering on the subject of "A Memorable Holiday" might look like the drawing on page 12.

This student may wish to brainstorm further on the Christmas he spent in the hospital with a case of appendicitis or perhaps on the Halloween he first experienced a house of horrors. By using clustering, he has recollected some important details about a number of holidays that may help him focus on an occasion he wants to describe in his paper.

5. The Boomerang

Still another variation on freewriting is the technique called the boomerang, named appropriately because, like the Australian stick, it invites your mind to travel over a subject from opposite directions to produce new ideas. It sends your mind flying away from your topic, but as it whirls back, it takes a different look at the topic.

Suppose, for example, members of your class have been asked to write about their major field of study, which in your case is General Arts. Begin by writing a statement that comes into your mind about majoring in General Arts, and then freewrite on that statement for five minutes. Then write a second statement that approaches the subject from an opposing point of view, and freewrite again for five minutes. Continue this pattern several times. Boomeranging, like looping, can help writers see their subject in a new way and consequently help them find an idea to write about.

Here's an abbreviated sample of boomeranging:

1. Majoring in General Arts is impractical in today's economy.

   [Freewrite for five minutes.]

2. Majoring in General Arts is practical in today's economy.

   [Freewrite for five minutes.]

3. General Arts funding should be increased on the federal level.

   [Freewrite for five minutes.]

4. General Arts funding should not be increased on the federal level.

   [Freewrite for five minutes.]

By continuing to "throw the boomerang" across your subject, you may not only find your focus but also gain insight into other people's views of your topic, which can be especially valuable if your paper will address a controversial issue or one that you feel is often misunderstood.

6. Cubing

Still another way to generate ideas is cubing. Imagine a six-sided cube that looks something like the figure on page 13.

Mentally, roll your subject around the cube and freewrite the answers to the questions that follow. Write whatever comes to mind for ten or fifteen minutes; don't concern yourself with the "correctness" of what you write.

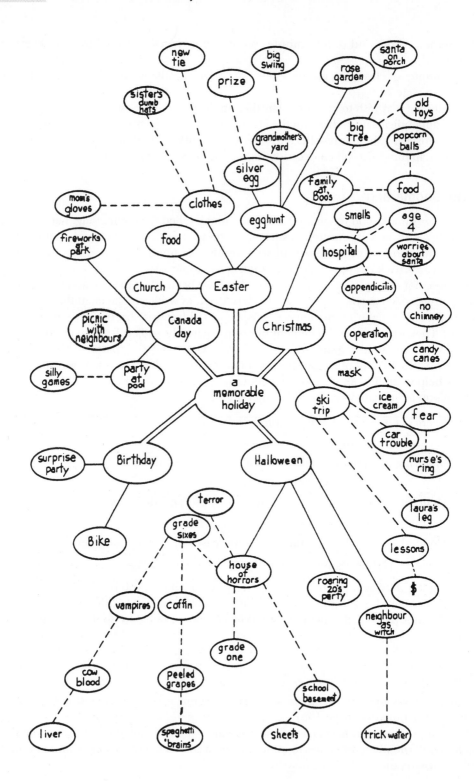

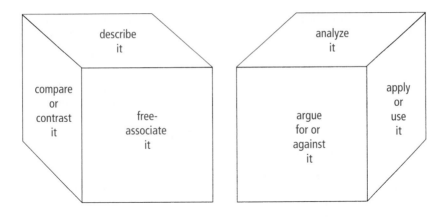

a. *Describe it:* What does your subject look like? What size, colours, textures does it have? Any special features worth noting?

b. *Compare or contrast it:* What is your subject similar to? What is your subject different from? In what ways?

c. *Free-associate it:* What does this subject remind you of? What does it call to mind? What memories does it conjure up?

d. *Analyze it:* How does it work? How are the parts connected? What is its significance?

e. *Argue for or against it:* What arguments can you make for or against your subject? What advantages or disadvantages does it have? What changes or improvements should be made?

f. *Apply it:* What are the uses of your subject? What can you do with it?

A student who had recently volunteered at a homeless shelter wrote the following responses about homelessness:

a. *Describe it:* When I went to the east side of town to volunteer at a homeless shelter, I felt I was in a different city. People were walking right through piles of garbage, and there were panhandlers everywhere. At the shelter, some of the people who lined up for a meal didn't seem to want to meet the eyes of the volunteers, though others were friendly. They ate eagerly and desperately.

b. *Compare or contrast it:* The situation of homeless people in my city is only a little different from that of homeless people in other parts of the world. For example, weather conditions are a hazard in many places, and adequate shelter becomes a necessity for survival. Where our homeless citizens have to deal with the dangers of the winter, the homeless in Brazil or Africa have to face the harsh summers.

c. *Free-associate it:* The regulars at the shelter made me think of some of the homeless people I'd met through my friend's social work in London. They were friendly and generous with what they had, and they were interesting people who made very shrewd observations about "regular" people who walked past them every day.

   d. *Analyze it:* How does a person become homeless? It can start with a small event, such as a missed mortgage payment or a layoff from a job. Banks and other creditors aren't patient forever, and an increasing number of people eventually lose their homes because of bank foreclosures on their properties.

   e. *Argue for or against it:* Homelessness is a social condition that is simply unacceptable today. Homeless shelters are only temporary solutions, and aren't very stable sources of support, as they depend so much on volunteers and varying government funding. Government organizations and grassroots organizations need to get together to find and implement practical solutions instead of attempting one isolated program here or there.

   f. *Apply it:* I will be doing more research into the causes of homelessness in my city by looking at any government documents about the subject that are in the public domain. I hope to find some causes for this problem, and to propose some possible solutions. Maybe I can get more of my fellow students involved!

After you've written your responses, see if any one or more of them give you an idea for a paper. The student who wrote the preceding responses decided she wanted to write an article for her campus newspaper encouraging people to volunteer at the shelter, not only to provide much-needed help but also to challenge their own preconceived notions about the homeless in her college town. Cubing helped her to realize she had something valuable to say about her experience and gave her a purpose for writing.

7. Interviewing

Another way to find a direction for your paper is through some informal interviewing or interactive brainstorming. Ask a classmate or friend to discuss your subject with you. Let your thoughts range over your subject as your friend asks you questions that arise naturally in the conversation. Or your friend might try asking what are called "reporter's questions" as she or he "interviews" you on your subject:

Who?	When?
What?	Why?
Where?	How?

Listen to what you have to say about your subject. What were you most interested in talking about? What did your friend want to know? Why? By talking about your subject, you may find that you have talked your way into an interesting focus for your paper. If, after the interview, you are still stumped, question your friend: if he or she had to publish an essay based on the information from your interview, what would that essay focus on? Why?

8. The Cross-Examination

If a classmate isn't available for an interview, try interviewing, or cross-examining, yourself. Ask yourself questions about your general subject, just as a lawyer might if you were on the witness stand. Consider using the five categories described on the next page, which are adapted from those suggested by Aristotle, centuries ago, to the orators of his day. Ask yourself as many questions in each category as you can think of, and then go on to the next category. Jot down brief notes to yourself as you answer.

Here are the five categories, plus six sample questions for each to illustrate the possibilities:

1. Definition
   a. How does the dictionary or encyclopedia define or explain this subject?
   b. How do most people define or explain it?
   c. How do I define or explain it?
   d. What do its parts look like?
   e. What is its history or origin?
   f. What are some examples of it?

2. Comparison and Contrast
   a. What is it similar to?
   b. What does it differ from?
   c. What does it parallel?
   d. What is it opposite to?
   e. What is it better than?
   f. What is it worse than?

3. Relationship
   a. What causes it?
   b. What are the effects of it?
   c. What larger group or category is it a part of?
   d. What larger group or category is it in opposition to?
   e. What are its values or goals?
   f. What contradictions does it contain?

4. Circumstance
   a. Is it possible?
   b. Is it impossible?
   c. When has it happened before?
   d. What might prevent it from happening?
   e. Why might it happen again?
   f. Who has been or might be associated with it?

5. Testimony
   a. What do people say about it?
   b. What has been written about it?
   c. What authorities exist on the subject?
   d. Are there any relevant statistics?
   e. What research has been done?
   f. Have I had any direct experience with it?

Some of the questions suggested here, or ones you think of, may not be relevant to or useful for your subject. But some may lead you to ideas you wish to explore in more depth, either in a discovery draft or by using another prewriting technique described in this chapter, such as looping or mapping.

9. Dramatizing the Subject

Some writers find it helpful to visualize their subject as if it were a drama or play unfolding in their minds. Kenneth Burke, a thoughtful writer himself, suggests that writers might think about human action in dramatists' terms and then see what sorts of new insights arise as the "drama" unfolds. Burke's dramatists' terms might be adapted for our use and pictured this way:

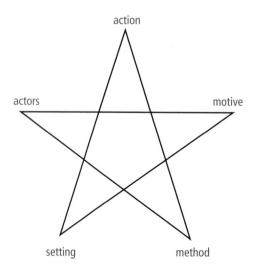

Just as you did in the cubing exercise, try mentally rolling your subject around the star and explore the possibilities that emerge. For example, suppose you want to write about the War of 1812 but you don't know what you want to say about this. Start thinking about this situation as a drama and jot down brief answers to such questions as these:

Action:	What happened?
	What were the results?
	What is going to happen?
Actors:	Who was involved in the action?
	Who was affected by the action?
	Who caused the action?
	Who was for it and who was opposed?
Motive:	What were the reasons behind the action?
	What forces motivated the actors to perform as they did?
Method:	How did the action occur?
	By what means did the actors accomplish the action?
Setting:	What was the time and place of the action?
	What did the place look like?
	What positive or negative feelings are associated with this time or place?

These are only a few of the dozens of questions you might ask yourself about your "drama." (If it helps, think of your "drama" as a murder mystery and answer the questions a police detective might ask: What happened here? To whom? Who did it? Why? With what? When? Where? and so on.)

You may find that you have a great deal to write about the combination of actor and motive but very little to say in response to the questions on setting or method. That's fine—simply use the "dramatists' approach" to help you find a specific topic or idea you want to write about.

If at any point in this stage of the writing process you are experiencing writer's block, you might turn to the suggestions for overcoming this common affliction that appear on pages 108–110 in Chapter 5. You might also find it helpful to read the section on keeping a journal, pages 27–29, because writing in a relaxed mood on a regular basis may be the best long-term cure for your writing anxiety.

■ After You've Found Your Focus

Once you think you've found the focus of your essay, you may be ready to compose a *working thesis statement,* an important part of your essay discussed in great detail in the next chapter. If you've used one of the prewriting exercises outlined in this chapter, by all means, hang onto it. The details and observations you generated as you focused your topic may be useful to you as you begin to organize and develop your body paragraphs.

■ PRACTISING WHAT YOU'VE LEARNED

A. Some of the subjects listed below are too broad for a 500-to-800-word essay. Identify those topics that might be treated in short papers and those that still need to be narrowed.

   1. The role of the modern university or college

   2. Canadian constitutional law and the homelessness problem in Canadian cities

   3. The characters of William Shakespeare

   4. Solar energy

   5. Modern heroism

   6. Anti-smoking laws

   7. Waste recyling programs

   8. Computers

   9. Independent artists and government funding

   10. Selecting the right bicycle

B. Select two of the large subjects that follow and, through looping or listing details or another prewriting technique, find focused topics that would be appropriate for essays of from three to five pages.

   1. music

   2. censorship

3. education

4. jobs

5. television commercials

6. politics

7. animals

8. childhood

9. pollution

10. athletics

■ Discovering Your Audience

Once you have a focused topic and perhaps some ideas about developing your essay, you need to stop a moment to consider your *audience*. Before you can decide what information needs to go into your essay and what should be omitted, you must know who will be reading your paper and why. Knowing your audience will also help you determine what *voice* you should use to achieve the proper tone in your essay.

Suppose, for example, you are attending a college or university organized on the three-term system, and you decide to write an essay arguing for a switch to the two-semester system. If your audience is composed of classmates, your essay will probably focus on the advantages to the student body, such as better opportunities for in-depth study in one's major, the ease of making better grades, and the benefits of longer midwinter and summer vacations. However, if you are addressing the Board of Governors, you might emphasize the power of the semester system to attract more students, cut registration costs, and use professors more efficiently. If your audience is composed of laypersons who know little about either system, you will have to devote more time to explaining the logistics of each one and then discuss the semester plan's advantages to the local merchants, realtors, restaurateurs, and so on. *In other words, such factors as the age, education, profession, experience, and interests of your audience can make a difference in determining which points of your argument to stress or omit, which ideas need additional explanation, and what kind of language to adopt.*

■ How to Identify Your Readers

To help you analyze your audience before you begin writing your working thesis statement and rough drafts, here are some steps you may wish to follow:

   1. First, see if your writing assignment specifies a particular audience (editors of a journal in your field or the Better Business Bureau of your town, for example) or a general audience of your peers (your classmates or readers of the local newspaper, for instance). Even if your assignment does not mention an intended audience, try to imagine one. Imagining specific readers will help you stick to your goal of communicating clearly, in engaging detail.

2. If a specific audience is designated, ask yourself some questions about their motivation or *reasons for reading* your essay.

- What do these readers want to learn?
- What do they hope to gain?
- Do they need your information to make a decision? Formulate a new plan? Design a new project?
- What action do you want them to take?
- Why would these readers want to listen to you?

The answers to such questions will help you find both your essay's purpose and its content. If, for example, you're trying to persuade an employer to hire you for a particular job, you certainly would write your application in a way that stresses the skills and training the company is searching for. You may have a fine hobby or wonderful family, but if your prospective employer–reader doesn't need to hear about that particular part of your life, toss it out of this piece of writing.

3. Next, try to discover what *knowledge* your audience has of your subject.

- What, if anything, can you assume that your readers already know about your topic?
- What background information might they need to know to understand a current situation clearly?
- What facts, explanations, or examples will best present your ideas? How detailed should you be?
- What terms need to be defined? Equipment explained?

Questions like these should guide you as you collect and discard information for your paper. An essay written to your colleagues in electrical engineering, for instance, need not explain commonly used technical instruments; to do so might even insult your readers. But the same report read by your composition classmates would probably need more detailed explanation in order for you to make yourself understood. Always put yourself in your readers' place and then ask: what else do they need to know to understand this point completely?

4. Once you have decided what information is necessary for your audience, dig a little deeper into your readers' identities. Pose some questions about their *attitudes* and emotional states.

- Are your readers already biased for or against your ideas in some way?
- Do they have positive or negative associations with your subject?
- Are they fearful or anxious, reluctant or bored?
- Do they have radically different expectations or interests?

It helps enormously to know the emotional attitudes of your readers toward your subject. Let's suppose you were arguing for the admission of a young child with AIDS into a local school system, and your audience was the parent–teacher organization. Some of your readers might be frightened or even hostile; knowing this, you would wisely begin your argument with a disarming array of information showing that no cases of AIDS have developed from the casual contact of schoolchildren. In other words, the more you know about your audience's attitudes before you begin writing, the more convincing your prose, because you will make the best choices about both content and organization.

5. Last, think of any *special qualities* that might set your audience apart from any other.

- Are they older or younger than your peers?
- Do they share similar educational experiences or training?
- Are they from a particular part of the world or country that might affect their perspective? Urban or rural?
- Are they in positions of authority?

Knowing special facts about your audience makes a difference, often in your choice of words and tone. You wouldn't, after all, use the same level of vocabulary addressing a group of students in grade 5 as you would writing to the children's teacher or principal. Similarly, your tone and word choice probably wouldn't be as formal in a letter to a friend as in a letter to the telephone company protesting your most recent bill.

Without question, analyzing your specific audience is an important step to take before you begin to shape your rough drafts. And before you move on to writing a working thesis, here are a few tips to keep in mind about *all* audiences, no matter who your readers are or what their reasons for reading your writing.

1. Readers don't like to be bored. Grab your readers' attention and fight to keep it. Remember the last dull movie you squirmed—or slept—through? How much you resented wasting not only your money but your valuable time as well? How you turned it off mentally and drifted away to somewhere more exciting? As you write and revise your drafts, keep imagining readers who are as intelligent—and busy—as you are. Put yourself in their place: would you find this piece of writing stimulating enough to keep reading?

2. Readers hate confusion and disorder. Can you recall a time when you tried to find your way to a party, only to discover that a friend's directions were so muddled you wound up hours later, out of gas, cursing in a wheat field? Or the afternoon you spent trying to follow a friend's notes for setting up a chemistry experiment, with explanations that twisted and turned as often as a wandering stray cat? Try to relive such moments of intense frustration as you struggle to make *your* writing clear and direct.

3. Readers want to think and learn (whether they realize it or not). Every time you write, you strike a bargain of sorts with your readers: in return for their time and attention, you promise to inform and interest them, to tell them something new, or to show them something familiar in a different light. You may enlighten them or amuse them or even try to frighten them—but they must feel, in the end, that they've received a fair trade. As you plan, write, and revise, ask yourself, "What are my readers learning?" If the honest answer is "nothing important," you may be writing only for yourself. (If you yourself are bored rereading your drafts, you're probably not writing for anybody at all.)

4. Readers want to see what you see, feel what you feel. Writing that is vague keeps your readers from fully sharing the information or experience you are trying to communicate. Clear, precise language—full of concrete details and specific examples—lets your readers know that you understand your subject and that you want them to understand it too. Even a potentially dull topic such as tuning a car can become engaging to a reader if the right details are provided in the right places: your terror as blue sparks leap under your nose when the wrong wire is touched, the depressing sight of the screwdriver squirming from your greasy fingers and disappearing into the oil pan, the sudden shooting pain when the wrench slips and turns your knuckles to raw hamburger. Get your readers involved and interested—and they'll listen to what you have to say. (Details also persuade your reader that you're an authority on your subject; after all, no reader likes to waste time listening to someone whose tentative, vague prose style announces "I only sort-of know what I'm talking about here.")

   5. Readers are turned off by writers with pretentious, phony voices. Too often inexperienced writers feel they must sound especially scholarly and/or scientific for their essays to be convincing. In fact, the contrary is true. When you use words without understanding their use and context, you assume a voice that is not yours. When you pretend to be someone you're not, you don't sound believable at all—you sound phony. Your readers want to hear what *you* have to say, and the best way to communicate with them is in a natural voice. This does not mean you can use slang or only simple and generic words. It means that you should use precise language that is a little more sophisticated than the words you use in conversations with friends, rather than using overblown jargon. You may believe that to write a good essay it is necessary to use a host of unfamiliar, unpronounceable, polysyllabic words gleaned from the pages of your thesaurus. Again, the opposite is true. Our best writers agree with Mark Twain, who once said, "Never use a twenty-five-cent word when a ten-cent word will do." In other words, avoid pretension in your writing just as you do in everyday conversation. Keep your writing balanced. Select simple, direct words you know and use frequently; keep your voice natural, sincere, and reasonable. But you also need to develop your vocabulary level so you can use more sophisticated words when appropriate, since using only simple and basic words won't be adequate for university- or college-level writing. Remember: you're writing a formal, not casual or personal essay. (For additional help choosing the appropriate words and the level of your diction, see Chapter 7.)

> ✓ **DON'T EVER FORGET YOUR READERS!** Thinking about them as you write will help you choose your ideas, organize your information effectively, and select the best words.

■ PRACTISING WHAT YOU'VE LEARNED

Find a piece of writing in a magazine or newspaper. Identify as specifically as you can the intended audience and main purpose of the selection. What is the intended audience and main purpose of the following selection? How did you arrive at your conclusions? Use the prompt questions in the above sections to guide you in these exercises.

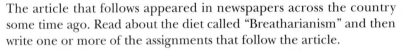

■ ASSIGNMENT

The article that follows appeared in newspapers across the country some time ago. Read about the diet called "Breatharianism" and then write one or more of the assignments that follow the article.

The Ultimate in Diet Cults: Don't Eat Anything at All

1   CORTE MADERA, CALIF.—Among those seeking enlightenment through diet cults, Wiley Brooks seemed to have the ultimate answer—not eating at all. He called himself a "Breatharian" and claimed to live on air, supplemented only by occasional fluids taken to counteract the toxins of urban environments.

2   "Food is more addictive than heroin," the tall, gaunt man told hundreds of people who paid $500 each to attend five-day "intensives," at which he would stand before them in a camel velour sweatsuit and talk for hours without moving, his fingers meditatively touching at their tips.

3   Brooks, 46, became a celebrity on the New Age touring circuit. ABC-TV featured him in October, 1980, as a weight lifter; he allegedly hoisted 1,100 pounds, about 10 times his own weight. He has also been interviewed on radio and in newspapers.

4   Those who went to his sessions during the past six months on the West Coast and in Hawaii were not just food faddists, but also physicians and other professionals who—though not necessarily ready to believe—thought this man could be onto something important. Some were convinced enough by what they saw to begin limiting their own diets, taking the first steps toward Breatharianism.

5   In his intensives, Brooks did not recommend that people stop eating altogether. Rather, he suggested they "clean their blood" by starting with the "yellow diet"—24 food items including grapefruit, papaya, corn products, eggs, chicken, fish, goat's milk, millet, salsa piquante (Mexican hot sauce) and certain flavors of the Häagen Dazs brand ice cream, including "rum raisin." These foods, he said, have a less toxic effect because, among other things, "their vibrational quality is yellow."

6   Last week, however, aspirants toward Breatharianism were shocked by reports that Brooks had been eating—and what's more, eating things that to health food purists are the worst kind of junk.

7   Word spread that during an intensive in Vancouver, Brooks was seen emerging from a 7-Eleven store with a bag of groceries. The next morning there were allegedly room service trays outside his hotel room, while inside, the trash basket held empty containers of chicken pot pie, chili and biscuits.

8   Kendra Wagner, regional Breatharian coordinator, said she herself had seen Brooks drinking a Coke. "When I asked him about it he said, 'That's how dirty the air is here,'" she explained. "We (the coordinators) sat down with Wiley after the training and said, 'We want you to tell us the truth.' He denied everything. We felt tricked and deceived."

9   As the rumors grew, some Breatharians confronted their leader at a lecture in San Francisco. Brooks denied the story and said that the true message of Breatharianism did not depend on whether he ate or not, anyway.

10   The message in his promotional material reads that "modern man is the degenerate descendant of the Breatharian," and that "living on air alone leads to perfect

health and perfect happiness." Though followers had the impression Brooks has not eaten for 18 years, his leaflets merely declare that "he does not eat, and seldom drinks any fluid. He sleeps less than seven hours a week and is healthier, more energetic and happier than he ever dreamed possible."

11 In a telephone interview, Brooks acknowledged that this assertion is not quite correct. "I'm sure I've taken some fruit, like an apple or an orange, but it's better in public to keep it simple." He again staunchly denied the 7-Eleven story.

12 Among those who have been on the yellow diet for months is Jim Collison, 24, who earlier tried "fruitarianism," fasting and other special regimens, and moved from Texas to the San Francisco Bay area just to be around the Breatharian movement. "Now I'm a basket case," he said. "My world revolved around Wiley's philosophy." He had thought Wiley "made the jump to where all of us health food fanatics were going," Collison said.

13 Other Brooks disciples, though disappointed, feel they nevertheless benefited from their experience. Said a physician who has been on the yellow diet for four months: "I feel very good. I still don't know what the truth is, but I do know that Wiley is a good salesman. So I'll be patient, keep an open mind and continue to observe."

14 "Breatharianism is the understanding of what the body really needs, not whether Wiley eats or doesn't," said James Wahler, 35, who teaches a self-development technique called "rebirthing," in Marin County. "I'm realizing that the less I eat the better I feel." He also suggested that Brooks may have lied for people's own good, to get them to listen.

15 "Everyone has benefited from what I'm saying," Brooks said. "There will be a food shortage and a lot of unhappy people when they realize that I was trying to save their lives."

Each of the assignments that follow is directed to a different audience, none of whom know much about Breatharianism. What information does each audience need to know? What kinds of details will be the most persuasive? What sort of organization will work best for each purpose and audience?

1. Write a brief radio advertisement for the five-day intensives. What appeals might persuade people to pay $500 each to attend a seminar to learn to eat air?

2. Assume you are a regional Breatharian coordinator. Write a letter to your city council petitioning for a parade permit that will allow members of your organization to parade down your main street in support of this diet and its lifestyle. What do council members need to know before they vote on such a permit?

3. You are a former Breatharian who is now unhappy with the diet and its unfulfilled promises. Write a report for the police calling for an investigation into the organization. Convince the investigators that the organization is defrauding local citizens and should be stopped.

After writing these assignments, you might exchange them with those written by some of your classmates. Which advertisements, petitions, and reports are the most persuasive and why?

■ Thinking Critically as a Writer

As a writer, you will be thinking critically in two important ways. First, you will need to think critically about any information you may be collecting to use as evidence in your essay. You will, for example, need to be a critical reader as you consider information from books, journals, or electronic sources. You almost certainly will need to be a critical listener as you hear other people talk about their experiences and beliefs.

As you draft your essay, you must become a critical thinker in a second way: you must become your own toughest reader–critic. To convince your readers that your essay has merit, you must stand back and assess objectively what you have written. Are your ideas clear not only to you but to your readers as well? Will readers find your opinions well developed, logical, and supported? In other words, even before you start writing, try role-playing one of your own most thoughtful critical readers, someone who will be closely examining the ideas and evidence in your essay before agreeing with its position.

Here are six suggestions to help you think critically as you draft and do early revisions:

1. Learn to distinguish fact from opinion. A *fact* is an accepted truth whose verification is not affected by its source. No matter who presents it, a fact remains true. We accept some statements as facts because we can test them personally (fire is hot) or because they have been verified frequently by others (penguins live in Antarctica). We accept as fact, for example, that Princess Diana was killed on August 31, 1997, in Paris, France, in a car accident. However, even though much investigation and debate have focused on the accident, the question of who was responsible for the accident is for many people still a matter of *opinion*. Some people believe that the accident was caused by a drunken chauffeur; others insist that the car's excessive speed was prompted by the paparazzi's relentless pursuit; still others claim that this was not an accident, but a conspiracy by the Palace to murder Diana. Opinions, then, are often based on personal feelings or beliefs or on one's interpretation of information. As you think about your evidence, be careful that you don't present your opinions as facts accepted by everyone. Opinions are debatable, and therefore you must always support them before your readers will be convinced.

2. Support your opinions with evidence. To support your opinions, you must offer evidence of one or more kinds. You have a variety of options to choose from. You might support one idea by using personal experiences. Or you might describe the experiences of friends or family. In another place, you might decide to offer detailed examples or to cite statistics or to quote an expert on your subject. You can also use hypothetical examples, researched material, vivid descriptions, reasoned arguments, revealing comparisons, case studies, or testimony of relevant participants, just to name a few other strategies. Consider your purpose and your audience, review the possibilities, and choose the most effective kind of support. The more convincing the support, the more likely your readers are to accept your opinions as true. (If you need to review some sample paragraphs developed by various types of evidence, turn to pages 58–62 of Chapter 3.)

3. Evaluate the strength of your evidence. As you choose your evidence, you should consider its value for the particular point it will support. Scrutinize the nature and source of your evidence carefully. If you are using examples, do they clearly illustrate your claim? Does this example or a different one (or both?) provide the best illustration of your particular point? Is description alone enough support here? Are your statistics or researched material from a reliable, current source? Was information from your research collected in a careful, professional way? Are your experts unbiased authorities from the field under discussion? Where did your experts obtain their information? (For example, are you claiming that crystals possess healing powers because a woman on a talk show said so and she sounded reasonable to you? Just how much do you know about the source of a particular website?) Asking yourself the kinds of questions posed here (and others suggested throughout Part Two of this textbook) will help you develop a critical eye for choosing the best evidence to support your opinions.

4. Use enough specific supporting evidence. Readers need to see strong, relevant supporting evidence throughout your essay. You must be sure, therefore, that you have enough clearly stated evidence for each of your major points. If you present, for instance, too few examples or only a vague reference to an event that supports one of your ideas, a reader may remain unconvinced or may even be confused. As you revise, ask yourself questions such as these: "Do I need to provide additional information here?" "Do I need more details to develop the supporting evidence already present?" "Is any of my evidence clouded by vague or fuzzy language?" If you feel additional supporting evidence or details are needed, take another look at any prewriting you did—or use one of the discovery techniques described in this chapter now to discover some new creative thoughts. For some topics, you may need to do more research or interviewing to find the information you need. (Writers occasionally need to prune ideas too, especially if they're repetitious or off the topic. But, in general, most early drafts are thin or overly general and will profit from more, rather than less, specific supporting evidence.)

5. Watch for biases and strong emotions that may undermine evidence. As you think critically about evidence you are using, monitor any biases and emotional attitudes that may distort information you wish to incorporate into your essay. If you are using personal experiences, for example, have you calmed down enough from your anger over your landlord's actions to write about the clash in a rational, persuasive way? In an essay criticizing a particular product, are you so familiar with the frustrating item that you are making ambiguous claims? (If you write, "The new instructions for use are more confusing than ever," have you shown that they were confusing in the first place? Or why they are more so now?) Be sensitive to any racial, ethnic, cultural, religious, or gender-based assumptions you or your sources may have. Opinions based on generalizations and stereotypes ("Japanese cars are good buys because Asians are more efficient workers than Canadians"; "Women should stay home because they are better with children than men") are not convincing to thinking readers.

6. Check your evidence for logical fallacies. Thinking critically about your drafts should help you support your ideas with reasonable, logical explanations and arguments. Logical fallacies are common errors in reasoning that good writers try to avoid. Those fallacies found most often today are explained on pages 279–281 in Chapter 10; reviewing them will enable you to identify problems in logic that might appear in the writing of others or in your own drafts.

7. Be aware of genres. The writing you do in university or college will be very different from that expected from your high-school assignments or in your personal life (e-mails, text messages, weblogs). Perhaps the biggest difference from other kinds of writing is that you'll be asked to reorient your focus away from personal writing. Even with general topics about summer vacations or cafeteria food, you will be expected to have an objective focus. This is easiest to achieve if you aim to do some outside research and try to imagine what academic subject would fit your topic. If you are writing about cafeteria food, for example, you could see what criteria a nutritionist might use to analyze this food, or find out how an economist would examine food pricing. If you are writing about your summer vacation, you could approach it from the point of view of a geographer, a historian, or a sociologist.

Critical thinking is not, of course, limited to the seven suggestions offered here. But by practising this advice, you will begin to develop and sharpen analytical skills that should improve any writing project.

© Giraudon/Art Resource, NY

The Letter, *1670, by Johannes Vermeer*

■ Keeping a Journal (Talking to Yourself *Does* Help)

Many professional writers carry small notebooks with them so they can jot down ideas and impressions for future use. Other people have kept daily logs or diaries for years to record their thoughts for their own enjoyment. In your composition class, you may find it useful to keep a journal that will help you with your writing process, especially in the early stages of prewriting. Journals can also help you to prepare for class discussions and to remember important course material.

You may have kept a journal in another class. There, it may have been called a daybook or learning log or some other name. Although the journal has a variety of uses, it frequently is assigned to encourage you to record your responses to the material read or discussed in class as well as your own thoughts and questions. Most often the journal is kept in a notebook you can carry with you; some writers with word processors may prefer to collect their thoughts in designated computer files. You can also work on a weblog. Even if a journal is not assigned in your composition class, it is still a useful tool.

Writers who have found journal writing effective advise trying to write a minimum of three entries a week, with each entry at least a half page. To keep your notebook organized, you might start each entry on a new page and date each entry you write. You might also leave the backs of your pages blank so that you can return and respond to an entry at a later date if you wish.

Uses of the Journal

Here are some suggested uses for your journal as you move through the writing process. You may want to experiment with a number of these suggestions to see which are the most productive for you.

1. Use the journal, especially in the first weeks of class, to confront your fears of writing, to conquer the blank page. Write anything you want to—thoughts, observations, notes to yourself, letters home, anything at all. Best your enemy by writing down that witty retort you thought of later and wished you had said. Write down questions and responses about the other subjects you've been learning, about the issues other students are talking about, or about the world issues you hear about. Write a self-portrait or make a list of all the subjects on which you are (or would like to become) an "authority." The more you write, the easier writing becomes—or at least, the easier it is to begin writing because, like a sword swallower, you know you have accomplished the act before and lived to tell about it.

2. Improve your powers of observation. Record interesting snippets of conversations you overhear or catalogue noises you hear in a ten-minute period in a crowded place, such as your student centre, a bookstore, or a mall. Eat something with multiple layers (a piece of fruit such as an orange) and list all the tastes, textures, and smells you discover. Look around your room and write down a list of everything that is yellow. By becoming sensitive to the sights, sounds, smells, and textures around you, you may find that your powers of description and explanation will expand, enabling you to help your reader "see" what you're talking about in your next essay.

3. Save your own brilliant ideas. Jot down those bright ideas that might turn into great essays. Or save those thoughts you have now for the essay you know is coming later in the semester, so you won't forget them. Expand or elaborate on any ideas you have; you might be able to convert your early thoughts into a paragraph when it's time to start drafting.

4. Save other people's brilliant ideas. Record interesting quotations, facts, and figures from other writers and thinkers. You may find some of this information useful in one of your later essays. It's also helpful to look at the ways other writers make their words emphatic, moving, and arresting so you can try some of their techniques in your own prose. (Important: Don't forget to note the source of any material you record, so if you do quote any of it in a paper later, you will be able to document it properly.)

5. Be creative. Write a poem or song or story or joke. Parody the style of someone you've heard or read. Become an inanimate object and complain to the humans around you (for example, what would a soft-drink machine like to say to those folks constantly beating on its stomach?). Become a little green creature from Mars and convince a human to accompany you back to your planet as a specimen of Earthlings (or be the invited guest and explain to the creature why you are definitely not the person to go). The possibilities are endless, so go wild.

6. Prepare for class. If you've been given a reading assignment (an essay or article or pages from a text, for instance), try a split-page entry. Draw a line down the middle of a page in your journal and on the left side of the page write a summary of what you've read or perhaps list the main points. Then on the right side of the same page, write your responses to the material. Your responses might be your personal reaction to the content (What struck you hardest? Why?), or it might be your agreement or disagreement with a particular point or two. Or the material might call up some long-forgotten idea or memory. By thinking about your class material both analytically and personally, you almost certainly will remember it for class discussion. You might also find that a good idea for an essay will arise as you think about the reading assignments in different ways.

7. Record responses to class discussions. A journal is a good place to jot down your reactions to what your teacher and your peers are saying in class. You can ask yourself questions ("What did Megan mean when she said . . .") or note any confusion ("I got mixed up when . . .") or record your own reactions ("I disagreed with Jamal when he argued that . . ."). Again, some of your reactions might become the basis of a good essay.

8. Focus on a problem. You can restate the problem or explore the problem or solve the problem. Writing about a problem often encourages the mind to flow over the information in ways that allow discoveries to happen. Sometimes, too, we don't know exactly what the problem is or how we feel about it until we write about it. (You can see the truth of this statement almost every week if you're a reader of advice columns such as "Dear Abby"—invariably someone will write a letter asking for help and end by saying, "Thanks for letting me write; I know now what I should do.")

9. Practise audience awareness. Write letters to different companies, praising or panning their product; then write advertising copy for each product. Become the third critic on a popular movie-review program and show the other two commentators why your review of your favourite movie is superior to theirs. Thinking about a specific audience when you write will help you plan the content, organization, and tone of each writing assignment.

10. Describe your own writing process. It's helpful sometimes to record how you go about writing your essays. How do you get started? How much time do you spend getting started? Do you write an "idea" draft or work from an outline? How do you revise? Do you write multiple drafts? These and many other questions may give you a clue to any problems you may have as you write your next essay. If, for example, you see that you're having trouble again and again with conclusions, you can turn to Chapter 4 for some extra help. Sometimes it's hard to see that there's a pattern in our writing process until we've described it several times.

11. Write a progress report. List all the skills you've mastered as the course progresses. You'll be surprised at how much you have learned. Read the list over if you're ever feeling frustrated or discouraged, and take pride in your growth.

12. Become sensitive to language. Keep a record of jokes and puns that play on words. Record people's weird-but-funny uses of language (overheard at the dorm cafeteria: "She was so skinny she was emancipated" and "I'm tired of being the escape goat"). Rewrite some of today's bureaucratic jargon or retread a cliché. Come up with new images of your own. Playing with language in fun or even silly ways may make writing tasks seem less threatening. (A newspaper recently came up with this language game: change, add, or subtract one letter in a word and provide a new definition. Example: intoxication/intaxication—the giddy feeling of getting a tax refund; graffiti/giraffiti—spray paint that appears on tall buildings; sarcasm/sarchasm—the gulf between the witty speaker and the listener who doesn't get it.)

13. Write your own textbook. Make notes on material that is important for you to remember. For instance, make your own grammar or punctuation handbook with only those rules you find yourself referring to often. Or keep a list of spelling rules that govern the words you misspell frequently. Writing out the rules in your own words and having a convenient place to refer to them may help you teach yourself quicker than studying any textbook (including this one).

These suggestions are some of the many uses you may find for your journal once you start writing in one on a regular basis. Obviously, not all the suggestions here will be appropriate for you, but some might be, so you might consider using a set of divider tabs to separate the different functions of your journal (one section for class responses, one section for your own thoughts, one for your own handbook, and so on).

You may find, as some students have, that the journal is especially useful during the first weeks of your writing course when putting pen to paper is often hardest. Many students, however, continue to use the journal throughout the entire course, and others adapt their journals to record their thoughts and responses to their other college or university courses and experiences. Whether you continue using a journal beyond this course is up to you, but consider trying the journal for at least six weeks. You may find that it will improve your writing skills more than anything else you have tried before.

★ CHAPTER 1 SUMMARY

Here is a brief summary of what you should know about the prewriting stage of your writing process:

1. Before you begin writing anything, remember that you have valuable ideas to tell your readers.

2. It's not enough that these valuable ideas are clear to you, the writer. Your single most important goal is to communicate those ideas clearly to your readers, who cannot know what's in your mind until you tell them.

3. Whenever possible, select a subject to write on that is of great interest to you, and always give yourself more time than you think you'll need to work on your essay.

4. Try a variety of prewriting techniques to help you find your essay's purpose and a narrowed, specific focus.

5. Review your audience's knowledge of and attitudes toward your topic before you begin your first draft; ask yourself questions such as "Who needs to know about this topic, and why?"

6. Examine the strength of your ideas by thinking critically: are you relying on personal opinion or on logical analysis of facts that can be proved by research and sources that are acceptable to your readers?

7. Consider keeping a journal to help you explore good ideas and possible topics for writing assignments in your composition class.

Chapter 2

The Thesis

■ What Is Critical Thinking?

Critical thinking means the ability to analyze and evaluate our own ideas and those of others. Because we are constantly bombarded today with all kinds of information and differing points of view, we need skills to examine ideas carefully before we accept or reject them.

Here's a common situation in which critical thinking comes into play: two of your friends are arguing over the use of fetal tissue in medical research. Each friend has many points to offer; each is presenting statistics, examples of actual case studies, the words of experts, and hypothetical situations that might arise. Many of the statistics and experts on one side of the argument seem to contradict directly the figures and authorities on the other side. Which side do you take? Why? Are there other points of view to consider? How can you know what to think?

Every day we are faced with just such decisions. We must be able to judge intelligently the merits of what we hear and read before we can feel confident about what we think of a particular issue. We must practise analyzing our beliefs and those held by others to evaluate the reasons for maintaining those views. To think critically about ideas doesn't mean being hostile or negative; it simply means that we need to examine opinions closely and carefully before we accept them. Without examining others' ideas or being conscious of our own reasons for taking the positions we do, we will not be able to write effectively.

■ Beginning To Write

The famous author Thomas Wolfe had a simple formula for beginning his writing: "Just put a sheet of paper in the typewriter and start bleeding." For some writers, the "bleeding" method works well. You may find that, indeed, you are one of those writers who must begin by freewriting or by writing an entire "discovery draft"* to find your purpose and focus—you must write yourself into your topic, so to speak. Other writers are more structured; they may prefer prewriting in lists, outlines, or cubes. Many writers start by writing responses to research notes so they have supporting facts for their arguments. There is no right or wrong way to find a topic or to begin writing; simply try to find the methods that work best for you.

Let's assume at this point that you have identified a topic you wish to write about—perhaps you found it by working through one of the prewriting activities mentioned in Chapter 1 or by writing in your journal. Perhaps you had an important idea you have been wanting to write about for some time, or perhaps the assignment in your class suggested the topic to you. Suppose that through one of these avenues you have focused on a topic and you have given some thought to a possible audience for your paper. You may now find it helpful to formulate a *working thesis*.

■ What Is a Thesis?

The thesis declares the main point or controlling idea of your entire essay. Frequently located near the beginning of a short essay, the thesis answers these questions: "What is the subject of this essay?" "What is the writer's opinion on this subject?" "What is the writer's purpose in this essay?" (To explain something? To argue a position? To move people to action? To entertain?). As you will see later in this chapter, the thesis or main point is expressed in a thesis statement. In other words, the thesis is the central *idea* of your essay, while the thesis statement is a sentence that articulates that idea. As you begin your essay, start with a "working thesis."

■ What Does a "Working Thesis" Do?

Consider a "working thesis" a statement of your main point in its trial or rough-draft form. Allow it to "work" for you as you move from prewriting through drafts and revision. Your working thesis may begin as a very simple sentence. For example, one of the freewriting exercises on nature in Chapter 1 (page 8) might lead to a working thesis such as "Our university needs an on-campus recycling centre." Such a working thesis states an opinion about the subject (the need for a centre) and suggests what the essay will do (give arguments for building such a centre on campus). Similarly, the prewriting list on running (page 7) might lead to a working thesis such as "Before beginning a successful program, novice

---

* If you do begin with a discovery draft, you may wish to turn at this point to the manuscript suggestions on pages 92–93 in Chapter 5.

runners must learn a series of warm-up and cool-down exercises." This statement not only tells the writer's opinion and purpose (the value of the exercises) but also indicates an audience (novice runners).

A working thesis statement can be your most valuable organizational tool. Once you have thought about your essay's main point and purpose, you can begin to draft your paper to accomplish your goals. *Everything in your essay should support your thesis.* Consequently, if you write your working thesis statement at the top of your first draft and refer to it often, your chances of drifting away from your purpose should be reduced.

If you want to write about a personal experience but are finding it difficult to come up with a clearly defined thesis idea, try asking yourself questions about the topic's significance or value (examples: Why is this topic important to me? What was so valuable about my year on the newspaper staff? What was the most significant lesson I learned? What was an unexpected result of this experience?). Often the answer to one of your questions will show you the way to a working thesis (example: Writing for the school newspaper teaches time-management skills that are valuable both in and out of class).

■ Can a "Working Thesis" Change?

It's important for you to know at this point that there may be a difference between the working thesis that appears in your rough drafts and your final thesis. As you begin drafting, you may have one main idea in mind that surfaced from your prewriting activities. But as you write, you may discover that what you really want to write about is different. Perhaps you discover that one particular part of your essay is really what you want to concentrate on (instead of covering three or four problems you have with your current job, for instance, you decide you want to explore in depth only the difficulties with your boss), or perhaps in the course of writing you find another approach to your subject more satisfying or persuasive (explaining how employees may avoid problems with a particular kind of difficult boss as opposed to describing various kinds of difficult bosses in your field).

Changing directions is not uncommon: *writing is an act of discovery.* Frequently we don't know exactly what we think or what we want to say until we write it. A working thesis appears in your early drafts to help you focus and organize your essay; don't feel it's carved in stone.

A warning comes with this advice, however. If you do write yourself into another essay—that is, if you discover as you write that you are finding a better topic or main point to make, consider this piece of writing a "discovery draft," that is, extended prewriting that has helped you find your real focus. Occasionally, your direction changes so slightly that you can rework or expand your thesis to accommodate your new ideas. But more frequently you may find that it's necessary to begin another draft with your newly discovered working thesis as the controlling idea. When this is the case, don't be discouraged—this kind of "re-seeing" or revision of your topic is a common practice among experienced writers (for more advice on revising as rethinking, see Chapter 5). Don't be tempted at this point to leave your original working thesis statement in an essay that has clearly changed its point, purpose, or approach—in other words, don't try to pass off an old head on the body of a new statue! Remember that ultimately you want your thesis to guide your readers rather than confuse them by promising an essay they can't find as they read on.

Guidelines for Writing a Good Thesis Statement

When you have decided on the direction of your essay, you will need to compose a more formal statement to represent your thesis. To help you draft your thesis statement, here is some advice:

A good thesis statement states the writer's clearly defined position on some subject. You must tell your reader what you think. Don't dodge the issue; present your position specifically and precisely. A worthwhile thesis statement needs to be contestable. In other words, you need to indicate that there are different positions about your topic. For example, if you were asked to write a thesis statement expressing your position on the differences in provincial laws that designate the legal minimum age to purchase or consume alcohol, the first three theses listed below would be confusing:

Poor	Many people have different opinions on whether there should be the same minimum age across the country for people to be permitted to drink alcohol, and I agree with some of them. [The writer's position on the issue is not clear to the reader.]
Poor	The question of whether we need the same legal drinking age across the country is a controversial issue in many provinces. [This statement might introduce the thesis, but the writer has still avoided stating a clear position on the issue.]
Poor	I want to give my position on the different drinking ages in different provinces and the reasons I feel this way. [What is the writer's position? The reader still doesn't know.]
Better	To ensure equal treatment of all citizens, our country needs to enforce the same legal drinking age across the country. [The writer clearly states a position that will be supported in the essay.]
Better	The legal minimum age for purchasing alcohol should be the same across Canada. [Again, the writer has asserted a clear position on the issue that will be argued in the essay. There is also room for disagreement and, thus, for an argument.]

A good thesis statement asserts one main idea. Many essays drift into confusion because the writer is trying to explain or argue two different, large issues in one essay. You can't effectively ride two horses at once; pick one main idea and explain or argue it in convincing detail. Here are some examples of how to do that:

Poor	The proposed no-smoking ordinance in our town will violate a number of our citizens' civil rights, and no one has proved secondary smoke is dangerous anyway. [This thesis statement contains two main assertions—the ordinance's violation of rights and secondary smoke's lack of danger—that require two different kinds of supporting evidence.]
Better	The proposed no-smoking ordinance in our town will violate our civil rights. [This essay will show the various ways the ordinance will infringe on personal liberties.]
Better	The most recent studies by the Canadian Surgeon General's office claiming that secondary smoke is dangerous to nonsmokers are

based on faulty research. [This essay will also focus on one issue: the validity of the studies on secondary smoke danger.]

Poor High-school athletes shouldn't have to maintain a certain grade-point average to participate in school sports, and the value of sports is often worth the lower academic average. [Again, this thesis statement moves in two different directions.]

Better High-school athletes shouldn't have to maintain a certain grade-point average to participate in school sports. [This essay will focus on one issue: reasons why a particular average shouldn't be required.]

Better For some students, participation in sports may be more valuable than achieving a high grade-point average. [This essay will focus on why the benefits of sports may sometimes outweigh those of academics.]

Incidentally, at this point you may recall from your high-school days a rule about always expressing your thesis in one sentence. Writing teachers often insist on this rule to help you avoid the double-assertion problem just illustrated. Although not all essays have one-sentence theses, many do, and it's a good habit to strive for in this early stage of your writing.

A good thesis statement has something worthwhile to say. Although it's true that almost any subject can be made interesting with the right treatment, some subjects are more predictable and therefore more boring than others. Before you write your thesis, think hard about your subject: does your position lend itself to stale or overly obvious ideas? For example, most readers would find the following theses tiresome unless the writers had some original method of developing their essays:

Poor Dogs have always been man's best friends. [This essay might be full of ho-hum clichés about dogs' faithfulness to their owners.]

Poor Friendship is a wonderful thing. [Again, watch out for tired truisms that restate the obvious.]

Poor Food in my dorm is horrible. [Although this essay might be enlivened by some vividly repulsive imagery, the subject itself is ancient.]

No matter what topic you are asked to write on in university, try to move away from too much personal reflection or experience. Personal material may be too restricted to be of general interest, and may not be appropriate for an academic writing context. It often helps to *universalize* the essay's thesis so your readers can also learn something about the general subject, while possibly learning something about you at the same time:

Poor The four children in my family have completely different personalities. [This statement may be true, but would anyone other than the children's parents really be fascinated with this topic?]

Better Birth order can influence children's personalities in startling ways. [The writer is wiser to offer this controversial statement, which is of more interest to readers than the preceding one because many readers have brothers and sisters of their own. The writer can then illustrate her claims with examples from her own family, and from other families, if she wishes. However, the writer should look to academic, published sources for the majority of her evidence.]

Poor   I don't like to take courses that are held in big lecture classes at this school. [Why should your reader care one way or another about your class preference?]

Better   Large lecture classes provide a poor environment for the student who learns best through interaction with both teachers and peers. [This thesis will allow the writer to present personal examples that the reader may identify with or challenge, without writing an essay that is exclusively personal.]

In other words, try to select a subject that will interest, amuse, challenge, persuade, or enlighten your readers. If your subject itself is commonplace, find a unique approach or an unusual, perhaps even controversial, point of view. If your subject is personal, ask yourself if the topic alone will be sufficiently interesting to readers; if not, think about universalizing the thesis to include your audience. Remember that a good thesis should encourage readers to read on with enthusiasm rather than invite groans of "Not this again" or shrugs of "So what."

A good thesis statement is limited to fit the assignment. Your thesis statement should show that you've narrowed your subject matter to an appropriate size for your essay. Don't allow your thesis to promise more of a discussion than you can adequately deliver in a short essay. You want an in-depth treatment of your subject, not a superficial one. Certainly you may take on important issues in your essays; don't feel you must limit your topics to local or personal subjects. But one simply cannot analyze the reasons for Canada's entry into the First World War or its role in peacekeeping missions in three to five pages. Focus your essay on an important part of a broader subject that interests you. (For a review of ways to narrow and focus your subject, see pages 6–17.)

Poor   Nuclear power should be banned as an energy source in this country. [Can the writer give the broad subject of nuclear power a fair treatment in three to five pages?]

Better   Because of its poor safety record during the past two years, the nuclear power plant should be closed. [This writer could probably argue the thesis in this focused statement in a short essay.]

Poor   The parking permit system at this college should be completely revised. [An essay calling for the revision of the parking permit system would involve discussion of permits for various kinds of students, faculty, administrators, staff, visitors, delivery personnel, disabled persons, and so forth. Therefore, the thesis represented by this statement is probably too broad for a short essay.]

Better   Because of the complicated application process, the parking permit system at this college penalizes disabled students. [This thesis is focused on a particular problem and could be argued in a short paper.]

Poor   Artists from the Maritimes have always contributed a lot to Canadian culture. ["Artists from the Maritimes," "a lot," and "culture" cover more ground than can be dealt with in one short essay.]

Better	Sarah McLaughlan has been a major influence in the development of a uniquely Canadian style followed by many singer–songwriters. [This thesis is more specifically defined.]

A good thesis statement is clear and specific. More than anything, a vague thesis statement reflects lack of clarity in the writer's mind and almost inevitably leads to an essay that talks around the subject but never makes a coherent point. Try to avoid words whose meanings are imprecise or those that depend largely on personal interpretation, such as "interesting," "good," and "bad."

Poor	The city is heading in the right direction. [What city does the writer refer to? What direction does the writer refer to? How is it "right"? For whom?]
Better	By re-designating more streets for bicyclists, Vancouver is taking a positive step toward solving both transportation and environmental problems. [This tells what the positive direction is and how it is being implemented.]
Poor	Registration is a big hassle. [No clear idea is communicated here. How much trouble is a "hassle"? Registration for what?]
Better	The alphabetical fee-paying system used for university and college registration is inefficient. [The issue is specified.]
Poor	Living in an apartment for the first time can teach you many things about taking care of yourself. ["Things" and "taking care of yourself" are both too vague—what specific ideas does the writer want to discuss? And who is the "you" the writer has in mind?]
Better	By living in an apartment, first-year university and college students can learn valuable lessons in financial planning and time management. [The thesis is now clearly defined and directed.]

A good thesis statement is easily recognized as the main idea and is often located in the first or second paragraph. Many students are hesitant to spell out a thesis by writing a thesis statement at the beginning of an essay. To quote one student, "I feel as if I'm giving everything away." Although you may feel uncomfortable "giving away" the main point so soon, the alternative of waiting until the last page to present your thesis can seriously weaken your essay.

Without an assertion of what you are trying to prove, your reader does not know how to assess the supporting details your essay presents. For example, if your roommate comes home one afternoon and points out that the roof on your apartment leaks, the rent is too high, and the closet space is too small, you may agree but you may also be confused. Does your roommate want you to call the owner or is this merely a gripe session? How should you respond? On the other hand, if your roommate first announces that he wants the two of you to look for a new place, you can put the discussion of the roof, rent, and closets into its proper context and react accordingly. Similarly, you write an essay to have a specific effect on your readers. You will have a better chance of producing this effect if readers easily and quickly understand what you are trying to do.

Granted, some essays whose position is unmistakably obvious from the outset can get by with a strongly *implied thesis,* and it's true that many essays, often those written by professional writers, are organized to build dramatically to a climax. You will also find that many essays written by professional writers do not have a thesis statement at all. But if you are an inexperienced writer, the best choice at this point still may be a direct statement of your main idea. It is, after all, your responsibility to make your purpose clear, with as little expense of time and energy on the readers' part as possible. Readers should not be forced to puzzle out your essay's main point—it's your job to tell them.

Remember: an essay is not a detective story, so don't keep your readers in suspense until the last minute. Until you feel comfortable with more sophisticated patterns of organization, plan to put your clearly worded thesis statement near the beginning of your essay.

■ Avoiding Common Errors in Thesis Statements

Here are five mistakes to avoid when forming your thesis statements:

1. Don't make your thesis merely an announcement of your subject matter or a description of your intentions. State an approach toward the subject.

Poor	The subject of this essay is my experience with a pet boa constrictor. [This is an announcement of the subject, not a thesis.]
Better	My pet boa constrictor, Sir Pent, was a much better bodyguard than my dog, Fang. [The writer states an opinion that will be explained and illustrated in the essay.]
Poor	I'm going to discuss boa constrictors as pets. [This represents a statement of intention but not a thesis.]
Better	Boa constrictors do not make healthy indoor pets. [The writer states a position that will be explained and defended in the essay.]

2. Don't merely state a fact. A thesis is an assertion of opinion that leads to discussion. Don't select an idea that is self-evident or dead-ended.

Poor	Child abuse is a terrible problem. [Yes, of course, who wouldn't agree that child abuse is terrible?]
Better	Child-abuse laws in this province are too lenient for repeat offenders. [This thesis will lead to a discussion in which supporting arguments and evidence will be presented.]
Poor	Advertisers often use attractive models in their advertisements to sell products. [True, but rather obvious. How could this essay be turned into something more than a list describing one advertisement after another?]
Better	A number of liquor advertisers, well known for using pictures of attractive models to sell their products, are now using special graphics to send subliminal messages to their readers. [This claim is controversial and will require persuasive supporting evidence.]
Better	Although long criticized for their negative portrayal of women in television commercials, the auto industry is just as often guilty of stereotyping men as brainless idiots unable to make a decision. [This thesis makes a point that may lead to an interesting discussion.]

3. Don't clutter your thesis with such expressions as "in my opinion," "I believe," and "in this essay I'll argue that. . . ." These unnecessary phrases weaken your thesis statement because they often make you sound timid or uncertain. This is your essay; therefore, the opinions expressed are obviously yours. Be forceful: speak directly, with conviction.

Poor	My opinion is that the federal government should devote more money to solar energy research.
Poor	My thesis states that the federal government should devote more money to solar energy research.
Better	The federal government should devote more money to solar energy research.
Poor	In this essay I will present lots of reasons why marijuana should not be legalized in Canada.
Better	Marijuana should not be legalized in Canada.

4. Don't be unreasonable. Making irrational or oversimplified claims will not persuade your reader that you have a thorough understanding of the issue. Don't insult any reader; avoid irresponsible charges, name-calling, and profanity.

Poor	Radical religious fanatics across the nation are trying to impose their right-wing views by censoring high-school library books. [Words such as "radical," "fanatics," "right-wing," and "censoring" will antagonize many readers immediately.]
Better	Only local school board members—not religious leaders or parents—should decide which books high-school libraries should order.
Poor	Too many corrupt books in our high-school libraries selected by liberal, atheistic educators are undermining the morals of our youth. [Again, some readers will be offended.]
Better	To ensure that high-school libraries contain books that reflect community standards, parents should have a voice in selecting new titles.

5. Don't express your thesis in the form of a question unless the answer is already obvious to the reader.

Poor	Why should every college student be required to take two years of foreign language?
Better	Chemistry majors should be exempt from the foreign-language requirement.

 REMEMBER: Many times writers "discover" a better thesis near the end of their first draft. That's fine—consider that draft a prewriting or focusing exercise and begin another draft, using the newly discovered thesis as a starting point.

■ PRACTISING WHAT YOU'VE LEARNED

A. Identify each of the following thesis statements as adequate or inadequate. If the thesis is weak or insufficient in some way, explain the problem.

1. I think *Schindler's List* is a really interesting movie that everyone should see.

2. Which clothes are better, Chinese imports or those made in Canada?

3. Current research says we should all take more Vitamin D supplements.

4. My essay will tell you how to apply for a college loan with the least amount of trouble.

5. More effective privacy laws need to be written and enforced as an increasing number of individuals are publicly humiliated through YouTube and other Internet sites.

6. Raising the cost of tuition will be a terrible burden on the students and won't do anything to help the quality of education at this school.

7. I can't stand to even look at people who are into body piercing, especially in their face.

8. Allowing private medical clinics will lead to a two-tiered medical system in this country.

B. Rewrite the following sentences so that each one is a clear thesis statement. Be prepared to explain why you changed the sentences as you did.

1. Being a Canadian soldier in the First World War was a negative experience.

2. Canadian literature has changed a lot over the last fifty years.

3. There are many advantages and disadvantages to going on strike.

4. The banning of public smoking has been one big headache.

5. In this paper I will debate the pros and cons of vegetarianism.

6. We need to do something about the injustices faced by poor people in this city.

7. In my opinion, Prince Edward Island is a fantastic place.

8. The Trudeau years had a tremendous effect on this country.

Narrow the subject and write one good thesis sentence each for five of the following topics:

1. A political or social issue
2. A job or profession
3. A recent scientific discovery
4. A historical process
5. A recent book or movie
6. A rule, law, or regulation
7. An environmental issue
8. A current fad or fashion

■ Using the Essay Map*

Many essays will benefit from the addition of an *essay map* (or, in classical terms, the "partitio"), a brief statement in the introductory paragraph introducing the major points to be discussed in the essay. This brief statement would be an addition to the thesis statement, sometimes within the same sentence and sometimes in a separate sentence. Where the thesis statement would articulate the essay's central idea, the essay map would be a statement indicating the main points that would develop the central idea. Consider the analogy of beginning a trip by checking your map to see where you are headed. Similarly, an essay map allows the readers to know in advance where you, the writer, will be taking them in the essay.

Let's suppose you have been assigned the task of praising or criticizing some aspect of your campus. You decide that your thesis will be "The Study Skills Centre is an excellent place for first-year students to receive help with basic courses." Although your thesis does take a stand ("excellent place"), your reader will not know why the Centre is helpful or what points you will cover in your argument. With an essay map added, the reader will have a brief but specific idea where the essay is going and how it will be developed:

Thesis

Essay map (underlined)

The Study Skills Centre is an excellent place for first-year students to receive help with basic courses. <u>The Centre's numerous free services, well-trained tutors, and variety of supplementary learning materials can often mean the difference between academic success and failure for many students.</u>

Thanks to the essay map, the reader knows that the essay will discuss the Centre's free services, tutors, and learning materials.

---

* We are indebted to Susan Wittig for this useful concept, introduced in *Steps to Structure: An Introduction to Composition and Rhetoric* (Cambridge, MA: Winthrop Publishers, 1975), pp. 125–126.

Here's another example—this time let's assume you have been frustrated trying to read articles that have been placed "on reserve" in your campus library, so you have decided to criticize your library's reserve facility:

Thesis

Essay map (underlined)

> The library's reserve facility is badly managed. <u>Its unpredictable hours, poor staffing, and inadequate space discourage even the most dedicated students.</u>

After reading the introductory paragraph, the reader knows the essay will discuss the reserve facility's problematic hours, staff, and space. In other words, the thesis statement defines the main purpose of your essay, and the essay map indicates the route you will take to accomplish that purpose.

The essay map often follows the thesis, but it can also appear before it. It is, in fact, frequently part of the thesis statement itself, as illustrated in the following examples:

Thesis with underlined essay map

> <u>Because of its free services, well-trained tutors, and useful learning aids,</u> the Study Skills Centre is an excellent place for students seeking academic help.

Thesis with underlined essay map

> For those students who need extra help with their basic courses, the Study Skills Centre is one of the best resources <u>because of its numerous free services, well-trained tutors, and variety of useful learning aids.</u>

Thesis with underlined essay map

> <u>Unreasonable hours, poor staffing, and inadequate space</u> make the library reserve facility difficult to use.

In addition to suggesting the main points of the essay, the map provides two other benefits. It provides a set of guidelines for organizing your essay and helps to keep you from wandering off into areas only vaguely related to your thesis. A clearly written thesis statement and essay map provide a skeletal outline for the sequence of paragraphs in your essay, frequently with one body paragraph devoted to each main point mentioned in your map. (Chapter 3, on paragraphs, will explain in more detail the relationships among the thesis, the map, and the body of your essay.) Note that the number of points in the essay map may vary, although three or four may be the number found most often in three- to five-page essays. (More than four main points in a short essay may result in underdeveloped paragraphs; see pages 61–62 for additional information.)

Some important advice: although essay maps can be helpful to both writers and readers, they can also sound too mechanical, repetitive, or obvious. If you choose to use a map, always strive to blend it with your thesis as smoothly as possible.

Poor

> The Study Skills Centre is a helpful place for three reasons. The reasons are its free services, good tutors, and lots of learning materials.

Better

> Numerous free services, well-trained tutors, and a variety of useful learning aids make the Study Skills Centre a valuable campus resource.

If you feel your essay map is too obvious or mechanical, try using it only in your rough drafts to help you organize your essay. Once you're sure it isn't necessary to clarify your thesis or to guide your reader, consider dropping it from your final draft.

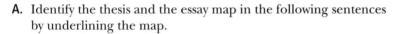

■ PRACTISING WHAT YOU'VE LEARNED

A. Identify the thesis and the essay map in the following sentences
by underlining the map.

1. *Citizen Kane* deserves to appear on a list of "Top Movies of All Times"
   because of its excellent ensemble acting, its fast-paced script, its classical
   focus on hubris, and its innovative editing.

2. Our province should double the existing fines for first-offence drunk
   drivers. Such a move would lower the number of accidents and increase
   the province's revenues for highway maintenance.

3. To guarantee sound construction, lower costs, environmental responsibility, and personalized design, more people should consider building
   their own log cabin home.

4. Apartment living is preferable to dorm living because it's cheaper, quieter,
   more private, and more luxurious.

5. Her spirit of protest and clever phrasing blended into unusual musical
   arrangements have made Joni Mitchell a successful recording artist for
   over thirty-five years.

6. Through unscrupulous uses of propaganda and secret assassination squads,
   Hitler was able to take control of an economically depressed Germany.

7. The new strike settlement will not radically reform the inequity in labour
   laws: job security, pay equity and benefit packages will continue to be
   serious issues.

8. Avocados make excellent plants for children. They're inexpensive to buy,
   easy to root, quick to sprout, and fun to grow.

B. Review the thesis statements you wrote for the Assignment on page 40. Write
an essay map for each thesis statement. You may place the map before or after
the thesis, or you may make it part of the thesis itself. Identify which part is the
thesis and which is the essay map by underlining the map.

■ ASSIGNMENT

Use one of the following quotations to help you think of a subject for an
essay of your own. Don't merely repeat the quotation itself as your thesis
statement but, rather, allow the quotation to lead you to your subject and a main point
of your own creation that is appropriately narrowed and focused. Don't forget to designate an audience for your essay, a group of readers who need or want to hear what you
have to say.

1. "It is never too late to be what one might have been"—George Eliot (Mary
   Ann Evans), nineteenth-century English novelist.

2. "It is amazing how complete is the delusion that beauty is goodness"—Leo Tolstoy, nineteenth-century Russian aristocrat and novelist.

3. "A nation without a literature is not a nation, and the quality of its literature is one of the standards by which a nation is judged now and will be judged in the future"—Robertson Davies, Canadian novelist.

4. "In this world there are only two tragedies. One is not getting what one wants, and the other is getting it"—Oscar Wilde, nineteenth-century Irish writer and wit.

5. "The prescription for fear is action"—Silken Laumann, Canadian Olympic champion.

6. "When a thing is funny, search it carefully for a hidden truth"—George Bernard Shaw, nineteenth- and twentieth-century Irish playwright.

7. "I am a great believer in luck, and I find the harder I work the more I have of it"—Stephen Leacock, twentieth-century Canadian economist and humorist.

8. "Noncooperation with evil is as much a moral obligation as is cooperation with good"—Martin Luther King, Jr., twentieth-century American statesman and civil rights activist.

9. "The essential lubricant for a free society is tolerance"—Lester B. Pearson, former Prime Minister of Canada.

10. "Few things are harder to put up with than the annoyance of a good example"—Mark Twain, nineteenth-century American writer and humorist.

11. "The new electronic independence recreates the world in the image of a global village"—Marshall McLuhan, Canadian communications theorist.

12. "You can discover more about a person in an hour of play than in a year of conversation"—Plato, early Greek philosopher.

13. "Power has direction: it is always exercised downwards, towards the weak"—Jean Vanier, Canadian founder of L'Arche movement.

14. "It is never too late to give up your prejudices"—Henry David Thoreau, nineteenth-century American writer and naturalist.

15. "We must never forget that, in the long run, a democracy is judged by the way the majority treats the minority"—Pierre Elliot Trudeau, former Canadian Prime Minister.

16. "Nobody can make you feel inferior without your consent"—Eleanor Roosevelt, American stateswoman.

17. "When a writer dies, he becomes his words"—Rosemary Sullivan, biographer.

Pierre Elliott Trudeau (1919–2000)

★ CHAPTER 2 SUMMARY

Here's a brief review of what you need to know about the thesis statement:

1. A thesis statement declares the main point of your essay; it tells the reader what clearly defined opinion you hold.

2. Everything in your essay should support your thesis statement.

3. A good thesis statement asserts one main idea, narrowed to fit the assignment, and is stated in clear, specific terms.

4. A good thesis statement makes a reasonable claim about a topic that is of interest to its readers as well as to its writer.

5. The thesis statement is often presented near the beginning of the essay, frequently in the first or second paragraph, or is so strongly implied that readers cannot miss the writer's main point.

6. A "working" or trial thesis is an excellent organizing tool to use as you begin drafting, because it can help you decide which ideas to include.

7. Because writing is an act of discovery, you may write yourself into a better thesis statement by the end of your first draft. Don't hesitate to begin a new draft with the new thesis statement.

8. Some writers may profit from using an essay map, a brief statement accompanying the thesis that introduces the supporting points discussed in the body of the essay.

Chapter 3

The Body Paragraphs

The middle—or *body*—of your essay is composed of paragraphs that support the thesis statement. They persuade your reader that the opinion you have expressed in your thesis is sensible, interesting and worthwhile, and they do so by

- citing examples
- explaining causes
- offering reasons
- citing authorities
- generally providing evidence and arguments.

Your essay will develop its thesis by discussing a few main ideas. You have probably encountered the five-paragraph model in the past, which looks a little like this:

- The introduction has a thesis sentence and three main reasons that back up that statement.
- Three body paragraphs follow, each representing one of the three main reasons.
- The conclusion repeats the introductory paragraph, with the addition of concluding phraseology, such as "therefore."

As you move into university- and college-level writing, you will be developing more sustained, complex and well-developed arguments in your essays. You will now have to adapt your essay development strategies to move beyond that five-paragraph structure.

As you plan your paper, try to divide up your essay into the sections that represent the ideas that support your thesis. You may find that just one paragraph per section will not be adequate for developing complete ideas, even if you're writing a short paper. So if you were to discuss Canada's policies on climate change, you would first want to identify the points you wanted to discuss, and then break those down into subsections. Under "public education," for example, you might want to discuss "classifications of target audiences" and "publicity campaigns." Each paragraph you write would discuss those related ideas before going on to the next section. Aim to focus on one point in each paragraph. If you try to discuss too many ideas within the same paragraph, your paragraph can become unfocused and lack unity. Some short paragraphs can be transition paragraphs or emphasis paragraphs, but generally, a new body paragraph signals a specific point in the discussion. That point is presented in the paragraph in the form of a topic sentence.

■ Planning the Body of Your Essay

Many writers like to have a plan before they begin drafting the body of their essay. To help you create a plan, first look at your thesis. If you used an essay map, as suggested in Chapter 2, you may find that the points mentioned there will provide the basis for the body paragraphs of your essay. For example, recall from Chapter 2 a thesis and essay map praising the Study Skills Centre: "Because of its free services, well-trained tutors, and useful learning aids, the Study Skills Centre is an excellent place for students seeking academic help." Your plan for developing the body of your essay might look like this:

Body paragraph one: discussion of free services

Body paragraph two: discussion of tutors

Body paragraph three: discussion of learning aids

At this point in your writing process you may wish to sketch in some of the supporting evidence you will include in each paragraph. You might find it helpful to go back to your prewriting activities (listing, looping, freewriting, mapping, cubing, and so on) to see what ideas surfaced then. Adding some examples and supporting details might make an informal outline of the Study Skills paper appear like this:

I. Free services
    A. Mini-course on improving study skills
    B. Tutoring ⟨ composition / math
    C. Weekly seminars ⟨ stress management / test anxiety / building vocabulary
    D. Testing for learning disabilities

II. Tutors
    A. Top graduate students in their fields
    B. Experienced teachers
    C. Some bilingual
    D. Have taken training course at Centre

III. Learning aids
   A. Supplementary texts
   B. Workbooks
   C. Audio-visual aids

Notice that this plan is an *informal* or *working outline* rather than a *formal outline*—that is, it doesn't have strictly parallel parts nor is it expressed in complete sentences. Unless your instructor requests a formal sentence or topic outline, don't feel you must make one at this early stage. Just consider using the informal outline to plot out a tentative plan that will help you start your first draft.

Here's an example of an informal outline at work: let's suppose you have been asked to write about your most prized possession—and you've chosen your 1966 Mustang, a car you have restored. You already have some ideas, but as yet they're scattered and too few to make an interesting, well-developed essay. You try an informal outline, jotting down your ideas thus far:

© Bettmann/CORBIS

   I. Car is special because it was a gift from Dad

   II. Fun to drive

   III. Looks great—new paint job

   IV. Engine in top condition

   V. Custom features

   VI. Car shows—fun to be part of

After looking at your outline, you see that some of your categories overlap and could be part of the same discussion. For example, your thoughts about the engine are actually part of the discussion of "fun to drive," and "custom features" are what make the car look great. Moreover, the outline may help you discover new ideas—custom features could be divided into those on the interior as well as those on the exterior of the car. The revised outline might look like this:

   I. Gift from Dad

   II. Fun to drive
      A. Engine
      B. Steering

   III. Looks great
      A. New paint job
      B. Custom features
         1. exterior
         2. interior

   IV. Car shows

You could continue playing with this outline, even moving big chunks of it around; for example, you might decide that what really makes the car so special is that it was a graduation gift from your dad, and that is the note you want to end on. So you move "I. Gift from Dad" down to the last position in your outline.

The important point to remember about an informal or working outline is that it is there to help you—not control you. The value of an outline is its ability to help you plan, to help you see logical connections between your ideas, and to help you see obvious places to add new ideas and details. (The informal outline is also handy to keep around in case you're interrupted for a long period while you're drafting; you can always check the outline to see where you were and where you were going when you stopped.) In other words, *don't be intimidated by the outline!*

Here's one more example of an informal outline, this time for the thesis and essay map on the library reserve facility, from Chapter 2:

Essay Map: Unpredictable hours, poor staffing, and inadequate space make the library's reserve facility difficult for students to use.

    I. Unpredictable hours
       A. Hours of operation vary from week to week
       B. Unannounced closures
       C. Closed on some holidays, open on others

    II. Poor staffing
       A. Uninformed personnel at reserve desk
       B. Too few on duty at peak times

    III. Inadequate space
       A. Room too small for number of users
       B. Too few chairs, tables
       C. Weak lighting

You may have more than three points to make in your essay. And, as explained earlier, you may need more than one paragraph to discuss a single point. For instance, you might discover that you need two paragraphs to explain fully the many services at the Study Skills Centre (for advice on splitting the discussion of a single point into two or more paragraphs, see pages 61–62). At this stage, you needn't bother trying to guess whether you'll need more than one paragraph per point; just use the outline to get going. Most writers don't know how much they have to say before they begin writing—and that's fine because writing itself is an act of discovery and learning.

When you are ready to begin drafting, read Chapter 5 for advice on composing and revising. Remember, too, that Chapter 5 contains suggestions for beating writer's block, should this condition arise while you are working on any part of your essay, as well as some specific hints on formatting your draft that may make revision easier (pages 89–93).

■ Composing the Body Paragraphs

There are many ways to organize and develop body paragraphs. Paragraphs developed by common patterns, such as example, comparison, and definition, will be discussed in specific chapters in Part Two; at this point, however, here are some comments about the general nature of all good body paragraphs that should help as you draft your essay.

REMEMBER: Most of the body paragraphs in your essay will profit from a focused *topic sentence*. In addition, body paragraphs should have adequate *development, unity,* and *coherence*.

■ The Topic Sentence

Most body paragraphs present one main point in your discussion, expressed in a *topic sentence*. The topic sentence of a body paragraph has three important functions:

1. It supports the thesis by clearly stating a main point in the discussion.

2. It announces what the paragraph will be about.

3. It controls the subject matter of the paragraph. The entire discussion—the examples, details, and explanations—in a particular paragraph must directly relate to and support the topic sentence.

Think of a body paragraph (or a single paragraph) as a kind of mini-essay in itself. The topic sentence is, in a sense, a smaller thesis. It too asserts one main idea on a limited subject that the writer can explain or argue in the rest of the paragraph. Like the thesis, the topic sentence should be stated in as specific language as possible.

To see how a topic sentence works in a body paragraph, study this sample:

Essay Thesis: The Study Skills Centre is an excellent place for students who need academic help.

Topic Sentence
1. The topic sentence supports the thesis by stating a main point (one reason that the Centre provides excellent academic help).
2. The topic sentence announces the subject matter of the paragraph (a variety of free services that improve basic skills).
3. The topic sentence controls the subject matter (all the examples—the mini-course, the tutoring, the seminars, and the testing—support the claim of the topic sentence).

The Centre offers students a variety of free services designed to improve basic skills. Those who discover their study habits are poor, for instance, may enroll in a six-week mini-course in study skills that offers advice on such topics as how to read a text, take notes, and organize material for review. Students whose math or writing skills are below par can sign up for free tutoring sessions held five days a week throughout each semester. In addition, the Centre presents weekly seminars on special topics such as stress management and overcoming test anxiety for those students who are finding university more of a nerve-wracking experience than they expected; other students can attend evening seminars in such worthwhile endeavours as spelling or vocabulary building. Finally, the Centre offers a series of tests to identify the presence of any learning disabilities, such as dyslexia, that might prevent a student from succeeding academically. With such a variety of free services, the Centre can help almost any student.

Here's another example from the essay on the library reserve:

Essay Thesis: The library's reserve facility is difficult for students to use.

Topic Sentence

1. The topic sentence supports the thesis by stating a main point (one reason that the facility is difficult to use).
2. The topic sentence announces the subject matter of the paragraph (the unpredictable hours).
3. The topic sentence controls the subject matter (all the examples—the changing hours, the sudden closures, the erratic holiday schedule—support the claim of the topic sentence).

The library reserve facility's unpredictable hours frustrate even the most dedicated students. Instructors who place articles on reserve usually ask students to read them by a certain date. Too often, however, students arrive at the reserve desk only to find it closed. The facility's open hours change from week to week: students who used the room last week on Tuesday morning may discover that this week on Tuesday the desk is closed, which means another trip. Perhaps even more frustrating are the facility's sudden, unannounced closures. Some of these closures allow staff members to have lunch or go on breaks, but, again, they occur without notice on no regular schedule. A student arrives, as I did two weeks ago, at the desk to find a "Be Back Soon" sign. In my case, I waited for nearly an hour. Another headache is the holiday schedule, which is difficult to figure out. For example, this year the reserve room was closed without advance notice on Remembrance Day but open on Easter; open during Winter Break but closed some days during Spring Break, a time many students use to catch up on their reserve assignments. Overall, the reserve facility would be much easier for students to use if it adopted a set schedule of operating hours, announced these times each semester, and maintained them.

Always be sure your topic sentences actually support the particular thesis of your essay. For example, the second topic sentence presented here doesn't belong in the essay promised by the thesis:

Thesis: The salmon fishing quota should be increased because it financially aids people in our province.

Topic Sentences

1. Fees for fishing licenses help pay for certain free, province-supported social services.
2. Controlled fishing helps keep the salmon population properly regulated.
3. Salmon fishing offers a means of obtaining free food for those people with low incomes.

Although topic sentence 2 is about salmon and may be true, it doesn't support the thesis's emphasis on financial aid and therefore should be tossed out of this essay.

Here's another example:

Thesis: During the last forty years, Canadian literature has actively embraced Canada's multicultural heritage.

Topic Sentences

1. Before the 1960s, even Canadian universities did not really acknowledge the existence of "CanLit."

2. Many immigrants whose first language isn't English have been writing some of the new classics of Canadian literature.

3. As a result, the patterns and rhythms of Canadian language have shifted in this new Canadian literature.

4. Two common and intertwining themes of this multicultural literature are linguistic and spatial identities.

Topic sentences 2, 3, and 4 all discuss the characteristics of multicultural Canadian literature. But topic sentence 1 focuses on the institutional legitimization of Canadian literature, rather than on its multicultural aspects. Although it does talk about Canadian literature, it doesn't illustrate the claim of this particular thesis.

Sometimes a topic sentence needs only to be rewritten or slightly recast to fit:

Thesis: The recent tuition hike may discourage students from attending our university.

Topic Sentences

1. Students already pay more here than at other schools in the province.
2. Out-of-province students will have to pay an additional "penalty" to attend.
3. Tuition funds should be used for scholarships.

As written, topic sentence 3 doesn't show why students won't want to attend the school. However, a rewritten topic sentence does support the thesis:

3. Because the tuition money will not be used for scholarships, some students may not be able to afford this higher priced school.

In other words, always check carefully to make sure that *all* your topic sentences clearly support your thesis's assertion.

Focusing Your Topic Sentence

A vague, fuzzy, or unfocused topic sentence most often leads to a paragraph that touches only on the surface of its subject or that wanders away from the writer's main idea. On the other hand, a topic sentence that is tightly focused and stated precisely will not only help the reader to understand the point of the paragraph but will also help you select, organize, and develop your supporting details.

Look, for example, at these unfocused topic sentences and their revisions:

Unfocused	Too many people treat animals badly in experiments. [What people? Badly how? What kinds of experiments?]
Focused	The cosmetic industry often harms animals in unnecessary experiments designed to test their products.

Unfocused	Grades are an unfair pain in the neck. [Again, the focus is too broad. All grades? Unfair how?]
Focused	A course grade based on one multiple-choice exam doesn't accurately measure a student's knowledge of the subject.
Unfocused	Getting the right job is important and can lead to rewarding experiences. [Note both vague language and a double focus—"important" and "can lead to rewarding experiences."]
Focused	Getting the right job can lead to an improved sense of self-esteem.

Before you practise writing focused topic sentences, you may wish to review the advice on composing good thesis statements (pages 32–39), as the same rules generally apply.

Placing Your Topic Sentence

Although the topic sentence most frequently occurs as the first sentence in the body paragraph, it also often appears as the second or last sentence. A topic sentence that directly follows the first sentence of a paragraph usually does so because the first sentence provides an introductory statement or some kind of "hook" to the preceding paragraph. A topic sentence frequently appears at the end of a paragraph that first presents particular details and then concludes with its central point. Here are two paragraphs in which the topic sentences do not appear first:

Introductory sentence

Topic sentence

Millions of Canadians watch the Canadian television channel, the Food Network. However, some of the most popular cooking programs come, not from Canada, but from England, a country traditionally associated with good manners and poor cuisine. *Gordon Ramsay, a respected and enormously successful chef and restaurateur, hosts a series of similar programs with titles such as Ramsay's Kitchen Nightmares and Hell's Kitchen.* In these programs, Ramsay certainly does demonstrate how to cook delicious foods made from fresh, local ingredients, thus exploding the stereotype that all British food is bland, boring, and unhealthy. But audiences really watch his programs for his demolition of the other great stereotype about the British: that they are infallibly well-behaved. Ramsay's episodes are each highly dramatic, as the star chef shouts at and insults all those around him, often reducing the mostly inexperienced chefs around him to tears. The combination of great recipes and pugnacious attitude appears to be a winning one.

In the preceding paragraph, the first sentence serves as an introduction leading directly to the topic sentence. In the following example, the writer places the topic sentence last to sum up the information in the paragraph:

Even during Grey Owl's lifetime, many newspaper editors and First Nations leaders knew that this Ojibway activist was really an Englishman named Archie Belaney. They also knew that he was a heavy drinker who had "married" five women, and abandoned his daughter. It was felt that Grey Owl's messages were only heard because of his authority as a clean-living "wild man" in tune with the land. The tacit agreement of his contemporaries to remain silent about his true identity may have allowed his messages about wilderness conservation to be taken seriously, and to influence future environmentalists. *If it is true that the man and his message were the same, should Grey Owl's passionate call to save and preserve the Canadian landscape and its animals be now discounted because we know*

Topic sentence   *that the "wild man" was also a representative of some of the worst vices of civilization?*

As you can see, the position of topic sentences largely depends on what you are trying to do in your paragraph. And it's true that the purposes of some paragraphs are so obvious that no topic sentences are needed. However, while you are building up your skills, you may want to practise putting your topic sentences first for a while to help you organize and unify your paragraphs.

Some paragraphs with a topic sentence near the beginning also contain a concluding sentence that makes a final, general comment based on the supporting details. The last sentence below, for example, re-emphasizes the main point of the paragraph.

Topic sentence   *Venice, a city with a rich historical past, faces a terrifying future.* The canals that charm visitors in the summer also signal the very real possibility that Venice will one day sink beneath the water. Each year, the rains make the canals overflow to flood the city a little more deeply than the year before. Already many of the ancient canalside palaces have begun to crumble and their occupants have been forced to move to higher storeys. For years, engineers have tried to put in defences, such as ingenious dams and other barriers to counteract the failing engineering that has been holding up the city in the first place. The urgency of the situation increases every year as scientists

Concluding sentence   measure the rising levels of water. *Effective solutions must be found soon, or Venice's time will run out.*

Warning: Although topic sentences may appear in different places in a paragraph, there is one common error you should be careful to avoid. Do *not* put a topic sentence at the end of one body paragraph that belongs to the paragraph that follows it. For example, let's suppose you were writing an essay discussing a job you had held recently, one that you enjoyed because of the responsibilities you were given, the training program you participated in, and the interaction you experienced with your coworkers. The body paragraph describing your responsibilities may end with its own topic sentence or with a concluding sentence about those responsibilities. However, that paragraph should not end with a sentence such as "Another excellent feature of this job was the training program for the next level of management." This "training program" sentence belongs in the *following* body paragraph as its topic sentence. Similarly, you would not end the paragraph on the training program with a topic sentence praising your experience with your coworkers.

If you feel your paragraphs are ending too abruptly, consider using a concluding sentence, as described previously. Later in this chapter you will also learn some ways to smooth the way from one paragraph to the next by using transitional devices and "idea hooks" (pages 68–72). For now, remember: do *not* place a topic sentence that introduces and controls paragraph "B" at the end of paragraph "A." In other words, always place your topic sentence in the paragraph to which it belongs, to which it is topic-related, not at the end of the preceding paragraph.

■ PRACTISING WHAT YOU'VE LEARNED

A. Point out the topic sentences in the following paragraphs; identify those paragraphs that also contain concluding sentences. Cross out any stray topic sentences that belong elsewhere.

1 Insulin, a widely available serum, is now the standard treatment for diabetes. But until 1922, when University of Toronto scientists Frederick Banting, John James Richard Macleod, Charles Best, and James Bertram Collip first tested insulin on human patients, diabetics could only expect blindness, lost limbs, and shortened life spans. The treatments of diabetes varied, often consisting of starvation diets, and were generally unsuccessful because doctors could not identify the exact cause of the body's sugar imbalance. Once Banting and his colleagues discovered insulin's role in converting sugar into energy, they focused on manufacturing this naturally occurring hormone so it could be administered to those patients who lacked it. The success of insulin was almost instantly evident, and, due to Banting and his colleagues' selfless decision not to patent it themselves, this life-saving medicine continues to be affordably manufactured for the millions of diabetic sufferers around the world.

2 Louis Riel, a controversial figure in Canadian history, and today acknowledged as the founder of Manitoba, was a hero to the Métis and to many French Canadians. But in English Canada, his First Nations ancestry and his Catholicism made all his actions and his motives suspect. For them, his status as a "half-breed" negated his many accomplishments, such as the securing of some French language rights and the establishment of Manitoba as a province. Although he was thrice elected to the House of Commons, he was never allowed to take his seat there. He was even exiled from Canada, partly due to his role in the execution of an English-Canadian soldier, and he became an American citizen. On his return to Canada, his continued agitation for fair land settlements for the Métis convinced John A. Macdonald's government to arrest and eventually take the controversial step of executing him. The dramatic end to Riel's life ensured this larger-than-life leader's position as an inspiration to Canadians for generations.

3 Almost every wedding tradition has a symbolic meaning that originated centuries ago. For example, couples have been exchanging rings to symbolize unending love for over a thousand years. Most often, the rings are worn on the third finger of the left hand, which was thought to contain a vein that ran directly to the heart. The rings in ancient times were sometimes made of braided grass, rope, or leather, giving rise to the expression "tying the knot." Another tradition, the bridal veil, began

when marriages were arranged by the families and the groom was not allowed to see his choice until the wedding. The tossing of rice at newlyweds has long signified fertility blessings, and the sweet smell of the bride's bouquet was present to drive away evil spirits, who were also diverted by the surrounding bridal attendants. Weddings may vary enormously today, but many couples still include ancient traditions to signify the beginning of their new life together.

4   Buying mountain gear that suits your individual abilities and needs is a tricky business. When you enter a big, well-equipped store of sporting goods, you may well be confused by the array of choices the store offers. The boots that promise the greatest durability and safety may not be comfortable on your feet, the most thoroughly insulated jacket might feel too tight on you for easy arm movement, and the wrap-around goggles you think look so smart on you might sit too heavily on the bridge of your nose. All of these are potential sources of discomfort at best and of actual hazard at the worst. Store assistants are not necessarily your best advisers in making your choices. Unless you have a helpful friend who is also an experienced climber or hiker, you will just have to trust your instinct and be prepared to get what really suits you by trial and—only too often—expensive error.

B. Rewrite these topic sentences so that they are clear and focused rather than fuzzy, too broad, or too informal.

   1. His party's policies have changed a lot in the last year.

   2. The performance turned out to be really great.

   3. The movie's special effects were incredible.

   4. The Canada Day celebration was more fun than ever before.

   5. The articles in this journal are useless.

C. Add topic sentences to the following paragraphs:

First, the airlines will keep putting up their ticket prices, which will mean fewer people will take international flights just for pleasure trips. Then cruise ship fares will be raised, and even local ferries will add higher and higher fuel surcharges to their regular prices, which will mean people will choose their travel destinations as well as their frequency more carefully. Travellers used to taking their RVs, trucks, and SUVs on road trips will find it difficult to go too far away, as the cost of gas will make a big difference to the amount they can spend on campground or hotel bills, food, and entertainment.

A 1950s felt skirt with Elvis's picture on it, for example, now sells for $150, and Elvis scarves go for as much as $200. Elvis handkerchiefs, originally 50 cents or less, fetch $150 in today's market, as do wallets imprinted with the singer's face. Original posters from the Rock King's movies can sell for $500, and cards from the chewing gum series can run $30 apiece. Perhaps one of the most expensive collectors' items is the Emene Elvis guitar that can cost a fan at least $1000, regardless of musical condition.

When successful playwright Jean Kerr once checked into a hospital, the receptionist asked her occupation and was told, "Writer." The receptionist said, "I'll just put down 'housewife.'" Similarly, when a British official asked W. H. Auden, the award-winning poet and essayist, what he did for a living, Auden replied, "I'm a writer." The official jotted down "no occupation."

In his novel *The Wars,* Timothy Findley mixes the historical with the fictional as he draws a sweeping portrait of the confusion of the First World War as seen through the eyes of a Canadian soldier, Robert Ross. That mixture of real and imagined creates a sense of authenticity that pulls the reader into the action, making him or her feel the same confusion and outrage as Ross at the waste, viciousness, and incompetence he sees around him. Pat Barker's *Regeneration* trilogy also looks at First World War experiences through the eyes of the individual, but she focuses the experiences through many individuals, rather than one. Like Findley, she uses historical research to create language, attitudes, and relationships that, in their socio-historical accuracy, are hauntingly immediate.

D. Write a focused topic sentence for five of the following subjects:

1. Job interviews
2. Museum design
3. Activism
4. Technology
5. Money
6. Internet and privacy
7. Music
8. Knowledge
9. Housing
10. Forensic crime solving

■ ASSIGNMENT

Review the thesis statements with essay maps you wrote for the practice exercise on page 43. Choose two, and from each thesis create at least three topic sentences for possible body paragraphs.

■ APPLYING WHAT YOU'VE LEARNED TO *YOUR* WRITING

If you currently have a working thesis statement you have written in response to an assignment in your composition class, try sketching out an outline or a plan for the major ideas you wish to include. After you write a draft, underline the topic sentences in your body paragraphs. Do your topic sentences directly support your thesis? If you find that they do not clearly support your thesis, you must decide if you need to revise your draft's organization or whether you have, in fact, discovered a new, and possibly better, subject to write about. If the latter is true, you'll need to re-draft your essay so that your readers will not be confused by a paper that announces one subject but discusses another. (See Chapter 5 for more information on revising your drafts.)

■ Paragraph Development

Possibly the most serious—and most common—weakness of all essays by novice writers is *the lack of effectively developed body paragraphs.* The information in each paragraph must adequately explain, exemplify, define, or in some other way support your topic sentence. Therefore, you must include *enough supporting information* or *evidence* in each paragraph to make your readers understand your topic sentence. Moreover, you must make the information in the paragraph clear and specific enough for the readers to accept your ideas.

The next paragraph is *underdeveloped.* Although the topic sentence promises a discussion of David Suzuki as a Cassandra figure, the paragraph does not provide enough specific supporting evidence (in this case, examples) to explain this view of the environmental activist.

> Although many people today see David Suzuki as the Canadian scientist most responsible for our awareness of environmental issues, in the 1980s and early 1990s, he was often more like Cassandra, the Trojan princess cursed with being disbelieved though she had the gift of foretelling the truth. Suzuki disseminated his message by television and through lectures all over the country. People finally began to listen when other scientists said the same things and the effects of global warming became too serious to ignore.

Rewritten, the paragraph might read as follows:

> Although many people today see David Suzuki as the Canadian scientist most responsible for our awareness of environmental issues, in the 1980s and early 1990s, he was often more like Cassandra, the Trojan princess cursed with being disbelieved though she had the gift of foretelling the truth. Even if he showed dried-up rivers, dying forests, and diseased animals on his television program, *The Nature of Things*, he was accused of being an alarmist who was manipulating data to feed his own paranoia. When, during lecture tours he spoke of the dangers of global warming, his opponents were quick to say that recent weather patterns were an anomaly, and were certainly not caused by human behaviour, as Suzuki claimed. However, as the effects of global warming began to touch people personally, especially with new patterns of extreme or unusual weather conditions, such as snow in Australia in summer, Suzuki's credibility began to increase. People finally began to listen when other scientists said the same things as Suzuki, and the effects of global warming became too serious to ignore.

The topic sentence promises a discussion of Suzuki's methods of making society aware of environmental issues and delivers just that by citing specific examples found in his television program and his lectures. The paragraph is, therefore, better developed.

The following paragraph offers reasons but no specific examples or details to support those claims:

> Living with my ex-roommate was unbearable. First, she thought everything she owned was the best. Second, she possessed numerous filthy habits. Finally, she constantly exhibited immature behaviour.

The writer might provide more evidence this way:

> Living with my ex-roommate was unbearable. First, she thought everything she owned, from clothes to cosmetics, was the best. If someone complimented my pants, she'd point out that her designer jeans looked better and would last longer because they were made of better material. If she borrowed my shampoo, she'd let me know that it didn't get her hair as clean and shiny as hers did. My hand cream wasn't as smooth; my sunscreen lotion wasn't as protective; not even my wire clothes hangers were as good as her padded ones! What's more, despite her pickiness about products, she had numerous filthy habits. Her dirty dishes remained in the sink for days before she felt the need to wash them. Piles of the "best" brand of tissues were regularly discarded from her upper bunk and strewn about the floor. Her desk and closets overflowed with heaps of dirty clothes, books, cosmetics, and whatever else she owned, and she rarely brushed her teeth (when she did brush, she left oozes of toothpaste in the sink). Finally, she constantly acted immaturely by throwing tantrums when things didn't go her way. A poor grade on an exam or paper, for example, meant books, shoes, or any other small object within her reach would hit the wall flying. Living with such a person taught me some valuable lessons about how not to win friends or keep roommates.

By adding more supporting evidence—specific examples and details—to this paragraph, the writer has a better chance of convincing the reader of the roommate's real character.

Where does evidence come from? Where do writers find their supporting information? Evidence comes from many sources. Personal experiences, memories, observations, hypothetical examples, reasoned arguments, facts, statistics, testimony from authorities, many kinds of studies and research—all these and more can help you make your points clear and persuasive. In the paragraph on David Suzuki, for example, the writer relied on recorded evidence from his television programs and public appearances. The paragraph on the obnoxious roommate was supported by examples gained through the writer's personal observation. The kind of supporting evidence you choose for your paragraphs depends on your purpose and your audience; as the writer, you must decide what will work best to make your readers understand and accept each important point in your discussion. Keep in mind that, generally, essays written for university- or college-level courses will be expected to use evidence from objective, published studies more than from personal experiences and memories, though these could be good starting points. (For advice on ways to think critically about evidence, see Chapter 5; for more information on incorporating research material into your essays, see Chapter 14.)

Having a well-developed paragraph is more than a matter of adding material or expanding length, however. The information in each paragraph must effectively explain or support your topic sentence. *Vague generalities or repetitious ideas are not convincing.* Look, for example, at the following paragraph, in which the writer offers only generalities:

> We ought to ban the use of cell phones in moving vehicles. Some people who have them think they're a really good idea but a lot of us don't agree. Using a phone while driving causes too many dangerous accidents to happen, and even if there's no terrible accident, people using them have been known to do some really stupid things in traffic. Drivers using phones are constantly causing

problems for other drivers; pedestrians are in big trouble from these people too. I think car phone use is getting to be a really dangerous nuisance and we ought to do something about it soon.

This paragraph is weak because it is composed of repetitious general statements using vague, unclear language. None of its general statements is supported with specific evidence. Why is car phone use not a "good" idea? How does it cause accidents? What are the "problems" and "trouble" the writer refers to? What exactly does "do something about it" mean? The writer obviously had some ideas in mind, but these ideas are not clear to the reader because they are not adequately developed with specific evidence and language.

By adding supporting examples and details, the writer might revise the paragraph this way:

Although cell phones may be a time-saving convenience for busy people, they are too distracting for use by drivers of moving vehicles, whose lack of full attention poses a serious threat to other drivers and to pedestrians. The simple act of dialling or answering a phone, for example, may take a driver's eyes away from traffic signals or other cars. Moreover, involvement in a complex or emotional conversation could slow down a driver's response time just when fast action is needed to avoid an accident. Last week I drove behind a man using his cell phone. As he drove and talked, I could see him gesturing wildly, obviously agitated with the other caller. His speed repeatedly slowed and then picked up, slowed and increased, and his car drifted more than once, on a street frequently crossed by schoolchildren. Because the man was clearly not in full, conscious control of his driving, he was dangerous. My experience is not isolated; a recent study by the Foundation for Traffic Safety has discovered that using a cell phone is far more distracting to drivers than listening to the radio or talking to a rider. With additional studies in progress, voters should soon be able to demand legislation to restrict phone use to passengers or to drivers when the vehicles are not in motion.

The reader now has a better idea why the writer feels such cell phone use is distracting and, consequently, dangerous. By using two hypothetical examples (looking away, slowed response time), one personal experience (observing the agitated man), and one reference to research (the safety study), the writer offers the reader three kinds of supporting evidence for the paragraph's claim.

After examining the following two paragraphs, decide which explains its point more effectively.

1   Competing in an Ironman triathlon is one of the most demanding feats known to amateur athletes. First, they have to swim many miles and that takes a lot of endurance. Then they ride a bicycle a long way, which is also hard on their bodies. Last, they run a marathon, which can be difficult in itself but is especially hard after the first two events. Competing in the triathlon is really tough on the participants.

2   Competing in an Ironman triathlon is one of the most demanding feats known to amateur athletes. During the first stage of the triathlon, the competitors must swim 3.9 km (2.4 miles) in the open ocean. They have to battle

the constantly choppy ocean, the strong currents, and the frequent swells. The wind is often an adversary, and stinging jellyfish are a constant threat. Once they have completed the ocean swim, the triathletes must ride 180 km (112 miles) on a bicycle. In addition to the strength needed to pedal that far, the bicyclists must use a variety of hand grips to assure the continued circulation in their fingers and hands as well as to ease the strain on the neck and shoulder muscles. Moreover, the concentration necessary to steady the bicycle as well as the attention to the inclines on the course and the consequent shifting of gears causes mental fatigue for the athletes. After completing these two gruelling segments, the triathletes must then run 42 km (26.2 miles), the length of a regular marathon. Dehydration is a constant concern as is the prospect of cramping. Even the pain and swelling of a friction blister can be enough to eliminate a contestant at this late stage of the event. Finally, disorientation and fatigue can set in and distort the athlete's judgment. Competing in an Ironman triathlon takes incredible physical and mental endurance.

The first paragraph contains, for the most part, repetitious generalities; it repeats the same idea (the triathlon is hard work) and gives few specific details to illustrate the point presented in the topic sentence. The second paragraph, however, does offer many specific examples and details—the exact distances, the currents, jellyfish, inclines, grips, blisters, and so forth—that help the reader understand why the event is so demanding.

Joseph Conrad, the famous novelist, once remarked that a writer's purpose was to use "the power of the written word to make you hear, to make you feel . . . before all, to make you *see*. That—and no more, and it is everything." By using specific details instead of vague, general statements, you can write an interesting, convincing essay. Ask yourself as you revise your paragraphs, "Have I provided enough information, presented enough clear, precise details to make my readers see what I want them to?" In other words, a well-developed paragraph effectively makes its point with *an appropriate amount of specific supporting evidence.* (Remember that a handwritten paragraph in a rough draft will look much shorter when it is typed. Therefore, if you can't think of much to say about a particular idea, you should gather more information or consider dropping it as a major point in your essay.)

■ Paragraph Length

"How long is a good paragraph?" is a question novice writers often ask. Like a teacher's lecture or a preacher's sermon, paragraphs should be long enough to accomplish their purpose and short enough to be interesting. In truth, there is no set length, no prescribed number of lines or sentences, for any of your paragraphs. In a body paragraph, your topic sentence presents the main point, and the rest of the paragraph must give enough supporting evidence to convince the reader. Although too much unnecessary or repetitious detail is boring, too little discussion will leave the reader uninformed, unconvinced, or confused.

Although paragraph length varies, beginning writers should avoid the one- or two-sentence paragraphs frequently seen in newspapers or magazine articles. (Journalists have their own rules to follow; paragraphs are shorter in newspapers because large masses of print in narrow columns are difficult to read quickly.) Essay writers do occasionally use the one-sentence paragraph, most often to produce some special effect, when the statement is especially dramatic or significant and needs to call attention to itself or when an emphatic transition is needed. For now, however, you should concentrate on writing well-developed body paragraphs.

One more note on paragraph length: sometimes you may discover that a particular point in your essay is so complex that your paragraph is growing far too long—well over a typed page, for instance. If this problem occurs, look for a logical place to divide your information and start a new paragraph. For example, you might see a convenient dividing point between a series of actions you're describing or a break in the chronology of a narrative or between explanations of arguments or examples. Just make sure you begin your next paragraph with some sort of transitional phrase or key words to let the reader know you are still discussing the same point as before ("Still another problem caused by the computer's faulty memory circuit is . . .").

■ PRACTISING WHAT YOU'VE LEARNED

Analyze the following paragraphs. Explain how you might improve the development of each one.

1. Grizzlies are supposed to be really fierce, but a lot of this is just a myth. Charlie Russell, a Canadian bear expert, has done a lot of field research in Russia. He has shown that bears are intelligent and affectionate, and if we just treat them well, they are responsive to humans.

2. Newspaper advice columns are pretty silly. The problems are generally stupid or unrealistic, and the advice is out of touch with today's world. Too often the columnist just uses the letter to make a smart remark about some pet peeve. The columns could be put to some good uses, but no one tries very hard.

3. Driving tests do not adequately examine a person's driving ability. Usually the person being tested does not have to drive very far. The test does not require the skills that are used in everyday driving situations. Supervisors of driving tests tend to be very lenient.

4. Nursing homes are often sad places. They are frequently located in ugly old buildings unfit for anyone. The people there are lonely and bored. What's more, they're sometimes treated badly by the people who run the homes. It's a shame something better can't be done for the elderly.

5. Freud's research methods were always controversial, but his theories were influential. People who disagreed with him, both then and later, were still influenced, if only to offer contrasting conclusions in response to his. Today, his theories are largely rejected, but people continue to use some of his terminology. His methods of gathering and interpreting evidence were seen to be unscientific.

A. Select two of the paragraphs from above and rewrite them, adding enough specific details to make well-developed paragraphs.

B. Select a topic on which you've done some research. Write a paragraph composed of generalities and vague statements. Exchange this paragraph with a classmate's, and, after consulting each other's research notes, turn each other's faulty paragraph into a clearly developed one.

C. Find at least two well-developed paragraphs in an essay or book; explain why you think the two paragraphs are successfully developed.

■ APPLYING **W**HAT **Y**OU'VE **L**EARNED TO *YOUR* **W**RITING

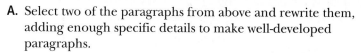

If you are currently drafting an essay, look closely at your body paragraphs. Find the topic sentence in each paragraph and circle the key words that most clearly communicate the main idea of the paragraph. Then ask yourself if the information in each paragraph effectively supports, explains, or illustrates the main idea of the paragraph's topic sentence. Is there enough information? If you're not sure, try numbering your supporting details. Are there too few to be persuasive? Are there too many details that then take you off topic or make your paragraph sound like a list? Does the paragraph present clear, specific supporting material that is directly connected with your topic sentence or does it contain too many vague generalities to be convincing? If you don't have enough evidence, where could you add more details to help the reader understand your ideas better and to make each paragraph more interesting? (For more help revising your paragraphs, see Chapter 5.)

■ Paragraph Unity

Every sentence in a body paragraph should relate directly to the main idea presented by the topic sentence. A paragraph must stick to its announced subject; it must not drift away into another discussion. In other words, a good paragraph has *unity*.

Examine the unified paragraph below; note that the topic sentence clearly states the paragraph's main point and that each sentence thereafter supports the topic sentence.

(1) In the early years of the twentieth century, a group of artists calling themselves the Group of Seven made it their active mission to modernize Canadian art and to give it its own, unique identity. (2) Though influenced by Impressionism, they still aimed to separate themselves from European schools of art. (3) They chose the Canadian landscape, both urban and natural, as their focus. (4) Yet it was not just their subject, but the boldness of execution, with

heavy brushstrokes, strong colours, and stylized shapes which defined their art. (5) The blend of the new artistic techniques inspired by the Impressionists and the use of their own landscape allowed the Group of Seven to redefine a Canadian artistic vision and, in turn, to influence several subsequent generations of Canadian artists.

The first sentence states the main idea, that the Group of Seven aimed to modernize and attempt to create specifically Canadian art, and the other sentences support this assertion:

Topic Sentence: The Group of Seven had a mission to create new and specifically Canadian art

- **(2)** influenced by Impressionists but still different from them and other European schools
- **(3)** focus on Canadian landscape
- **(4)** subject, bold execution, heavy brushstrokes, strong colours, stylized shapes
- **(5)** blend of Impressionist techniques and Canadian landscape created new, uniquely Canadian and influential art

Now look at the next paragraph, in which the writer strays from his original purpose:

(1) Cigarette smoke is unhealthy even for people who don't have the nicotine habit themselves. (2) Secondhand smoke can cause asthmatics and sufferers of sinusitis serious problems. (3) Doctors regularly advise heart patients to avoid confined smoky areas because coronary attacks might be triggered by the lack of clean air. (4) Moreover, having the smell of smoke in one's hair and clothes is a real nuisance. (5) Even if a person is without any health problems, exhaled smoke doubles the amount of carbon monoxide in the air, a condition that may cause lung problems in the future.

Sentence 4 refers to smoke as a nuisance and therefore does not belong in a paragraph that discusses smoking as a health hazard to nonsmokers.

Sometimes a large portion of a paragraph will drift into another topic. In the paragraph below, did the writer wish to focus on the metaphor of bingo, on injustice, or on Highway's knowledge of life on a reservation?

Thomson Highway's play *The Rez Sisters* examines the lives of a group of women who live on a reservation in Ontario. They are all connected in some way, not only by blood, marriage, poverty or trauma, but by their dreams of going to the "biggest bingo in the world," held in Toronto. While this goal initially appears humorous and trivial, it reveals itself to be a profound metaphor for life. As long as that dream is possible, all is possible, whether it is the acquisition of a new toilet or a new life away from the cycles of poverty and limited choices on the reservation. When the women do finally achieve this dream, and some even win at the bingo game, there is a sense that a few injustices in these women's lives have been redressed. Highway's choice of the bingo game as a central activity in this community reflects his intimate knowledge of reservation life.

Note shift from the topic of the significance of the dream of going to the bingo game

There are many ideas in this paragraph. The idea of bingo as "a profound metaphor for life" could be the central idea of this paragraph and explained in more detail, and the idea of injustice might be brought up earlier. The writer seems to move in a different direction by talking about Highway's authority on this subject at the end of the paragraph.

Also beware of a tendency to end your paragraph with a new idea. A new point calls for an entirely new paragraph. For example, the following paragraph focuses on the financial success of publishers of the Harry Potter novels; the last sentence, on Rowling's effect on readers, should be omitted or moved to a paragraph on her influence on revitalizing reading as an activity for young people.

> The Harry Potter novels, written by British author J.K. Rowling, have been the publishing phenomenon of the turn of the twenty-first century. The history of their publication is almost legendary: when Rowling initially submitted the manuscript of *Harry Potter and the Philosopher's Stone* to major publishers, they didn't want to take a chance, and she was rejected. Fortunately, some smaller publishers, including Canada's Raincoast Books, saw a potential the big publishing houses missed, and their initial faith in Rowling won them exclusive contracts to publish the entire series of seven books. It is not just the publication of the original texts or of their translations or of the brief supplemental texts written by Rowling herself that has made the publishers' fortunes. There is a great deal of supplemental merchandise (unrelated to the film merchandise), such as trading cards and bookmarks that has added to the publishers' profits.
>
> Breaks unity *Rowling is perhaps the most popular and successful living children's author today, and her books have influenced many young people to start reading again.*

In general, think of paragraph unity in terms of the diagram below:

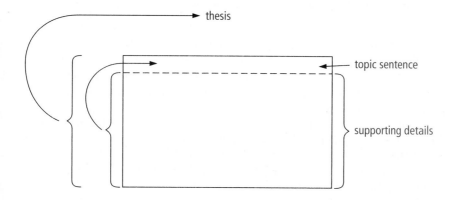

The sentences in the paragraph support the paragraph's topic sentence; the paragraph, in turn, supports the thesis statement.

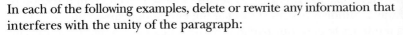

■ PRACTISING WHAT YOU'VE LEARNED

In each of the following examples, delete or rewrite any information that interferes with the unity of the paragraph:

1 Conservation means the proper use of nature's resources. The problem with industrial society is that people will simply not cut back on their consumption, and manufacturers, particularly those who produce luxury goods such as cosmetics or special fabrics or even coffee-table books, will keep tempting consumers with an ever-expanding array of goods that we don't really need. Last year alone saw the publication of over a thousand books and articles detailing the destruction of animal habitats. A great irony, however, is that those who cry foul over clear-cutting see no self-contradiction in churning out thousand page briefs exhorting others to conserve our forests. Not that capitalist greed is a minor evil. Who cares for nature's laws when another cent can be made by dumping mine runoffs in a mountain stream? Community groups, such as one in Coquitlam, British Columbia, routinely spend hundreds of hours cleaning up forest paths. But isn't it a shame that even lovers of the Great Canadian Outdoors think nothing of chopping down an acre of first-growth forest if that opens up a better view of the lake?

2 Health food is nothing but a silly fad encouraged by people who are trying to sell you some tasteless mush. Imagine having to buy a single apple for a whole two dollars! My neighbourhood in Montreal boasts of over a dozen "nutrition priority" food stores where every customer looks sick with anxiety and spends hundreds of dollars in search of a healthy life. Yet, to get to the store many of them drive no more than a couple of blocks, which actually works not only against the environment but their own muscle tone. People don't seem to realize that our car-dependency is as much to blame for our children's obesity as French fries.

3 As late as the 1870s, a Christian missionary in British Columbia was reporting in the *Boys' Own Magazine* that he had been present at a cannibal feast in a First Nations village. Incredible as this may sound, such was the stereotype of Native people fostered by British colonists in their quest to validate their territorial ambitions. The history of Canada's indigenous people is full of misrepresentation. No doubt many missionaries dedicated their lives to providing medical and educational services to Native peoples, and many admired their hardihood and bravery, but the religious zeal of the missionaries viewed the animistic faiths of communities such as the Haida and the Salish with revulsion and marked them as irrevocably debased. Ultimately, though, it was the need for political mastery that determined missionary intervention in indigenous culture.

4 The western provinces have often led the way in recognizing women's roles in politics. Nellie McClung, arguably the most significant activist in the history of women's suffrage in Canada, first started her long campaign for the vote when she lived in Winnipeg. She wrote a novel in 1908. She was well-known for her inspiring speeches and her tireless work to achieve women's rights. It was here in Winnipeg that she publicized her daring political stance by playing the role of Manitoba Premier Sir

Rodmond Roblin in the mock "Women's Parliament," an event sponsored by the Canadian Women's Press. Eventually, after moving to Edmonton in 1915, she joined four other Albertan women, Emily Murphy, Henrietta Muir Edwards, Louise McKinney, and Irene Parlby, to take on the government in the landmark "Persons Case," in which women were finally established as persons under the law under the British North America Act in 1929. McClung went on to fight for many other issues, including old age pensions and factory safety. She wrote a newspaper column. She also won a seat in the Alberta Legislature even before the Persons Case, and she had a voice in her province's parliament for five years.

■ APPLYING WHAT YOU'VE LEARNED TO *YOUR* WRITING

If you have written a draft of an essay, underline the topic sentence in each body paragraph and circle the key words. For example, if in an essay on Canada's growing health consciousness one of your topic sentences reads "In an effort to improve their health, Canadians have increased the number of vitamins they consume," you might circle "Canadians," "increased," and "vitamins." Then look closely at your paragraph. All the information in that paragraph should support the idea expressed in your topic sentence; nothing should detract from the idea of showing that Canadians have increased their vitamin consumption. A good way to make a sentence "about" something is to put your main idea close to the beginning of the sentence. Now study the paragraphs in your draft, one by one. Cross out any sentence or material that interferes with the ideas in your topic sentences. If one of your paragraphs begins to drift away from its topic-sentence idea, you will need to rethink the purpose of that paragraph and rewrite so that the reader will understand what the paragraph is about. (For additional help revising your drafts, turn to Chapter 5.)

■ Paragraph Coherence

In addition to unity, *coherence* is essential to a good paragraph. Coherence means that all the sentences and ideas in your paragraph flow together to make a clear, logical point about your topic. Your paragraph should not be a confusing collection of ideas set down in random order. The readers should be able to follow what you have written and see easily and quickly how each sentence grows out of, or is related to, the preceding sentence. To achieve coherence, you should have a smooth connection or transition between the sentences in your paragraphs.

There are five important means of achieving coherence in your paragraphs:

1. A natural or easily recognized order
2. Transitional words and phrases
3. Repetition of key words
4. Substitution of pronouns for key nouns
5. Parallelism

These transitional devices are similar to the couplings between railroad cars; they enable the controlling engine to pull the train of thought along as a unit.

A Recognizable Ordering of Information

Without consciously thinking about the process, you may often organize paragraphs in easily recognized patterns that give the reader a sense of logical movement and order. Four common patterns of ordering sentences in a paragraph are discussed next.

The Order of Time

Some paragraphs are composed of details arranged in chronological order. You might, for example, explain the process of changing an oil filter on your car by beginning with the first step, draining the old oil, and concluding with the last step, installing the new filter. Here is a paragraph on black holes in which the writer chronologically orders her details:

> A black hole in space, from all indications, is the result of the death of a star. Scientists speculate that stars were first formed from the gases floating in the universe at the beginning of time. In the first stage in the life of a star, the hot gas is drawn by the force of gravity into a burning sphere. In the middle stage— our own sun being a middle-aged star—the burning continues at a regular rate, giving off enormous amounts of heat and light. As it grows old, however, the star eventually explodes to become what is called a nova, a superstar. But gravity soon takes over again, and the exploded star falls back in on itself with such force that all the matter in the star is compacted into a mass no larger than a few miles in diameter. At this point, no heavenly body can be seen in that area of the sky, as the tremendous pull of gravity lets nothing escape, not even light. A black hole has thus been formed.

The Order of Space

When your subject is a physical object, you should select some orderly means of describing it: from left to right, top to bottom, inside to outside, and so forth. For example, you might describe a sculpture as you walk around it from front to back. Below is a paragraph describing a politician in which the writer has ordered the details of his description in a head-to-feet pattern.

> Steve was pure politician. His grey hair was always impeccably cut, and his matching eyes gave him a look of distinction until you realized those piercing looks were just a result of short-sightedness. He was rarely seen without a tie in tasteful dark colours, even when he was wearing otherwise casual clothes. His dark-coloured suits were well tailored and unobtrusively cut, so that he seemed elegant and at his ease at the same time. His self-confidence was most obviously on display, however, when, as he often did, he wore his signature silver cufflinks, which bore a tiny letter "S" engraved in diamonds.

Deductive Order

A paragraph ordered deductively moves from a generalization to particular details that explain or support the general statement. Perhaps the most common pattern of all paragraphs, the deductive paragraph begins with its topic sentence and proceeds to its supporting details, as illustrated in the following example:

> Despite the universally accepted truth that crime is steadily increasing in our society, some social historians suggest that the human species has, in fact, become less violent as it has evolved. None of the following behaviours are legally or even socially acceptable today. For example, while Shakespeare's company was performing during the sixteenth century, bear-baiting, or torturing a bear, was a common amusement in London, and raised no outcry. As Victor Hugo famously recorded, a nineteenth-century Frenchman could go to prison for years, or even be executed, for stealing bread. Heavy corporal punishment of children, both in homes and in schools, was the norm in many countries well into the twentieth century.

Inductive Order

An inductive paragraph begins with an examination of particular details and then concludes with a larger point or generalization about those details. Such a paragraph often ends with its topic sentence, as does the following paragraph on Little League hockey:

> At too many junior hockey games, one or another adult creates a minor scene by yelling rudely at an umpire or a coach. Similarly, it is not uncommon to hear adults whispering loudly to one another in the stands over which child should have made a missed goal. Perhaps the most astounding spectacle of all, however, is an irate parent or coach yanking a child off the ice after a bad play for a humiliating lecture in front of the whole team. Sadly, junior hockey today often seems intended more for childish adults than for the children who actually play it.

Transitional Words and Phrases

Some paragraphs may need internal transitional words to help the reader move smoothly from one thought to the next so that the ideas do not appear disconnected or choppy.

Here is a list of common transitional words and phrases and their uses:

giving examples	for example, for instance, specifically, in particular, namely, another, other
additions	also, as well as, in addition, moreover, furthermore
reasons	as a result of, because, the reason . . . is that
comparison	similarly, not only . . . but also, in comparison
contrast	although, but, while, in contrast, however, though, on the other hand
sequence	first . . . second . . . third, finally, moreover, also, in addition, next, then, after, furthermore, and
results	therefore, thus, consequently, as a result
changing direction	but, however, nonetheless, in contrast, on the other hand

Notice the difference the use of transitional words makes in the paragraphs below:

> Working in the neighbourhood grocery store as a checker was one of the worst jobs I've ever had. In the first place, I had to wear an ugly, scratchy uniform cut at least eight centimetres (three inches) too short. My schedule of working hours was another inconvenience; because my hours were changed each week, it was impossible to make plans in advance, and getting a day off was out of the question. In addition, the lack of working space bothered me. Except for a half-hour lunch break, I was restricted to less than a square metre of room behind the counter and consequently felt as if I were no more than a cog in the cash register.

The same paragraph rewritten without transitional words sounds choppy and childish:

> Working in the neighbourhood grocery store as a checker was one of the worst jobs I've ever had. I had to wear an ugly, scratchy uniform. It was cut at least eight centimetres (three inches) too short. My schedule of working hours was inconvenient. My hours changed each week. It was impossible to make plans in advance. Getting a day off was out of the question. The lack of working space bothered me. Except for a half-hour break, I was restricted to less than a square metre of room behind the counter. I felt like a cog in the cash register.

Although transitional words and phrases are useful in bridging the gaps between your ideas, don't overuse them. Not every sentence needs a transitional phrase, so use one only when the relationship between your thoughts needs clarification. It's also a mistake to place the transitional word in the same position in your sentence each time. Look at the paragraph that follows:

> It's a shame that every high-school student isn't required to take a course in first aid. *For example*, you might need to treat a friend or relative for drowning during a family picnic. Or, *for instance*, someone might break a bone or receive a snakebite on a camping trip. *Also*, you should always know what to do for a common cut or burn. *Moreover*, it's important to realize when someone is in shock. *However*, very few people take the time to learn the simple rules of first aid. *Thus*, many injured or sick people suffer more than they should. *Therefore*, everyone should take a first aid course in school or through the St. John Ambulance.

As you can see, a series of sentences each beginning with a transitional word quickly becomes repetitious and boring. To hold your readers' attention, use transitional words only when necessary to avoid choppiness, and vary their placement in your sentences.

Repetition of Key Words

Important words or phrases (and their synonyms) may be repeated throughout a paragraph to connect the thoughts into a coherent statement:

> One of the most common, and yet most puzzling, phobias is the *fear* of *snakes*. It's only natural, of course, to be afraid of a poisonous *snake*, but many people are just as frightened of the harmless varieties. For such people, a tiny

green grass *snake* is as terrifying as a cobra. Some researchers say this unreasonable *fear* of any and all *snakes* is a legacy left to us by our cave-dwelling ancestors, for whom these *reptiles* were a real and constant danger. Others maintain that the *fear* is a result of our associating the *snake* with the notion of evil, as in the Garden of Eden. Whatever the reason, the fact remains that for many otherwise normal people, the mere sight of a *snake* slithering through the countryside is enough to keep them city dwellers forever.

The repeated words "fear" and "snake" and the synonym "reptile" help tie one sentence to another so that the reader may follow the ideas easily.

Pronouns Substituted for Key Nouns

A pronoun is a word that stands for a noun. In your paragraph you may use a key noun in one sentence and then use a pronoun in its place in the following sentences. The pronoun "it" often replaces "shark" in the description that follows:

(1) The great white shark is perhaps the best equipped of all the ocean's predators. (2) *It* can grow up to 6.4 m (twenty-one feet) and weigh 2,722 kg (three tons), with 5-cm (two-inch) teeth that can replace themselves within twenty-four hours when damaged. (3) The shark's sense of smell is so acute *it* can detect 28.4 mL (one ounce) of fish blood in 28,400,00 mL (a million ounces) of water. (4) In addition, *it* can sense vibrations from 183 m (six hundred feet) away.

Sentences 2, 3, and 4 are tied to the topic sentence by the use of the pronoun "it."

Parallelism

Parallelism in a paragraph means using the same grammatical structure in several sentences to establish coherence. The repeated use of similar phrasing helps tie the ideas and sentences together. Next, for example, is a paragraph predominantly unified by its use of grammatically parallel sentences:

(1) The natural wonders of Vancouver offer something for everyone. (2) If you are the kind who likes to go skiing, a visit to Grouse Mountain will satisfy you. (3) If, on the other hand, you demand a bright sun to bake your skin a golden brown, visit any of the fourteen beaches dotting the city. (4) And for hardier souls, who ask from nature a show of force, the rapids of the Squamish River regularly challenge canoeists with unpredictable currents. (5) Finally, if you are the relaxed type, by all means stay in downtown Vancouver, where the sun may shine bravely at any time throughout the most torrential rainstorm.

The parallel structures of sentences 2, 3, and 5 ("if you" + verb) keep the paragraph flowing smoothly from one idea to the next.

Using a Variety of Transitional Devices

Most writers use a combination of transitional devices in their paragraphs. In the following example, three kinds of transitional devices are circled. See if you can identify each one.

(Transitions) are the (glue) that holds a (paragraph) together. These devices lead the reader from sentence to (sentence), smoothing over the (gaps) between by indicating the (relationship) between the (sentences). If this (glue) is missing, the (paragraph) will almost inevitably sound choppy or childish, even if every (sentence) in (it) responds to a single (topic) commitment. (However), (transitions) are not substitutes for (topic) unity: like most (glue), (they) are most effective when joining similar objects, (or, in this case), similar ideas. (For example), in a (paragraph) describing a chicken egg, no (transition) could bridge the (gap) created by the inclusion of the (sentence) concerned with naval losses in the First World War. (In other words), (transitions) can call attention to the (topic) (relationships) between (sentences), but (they) cannot create those (relationships).

Transitional words   repetition of pronouns   repetition of key words

---

■ PRACTISING WHAT YOU'VE LEARNED

A. Identify each of the following paragraphs as ordered by time, space, or parallelism:

1 My apartment is so small that it will no longer hold all my possessions. Every day when I come in the door, I am shocked by the clutter. The wall to my immediate left is completely obscured by art and movie posters that have become so numerous they often overlap, hiding even each other. Along the adjoining wall is my sound system: CDs are stacked several feet high on two long, low tables. The big couch that runs across the back of the room is always piled so high with schoolbooks and magazines that a guest usually ends up sitting on the floor. To my right is a large sliding glass door that opens onto a balcony—or at least it used to, before it was permanently blocked by my tennis gear, golf clubs, and mountain bike. Even the tiny closet next to the front door is bursting with clothes, both clean and dirty. I think the time has come for me to move.

2 Once-common acts of greeting may be finding renewed popularity after three centuries. According to one historian, kissing was at the height of its popularity as a greeting in seventeenth-century England, when ladies and gentlemen of the court often saluted each other in this affectionate manner. Then the country was visited

by a strange plague, whose cause was unknown. Because no one knew how the plague was spread, people tried to avoid physical contact with others as much as possible. Both kissing and the handshake went out of fashion and were replaced by the bow and curtsy, so people could greet others without having to touch them. The bow and curtsy remained in vogue for over a hundred years, until the handshake—for men only—returned to popularity in the nineteenth century. Today, both men and women may shake hands upon meeting others, and kissing as a greeting is making a comeback—especially among the jet setters and Hollywood stars.

3 Students have diverse ways of preparing for final exams. Some stay up the night before, trying to cram into their brains what they avoided all term. Others pace themselves, spending a little time each night going over the notes they took in class that day. Still others just cross their fingers, assuming they absorbed enough along the way from lectures and readings. In the end, though, everyone hopes the tests are easy.

B. Circle and identify the transitional devices in the following paragraphs:

Each year I follow a system when preparing firewood to use in my stove. First, I hike about 1.61 km (a mile) from my house with my bow saw in hand. I then select three good-sized oak trees and mark them with orange ties. Next, I saw through the base of each tree about 60 cm (two feet) from the ground. After I fell the trees, not only do I trim away the branches, but I also sort the scrap from the usable limbs. I find cutting the trees into manageable-length logs is too much for one day; however, I roll them off the ground so they will not begin to rot. The next day I cut the trees into 2.44-m (eight-foot) lengths, which allows me to handle them more easily. Once they are cut, I roll them along the fire lane to the edge of the road, where I stack them neatly but not too high. The next day I borrow my uncle's van, drive to the pile of logs, and load as many logs as I can, thus reducing the number of trips. When I finally have all the logs in my backyard, I begin sawing them into 47-cm (eighteen-inch) lengths. I create large piles that consequently have to be split and finally stacked. The logs will age and dry until winter when I will make daily trips to the woodpile.

When Canadian women began playing Canada's unofficial national sport at the turn of the twentieth century, they were often criticized for being unfeminine. Appropriate

Glenbow Archives NA-1438-5

Women's Hockey Game, Banff, Alberta *(ca. 1904–1905),* *Anonymous* leisure activities for women included flower arranging and sewing, both activities with a domestic focus. Men's leisure activities, on the other hand, were seen to be more appropriate when focused on the outdoors. In these social expectations, we see the conventional thinking that women belonged in the private sphere, while men belonged in the public. Where men were praised for throwing themselves spectacularly onto the ice to save a goal, comparable actions by female goalkeepers were seen as ungainly and undignified. Men and women's legs were equally protected from the cold by heavy woollen tights, but if a woman's skirt moved during the action to reveal some ankle, she was deliberately drawing attention to herself. However, the sight of a man's ankle meant only that he was playing energetically.

C. The following paragraph lacks common transitional devices. Fill in each blank with the appropriate transitional word or key word.

Scientists continue to debate the cause of the dinosaurs' disappearance. One group claims the _____ vanished after a comet smashed into the Earth; dust and smoke _____ blocked the sun for a long time. _____ of no direct sunlight, the Earth underwent a lengthy "winter," far too cold for the huge _____ to survive. A University of California paleontologist, _____ , disputes this claim. He argues that _____ we generally think of _____ living in swampy land, fossils found in Alaska show that _____ could live in cold climates _____ warm ones. _____ group claims that the _____ became extinct following an intense period of global volcanic activity. _____ to killing the _____ themselves, these scientists _____ believe the volcanic activity killed much of the plant life that the _____ ate and, _____ , many of the great _____ who survived the volcanic eruptions starved to death. Still _____ groups of _____ claim the _____ were destroyed by acid rain, by a passing "death star," _____ even by visitors from outer space.

D. The sentences in each of the following exercises are out of order. By noting the various transitional devices, you should be able to arrange each group of sentences into a coherent paragraph.

Paragraph 1: How to Purchase a New Car

- If you're happy with the car's performance, find out about available financing arrangements.

- Later, at home, study your notes carefully to help you decide which car fits your needs.

- After you have discussed various loans and interest rates, you can negotiate the final price with the salesperson.

- A visit to the showroom also allows you to test-drive the car.

- Once you have agreed on the car's price, feel confident you have made a well-chosen purchase.

- Next, a visit to a nearby showroom should help you select the colour, options, and style of the car of your choice.

- First, take a trip to the library to read the current auto magazines.

- As you read, take notes on models and prices.

Paragraph 2: Henry VIII and the Problems of Succession

- After Jane, Henry took three more wives, but all these marriages were childless.

- Jane did produce a son, Edward VI, but he died at age fifteen.

- The problem of succession was therefore an important issue during the reign of Henry VIII.

- Still hoping for a son, Henry beheaded Anne and married Jane Seymour.

- Thus, despite his six marriages, Henry failed in his attempts to produce a male heir for the British throne.

- In sixteenth-century England it was considered essential for a son to assume the throne.

- Henry's first wife, Catherine of Aragon, had only one child, the Princess Mary.

- Anne and Henry also produced a daughter, the future Queen Elizabeth I.

- Consequently, he divorced Catherine and married Anne Boleyn.

■ Paragraph Sequence

The order in which you present your paragraphs is another decision you must make. In some essays, the subject matter itself will suggest its own order.* For instance, in an essay designed to instruct a beginning runner, you might want to discuss the necessary equipment—good running shoes, loose-fitting clothing, and a sweatband—before moving to a discussion of where to run and how to run. Other essays, however, may not suggest a natural order, in which case you must decide which order will most effectively reach and hold the attention of your audience. Frequently, writers withhold their strongest point until last. (Lawyers often use this technique; they first present the jury with the weakest

---

* For more information on easily recognized patterns of order, see pages 68–69.

arguments, then pull out the most incriminating evidence—the "smoking pistol." Thus the jury members retire with the strongest argument freshest in their minds.) Sometimes, however, you'll find it necessary to present one particular point first so that the other points make good sense. Study your own major points and decide which order will be the most logical, successful way of persuading your reader to accept your thesis.

■ Transitions between Paragraphs

As you already know, each paragraph usually signals a new major point in your discussion. These paragraphs should not appear as isolated blocks of thought but rather as parts of a unified, step-by-step progression. To avoid a choppy essay, link each paragraph to the one before it with *transitional devices*. Just as the sentences in your paragraphs are connected, so are the paragraphs themselves; therefore, you can use the same transitional devices suggested on pages 69–71.

The first sentence of most body paragraphs frequently contains the transitional device. To illustrate this point, here are some topic sentences lifted from the body paragraphs of a student essay criticizing a popular sports car, renamed the 'Gator to protect the guilty and to prevent lawsuits. The transitional devices are italicized.

Thesis: The 'Gator is one of the worst cars on the market.

- When you buy a 'Gator, you buy physical inconvenience. [repetition of key word from thesis]

- *Another* reason the 'Gator is a bad buy is the cost of insurance. [transitional word, key word]

- You might overlook the *inconvenient* size and exorbitant *insurance* rates if the 'Gator were a strong, reliable car, *but* this automobile constantly needs repair. [key words from preceding paragraphs, transitional word]

- When you decide to sell this *car*, you face *still another* unpleasant surprise: the extremely low resale value. [key word, transitional phrase]

- The most serious drawback, *however*, is the 'Gator's safety record. [transitional word, key word]

Sometimes, instead of using transitional words or repetition of key words or their synonyms, you can use an *idea hook*. The last idea of one paragraph may lead you smoothly into your next paragraph. Instead of repeating a key word from the previous discussion, find a phrase that refers to the entire idea just expressed. If, for example, the previous paragraph discussed the highly complimentary advertising campaign for the 'Gator, the next paragraph might begin, "This view of the 'Gator as an economy car is ridiculous to anyone who's pumped a week's salary into this gas guzzler." The phrase "this view" connects the idea of the first paragraph with the one that follows. Idea hooks also work well with transitional words: "This view, however, is ridiculous. . . ."

If you do use transitional words, don't allow them to make your essay sound mechanical. For example, a long series of paragraphs beginning "first . . . second . . . third . . ." quickly becomes boring. Vary the type and position of your transitional devices so that your essay has a subtle but logical movement from point to point.

■ APPLYING WHAT YOU'VE LEARNED TO *YOUR* WRITING

If you are currently working on a draft of an essay, check each body paragraph for coherence, the smooth connection of ideas and sentences in a logical, easy-to-follow order. You might try placing brackets around key words, pronouns, and transitional words that carry the reader's attention from thought to thought and from sentence to sentence. Decide whether you have enough ordering devices, placed in appropriate places, or whether you need to add (or delete) others. (For additional help revising your drafts, turn to Chapter 5.)

CHAPTER 3 SUMMARY

Here is a brief restatement of what you should know about the paragraphs in the body of your essay:

1. Each body paragraph usually contains one major point in the discussion promised by the thesis statement.

2. Each major point is presented in the topic sentence of a paragraph.

3. Each paragraph should be adequately developed with clear supporting detail.

4. Every sentence in the paragraph should support the topic sentence.

5. There should be an orderly, logical flow from sentence to sentence and from thought to thought, ensured by the use of transitional words and phrases.

6. The sequence of your essay's paragraphs should be logical and effective.

7. There should be a smooth flow from paragraph to paragraph, achieved by transitional words or phrases, or idea hooks.

8. The body paragraphs should successfully persuade your reader that the position taken in your thesis is valid.

Chapter 4

Beginnings and Endings

As you work on your rough drafts, you might think of your essay as a coherent, unified whole composed of three main parts: the introduction (lead-in, thesis, and essay map), the body (paragraphs with supporting evidence), and the conclusion (final address to the reader). These three parts should flow smoothly into one another, presenting the reader with an organized, logical discussion. The following pages will suggest ways to begin and end. It will also show you how to name your essay effectively.

■ How to Write a Good Lead-in

The first few sentences of your essay are particularly important; first impressions, as you know, are lasting ones. The beginning of your essay, then, must catch your readers' attention and make them want to keep reading. Recall the way you read a magazine: if you are like most people, you probably skim the magazine, reading a paragraph or two of each article that looks promising. If the first few paragraphs hold your interest, you read on. When you write your own introductory paragraph, assume that you have only a few sentences to attract your readers. So, you must pay particular attention to making those first lines especially interesting and well written.

In some essays, your thesis statement alone may be controversial or striking enough to capture the readers. At other times, however, you will want to use the introductory device called a *lead-in*.* The lead-in (1) catches the reader's attention; (2) announces the subject matter and tone of your essay (humorous, satiric, serious, etc.); and (3) sets up, or leads into, the presentation of your thesis and essay map. You need to make sure, however, that your lead-in is not vague or unfocused, that it isn't just "filler" material that gives you some breathing space before you come to your real point. As you choose a lead-in, think about the goal of your essay. Are you trying to persuade someone to take an action or to agree with you about a particular point of view? Are you trying to analyze how something works? Are you trying to explain a process, to narrow down or define a broad idea? Each of the following suggestions for lead-ins will work best if you make your choice according to your essay's specific goals.

Here are some suggestions for and examples of lead-ins:

1. A paradoxical or intriguing statement

    "Eat two chocolate bars and call me in the morning," says the psychiatrist to his patient. Such advice sounds like a sugar fanatic's dream, but recent studies have indeed confirmed that chocolate positively affects depression and anxiety.

2. An arresting statistic or shocking statement

    A special report released by the Canadian Cancer Society in April 2007 announces some unexpectedly positive news: the death rate from breast cancer for Canadian women has fallen by 25 percent since 1986.

3. A question

    It has become common practice for many Western countries to blame political instability in the Middle East for the increasing threat of terrorist attacks from Islamic militants. That instability, it is implied, has arisen as a result of incompetence by the governments of Middle Eastern countries, an incompetence at which Western countries shake their heads complacently. But is local governmental incompetence the only reason for the troubles of these nations, or for the rise of militant groups?

4. A quotation or literary allusion

    After he was made a *Chévalier* of the Order of Arts and Letters in France, Canadian artist Charles Pachter mourned his comparative lack of celebrity in his native country, saying, "The French treat artists the way Canadians treat hockey players."

---

* Do note that for some writing assignments, such as many scholarly papers and certain kinds of technical reports, attention-grabbing lead-ins are not appropriate. Frequently, these reports are directed toward particular professional audiences and have their own designated format; they often begin, for example, with a statement of the problem under study or with a review of pertinent information or research.

5. A relevant story, joke, or anecdote

> During an election debate, Canada's first prime minister, Sir John A. Macdonald, was so drunk that he began vomiting violently on stage while his opponent was speaking. Recovering quickly, Macdonald told the crowd, "See how my opponent's ideas disgust me." Such ability to turn a disaster into a triumph is indispensable not only in politics but equally in business, war, and even the food and entertainment industry.

6. A description, often used for emotional appeal

> With one eye blackened, one arm in a cast, and third-degree burns on both her legs, the pretty, blond two-year-old seeks corners of rooms, refuses to speak, and shakes violently at the sound of loud noises. Tammy is not the victim of a war or a natural disaster; rather, she is the helpless victim of her parents, one of the thousands of children who suffer daily from Canada's hidden crime, child abuse.

7. A factual statement or a summary who-what-where-when-why lead-in

> Rising concerns about the twin evils of obesity and consumer indoctrination finally resulted in the banning of junk food at British Columbia's elementary schools in 2007.

8. An analogy or comparison

> In the eighteenth century Irish writer Jonathan Swift represented British society as cannibals in their greedy exploitation of his country's poor, though the Irish, in allowing themselves to be victimized, did not escape his scorn either. In the twentieth century, Ojibway writer Basil Johnston was equally critical of the relationship between the exploiter and the exploited as he drew an analogy between giant corporations and the weendigo, a mythical monster that feeds on the foolish and the sinful.

9. A contrast

> I used to search for toast in the supermarket. I used to think "blackened"—as in blackened Cajun shrimp—referred to the way I cooked anything in a skillet. "Poached" could only have legal ramifications. But all that has changed! Attending a class in basic cooking this summer has transformed the way I purchase, prepare, and even talk about food.

10. Statement of a problem or a popular misconception

> It is widely acknowledged by the Canadian public that the conservation of natural resources must be a priority today. Yet the number of Canadians enrolled in agriculture, natural resources, or conservation studies in universities has fallen significantly since 2000.

11. A catalogue of relevant examples

> A 91-kg (two-hundred-pound) teenager quit school because no desk would hold her. A 136-kg (three-hundred-pound) chef who could no longer stand on his feet was fired. A 159-kg (three-hundred-fifty-pound) truck driver broke furniture in his friends' houses. All these people are now living healthier, happier, and thinner lives, thanks to the remarkable intestinal bypass surgery first developed in 1967.

12. A personal experience

> I realized times were changing for women when I overheard my six-year-old nephew speaking to my sister, a prominent Toronto lawyer. As we left her elaborate, luxurious office one evening, Tommy looked up at his mother and queried, "Mommy, can little boys grow up to be lawyers too?"

Thinking of a good lead-in is often difficult when you sit down to begin your essay. Many writers, in fact, skip the lead-in until the first draft is written. They compose their working thesis first and then write the body of the essay, saving the lead-in and conclusion for last. As you write the middle of your essay, you may discover an especially interesting piece of information you might want to save to use as your lead-in.

■ Avoiding Errors in Lead-ins

In addition to the previous suggestions, here is some advice to help you avoid common lead-in errors:

Make sure your lead-in introduces your thesis. A frequent weakness in introductory paragraphs is an interesting lead-in but no smooth or clear transition to the thesis statement. To avoid a gap or awkward jump in thought in your introductory paragraph, you may need to add a connecting sentence or phrase between your lead-in and thesis. Study the paragraph below, which uses a comparison as its lead-in. The italicized transitional sentence takes the reader from a comment on medical scientists of an earlier age to another kind of scientist in the present age, smoothly preparing the reader for the thesis that follows, warning the reader about the cost of inaction.

Lead-in	When mid-twentieth-century medical scientists were warning people about the health hazards of secondhand smoke, few were ready to
Transitional sentence	listen. *Now social scientists are calling attention to this generation's growing dependency on computers and the erosion of social relations,* but we are refusing to listen. Unless parents and educators find the will
Thesis	to engage our youth in human interaction, we will soon have a society peopled by alienated individuals who owe neither interest in nor responsibility to one another.

Keep your lead-in brief. Long lead-ins in short essays often give the appearance of a tail wagging the dog. Use a brief, attention-catching hook to set up your thesis; don't make your introduction the biggest part of your essay.

Don't begin with an apology or complaint. Such statements as "It's difficult to find much information on this topic . . ." and "This controversy is hard to understand, but . . ." do nothing to entice your reader.

Don't assume your audience already knows your subject matter. Identify the pertinent facts even though you know your instructor knows the assignment. ("The biggest problem with the new requirement . . ." What requirement?) If you are writing about a particular piece of literature, identify the title of the work and its author, using the writer's full name in the first reference.

Stay clear of overused lead-ins. If composition instructors had a nickel for every essay that began with a dry dictionary definition, they could all retire to Bermuda. Leave *Webster's* alone and find a livelier way to begin. Asking a question as your lead-in is becoming overworked too, so use it only when it is obviously the best choice for your opener.

> ■ **PRACTISING WHAT YOU'VE LEARNED**
>
> Find three good lead-ins from essays, magazine articles, or newspaper feature stories. Identify the kinds of lead-ins you found, and tell why you think each effectively catches the reader's attention and sets up the thesis.

■ How to Write a Good Concluding Paragraph

Like a good story, a good essay should not stop in the middle. It should have a satisfying conclusion, one that gives the reader a sense of completion on the subject. Don't allow your essay to drop off or fade out at the end—instead, use the concluding paragraph to emphasize the validity and importance of your thinking. Remember that the concluding paragraph is your last chance to convince the reader. (As one cynical but realistic student pointed out, the conclusion may be the last part of your essay the teacher reads before putting a grade on your paper.) Therefore, make your conclusion count.

Some people feel that writing an essay shares a characteristic with a romantic fling—both activities are frequently easier to begin than they are to end. If you find, as many writers do, that you often struggle while searching for an exit with the proper emphasis and grace, here are some suggestions, by no means exhaustive, that might spark some good ideas for your conclusions:

1. A restatement of the thesis and the essay's major points (most useful in long essays)

> The destruction of the rainforests must be stopped. Although developers protest that they are bringing much-needed financial aid into these traditionally poverty-stricken areas, no amount of money can compensate for what is being lost. Without the rainforests, we not only are contributing to the global warming of the entire planet, we are losing indigenous trees and plants that might someday provide new medicines or vaccines for diseases. Moreover, the displacement of indigenous peoples by corporation-run ranches robs the world of

cultural diversity. For the sake of the planet's well-being, Project Rainforest should be implemented.

2. An evaluation of the importance of the essay's subject

These amazing, controversial photographs of the comet will continue to be a subject of debate because, according to some scientists, they yield the most important clues yet revealed about the origins of our universe.

3. A statement of the essay's broader implications

Because these studies of feline leukemia may someday play a crucial role in the discovery of a cure for AIDS in human beings, the experiments, as expensive as they are, must continue.

4. A call to action

The specific details surrounding the death of Second World War hero Raoul Wallenberg are still unknown. Although Russia has recently admitted—after fifty years of denial—that Wallenberg was murdered by the KGB in 1947, such a confession is not enough. We must write our parliamentary representatives today urging their support for the new Swedish commission investigating the circumstances of his death. No hero deserves less.

5. A warning based on the essay's thesis

Understanding the politics that led to the rise of Nazism is essential for all the world's peoples. Without such knowledge, the frightful possibility exists that somewhere, sometime, institutionalized hatred and oppression may overwhelm a nation—and indeed, the world—again.

6. A quotation from an authority or someone whose insight emphasizes the main point

Even though I didn't win the fiction contest, I learned so much about my own powers of creativity and about myself. I'm proud that I pushed myself in new directions. I know now what was meant by Robertson Davies when he said that "Being an author is a state of mind, and it cannot be changed."

7. An anecdote or witticism that emphasizes or sums up the point of the essay

The most hardheaded people are usually the first to fall for a con man's spiel, for it is human nature to go for the deal of a lifetime. As Irish dramatist and wit Oscar Wilde said, "I can resist everything but temptation."

Oscar Wilde (1854–1900)

© Bettmann/CORBIS

8. An image or description that lends finality to the essay

> Bare, leafless trees stand stark against the grey sky, a thin rain dripping off sooty roofs like a dirty curtain barely hiding the mean shacks of the shantytown. Another day dies in the empire of coal.

(For another brief image that captures the essence of an essay, see also the "open house" scene that concludes "To Bid the World Farewell," page 198.)

9. A rhetorical question that makes the readers think about the essay's main point

> No one wants to see hostages put in danger. But what nation can afford to let terrorists know they can get away with murder?

10. A forecast based on the essay's thesis

> Soap operas will continue to be popular not only because they distract us from our daily chores but also because they present life as we want it to be: fast-paced, glamorous, and full of exciting characters.

■ Avoiding Errors in Conclusions

Try to omit the following common errors in your concluding paragraphs:

Avoid a mechanical ending. One of the most frequent weaknesses in student essays is the conclusion that merely restates the thesis, word for word. A brief essay of from five hundred to seven hundred and fifty words rarely requires a flat, point-by-point conclusion—in fact, such an ending often insults the readers' intelligence by implying that their attention spans are extremely short. Only after reading long essays do most readers need a precise recap of all the writer's main ideas. Instead of recopying your thesis and essay map, try finding an original, emphatic way to conclude your essay—or as a well-known newspaper columnist described it, a good ending should snap with grace and authority, like the close of an expensive sports car door.

Don't introduce new points. Treat the major points of your essay in separate body paragraphs rather than in your exit.

Don't tack on a conclusion. There should be a smooth, logical flow of thought from your last body paragraph into your concluding statements.

Don't change your stance. Sometimes writers who have been critical of something throughout their essays will soften their stance or offer apologies in their last paragraph. For instance, a writer arguing against the government's carbon tax might abruptly conclude with statements that declare the tax may not be so bad after all, that maybe the government will use the revenue from the tax to make people's lives better, or that maybe the tax will significantly slow down climate change. Such reneging may seem polite, but actually it undercuts the thesis and confuses the reader who has taken the writer's criticisms seriously. Instead of contradicting themselves, writers should stand their ground, forget about puffy clichés or "niceties," and find an emphatic way to conclude that is consistent with their thesis.

Avoid trite, overused expressions. Don't begin your conclusions by declaring, "in conclusion," "in summary," or "as you can see, this essay proves my thesis that. . . ." End your essay so that the reader clearly senses completion; don't merely announce that you're finished.

■ **PRACTISING WHAT YOU'VE LEARNED**

Find three good concluding paragraphs. Identify each kind of conclusion and tell why you think it is an effective ending for the essay or article.

■ How to Write a Good Title

As in the case of lead-ins, your title may be written at any time, but many writers prefer to finish their essays before naming them. A good title is similar to a good newspaper headline in that it attracts the readers' interest and makes them want to investigate the essay. Like the lead-in, the title also helps announce the tone of the essay. An informal or humorous essay, for instance, might have a catchy, funny title. Some titles show the writer's wit and love of wordplay; a survey of recent magazines revealed these titles: "Bittersweet News about Saccharin," "Coffee: New Grounds for Concern," and "The Scoop on the Best Ice Cream." A scholarly essay, on the other hand, tends to use more formal language and tone: "Colonial Anxieties and Post-Colonial Desires: Theatre as a Space of Translations," "Tradition, Change, and the Idea of Progress in Feminist Legal Thought," and "Form, Ideology, and *The Secret Agent.*"

On the other hand, a serious, informative essay should have a more formal title that suggests its content as clearly and specifically as possible. Let's suppose, for example, that you are researching the meaning of colour in dreams, and you see an article in a database list titled merely "Dreams." You don't know whether you should bother to read it. To avoid such confusion in your own essay and to encourage readers' interest, always use a specific title: "Interpreting Animal Imagery in Dreams," "Dream Research: An Aid to Diagnosing Depression," and so forth. Moreover, if your subject matter is controversial, let the reader know which side you're on (for example, "The Advantages of Solar Power"). Never substitute a mere label, such as " Politics" or "Cancer Research," for a meaningful title. And never, never label your essays "Theme One" or "Comparison and Contrast Essay." In all your writing, including the title, use your creativity to attract the readers' attention and to invite their interest in your ideas.

If you're unsure about how to present your title, here are two basic rules:

1. Your own title should *not* be underlined or put in quotation marks. It should be written at the top of page one of your essay or on an appropriate cover sheet with no special marks of punctuation.

2. Only the first word and the important words of your title should be capitalized. Generally, do not capitalize such words as "an," "and," "a," or "the," or prepositions, unless they appear as the first word of the title.

■ **ASSIGNMENT**

Select any three of the student or professional essays in this text; give the first one a new title; the second, an interesting lead-in; the third, a different conclusion. Why are your choices as effective as (or even better than) those of the original writers?

■ **APPLYING WHAT YOU'VE LEARNED TO *YOUR* WRITING**

Look at the draft of an essay you are currently working on and ask yourself these questions:

- Does the opening of my essay make my reader want to continue reading? Does the lead-in smoothly set up my thesis or do I need to add some sort of transition to help move the reader to my main idea? Is the lead-in appropriate to the tone and length of my essay?

- Does the closing of my essay offer an emphatic ending, one that is consistent with my essay's purpose? Have I avoided a mechanical, trite, or tacked-on closing paragraph? Have I refrained from adding a new point in my conclusion that belongs in the body of my essay or in another essay?

- Does my title interest my reader? Are its content and tone appropriate for this particular essay?

If you have answered "no" to any of the above questions, you should continue revising your essay. (For more help revising your essay, turn to Chapter 5.)

 CHAPTER 4 SUMMARY

Here is a brief restatement of what you should remember about writing introductions, conclusions, and titles:

1. Many essays will profit from a lead-in, the first sentences of the introductory paragraph that attract the reader's attention and smoothly set up the thesis statement.

2. Essays should end convincingly, without being repetitious or trite, with thoughts that emphasize the writer's main purpose.

3. Titles should invite the reader's interest by indicating the general nature of the essay's content and its tone.

Chapter 5

Drafting and Revising: Creative Thinking, Critical Thinking

There is no good writing, only rewriting.
—JAMES THURBER

When I say writing, O, believe me, it is rewriting that I have chiefly in mind.
—ROBERT LOUIS STEVENSON

The absolute necessity of revision cannot be overemphasized. All good writers rethink, rearrange, and rewrite large portions of their prose. The French novelist Colette, for instance, wrote everything over and over. In fact, she often spent an entire morning working on a single page. Hemingway, to cite another example, rewrote the ending to *A Farewell to Arms* thirty-nine times "to get the words right." Although no one expects you to make thirty-nine drafts of each essay, the point is clear: writing well means revising. **All good writers revise their writing.**

To help you sharpen your thinking and revision skills, this chapter will suggest a step-by-step method of self-questioning designed to help you achieve your writing goals.

■ What Is Revision?

Revision isn't just proofreading for grammatical or typing errors. It is a *thinking process* that occurs any time you are working on a writing project. It means looking at your writing with a "fresh eye"—that is, re-seeing your writing in ways that will enable you to make more effective choices throughout your essay. Revision often entails rethinking what you have written and asking yourself questions about its effectiveness; it involves discovery as well as change. As you write, new ideas surface, prompting you to revise what you have planned or have just written. Or perhaps these new ideas will cause changes in earlier parts of your essay. In some cases, your new ideas will encourage you to begin an entirely new draft with a different focus or approach. Revision means making important decisions about the best ways to focus, organize, develop, clarify, and emphasize your ideas.

■ When Does Revision Occur?

Revision, as previously noted, occurs throughout your writing process. Early on, you are revising as you sort through ideas to write about, and you almost certainly revise as you define your purpose and audience, and sharpen your thesis. Some revising may be done in your head, and some may be on paper or computer screen as you plan, sketch, or "discovery-write" your ideas. Later, during drafting, revision becomes more individualized and complex. Many writers find themselves sweeping back and forth over their papers, writing for a bit and then rereading what they have written, making changes, and then moving ahead. Some writers like to revise "lumps," or pieces of writing, perhaps reviewing one major idea or paragraph at a time. Frequently, writers discover that a better idea is occurring almost at the very moment they are putting another thought on paper. And virtually all writers revise after "re-seeing" a draft in its entirety.

Revision, then, occurs before drafting, during drafting, between parts of drafts, and at the ends of drafts. You can revise a word, a sentence, a paragraph, or an entire essay. If you are like most writers, you sometimes revise almost automatically as you write (deleting one word or line and quickly replacing it with another as you move on, for example), and at other times you revise very deliberately (for example, concentrating on a conclusion you know is weak). Revision is "rethinking," and that activity can happen any time, in many ways, in any part of your writing.

■ Myths about Revision

If revision is rethinking, what is it not? Three misconceptions about revision are listed here.

1. Revision Is Not Autopsy

Revision is not an isolated stage of writing that occurs *only* after your last draft is written or right before your paper is due. Revising is not merely a postmortem procedure, to be performed only after your creative juices have ceased to flow. Good writing, as Thurber noted, *is* revision, and revision occurs throughout the writing process.

2. Revision Is Not Limited to Editing or Proofreading

Too many writers mistakenly equate revision with editing and proofreading. *Editing* means revising for "surface errors"—mistakes in spelling, grammar, punctuation, sentence sense, and word choice. Certainly, good writers comb their papers for such errors, and they edit their prose extensively for clarity, conciseness, and emphasis, too. *Proofreading* to search out and correct errors and typos that distort meaning or distract the reader is also important. Without question, both editing and proofreading are essential to a polished paper. But revision is not *limited* to such activities. It includes them, but also encompasses those larger, global changes writers may make in purpose, focus, organization, and development. Writers who revise effectively not only change words and catch mechanical errors but also typically add, delete, rearrange, and rewrite large chunks of prose. In other words, revision is not cosmetic surgery on a body that may need major resuscitation.

3. Revision Is Not Punishment or Busywork

At one time or another, most of us have found ourselves guilty of racing too quickly through a particular job and then moving on. And perhaps just as often we have found ourselves redoing such jobs because the results were so disappointing. Some people may regard revising in a similar light—as the repeat performance of a job done poorly the first time. But that attitude isn't productive. Revising isn't punishment for failing to produce a perfect first draft. Rarely, if ever, does anyone—even our most admired professional writers—produce the results he or she wants without revising.* Remember that revising is not a tacked-on stage nor is it merely a quick touchup; it's an integral part of the entire writing process itself. It's an ongoing opportunity to discover, remember, re-shape, and refine your ideas.

If you've ever created something you now treasure—a piece of jewellery, furniture, painting, or music—recall the time you put into it. You probably thought about it from several angles, experimented with it, crafted it, worked it through expected and unexpected problems, and smoothed out its minor glitches, all to achieve the results you wanted. Similarly, with each revision you make, your paper becomes clearer and more satisfying to you and to your readers. With practice, you will produce writing you are proud of—and you will discover that revising has become not only an essential but also a natural part of your writing process.

■ Can I Learn to Improve My Revision Skills?

Because revision is such a multifaceted and individual activity, no textbook can guide you through all the rethinking you may do as you move through each sentence of every writing project. But certainly you can learn to improve your ability to think creatively and critically about your prose.

■ Preparing to Draft: Some Time-Saving Hints

Before you begin drafting (either a "discovery" draft or a draft from your working thesis), remember this important piece of advice: no part of your draft is sacred or permanent. No matter what you write at this point, you can always change it. Drafting is discovering and

---

* All of us have heard stories about famous essays or poems composed at one quick sitting. Bursts of creativity do happen. But it's also highly likely that authors of such pieces revise extensively in their heads before they write. They rattle ideas around in their brains for such a prolonged period that the actual writing does in fact flow easily or may even seem "dictated" by an inner voice. This sort of lengthy internal "cooking" may work well at various times for you too, but it might be risky to expect this to be a consistently reliable method.

recollecting as well as developing ideas from your earlier plans. Take the pressure off yourself: no one expects blue-ribbon prose in early drafts. (If you can't seem to get going or if you do become stuck along the way, try turning to pages 108–110 of this chapter for suggestions to help you confront your case of writer's block.)

At this point, too, you might consider the actual format of your drafts. Because you will be making many changes in your writing, you may find revising less cumbersome and time-consuming if you prepare your manuscripts as described below. (If you do not have access to a computer, please refer to "Working with Pen and Paper" below.)

On your computer you can compose and store your prewriting activities, journal entries, notes, or good ideas in various files until you need to recall certain information. Make sure you name your files clearly, though, as it is easy to lose track of your documents if they only have generic titles like "notes.doc" or "paperfiles.doc." You can easily produce extra copies of your drafts from your printer (or from more publicly available printers at your school or from a copy service). When you write multiple drafts, number each draft so you can track the progress of your essay. Spell checkers and dictionaries may help you correct many of your errors and typos, but look at the warnings about spell checkers and dictionaries later in this chapter, so you can use these tools without making inadvertent mistakes.

But the most important use of the computer to a writer may be what it can do as you draft and revise your prose. At your command, a word-processing program enables you to add, delete, or change words easily; it allows you to move words, sentences, and even paragraphs or larger pieces of your essay. On a computer, for example, you can try out different ideas by dropping the cursor below what you have written and phrasing your idea in another way. With some programs, you can even compare drafts side by side or with special "windows" that help you see your choices more clearly. In other words, computers can help us as writers do the kind of deep structure revision necessary to produce our best, most effective prose—the kind of major changes that, in the past, we may have been hesitant to make because of the time involved in re-copying or re-typing major portions of our drafts.

Here are a few suggestions for drafting and revising your essay on a computer:

1. Devise a system of symbols (circles, stars, checks, asterisks, etc.) that will remind you of changes you want to make later. For example, if you're in hot pursuit of a great idea but can't think of the exact word you want, put down a word that's close, circle it (or type three XXXs by it), and go on, so that your thinking is not derailed. Similarly, a check in the margin might mean "return to this tangled sentence." A question mark might mean a fuzzy idea, and a star, a great idea that needs expanding. A system of symbols can save you from agonizing over every inch of your essay while you are still trying to discover and clarify your ideas. You can also write an easily searchable word or phrase, such as "Revise," "Look Again," and so on. If this is in bold font, it will stand out, whether on the screen or on a printed draft, which can make your revision easier.

2. If your ideas are flowing well but you realize you need more supporting evidence for some of your points, consider leaving some blank spots to fill in later. For example, let's say you are writing about the role of television in the federal elections; your ideas are good but in a particular body paragraph you decide some statistics on commercial frequency would be most convincing. Or perhaps you need to cite an example of a particular kind of advertisement but you just can't

think of a good one at that moment. Leave a spot, perhaps marked by an underscore line, for the piece of evidence with a key word or two to remind you of what's needed, and keep writing. Later, when you come back to that spot, you can add the appropriate support; if you can't find or think of the right supporting evidence to insert, you may decide to omit that point.

3. If you aren't sure whether you're going to use some material in a particular section, highlight or put brackets around that material, because you may want to use it elsewhere. Or consider moving a larger chunk of prose to a "holding page" or to the end of the current draft so you can take another look at it later.

Some Reminders about Potential Problems

Although computers have made composing and revising easier and more effective for many writers, such technology provides its own special temptations and potential problems. The suggestions below should help you avoid some of these:

1. To avoid the "agony of delete," always "save" what you have composed every ten minutes or so, and do print out a copy after each drafting session in case your system crashes or gobbles your work. Remember that all sorts of events, from electrical storms to carpet cleaning, have caused the tiny leprechauns in computers to behave badly; having "hard" (printed) copies of your notes and latest revisions will help you reconstruct your work should disaster strike. (Also, if you are working on multiple writing tasks, as most students are, or if you are just the forgetful type, develop the habit of noting on each print copy the name you have given the file. Doing so may save you from a frustrating search through your list of existing documents, especially if several days have elapsed between drafts.)

2. Do learn to use the editing tools that your word-processing program offers. For example, the "word count" command can help writers who want to trim the fat from their essays. Even word choice can be assisted by computer tools. In addition to making changes and moving text, most programs offer a dictionary to help you check the proper spelling, meaning, and use of your words; a thesaurus may help you expand your vocabulary, avoid repetition of words, or find just the right word to express the shade of meaning you want. But be aware that many spell-checker programs do not use Canadian spelling, so have a good print dictionary (*Canadian Oxford, Gage Canadian,* etc.) Also, make sure you use a thesaurus carefully—don't just make a random pick out of a list of synonyms, but look at connotations and exact definitions.

   One of the most prized tools the computer offers writers is the spell checker. For poor spellers and bad typists, the invention of the spell checker ranks right up there with penicillin as a boon to humankind. The spell checker performs minor miracles as it asks writers to reconsider certain words as typed on the page. If you have a spell checker available, by all means, run it! But be aware of its limitations: spell checkers only highlight words whose order of assembled letters they do not recognize or whose capitalization they question. They do not recognize confused words (its/it's; you're/your; their/there; to/too), incorrect usage of words, or typos that are correctly spelled words. To underscore this point, here's a sample of writing that any spell checker would happily pass over:

Eye have a knew spell checker
That tells me wrong from write;
It marks four me miss steaks
My ayes kin knot high lite.

I no its let her perfect,
Sew why due I all ways get
Re quests to proof reed bet her
Win my checker says I'm set?

The message of this brilliantly crafted poem? Don't rely on your spell checker to catch all the errors in your final draft! Learn to edit, question your word choice, and proofread carefully with your own eyes and brain. (The same advice holds true for grammar check and "style" programs, too. Although such programs have improved over the past several years, they are still limited in their ability to catch errors and see distinctions among usage and punctuation choices. Such programs may help you take a second look at your grammatical decisions, but do not rely on *any* computer program to do your editing and proofreading work for you!)

3. Use the computer to help you double check for your own common errors. By using the "search," "find," or similar command, many writers can highlight words they know they frequently misuse. For example, on a final sweep of editing, you might take one last look at each highlighted "its" you wrote to determine whether the usage truly calls for the possessive pronoun "its" or rather should be the contraction for "it is" (it's). Or perhaps you have an ongoing struggle with the uses of "affect" and "effect" and know that you have used these words often in your essay of causal analysis. Reviewing your word-choice decisions in the proofreading stage could make an important difference to your readers, who wish to travel smoothly through the ideas in your essay without annoying errors flagging down their attention. Also consider searching for and replacing words that you know you overuse or those that are lazy or vague. For example, until you break yourself of the habit, highlight any use of the word "thing." In each case, are you really discussing an unknown quantity—or do you need to press yourself to find a more specific or vivid word to communicate what you mean?

4. Even if you are comfortable drafting on your computer, resist doing all your work there. It's a good idea from time to time to read your screen version in its printed form—the format your readers will most likely see. Many—if not most—writers move back and forth multiple times between the computer screen and printed copies of their drafts. Experiment to discover the best ways for you to revise. Remember that a neatly printed draft can look professional but still need much rethinking, restructuring, and polishing!

Working with Pen and Paper

1. If you are handwriting your first drafts, always write on one side of your paper only, in case you want to cut and tape together portions of drafts or you want to

experiment with interchanging parts of a particular draft. (If you have written on both sides, you may have to re-copy the parts of your essay you want to save; your time is better spent creating and revising.)

2. Leave big margins on *both* sides of any handwritten pages so you can add information later or jot down new ideas as they occur. (Some writers also skip lines for this reason. If you choose to write on every other line, however, do remember that you may not be getting a true picture of your paragraph development or essay length. A handwritten double-spaced body paragraph, for example, may appear skimpy in your typed final copy.)

3. If you do decide to rewrite or omit something—a sentence or an entire passage—in a handwritten draft, mark a single "X" or line through it lightly. Don't scratch it out or destroy it completely; you may realize later that you want to reinsert the material there or move it to another, better place.

4. If you begin with a handwritten draft, do eventually work on a **printed** copy. Frankly, the more compact spacing of printed prose allows you to see more clearly the relationship of the parts in your essay, making it easier for you to organize and develop your ideas. It is also far more likely that you will catch spelling and other mechanical errors in a printed draft.

5. Just as you would back up your files on your computer, keep your notes, outlines, drafts, and an extra copy of your final paper. Never burn your bridges—or your manuscripts! Sometimes essays change directions, and writers find they can return to prewriting or earlier drafts to recover ideas, once rejected, that now work well. Drafts also may contain ideas that didn't work in one paper but that look like great starts for another assignment. Tracking revisions from draft to draft can give writers a sense of accomplishment and insight into their composing processes. Drafts can be good insurance in case final copies of papers are lost or accidentally destroyed. If professors wish to see the progress of your work, you can show it easily through your drafts.

■ Writing Centres, Computer Labs, and Computer Classrooms

Today many schools have professionally staffed writing centres and computer labs open to composition students. The writing centre or laboratory computers may have a variety of software designed to help you brainstorm, focus your ideas, organize a working structure, compose your drafts, revise your essay, and proofread. These computers may also help you research a topic by allowing you to check information available in your campus library as well as providing access to other libraries and sources on the Internet. Many writing centres have special tutors on hand to answer your questions about your drafts, as well as to explain effective uses of the available computer programs. In addition, some schools now have labs and special classrooms in which the computers are part of a network, linked together so that a specific group of writers may communicate with each other and/or with their instructor. In such a lab or classroom, for example, students might read each other's drafts and make suggestions or post comments about a current reading assignment on an electronic bulletin board for their classmates to consider.

■ A Revision Process for Your Drafts

Let's assume at this point that you have completed a draft, using the first four chapters of this book as a guide. You feel you've chosen an interesting topic and collected some good ideas. Perhaps the ideas came quickly or perhaps you had to coax them. No matter how your thoughts came, they're now in print—you have a draft with meaning and general order, although it's probably much rougher in some spots than in others. Now it's time to "re-see" this draft in a comprehensive way.

But wait. If possible, put a night's sleep or at least a few hours between this draft and the advice that appears on the next few pages. All writers become tired when they work on any project for too long at one sitting, and then they lose a sense of perspective. When you've looked at a piece of prose again and again, you may begin to read what's written in your head instead of what's on the page—that is, you may begin to "fill in" for yourself, reading into your prose what you meant to say rather than what your reader will actually see. Always try to start your writing process early enough to give yourself a few breaks from the action. You'll find that you will be better able to evaluate the strengths and weaknesses of your prose when you are fresh.

When you do return to your draft, *don't try to look at all the parts of your paper, from ideas to organization to mechanics, at the same time.* Trying to re-see everything at once is rarely possible and will only overload and frustrate you. It may cause you to overlook some important part of your paper that needs your full attention. Overload can also block your creative ideas. Therefore, instead of trying to revise an entire draft in one swoop, break your revising process into a series of smaller, more manageable steps. Here is a suggested process:

I.	rethink	purpose, thesis, and audience
II.	rethink	ideas and evidence
III.	rethink	organization
IV.	rethink	clarity and style
V.	edit	grammar, punctuation, and spelling
VI.	proofread	entire essay

IMPORTANT: Please note that these steps are not necessarily distinct, nor must you always follow this suggested order. You certainly might, for instance, add details to a paragraph when you decide to move or reorder it. Or you might replace a vague word with a specific one after thinking about your audience and their needs. After strengthening a particular point, you might decide to offer it last, and therefore rearrange the order of your paragraphs. In other words, the steps offered above are not part of a forced march—they are here simply to remind you to rethink and improve any part of your essay that needs work.

Now let's look at each of the steps in the revision process suggested above in more detail.

I. Revising for Purpose, Thesis, and Audience

To be effective, writers need a clear sense of purpose and audience. Their essays must present (or clearly imply) a main idea or thesis designed to fulfill that purpose and to inform their audience. As you reread your draft, ask yourself the following questions:

- Have I fulfilled the objectives of my assignment? (For example, if you were asked to analyze the causes of a problem, did you merely describe or summarize it instead?)

- Did I follow directions carefully? (If I was given a three-part assignment, did I treat all parts as requested?)

- Did I understand what genre of essay I was supposed to write? (If I was asked to support my argument with research, did I do that research? Did I do enough research or choose appropriate sources? If I was asked to write a formal, academic and objective essay, did I include too much personal material or informal language?)

- Did I understand the purpose of the assignment? (Demonstrate my knowledge of the subject? Demonstrate critical reasoning skills? Showcase my writing skills?)

- Do I understand the purpose of my essay? Am I trying to inform, persuade, or amuse my readers? Spur them to action? Convince them to change their minds? Give them a new idea? Am I myself clear about my exact intent—what I want to do or say—in this essay?

- Does my essay reflect my clearly understood purpose by offering an appropriately narrowed and focused thesis? (After reading through your essay once, could a reader easily state its purpose and main point?)

- Have I distinguished between fact, argument, and opinion?

- Do I have a clear picture of my audience—their character, knowledge, and expectations?

- Have I addressed both my purpose and my readers' needs by selecting appropriate strategies of development for my essay? (For example, would it be better to write an essay primarily developed with examples illustrating the community's need for a new hospital or should I present a more formal argument that also rebuffs objections to the project? Should I narrate the story of my accident or analyze its effects on my family or examine the process by which a new traffic law was established in my city as a result of my accident?)

If you feel that your draft needs work in any of these areas, make changes. You might find it helpful to review Chapters 1 and 2 of this text to guide you as you revise.

II. Revising for Ideas and Evidence

If you're satisfied that your purpose and thesis are clear to your readers, begin to look closely at the development of your essay's ideas.

You want your readers to accept your thesis. To achieve this goal, you must offer body paragraphs whose major points clearly support that main idea. As you examine the body of your essay, you might ask yourself questions such as these:

- Is there a clear relationship between my thesis and each of the major points presented in the body of my essay? That is, does each major point in my essay further my readers' understanding, and thus their acceptance, of my thesis's general claim?

- Did I write myself into a new or slightly different position as I drafted my essay? If so, do I need to begin another draft with a new working thesis?

- Have I included all the major points necessary to the readers' understanding of my subject or have I omitted pertinent ones? (On the other hand, have I inserted major ideas that aren't relevant or that actually belong in a different essay?)
- Are my major points located and stated clearly in specific language so readers can easily see what position I am taking in each part of my discussion?

If you are happy with your choice and presentation of the major ideas in the body of your essay, it's time to look closely at the evidence you are offering to support those ideas (which, in turn, support the claim of your thesis). To choose the best supporting evidence for their major points, effective writers use *critical thinking skills*.

III. Revising for Organization

In reality, you have probably already made several changes in the order and organization of ideas in your draft. As noted before, it's likely that when you thought about your essay's meaning—its major points and their supporting evidence—you also thought about the arrangement of those ideas. As you take another look at your draft's organization, use these questions as a guide:

- Am I satisfied with the organizational strategy I selected for my purpose? (For example, would an essay primarily developed by comparison and contrast achieve your purpose better than a narrative approach?)
- Are my major points ordered in a logical, easy-to-follow pattern? Would readers understand my thinking better if certain paragraphs or major ideas were rearranged? Added? Divided? Omitted? Expanded?
- Are my major points presented in topic sentences that state each important idea clearly and specifically? (If any of your topic sentences are implied rather than stated, are you absolutely, 100 percent sure that your ideas cannot be overlooked or even slightly misunderstood by your readers?)
- Is there a smooth flow between my major ideas? Between paragraphs? Within paragraphs? Have I used enough transitional devices to guide the reader along?
- Are any parts of my essay out of proportion? Are they too long or too brief to do their job effectively?
- Do my title and lead-in draw readers into the essay and toward my thesis?
- Does my conclusion end my discussion thoughtfully? Emphatically, or memorably?

Don't be afraid to restructure your drafts. Most good writers rearrange and recast large portions of their prose. Reviewing Chapters 3 and 4 may help you address questions on organization, beginnings, or endings.

IV. Revising for Clarity and Style

As you've revised for purpose, ideas, and organization, you have also taken steps to clarify your prose. Making a special point now of focusing on sentences and word choice will ensure your readers' complete understanding of your thinking. Read through your draft, asking these kinds of questions:

- Is each of my sentences as clear and precise as it could be for readers who do not know what I know? Are there sentences that contain misplaced words or convoluted phrases that might cause confusion?

- Are there any sentences that are unnecessarily wordy? Is there deadwood that could be eliminated? (Remember that concise prose is more effective than wordy "fat" prose, because readers can more easily find and follow key ideas and terms. Nearly every writer has a wordiness problem that chokes communication, so now is the season to prune.)

- Do any sentences run on for too long to be fully understood? Can any repetitive or choppy sentences be combined to achieve clarity and a pleasing variation of sentence style? (To help you decide if you need to combine sentences, you might try this experiment. Select a body paragraph and count the number of words it contains. Then count the number of sentences; divide the number of words by the number of sentences to discover the average number of words per sentence. If your score is less than fifteen to eighteen, you may need to combine *some* sentences. Good prose offers a variety of sentence lengths and patterns.)

- Are all my words and their connotations accurate and appropriate?

- Can I clarify and energize my prose by adding "showing" details and by replacing bland, vague words with vivid, specific ones? By using active verbs rather than passive ones?

- Can I eliminate any pretentious or unnecessary jargon or language that's inappropriate for my audience? Replace clichés and trite expressions with fresh, original phrases?

- Is my voice authentic, or am I trying to sound like someone else? Is my tone reasonable, honest, and consistent?

The issues raised by these questions—and many others—are discussed in detail in Chapters 6 and 7, on effective sentences and words, which offer more advice on clarifying language and improving style.

V. Editing for Errors

Writers who are proud of the choices they've made in content, organization, and style are, to use a baseball metaphor, rounding third base and heading for home. But there's more to be done. Shift from a baseball metaphor to car maintenance for a moment. All good essays are not only fine-tuned but also waxed and polished—they are edited and proofread repeatedly for errors until they shine. To help you polish your prose by correcting errors in punctuation, grammar, spelling, and diction, here are some hints for effective editing:

Read aloud. In addition to repeatedly reading your draft silently, reading your draft aloud is a good technique because it allows your ears to hear ungrammatical "clunks" or unintended gaps in sense or sound you may otherwise miss. (Reading aloud may also flag omitted words. If, for example, the mother had reread this note to her child's teacher, she might have noticed a missing word: "Please excuse Ian for being. It was his father's fault.")

Know your enemies. Learn to identify your particularly troublesome areas in punctuation and grammar and then read through your draft for one of these problems at a time: once for fragments, once for comma splices, once for run-ons, and so on. (If you try to look for too many errors at each reading, you'll probably miss quite a few.)

Read backwards. Try reading your draft one sentence at a time starting at the *end* of your essay and working toward the beginning. Don't read each sentence word-for-word backwards—just read the essay one sentence at a time from back to front. When writers try to edit (or proofread) starting at the beginning of their essays, they tend to begin thinking about the ideas they're reading rather than concentrating on the task of editing for errors. By reading one sentence at a time from the back, you will find that the sentences will still make sense but that you are less likely to wander away from the job at hand.

Learn some tricks. There are special techniques for treating some punctuation and grammar problems. If you have trouble, for example, with comma splices, turn to the FANBOYS hint on page 129. If fragments plague your writing, try the "it is true that" test explained on page 488. Consider designating a special part of your journal or class notebook to record, in your own words, these tricks and other useful pieces of advice so that you can refer to them easily and often.

Eliminate common irritants. Review your draft for those diction and mechanical errors many readers find especially annoying because they often reflect sheer carelessness. For example, look at these frequently confused words: *it's/its, your/you're, there/their/they're, who's/whose* (other often-confused words are listed on pages 136–137). Some readers are ready for a national march to protest the public's abandonment of the apostrophe, the Amelia Earhart of punctuation. (Apostrophes *can* change the meaning of sentences: "The teacher called the students names." Was the instructor being rude or just taking roll?)

Use your tools. Keep your dictionary handy to check the spelling, usage, and meanings of words in doubt. A thesaurus can also be useful if you can restrain any tendencies you might have for growing overly exotic prose. If you are using a word processor with a spell checker, by all means run it after your last revisions are completed. Do remember, as noted earlier in this chapter, that such programs only flag words whose spelling they don't recognize; they will not alert you to omitted or confused words (*affect/effect*), nor will they signal when you've typed in a wrong, but correctly spelled, word (*form* for *from*).

Use Part Four of this text to help resolve any questions you may have about grammar, mechanics, and spelling. Advice on untangling sentences and clarifying word choice in Chapters 6 and 7 may be useful too.

VI. Proofreading

Proofread your final draft several times, putting as much time between the last two readings as possible. Fresh eyes catch more typographical or careless errors. Remember that typing errors—even the simple transposing of letters—can change the meaning of an entire thought and occasionally bring unintended humour to your prose. (Imagine, for example, the surprise of restaurant owners whose new lease instructed them to "Please sing the terms of the agreement." Or consider the ramifications of the newspaper advertisement offering "Great dames for sale" or the 1716 Bible whose advice "sin no more" was misprinted as "sin on more.")

Make sure, too, that your paper looks professional before you turn it in. You wouldn't, after all, expect to be taken seriously if you went to an executive job interview dressed in cut-offs. Turning in a paper with a coffee stain or ink smear on it has about the same effect as a blob of spinach in your teeth—it distracts folks from hearing what you have to say. If your final draft has typos or small blemishes, you may use correction fluid to conceal them; if you've patched so frequently that your paper resembles the medicine-dotted face of a kindergartener with chicken pox, reprint or photocopy your pages for a fresh look.

Check to be sure you've formatted your paper exactly as your assignment requested. Some instructors ask for a title page; others want folders containing all your drafts and prewriting. Most instructors appreciate typed papers with pages that are numbered, ordered correctly, paper clipped or stapled, with clean edges (no sheets violently ripped from a spiral notebook still dribbling angry confetti down one side; no pages mutilated at the corners by the useless "tear-and-fold-tab" technique). Putting your name on each page will identify your work if papers from a particular class are accidentally mixed up.

 As it's often been said, essays are never really done—only due. Take a last reading using the checklist that follows, make some notes on your progress as a writer and thinker, and congratulate yourself on your fine efforts and accomplishment.

■ A Final Checklist for Your Essay

If you have written an effective essay, you should be able to answer "yes" to the following questions:

1. Do I feel I have something important to say to my reader?

2. Am I sincerely committed to communicating with my reader and not just with myself?

3. Have I considered my audience's needs? (See Chapter 1.)

4. Do my title and lead-in attract the reader's attention and help set up my thesis? (See Chapter 4.)

5. Does my thesis statement assert one main, clearly focused idea? (See Chapter 2.)

6. Does my thesis and/or essay map give the reader an indication of what points the essay will cover? (See Chapter 2.)

7. Do my body paragraphs contain the essential points in the essay's discussion, and are those points expressed in clearly stated or implied topic sentences? (See Chapter 3.)

8. Is each major point in my essay well developed with enough detailed supporting evidence? (See Chapter 3.)

9. Does each body paragraph have unity and coherence? (See Chapter 3.)

10. Are all the paragraphs in my essay smoothly linked in a logical order? (See Chapter 3.)

11. Does my concluding paragraph provide a suitable ending for the essay? (See Chapter 4.)

12. Are all my sentences clear, concise, and coherent? (See Chapter 6.)

13. Are my words accurate, necessary, and meaningful? (See Chapter 7.)

14. Have I edited and proofread for errors in grammar, punctuation, spelling, or typing? (See Part Four.)

And most important:

15. Has my essay been effectively revised so that I am proud of this piece of writing?

■ PRACTISING WHAT YOU'VE LEARNED

The draft of the student essay below has been annotated by its own writer according to some—*but not all*—of the questions presented in this chapter's discussion of revision. As you read the draft and the writer's marginal comments, think of specific suggestions you might offer to help this writer improve her essay. What other changes, in addition to the ones mentioned here, would you encourage this writer to make? What strengths do you see in this draft?

DORM LIFE

My title and lead-in are too bland to attract readers' attention. There are some problems with parallelism.

Would my thesis be clearer if I said what I did find? This paragraph's last sentence sounds a bit pompous.

Dorm life is not at all what I had expected it to be. I had anticipated meeting friendly people, quiet hours for studying, eating decent food, and having wild parties on weekends. My dreams, I soon found out, were simply illusions, erroneous perceptions of reality.

My roommate, Kathy, and I live in Holland Hall on the third floor. The people on our dorm floor are about as unfriendly as they can possibly be. I wonder whether or not they're just shy and afraid or if they are simply snobs. Some girls, for example, ignore my roommate and me when we say "hello." Occasionally, they stare straight ahead and act like we aren't even there. Other girls respond, but it's as if they do it out of a sense of duty rather than being just friendly. The guys seem nice, but some are just as afraid or snobby as the girls.

I remember signing up for "quiet hours" when I put in my application for a dorm room last December. Unfortunately, I was assigned to a floor that doesn't have any quiet hours at all. I am a person who requires peace and quiet when

My supporting examples could use more "showing" details so the readers can really see the unfriendliness. I should revise colloquial words like "snobby." Phrases like "wee hours" sound anachronistic and clichéd.

Contradicts my point

This paragraph has some specific details but it rambles and repeats ideas. Needs tighter organization.

Contradicts my ¶'s point

This paragraph doesn't support my thesis claim—do I mean the dorm has no good parties or not enough parties? Rethink so my point is clear.

As stated, this topic sentence contradicts my thesis.

studying or reading. The girls in all the rooms around us love to stay up until early in the morning and yell and turn up their music full blast. They turn music on at about eight o'clock at night and turn it off early in the morning. There is always at least one girl who has music playing at maximum volume. Now, I am very appreciative of music, but listening to heavy metal until three in the morning isn't really my idea of what music is. The girls right across from us usually play Bonnie Raitt or the Dixie Chicks and I enjoy them. On the other hand, though, the girls on either side of our room love to listen to Metallica or Linkin Park into the wee hours of the morning. It is these girls who run up and down the hall, yell at each other, laugh obnoxiously, and try to attract attention. All this continuous racket makes it nearly impossible to study, read, or get any sleep. Kathy and I usually end up going to the library or student cafeteria to study. As far as sleep goes, it doesn't matter what time we go to bed, but rather it depends on how noisy it is, and how late the music is on. Sometimes the noise gets so loud and goes on for so long that even when it stops, my ears are ringing and my stomach keeps churning. It is on nights like this that I never go to sleep. I wish the people here were a little more considerate of the people around them.

Parties, on weekends, are supposedly the most important part of dorm life. Parties provide the opportunity to meet others and have a good time. Holland Hall has had two parties that are even worth mentioning. One of them was a Fifties dance held in the courtyard approximately three weeks ago. Unfortunately, all the other dormitories, the fraternities, and the sororities heard about it, and by eight o'clock at night there were masses of people. It was so packed that it was hard to move around. The other party, much to my dismay, turned out to be a luau party. I do not really care for roast pig, and my stomach turned from the scent of it when I entered the room. Our floor never has parties. Everyone leaves their doors open, turns up the music, and yells back and forth. I suppose that there will be more floor parties once everyone becomes adjusted to this life and begins to socialize.

Dorm food is what I anticipated it would be, terrible, and I was right, it is awful. Breakfast is probably the hardest meal to digest. The bacon and sausage are cold, slightly uncooked, and very greasy. Sometimes, it's as though I am eating pure grease. The eggs look and taste like nothing I ever had

Some good examples—could I use even more descriptive language?

Unity?

Can I conclude emphatically without switching positions?

before. They look like plastic and they are never hot. I had eggs once and I vowed I would never have another one as long as I lived in Holland Hall. The most enjoyable part of breakfast is the orange juice. It's always cold and it seems to be fresh. No one can say dorm food is totally boring because the cooks break up the monotony of the same food by serving "mystery meat" at least once every two weeks. This puts a little excitement in the student's day because everyone cracks jokes and wonders just what's in this "mystery meat." I think a lot of students are afraid to ask, fearful of the answer, and simply make snide remarks and shovel it in.

All in all, I believe dorm life isn't too great, even though there are some good times. Even though I complain about dorm food, the people, the parties, and everything else, I am glad I am here. I am happy because I have learned a lot about other people, responsibilities, consideration, and I've even learned a lot about myself.

■ Benefiting from Revision Workshops

Many writing courses today include revision workshops in which students comment helpfully on one another's drafts. This sort of revision activity may also be called *peer editing, classroom critique,* or *reader review*. Peer workshops may be arranged in a variety of ways, though frequently students will work in pairs or in small groups of from three to five. Sometimes writers will simply talk about their papers or read them aloud; at other times students will be asked to write suggestions on one another's drafts. Sometimes instructors will give student reviewers a list of questions to answer; at other times, the writers themselves will voice their concerns directly to their reviewers. Structured in many effective ways, peer workshops can be extremely valuable to writers, who will invariably profit from seeing their drafts from a reader's point of view.

Students taking part in revision workshops for the first time often have questions about the reviewing process. Some student reviewers may feel uneasy about their role, wondering, "What if I can't think of any suggestions for the writer? How can I tell someone that the essay is really terrible? What if I sense something's wrong but I'm not sure what it is—or how to fix it?" Writers, too, may feel apprehensive or even occasionally defensive about receiving criticism of their papers. Because these concerns are genuine and widespread, here is some advice to help you get the most out of your participation in revision workshops, in the role of writer or reviewer.

When you are the writer:

1. **Develop a constructive attitude.** Admittedly, receiving criticism—especially on a creation that has required hard work—can sometimes be difficult, particularly if your self-image has become mixed up with your drafts. Try to realize that your reviewer is not criticizing

you personally but rather is trying to help you by offering fresh insights. All drafts can be improved, and no writer need feel embarrassed about seeking or receiving advice. (Take comfort in the words of writer Somerset Maugham: "Only the mediocre person is always at his best.") See the workshop as a non-threatening opportunity to reconsider your prose and improve your audience awareness.

2. Come prepared. If your workshop structure permits, tell your reviewer what sort of help you need at this point in your drafting or revising process. Ask for suggestions to fix a particularly troublesome area or ask for feedback on a choice you've made but of which you are feeling unsure. Don't hesitate to ask your reviewer for assistance with any part of your essay.

3. Evaluate suggestions carefully. Writing isn't math: most of the time there are no absolutely right or wrong answers—just better or worse rhetorical choices. That is, there are many ways to communicate an idea to a set of readers. You, as the writer, must decide on an effective way, the way that best serves your purpose and your readers' needs. Sometimes your reviewer will suggest a change that is brilliant or one so obviously right you will wonder why in the world you didn't think of it yourself. At other times you may weigh your reviewer's suggestion and decide that your original choice is just as good or perhaps even better. Be open to suggestions, but learn to trust yourself as well.

4. Find the good in bad advice. Occasionally you may have a reviewer who seems to miss a crucial point or misunderstands your purpose entirely, whose suggestions for revising your paper seem uniformly unproductive for one reason or another. You certainly shouldn't take bad advice—but do think about the issues it raises. Although it's helpful to receive a dynamite suggestion you can incorporate immediately, the real value of a revision workshop is its ability to encourage you to rethink your prose. Readers' responses (yes, even the bizarre ones) challenge writers to take still another look at their rhetorical choices and ask themselves, "Is this clear after all? Does this example really work here? Did something in my essay throw this reader off the track?" Revision workshops offer you benefits, even if you ultimately decide to reject many of your reviewer's suggestions.

When you are the reviewer:

1. Develop a constructive attitude. Sometimes it's hard to give honest criticism—most of us are uncomfortable when we think we might hurt someone's feelings—but remember that the writer has resolved to develop a professional attitude too. The writer expects (and is sometimes desperately begging for) sincere feedback, so be honest as you offer your best advice.

2. Be clear and specific. Vague or flippant responses ("This is confusing."; "Huh?") don't help writers know what or how to revise. Try putting some of your comments into this format: your response to X, the reason for your response, a request for change, and, if possible, a specific suggestion for the change. ("I'm confused when you say you enjoy some parts of breakfast because this seems to contradict your thesis claim of 'wretched dorm food.' Would it be clearer to modify your thesis to exclude breakfast or to revise this paragraph to include only discussion of the rubbery eggs?")

3. Address important issues. Unless you have workshop directions that request certain tasks, read through the draft entirely at least once and then comment on the larger issues first. Writers want to know if they are achieving their overall purpose, if their thesis is clear and convincing, if their major points and evidence make sense, and if their paper seems logical and ordered. Editing tips are fine, too, but because workshops encourage authors to rewrite large portions of their prose, attention to minor details may be less valuable early on than feedback on ideas, organization, and development. (Of course, an editing workshop later in the revision process may be exclusively focused on sentence and word problems. Workshops may be designed to address specific problems that writers face.)

4. Encourage the writer. Writers with confidence write and revise better than insecure or angry writers. Praise honestly wherever you can, as specifically as you can. When weaknesses do appear, show the writer that you know she or he is capable of doing better work by linking the weakness to a strength elsewhere in the draft. ("Could you add more 'showing' details here so that your picture of the dentist is as vivid as your description of the nurse?") Substitute specific responses and suggestions for one-word labels such as "awk" (awkward) or "unclear." Even positive labels don't always help writers repeat effective techniques. ("Good!" enthusiastically inscribed in the margin by a well-developed paragraph feels nice but might cause the writer to wonder, "'Good' what? Good point? Good supporting evidence? Good detail? How can I do 'good' again if I don't know exactly what it is?")

5. Understand your role as critical reader. Sometimes it's easy for a reviewer to take ownership of someone else's paper. Keep the writer's purpose in mind as you respond; don't insist on revisions that produce the essay that's in *your* head. Be sensitive to your own voice and language as a reviewer. Instead of making authoritative pronouncements that might offend, ask reader-based questions ("Will all your readers know the meaning of this technical term?" "Would some readers profit from a brief history of this controversy?"). If you're unsure about a possible error, request verification ("Could you recheck this quotation? Its wording here is confusing me because . . ."). Practise offering criticism in language that acknowledges the writer's hard work and accentuates the positive nature of revision ("Would citing last year's budget figures make your good argument against the fish market even stronger?").

Last, always look over your own draft in light of the insightful suggestions you are offering your classmates. You may feel at first that it is far simpler to analyze someone else's writing than your own. As you participate in revision workshops, however, you will find it increasingly easy to transfer those same critical reading skills to your own work. Becoming a good reader–reviewer for your composition colleagues can be an important part of your training as a first-rate writer.

■ **PRACTISING WHAT YOU'VE LEARNED**

A. Assume that the essay below is a draft written by one of your classmates who has asked you for help during a class workshop. He knows his draft needs extensive revision. Help him out by telling him what he might do in another draft to accomplish his purpose more effectively and better address his audience. Be specific and constructive.

What is his purpose? Has he made the best choices in organization, selection and development of ideas, paragraph structure, grammar, and diction? Does he use fresh images? How effective is his title in its content and its form? What is his thesis? Does he follow it through adequately? Are you satisfied with his evidence or with his logic? (See Chapter 10 for discussion on logic and evidence.) When he uses specific examples, how careful is he with citation and the credibility of his sources? (See Chapter 14 on research and citations.) Does he consider his audience carefully? Discuss why and how his essay needs revision.

DRUGS ARE NOT GOOD BECAUSE THEY CAUSE PAIN

On the rocky road of life there are many problems. Some are very bad and some are less bad. My problem in this essay is drugs because its very important. Drugs cause so much pain in people's lives and I definately want to focus on this. There are many kinds of drugs that have changed over a period of time. In English literature lots of fictional characters took drugs and real poets like Coleridge and De Quincey. As well, Sherlock Holmes. For these people in literature, drugs were a door to creativity. But all of them paid a huge price for it. Aldous Huxley, in his influential and amazing book, Brave New World, talked about the dangers of soma, a fictional drug that allowed some people in this world to control the others. He took hallucinogens himself, as it says in Wikipedia. But basically, drugs cause pain. In the essay we read in class the history of drug use for humans was traced. This proves drugs have been around from the dawn of time. People need to be educated about drugs.

Alot of people are using street drugs today. There are many kinds of these and people can get them from many different places: they have many street names. New formulations of street drugs come out everyday. Some started out as prescription meds but they got transformed somehow. All of them are pricey, and the cost is high for people like for Coleridge. Some research has been done on this in university studies, and police studies have proved this too. This proves drugs are everywhere.

Henceforth, people shouldn't take drugs. Not even just as an experiment. Not just young people but older people can get hooked and become enslaved Look at the celebrities on TV, how they're effected and their wealthy. In a study at Concordia University, they found anywhere from 25% to 85% of people go on to more addictive drugs even if they start with marijuana, so that shouldn't be legalized probably. Marijuana smells really bad, and you can be found out if your using it. Except for medical reasons marijuana is ok. Sometimes, drugs can take away pain.

The principle reason why people take drugs is because they want to have fun, and some want to solve problems. Some people even want to be creative like English poets. But drugs cause pain, they don't solve problems. These people are misguided. However, they should accept the road of life isn't smooth. Instead of depending on chemicals, they should depend on family and friends. We should all stand shoulder to shoulder to help our friends if they need us. We don't want our friends to be slaves to drugs, because freedom is important in our democracy today.

Though I'm not an expert, in my personal opinion people need more education about drugs and the pain they can cause. There are some great resources and programs in countries all over the world. For example, safe injection sites in places like Vancouver. Which are really amazing, even with funding shortages from the government. Also, in Albania, there are youth involvement programs were youth become peer educators, and in Vietnam, there are stickers on motorcycles that say, "Fill me up with gas, not drugs." Some countries target prison populations first in they're education programs. These organizations are all giving 110% to educating the public and solving the threat of drugs. Which shows education works. This is a different way of being creative and solving problems than taking drugs.

Therefore, down with drugs! Everyone deserves a helping hand and to be free. We should learn the best from literature and leave the rest. No man needs to be a slave to drugs—male or female!

B. Continue to practise your revision skills by writing a one-to-two-page evaluation of the essay that follows. Using your best critical thinking skills, offer some constructive marginal comments and questions that will guide this writer through an effective revision process. Are the paragraphs unified and adequately developed? Is the organization of ideas the most effective? Do the ideas flow well? Is the focus clear? Are you satisfied with the writer's use of evidence? Are you convinced by her argument? Do you feel you know more about the issue now? How could this essay be improved?

News Media and Responsibility

Over the last forty years, news agencies all over the world have become increasingly less responsible about the way they report news. Often, the most sensational aspect of a "news story" is highlighted, which relegates contextual or other important facts to a minor position, thus providing an inaccurate perspective on that story. Sometimes, reporters try to find analogies with other news items, even if those analogies are only superficially accurate. Again, this can seriously misrepresent the story. Probably the most serious example of irresponsibility comes from a tendency to jump the gun with a story without checking the facts carefully. When they don't know facts about a story, they start to speculate.

Strikes can certainly have their sensational aspects. Minor clashes can occur between strikers, management, strike breakers and members of the general public. The strike action can escalate as a strike continues. Striking workers can make strident public speeches condemning management. Management can respond by outlining the outrageous demands of the strikers. But when only the clashes or insulting language are reported, there can be a huge misconception about the causes of the strike, the progress of the strike and the nature of the strikers. These sensational aspects of a crisis situation can make entertaining news, but news agencies are responsible for reporting in as balanced, fair and accurate a manner as possible. The real issues faced by strikers and those they affect need to be explained clearly and without judgement.

News agencies are increasingly allowing reporters to show emotions that are socially approved or to use words that represent those emotions. The job of a reporter is to report the news objectively, not to guide the audience in how to respond to the news.

When a building in a local university campus last year was suddenly shut down in the middle of the day and students and faculty were trapped in the building for hours, the instant reaction of the media was to assume a school shooter was on the loose. Without knowing facts, since the RCMP was giving very little information, reporters began to present long reports on what they saw as analogous situations, complete with profiles of school assassins in other North American cities, footage of actual school shootings, and so on. The actual footage at the campus was quite tame, so they simply substituted footage they found more interesting. Although they did note that the sensational footage was from other situations, they blurred the line between what was actually happening, and the apparently more interesting and newsworthy occurrences elsewhere.

One of the biggest news events of the last part of the twentieth century was the death of Princess Diana. Without checking the facts, news agencies scrambled to be first to say she was in an accident, she was dead, she was not dead but injured, she had walked away from the accident, and so on. They also scrambled to blame the paparazzi for the accident, and then to suggest there was a conspiracy to murder her. What proof did they have? Why was getting the news reported first more important than reporting accurate news?

Recently, a number of tennis shoes containing dismembered human feet have washed up on the shores of British Columbia. None of these have been matched to missing persons, and the number of shoes recovered, have suggested they must be connected in some way. This is certainly a sensational mystery, but the operative word is mystery. When the American television host Nancy Grace picked up on this story, she immediately brought in several experts in law and forensic science to talk about this story. Neither Grace nor the panel experts appeared to have any more solid information than any other news agency, so they filled up the airtime with speculations about what the shoes *might* mean. Members of the public called in to add their speculations to the discussion. The result was that all kinds of wild speculations went out to the general public, and though no consensus was reached, the audience was left with the vague idea that perhaps a mysterious, unreported plane crash was the cause or that a serial killer was on the loose. There was no credible proof of any of these theories.

Most audience members never stop to think about the ways in which their understanding of the world is being manipulated by news media. The general public should become aware of media irresponsibility, and demand more stringent codes of conduct. The first step should be to set up an independent board that evaluates news reporting.

Select a body paragraph from "Dorm Life" (pages 100–102), "Drugs Are Not Good Because They Cause Pain" (pages 105–106), or "News Media and Responsibility" (pages 106–107) and revise it, making any changes in focus, organization, development, sentence construction, or word choice you think necessary. (Feel free to elaborate on, eliminate, or change the content to improve the paragraph's effectiveness.) Once you've practised with the body paragraph, revise (or rewrite!) the whole essay, making any changes necessary. Use the revision guidelines in this chapter to help you.

■ Some Last Advice: How to Play with Your Mental Blocks

Every writer, sooner or later, suffers from some form of writer's block, the inability to think of or organize ideas. Symptoms may include sweaty palms, pencil chewing, and a pronounced tendency to sit in corners and weep. Although not every "cure" works for everyone, here are a few suggestions to help minimize your misery:

Try to give yourself as much time as possible to write your essay. Don't try to write the entire paper in one sitting. By doing so, you place yourself under too much pressure. Writer's block often accompanies the "up against the wall" feeling that strikes at 2:00 a.m. the morning your essay is due at 9:00. Rome wasn't constructed in a day, and neither are most good essays.

Sometimes writer's block makes you want to . . .

Because most of us have had more experience talking than writing, try verbalizing your ideas. Sometimes it's helpful to discuss your ideas with friends or classmates. Their questions and comments (not to mention their sympathy for your temporary block) will often trigger the thoughts you need to begin writing again. Or you might try talking into a recorder so you can hear what you want to say.

When an irresistible force meets an immovable object, something's going to give. Conquer the task: break the paper into manageable bits. Instead of drooping with despair over the thought of a ten-page research paper, think of it as a series of small parts (explanation of the problem, review of current research, possible solutions, etc.). Then tackle one part at a time and reward yourself when that section's done.

The Scream, *1893, by Edvard Munch*

Get the juices flowing and the pen moving. Try writing the easiest or shortest part of your essay first. A feeling of accomplishment may give you the boost of confidence you need to undertake the other, more difficult sections. If no part looks easy or inviting, try more prewriting exercises, as described in Chapter 1, until you feel prepared to begin the essay itself.

Play "Let's Make a Deal" with yourself. Sometimes we just can't face the failure that we are predicting for ourselves. Strike a bargain with yourself: promise yourself that you are only going to work on your paper for twenty minutes—absolutely, positively only twenty minutes, not a second more, no sir, no way. If in twenty minutes, you're on to something good, ignore your promise to yourself and keep going. If you're not, then leave and come back for another twenty-minute session later (if you started early enough, you can do this without increasing your anxiety).

Give yourself permission to write nonsense. Take the pressure off yourself by agreeing in advance to tear up the first page or two of whatever you write. You can always change your mind if the trash turns out to be treasure; if it isn't, so what? You said you were going to tear it up anyway.

Imagine that your brain is a water faucet. If you're like most people, you've probably lived in a house or apartment containing a faucet that needed to run a few minutes before the hot water came out. Think of your brain in the same way, and do some other, easier writing task to warm up. Write a letter, send an e-mail, make a grocery list, copy notes, whatever, to get your brain running. When you turn to your essay, your ideas may be hotter than you thought.

Remove the threat by addressing a friendly face. Sometimes we can't write because we are too worried about what someone else will think about us or maybe we can't write because we can't figure out who would want to read this stuff anyway. Instead of writing into a void or to an audience that seems threatening, try writing to a friend. Imagine what that friend's responses might be and try to elaborate or clarify wherever necessary. If it helps, write the first draft as a letter ("Dear Clyde, I want to tell you what happened to me last week . . ."), and then redraft your ideas as an essay when you've found your purpose and focus, making whatever changes in tone or development are necessary to fit your real audience.

If writer's block does hit, remember that it is a temporary stop, not a permanent one. Other writers have had it—and survived to write again. Try leaving your draft and taking a walk outdoors or at least into another room. Think about your readers—what should they know or feel at this point in your essay? As you walk, try to complete this sentence: "What I am trying to say is. . . ." Keep repeating this phrase and your responses aloud until you find the answer you want.

Sometimes while you're blocked at one point, a bright idea for another part of your essay will pop into your head. If possible, skip the section that's got you stuck and start working on the new part. (At least jot down the new idea somewhere, so it won't be lost when you need it later.)

Change partners and dance. If you're thoroughly overcome by the vast white wasteland on the desk (or screen) before you, get up and do something else for a while. Exercise, balance your chequebook, or put on music and dance. (Mystery writer Agatha Christie claimed she did her best planning while washing the dishes.) Give your mind a break and refresh your spirit. When you come back to the paper or computer, you may be surprised to discover that your subconscious writer has been working while the rest of you played.

Here's the single most important piece of advice to remember: relax. No one—not even the very best professional writer—produces perfect prose every time pen hits paper or fingers strike the keyboard. If you're blocked, you may be trying too hard; if your expectations of your first draft are too high, you may not be able to write at all for fear of failure. You just might be holding yourself back by being a perfectionist at this point. You can always revise and polish your prose in another draft—the first important step is jotting down your ideas. Remember that once the first word or phrase appears on your blank page or screen, a major battle has been won.

CHAPTER 5 SUMMARY

Here is a brief summary of what you should remember about revising your writing:

1. Revision is an activity that occurs in all stages of the writing process.

2. All good writers revise their prose extensively.

3. Revision is not merely editing or last-minute proofreading; it involves important decisions about the essay's ideas, organization, and development.

4. To revise effectively, novice writers might review their drafts in steps to avoid the frustration that comes with trying to fix everything at once.

5. Most writers experience writer's block at some time but live through it to write again.

Chapter 6

Effective Sentences

An insurance agent was shocked to open his mail one morning and read the following note from one of his clients: "In accordance with your instructions, I have given birth to twins in the enclosed envelope." Perhaps he may have been as astonished as the patrons of a health club who learned that "Guest passes will not be given to members until the manager has punched each of them first." However, he may not have been more surprised than the congregation who read this announcement in their church bulletin: "There will be a discussion tomorrow on the problem of adultery in the minister's office."

Certainly, there were no babies born in an envelope, nor was there adultery in the minister's office, and one doubts that the club manager was planning to assault the membership. But the implications (and the unintended humour) are nevertheless present—solely because of the faulty ways in which the sentences were constructed.

To improve your own writing, you must express your thoughts in clear, coherent sentences that produce precisely the reader response you want. Effective sentences are similar to the threads in a piece of knitting or weaving: each thread helps form the larger design; if any one thread becomes tangled or lost, the pattern becomes muddled. In an essay, the same is true: if any sentence is fuzzy or obscure, the reader may lose the point of your discussion and in some cases never bother to regain it. Therefore, to hold your readers, you must concentrate on writing informative, effective sentences that continuously clarify the purpose of your essay.

Many problems in sentence clarity involve errors in grammar, punctuation, word choice, and usage; the most common of these errors are discussed in Chapter 7, "Word Logic," and throughout Part Four, the handbook section of this text. In this chapter you'll find some general suggestions for writing clear, concise, engaging sentences. However, *don't try to apply all the rules to the first draft of your essay*. Revising sentences before your ideas are firmly in place may mean you have to redo your work if your essay's stance or structure changes. Concentrate your efforts in early drafts on your thesis, the development of your important supporting points, and the essay's general organization. Then, in a later draft, rework your sentences so that each one is informative and clear. Your reader reads only the words on the page, not those in your mind—so it's up to you to make sure the sentences in your essay express the thoughts in your head as closely and vividly as possible.

 REMEMBER: All good writers revise and polish their sentences.

■ Developing a Clear Style

When you are ready to revise the sentences in your rough draft for clarity, try to follow the following five rules.

Give Your Sentences Content

Fuzzy sentences are often the result of fuzzy thinking. When you examine your sentences, ask yourself, "Do I know what I'm talking about here? Are my sentences vague or confusing because I'm really not sure what my point is or where it's going?" Look at this list of content-poor sentences taken from student essays. How could you put more information into each one?

> If you were to observe a karate class, you would become familiar with all the aspects that make it up.

> The meaning of the poem isn't very clear the first time you read it, but after several readings, the poet's meaning comes through.

> One important factor that is the basis for determining a true friend is the ability that person has for being a real human being.

> Listening is important because we all need to be able to sit and hear all that is said to us.

Don't pad your paragraphs with sentences that run in circles, leading nowhere; rethink your ideas and revise your writing so that every sentence—like each brick in a wall—contributes to the construction of a solid discussion. In other words, commit yourself to a position and make each sentence contain information pertinent to your point; leave the job of padding to mattress manufacturers.

Sometimes, however, you may have a definite idea in mind but still continue to write "empty sentences"—statements that, alone, do not contain enough information to make a specific point in your discussion. Frequently, an empty sentence may be revised by combining it with the sentence that follows, as shown in the examples here. The empty, or overly general, sentences are underlined.

Poor   <u>There are many kinds of beautiful tropical fish.</u> The kind most popular with aquarium owners is the angelfish.

Better	Of the many kinds of beautiful tropical fish, the angelfish is the most popular with aquarium owners.
Poor	Susanna Moodie and Catherine Parr Traill were two sisters. They moved to Canada in the early nineteenth century. They wrote lively accounts about their experiences as new settlers in Canada.
Better	Early nineteenth-century pioneers Susanna Moodie and her sister Catherine Parr Traill both wrote lively accounts of their adventures as new Canadian settlers.
Poor	There is a very successful Internet shopping site called Abe Books. Its profits increase every year.
Better	The profits of the successful Internet shopping site, Abe Books, increase every year.

For more help on combining sentences, see pages 129–131.

Make Your Sentences Specific

In addition to containing an informative, complete thought, each of your sentences should give readers enough clear details for them to "see" the picture you are creating. Sentences full of vague words produce blurry, boring prose and drowsy readers. Remember your reaction the last time you asked a friend about a recent vacation? If the only response you received was something like, "Oh, it was great—a lot of fun," you probably yawned and proceeded quickly to a new topic. But if your friend had begun an exciting account of a wilderness rafting trip, with detailed stories about narrow escapes from freezing white water, treacherous rocks, and uncharted whirlpools, you'd probably have stopped and listened. The same principle works in your writing—clear, specific details are the only sure way to attract and hold the reader's interest. Therefore, make each sentence contribute something new and interesting to the overall discussion.

The following examples first show sentences far too vague to sustain anyone's attention. Rewritten, these sentences contain specific details that add clarity and interest:

Vague	She went home in a bad mood. [What kind of a bad mood? How did she act or look?]
Specific	She stomped home, hands jammed in her pockets, angrily kicking rocks, dogs, small children, and anything else that crossed her path.
Vague	His neighbour bought a really nice old desk. [Why nice? How old? What kind of desk?]
Specific	His neighbour bought a solid-oak rolltop desk made in 1885 that contains a secret drawer triggered by a hidden spring.
Vague	My roommate is truly horrible. ["Horrible" in what ways? To what extent? Do you "see" this person?]
Specific	My thoughtless roommate leaves dirty dishes under the bed, sweaty clothes in the closet, and toenail clippings in the sink.

For more help selecting specific "showing" words, see pages 144–145 in Chapter 7.

Avoid Over-Packing Your Sentences

Because our society is becoming increasingly specialized and highly technical, we tend to equate complexity with excellence and simplicity with simple-mindedness. This assumption is unfortunate, because it often leads to a preference for unnecessarily complicated and even contorted writing. In a recent survey, for example, a student who was asked to choose the most impressive writing sample out of a series of paragraphs chose a sample of bureaucratic hogwash over several well-written paragraphs, explaining his choice by saying that it must have been better because he didn't understand it.

Our best writers have always worked hard to present their ideas simply and specifically so that their readers could easily understand them. Mark Twain, for instance, once praised a young author this way: "I notice that you use plain simple language, short words, and brief sentences. This is the way to write English. It is the modern way and the best way. Stick to it." And when a critic asked Hemingway to define his theory of writing, he replied, "[I] put down what I see and what I feel in the best and simplest way I can tell it."

In your own writing, therefore, work for a simple, direct style. Avoid sentences that are over-packed (too many ideas or too much information at once) as in the following example on racquetball:

> John told Phil that to achieve more control over the ball, he should practise flicking or snapping his wrist, because this action is faster in the close shots and placing a shot requires only a slight change of the wrist's angle instead of an acute movement of the whole arm, which gives a player less reaction time.

To make the over-packed sentence easier to understand, try dividing the ideas into two or more sentences:

> John told Phil that to achieve more control over the ball, he should practice flicking or snapping his wrist, because this action is faster in the close shots. Placing a shot requires only a slight change of the wrist's angle instead of an acute movement of the whole arm, which gives a player less reaction time.

Don't ever run the risk of losing your reader in a sentence that says too much to comprehend in one bite. This confusing notice, for example, came from a well-known credit card company:

> The Minimum Payment Due each month shall be reduced by the amounts paid in excess of the Minimum Payment Due during the previous three months which have not already been so applied in determining the Minimum Payment Due in such earlier months, unless you have exceeded your line of credit or have paid the entire New Balance shown on your billing statement.

Or consider the confusion of soccer players whose coach warned them in this manner:

> It is also a dangerous feeling to consider that where we are in the league is of acceptable standard because standard is relevant to the standards we have set, which thereby may well indicate that we have not aspired to the standard which we set ourselves.

Try for a straightforward construction as well; these sentences by British television character Sir Humphrey Appleby, for example, take far too many twists and turns for anyone to follow them easily on the first reading:

> Minister, the traditional allocation of executive responsibilities has always been so determined as to liberate the ministerial incumbent from the administrative minutiae by devolving the managerial functions to those whose experience and qualifications have better formed them for the performance of such humble offices, thereby releasing their political overlords for the more onerous duties and profound deliberations which are the inevitable concomitant of their exalted position.

> Well it was a conversation to the effect that, in view of the somewhat nebulous and inexplicit nature of your remit, and the arguably marginal and peripheral nature of your influence on the central deliberations and decisions within the political process, there could be a case for restructuring their action priorities in such a way as to eliminate your liquidation from their immediate agenda.

If any sentences in your rough draft are over-packed or contorted, try rephrasing your meaning in shorter sentences and then combining thoughts where most appropriate. (Help with sentence variety may be found on pages 126–128 of this chapter.)

Pay Attention to Word Order

The correct word order is crucial for clarity. Always place a modifier (a word or group of words that affects the meaning of another word) near the word it modifies. The position of a modifier can completely change the meaning of your sentence; for example, each sentence presented here offers a different idea because of the placement of the modifier "only."

1. Mitsuko said she loves only me.
   [Mitsuko loves me and no one else.]

2. Only Mitsuko said she loves me.
   [No other person said she loves me.]

3. Mitsuko only said she loves me.
   [Mitsuko said she loves me, but said nothing other than that.]

4. Mitsuko said only she loves me.
   [Mitsuko says no one else loves me.]

To avoid confusion, therefore, place your modifiers close to the words or phrases they describe.

A modifier that seems to modify the wrong part of a sentence is called "misplaced." Not only can misplaced modifiers change or distort the meaning of your sentence, they can also provide unintentional humour, as illustrated by the following excerpt from the 1929 Marx Brothers' movie *Coconuts:*

Woman: There's a man waiting outside to see you with a black mustache.

Groucho: Tell him I've already got one.

Of course, the woman didn't mean to imply that the man outside was waiting with (that is, accompanied by) a mustache; she meant to say, "There's a man with a black mustache who is waiting outside."

A poster advertising a lecture on campus provided this opportunity for humour: "Professor Elizabeth Sewell will discuss the latest appearance of Halley's Comet in room 104." Under the announcement a local wit had scribbled, "Shall we reserve room 105 for the tail?" Or take the case of this startling headline: "Calf Born to Rancher with Two Heads."

Here are some other examples of misplaced modifiers:

Misplaced	Dilapidated and almost an eyesore, Shirley bought the old house to restore it to its original beauty. [Did the writer mean that Shirley needed a beauty treatment?]
Revised	Shirley bought the old house, which was dilapidated and almost an eyesore, to restore it to its original beauty.
Misplaced	Because she is now thoroughly housebroken, Sarah can take her dog almost anywhere she goes. [Did the writer mean that Sarah once had an embarrassing problem?]
Revised	Because she is now thoroughly housebroken, Sarah's dog can accompany her almost anywhere she goes.
Misplaced	Three family members were found bound and gagged by the grandmother. [Did the writer mean that the grandmother had taken up a life of crime?]
Revised	The grandmother found the three family members who had been bound and gagged.
Misplaced	The lost child was finally found wandering in a frozen farmer's field. [Did the writer mean to say that the farmer was that cold?]
Revised	The lost child was finally found wandering in a farmer's frozen field.

In each of the preceding examples the writer forgot to place the modifying phrase so that it modifies the correct word. In most cases, a sentence with a misplaced modifier can be corrected easily by moving the word or phrase closer to the word that should be modified.

In some sentences, however, the word being modified is missing entirely. Such a phrase is called a "dangling modifier." Think of these phrases as poor orphans, waiting out in the cold, without a parent to accompany them. Most of these errors may be corrected by adding the missing "parent"—the word(s) described by the phrase. Here are some examples followed by their revisions:

Dangling	Waving farewell, the plane began to roll down the runway. [Did the writer mean the plane was waving farewell?]
Revised	Waving farewell, <u>we</u> watched as the plane began to roll down the runway.
Dangling	After spending hours planting dozens of strawberry plants, the gophers came back to the garden and ate every one of them. [Did the writer mean that the gophers had a good meal after putting in such hard work?]

Revised	After spending hours planting dozens of strawberry plants, Kim realized that the gophers had come back to the garden and eaten every one of them.
Dangling	While telling a joke to my roommate, a cockroach walked across my soufflé. [Did the writer mean that the cockroach was a comedian?]
Revised	While telling a joke to my roommate, <u>I</u> noticed a cockroach walking across my soufflé.
Dangling	Having tucked the children into bed, the cat was put out for the night. [Did the writer mean that the family pet had taken up nanny duties?]
Revised	Having tucked the children into bed, <u>Mother and Father</u> put the cat out for the night.

Misplaced and dangling modifiers (and many other kinds of sentence errors) often occur as you write your first "idea" or discovery drafts. Later, when you are satisfied with your content and organization, you can smooth out these confusing or unintentionally humorous constructions. At first you may agree with well-known essayist Annie Dillard, who notes that writing sometimes feels like alligator wrestling: "With your two bare hands, you hold and fight a sentence's head while its tail tries to knock you over." By practising good revision skills, however, you soon should be able to wrestle your sentence problems to the ground. (For additional examples of misplaced and dangling modifiers, see page 486 in Part Four.)

Avoid Mixed Constructions and Faulty Predication

Sometimes you may begin with a sentence pattern in mind and then shift, mid-sentence, to another pattern—a change that often results in a generally confusing sentence. In many of these cases, you will find that the subject of your sentence simply doesn't fit with the rest of the sentence (the predicate). Look at the following examples and note their corrections:

Faulty	Financial aid is a growing problem for many college students. [Financial aid itself isn't a problem; rather, it's the lack of aid.]
Revised	College students are finding it harder to obtain financial aid.
Faulty	Pregnant cows are required to teach a portion of two courses in Animal Science, AS100 (Breeding of Livestock) and AS200 (Problems in Reproduction of Cattle). [Obviously, the cows will not be the instructors for the classes.]
Revised	The Animal Science Department needs to purchase pregnant cows for use in two courses, AS100 (Breeding of Livestock) and AS200 (Problems in Reproduction of Cattle).
Faulty	Love is when you start rehearsing dinner-date conversation before breakfast. [A thing is never a "when" or a "where"; rewrite all "is when" or "is where" constructions.]
Revised	You're in love if you start rehearsing dinner-date conversation before breakfast.

Faulty	My math grade is why I'm so depressed.
Revised	I'm so depressed because of my math grade. [A grade is not a "why"; rewrite "is why" constructions.]
Faulty	"Fans, don't fail to miss tomorrow's game." [A contorted line from Dizzy Dean, baseball star and sportscaster.]
Revised	"Fans, don't miss tomorrow's game."

Many mixed constructions occur when a writer is in a hurry; read your rough drafts carefully to see if you have sentences in which you started one pattern but switched to another. (For more help on faulty predications and mixed constructions, see pages 493–494 in Part Four.)

■ Developing a Concise Style

Almost all writing suffers from wordiness—the tendency to use more words than necessary. When useless words weigh down your prose, the meaning is often lost, confused, or hidden. Flabby prose calls for a reducing plan: put those obese sentences on a diet by cutting out unnecessary words, just as you avoid too many fatty foods to keep yourself at a healthy weight. Mushy prose is ponderous and boring; crisp, to-the-point writing, on the other hand, is both accessible and pleasing. Beware, however, a temptation to over-diet— you don't want your prose to become so thin or brief that your meaning disappears completely. Therefore, cut out only the *inessential* words and phrases.

Wordy prose is frequently the result of using one or more of the following: (1) deadwood constructions, (2) redundancies, (3) passive verbs, and (4) pretentious diction.

Avoid Deadwood Constructions

Always try to cut useless "deadwood" from your sentences. Having a clear, concise style does not mean limiting your writing to choppy, childish Dick-and-Jane sentences; it only means that all unnecessary words, phrases, and clauses should be deleted. Here are some sentences containing common deadwood constructions and ways they may be pruned:

Poor	The *reason* the starving novelist drove eighty kilometres to a new restaurant was *because* it was serving his favourite chicken dish, Pullet Surprise. ["The reason . . . was because" is both wordy and ungrammatical. If you have a reason, you don't need a "reason because."]
Revised	The starving novelist drove eighty kilometres to a new restaurant because it was serving his favourite chicken dish, Pullet Surprise.
Poor	The land settlement *was an example where* my client, Ms. Patti O. Furniture, did not receive fair treatment.
Revised	The land settlement was unfair to my client, Ms. Patti O. Furniture.
Poor	Because *of the fact that* his surfboard business failed after only a month, my brother decided to leave Saskatchewan.
Revised	Because his surfboard business failed after only a month, my brother decided to leave Saskatchewan.

Other notorious deadwood constructions include the following:

regardless of the fact that	(use "although")
due to the fact that	(use "because")

the reason is that	(omit)
as to whether or not to	(omit "as to" and "or not")
at this point in time	(use "now" or "today")
it is believed that	(use a specific subject and "believes")
concerning the matter of	(use "about")
by means of	(use "by")
these are the kinds of . . . that	(use "these" plus a specific noun)
on account of	(use "because")

Watch a tendency to tack on empty "fillers" that stretch one word into a phrase:

Wordy	Each candidate will be evaluated *on an individual basis.*
Concise	Each candidate will be evaluated *individually.*
Wordy	Television does not portray violence in a *realistic fashion.*
Concise	Television does not portray violence *realistically.*
Wordy	The Quebec ice storm produced a *crisis-type situation.*
Concise	The Quebec ice storm produced a *crisis.*

To retain your reader's interest and improve the flow of your prose, trim all the fat from your sentences.

"There are," "It is." These introductory phrases are often space wasters. When possible, omit them or replace them with specific subjects, as shown in the following:

Wordy	*There are* ten dental students on Full-Bite Scholarships attending this university.
Revised	Ten dental students on Full-Bite Scholarships attend this university.
Wordy	*It is* true that the County Fair still offers many fun contests, including the ever-popular map fold-off.
Revised	The County Fair still offers many fun contests, including the ever-popular map fold-off.

"Who" and "which" clauses. Some "who" and "which" clauses are unnecessary and may be turned into modifiers placed before the noun:

Wordy	The getaway car, *which* was stolen, turned the corner.
Revised	The stolen getaway car turned the corner.
Wordy	The chef, *who was* depressed, ordered his noisy lobsters to simmer down.
Revised	The depressed chef ordered his noisy lobsters to simmer down.

When adjective clauses are necessary, the words "who" and "which" may sometimes be omitted:

Wordy	Fiona Drews, *who* is a local artist, was delighted to hear that she had won a fellowship, *which is* sponsored by the Banff Centre for the Arts.
Revised	Fiona Drews, a local artist, was delighted to hear she had won a Banff Centre for the Arts fellowship.

"To be." Most "to be" phrases are unnecessary and ought not to be. Delete them every time you can.

Wordy	She seems *to be* angry.
Revised	She seems angry.
Wordy	Herb's charisma-bypass operation proved *to be* successful.
Revised	Herb's charisma-bypass operation proved successful.
Wordy	The new mayor wanted her archenemy, the local movie critic, *to be* arrested.
Revised	The new mayor wanted her archenemy, the local movie critic, arrested.

"Of" and infinitive phrases. Many "of" and infinitive ("to" plus verb) phrases may be omitted or revised by using possessives, adjectives, and verbs, as shown below:

Wordy	At the *time of registration*, students are required *to make* payment *of their library fees.*
Revised	At registration students must pay their library fees.
Wordy	The producer fired the mother *of the director of the movie.*
Revised	The producer fired the movie director's mother.

Including deadwood phrases makes your prose puffy; streamline your sentences to present a simple, direct style.

Avoid Redundancy

Many flabby sentences contain *redundancies* (words that repeat the same idea or whose meanings overlap). Consider the following examples, currently popular in the Department of Redundancy Department:

In this *day and age*, people expect to live at least seventy years. ["Day" and "age" present a similar idea. "Today" is less wordy.]

He repeated the winning bingo number *over again*. ["Repeated" means "to say again," so there is no need for "over again."]

The *group* consensus *of opinion* was that the pizza crust tasted like cardboard. ["Consensus" means "collective opinion," so it's unnecessary to add "group" or repeat "opinion."]

She thought his hot-lava necklaces were *really very* unique. [Because "unique" means "being the only one of its kind," the quality described by "unique" cannot vary in degree. Avoid adding modifiers such as "very," "most," or "somewhat" to the word "unique."]

Some other common redundancies include:

reverted ~~back~~	~~new~~ innovation
reflected ~~back~~	red ~~in colour~~
retreated ~~back~~	burned ~~down~~ up

fell ~~down~~	~~pair of~~ twins~~/two~~ twins
climb ~~up~~	~~resulting~~ effect (or "result")
a ~~true~~ fact	~~final~~ outcome
large ~~in size~~	at this point ~~in time~~ (or "now")
joined ~~up~~	8 p.m. ~~at night~~

Carefully Consider Your Passive Verbs

When the subject of the sentence performs the action, the verb is *active;* when the subject of the sentence is acted on, the verb is *passive*. You can recognize some sentences with passive verbs because they often contain the word "by," telling who performed the action.

Passive	The wedding date *was announced* by the young couple.
Active	The young couple *announced* their wedding date.
Passive	His letter of resignation *was accepted* by the Board of Trustees.
Active	The Board of Trustees *accepted* his letter of resignation.
Passive	The demonstration *was attended* by a group of local senior activists, the Grumpy Grannies.
Active	The local senior activist group, the Grumpy Grannies, *attended* the demonstration.

In addition to being wordy and weak, passive sentences often disguise the performer of the action in question. You might have heard a politician, for example, say something similar to this: "It was decided this year to give all the city councillors an increase in salary." The question of *who* decided to raise salaries remains foggy—perhaps purposefully so. In your own prose, however, you should strive for clarity and directness; therefore, use active verbs as often as you can except when you wish to stress the person or thing that receives the action, as shown in the following samples:

Their first baby was delivered September 30, 1980, by a local midwife.

The elderly man was struck by a drunk driver.

Special note: Authorities in some professional and technical fields still prefer the passive construction because they wish to put emphasis on the experiment or process rather than on the people performing the action. If the passive voice is preferred in your field, you should abide by that convention when you are writing reports or papers for your professional colleagues.

Avoid Pretentiousness

Another enemy of clear, concise prose is *pretentiousness*. Pompous, inflated language surrounds us, and because too many people think it sounds learned or official, we may be tempted to use it when we want to impress others with our writing. But as George Orwell, author of *1984*, noted, an inflated style is like "a cuttlefish squirting out ink." If you want your prose easily understood, write as clearly and plainly as possible.

To illustrate how confusing pretentious writing can be, here is a copy of a U.S. government memo announcing a blackout order, issued in 1942 during World War II:

> Such preparations shall be made as will completely obscure all Federal buildings and non-Federal buildings occupied by the Federal government during an air raid for any period of time from visibility by reason of internal or external illumination.

American President Franklin Roosevelt intervened and rewrote the order in plain English, clarifying its message and reducing the number of words by half:

> Tell them that in buildings where they have to keep the work going to put something across the windows.

By translating the obscure original memo into easily understandable language, Roosevelt demonstrated that a natural prose style can communicate necessary information to readers more quickly and efficiently than bureaucratic jargon. (For more advice on ridding your prose of jargon, see pages 147–149 in Chapter 7.)

> ✓ **REMEMBER:** In other—shorter—words, to attract and hold your readers' attention, to communicate clearly and quickly, make your sentences as informative, straightforward, specific, and concise as possible.

▪ PRACTISING WHAT YOU'VE LEARNED

A. The following sentences are vague, "empty," over-packed, or confused. Rewrite each one so that it is clear and specific, combining or dividing sentences and adding content as necessary. As you add content and consider style, also consider the context in which this sentence would appear. Are you writing a formal essay or a personal essay? What would be appropriate for a college- or university-level essay?

1. Roger was an awesome guy who was really a big part of his company.

2. There's a new detective show on television. It stars Phil Noir and is set in the 1940s.

3. Sanjay's room is always a huge disaster.

4. The book *Biofeedback: How to Stop It* is a good one because of all the ideas the writer put into it.

5. I can't help but wonder whether or not he isn't unwelcome.

6. Afraid poor repair service will ruin your next road trip? Come to the Fix-It Shop and be sure. If your car has a worn-out part, we'll replace it with one just like it.

7. I've signed up for a course at my local community college. It is "Cultivating the Mould in Your Refrigerator for Fun and Profit."

8. For some people, reading your horoscope is a fun way to learn stuff about your life, but some people think it's too weird, even though the others don't.

9. I'm not sure but I think that Lois is the author of *The Underachiever's Guide to Very Small Business Opportunities* or is she the writer of *Whine Your Way to Success* because I know she's written several books since she's having an autograph party at the campus bookstore either this afternoon or tomorrow.

10. Upon being asked if she would like to live forever, one contestant in the 1994 Miss USA contest replied: "I would not live forever, because we should not live forever, because if we were supposed to live forever, then we would live forever, but we cannot live forever, which is why I would not live forever."

B. The following sentences contain misplaced words and phrases as well as other faulty constructions. Revise them so that each sentence is clear.

1. If you are accosted in the subway at night, you should learn to escape harm from the police.

2. The bride was escorted down the aisle by her stepfather wearing an antique family wedding gown.

3. Almost dead for five years now, I miss my dog so much.

4. For sale: unique gifts for that special, hard-to-find person in your life.

5. The reason why I finally got my leg operated on over Thanksgiving break is because it had been hanging over my head for years.

6. We need to hire two three-year-old teachers for preschool kids who don't smoke.

7. The story of Rip Van Winkle is one of the dangers endured by those who oversleep.

8. We gave our waterbed to friends we didn't want anymore.

9. People who are allergic to chocolate and children under six should not be given the new vaccine.

10. At 7:00 a.m., Kate starts preparing for another busy day as an executive in her luxurious bathroom.

C. The following sentences are filled with deadwood, redundancies, awkward phrases, and passive constructions. Rewrite each one so that it is concise and direct.

1. In point of fact, the main reason he lost the editing job was primarily because of his being too careless and sloppy in his proofreading work.

2. It was revealed to us by staff members today that there were many adults at the company picnic throwing their trash on the ground as well as their children.

3. My brother Austin, who happens to be older than me, can't drive to work this week due to the fact that he was in a wreck in his car at 2:00 a.m. early Saturday morning.

4. In this modern world of today, we often criticize or disapprove of advertising that is thought to be damaging to women by representing them in an unfair way.

5. When the prosecution tried to introduce the old antique gun, this was objected to by the attorney defending the two twin brothers.

6. It seems to me in my opinion that what the poet is trying to get across to the reader in the poem "Now Is the Winter of Our Discount Tent" is her feeling of disgust with camping.

7. We very often felt that although we expressed our deepest concerns and feelings to our boss, she often just sat there and gave us the real impression that she was taking what we said in a very serious manner although, in our opinion, she did not really and truly care about our concerns.

8. It is a true fact that certainly bears repeating over and over again that learning computer skills and word processing can help you perform in a more efficient way at work and school and also can save you lots of time in daily life too.

9. Personally, I believe that there are too many people who go to eat out in restaurants who always feel they must continually assert their superior natures by acting in a rude, nasty fashion to the people who are employed to wait on their tables.

10. In order to enhance my opportunities for advancement in the workplace at this point in time, I arrived at the decision to seek the hand of my employer's daughter in the state of matrimony.

■ ASSIGNMENT

Write a paragraph of at least five sentences as clearly and concisely as you can. Then rewrite this paragraph, filling it with as many vague words, redundancies, and deadwood constructions as possible. Exchange this rewritten paragraph for a similarly faulty one written by a classmate; give yourselves fifteen minutes to "translate" each other's sentences into effective prose. Compare the translations to the original paragraphs. Which version is clearer? Why?

■ Developing a Lively Style

Good writing demands clarity and conciseness—but that's not all. Good prose must also be lively, engaging, and interesting. It should excite, intrigue, and charm; each line should seduce the reader into the next. Consider, for example, a dull article you've read lately. It may have been written clearly, but perhaps it failed to interest or inform because of its insufferably bland tone; by the time you finished a few pages, you had discovered a new cure for insomnia.

You can prevent your readers from succumbing to a similar case of the blahs by developing a vigorous prose style that continually surprises and pleases them. As one writer has pointed out, all subjects—with the possible exceptions of sex and money—are dull until somebody makes them interesting. As you revise your rough drafts, remember: bored readers are not born but made. Therefore, here are some practical suggestions to help you transform ho-hum prose into lively sentences and paragraphs:

Use specific, descriptive verbs. Avoid bland verbs that must be supplemented by modifiers.

Bland	His fist *broke* the window *into many little pieces.*
Better	His fist *shattered* the window.
Bland	The Doukhobors *were moved* from their settlements over and over again.
Better	The government agencies *hounded* the Doukhobors from settlement to settlement.
Bland	The exhausted runner *went* up the last hill *in an unsteady way.*
Better	The exhausted runner *staggered* up the last hill.

To cut wordiness that weighs down your prose, try to use an active verb instead of a noun plus a colourless verb such as "to be," "to have," "to get," "to do," and "to make." Avoid unnecessary uses of "got."

Wordy	At first the players and managers *had an argument* over the money, but finally they *came to an agreement that got* the contract dispute settled.
Better	At first the players and managers *argued* over the money, but finally they *settled* the contract dispute.
Wordy	The executives *made the decision* to *have another meeting* on Tuesday.
Better	The executives *decided* to *meet again* on Tuesday.
Wordy	Victor Frankenstein made many experiments on cadavers that he stole, which led to the creation of a monstrous creature that committed murder.
Better	Victor Frankenstein's frequent experiments on stolen cadavers led him to create a monstrous, murderous creature.

Use specific, precise modifiers that help the reader see, hear, or feel what you are describing. Adjectives such as "good," "bad," "many," "more," "great," "a lot," "important," and "interesting" are too vague to paint the reader a clear picture. Similarly, the adverbs "very," "really," "too," and "quite" are overused and add little to sentence clarity. The following are examples of weak sentences and their revisions:

Imprecise	The potion changed the scientist into a *really old* man.
Better	The potion changed the scientist into a *one-hundred-year-old* man.
Imprecise	Ali is a very *interesting* person.
Better	Ali is *witty, intelligent,* and *talented.*

Imprecise	The vegetables tasted *funny*.
Better	The vegetables tasted *like moss mixed with Krazy Glue*.

(For more advice on using specific, colourful words, see pages 144–146 in Chapter 7.)

Emphasize people when possible. Try to focus on human beings rather than abstractions whenever you can. Next to our fascinating selves, we most enjoy hearing about other people. Although all the sentences in the first paragraph below are correct, the second one is clearer and more useful because the over-packed sentences have been eliminated and the various examples have been summarized into categories.

Original	A student may be placed on financial hold as a result of outstanding indebtedness to the University, including tuition fees, student fees, parking fines, library fines, housing and conference fees. When a student has been placed on financial hold, no subsequent registration activity will be allowed and no transcripts of academic record or graduation diploma will be issued. The Department of Housing and Conferences may refuse admission to residences and may withdraw privileges, including dining privileges, requiring a resident to vacate the premises; Parking and Access Control Services may withdraw parking privileges and may tow vehicles; and the UBC Library may withdraw borrowing privileges and access to its collection of electronic information. (University of British Columbia fee regulation)
Revised	A student may be barred from registration or from getting transcripts, and from all university services, such as housing, parking and library privileges, until all fees and fines are paid.

Here's a similar example with a bureaucratic focus rather than a personal one:

Original	The salary deflations will most seriously impact the secondary educational profession.
Revised	High-school teachers will suffer the biggest salary reductions.

Obviously, the revised sentence is the more easily understood of the two because the reader knows exactly who will be affected by the pay cuts. In your own prose, wherever appropriate, try to replace vague abstractions, such as "society," "culture," "administrative concerns," "programmatic expectations," and so forth, with the human beings you're thinking about. In other words, remember to talk *to* people *about* people.

Vary your sentence style. The only torture worse than listening to someone's nails scraping across a blackboard is being forced to read a paragraph full of identically constructed sentences. To illustrate this point, the following are a few sentences composed in the all-too-common "subject + predicate" pattern:

> The Canadians were loyal to the British. The Canadians had a strong strategy. The Canadians were well trained. The Canadian soldiers advanced across the border. The Canadian forces then attacked the American outposts. The Canadian generals then decided to march on to Washington.

Excruciatingly painful, yes? Each of us has a tendency to repeat a particular sentence pattern (though the choppy "subject + predicate" is by far the most popular); you can often detect your own by reading your prose aloud. To avoid overdosing your readers with the same pattern, vary the length, arrangement, and complexity of your sentences. Of course, this doesn't mean that you should contort your sentences merely for the sake of illustrating variety; just read your rough draft aloud, listening carefully to the rhythm of your prose so you can revise any monotonous passages or disharmonious sounds. (Try also to avoid the hiccup syndrome, in which you begin a sentence with the same word that ends the preceding sentence "Most high-school students read the Canadian classic, *Who Has Seen the Wind*, by W.O. Mitchell. Mitchell wrote about life in a small prairie town.")

Avoid overuse of any one kind of construction in the same sentence. Don't, for example, pile up too many negatives, "who" or "which" clauses, and prepositional or infinitive phrases in one sentence.

He *couldn't* tell whether she *didn't* want him to go or *not*.

I gave the money to my brother, *who* returned it to the bank president, *who* said the decision to prosecute was up to the sheriff, *who* was out of town.

I went to the florist *for* my roommate *for* a dozen roses *for* his date.

Try also to avoid stockpiling nouns, one on top of another, so that your sentences are difficult to read. Although some nouns may be used as adjectives to modify other nouns ("stealth bomber," "gasoline pump," "food processor"), too many nouns grouped together sound awkward and confuse readers. If you have run too many nouns together, try using prepositional phrases ("an income tax bill discussion" becomes "discussion of an income tax bill"), or changing the order or vocabulary of the sentence:

Confusing	The legislators are currently considering the *liability insurance multiple-choice premium proposal.*
Clearer	The legislators are currently considering the proposal that suggests *multiple-choice premiums* for *liability insurance.*
Confusing	We're concerned about the low *female labour force participation figures* in our department.
Clearer	We're concerned about the low *number of women working* in our department.

Don't change your point of view between or within sentences. If, for example, you begin your essay discussing students as "they," don't switch midway—or mid-sentence—to "we" or "you."

Inconsistent	Students pay tuition, which should entitle *them* to some voice in the university's administration. Therefore, *we* deserve one student on the Board of Regents.
Consistent	Students pay tuition, which should entitle *them* to some voice in the university's administration. Therefore, *they* deserve one student on the Board of Regents.

Inconsistent	*I* like my photography class because *we* learn how to restore *our* old photos and how to take better colour portraits of *your* family.
Consistent	*I* like my photography class because *I'm* learning how to restore *my* old photos and how to take better colour portraits of *my* family.

Perhaps this is a good place to dispel the myth that the pronoun "I" should never be used in an essay; on the contrary, many of our best essays have been written in the first person. Some of your former teachers may have discouraged the use of "I" for these two reasons: (1) personal opinion does not belong in the formal essay and (2) writing in the first person often produces too many empty phrases, such as "I think that" and "I believe that." At times you will find you need to use the first person: if the personal point of view is appropriate in a particular assignment, you may use the first person in moderation, making sure that every other sentence doesn't begin with "I" plus a verb. Your instructor will guide you toward the most appropriate choice for the assignment you have been given, so don't hesitate to clarify your assignment's genre and requirements before you decide on using the first person.

▪ PRACTISING WHAT YOU'VE LEARNED

Replace the following underlined words so that the sentences are clear and vivid. In addition, rephrase any awkward constructions or unnecessarily abstract words you find.

1. Judging from the <u>crazy</u> sound of the reactor, it isn't obvious to me that nuclear power as we know it today isn't a technology with a less than wonderful future.

2. The City Council felt <u>bad</u> because the revised tourist development activities grant fund application form letters were mailed without stamps.

3. To see the film *Juno* with my mother was <u>most interesting</u>.

4. For sale: <u>very nice</u> antique bureau suitable for ladies or gentlemen with thick legs and extra-large side handles.

5. There are many <u>things</u> people shouldn't eat, especially the elderly.

6. My roommate is <u>sort of different</u>, but he's a <u>good</u> guy at heart.

7. After reading the <u>great</u> new book *The Looter's Guide to Riot-Prone Cities*, Eddie <u>asked to have</u> a transfer <u>really soon</u>.

8. The wild oats soup was <u>fantastic</u>, so we drank <u>a lot of it very fast</u>.

9. When his new cat Chairman Meow won the pet show, owner Warren Peace got <u>pretty excited</u>.

10. The new diet made me feel awful, and <u>it did many horrible things</u> to my body.

Find a short piece of writing you think is too bland, boring, vague, or confusing. (Possible sources: your college or university catalogue, a business contract, a form letter, an article in a community paper, or your student health insurance policy.) Write a well-written paragraph to identify the sample's major problems and offer some specific suggestions for improving the writing. (If time permits, read aloud several of the samples and vote one the winner of the Most Lifeless Prose Award.)

■ Developing an Emphatic Style

Some words and phrases in your sentences are more important than others and, therefore, need more emphasis. Three ways to vary emphasis are by (1) word order, (2) coordination, and (3) subordination.

Word Order

The arrangement of words in a sentence can determine which ideas receive the most emphasis. To stress a word or phrase, place it at the end of the sentence or at the beginning of the sentence. Accordingly, a word or phrase receives least emphasis when buried in the middle of the sentence. Compare the following examples, in which the word "murder" receives varying degrees of emphasis:

Least emphatic	For Colonel Mustard *murder* was the only solution.
Emphatic	*Murder* was Colonel Mustard's only solution.
Most Emphatic	Colonel Mustard knew only one solution: *murder.*

Another use of word order to vary emphasis is *inversion,* taking a word out of its natural or usual position in a sentence and relocating it in an unexpected place.

Usual order	Parents who give their children both roots and wings are *wise.*
Inverted order	*Wise* are the parents who give their children both roots and wings.

Not all your sentences will contain words that need special emphasis; good writing generally contains a mix of some sentences in natural order and others rearranged for special effects.

Coordination

When you want to stress two closely related ideas equally, coordinate them.* In coordination, you join two sentences with a coordinating conjunction. To remember the coordinating conjunctions ("for," "and," "nor," "but," "or," "yet," "so"), think of the acronym FANBOYS; then always join two sentences with a comma and one of the FANBOYS. Here are two samples:

Choppy	The most popular girl's name today is Emily.
	The most popular boy's name today is Jacob.

---

* To remember that the term "coordination" refers to equally weighted ideas, think of other words with the prefix "co" such as "copilots," "coauthors," or "cooperation."

Coordinated	The most popular girl's name today is Emily, *and* the most popular boy's name is Jacob.
Choppy	Imelda brought home a pair of ruby slippers. Ferdinand made her return them.
Coordinated	Imelda brought home a pair of ruby slippers, *but* Ferdinand made her return them.

You can use coordination to show a relationship between ideas and to add variety to your sentence structures. Be careful, however, to select the right words while linking ideas, unlike the sentence that appeared in a church newsletter: "The ladies of the church have discarded clothing of all kinds, and they have been inspected by the minister." In other words, writers often need to slow down and make sure their thoughts are not joined in unclear or even unintentionally humorous ways: "For those of you who have children and don't know it, we have a nursery downstairs."

Sometimes when writers are in a hurry, they join ideas that are clearly related in their own minds, but whose relationship is confusing to the reader:

Confusing	My laboratory report isn't finished, and today my sister is leaving for a visit home.
Clear	I'm still working on my laboratory report, so I won't be able to catch a ride home with my sister who's leaving today.

You should also avoid using coordinating conjunctions to string too many ideas together like linked sausages:

Poor	We went inside the famous cave and the guide turned off the lights and we saw the rocks that glowed.
Revised	After we went inside the famous cave, the guide turned off the lights so we could see the rocks that glowed.

Subordination

Some sentences contain one main statement and one or more less emphasized elements; the less important ideas are subordinate to, or are dependent on, the sentence's main idea.* Subordinating conjunctions introducing dependent clauses show a variety of relationships between the clauses and the main part of the sentence. Here are four examples of subordinating conjunctions and their uses:

1. To show time without subordination	Superman stopped changing his clothes. He realized the phone booth was made of glass.
with subordination	Superman stopped changing his clothes *when* he realized the phone booth was made of glass.
2. To show cause without subordination	The sub-prime mortgage crisis in the United States is more serious than anticipated. It has affected the economies of other countries as well.

---

* To remember that the term "subordination" refers to sentences containing dependent elements, think of such words as "a subordinate" (someone who works for someone else) or a post office "substation" (a branch of the post office less important than the main branch).

with subordination	*Because* the sub-prime mortgage crisis in the United States is more serious than anticipated, other countries' economies have been affected as well.
3. To show condition without subordination	Susan ought to study the art of tattooing. She will work with colourful people.
with subordination	*If* Susan studies the art of tattooing, she will work with colourful people.
4. To show place without subordination	Bulldozers are smashing the old movie theatre. That's the place I first saw Leonardo DiCaprio cry "I'm the king of the world!"
with subordination	Bulldozers are smashing the old movie theatre *where* I first saw Leonardo DiCaprio cry "I'm the king of the world!"

Subordination is especially useful in ridding your prose of choppy Dick-and-Jane sentences and those "empty sentences" discussed on pages 112–113. Here are some examples of choppy, weak sentences and their revisions, which contain subordinate clauses:

Choppy	Lew makes bagels on Tuesday. Lines in front of his store are a block long.
Revised	When Lew makes bagels on Tuesday, lines in front of his store are a block long.
Choppy	I have fond memories of Stanley Park. My husband and I met there.
Revised	I have fond memories of Stanley Park because my husband and I met there.

Effective use of subordination is one of the marks of a sophisticated writer, because it presents adequate information in one smooth flow instead of in monotonous drips. Subordination, like coordination, also adds variety to your sentence construction.

Generally, when you subordinate one idea, you emphasize another, so to avoid the tail-wagging-the-dog problem, put your important idea in the main clause. Also, don't let your most important idea become buried under an avalanche of subordinate clauses, as in the sentence that follows:

When he was told by his boss, *who* had always treated him fairly, *that* he was being fired from a job *that* he had held for twenty years at a factory *where* he enjoyed working *because* the pay was good, Henry felt angry and frustrated.

Practise blending choppy sentences by studying the following sentence-combining exercise. In this exercise, a description of a popular movie has been chopped into simple sentences and then combined into one complex sentence.

1. *Spiderman* (2002)
Peter Parker gets bitten by a radioactive spider.
He gains special powers.
He can spin webs.
He can swing between tall buildings.
So he starts to fight crime.

He wears a masked costume.

But he is misunderstood.

A radioactive spider's bite gives Peter Parker special powers that enable him to start fighting crime by spinning webs and swinging from tall buildings; however, he is misunderstood because of his masked costume.

2. *King Kong* (1933)

A showman goes to the jungle.

He captures an ape.

The ape is a giant.

The ape is taken to New York City.

He escapes.

He dies fighting for a young woman.

He loves her.

She is beautiful.

A giant ape, captured in the jungle by a showman, is taken to New York City, where he escapes and dies fighting for the beautiful young woman he loves.

3. *Austin Powers: International Man of Mystery* (1997)

Austin Powers is a British spy.

He is very cool.

He is put in cryogenic stasis in the 1960s.

He is thawed in the 1990s.

Austin is now outdated.

That makes him doubt himself.

He fights a supervillain.

The supervillain wants to rule the world.

Austin conquers the supervillain's plans.

Austin regains confidence.

After Austin Powers, a cool spy from the 1960s is thawed from cryogenic stasis, he is filled with self doubt because he is now outdated, but he regains his self-confidence once he successfully fights a supervillain's plans to rule the world.

Please note that the sentences in these exercises may be combined effectively in a number of ways. For instance, the description of *King Kong* might be rewritten this way: "After a showman captures him in the jungle, a giant ape escapes in New York City but dies fighting for the love of a beautiful young woman." How might you rewrite the other two sample sentences?

■ PRACTISING WHAT YOU'VE LEARNED

A. Revise the following sentences so that the underlined words receive more emphasis.

1. A remark attributed to nineteenth-century wit <u>Oscar Wilde</u> is "I have put my talent into my work, but my genius into my life."

2. According to recent polls, <u>television</u> is where most Canadians get their news.

3. Of all the world's problems, it is <u>hunger</u> that is most urgent.

4. I enjoyed visiting many foreign countries last year, with <u>Greece</u> being my favourite of all of them.

5. The annoying habit of <u>knuckle-cracking</u> is something I can't stand.

B. Combine the following sentences using coordination or subordination.

1. The guru rejected his dentist's offer of novocaine. He could transcend dental medication.

2. John failed his literature test. John incorrectly identified Margaret Atwood as the author of the classic novel *Sense and Sensibility*.

3. Ben's house burned. He dialled a "9." He couldn't find "11" on the dial.

4. The police had only a few clues. They suspected Jean and David had strangled each other in a desperate struggle over control of the thermostat.

5. Dave's favourite movie is *Sorority Babes in the Slimeball Bowl-O-Rama* (1988). A film critic called it "a pinhead chiller."

6. We're going to the new Psychoanalysis Restaurant. Their menu includes banana split personality, repressed duck, shrimp basket case, and self-expresso.

7. Kato lost the junior high spelling bee. He could not spell *DNA*.

8. Colorado hosts an annual BobFest to honour all persons named Bob. Events include playing softbob, bobbing for apples, listening to bob-pipes, and eating bob-becue.

9. The earthquake shook the city. Louise was practising primal-scream therapy at the time.

10. In 1789 many Parisians bought a new perfume called "Guillotine." They wanted to be on the cutting edge of fashion.

C. Combine the following simple sentences into one complex sentence. See if you can guess the name of the books or movies described in the sentences. (Answers appear on page 135.)

1. A boy runs away from home.
   His companion is a runaway slave.
   He lives on a raft.
   The raft is on the Mississippi River.
   He has many adventures.
   The boy learns many lessons.
   Some lessons are about human kindness.
   Some lessons are about friendship.

2. An orphaned girl is adopted.
   She is adopted by mistake.
   She is adopted by a brother and sister.
   They live in a small town on Prince Edward Island.
   The girl is imaginative.
   The girl is impractical.
   The girl has many amusing adventures.
   The girl is finally accepted by the community.

3. A scientist is obsessed.
   He wants to recreate life.
   He creates a monster.
   The monster rebels against the scientist.
   The monster kills his creator.
   The villagers revolt.
   The villagers storm the castle.

■ ASSIGNMENT

A. Make up your own sentence-combining exercise by finding or
   writing one-sentence descriptions of popular or recent movies,
   books, or television shows. Divide the complex sentences into simple sentences
   and exchange papers with a classmate. Give yourselves ten minutes to combine
   sentences and guess the titles.

B. The following two paragraphs are poorly written because of their choppy,
   wordy, and monotonous sentences. Rewrite each passage so that it is clear,
   lively, and emphatic.

   1. Publishers try to guess what kinds of books children will like. The adults who
      buy books for children also try to imagine what those children will like. But
      they also think of what kinds of lessons children need to learn. So they look
      for books that represent certain morals and books that teach certain kinds of
      lessons. This attitude also affects authors, who may have to change their
      approaches to a story or who may not even get a story published because it
      represents an idea publishers or parents think is not acceptable. This attitude
      toward children's books is a kind of censorship since children can only have
      access to the books adults purchase or get for them from the library.

   2. In this modern world of today, man has come up with another new invention.
      This invention is called the "Talking Tombstone." It is made by the Gone-But-
      Not-Forgotten Company, which is located in Burbank, California. This com-
      pany makes a tombstone that has a device in it that makes the tombstone
      appear to be talking aloud in a realistic fashion when people go close by it.
      The reason is that the device is really a recording machine that is turned on
      due to the simple fact of the heat of the bodies of the people who go by. The
      closer the people get, the louder the sound the tombstone makes. It is this
      device that individual persons who want to leave messages after death may

utilize. A hypochondriac, to cite one example, might leave a recording of a message that says over and over again in a really loud voice, "See, I told you I was sick!" It may be assumed by one and all that this new invention will be a serious aspect of the whole death situation in the foreseeable future.

■ APPLYING WHAT YOU'VE LEARNED TO *YOUR* WRITING

If you have drafted a piece of writing and are satisfied with your essay's ideas and organization, begin revising your sentences for clarity, conciseness, and emphasis. As you move through your draft, think about your readers. Ask yourself, "Are any of my sentences too vague, over-packed, or contorted for my readers to understand? Can I clarify any of my ideas by using more precise language or by revising confusing sentence constructions?

If you can't easily untangle a jumbled sentence, try following the sentence-combining exercise described on pages 133–134 of this chapter—but in reverse. Instead of combining ideas, break your thought into a series of simpler sentences. Think about what you want to say and put the person or thing of importance in the *subject* position at the beginning of the sentences. Then select a verb and a brief phrase to complete each of the sentences. You will most likely need several of these simpler constructions to communicate the complexity of your original thought. Once you have your thought broken into smaller, simpler units, carefully begin to combine some of them as you strive for clarity and sentence variety.

Remember that it's not enough for you, the writer, to understand what your sentences mean—your readers must be able to follow your ideas too. When in doubt, always revise your writing so that it is clear, concise, and inviting. (For more help, turn to Chapter 5, on revision.)

★ CHAPTER 6 SUMMARY

Here is a brief summary of what you should remember about writing effective sentences:

1. All good writers revise and polish their sentences.

2. You can help clarify your ideas for your readers by writing sentences that are informative, straightforward, and precise.

3. You can communicate your ideas more easily to your readers if you cut out deadwood, redundancies, passive verbs, and pretentious language.

4. You can maintain your readers' interest in your ideas if you cultivate an engaging style offering a variety of pleasing sentence constructions.

---

* Answers to sentence-combining exercise (pp. 133–134)

1. Huckleberry Finn
2. Anne of Green Gables
3. Frankenstein

Chapter 7

Word Logic

The English language contains over a half million words—quite a selection for you as a writer to choose from. But such a wide choice may make you feel like a hungry person confronting a six-page, fancy French menu. Which choice is best? How do I choose? Is the choice so important?

Word choice can make an enormous difference in the quality of your writing for at least one obvious reason: if you substitute an incorrect or vague word for the right one, you risk being misunderstood. Confucius made the same point: "If language is incorrect, then what is said is not meant. If what is said is not meant, then what ought to be done remains undone." It isn't enough that you know what you mean; you must transfer your thoughts onto paper in the proper words so that others clearly understand your ideas.

To help you avoid possible paralysis from indecision over word choice, this chapter offers some practical suggestions for selecting words that are not only accurate and appropriate but also memorable and persuasive.

■ Selecting the Correct Words

Accuracy: Confused Words

Unless I get a bank loan soon, I will be forced to lead an *immortal* life.

Dobermans make good pets if you train them with enough *patients*.

He dreamed of eating *desert* after *desert*.

She had dieted for so long that she had become *emancipated*.

The young man was completely in *ah* of the actress's beauty.

Socrates died from an overdose of *wedlock*.

The preceding sentences share a common problem: each one contains an error in word choice. In each sentence, the italicized word is incorrect, causing the sentence to be nonsensical or silly. (Consider a sign recently posted in a local nightspot: "No miners allowed." Did the owner think the lights on their hats would bother the other customers? Did the student with "duel majors" imagine that his two areas of study were squaring off with pistols at twenty paces?) To avoid such confusion in word choice, check your words for *accuracy*. Select words whose precise meaning, usage, and spelling you know; consult your dictionary for any words whose definitions (or spellings) are fuzzy to you. As Mark Twain noted, the difference between the right word and the wrong one is the difference between lightning and the lightning bug.

Here is a list of words that are often confused in writing. Use your dictionary to determine the meanings or usage of any word unfamiliar to you.

its/it's	lead/led	choose/chose
to/too/two	cite/sight/site	accept/except
there/their/they're	affect/effect	council/counsel
your/you're	good/well	reign/rein
complement/compliment	who's/whose	lose/loose
stationary/stationery	lay/lie	precede/proceed
capitol/capital	than/then	illusion/allusion
principal/principle	insure/ensure	farther/further

Special note: Some "confused" words don't even exist! Here are four commonly used non-existent words and their correct counterparts:

No Such Word or Spelling	Use Instead
irregardless	regardless
allready	already *or* all ready
alot	a lot
its'	its or it's

Accuracy: Idiomatic Phrases

Occasionally you may have an essay returned to you with words marked "awkward diction" or "idiom." In English, as in all languages, we have word groupings that seem governed by no particular logic except the ever-popular "that's-the-way-we-say-it" rule. Many of these idiomatic expressions involve prepositions that novice writers sometimes confuse or misuse. Some common idiomatic errors and their corrected forms are listed here.

regardless ~~to~~ of	different ~~than to~~ from	relate ~~with~~ to
insight ~~of~~ into	must ~~of~~ have known	capable ~~to~~ of
similar ~~with~~ to	superior ~~than~~ to	aptitude ~~toward~~ for

| comply ~~to~~ with | ~~to~~ in my opinion | prior ~~than~~ to |
| off ~~of~~ | meet ~~to~~ her standards | should ~~of~~ have |

To avoid idiomatic errors, consult your dictionary and read your essay aloud; often your ears will catch mistakes in usage that your eyes have overlooked.*

Levels of Language

In addition to choosing the correct word, you should also select words whose status is suited to your purpose and audience. For convenience here, language has been classified into five categories, or levels, of usage: (1) colloquial, (2) informal, (3) semi-formal, (4) formal, and (5) academic or professional.

Colloquial language is the kind of speech you use most often in face-to-face, e-mail, and text-message conversation with your friends, classmates, and family. It may not always be grammatically correct ("It's me"); it may include fragments, contractions, some slang, words identified as nonstandard by the dictionary (such as "yuck" or "lousy"), and shortened or abbreviated words ("grad school," "photos," "TV"). Colloquial speech is everyday language, and although you may use it in some writing (personal letters, journals, memos, and so forth), you should think carefully about using colloquial language in college and university essays or in professional letters, reports, or papers, because such a choice implies a casual relationship between writer and reader. Be particularly vigilant about your audience if you are sending an e-mail or text message to a person with whom you have a formal relationship; it is not appropriate to use slang, abbreviations, computer jargon, and computer shorthand like a smiley face—:-)—or incorrect grammar, just because your message is being sent electronically.

Informal language is used in conversations with people who aren't in your close circle of friends and family, but who still have an informal relationship with you. You would use this language to speak to your local librarian, perhaps, or to write a letter to the editor of your local paper. You will often see informal language used in magazines and newspaper articles, as well as in broadcast news reports.

Semi-formal language is called for in many college and undergraduate university assignments. The tone is more formal than in colloquial writing or speech; no slang or nonstandard words are permissible. Semi-formal writing consistently uses correct grammar; fragments are used for special effect or not at all. Authorities disagree on the use of contractions in semi-formal writing: some say avoid them entirely; others say they're permissible; still others advocate using them only to avoid stilted phrases ("Let's

---

* You may not immediately recognize what's wrong with words your instructor has labelled "awkward diction" or "idiom." If you're uncertain about an error, ask your instructor for clarification; after all, if you don't know what's wrong with your prose, you can't avoid the mistake again. To illustrate this point, here's a true story: A bright young woman was having trouble with prepositional phrases in her essays, and although her professor repeatedly marked her incorrect expressions with the marginal note "idiom," she never improved. Finally, one day near the end of the term, she approached her professor in tears and wailed, "Professor Jones, I know I'm not a very good writer, but must you write 'idiot,' 'idiot,' 'idiot' all over my papers?" The moral of this story is simple: it's easy to misunderstand a correction or misread your instructor's writing. Because you can't improve until you know what's wrong, always ask when you're in doubt.

go," for example, is preferable to "Let us go"). A balance of straightforward words ("indifferent" or "spacious," for example) with specialized or advanced words ("tenacious" or "doctrinal") should be the goal in semi-formal writing. Most, if not all, of your essays in college or university classes will be written in semi-formal language.

Formal language is found in important documents and in serious, often ceremonial, speeches. Characteristics include an elevated—but not pretentious—tone, no contractions, and correct grammar. Formal writing often uses inverted word order and balanced sentence structure. John F. Kennedy's 1960 Inaugural Address, for example, was written in a formal style ("Ask not what your country can do for you; ask what you can do for your country"). Most people rarely, if ever, need to write formally. If you are called on to do so, however, be careful to avoid diction that sounds pretentious, pompous, or phony.

Academic or professional language. Much of the professional writing you will encounter will come from academic or professional journals, such as journals of economics or medicine. This language uses sophisticated and complex sentences as well as a great deal of specialized language, with words such as "hegemony," "ontological," or "macroeconomic." While it can be all too easy for academic writers to fall into the trap of using jargon and obscuring their ideas, successful academic writing is able to express complex ideas accurately and clearly, precisely because of the use of specialized diction. Be patient as you build up your skill in scholarly language. It's better to use straightforward, simple language than to pad your essay with scholarly vocabulary that is used incorrectly.

Tone

Tone is a general word that describes writers' attitudes toward their subject matter and audience. There are as many different kinds of tones as there are emotions. Depending on how the writer feels, an essay's "voice" may sound lighthearted, indignant, sarcastic, or solemn, to name but a few of the possible choices. In addition to presenting a specific attitude, a good writer gains credibility by maintaining a tone that is generally reasonable, sincere, and authentic.

Although it is impossible to analyze all the various kinds of tones one finds in essays, it is nevertheless beneficial to discuss some of those that repeatedly give writers trouble. Here are some tones that should be used carefully or avoided altogether:

Invective

Invective is unrestrained anger, usually expressed in the form of violent accusation or denunciation. Let's suppose, for example, you hear a friend argue, "Anyone who votes for Joe Smith is a fascist pig." If you are considering Smith, you are probably offended by your friend's abusive tone. Raging emotion, after all, does not sway the opinions of intelligent people; they need to hear the facts presented in a calm, clear discussion. Therefore, in your own writing, aim for a reasonable tone. You want your readers to think, "Now here is someone with a good understanding of the situation, who has evaluated it with an unbiased, analytical mind." Keeping a controlled tone doesn't mean you shouldn't feel strongly about your subject—on the contrary, you certainly should—but you should realize that a hysterical or outraged tone defeats your purpose by causing you to sound irrational and therefore untrustworthy. For this reason, you should avoid using profanity in your essays; the shock value of an obscenity may not be worth what you might lose in credibility. The most effective way to make your point is by persuading, not offending, your reader.

Sarcasm

In most of your writing you'll discover that a little sarcasm—bitter, derisive remarks—goes a long way. Like invective, too much sarcasm can damage the reasonable tone your essay should present. Instead of saying, "You can recognize the supporters of the new tax law by their horns and tails," give your readers the reasons for your belief that the tax bill is flawed. Sarcasm can be effective, but realize that it often backfires by causing the writer to sound like a childish name-caller rather than a judicious commentator.

Irony

Irony is a figure of speech whereby the writer or speaker says the opposite of what is meant; for the irony to be successful, however, the audience must understand the writer's true intent. For example, if you have slopped to school in a rainstorm and your drenched instructor enters the classroom saying, "Ah, nothing like this beautiful, sunny weather," you know that your instructor is being ironic. Perhaps one of the most celebrated thrusts of irony was delivered in 1938 by Sigmund Freud, the famous Viennese psychiatrist, who was arrested by the Nazis. After being harassed by the Gestapo, he was released on the condition that he sign a statement swearing he had been treated well by the secret police. Freud signed it, but he added a few words after his signature: "I can heartily recommend the Gestapo to anyone." Looking back, we easily recognize Freud's jab at his captors; the Gestapo missed the irony and let him go.

Although irony is often an effective device, it can also cause great confusion, especially when it is written rather than spoken. Unless your readers thoroughly understand your position in the first place, they may become confused by what appears to be a sudden contradiction. Irony that is too subtle, too private, or simply out of context merely complicates the issue. Therefore, you must make certain that your reader has no trouble realizing when your tongue is firmly embedded in your cheek. And unless you are assigned to write an ironic essay (in the same vein, for instance, as Swift's "A Modest Proposal"), don't overuse irony. Like any rhetorical device, its effectiveness is reduced with overkill.

Flippancy or Cuteness

If you sound too flip, hip, or bored in your essay ("People with IQs lower than their sunscreen number will object . . ."), your readers will not take you seriously and, consequently, will disregard whatever you have to say. Writers suffering from cuteness will also antagonize their readers. For example, let's assume you're assigned the topic "Which Person Did the Most to Arouse the Labouring Class in Twentieth-Century England?" and you begin your essay with a discussion of the man who invented the alarm clock. Although that joke might be funny in an appropriate situation, it's not likely to impress your reader, who's looking for serious commentary. How much cuteness is too much is often a matter of taste, but if you have any doubts about the quality of your humour, leave it out. Also, omit personal messages or comic asides to your reader (such as "Ha, ha, just kidding!" or "I knew you'd love this part"). Humour is often effective, but the writer needs to remember that the purpose of any essay is to persuade an audience to accept your thesis, not merely to entertain with freestanding jokes. In other words, if you use humour, make sure it is appropriate for your subject matter and that it works to help you make your point.

Sentimentality

Sentimentality is the excessive show of cheap emotions—"cheap" because they are not deeply felt but evoked by clichés and stock, tear-jerking situations. In the nineteenth century, for example, a typical melodrama played on the sentimentality of the audience by presenting a black-hatted, cold-hearted, mustache-twirling villain tying a golden-haired, pure-hearted "Little Nell" to the railroad tracks after driving her ancient, sickly mother out into a snowdrift. Today, politicians (among others) often appeal to our sentimentality by conjuring up vague images they feel will move us emotionally rather than rationally to take their side: "My friends," says Premier Stereotype, "my party and I represent all that is good and decent in this fine nation of ours, a nation built by the hard work and courage of men like my grandfather, a Saskatchewan farmer; a nation blessed in its many natural resources of mountains, rivers and prairies, and strengthened by the diversity of its peoples. I promise you today, that if you vote for me, we will keep our country the model of harmony, prosperity and freedom that is admired by the world." Such gush is hardly convincing; good writers and speakers use evidence and logical reason to persuade their audience. In personal essays, guard against becoming too carried away with emotion, as did this student: "My dog, Cuddles, is the sweetest, cutest, most precious little puppy dog in the whole wide world, and she will always be my best friend." In addition to sending the reader into sugar shock, this description fails to present any specific reasons why anyone should appreciate Cuddles. Here's another example that uses vague, generic, and sentimental phrasing: "We are blessed to have the medical professionals who volunteer with Doctors Without Borders because they are the kind of heroes we all look up to and dream of being every day; they are the best examples of human beings in the whole of the universe." In other words, be sincere in your writing, but don't lose so much control of your emotions that you become mushy or maudlin.

Preachiness

Even if you are so convinced of the rightness of your position that a burning bush couldn't change your mind, try not to sound smug about it. No one likes to be lectured by someone perched atop the mountain of morality. Instead of preaching, adopt a tone that says, "I believe my position is correct, and I am glad to have this opportunity to explain why." Then give your reasons and meet objections in a positive but not holier-than-thou manner.

Pomposity

The "voice" of your essay should sound reasonably natural; don't *strain* to sound scholarly, scientific, or sophisticated. If you write "My summer sojourn through the Western provinces of this grand country was immensely pleasurable" instead of "My vacation last summer in the Rockies was really enjoyable," you sound merely phony, not dignified and learned. Select only words you know and can use easily. Never write anything you wouldn't say in an intelligent classroom conversation. (For more information on correcting pretentious writing, see pages 121–122 in Chapter 6 and pages 148–149 in this chapter.)

 To achieve the appropriate tone, be as sincere, forthright, and reasonable as you can. Let the tone of your essay establish a basis of mutual respect between you and your reader.

Connotation and Denotation

A word's *denotation* refers to its literal meaning, the meaning defined by the dictionary; a word's *connotation* refers to the emotional associations surrounding its meaning. For example, "home" and "residence" both may be defined as the place where one lives, but "home" carries connotations of warmth, security, and family that "residence" lacks. Similarly, "old" and "antique" have similar denotative meanings, but "antique" has the more positive connotation because it suggests something that also has value. Reporters and journalists do the same job, but the latter name somehow seems to indicate someone more sophisticated and professional. Because many words with similar denotative meanings do carry different connotations, good writers must be careful with their word choice. *Select only words whose connotations fit your purpose.* If, for example, you want to describe your grandmother in a positive way as someone who stands up for herself, you might refer to her as "assertive" or "feisty"; if you want to present her negatively, you might call her "aggressive" or "pushy."

In addition to selecting words with the appropriate connotations for your purpose, be careful to avoid offending your audience with particular connotations. For instance, if you were trying to persuade a group of politically conservative university administrators to accept your stand on a more extensively subsidized tuition system, you would not want to refer to your opposition as "right-wingers" or "reactionaries," extremist terms that have negative connotations. Remember, you want to inform and persuade your audience, not antagonize them.

You should also be alert to the use of words with emotionally charged connotations, especially in advertising and propaganda of various kinds. Car manufacturers, for example, have often used names of swift, bold, or graceful animals (Jaguar, Cougar, Impala) to sway prospective buyers; cosmetic manufacturers in recent years have taken advantage of the trend toward lighter makeup by associating such words as "nature," "natural," and "healthy glow" with their products. Diet-conscious Canadians are now deluged with "light" and "locally grown" food products. Politicians, too, are heavy users of connotation; they often drop in emotionally positive, but virtually meaningless, words and phrases such as "defender of family values," "friend of the common man," and "visionary" to describe themselves, while tagging their opponents with such negative, emotionally charged labels as "radical," "elitist," and "anti-family." Intelligent readers, like intelligent voters and consumers, want more than emotion-laden words; they want facts and logical argument. Therefore, as a good writer, you should use connotation as only one of many persuasive devices to enhance your presentation of evidence; never depend solely on an emotional appeal to convince your audience that your position—or thesis—is correct.

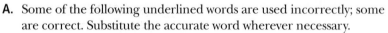

■ PRACTISING WHAT YOU'VE LEARNED

A. Some of the following underlined words are used incorrectly; some are correct. Substitute the accurate word wherever necessary.

1. Vacations of <u>to</u> weeks with <u>to</u> friends are always <u>to</u> short, and although <u>you're</u> <u>to</u> tired <u>to</u> return to work, <u>your</u> <u>to</u> broke not <u>to</u>.

2. The professor, <u>whose</u> famous for his <u>photogenic</u> memory, graciously <u>excepted</u> a large <u>amount</u> of <u>complements</u>.

3. <u>Its</u> <u>to</u> bad you don't like <u>they're</u> new Popsicle stick sculpture since <u>their</u> giving it <u>to</u> you for <u>you're</u> birthday.

4. The finances of the chicken ranch are in <u>fowl</u> shape because the hens are <u>lying</u> down on the job.

5. Sara June said she deserved an "A" in math, <u>irregardless</u> of her 59 average in the <u>coarse</u>, but her arguments were in <u>vein</u>.

6. Does the pamphlet "Ridding Your Home of Pesky <u>Aunts</u>" belong in the domestic-relations area of the public library?

7. Did the school <u>principal</u> <u>loose</u> <u>you're</u> heavy <u>medal</u> CD and <u>it's</u> case <u>too</u>?

8. The new city <u>counsel</u> parade ordinance will <u>effect</u> everyone in the <u>capitol</u> city <u>except</u> members of the Lawn Chair Marching Band.

B. The following sentences contain words and phrases that interfere with the sincere, reasonable tone good writers try to create. Rewrite each sentence, replacing sentimentality, cuteness, and pretentiousness with more appropriate language.

1. The last dying rays of day were quickly ebbing in the west as if to signal the feline to begin its lonely vigil.

2. Because of seasonal unproductivity, it has been deemed an unfortunate fiscal necessity to terminate your valuable association with our store in order to meet our projected growth estimates.

3. I was desirous of acquiring knowledge about members of our lower income brackets.

4. If the bill to legalize marijuana is passed, we can safely assume that the whole country will soon be going to pot (Heh, heh!).

5. I just love to look at those little critters with their itty-bitty mousy eyes.

C. In each of the following groups of words, identify the words with the most pleasing and least positive (or even negative) connotations.

1. dull/drab/quiet/boring/colourless/serene

2. slender/slim/skinny/thin/slight/anorexic

3. famous/notorious/well known/infamous

4. wealthy/opulent/rich/affluent/privileged

5. teacher/instructor/educator/professor/lecturer

D. Replace the underlined words in the following sentences with words arousing more positive feelings:

1. The <u>stench</u> from Jean's kitchen meant dinner was ready and was about to be served.

2. My neighbour was a <u>weird old guy</u> known for finding <u>cheap deals</u> on the Internet.

3. The sonnet form has <u>rigid</u> rules.

4. His <u>obsession</u> with his yard pleased the city's beautification committee.

5. The <u>slick</u> car salesman made a <u>pitch</u> to the <u>old geezer</u> who walked in the door.

6. Textbook writers admit to having a few <u>bizarre</u> habits.

7. Carol was a <u>mediocre</u> student.

8. His <u>odd</u> clothes made Mary think he was a <u>bum</u>.

9. The High Priest explained his tribe's <u>superstitions</u>.

10. Many of the board members were amazed to see how Algernon <u>dominated</u> the meeting.

■ Selecting the Best Words

In addition to selecting the correct word and appropriate tone, good writers also choose words that firmly implant their ideas in the minds of their readers. The best prose not only makes cogent points but also states these points memorably. To help you select the best words to express your ideas, the following is a list of do's and don'ts covering the most common diction (word choice) problems in students' writing today.

Do make your words as precise as possible. Always choose vigorous, active verbs and colourful, specific nouns and modifiers. "The big tree was hit by lightning," for example, is not as informative or interesting as "Lightning splintered the neighbours' thirty-foot oak." *Don't* use words whose meanings are unclear.

Vague Verbs

Unclear	She *got involved* in a lawsuit. [How?]
Clear	She is suing her dentist for filling the wrong tooth.
Unclear	Tom can *relate* to Jennifer. [What's the relationship?]
Clear	Tom understands Jennifer's financial problem.
Unclear	He won't *deal* with his ex-wife. [In what way?]
Clear	He refuses to speak to his ex-wife.
Unclear	Clyde *participated* in an off-Broadway play. [How?]
Clear	Clyde held the cue cards for the actors in an off-Broadway play.

Vague Nouns

Unclear	The burglar took several valuable *things* from our house.* [What items?]
Clear	The burglar took a *flatscreen television, laptop computer,* and a *microwave oven* from our house.

---

* Advice that bears repeating: banish the word "thing" from your writing. In nine out of ten cases, it is a lazy substitute for some other word. Unless you mean a nameless inanimate object, replace "thing" with the specific word it represents.

Unclear	When I have my car serviced, there is always *trouble.* [What kind?]
Clear	When I have my car serviced, *the mechanics always find additional repairs and never have the car ready when it is promised.*
Unclear	When I have *problems,* I always call my friends for advice. [What problems?]
Clear	*If my girlfriend breaks up with me, my roof needs repairing, or my dog needs surgery,* I always call my friends for advice.
Unclear	I like to have *fun* while I'm on vacation. [What sort of activities?]
Clear	I like to *eat in fancy restaurants, fly stunt kites,* and *walk along the beach* when I'm on vacation.

Vague Modifiers

Unclear	His *terrible* explanation left me *very* confused. [Why "terrible"? How confused?]
Clear	His *disorganized* explanation left me *too confused to begin the project.*
Unclear	The boxer hit the punching bag *really* hard. [How hard?]
Clear	The boxer hit the punching bag *so hard it split open.*
Unclear	*Casablanca* is a *good* movie *with something for everyone.* [Why "good" and for everyone?]
Clear	*Casablanca* is a *witty, sentimental* movie that *successfully combines an adventure story and a romance.*

To help you recognize the difference between general and specific language, consider the following series of words:

General → → → → → → → → → → → → → → → → → → → **Specific**

food→snack food→chips→potato chips→Red Hot Jalapeño Potato Chips

car→red car→red sports car→classic red Corvette→1966 red Corvette convertible

building→house→old house→big old fancy house→19th-century Victorian mansion

The preceding examples illustrate varying degrees of generality, with the words becoming more specific as they move to the right. Sometimes in your writing you will, of course, need to use general words to communicate your thought. However, most writers need practice finding specific language to substitute for bland, vague, or overly general diction that doesn't clearly present the precise picture the writer has in mind. For instance, look at the difference between these two sentences:

- My date arrived at the restaurant in an older car and then surprised us by ordering snack food.
- My date arrived at the restaurant in a rusted-out, bumperless '52 Cadillac DeVille and then surprised us by ordering only a small bowl of organic cheesy puffs.

Which description better conveys the start of an unusual evening? Which sentence would make you want to hear more?

Not all occasions call for specific details, to be sure. Don't add details that merely clutter if they aren't important to the idea or mood you are creating. If all your readers need to know is "I ate dinner alone and went to bed early," you don't need to write "Alone, I ate a dinner of lasagna, green salad, and ice cream before putting on my Gap cowgirl pyjamas and going to sleep under my yellow comforter at nine o'clock."

Most of the time, however, writers can improve their drafts by giving their language a close look, considering places where a vigorous verb or a "showing" adjective or a specific noun might make an enormous difference to the reader. As you revise and polish your own essays, ask yourself if you can clarify and enliven your writing by replacing dull, lifeless words with engaging, vivid, specific ones. Challenge yourself to find the best words possible—it's a writing habit that produces effective, reader-pleasing results. (For more help converting vague sentences to clear, inviting prose, see pages 112–118 in Chapter 6.)

Do make your word choices as fresh and original as possible. Instead of saying, "My hometown is very quiet," you might say, "My hometown's definition of an orgy is a light burning after midnight." In other words, if you can make your readers admire and remember your prose, you have a better chance of persuading them to accept your ideas.

Avoid clichés. Conversely, to avoid ho-hum prose, *don't* fill your sentences with clichés and platitudes—overworked phrases that cause your writing to sound lifeless and trite. Although we use clichés in everyday conversation, good writers avoid them in writing because (1) they are often vague or imprecise (Just how pretty is "pretty as a picture"?) and (2) they are used so frequently that they rob your prose style of personality and uniqueness ("It was raining cats and dogs"—does that phrase help your reader "see" the particular rainstorm you're trying to describe?).

Novice writers often include trite expressions because they do not recognize them as clichés; therefore, here is a partial list (there are literally thousands more) of phrases to avoid. Instead of using a cliché, try substituting an original phrase to describe what you see or feel. Never try to disguise a cliché by putting it in quotation marks—a baboon in dark glasses and a wig is still a baboon.

crack of dawn	needle in a haystack	gentle as a lamb
a crying shame	bed of roses	blind as a bat
white as a sheet	cold as ice	strong as an ox
depths of despair	hard as nails	sober as a judge
dead of night	white as snow	didn't sleep a wink
shadow of a doubt	almighty dollar	face the music
hear a pin drop	busy as a bee	out like a light
blessed event	to make a long story short	the last straw
first and foremost	pale as a ghost	solid as a rock
dawn of time	the writing on the wall	shoulder to shoulder
this day and age	point in time	clear as mud
today's society	go with the flow	until and unless

It would be impossible, of course, to memorize all the clichés and trite expressions in our language, but do check your prose for recognizable, overworked phrases so that your words will not be predictable and, consequently, dull. If you aren't sure if a phrase is a cliché—but you've heard it used frequently—your prose will probably be stronger if you substitute an original phrase for the suspected one.

Some overused words and phrases might better be called "Insta-Prose" rather than clichés. Similar to those instant "just add water and stir" food mixes on grocery shelves, Insta-Prose occurs when writers grab for the closest words within thought-reach rather than taking time to create an original phrase or image. It's easy, for example, to recognize such overused phrases as "last but not least," "easier said than done," "each and every," and "when all was said and done." But Insta-Prose may pop up in essays almost without a writer's awareness. For instance, using your very first thoughts, fill in the blanks in the following sentence:

After years of service, my old car finally _____, _____, and _____ by the side of the road.

If your immediate responses were the three words printed at the bottom of page 157, don't be surprised! Most people who have taken this simple test responded that way too, either entirely or in part. So what's the problem, you might ask. The writer describing the car wanted her readers to see *her* particular old car, not some bland image identically reproduced in her readers' minds. To show readers her car—as opposed to thousands of other old cars—she needs to substitute specific, "showing" language for the Insta-Prose.* (Retest yourself: what might she have said about this car that would allow you, the reader, to see what happened that day?)

As a writer, you also want your readers to "see" your specific idea and be engaged by your prose, rather than skipping over canned bland images. When you are drafting for ideas early in the writing process, Insta-Prose pours out—and that's as expected, because you are still discovering your thoughts. But, later, when you revise your drafts, be sensitive to predictable language in all its forms. Stamp out Insta-Prose! Cook up some fresh language to delight your reader!

Don't use trendy expressions or slang in your essays. Slang generally consists of commonly used words made up by special groups to communicate among themselves. Slang has many origins, from sports to space travel; for example, surfers gave us the expression "to wipe out" (to fail), soldiers lent "snafu" (from the first letters of "situation normal—all fouled up"), and astronauts provided "A-OK" (all systems working).

Although slang often gives our speech colour and vigour, it is unacceptable in most writing assignments for several reasons. First, slang is often part of a private language understood only by members of a particular professional, social, or age group. Second, slang often presents a vague picture or one that changes meanings from person to person or from context to context. More than likely, each person has a unique definition for a particular slang expression, and, although these definitions may overlap, they are not precisely the same. Consequently, your reader could interpret your words in one way whereas you mean them in another, a dilemma that might result in total miscommunication.

Too often, beginning writers rely on vague, popular phrases ("The party was way awesome") instead of thinking of specific words to explain specific ideas. Slang expressions frequently contain non-traditional grammar and diction that is inappropriate for college and

---

* Some prose is so familiar that it is now a joke. The phrase "It was a dark and stormy night," the beginning of an 1830 Edward George Bulwer-Lytton novel, has been parodied in the Peanuts comic strip (plagiarized without shame by Snoopy). It has also prompted a bad-writing contest sponsored since 1982 by the English Department at San José State University, in which entrants are challenged to "compose the opening sentence to the worst of all possible novels."

university work. Moreover, slang becomes dated quickly, and almost nothing sounds worse than yesterday's "in" expressions. (Can you seriously imagine calling a friend "Daddy-O" or telling someone you're "feelin' groovy"?)

Try to write so that your prose will be as fresh and pleasing ten years from now as today. Don't allow slang to give your writing a tone that detracts from a serious discussion. Putting slang in quotation marks isn't the solution—omit the slang and use precise words instead.

Do select simple, direct words your readers can easily understand. Don't use pompous or pseudo-sophisticated language in place of plain speech. Don't use a thesaurus to pad your writing or to try and sound impressive. Wherever possible, avoid *jargon*—that is, words and phrases that are unnecessarily technical, pretentious, or abstract.

Be sure you know your target audience when you are choosing whether to use technical language—terms specific to one area of study or specialization—or not. An academic and specialist audience would expect you to use language specific to its field. But technical jargon should be omitted or clearly defined in essays directed to a general audience because such language is often inaccessible to anyone outside the writer's particular field. By now most of us are familiar with bureaucratese, journalese, and psychobabble, in addition to gobbledygook from business, politics, advertising, and education. If, for example, you worry that "a self-actualized person such as yourself cannot transcend either your hostile environment or your passive-aggressive behaviour to make a commitment to a viable lifestyle and meaningful interpersonal relationships," you are indulging in psychological or sociological jargon; if you "review existing mechanisms of consumer input, throughput, and output via the consumer communications channel module," you are speaking business jargon. Although most professions do have their own terms, you should limit your use of specialized language to writing aimed solely at your professional colleagues; always try to avoid technical jargon in prose directed at a general audience.

Today the term "jargon" also refers to prose containing an abundance of abstract, pretentious, multi-syllabic words. The use of this kind of jargon often betrays a writer's attempt to sound sophisticated and intellectual; actually, it only confuses meaning and delays communication. Here, for instance, is a sample of incomprehensible jargon from a university president who obviously prefers twenty-five-cent words to simple, straightforward, nickel ones: "We will divert the force of this fiscal stress into leverage energy and pry important budgetary considerations and control out of our fiscal and administrative procedures." Or look at the thirty-eight-word definition of "exit" written by an Occupational Health and Safety bureaucrat: "That portion of a means of egress which is separated from all spaces of the building or structure by construction or equipment as required in this subpart to provide a protected way of travel to the exit discharge." Such language is not only pretentious and confusing but almost comic in its wordiness.

Legal jargon, complicating even the smallest transaction, has become so incomprehensible that some lawmakers and consumers have begun to fight back. Today in Texas, for example, any firm lending $500 or less must use a model plain-English contract or submit its contract for approval to the Office of Consumer Credit. The new, user-friendly contract replaces "Upon any such default, and at any time thereafter, Secured party may declare the entire balance of the indebtedness secured hereby, plus any other sums owed hereunder, immediately due and payable without demand or notice, less any refund due, and Secured Party shall have all the remedies of the Uniform Commercial Code" with a clear, easy-to-understand statement: "If I break any of my promises in this document, you can demand that I immediately pay all that I owe." Hooray for the gobbledygook squashers in the Lone Star State!

To avoid such verbal litter in your own writing, follow these rules:

1. Always select the plainest, most direct words you know.

   Jargon   The editor wanted to halt the proliferation of the product because she discovered an error on the page that terminates the volume.

   Revised   The editor wanted to stop the publishing process because she found an error on the last page of the book.

2. Replace nominalizations (nouns that are made from verbs and adjectives, usually by adding endings such as *-tion, -ism, -ness,* or *-al*) with simpler verbs and nouns.

   Jargon   The departmental head has come to the recognition that the utilization of verbose verbalization renders informational content inaccessible.

   Revised   The head of the department recognizes that wordiness confuses meaning.

3. Avoid adding *-ize* or *-wise* to verbs and adverbs.

   Jargon   *Weatherwise,* it looked like a good day to *finalize* her report on wind tunnels.

   Revised   The day's clear weather would help her finish her report on wind tunnels.

4. Drop out meaningless tack-on words such as "factor," "aspect," and "situation."

   Jargon   The convenience *factor* of the neighbourhood grocery store is one *aspect* of its success.

   Revised   The convenience of the neighbourhood grocery store contributes to its success.

Remember that good writing is clear and direct, never wordy, cloudy, or ostentatious. (For more hints on developing a clear style, see pages 112–118 in Chapter 6.)

Use inclusive language. Take special care to consider another emotionally charged aspect of diction. Most people will agree that language helps shape thought. Consequently, writers should avoid using any language that promotes demeaning stereotypes. Over the last forty years in particular, as Western societies have attempted to become more sensitive toward human experience and more accepting of difference, language has been adapted. Inclusive language is applied to many areas of human relationships and existence. Words like "mailman" are becoming outdated and even offensive, like "authoress," "cripple," and "Red Indian," which are words that aren't used anymore. Make sure, however, that you use words that convey meaning clearly and precisely, and that you don't mislead or confuse your audience by using vague terms that could mean anything (such as "physically challenged").

Avoid sexist language. Writers should avoid using any language that promotes demeaning stereotypes. Sexist language, in particular, often subtly suggests that either men or women, depending on the context, are less rational, intelligent, or capable of handling certain tasks or jobs. To make your writing as accurate and unbiased as possible, here are some simple suggestions for writing nonsexist prose:

1. Try using plural nouns to eliminate the need for the singular pronouns "he" and "she."

Original	Today's *doctor* knows *he* must carry extra malpractice insurance.
Revision	Today's *doctors* know *they* must carry extra malpractice insurance.

2. Try substituting gender-neutral occupational titles for those ending in "man" or "woman."

Original	The *fireman* and the *saleslady* watched the *policeman* arrest the former *chairman* of the Physics Department.
Revision	The *firefighter* and the *sales clerk* watched the *police officer* arrest the former *chair* of the Physics Department.

3. Don't contribute to stereotyping by assigning particular roles solely to men or women.

Original	*Mothers* concerned about the possibility of Reye's syndrome should avoid giving aspirin to their sick children.
Revision	*Parents* concerned about the possibility of Reye's syndrome should avoid giving aspirin to their sick children.

4. Try substituting such words as "people," "persons," "one," "voters," "workers," "students," and so on, for "man" or "woman."

Original	Any *man* who wants to become a corporation executive before the age of thirty should buy this book.
Revision	*Anyone* who wants to become a corporation executive before the age of thirty should buy this book.

5. Don't use inappropriate diminutives.

Original	In the annual office picture, the photographer asked the men to stand behind the *girls*.
Revision	In the annual office picture, the photographer asked the men to stand behind the *women*.

6. Consider avoiding words that use "man" to describe the actions or characteristics of a group ("man the barricades") or that refer to people in general.

Original	Rebuilding the space shuttle will call for extra money and *manpower*, but such an endeavour will benefit *mankind* in the generations to come.
Revision	Rebuilding the space shuttle will call for extra money and *employees*, but such an endeavour will benefit future *generations*.

7. Be consistent in your treatment of men's and women's names, marital status, professional titles, and physical appearances.

Original	Neither Tom Thomson, the wilderness painter, nor *Miss* Emily Dickinson, the *spinster poetess* of Amherst, gained fame or fortune in their lifetimes.
Revision	Neither Tom Thomson, the wilderness painter, nor Emily Dickinson, the *poet*, gained fame or fortune in their lifetimes.

8. If a situation demands multiple hypothetical examples, consider including references to both genders, when appropriate.

Original	In a revision workshop, one writer may request help with *his* concluding paragraph. Another writer may want reaction to *his* essay's introduction.
Revision	In a revision workshop, one writer may request help with *his* concluding paragraph. Another writer may want reaction to *her* essay's introduction.

Revising your writing to eliminate certain kinds of gender-specific references does not mean turning clear phrases into awkward or confusing jumbles of "he/she told him/her that the car was his/hers." By following the previous suggestions, you should be able to make your prose both clear and inoffensive to all members of your audience.*

Do call things by their proper names. Don't sugarcoat your terms by substituting *euphemisms*—words that sound nice or pretty applied to subjects some people find distasteful. For example, you've probably heard someone say "She passed away" instead of "She died," or "He was under the influence of alcohol" instead of "He was drunk." Flight attendants refer to a "water landing" rather than an ocean crash. Often, euphemisms are used to soften names of jobs: "sanitary engineer" for garbage collector, "field representative" for salesperson, "information processor" for typist, and so forth.

Some euphemisms are dated and now seem plain silly: in Victorian times, for example, the word "leg" was considered unmentionable in polite company, so people spoke of "piano limbs" and asked for the "first joint" of a chicken. The phrases "white meat" and "dark meat" were euphemisms some people used to avoid asking for a piece of chicken breast or thigh.

Today, euphemisms still abound. Though our generation is perhaps more direct about sex and death, many current euphemisms gloss over unpleasant or unpopular business, military, and political practices. Some stockbrokers, for example, once referred to an October market crash as "a fourth-quarter equity retreat," and General Motors didn't really shut down one of its plants—the closing was merely a "volume-related production schedule adjustment." Similarly, Chrysler didn't lay off workers; it simply "initiated a career alternative enhancement program." Nuclear power plants no longer have dumps; they have "containment facilities" with radiation "migration" rather than leaks, and "inventory discrepancies" rather than thefts of plutonium. Simple products are now complex technology: clocks are "analog temporal displacement monitors," toothbrushes are "home plaque removal instruments," sinks are part of the "hygienic hand-washing media," and pencils are "portable handheld communications inscribers." Vinyl is now "vegetarian leather."

Euphemisms abound in governments and official agencies when those in charge try to hide or disguise the truth from the public. On the national level, a former budget director gave us "revenue enhancements" instead of new taxes, and a former Minister for Social Services once tried to camouflage cuts in social services by calling them "advance downward adjustments." It is now common to refer to job cuts as "downsizing." Wiretaps once became "technical collection sources" used by "special investigators units" instead of burglars, and plain

---

* Some writers now use "s/he" to promote gender inclusivity in their informal prose. Be aware, however, that this usage is non-traditional and not accepted universally. Always check with your instructors, or the publication for which you are writing, for the appropriate and preferred style.

lying became on one important occasion merely "plausible deniability." Other lies or exaggerations have been "strategic misrepresentations," and convenient "reality augmentations." Interestingly enough, even government staff members in charge of prettying up the truth for the public have earned their own euphemistic title: "spin doctors."

Perhaps the U.S. military, however, is the all-time winner of the "substitute-a-euphemism" contest. Over the years, the military has used a variety of words, such as "neutralization," "pacification," and "liberation," to mean the invasion and destruction of other countries and governments. During the first Gulf War with Iraq, for example, bombs that accidentally fell on civilians were referred to as "incontinent ordnance," with the dead becoming "collateral damage." Earlier, to avoid publicizing a retreat, the military simply called for "backloading our augmentation personnel." On the less serious side, the U.S. Navy changes ocean waves into "climatic disturbances at the air–sea interface," and the Army, not to be outdone, transforms the lowly shovel into a "combat emplacement evacuator."

Although many euphemisms seem funny and harmless, too many of them are not because people—often those with power to shape public opinion—have intentionally designed them to obscure the reality of a particular situation or choice of action. Because euphemisms can be used unscrupulously to manipulate people, you should always avoid them in your own prose and be suspicious of them in the writing of others. As Aldous Huxley, author of *Brave New World*, noted, "[a]n education for freedom is, among other things, an education in the proper uses of language."

In addition to weakening the credibility of one's ideas, euphemisms can make prose unnecessarily abstract, wordy, pretentious, or even silly. For a clear and natural prose style, use terms that are straightforward and simple. In other words, call a spade a spade, not "an implement for intervention in horticultural environments."

Do enliven your writing with figurative language, when appropriate. Figurative language produces pictures or images in a reader's mind, often by comparing something unfamiliar to something familiar. The two most common figurative devices are the simile and the metaphor. A *simile* is a comparison between two people, places, feelings, or things, using the word "like" or "as"; a more forceful comparison, omitting the word "like" or "as," is a *metaphor*. Here are two simple examples:

Simile	George eats his meals like a hog.
Metaphor	George is a hog at mealtime.

In both sentences, George, whose eating habits are unfamiliar to the reader, is likened to a hog, an animal whose sloppy manners are generally well known. By comparing George to a hog, the writer gives the reader a clear picture of George at the table. Figurative language not only can help you present your ideas in clear, concrete, economical ways but also can make your prose more memorable—especially if the image or picture you present is a fresh, arresting one. Most importantly, metaphors and similes enable us to discover and see things differently. Here are some examples of striking images designed to catch the reader's attention, to clarify the writer's point, and to open up new perspectives:

- An hour away from him felt like a month in the country.

- The angry accusation flew like a spear: once thrown, it could not be retrieved and it cut deeply.

- Out of the night came the convoy of brown trucks, modern-day buffalo thundering single file across the prairie, eyes on fire.

- Behind her broad polished desk, Matilda was a queen bee with a swarm of office drones buzzing at her door.
- The factory squatted on the bank of the river like a huge black toad.

Sometimes, in appropriate writing situations, exaggerated similes and metaphors may be used humorously to underscore a particular point: "I felt so stupid that day. I'm sure my colleagues thought my brain was so small that if they placed it on the head of a pin, it would roll around like a marble on a six-lane highway."

Figurative language can spice up your prose, but like any spice, it can be misused, thus spoiling your soup. Therefore, don't overuse figurative language; not every point needs a metaphor or simile for clarity or emphasis. Too many images are confusing. Moreover, don't use stale images. (Clichés—discussed on pages 146–147 —are often tired metaphors or similes: snake in the grass, hot as fire, quiet as a mouse, etc.) If you can't catch your readers' attention with a fresh picture, don't bore them with a stale one.

Mixed metaphors. Finally, don't mix images—this too often results in a confusing or unintentionally comic scene. For example, a politician once responded to a question about city fiscal requirements this way: "I think the proper approach is to go through this Garden of Gethsemane that we're in now, give birth to a budget that will come out of it, and then start putting our ducks in order with an appeal and the backup we would need to get something done at the provincial level." Or consider the defence attorney who didn't particularly like his client's plea-bargaining deal but nevertheless announced, "Given the attitude of the normal jury on this type of crime, I feel we would be paddling up a stream behind the eight ball." Perhaps a newspaper columnist wins the prize for confusion with this triple-decker: "The city councillors also were miffed at their union counterparts because they have refused to bite the bullet that now seems to have grown to the size of a millstone to the councillors whose necks are on the line."

Think of figurative language as you might regard a fine cologne on the person sitting next to you in a crowded theatre: just enough is engaging; too much is overpowering.

(For more discussion of similes, metaphors, and other figurative language, see pages 306–307 in Chapter 11.)

Do vary your word choice so that your prose does not sound wordy, repetitious, or monotonous. Consider the following sentence:

> According to child psychologists, depriving a child of artistic stimulation in the earliest stages of childhood can cause the child brain damage.

Reworded, the following sentence eliminates the tiresome, unnecessary repetition of the word "child":

> According to child psychologists, depriving infants of artistic stimulation can cause brain damage.

By omitting or changing repeated words, you can add variety and crispness to your prose. Of course, don't ever change your words or sentence structure to achieve variety at the expense of clarity or precision; at all times, your goal is to make your prose clear to your readers.

Do remember that wordiness is a major problem for all writers, even the professionals. State your thoughts directly and specifically in as few words as necessary to communicate your meaning clearly. In addition to the advice given here on avoiding wordy or vague jargon, euphemisms, and clichés, you might also review the sections on simplicity and conciseness in Chapter 6.

THE MOST IMPORTANT KEY TO EFFECTIVE WORD CHOICE IS REVISION.

As you write your first draft, don't fret about selecting the best words to communicate your ideas; in later drafts, one of your main tasks will be replacing the inaccurate or imprecise words with better ones. (Dorothy Parker, famous for her witty essays, once lamented, "I can't write five words but that I change seven.") All good writers rewrite, so revise your prose to make each word count.

■ **PRACTISING WHAT YOU'VE LEARNED**

A. Underline the vague nouns, verbs, and modifiers in the sentences that follow. Then rewrite each sentence so that it says something clear and specific. You can choose your own context.

1. The experiment had very bad results.

2. The speaker came up with some odd items.

3. The house was big, old, and ugly.

4. The man was a nice guy with a good personality.

5. I felt that the whole ordeal was quite an experience.

6. The machine we got was missing a few things.

7. The play wasn't really anything special.

8. The classroom material was interesting.

9. The child made a lot of very loud noises.

10. The cost of the unusual meal was amazing.

B. Rewrite the following sentences, eliminating all clichés, slang, mixed metaphors, euphemisms, and sexist language you find.

1. When our mother didn't return from the little girl's room, we agreed she was slow as molasses.

2. Anyone who wants to be elected the next Member of Parliament for our riding must clearly recognize that our tourist industry is sitting on a launching pad, ready to flex its muscles, and become a dynamo.

3. It goes without saying that all of us silver foxes over the ripe old age of sixty-five should exercise our most sacred democratic privilege in every election.

4. The automobile company sent a complimentary letter warning that driving their pre-owned 2002 cars with the factory-installed set of bearings could adversely affect vehicle control.

5. After all is said and done, agricultural producers may be forced to relocate to urban environments settling in substandard housing with other members of the disadvantaged class until the day they expire.

6. The city councilman was stewing in his juices when he learned that his goals-impaired son had been arrested for fooling around with the funds for the fiscal underachievers' home.

7. Each commander realizes that he may one day be called upon to use the peacekeepers to depopulate an emerging nation in a lethal intervention.

8. Although Jack once regarded her as sweet and innocent, he knew then and there that Jill was really a wolf in sheep's clothing with a heart of stone.

C. Rewrite the following sentences, replacing the jargon and cloudy language with clear, precise words and phrases.

1. To maintain a state of high-level wellness, one should use a wooden inter-dental stimulator at least once a day and avoid spending time at fake-bake salons.

2. According to the military, one should not attempt a pre-dawn vertical insertion without an aerodynamic personnel decelerator because it could lead to sudden deceleration trauma upon landing.

3. Air Canada's passengers can now arrive and depart planes on customer conveyance mobile lounges.

4. If you are in the armed services, you should avoid receiving a ballistically induced aperture in the subcutaneous environment that might lead to your being terminated with extreme prejudice.

5. An internal memo at a large corporation recently announced: "In consideration of the perceived growth of the institutional health support workforce in corporate environments and the resultant requirements of personnel identity facilitation, managerial decision-making in the material procurement sector has been energized optimally to reformulate the paradigms of the acquisition process."

6. At a 2003 press conference on the war in Iraq, U.S. Defense Secretary Donald Rumsfeld announced the following: "Reports that say something hasn't happened are always interesting to me, because as we know, there are known knowns, there are things we know we know. We also know there

are known unknowns; that is to say we know there are some things we do not know. But there are also unknown unknowns—the ones we don't know we don't know."*

7. The employee was outplaced for a lack of interpersonal skills and for failing to optimize productivity.

8. My institute of higher learning announced today that its academic evaluation program had been delayed and in all probability indefinitely postponed due to circumstances relating to financial insolvency.

9. All of us could relate to Zhang Wei's essay on the significant educational factors involved in the revenue enhancement tax-base erosion control program.

10. In a recent report by the Canadian government's Department of National Defence, the American pilot who killed a Canadian soldier in a "friendly fire" incident was reprimanded for losing his "situational awareness," and for using the wrong "visual reference point" for his "objective area." In other words, he killed an ally by mistake because he couldn't see clearly, and shot the wrong target.

---

*Incidentally, this comment won Rumsfeld the "Foot in Mouth" prize for the most confusing public statement of the year, awarded by Britain's Plain English Campaign, a group dedicated to ridding the language of jargon and legalese.

▪ ASSIGNMENT

A. The following two quotes are taken from the 2007 annual report of the U.S. Department of Defense's Chemical and Biological Defense Program. See if you can translate the bureaucratese into clear, straightforward language.

1. It is extremely difficult to collect reliable intelligence on WMD programs and activities, which are closely guarded secrets. The prevalence of dual-use technologies and legitimate civilian applications means CB research efforts are easy to conceal and difficult to detect and monitor. Based on the demonstrated ease with which uncooperative states and nonstate actors can conceal WMD programs and related activities, the United States, its allies, and its partners must expect further intelligence gaps and surprises. Consequently, the United States must couple responses to known and validated threats with an aggressive and adaptive capability development process that anticipates potential novel and emerging threats.

2. Partnerships typically begin with an exchange of technical information through an information exchange annex, of which more than fifty currently

exist. When synergies are identified, these exchanges may lead to the development of a Memorandum of Understanding or Program Agreement, which support more extensive international collaborative activities.

B. Fill in the blanks with colourful, precise words. Make the paragraph as interesting, exciting, or humourous as you can. Avoid clichés and Insta-Prose (those predictable phrases that first come to mind). Make your responses original and creative.

As midnight approached, Janet and Brad _____ toward the _____ mansion to escape the _____ storm. Their _____ car had _____ on the road nearby. The night was _____, and Brad _____ at the shadows with _____ and _____. As they _____ up the _____ steps to the _____ door, the _____ wind was filled with _____ and _____ sounds. Janet _____ on the door, and moments later, it opened to reveal the _____ scientist, with a face like a _____ Brad and Janet _____ at each other and then _____ (complete this sentence and then end the paragraph and the story).

■ APPLYING WHAT YOU'VE LEARNED TO *YOUR* WRITING

If you have drafted a piece of writing and you are satisfied with the development and organization of your ideas, you may want to begin revising your word choice. First, read your draft for accuracy, looking up in your dictionary any words you suspect may have been used incorrectly. Then, focus your attention on your draft's tone, on the "voice" your words are creating. Have you selected the right words for your purpose, subject, and audience?

If you need a word with a slightly different connotation, use your thesaurus to suggest choices (for example, is the person you're discussing best described as smart, intellectual, studious, or wise?). Next, go on a Bland Verb Hunt. Try to replace at least five colourless vague or passive verbs (such as "are," "get," or "make") with active, vivid ones. Revise vague nouns ("thing") and dull, generic adjectives ("very," "really"); if you're stuck, think of words with strong sensory appeal (sight, smell, taste, sound, touch) to enliven your prose. Last, mine-sweep for any clichés, slang, or jargon. Make each word count: each choice should clarify, not muddy, your meaning.

Answer for page 147:

Most people respond with "coughed, sputtered, and died."

CHAPTER 7 SUMMARY

Here is a brief restatement of what you should remember about word choice:

1. Consult a dictionary if you are in doubt about the meaning or usage of a particular word.

2. Choose words that are appropriate for your purpose and audience.

3. Choose words that are clear, specific, and fresh rather than vague, bland, or clichéd.

4. Avoid language that is sexist, trendy, or that tries to disguise meaning with jargon or euphemisms.

5. Work for prose that is concise rather than wordy, precise rather than foggy.

Chapter 8

The Reading–Writing Connection

It's hardly surprising that good readers often become good writers themselves. Even if you haven't been a reader in the past, it's never too late to start. Good readers note effectiveness in the writing of others and use these observations to help clarify their own ideas and rhetorical choices about organization, development, and style. Analogies abound in every skill: singers listen to vocalists they admire, tennis players watch championship matches, actors evaluate their colleagues' award-winning performances, medical students observe famous surgeons, all with an eye to improving their own craft. Therefore, to help you become a better writer, your instructor may ask you to study some of the professional essays included in other sections of this text. Learning to read these essays analytically will help when you face your own writing decisions. To sharpen your reading skills, follow the steps suggested in this chapter. After practising these steps several times, you should discover that the process is becoming a natural part of your reading experience.

■ How Can Reading Well Help Me Become a Better Writer?

Close reading of the professional essays in this text should help you become a better writer in several ways. First, understanding the opinions expressed in these essays may spark interesting ideas for your own essays; second, discovering the various ways other writers have organized and explained their material should give you some new ideas about selecting your own strategies and supporting evidence. Familiarizing yourself with the effective stylistic devices and diction of other writers may also encourage you to use language in ways you've never tried before.

Perhaps most important, analyzing the prose of others should make you more aware of the writing process itself. Each writer represented in this text faced a series of decisions regarding the most effective rhetorical strategies to use. They must choose organization, development, and style very carefully, just as you do when you write. By asking questions (Why did the writer begin the essay this way? Why compare this event to that one? Why use a personal example in that paragraph?), you will begin to see how the writer put the essay together—and that knowledge will help you plan and shape your own essay. Questioning the rhetorical choices of other writers should also help you revise your prose, because it promotes the habit of asking yourself questions that consider the reader's point of view (Does the point in paragraph three need more evidence to convince my reader? Will the reader be confused if I don't add a smoother transition from paragraph four to five? Does the conclusion fall flat?).

In other words, the skills you practise as an analytical reader are those you'll use as a good writer.

■ How Can I Become an Analytical Reader?

Becoming an analytical reader who is conscious of an author's rhetorical strategies may, at first, demand more time—and involvement—than you have previously devoted to a reading assignment. Analytical reading requires more than allowing your eyes to pass over the words on the page; it's not like channel-surfing through late-night television shows, stopping here or there as interest strikes. Analytical reading asks you not only to understand the writer's ideas, but also to consider *how* those ideas were presented, *why* the writer presented them that way, and whether that presentation was *effective*. Consequently, to improve your understanding of the reading–writing connection, you should plan on two readings of the assigned essay, some note-taking, and some marking of the text (called *annotating*). This procedure may seem challenging at first, but the benefits to you as both reader and writer will be well worth the extra minutes.

Steps to Reading Well

1. Before you begin the essay itself, note the *publication information* and *biographical data* on the author in the paragraph that precedes each selection in this text. Where and when was the essay originally published? Was it directed toward a particular or a general audience? Was it written in response to some event or controversy? Is the essay still timely or is it dated? Does the author seem qualified to write about this subject? Does the introduction offer any other information that might help you assess the essay's effectiveness?

2. Next, note the *title* of the essay. Does it draw you into the essay? Does it suggest a particular tone or image?

3. You're now ready to begin your first reading of the essay. Some readers like to read through the essay without stopping; others feel comfortable at this point underlining a few main ideas or making checks in the margins. You may also have to make a dictionary stop if words you don't know appear in key places in the essay. Many times you can figure out definitions from context—that is, from the words and ideas surrounding the unknown word—but don't miss the point of a major part of an essay because of failure to recognize an important word, especially if that word is repeated or emphasized in some way.

When you finish this reading, write a sentence or two summarizing your general impression of the essay's content or ideas. Consider the author's *purpose:* What do you think the writer was trying to do? Overall, how well did he or she succeed? (A typical response might be "argued for tuition hike—unconvincing, boring—too many confusing statistics.")

Now prepare to take another, closer look at the essay. Make some notes in the margins or in another convenient place as you respond to the following questions. Remember that analytical reading is not a horse race: there are no trophies for finishing quickly! Fight the bad habit of galloping at breakneck speed through an essay; slow down to admire the verbal roses the writer has tried to place in your path.

4. Look at the *title* (again) and at the essay's *introductory paragraph(s).* Did they effectively set up your expectations? Introduce the essay's topic, main idea, tone? (Would some other title or introductory "hook" have worked better?)

5. Locate the writer's main point or *thesis;* this idea may be stated plainly or it may be clearly implied. If you didn't mark this idea on your first reading, do so now by placing a "T" in the margin so you can refer to the thesis easily. (If the thesis is implied, you may wish to mark places that you think most clearly indicate the writer's stance.)

6. As you reread the essay, look for important statements that support or illustrate the thesis. (As you know, these are often found as *topic sentences* occurring near the beginning or end of the body paragraphs.) Try numbering these supporting points or ideas and jotting a key word by each one in the margin.

7. As you identify each important supporting point, ask yourself how the writer develops, explains, or argues that idea. For example, does the writer clarify or support the point by providing examples, testimony, or statistics? By comparing or contrasting one idea to another? By showing a cause–effect relationship? Some other method? A combination of methods? A writer may use one or many methods of development, but each major point in an essay should be explained clearly and logically. Make brief marginal notes to indicate how well you think the writer has succeeded ("convincing example," "generalization without support," "questionable authority cited," "good comparison," etc.). Practise using marginal symbols, such as stars (for especially effective statements, descriptions, arguments) or question marks (for passages you think are confusing, untrue, or exaggerated). Make up your own set of symbols to help yourself remember your evaluations of the writer's ideas and techniques. Consult page 90 for a more extended discussion on shorthand symbols.

8. Look back over the essay's general *organization.* Did the writer use one of the expository, descriptive, narrative, or argumentative strategies (discussed in Part Two of this book) to structure the essay? Some combination of strategies? Was this choice effective? (Always consider alternate ways: Would another choice have allowed the writer to make his or her main point more emphatically? Why or why not?)

9. Does the essay flow logically and coherently? If you are having trouble with *unity* or *coherence* in your own essays, look closely at the transitional devices used in a few paragraphs; bracketing transitional words or phrases you see might show you how the writer achieved a sense of unity and flow.

10. Consider the writer's *style* and the essay's *tone.* Does the writer use figurative language in an arresting way? Specialized diction for a particular purpose? Repetition of words or phrases? Any especially effective sentence patterns? Does the writer's tone of voice come through clearly? Is the essay serious, humorous, angry, consoling, happy, sad, sarcastic, or something else? Is the tone appropriate for the purpose and audience of this essay? Writers use a variety of stylistic devices to create prose that is vivid and memorable; you might mark new uses of language you would like to try in essays of your own.

Now is also the time to look up meanings of any words you felt you could skip during your first time through the essay, especially if you sense that these words are important to the writer's tone or use of imagery.

Once you have completed these steps and added any other comments that seem important to the analysis of the essay, review your notes. Is this an effective essay? Is the essay's thesis explained or supported adequately with enough logically developed points and evidence? Is the essay organized as effectively as it could have been? What strengths and weaknesses did you find after this analytical reading? Has your original evaluation of this essay changed in any way? If so, write a new assessment, adding any other notes you want to help you remember your evaluation of this essay.

Finally, after this close reading of the essay, did you discover any new ideas, strategies, or techniques you might incorporate into *your* current piece of writing?

■ Sample Annotated Essay

Here is a professional essay annotated according to the steps listed on the previous pages.

■ Don't You Think It's Time to Start Thinking? —————— *title forecasts thesis*

Northrop Frye

Northrop Frye (1912–1991) taught at the University of Toronto, and was one of the most respected literary critics of the twentieth century. This article was originally published in *The Toronto Star* in 1986, and has been reprinted often.

educator

general audience

1   A student often leaves high school today without any sense of language as a structure. He may also have the idea that reading and writing are elementary skills that he mastered in childhood, never having grasped the fact that there are differences in levels of reading and writing as there are in mathematics between short division and long division.

2   Yet, in spite of his limited verbal skills, he firmly believes that he can think, that he has ideas, and that if he is just given the opportunity to express them he will be all right. Of course, when you look at what he's written you find it doesn't make any sense. When you tell him this he is devastated.

3   Part of his confusion here stems from the fact that we use the word "think" in so many bad, punning ways. Remember James Thurber's Walter Mitty who was always dreaming great dreams of glory. When his

Introduction briefly presents subject: students leave high school without a good understanding of how language functions; anticipates direction of argument; straightforward and clear, informal language

Students have confused ideas they can't communicate; critical, even condescending tone; use of allusion

wife asked him what he was doing he would say, "Has it ever occurred to you that I might be thinking?"

4   But of course, he wasn't thinking at all. Because we use it for everything our minds do, worrying, remembering, daydreaming, we imagine that thinking is something that can be achieved without any training. But again, it's a matter of practice. How well we can think depends on how much of it we have already done. Most students need to be taught, very carefully and patiently, that there is no such thing as an inarticulate idea waiting to have the right words wrapped around it.

5   They have to learn that ideas do not exist until they have been incorporated into words. Until that point you don't know whether you are pregnant or just have gas on the stomach.

6   The operation of thinking is the practice of articulating ideas until they are in the right words. And we can't think at random either. We can only add one more idea to the body of something we have already thought about. Most of us spend very little time doing this, and that is why there are so few people whom we regard as having any power to articulate at all. When such a person appears in public life, like Mr. Trudeau, we tend to regard him as possessing a gigantic intellect.

7   A society like ours doesn't have very much interest in literacy. It is compulsory to read and write because society must have docile and obedient citizens. We are taught to read so that we can obey the traffic signs and to cipher so that we can make out our income tax, but development of verbal competency is very much left to the individual.

8   And when we look at our day-to-day existence we can see that there are strong currents at work against the development of powers of articulateness. Young adolescents today often betray a curious sense of shame about speaking articulately, of framing a sentence with a period at the end of it.

9   Part of the reason for this is the powerful anti-intellectual drive which is constantly present in our society. Articulate speech marks one out as an individual, and in some settings this can be rather dangerous because people are often suspicious and frightened of articulateness. So if you say as little as possible and use only stereotyped, ready-made phrases you can hide yourself in the mass.

10   Then there are various epidemics sweeping over society which use unintelligibility as a weapon to preserve the present power structure. By making things as unintelligible as possible, to as many people as possible, you can hold the present power structure together. Understanding and articulateness lead to its destruction. This is the kind of thing that George Orwell was talking about, not just in *Nineteen Eighty-Four*, but in all his work on language. The kernel of everything reactionary and tyrannical in society is the impoverishment of the means of verbal communication.

11   The vast majority of things we hear today are prejudices and clichés, simply verbal formulas that have no thought behind them but are put up as pretence of thinking. It is not until we realize these things conceal

Categorizes and redefines ideas and thinking;

*Thesis: ideas only exist when they are articulated

Cultural context: explains and defends need for his argument—well-articulated ideas are rare—transition to Canadian context with specific example; leads to point about language and power in paragraphs 6 and 7 while continuing main point about importance of articulate thought and personal responsibility

1. Cultural context: Our society does not encourage anything beyond basic, practical literacy

2.Cultural context: linguistic competence actually carries stigma; "ready-made phrases"— allusion to Orwell's essay, "Politics and the English Language"

3.Central point: Language is connected to political power; Orwell allusion used—creates continuity with previous paragraph

*4. Evaluates modern ideas in general—no specific examples

meaning, rather than reveal it, that we can begin to develop our own powers of articulateness.

12   The teaching of humanities is, therefore, a militant job. Teachers are faced not simply with a mass of misconceptions and unexamined assumptions. They must engage in a fight to help the student confront and reject the verbal formulas and stock responses, to convert passive acceptance into active, constructive power. It is a fight against illiteracy and for the maturation of the mental process, for the development of skills which once acquired will never become obsolete.

Conclusion identifies possible solutions, calls for action; use of advanced diction

First impression: Frye suggests that in modern Canadian society, the level of thinking has degenerated, which has resulted in the loss of an individual's abilities and of much individual power.

Notes: Frye uses contrasting paragraphs, analogies, specific examples, literary allusions, analysis, and definition to develop his argument. A larger number of specific examples might have supported his argument even more strongly.

Personal response: I agree with Frye, though his somewhat polemical tone might alienate some of the young people who seem to be the particular targets of his criticism.

■ PRACTISING WHAT YOU'VE LEARNED

Select one of the professional essays reprinted in this text and annotate it according to the steps described in this chapter. Note at least one strength in the essay that you would like to incorporate into your own writing.

■ ASSIGNMENT

Select one of the professional essays in this text to read analytically and annotate. Then write a one-page explanation of the essay's major strengths (or weaknesses), showing how the writer's rhetorical choices affected you, the reader.

■ Writing a Summary

Frequently, writing teachers will ask students to read an essay and briefly summarize it. A *summary* is an objective, condensed version of a reading selection, containing the author's main ideas. You will still need to use your analytical skills, however, in order to pick out the key points in any piece of writing. Although summaries are always more concise than the original texts, the length of a particular summary often depends on the length and complexity of the original reading and the purpose of the summary.

Learning to summarize reading material is a valuable skill, useful in many post-secondary courses and in professional work. In one of your college or university classes, for example, your instructor might ask you to summarize an article pertinent to an upcoming lecture or class discussion, thus ensuring that you have thoroughly understood the information; at other times, you may need to summarize material for your own research. On your job, you might want to share a summary of an important report with colleagues, or you might be asked to present a summary of project results to your boss.

Because summarizing is such a useful skill, here are a few guidelines:

1. Read the selection carefully, as many times as it takes for you to understand and identify the author's thesis and main ideas. You might underline or take notes on the key ideas as you read. Use the suggestions in the previous pages of this chapter to help you.

2. When you begin to draft your summary, always include the author's name and the title of the original text in your first sentence. Many times, it's important to include the source of the work and its publication date too.

3. Using your own words, present the author's thesis and other main ideas in a few concise sentences. Do not merely copy sentences directly from the original text, as this can constitute plagiarism, even if you give the page number (see more on plagiarism in Chapter 14). A summary is not a collection of quoted sentences from the original. Use your own words to convey the main ideas as clearly and concisely as possible.

4. Omit all references to the supporting examples, long descriptions, and details in the selection, unless you have been instructed to include these. Try to articulate the core idea of each paragraph of the essay. Look out for wordy sentences and empty phrasing, both in your own writing and in the essay you are summarizing.

5. If, for clarity or emphasis, you do need to include an exact word or phrase from the original text, be certain to enclose the words in quotation marks. When you're taking notes, don't forget to write down page numbers where applicable, so you don't forget where you got your quotes, and so readers can find those quotes if necessary.

6. Do not give your own opinion or interpretation of the material you are summarizing. Your goal is an objective, accurate, condensed overview of the selection that does not reveal your attitude toward the ideas presented.

To illustrate the preceding guidelines, here is a brief summary of the essay that appears on pages 162–164 of this chapter.

In *The Toronto Star* essay "Don't You Think It's Time to Start Thinking?" Northrop Frye, a leading twentieth-century thinker, argues that youth today do not know how to form or articulate ideas. He blames their incompetence and uncaring attitudes on a society that devalues thinking to such a point that articulate thinkers are either seen as geniuses worthy of adulation or, more often, anomalies who pose a danger to existing power structures. Frye urges teachers to arm their students in critical thinking so young people can see through false and empty ideas, and thus convert from passive victims to active participants in society.

Note that the writer of the summary did not offer her opinion of Frye's argument, but, instead, objectively presented the essay's main ideas.

For additional discussion clarifying the difference between *summary* and *paraphrase*, see pages 377–378 in Chapter 14. For suggestions on writing the assignment known as the "summary-and-response essay," see pages 417–419 in Chapter 15; this section also contains a sample student paper written in response to Northrop Frye's essay "Don't You Think It's Time to Start Thinking?"

■ PRACTISING WHAT YOU'VE LEARNED

Read one of the professional essays in this textbook and annotate it according to the steps outlined earlier in this chapter. After you are sure you clearly understand the author's thesis and main ideas, write a one-paragraph summary of the essay. Use your own words to convey the essay's main ideas, but remember to remain objective in your summary.

■ Benefiting from Class Discussions

If you have been practising the steps for close reading of essays, you are on your way to becoming a better writer. By analyzing the rhetorical choices of other writers, you are gathering new ideas and techniques as well as improving your ability to look thoughtfully at your own drafts. To continue this progress, your composition instructor may devote class time to discussing sample professional or student essays that appear in this text.

Active participation in these discussions will contribute to your growth as a writer as you share ideas about effective prose with your classmates. To benefit from such discussions, consider the following suggestions for improving your classroom skills.

During the class period, your instructor may ask for responses to questions that follow selected essays in this text or he or she may pose new questions. If you've prepared by closely reading and annotating the assigned essay as outlined on pages 162–164, you should be able to join these discussions. Listen carefully to your classmates' opinions; offer your own insights and be willing to voice agreement or polite disagreement. If participating in class makes you so nervous you fear you will break out in spots, prepare one or two comments out of class in such clear detail that speaking about them will be easier for you, and then volunteer when those topics arise in the discussion. Don't hesitate to ask questions or request additional explanations; remember that if you don't understand something, it's a good bet others in the class are puzzled too.

As discussion of a sample essay unfolds, practise thinking critically on two levels. First, think of the essay as a draft in which the writer made certain choices to communicate meaning, just as you do in your essays. Trading ideas with your classmates may help you see why the writer chose as he or she did—and whether those decisions work effectively. As you gain a clear understanding of the strengths and weaknesses in the sample essay, move to the second level by considering the choices you are making in your own writing. For example, if you struggle with conclusions to your essays, listen attentively to the discussion of the writer's choice and then consider whether this kind of ending might work in your essay. If a writer has failed to provide enough examples or details to illustrate a particular point, think about a paragraph in your current rough draft. Do you now see a similar problem in need of revision? In other words, as you and your classmates analyze essays in class, *actively make the essential connection between the samples and your own work.*

To remember important points in any class discussion, sharpen your note-taking skills. If you use a notebook for this course, you may find it helpful to leave a wide margin on the left side of your paper, giving yourself space to write key words, questions, or ideas for your own writing. Start each day's notes on a new page with the day's date to help you locate material later. Acquire the habit of stapling or taping handouts to blank pages that immediately follow notes from a particular class period (handouts stuck in your textbook or in your backpack are easily lost). As you take notes, pay special attention to any words your instructor considers significant enough to write on the board and to those concepts that merit treatment in handouts or other visual aids (transparencies, slides, PowerPoint presentations, etc.). Be sensitive to the verbal cues your instructor uses to emphasize essential material (words such as "key terms," "main reasons," and "central idea," as well as repetition and even a raised voice).

Because class discussion often moves quickly, you'll need to develop a shorthand method of note-taking. Some students write out an important term the first time (development) and then abbreviate it thereafter (dev). You can devise your own system of symbols, but included here are some abbreviations common to note-taking you may find handy. Most of these abbreviations are for notes only, although some (such as e.g., i.e., cf., and ca.) may be used in college and professional writing; consult your instructor or the appropriate style manual if you are in doubt.

b/c = because	→ = causes, leads to, produces
b/4 = before	cf. = compare
w/ = with	↑ = increases, higher than
w/o = without	↓ = decreases, lower than
w/i = within	esp. = especially
e.g. = for example	re = regarding
i.e. = that is	ca. = approximately (use with dates or figures)
& = and	∴ = therefore
@ = at	≠ = not equal to, not the same, differs from
# = number	N.B. = "nota bene," Latin for "note well"

Later, after class, you may want to underline, star, or highlight important material. Fill in any gaps and rewrite any illegible words now before you forget what you meant. Use the wide left-hand margin to make some notes about applying the ideas and techniques discussed in class to your own writing. Reread these notes before you begin drafting or revising your essay. Make sure, however, that you never use note-taking abbreviations in any serious draft; you should certainly not use them in any formally submitted writing.

Here's the last, and possibly most important, piece of advice for every student of writing: *attend every class session*! There is a logical progression in all composition courses; each day's lesson emphasizes and builds on the previous one. By conscientiously attending every class discussion and actively participating in your own learning process, you *will* improve your writing skills.

Chapter 8 Summary

1. Reading and analyzing essays can improve your writing skills.

2. Learning to recognize and evaluate the strategies and stylistic techniques of other writers will help you plan and shape your own essays.

3. Reading analytically takes time and practice but is well worth the extra effort.

4. Learning to summarize reading material accurately and objectively is an important skill, useful in school and at work.

5. Active participation in class discussions of sample essays can help you strengthen your own writing.

Part One Summary: The Basics of the Short Essay

Here are ten suggestions to keep in mind while you are working on the rough drafts of your essay:

1. Be confident that you have something important and interesting to say.

2. Identify your particular audience and become determined to communicate effectively with them.

3. Use prewriting techniques to help you focus on one main idea that will become the thesis of your essay.

4. Organize your essay's points logically, in a persuasive and coherent order.

5. Develop each of your ideas with enough evidence and specific details.

6. Delete any irrelevant material that disrupts the smooth flow from idea to idea.

7. Compose sentences that are clear, concise, and informative; choose accurate, vivid words.

8. Improve your writing by learning to read analytically.

9. Revise your prose.

10. Revise your prose!

Part 2

Purposes, Modes, and Strategies

Communication may be divided into four types (or "modes" as they are often called): exposition, argumentation, description, and narration. Although each one will be explained in greater detail in this section of the text, the four modes may be defined briefly as follows:

Exposition
The writer intends to explain or inform.

Argumentation
The writer intends to convince or persuade.

Description
The writer intends to create in words a picture of a person, place, object, or feeling.

Narration
The writer intends to tell a story or recount an event.

Although we commonly refer to exposition, argumentation, description, and narration as the basic types of prose, in reality it is difficult to find any one mode in a pure form. In fact, almost all essays are combinations of two or more modes; it would be virtually impossible, for instance, to write a story—narration—without including description or to argue without also giving some information. Nevertheless, by determining a writer's main purpose, we can usually identify an essay or prose piece as primarily exposition, argumentation, description, or narration. In other words, an article may include a brief description of a new mousetrap, but if the writer's main intention is to explain how the trap works, then we may designate the essay as exposition. In most cases, the primary mode of any essay will be readily apparent to the reader.

In Part Two of this text, you will study each of the four modes in detail and learn some of the patterns of development, called *strategies,* that will enable you to write the kind of prose most frequently demanded in college and professional work. Mastering the most common prose patterns in their simplest forms now will help you to successfully assess and organize any kind of complex writing assignment you may face in the future. Chapter 13 concludes this section by discussing the more complex essay, developed through use of multiple strategies. ∎

Chapter 9

Exposition

Exposition refers to prose whose primary purpose is giving information. Some familiar examples of expository writing include encyclopedias, dictionaries, news magazines, and textbooks. In addition, much of your own university work may be classified as exposition: political analyses, laboratory and business reports, and most essay exams, to cite only a few of the possibilities.

Although expository writing does present information, a good expository essay is more than a collection of facts, figures, and details. First, each essay should contain a thesis statement clarifying the writer's purpose and position. Then the essay should be organized so that the body paragraphs explain and support that thesis. In an expository essay the writer says, in effect, here are the facts *as I see them;* therefore, the writer's main purpose is not only to inform the readers but also to convince them that this essay explains the subject matter in the clearest, most truthful way.

■ The Strategies of Exposition

There are a variety of ways to organize an expository essay, depending on your purpose. The most common strategies, or patterns, of organization include development by *example, process analysis, comparison and contrast, definition, classification,* and *causal analysis.* However, an essay is rarely developed completely by a single strategy (an essay developed by comparison and contrast, for instance, may also contain examples; a classification essay may contain definitions, and so forth); therefore, as in the case of the four modes, we identify the kind of expository essay by its *primary* strategy of development. To help you understand every expository strategy thoroughly before going on to the next, each is presented here separately. Each discussion section follows a similar pattern, which includes explanation of the strategy, advice on developing your essay, a list of essay topics, a topic proposal sheet, a revision checklist, sample essays (by students and by professional writers), and a progress report.

■ Strategy One: Development by Example

Perhaps you've heard a friend complain lately about politicians: "Politicians are all corrupt and they don't care about the people who vote for them!" she cries. Your natural response might be to question your friend's rather broad accusation: "What makes you say politicians don't care about people? What do they do that's corrupt?" Your friend might then respond with specific examples of corrupt politicians: she names one who has used campaign funds for vacations, another one who has taken a bribe from a large corporation, and yet another one who has passed legislation that has demonstrated a conflict of interest. By citing several examples, your friend clarifies and supports her general criticism of politicians, thus enabling you to understand her point of view.

Examples in an essay work precisely the same way as in the hypothetical story above: they *support, clarify, interest,* and *persuade.*

In your writing assignments, you might want to assert that dorm food is cruel and inhuman punishment, that recycling is a profitable habit, or that the cost of housing is rising dramatically. But without some carefully chosen examples to show the truth of your statements, these remain unsupported generalities or mere opinions. Your task, then, is to provide enough specific examples to support your general statements and to make them both clear and convincing. Here is a statement offering the reader only hazy generalities:

> Our locally supported TV channel presents a variety of excellent educational shows. The shows are informative on lots of different subjects for both children and adults. The information they offer makes Channel 19 well worth the public funds that support it.

Rewritten, the same paragraph explains its point clearly through the use of specific examples:

> Our locally supported TV channel presents a variety of excellent educational shows. For example, young children can learn their alphabet and numbers from *Sesame Street;* imaginative older children can be encouraged to create by watching *Kids' Writes,* a show on which four hosts read and act out stories written and sent in by youngsters from eight to fourteen. Adults may enjoy learning about antiques and collectibles from a program called *The Collector;* each week the show features an in-depth look at buying, selling, trading, and displaying collectible items, from Depression glass to teddy bears to Haida art. Those folks wishing to become handy around the home can use information on repairs from plumbing to wiring on *This Old House,* while the non-musical can learn the difference between scat singing and arias on such programs as *Jazz!*

and *Opera Today*. And the money-minded can profit from the tips dropped by stockbrokers who appear on *Wall Street Week*. The information offered makes these and other educational shows on Channel 19 well worth the public funds that support the station.

Although the preceding example is based on real shows, you may also use personal experiences, hypothetical situations, anecdotes, research material, facts, testimony, or any combination thereof, to explain, illustrate, or support the points in your essays.

In some cases you may find that a series of short examples fits your purpose, illustrating clearly the idea you are presenting to your reader:

In the earlier years of Hollywood, actors aspiring to become movie stars often adopted new names that they believed sounded more attractive to the public. Frances Ethel Gumm, for instance, decided to change her name to Judy Garland long before she flew over any rainbows, and Alexander Archibald Leach became Cary Grant on his way from England to America. Alexandra Cymboliak and Merle Johnson, Jr., might not have set teenage hearts throbbing in the early 1960s, but Sandra Dee and Troy Donahue certainly did. And while some names were changed to achieve a smoother flow (Frederic Austerlitz to Fred Astaire, for example), some may have also been changed to ensure a good fit on movie theatre marquees as well as a place in their audience's memory: the little Turner girl, Julia Jean Mildred Frances, for instance, became just Lana.

Or you may decide that two or three examples, explained in some detail, provide the best support for your topic rather than a series of short examples. In the paragraph that follows, the writer chose to develop two examples to illustrate her point about the unusual dog her family owned when she was a young girl in the late 1970s:

Our family dog Sparky always let us know when he wasn't getting enough attention. For instance, if he thought we were away from home too much, he'd perform his record trick. While we were out, Sparky would push an album out of the record rack and then tap the album cover in just such a way that the record would roll out. Then he would chomp the record! We'd return to find our favourite LP (somehow, always our current favourite) chewed into tiny bits of black vinyl scattered about the room. Another popular Sparky trick was the cat-sit. If the family was peacefully settled on the porch, not playing with him, Sparky would grab the family cat by the ear and drag her over to the steps, whereupon he would sit on top of her until someone paid attention to him. He never hurt the cat; he simply sat on her as one would sit on a fine cushion, with her head poking out under his tail, and a silly grin on his face that said, "See, if you'd play with me, I wouldn't get into such mischief."

You may also find that in some cases, one long, detailed example (called an *extended example*) is more useful than several shorter ones. If you were writing a paragraph urging the traffic department to install a stop sign at a particularly dangerous corner, you probably should cite numerous examples of accidents there. On the other hand, if you were praising a certain kind of local architecture, you might select one representative house and discuss it in detail. In the following paragraph, for instance, the writer might have supported his main point by citing a number of cases in which lives had been saved by seat belts; he chose instead to offer one detailed example, in the form of a personal experience:

> Wearing seat belts can protect people from injury, even in serious accidents. I know because seat belts saved me and my Dad two years ago when we were driving to see my grandparents who live in Peggy's Cove. Because of the distance, we had to travel late on a rainy, foggy Saturday night. My Dad was driving, but what he didn't know was that there was a car a short way behind us driven by a drunk driver who was following our car's tail lights in order to keep himself on the road. About midnight, my Dad decided to check the map to make sure we were headed in the right direction, so he signalled, pulled over to the shoulder, and began to come to a stop. Unfortunately for us, the drunk driver didn't see the signal and moved his car over to the shoulder thinking that the main road must have curved slightly since our car had gone that way. As Dad slowed our car, the other car plowed into us at a speed estimated later by the police as over eighty miles an hour. The car hit us like Babe Ruth's bat hitting a slow pitch; the force of the speeding car slammed us hard into the dashboard, but not through the windshield and out onto the rocky shoulder, because, lucky for us, we were wearing our seat belts. The highway patrol, who arrived quickly on the scene, testified later at the other driver's trial that without question my Dad and I would have been seriously injured, if not killed, had it not been for our seat belts restraining us in the front seat.

The story of the accident illustrates the writer's claim that seat belts can save lives; without such an example, the writer's statement would be only an unsupported generalization.

In addition to making general statements specific and thus more convincing, good examples can explain and clarify unfamiliar, abstract, or difficult concepts for the reader. For instance, Newton's law of gravity might be more easily understood once it is explained through the simple, familiar example of an apple falling from a tree.

Moreover, clear examples can add vivid details to your prose that hold the reader's attention while you explain your points. A general statement decrying animal abuse, for instance, may be more effective accompanied by several examples detailing the brutal treatment of one particular laboratory's research animals.

The use of good examples is not, however, limited only to essays primarily developed by example. In reality, you will probably use examples in every essay you write. You couldn't, for instance, write an essay classifying kinds of popular movies without including examples to help identify your categories. Similarly, you couldn't write an essay defining the characteristics of a good lab assistant or comparing two kinds of cars without ample use of specific examples. To illustrate the importance of examples in all patterns of essay development, here are two excerpts from student essays reprinted in other parts of this textbook. The first excerpt comes from an essay classifying Canadian children's literature. Here, the writer uses one central, extended example, and three briefer examples to illustrate her discussion of a particular era:

> By the time they reached the twentieth century, some Canadian writers were acknowledging the reality that neither children nor their lives were necessarily ideal. The story of *Anne of Green Gables*, published at the beginning of the twentieth century, became a counter-model to the idealized girls in many girls'

stories popular in the previous century. This absent-minded fantasizer who was hopeless at domestic tasks not only avoided a terrible end, but was rewarded by love and enthusiastic inclusion into her community. Her unorthodox family, consisting of a set of elderly unmarried siblings, was also a departure, as it remained unorthodox till the end, while successfully and unexpectedly providing stability. Anne's story (which was continued in a series of books) anticipated a wider Western trend to examine the breakdown of earlier societal norms, particularly in the context of the family. This type of story, in which a child attempts to survive in and make sense of unusual family configurations, became particularly popular from the 1960s onward, sometimes in combination with some of the earlier literary themes, such as the connection with land. The books of Sarah Ellis and Susan Juby, for example, examine the lives of today's Canadian children, who must cope with divorced or absent parents, poverty and homelessness. This twin interest in unexpected family units that must survive a harsh environment is evident even in Monica Dickens' science fiction *Isis Trilogy*. In many of these stories, it is a young girl who is the focal point. Thanks to Anne Shirley of Green Gables, these girls are able to draw strength and respect from skills that are not limited to the domestic sphere.

Another student uses a personal example to help her support a point in her essay that contrasts a local food co-op to a big chain grocery store (pages 210–213). By using her friend's experience as an example, the writer shows the reader how a co-op may assist local producers in the community:

> Direct selling offers two advantages for producers: they get a better price for their wares than by selling them through a middleman, and at the same time they establish an independent reputation for their business, which can be immensely valuable to their success later on. On Salt Spring Island, for example, Luna tofu (bean curd) stands out as an excellent illustration of this kind of mutual support. Several years ago my friend Gillie Campbell began making tofu in small batches to sell to the co-op as a way to earn a part-time income as well as to contribute to the co-op. Her enterprise has now grown so well that last year her husband quit his job to go into business with her full time. She currently sells to distributors and independent stores from here to St. John's; even Grocery Giant, who earlier would not consider selling her tofu even on a trial basis, is now thinking about changing its policy.

Learning to support, explain, or clarify your assertions by clear, thoughtful examples will help you develop virtually every piece of writing you are assigned, both in school and on the job. Development by example is the most widely used of all the expository strategies and by far the most important.

Developing Your Essay

An essay developed by example is one of the easiest to organize. In most cases, your first paragraph will present your thesis; each body paragraph will contain a topic sentence and as many effectively arranged examples as necessary to explain or support each major point; and your last paragraph will conclude your essay in some appropriate way. Although the general organization is fairly simple, you should revise the examples in your rough draft by asking these questions:

Are all my examples relevant? Each specific example should support, clarify, or explain the general statement it illustrates; each example should provide readers with additional insight into the subject under discussion. In an essay on Canadian political corruption, examples of corrupt Japanese politicians aren't directly relevant. Keep the purpose of your paragraphs in mind: don't wander off into an analysis of the causes of theft if you are only supposed to show examples of it on your campus. Keep your audience in mind too; which examples will provide the kinds of information that your particular readers need to understand your point?

Are my examples well chosen? To persuade your readers to accept your opinion, you should select those examples that are the strongest and most convincing. Let's say you were writing a research paper exposing a government agency's wastefulness. To illustrate your claim, you would select those cases that most obviously show gross or ridiculous expenditures rather than asking your readers to consider some unnecessary but minor expenses. And you would try to select cases that represent recent or current examples of wastefulness rather than discussing expenditures too dated to be persuasive. In other words, when you have a number of examples to choose from, evaluate them and then select the best ones to support your point.

Are there enough examples to make each point clear and persuasive? Put yourself in your reader's place: Would you be convinced with three brief examples? Five? One extended example? Two? Use your own judgment, but be careful to support or explain your major points adequately. It's better to risk over-explaining than to leave your reader confused or unconvinced.

Problems to Avoid

By far, the most common weakness in essays developed by example is a lack of specific detail. Too often novice writers present a sufficient number of relevant, well-chosen examples, but the illustrations themselves are too general, vague, or brief to be helpful. Examples should be clear, specific, and adequately detailed so that the reader receives the full persuasive impact of each one. For instance, in an essay claiming that professional hockey has become too violent, don't merely say, "Too many players were hurt last year." Such a statement only hints; it lacks enough development to be fully effective. Go into more detail by giving actual examples of jammed fingers, wrenched backs, fractured legs, crushed kneecaps, and broken dreams. Present these examples in specific, vivid language; once your readers begin to "see" that ice covered with blood and bruised bodies, you'll have less trouble convincing them that your point of view is accurate. (For more help incorporating specific details into your paragraph development, review pages 58–61 in Chapter 3.)

The second biggest problem in example essays is the lack of coherence. The reader should never sense an interruption in the flow of thought from one example to the next in paragraphs containing more than one example. Each body paragraph of this kind should be more than a topic sentence and a choppy list of examples. You should first arrange the examples in an order that best explains the major point presented by your topic sentence; then carefully check to make sure each example is smoothly connected in thought to the statements preceding and following it. You can avoid a listing effect by using transitional devices where necessary to ensure easy movement from example to example and from point to point. A few common transitional words often found in essays of example include "for instance," "for example," "to illustrate," "another," and "in addition." (For a list of other transitional words and additional help on writing coherent paragraphs, review pages 67–72 in Chapter 3.)

The third biggest problem in example essays is drawing misleading conclusions from insufficient evidence. Beware of drawing conclusions from too few examples or examples that aren't representative. Your examples must stand in for the usual, not the exceptional. You might want to make the argument that university or college education is unnecessary for success, but if your only example is Bill Gates, the founder of Microsoft, then he is merely an exception, rather than a representative example. You could also draw misleading conclusions about the nature of Renaissance poetry in general if you're only using examples of poetry by Shakespeare, since there were many other poets in the sixteenth and seventeenth centuries.

■ ESSAY TOPICS

Use the following broad statements to help you discover, narrow down, and focus an essay topic of your own design. What are the most effective examples you can use to develop this essay? Use the above suggestions to guide you in your choices. For additional ideas, turn to the "Suggestions for Writing" section following the professional essay (pages 184–185).

1. Heroes today are merely media creations rather than truly admirable people.

2. Francophone Canadian literature does/does not use the same themes as anglophone Canadian literature.

3. High schools do/do not adequately prepare students for college or university

4. Immigration policies should/should not give priority to refugees from countries undergoing current conflicts.

5. The willingness to undertake adventure is a necessary part of a happy existence.

6. This is the most influential Canadian of the past one hundred years.

7. Double standards still exist in society's treatment of those unable to take care of themselves.

8. Consumers are often at the mercy of unscrupulous companies.

9. Modern technology can produce more inconvenience than convenience.

10. Visits to the doctor/dentist/veterinarian can prove more traumatic than the illness.

11. Many required courses are/are not relevant to a student's education.

12. Failure is a better teacher than success.

13. Overprescription of drugs to behaviourally challenged children can create a new set of problems.

14. In its war on drug use, the government will/will not have to avoid many ethical pitfalls.

15. Many commonly used cleaning products contain toxic chemicals that can cause allergic reactions.

16. Economists' models for measuring happiness are/are not flawed.

A Topic Proposal for Your Essay

Selecting the right subject matter is important to every writer. To help you clarify your ideas and strengthen your commitment to your topic, here is a proposal sheet that asks you to describe some of your preliminary ideas about your subject before you begin drafting. Although your ideas may change as you draft (they will almost certainly become more refined), thinking through your choice of topic now may help you avoid several false starts.

1. In a few words, identify the subject of your essay as you have narrowed and focused it for this assignment. Write a rough statement of your opinion or attitude toward this topic.

2. Why are you interested in this topic? Do you have a personal or professional connection to the subject? State at least one reason for your choice of topic.

3. Is this a significant topic of interest to others? Why? Who specifically might find it interesting, informative, or entertaining?

4. Describe in one or two sentences the primary effect you would like to have on your audience. After they read your essay, what do you want your audience to think, feel, or do? (In other words, what is your purpose in writing this essay?)

5. Writers use examples to explain and clarify their ideas. Briefly list two or three examples you might develop in your essay to support discussion of your chosen topic.

6. What difficulties, if any, might this topic present during your drafting? For example, do you know enough about this topic to illustrate it with specific rather than vague examples? Might the topic still be too broad or unfocused for this assignment? Revise your topic now or make notes for an appropriate plan of action to resolve any difficulties you foresee.

■ Sample Student Essay

Study the use of specific examples in the brief student essay that follows. If the writer were to revise this essay, where might he add more examples or details?

RIVER RAFTING TEACHES WORTHWHILE LESSONS

1   Sun-warmed water slaps you in the face, the blazing sun beats down on your shoulders, and canyon walls speed by as you race down rolling waves of water. No experience can equal that of river rafting. In addition to being fun and exciting, rafting has many educational advantages as well, especially for those involved in school-sponsored rafting trips. River trips teach students how to prevent some of the environmental destruction that concerns the park officials, and, in addition, river trips teach students to work together in a way few other experiences can.

2   The most important lesson a rafting trip teaches students is respect for the environment. When students are exposed to the outdoors, they can better learn to appreciate its beauty and feel the need to preserve it. For example, I went on a rafting trip three summers ago with the biology department at my high school. Our trip lasted seven days down the Nimpkish River through the challenging Carnage Canyon in British Columbia. After the first day of rafting, I found myself surrounded by steep canyon walls and saw virtually no evidence of human life. The starkly beautiful, unspoiled atmosphere soon became a major influence on us during the trip. By the second day I saw classmates, whom I had previously seen fill an entire room with candy wrappers and empty soda cans, voluntarily inspecting our campsite for trash. And when twenty-four high school students sacrifice washing their hair for the sake of a suds-less and thus healthier river, some new, better attitudes about the environment have definitely been established.

3   In addition to the respect for nature a rafting trip encourages, it also teaches the importance of group cooperation. Since school-associated trips put students in command of the raft, the students find that in order to stay in control, each member must be reliable,

Margin notes:

Paragraphs in the Sample Student Essays are numbered for ease of discussion; do not number your own paragraphs.

Introduction: A description

Thesis

Essay map

Topic sentence one: Trip teaches respect for environment

Two brief examples illustrating respect:
1. Cleaning up trash
2. Forgoing suds in river

Topic sentence two: Trip teaches cooperation

Two examples of the need for cooperation:

1. Difficulties in paddling raft

be able to do his or her own part, and be alert to the actions of others. These skills are quickly learned when students see the consequences of noncooperation. Usually this occurs the first day, when the left side of the raft paddles in one direction, and the right the other way, and half the crew ends up seasick from going in circles. An even better illustration is another experience I had on my river trip. Because an upcoming rapid was usually not too rough, our instructor said a few of us could jump out and swim in it. Instead of deciding as a group who should go, though, five eager swimmers bailed out. This left me, our angry instructor, and another student to steer the raft. As it turned out, the rapid was fairly rough, and we soon found ourselves heading straight for a huge hole (a hole is formed from swirling funnel-like currents and can pull a raft under). The combined effort of the three of us was not enough to get the raft completely clear of the hole, and the

2. A near accident

raft tipped up vertically on its side, spilling us into the river. Luckily, no one was hurt, and the raft did not topple over, but the near loss of our food rations for the next five days, not to mention the raft itself, was enough to make us all more willing to work as a group in the future.

Conclusion: Importance of lessons

4   Despite the obvious benefits rafting offers, the number of river permits issued to school groups continues to decline because of financial cutbacks. It is a shame that those in charge of these cutbacks do not realize that in addition to having fun and making discoveries about themselves, students are learning valuable lessons through rafting trips—lessons that may help preserve the rivers for future rafters.

Professional Essay*

■ Narrate or Die: Why Scheherezade Keeps on Talking

A. S. Byatt

A. S. Byatt is an English novelist whose best-known novels, *Possession* and *Angels and Insects,* have both been made into films. Byatt's writes complex narratives that often interweave past and present as the main characters enter their quest for self-knowledge. The following essay was published in the *New York Times Magazine* in 1999.

1   The best story ever told? Perhaps the story of the two brothers, both kings, who found that their wives were unfaithful, took bloody vengeance, and set out into the world to travel until they found someone less fortunate than they were. They encountered a demon who kept a woman in a glass chest with four locks; she came out while he slept and showed them 98 rings she collected from chance lovers and insisted on having sex with the princes to make it a round 100. The princes decided that the demon was more unfortunate than they were and returned to their kingdoms. There the elder brother, Shahryar, still angry over his wife's betrayal, instituted a reign of terror, marrying a virgin each day and handing her to his vizier for execution at dawn. The vizier's daughter Shahrazad, a woman both wise and learned, beseeched her father to give her to the king. On the wedding night, the bride asked that her younger sister, Dinarzad, might sleep under the bed, so that when the king had "finished with Shahrazad," the younger girl, as the sisters had agreed, might ask Shahrazad to tell a story to while away the time until dawn. When dawn came, the story was not finished, and the curious king stayed execution for a night. Shahrazad continued to tell tales, which gave rise to other tales, all of which were unfinished at dawn. The king's narrative curiosity kept Shahrazad alive, day after day. She narrated a stay of execution. A space in which she bore three children. And in the end, the king removed the sentence of death, and they lived happily ever after.

2   This story has everything a tale should have. Sex, death, treachery, vengeance, magic, humour, warmth, wit, surprise and a happy ending. Though it appears to be a story against women, it actually marks the creation of one of the strongest and cleverest heroines in world literature. Shahrazad, who has been better known in the West as Scheherazad, triumphs because she is endlessly inventive and keeps her head. The stories in "The Thousand and One Nights" (interchangeably known as "The Arabian Nights") are stories about storytelling without ever ceasing to be stories about love and life and death and money and money and food and other human necessities. Narration is as much a part of human nature as breath and the circulation of blood. Modernist literature tried to do away with storytelling, which it thought vulgar, replacing it with flashbacks, epiphanies, streams of consciousness. But storytelling is intrinsic to biological time, which we cannot escape. Life, Pascal said, is like living in a prison from which every day fellow prisoners are taken away to be executed. We are all, like Scheherazade, under sentence of death, and we all think of our lives as narratives, with beginnings, middles and ends.

---

* To help you read this essay analytically, review pages 160–162 in Chapter 8.

3   Storytelling in general, and "The Thousand and One Nights" in particular, consoles us for endings with endless new beginnings. I have just finished my own telling of the frame story with the European fairy tale ending, "they lived happily ever after," which is a consolatory false eternity, for no one does, except in the endless repetitions of storytelling. Stories keep part of us alive after the end of the story, and there is something very moving about Scheherazade entering on the happiness ever after, not at her wedding, but after 1,001 tales and three children.

4   Great stories, and great story collections, are shape shifters. "The Thousand and One Nights," with its roots in Persia and India, has probably been circulating in one form or another since the ninth century. It first appeared in Europe in the French translation of Antoine Galland between 1704–1717. He used a 14th-century Syrian text but adapted and rewrote and added for French taste—it is possible that both Aladdin and Ali Baba as we read them originate with the Frenchman. Subsequent translators took liberties, or used their imaginations. Richard Burton invented a curious Victorian-medieval style. Joseph Charles Madrus, in 1899, according to Robert Irwin, whose "Companion to the Arabian Nights" is gripping and indispensable, "reshaped the 'Nights' in such a manner that the stories appear to have been written by Oscar Wilde or Stéphane Mallarmé."

5   Eastern and Western literature contain other related collections of interlinked tales—"Katha Sarit Sagara" ("The Ocean of Story"), Ovid's "Metamorphoses," Chaucer's "Canterbury Tales" and Boccaccio's "Decameron," whose frame story has its characters defying the Black Death by retreating to the country and telling tales. Out of such works came 19th-century Gothic fantasy and the intricate, paranoid nightmare plottings of such story webs as "The Crying of Lot 49" and Lawrence Norfolk's "Lempriere's Dictionary." Collections of tales talk to one another and borrow from one another; motifs glide from culture to culture, century to century. If the origin of stories is the human ability to remember the past, speculate about beginnings and imagine the ending, it doesn't follow that the search for any "pure" or undisputed origin for any story will lead to definiteness.

6   Scheherazade's tales have lived on, like germ cells, in many literatures. Dickens, who became the master of serial narration and endless beginnings, comforted his lonely and miserable childhood with "The Arabian Nights," living in their world and learning their craft. In British Romantic poetry, "The Arabian Nights" stood for the wonderful against the mundane, the imaginative against the prosaically and reductively rational. Coleridge said his mind had been "habituated to the vast" by his early reading of "Romances, & Relations of Giants and Magicians, & Genii." He used the tale of an angry and vengeful Djinn whose invisible child had been killed by a thrown date stone as an example of pure chance or fate. Wordsworth, in the fifth book of his "Prelude," describes his childhood treasure as "a little yellow, canvas-covered book,/ A slender abstract of the Arabian tales," and the "promise scarcely earthly" of his discovery that there were four large volumes of the work.

7   Various Western writers have been tempted to write the 1,002nd tale. Edgar Allan Poe's Scheherazade makes the mistake of telling her aging husband about modern marvels like steamships, radio and the telegraph. He finds these true tales so incredible that he concludes she has lost her touch and has her strangled after all. Poe is a combative and irreverent Yankee at the Persian court. Joseph Roth's Scheherazade resides in the decadent days of the Austrian Empire; while John Barth, in his "Dunyazadiad,"

appears in person as a balding, bespectacled genie who tells the nervous Scheherazade the tales she will tell because he has read them in the future and she is his heroine— thus creating another false eternity, a circular time loop, in which storytellers hand on stories of storytellers.

8   Then there are the modern Oriental fabulists, Naguib Mahfouz and Salman Rushdie, both threatened with death for storytelling. Mahfouz's "Arabian Nights and Days" is a collection of magical tales with a political edge and a spiritual depth. His stories rework "The Thousand and One Nights": his Shahriyar slowly learns about justice and mercy, the Angel of Death is a bric-a-brac merchant and genies play tricks with fate. Salman Rushdie's narratives are intertwined with the storytelling of the "Nights." "Haroun and the Sea of Stories" pits a resourceful child, Haroun, against the evil Khattam-Shud, who wants to drain the ocean of the streams of story, which are alive, and replace it with silence and darkness. Rushdie's tale, like Scheherazade's, equates storytelling with life, but his characters and wit owe as much to "Western fantasies"—"Alice in Wonderland" and "The Wizard of Oz"—as they do to "The Thousand and One Nights." Another cross-fertilization, another conversation.

9   Rushdie's sea of stories is "the biggest library in the universe." Jorge Luis Borges, to whom libraries, labyrinths and books were all images of infinity, wrote in "The Garden of Forking Paths" of "That night which is at the middle of the 'Thousand and One Nights' when Scheherazade (through a magical oversight of the copyist) begins to repeat her stories over again . . ." This circular tale fascinated Italo Calvino. It also inspired him, for his "If on a Winter's Night a Traveller" is the endless tale of a lost reader who starts a book only to find that the rest is missing; when he replaces the book he finds that it has a new beginning. This novel contains a novelist—as Borges's tale contains Scheherazade within Scheherazade—who wants to write a book that will contain only the pure pleasure of anticipation of the beginning, "a book that is only an incipit," a book with no ending, perhaps like "The Arabian Nights."

10   Marcel Proust saw himself as Scheherazade, in relation to both sex and death. At the end of the almost endless novel, "Remembrance of Things Past," he writes a triumphant meditation on the presence of death, which has in fact driven him to create his great and comprehensive book, the book of his life. At one point he even personifies this presence of death as "le sultan Sheriar," who might or might not put a dawn end to his nocturnal writing. Malcolm Bowie, in "Proust Among Stars," comments that "the big book of death-defying stories" with which Proust's novel compares itself is no Boccaccio's "Decameron," in which death appears as a "horrifying initial trigger to tale-telling," but the "Nights," where stories are life. "Narrate or die," for Proust's narrator as for Scheherazade, is the imperative. "By mere sentences placed end on end, one's sentence is commuted for a while, and the end is postponed."

11   The Judeo-Christian culture is founded on a linear narrative in time. It moves forward from creation through history, to redemption in the Christian case, and looks forward to the promised end, when time and death will cease to be. The great novels of Western culture, from "Don Quixote" to "War and Peace," from "Moby Dick" to "Dr. Faustus," were constructed in the shadow of this story. People are excited by millennial events as images of beginnings and endings. There is a difference between these great, portentous histories and small tales that are handed down like gifts for delight and contemplation.

12   Storytellers like Calvino and Scheherazade can offer readers and listeners an infinity of incipits, and illusion of inexhaustibility. Calvino's imaginary novelist sits and stares

at a cartoon of Snoopy, sitting at a typewriter, with the caption "It was a dark and stormy night," the beginning of a circular shaggy-dog story. Both cartoons and soap operas are versions of Scheherazade's tale telling, worlds in which death and endings are put off indefinitely—and age too, in the case of Charlie Brown.

13   High modernism escaped time with epiphanic visions of timeless moments, imagined infinities that have always seemed to me strained, for they fail to offer any counter to fear and death. But the small artifices of elegant, well-made tales and the vulgar satisfaction of narrative curiosity do stand against death. The romantic novelist Georgette Heyer kept few fan letters, but I saw two: one from a man who had laughed at one of her comic fops on the trolley going to a life-threatening operation, and one from a Polish woman who had kept her fellow prisoners alive during the war by reciting, night after night, a Heyer novel she knew by heart.

14   During the bombardment of Sarajevo in 1994, a group of theatre workers in Amsterdam commissioned tales, from different European writers, to be read aloud, simultaneously, in theatres in Sarajevo itself and all over Europe, every Friday until the fighting ended. This project pitted storytelling against destruction, imaginative life against real death. It may not have saved lives, but it was a form of living energy. It looked back to "The Thousand and One Nights" and forward to the millennium. It was called Scheherazade 2001.

Questions on Content, Structure, and Style

1. Why does Byatt begin her essay with a question which she answers right away with an extended example?

2. What is Byatt's thesis? Is it specifically stated or clearly implied?

3. What examples does Byatt offer to illustrate her belief that storytelling is vital to our lives? Are there enough well-chosen examples to make her position clear?

4. What is the effect, according to Byatt, of Eastern stories on the Western narrative imagination? In what ways does she show this effect?

5. Does Byatt use enough details in her examples to make them clear, vivid, and persuasive? Point out some of her details to support your answer.

6. What does Byatt gain by using quotations in some of her examples?

7. How does Byatt defend her argument? How does she clarify her claims?

8. Characterize the tone of Byatt's essay. Is it appropriate for her purpose and for her intended audience? Why or why not?

9. Evaluate Byatt's conclusion. Does it effectively wrap up the essay?

10. Do you agree or disagree with Byatt? What examples could you offer to support your position?

Suggestions for Writing

Try using A. S. Byatt's essay "Narrate or Die: Why Scheherezade Keeps on Talking" as a stepping stone, moving from one or more of her ideas to a subject for your own essay. For instance, you might write an essay based on your own historical and/or sociological research that illustrates or challenges Byatt's view that stories are what give us the ability to survive. Perhaps Byatt's claim that Eastern storytelling has influenced major Western writers might lead you to an essay based on your research and observations on this provocative idea. You can also look for essays that challenge Byatt's ideas about the importance of the story. Look through Byatt's essay once more to find other springboard ideas for *your* writing.

Vocabulary*

vizier (1)	consolatory (3)	motif (5)
epiphanies (2)	eternity (3)	prosaically (6)
intrinsic (2)	intricate (5)	reductively (6)
habituated (6)	vengeful (6)	combative (7)
irreverent (7)	fabulist (8)	bric-a-brac (8)
resourceful (8)	labyrinths (9)	infinity (9)
incipit (9)	portentous (11)	artifices (12)

▪ A REVISION WORKSHEET

As you write your rough drafts, consult Chapter 5 for guidance through the revision process. In addition, here are a few questions to ask yourself as you revise your example essay:

1. Is the essay's thesis clear to the reader?

2. Do the topic sentences support the thesis?

3. Does each body paragraph contain examples that effectively illustrate the claim of the topic sentence rather than offering mere generalities?

4. Are there enough well-chosen examples to make each point clear and convincing?

5. Is each example developed in enough specific detail? Where could more details be added? Could you use more precise language?

6. If a paragraph contains multiple examples, are they arranged in the most effective order, with a smooth transition from one to another?

7. If a paragraph contains an extended example, does the discussion flow logically and with coherence?

After you've revised your essay extensively, you might exchange rough drafts with a classmate and answer these questions for each other, making specific suggestions for improvement wherever appropriate. (For advice on productive participation in classroom workshops, see pages 102–104 in Chapter 5.)

---

* Numbers in parentheses following vocabulary words refer to paragraphs in the essay.

Reviewing Your Progress

After you have completed your essay developed by examples, take a moment to measure your progress as a writer by responding to the following questions. Such analysis will help you recognize growth in your writing skills and may enable you to identify areas that are still problematic.

1. What is the best feature of your essay? Why?

2. After considering your essay's supporting examples, which one do you think most effectively explains or illustrates your ideas? Why?

3. What part of your essay gave you the most trouble? How did you overcome the problem?

4. If you had more time to work on this essay, what would receive additional attention? Why?

5. What did you learn about your topic from writing this essay? About yourself as a writer?

■ Strategy Two: Development by Process Analysis

Process analysis identifies and explains what steps must be taken to complete an operation or procedure. There are two kinds of process analysis essays: directional and informative.

A *directional process* tells the reader how to do or make something. In simple words, it gives directions. You are more familiar with directional process than you might think; when you open a telephone book, for example, you see the pages in the front explaining how to make a three-way long-distance call. When you tell friends how to find your house, you're asking them to follow a directional process. On your computer, you can learn how to transfer files or download attachments or any one of hundreds of other options by following step-by-step directions often found on a "Help" menu. The most widely read books in North American libraries fall into the how-to-do-it (or how-to-fix-it) category: how to wire a house, how to repair a car, how to play winning poker, how to become a millionaire overnight, and so forth. And almost every home contains at least one cookbook full of recipes providing directions for preparing various dishes. (Even Part One of this text is, in detailed fashion, a directional process telling how to write a short essay, beginning with the selection of a topic and concluding with advice on revision.)

An *informative process* tells the reader how something is or was made or done or how something works. Informative process differs from directional process in that it is not designed primarily to tell people how to do it; instead, it describes the steps by which someone other than the reader does or makes something (or how something was made or done in the past). For example, an informative process essay might describe how scientists discovered polio vaccine, how a bill passes through Parliament, how a fossil sample is cleaned, how a cell goes through mitosis, or how an engine propels a jet. In other words, this type of essay gives information on processes that are not intended to be—or cannot be—duplicated by the individual reader.

Developing Your Essay

Of all the expository essays, students usually agree that the process paper is the easiest to organize, mainly because it is presented in simple, chronological steps. To prepare a well-written process essay, however, you should remember the following advice:

Select an appropriate subject. First, make sure you know your subject thoroughly; one fuzzy step could wreck your entire process. Second, choose a process that is simple and short enough to describe in detail. In a 500-to-800-word essay, for instance, it's better to describe how to build a ship in a bottle than how to construct a life-size replica of Noah's Ark. On the other hand, don't choose a process so simple-minded, mundane, or mechanical that it insults your readers' intelligence or bores them silly. (Some years ago at a large university, first-year students were asked to write a process essay on "How to Sharpen a Pencil"; with the assignment of such stirring, creative topics, it's a wonder that particular English department produced any majors at all that year.)

Describe any necessary equipment and define special terms. In some process essays, you will need to indicate what equipment, ingredients, or tools are required. Such information is often provided in a paragraph following the thesis, before the process itself is described; in other cases, the explanation of proper equipment is presented as the need arises in each step of the process. As the writer, you must decide which method is best for your subject. The same is true for any terms that need defining. Don't lose your reader by using terms only you, the specialist, can comprehend. Always remember that you're trying to tell people about a process they don't understand.

State your steps in a logical, chronological order. Obviously, if someone wanted to know how to bake bread, you wouldn't begin with "Put the prepared dough in the oven." Start at the beginning and carefully follow through, step by step, until the process is completed. Don't omit any steps or directions, no matter how seemingly insignificant. Without complete instructions, for example, the would-be baker might end up with a gob of dough rather than a loaf of bread—simply because the directions didn't say to heat the oven to a certain temperature.

Explain each step clearly, sufficiently, and accurately. If you've ever tried to assemble a child's toy or a piece of furniture, you probably already know how frustrating—and infuriating—it is to work from vague, inadequate directions. Save your readers from tears and tantrums by describing each step in your process as clearly as possible. Use enough specific details to distinguish one step from another. As the readers finish each step, they should know how the subject matter is supposed to look, feel, smell, taste, or sound at that stage of the process. You might also explain why each step is necessary ("Cutting back the young avocado stem is necessary to prevent a spindly plant"; "Senator Snort then had to win over the chair of the Arms Committee to be sure his bill would go to the Senate floor for a vote"). In some cases, especially in directional processes, it's helpful to give warnings ("When you begin tightrope walking, the condition of your shoes is critical; be careful the soles are not slick") or descriptions of errors and how to rectify them ("If you pass a white church, you've gone a block too far, so turn right at the church and circle back on Candle Lane"; "If the sauce appears grey and thin, add one teaspoon more of cornstarch until the gravy is white and bubbly").

Organize your steps effectively. If you have a few big steps in your process, you probably will devote a paragraph to each one. On the other hand, if you have several small steps, you should organize them into a few manageable units. For example, in the essay "How to

Prepare Fresh Fish," the list of small steps on the left has been grouped into three larger units, each of which becomes a body paragraph:

1. scaling	I. Cleaning
2. beheading	A. scaling
3. gutting	B. beheading
4. washing	C. gutting
5. seasoning	II. Cooking
6. breading	A. washing
7. frying	B. seasoning
8. draining	C. breading
9. portioning	D. frying
10. garnishing	III. Serving
	A. draining
	B. portioning
	C. garnishing

In addition, don't forget to use enough transitional devices between steps to avoid the effect of a mechanical list. Some frequently used linking words in process essays include the following:

next	first, second, third, etc.
then	at this point
now	following
to begin	when
finally	at last
before	afterward

Vary your transitional words sufficiently so that your steps are not linked by a monotonous repetition of "and then" or "next."

Problems to Avoid

Don't forget to include a thesis. You already know, of course, that every essay needs a thesis, but the advice bears repeating here because for some reason some writers often omit the statement in their process essays. Your thesis might be (1) your reason for presenting this process—why you feel it's important or necessary for the readers to know it ("Because rescue squads often arrive too late, every adult should know how to administer CPR to accident victims") or (2) an assertion about the nature of the process itself ("Needlepoint is a simple, restful, fun hobby for both men and women"). Here are some other subjects and sample theses:

- The restoration of antique paintings is an exacting process.
- The rise in interest rates wasn't altogether unexpected.
- The socialization of older students who go into undergraduate programs is not as difficult as we anticipate.

- The acquisition of new language skills becomes more challenging as people get older.

- Challenging a speeding ticket is a time-consuming, energy-draining, but financially rewarding endeavour.

- The series of public protests that led to the return of the traditional Coca-Cola was an unparalleled success in the history of North American consumerism.

Presenting a thesis and referring to it appropriately gives your essay unity and coherence, as well as ensuring against a monotonous list of steps.

Pay special attention to your conclusion. Don't allow your essay to grind to an abrupt halt after the final step. You might conclude the essay by talking of the significance of the completed process or by explaining other uses it may have. Or, if it is appropriate, finish your essay with an amusing story or emphatic comment. However you conclude, leave the reader with a feeling of satisfaction, with a sense of having completed an interesting procedure. (For more information on writing good conclusions, see pages 82–85.)

■ Essay Topics

Here are suggested topics for both directional and informative process essays. Some of the topics may be used in humorous essays, such as "How to Flunk a Test," "How to Remain a Bench Warmer," or "How to Say Nothing in Eight Hundred Words." For additional ideas, turn to the "Suggestions for Writing" sections following the professional essays (pages 199–200 and page 203).

1. How you arrived at a major decision or solved an important problem
2. How to choose your university or college major
3. How to succeed or fail in a job interview (or in some other important endeavour)
4. How to buy a computer, CD player, camera, or other recreational product
5. How a popular product or fad originated or grew
6. How to manage stress, stage fright, homesickness, or an irrational fear
7. How something in nature works or was formed
8. How a company makes or sells a product
9. How a piece of equipment or a machine works
10. How to analyze chemical samples
11. How to get in shape/develop physical fitness
12. How to evaluate credibility in information sources such as the Internet
13. How a historical event occurred or an important law was passed (e.g., Canadian Constitution, Goods and Services Tax, Terry Fox's marathon)

14. How to earn money quickly or easily (and legally)

15. How a famous invention or discovery occurred

16. How to lodge a complaint and win

Terry Fox, whose attempt at a one-legged marathon across the country raised cancer research funding and cancer awareness in Canada.

A Topic Proposal for Your Essay

Selecting the right subject matter is important to every writer. To help you clarify your ideas and strengthen your commitment to your topic, here is a proposal sheet that asks you to describe some of your preliminary ideas about your subject before you begin drafting. Although your ideas may change as you write (they will almost certainly become more refined), thinking through your choice of topic now may help you avoid several false starts.

1. What process will you explain in your essay? Is it a directional or an informative process? Can you address the complexity of this process in a short essay?

2. Why did you select this topic? Are you personally or professionally interested in this process? Cite at least one reason for your choice.

3. Why do you think this topic would be of interest to others? Who might find it especially informative or enjoyable?

4. Describe in one or two sentences the ideal response from your readers. What would you like them to do or know after reading about your topic?

5. List at least three of the larger steps or stages in the process.

6. What difficulties might this topic present during your drafting? Will this topic require any additional research on your part?

■ Sample Student Essay

The following essay is on a directional process telling readers how to run a successful garage sale. To make the instructions clear and enjoyable, the writer described seven steps and offered many specific examples, details, and warnings.

CATCHING GARAGE SALE FEVER

1   Ever need some easy money fast? Do you need it to repay those incredible overdue library fines you ran up writing your last research paper? Perhaps you need it to raise money for that much-needed vacation to Mexico you put on your credit card last reading week. Maybe you feel you simply have to clear out some junk before the piles block the remaining sunlight from your windows? Whether the problem is cash flow or trash flow, you can solve it easily by holding what is fast becoming a popular Canadian sport: the weekend garage sale. As a veteran of some half-dozen successful ventures, I can testify that garage sales are the easiest way to make quick money, with a minimum of physical labour and the maximum of fun.

Introduction: A series of questions to hook the reader

Thesis

2   Most garage sale "experts" start getting ready at least two weeks before the sale by taking inventory. Look through your closets and junk drawers to see if you actually have enough items to make a sale worthwhile. If all you have is a mass of miscellaneous small items, think about waiting or joining a friend's sale, because you do need at least a couple of larger items (furniture is always a big seller) to draw customers initially. Also, consider whether the season is appropriate for your items: sun dresses and shorts, for example, sell better in the spring and summer; coats and boots in the fall. As you collect your items, don't underestimate the "saleability" of some of your junk—the hideous purple china bulldog Aunt Clara gave you for Christmas five years ago may be perfect for someone's Ugly Mutt Collection.

Step one: Taking inventory

3   As you sort through your closets, begin thinking about the time and place of your sale. First, decide if you want a one- or two-day sale. If you opt for only one day, Saturdays are generally best because most people are free that day. Plan to start early—by 8 a.m. if possible—because the experienced buyers get up and get

Step two: Deciding when and where

going so they can hit more sales that way. Unless you have nothing else to do that day, plan to end your sale by mid-afternoon; most people have run out of buying energy (or money) by 3 p.m. Deciding on the location of your sale depends, of course, on your housing situation, but you still might need to make some choices. For instance, do you want to put your items out in a driveway, a front yard, or actually in the garage (weather might affect this decision)? Perhaps you want to put them on a side yard because it gets more passersby? Wherever you decide, be sure that there are plenty of places for customers to park close by without blocking your neighbours' driveways.

Step three: Advertising the sale

4   Unless you live in a very small town or on a very busy street, you'll probably want to place an inexpensive advertisement in the "garage sale" column of your local newspaper, scheduled to run a day or two before, and the day of, your sale. Your advertisement should tell the times and place of the sale (give brief directions or mention landmarks if the location is hard to find) as well as a short list of some of your items. Few people will turn out for "household goods" alone; some popular items include bookcases, antiques, books, fans, jewellery, toys, baby equipment, and name-brand clothes. One other piece of advice about the advertisement copy: it

A warning

should include the phrase "no early sales" unless you want to be awakened at 6:30 a.m., as I was one Saturday, by a bunch of semi-pro garage sale buyers milling restlessly around in your yard, looking like zombies out of a George Romero horror movie. In addition to your newspaper advertisement, you may also wish to put up posters in places frequented by lots of people; laundromats and grocery stores often have bulletin boards for such announcements.

Another warning

You can also put up signs on nearby well-travelled streets, but one warning: in some towns it's illegal to post anything on utility poles or traffic signs, so be sure to check your local ordinances first.

5   Tagging your items with their prices is the least fun, and it can take a day or a week depending on how many items you have and how much time each day you can devote to the project. You can buy sheets of little white stickers or use pieces of masking tape to stick on the prices, but if you want to save time, consider grouping some items and selling them all for the same price—all shirts, for example, are 50 cents. Be realistic about your prices; the handcrafted rug from Greece may have been expensive and important to you, but to others, it's a worn doormat. Some experts suggest pricing your articles at about one-fourth their original value, unless you have special reasons not to (an antique or a popular collectors' item, for instance, may be more valuable now than when you bought it). Remember that you can always come down on your prices if someone is interested in a particular item.

Step four: Pricing the merchandise

6   By the day before your sale you should have all your items clean and tagged. One of the beauties of a garage sale is that there's very little equipment to collect. You'll need tables, benches, or boards supported by bricks to display your goods; a rope tied from side to side of your garage can double as a clothes rack. Try to spread out your merchandise rather than dumping articles in deep boxes; customers don't want to feel like they're rummaging through a trash barrel. Most important, you'll need a chair and a table to hold some sort of money box, preferably one with a lock. The afternoon before the sale, take a trip to the bank if you need to, to make sure you have enough one-dollar bills and coins to make plenty of change. The evening before the sale, set up your items on your display benches in the garage or indoors near the site of your sale so that you can quickly set things out in the morning. Get a good night's sleep so you can get up to open on time: the early bird does get the sales in this business.

Step five: Setting up your sale

A note on equipment

Step six: Running the sale   **7**   The sale itself is, of course, the real fun. Half the enjoyment is haggling with the customers, so be prepared to joke and visit with the shoppers. Watching the different kinds of people who show up is also a kick—you can get a cross section from university students on a tight budget to harried mothers toting four kids to real eccentrics in fancy cars who will argue about the price of a 75-cent item (if you're a creative writer, don't forget to take notes for your next novel). If the action slows in the afternoon, you can resort to a half-price or two-for-one sale by posting a large sign to that effect; many shoppers can't resist a sale at a sale!

Step seven: Closing up   **8**   By late afternoon you should be richer and junk-free, at least to some extent. If you do have items left after the half-price sale, decide whether you want to box them up for the next sale or drop them by a charitable organization such as the Salvation Army thrift stores (some organizations will even pick up your donations; others have convenient drop boxes). After you've taken your articles inside, don't forget to take down any signs you've posted in the neighbourhood; old, withered garage sale signs fluttering in the breeze are an eyesore. Last, sit down and count your profits, so you can go out in the evening to celebrate a successful business venture.

Conclusion: A summary of the benefits and a humorous warning   **9**   The money you make is, of course, the biggest incentive for having one or two sales a year. But the combination of money, clean closets, and memories of the characters you met can be irresistible. Garage sales can rapidly get in your blood; once you hold a successful one, you're tempted to have another as soon as the junk starts to mount up. And having sales somehow leads to attending them too, as it becomes fun to see what other folks are selling at bargain prices. So be forewarned: you too can be transformed into a garage sale junkie, travelling with a now-popular car bumper sticker that proudly proclaims to the world: "Caution! I brake for garage sales!"

■ Professional Essays*

Because there are two kinds of process essays, informative and directional, this section presents two professional essays to illustrate each type.

I. The Informative Process Essay

■ To Bid the World Farewell

Jessica Mitford

As an investigative reporter, Jessica Mitford wrote many articles and books, including *Kind and Unusual Punishment: The Prison Business* (1973), *A Fine Old Conflict* (1977), *Poison Penmanship* (1979), and *The American Way of Birth* (1979). This essay is from her best-selling book *The American Way of Death* (1963), which scrutinizes the funeral industry.

1   Embalming is indeed a most extraordinary procedure, and one must wonder at the docility of Americans who each year pay hundreds of millions of dollars for its perpetuation, blissfully ignorant of what it is all about, what is done, how it is done. Not one in ten thousand has any idea of what actually takes place. Books on the subject are extremely hard to come by. They are not to be found in most libraries or bookshops.

2   In an era when huge television audiences watch surgical operations in the comfort of their living rooms, when, thanks to the animated cartoon, the geography of the digestive system has become familiar territory even to the nursery school set, and in a land where the satisfaction of curiosity about almost all matters is a national pastime, the secrecy surrounding embalming can, surely, hardly be attributed to the inherent gruesomeness of the subject. Custom in this regard has within this century suffered a complete reversal. In the early days of American embalming, when it was performed in the home of the deceased, it was almost mandatory for some relative to stay by the embalmer's side and witness the procedure. Today, family members who might wish to be in attendance would certainly be dissuaded by the funeral director. All others, except apprentices, are excluded by law from the preparation room.

3   A close look at what does actually take place may explain in large measure the undertaker's intractable reticence concerning a procedure that has become his major *raison d'être*. Is it possible he fears that public information about embalming might lead patrons to wonder if they really want this service? If the funeral men are loath to discuss the subject outside the trade, the reader may, understandably, be equally loath to go on reading at this point. For those who have the stomach for it, let us part the formaldehyde curtain. . . .

4   The body is first laid out in the undertaker's morgue—or rather, Mr. Jones is reposing in the preparation room—to be readied to bid the world farewell.

5   The preparation room in any of the better funeral establishments has the tiled and sterile look of a surgery, and indeed the embalmer-restorative artist who does his chores there is beginning to adopt the term "dermasurgeon" (appropriately corrupted by

---

* To help you read this essay analytically, review pages 160–162 in Chapter 8.

some mortician-writers as "demisurgeon") to describe his calling. His equipment, consisting of scalpels, scissors, augers, forceps, clamps, needles, pumps, tubes, bowls and basins, is crudely imitative of the surgeon's as is his technique, acquired in a nine- or twelve-month post-high-school course in an embalming school. He is supplied by an advanced chemical industry with a bewildering array of fluids, sprays, pastes, oils, powders, creams, to fix or soften tissue, shrink or distend it as needed, dry it here, restore the moisture there. There are cosmetics, waxes and paints to fill and cover features, even plaster of Paris to replace entire limbs. There are ingenious aids to prop and stabilize the cadaver: a Vari-Pose Head Rest, the Edwards Arm and Hand Positioner, the Repose Block (to support the shoulders during the embalming), and the Throop Foot Positioner, which resembles an old-fashioned stocks.

6   Mr. John H. Eckels, president of the Eckels College of Mortuary Science, thus describes the first part of the embalming procedure: "In the hands of a skilled practitioner, this work may be done in a comparatively short time and without mutilating the body other than by slight incision—so slight that it scarcely would cause serious inconvenience if made upon a living person. It is necessary to remove the blood, and doing this not only helps in the disinfecting, but removes the principal cause of disfigurement due to discoloration."

7   Another textbook discusses the all-important time element: "The earlier this is done, the better, for every hour that elapses between death and embalming will add to the problems and complications encountered. . . ." Just how soon should one get going on the embalming? The author tells us, "On the basis of such scanty information made available to this profession through its rudimentary and haphazard system of technical research, we must conclude that the best results are to be obtained if the subject is embalmed before life is completely extinct—that is, before cellular death has occurred. In the average case, this would mean within an hour after somatic death." For those who feel that there is something a little rudimentary, not to say haphazard, about this advice, a comforting thought is offered by another writer. Speaking of fears entertained in early days of premature burial, he points out, "One of the effects of embalming by chemical injection, however, has been to dispel fears of live burial." How true; once the blood is removed, chances of live burial are indeed remote.

8   To return to Mr. Jones, the blood is drained out through the veins and replaced by embalming fluid pumped in through the arteries. As noted in *The Principles and Practices of Embalming*, "every operator has a favorite injection and drainage point—a fact which becomes a handicap only if he fails or refuses to forsake his favorites when conditions demand it." Typical favorites are the carotid artery, femoral artery, jugular vein, subclavian vein. There are various choices of embalming fluid. If Flextone is used, it will produce a "mild flexible rigidity. The skin retains a velvety softness, the tissues are rubbery and pliable. Ideal for women and children." It may be blended with B. and G. Products Company's Lyf-Lyk tint, which is guaranteed to reproduce "nature's own skin texture . . . the velvety appearance of living tissue." Suntone comes in three separate tints: Suntan; Special Cosmetic Tint, a pink shade "especially indicated for young female subjects"; and Regular Cosmetic Tint, moderately pink.

9   About three to six gallons of a dyed and perfumed solution of formaldehyde, glycerin, borax, phenol, alcohol and water is soon circulating through Mr. Jones, whose mouth has been sewn together with a "needle directed upward between the upper lip and gum and brought out through the left nostril," with the corners raised slightly

"for a more pleasant expression." If he should be bucktoothed, his teeth are cleaned with Bon Ami and coated with colorless nail polish. His eyes, meanwhile, are closed with flesh-tinted eye caps and eye cement.

10   The next step is to have at Mr. Jones with a thing called a trocar. This is a long, hollow needle attached to a tube. It is jabbed into the abdomen, poked around the entrails and chest cavity, the contents of which are pumped out and replaced with "cavity fluid." This done, and the hole in the abdomen sewn up, Mr. Jones' face is heavily creamed (to protect the skin from burns which may be caused by leakage of the chemicals), and he is covered with a sheet and left unmolested for a while. But not for long—there is more, much more, in store for him. He has been embalmed, but not yet restored, and the best time to start the restorative work is eight to ten hours after embalming, when the tissues have become firm and dry.

11   The object of all this attention to the corpse, it must be remembered, is to make it presentable for viewing in an attitude of healthy repose. "Our customs require the presentation of our dead in the semblance of normality . . . unmarred by the ravages of illness, disease or mutilation," says Mr. J. Sheridan Mayer in his *Restorative Art*. This is rather a large order since few people die in the full bloom of health, unravaged by illness and unmarked by some disfigurement. The funeral industry is equal to the challenge: "In some cases the gruesome appearance of a mutilated or disease-ridden subject may be quite discouraging. The task of restoration may seem impossible and shake the confidence of the embalmer. This is the time for intestinal fortitude and determination. Once the formative work is begun and affected tissues are cleaned or removed, all doubts of success vanish. It is surprising and gratifying to discover the results which may be obtained."

12   The embalmer, having allowed an appropriate interval to elapse, returns to the attack, but now he brings into play the skill and equipment of sculptor and cosmetician. Is a hand missing? Casting one in plaster of Paris is a simple matter. "For replacement purposes, only a cast of the back of the hand is necessary; this is within the ability of the average operator and is quite adequate." If a lip or two, a nose or an ear should be missing, the embalmer has at hand a variety of restorative waxes with which to model replacements. Pores and skin texture are simulated by stippling with a little brush, and over this cosmetics are laid on. Head off? Decapitation cases are rather routinely handled. Ragged edges are trimmed, and head joined to torso with a series of splints, wires and sutures. It is a good idea to have a little something at the neck—a scarf or high collar—when time for viewing comes. Swollen mouth? Cut out tissue as needed from inside the lips. If too much is removed, the surface contour can easily be restored by padding with cotton. Swollen necks and cheeks are reduced by removing tissue through vertical incisions made down each side of the neck. "When the deceased is casketed, the pillow will hide the suture incisions . . . as an extra precaution against leakage, the suture may be painted with liquid sealer."

13   The opposite condition is more likely to present itself—that of emaciation. His hypodermic syringe now loaded with massage cream, the embalmer seeks out and fills the hollowed and sunken areas by injection. In this procedure the backs of the hands and fingers and the under-chin area should not be neglected.

14   Positioning the lips is a problem that recurrently challenges the ingenuity of the embalmer. Closed too tightly, they tend to give a stern, even disapproving expression. Ideally, embalmers feel, the lips should give the impression of being ever so slightly parted, the upper lip protruding slightly for a more youthful appearance. This takes

some engineering, however, as the lips tend to drift apart. Lip drift can sometimes be remedied by pushing one or two straight pins through the inner margin of the lower lip and then inserting them between the two front teeth. If Mr. Jones happens to have no teeth, the pins can just as easily be anchored in his Armstrong Face Former and Denture Replacer. Another method to maintain lip closure is to dislocate the lower jaw, which is then held in its new position by a wire run through holes which have been drilled through the upper and lower jaws at the midline. As the French are fond of saying, *il faut souffrir pour être belle.**

15   If Mr. Jones has died of jaundice, the embalming fluid will very likely turn him green. Does this deter the embalmer? Not if he has intestinal fortitude. Masking pastes and cosmetics are heavily laid on, burial garments and casket interiors are color-correlated with particular care, and Jones is displayed beneath rose-colored lights. Friends will say, "How *well* he looks." Death by carbon monoxide, on the other hand, can be rather a good thing from the embalmer's viewpoint: "One advantage is the fact that this type of discoloration is an exaggerated form of a natural pink coloration." This is nice because the healthy glow is already present and needs but little attention.

16   The patching and filling completed, Mr. Jones is now shaved, washed and dressed. Cream-based cosmetic, available in pink, flesh, suntan, brunette and blond, is applied to his hands and face, his hair is shampooed and combed (and, in the case of Mrs. Jones, set), his hands manicured. For the horny-handed son of toil special care must be taken; cream should be applied to remove ingrained grime, and the nails cleaned. "If he were not in the habit of having them manicured in life, trimming and shaping is advised for better appearance—never questioned by kin."

17   Jones is now ready for casketing (this is the present participle of the verb "to casket"). In this operation his right shoulder should be depressed slightly "to turn the body a bit to the right and soften the appearance of lying flat on the back." Positioning the hands is a matter of importance, and special rubber positioning blocks may be used. The hands should be cupped slightly for a more lifelike, relaxed appearance. Proper placement of the body requires a delicate sense of balance. It should lie as high as possible in the casket, yet not so high that the lid, when lowered, will hit the nose. On the other hand, we are cautioned, placing the body too low "creates the impression that the body is in a box."

18   Jones is next wheeled into the appointed slumber room where a few last touches may be added—his favorite pipe placed in his hand or, if he was a great reader, a book propped into position. (In the case of little Master Jones a Teddy bear may be clutched.) Here he will hold open house for a few days, visiting hours 10 a.m. to 9 p.m.

Questions on Content, Structure, and Style

1. By studying the first three paragraphs, summarize both Mitford's reason for explaining the embalming process and her attitude toward undertakers who wish to keep their patrons uninformed about this procedure.

2. Does Mitford use enough specific details to help you visualize each step as it occurs? Point out examples of details that create vivid descriptions by appealing to your sense of sight, smell, or touch.

---

* "One must suffer to be beautiful."

3. How does the technique of using the hypothetical "Mr. Jones" make the explanation of the process more effective? Why didn't Mitford simply refer to "the corpse" or "a body" throughout her essay?

4. What is Mitford's general attitude toward this procedure? The overall tone of the essay? Study Mitford's choice of words and then identify the tone in each of the following passages:

> "The next step is to have at Mr. Jones with a thing called a trocar." (10)*

> "The embalmer, having allowed an appropriate interval to elapse, returns to the attack. . . ." (12)

> "Friends will say, 'How *well* he looks.'" (15)

> "On the other hand, we are cautioned, placing the body too low 'creates the impression that the body is in a box.'" (17)

> "Here he will hold open house for a few days, visiting hours 10 a.m. to 9 p.m." (18)

> What other words and passages reveal Mitford's attitude and tone?

5. Why does Mitford repeatedly quote various undertakers and textbooks on the embalming and restorative process ("'needle directed upward between the upper lip and gum and brought out through the left nostril'")? Why is the quotation in paragraph 7 that begins "'On the basis of such scanty information made available to this profession through its rudimentary and haphazard system of technical research'" particularly effective in emphasizing Mitford's attitude toward the funeral industry?

6. What does Mitford gain by quoting euphemisms used by the funeral business, such as "dermasurgeon," "Repose Block," and "slumber room"?

7. What are the connotations of the words "poked," "jabbed," and "left unmolested" in paragraph 10? What effect is Mitford trying to produce with the series of questions (such as "Head off?") in paragraph 12?

8. Does this process flow smoothly from step to step? Identify several transitional devices connecting the paragraphs.

9. Evaluate Mitford's last sentence. Does it successfully sum up the author's attitude and conclude the essay?

10. By supplying information about the embalming process, did Mitford change your attitude toward this procedure or toward the funeral industry? Are there advantages Mitford fails to mention?

11. Who is the audience for this essay?

Suggestions for Writing

Try using Jessica Mitford's "To Bid the World Farewell" as a stepping stone to your own writing. Mitford's graphic details and disparaging tone upset some readers who feel funerals are important for the living. If you agree, consider writing an essay that challenges

---

* Numbers in parentheses following quoted material and vocabulary words refer to paragraphs in the essay.

Mitford's position. Or adopt Mitford's role as an investigative reporter exposing a controversial process. For example, how is toxic waste disposed of at the student health centre? What happens to unclaimed animals at your local shelter? Or try a more lighthearted investigation: just how do they obtain that mystery meat served in the dorm cafeteria? Use Mitford's vivid essay as a guide as you present your discoveries.

Vocabulary

docility (1)	*raison d'être* (3)	pliable (8)
perpetuation (1)	ingenious (5)	semblance (11)
inherent (2)	cadaver (5)	ravages (11)
mandatory (2)	somatic (7)	stippling (12)
intractable (3)	rudimentary (7)	emaciation (13)
reticence (3)	dispel (7)	

II. The Directional Process Essay

■ "How to Live to Be 200"

Stephen Leacock

Stephen Leacock, the head of McGill University's Economics department for twenty-eight years, was as beloved a humourist in Canada as Mark Twain was in the United States. Although he wrote over sixty books, both academic and non-academic, he is best known for humourous works such as *Literary Lapses* (1910), *Sunshine Sketches of a Little Town* (1912), and *My Remarkable Uncle and Other Sketches* (1942). Leacock was so funny when he was giving readings to audiences that once an audience member died from laughing.

1   Twenty years ago I knew a man called Jiggins, who had the Health Habit.

2   He used to take a cold plunge every morning. He said it opened his pores. After it he took a hot sponge. He said it closed his pores. He got so that he could open and shut his pores at will.

3   Jiggins used to stand and breathe at an open window for half an hour before dressing. He said it expanded his lungs. He might, of course, have done it in a shoe store with a boot-stretcher, but after all it cost him nothing this way, and what is half an hour?

4   After he had got his undershirt on, Jiggins used to hitch himself up like a dog in harness and do Sandow exercises. He did them forwards, backwards, and hind-side up.

5   He could have got a job as a dog anywhere. He spent all his time at this kind of thing. In his spare time at the office, he used to lie on his stomach on the floor and see if he could lift himself up with his knuckles. If he could, then he tried some other way until he found one that he couldn't do. Then he would spend the rest of his lunch hour on his stomach, perfectly happy.

6   In the evenings in his room he used to lift iron bars, cannon-balls, heave dumb-bells, and haul himself up to the ceiling with his teeth. You could hear the thumps half a mile.

7   He liked it.

8   He spent half the night slinging himself around the room. He said it made his brain clear. When he got his brain perfectly clear, he went to bed and slept. As soon as he woke, he began clearing it again.

9   Jiggins is dead. He was, of course, a pioneer, but the fact that he dumb-belled himself to death at an early age does not prevent a whole generation of young men from following in his path.

10   They are ridden by the Health Mania.

11   They make themselves a nuisance.

12   They get up at impossible hours. They go out in silly little suits and run Marathon heats before breakfast. They chase around barefoot to get the dew on their feet. They hunt for ozone. They bother about pepsin. They won't eat meat because it has too much nitrogen. They won't eat fruit because it hasn't any. They prefer albumen and starch and nitrogen to huckleberry pie and doughnuts. They won't drink water out of a tap. They won't eat sardines out of a can. They won't use oysters out of a pail. They won't drink milk out of a glass. They are afraid of alcohol in any shape. Yes sir, afraid. "Cowards."

13   And after all their fuss they presently incur some simple old-fashioned illness and die like anybody else.

14   Now people of his sort have no chance to attain any great age. They are on the wrong track.

15   Listen. Do you want to live to be really old, to enjoy a grand, green, exuberant, boastful old age and to make yourself a nuisance to your whole neighbourhood with your reminiscences?

16   Then cut out all this nonsense. Cut it out. Get up in the morning at a sensible hour. The time to get up is when you have to, not before. If your office opens at eleven, get up at ten-thirty. Take your chance on ozone. There isn't any such thing anyway. Or, if there is, you can buy a Thermos bottle full for five cents, and put it on your shelf in your cupboard. If your work begins at seven in the morning, get up at ten minutes to, but don't be liar enough to say that you like it. It isn't exhilarating, and you know it.

17   Also, drop all that cold-bath business. You never did it when you were a boy. Don't be a fool now. If you must take a bath (you don't really need to), take it warm. The pleasure of getting out of a cold bed and creeping into a hot bath beats a cold plunge to death. In any case, stop gassing about your tub and your "shower," as if you were the only man who ever washed.

18   So much for that point.

19   Next, take the question of germs and bacilli. Don't be scared of them. That's all. That's the whole thing, and if you once get on to that you never need to worry again.

20   If you see a bacilli, walk right up to it, and look it in the eye. If one flies into your room, strike at it with your hat or with a towel. Hit it as hard as you can between the neck and the thorax. It will soon get sick of that.

21   But as a matter of fact, a bacilli is perfectly quiet and harmless if you are not afraid of it. Speak to it. Call out to it to "lie down." It will understand. I had a bacilli once, called Fido, that would come and lie at my feet while I was working. I never knew a more affectionate companion and when it was run over by an automobile, I buried it in the garden with genuine sorrow.

22   (I admit this is an exaggeration. I don't really remember its name; it may have been Robert.)

23   Understand that it is only a fad of modern medicine to say that cholera and typhoid and diphtheria are caused by bacilli and germs; nonsense. Cholera is caused by a frightful pain in the stomach, and diphtheria is caused by trying to cure a sore throat.

24   Now take the question of food.

25   Eat what you want. Eat lots of it. Yes, eat too much of it. Eat till you can just stagger across the room with it and prop it up against a sofa cushion. Eat everything you like until you can't eat anymore. The only test is, can you pay for it? If you can't pay for it, don't eat it. And listen—don't worry as to whether your food contains starch, or albumen, or gluten, or nitrogen. If you are a damn fool enough to want these things, go and buy them and eat all you want of them. Go to a laundry and get a bag of starch, and eat your fill of it. Eat it, and take a good long drink of glue after it, and a spoonful of Portland cement. That will gluten you, good and solid.

26   If you like nitrogen, go and get a druggist to give you a canful of it at the soda counter, and let you sip it with a straw. Only don't think that you can mix all these things up with your food. There isn't any nitrogen or phosphorus or albumen in ordinary things to eat. In any decent household all that sort of stuff is washed out in the kitchen sink before the food is put on the table.

27   And just one word about fresh air and exercise. Don't bother with either of them. Get your room full of good air, then shut up the windows and keep it. It will keep for years. Anyway, don't keep using your lungs all the time. Let them rest. As for exercise, if you have to take it, take it and put up with it. But as long as you have the price of a hack and can hire other people to play baseball for you and run races and do gymnastics when you sit in the shade and smoke and watch them—great heavens, what more do you want?

Questions on Content, Structure, and Style

1. Why does Leacock begin with the example of "Jiggins?"

2. Overall, what is the tone of the essay? At what point was this tone clear to you?

3. In his section about confronting the bacilli, what kind of literary device does Leacock use? Throughout the essay, how does Leacock's anecdotal style affect the reader's understanding of and attitude toward the process?

4. What are the steps in this process? By what criteria are these steps judged?

5. What "equipment" is necessary for this process?

6. Point out some of the most effective examples and details Leacock uses to illustrate and clarify the steps in his process.

7. Effective process analysis sometimes offers readers warnings and advice on what not to do. How does Leacock make use of this technique?

8. How does Leacock make clear the transition from one step in the process to the next?

9. Identify some of Leacock's uses of old-fashioned, colloquial language and exaggeration. What do these uses of language add to the tone and real purpose of this essay?

10. Evaluate Leacock's instruction-filled conclusion with the rhetorical question in the last line. Do you find the conclusion effective for this process essay? Why or why not?

11. Who is the audience for this essay?

Suggestions for Writing

Try using Stephen Leacock's humorous process essay, "How to Live to be 200," as a stepping stone to your own writing. Select an activity that you think is a fad or which you think is misguided and ineffectual, and defend your position by explaining its intricate steps in a humorous or "mock heroic" process essay; for example, how to lose weight by eating all the fat you like, or how to get a contestant thrown off a national television competition by going on a hunger strike. Consider using language lifted from a sport or another art form to add to the comic effect. (For example, might the steps you must take to arrive at your 8 a.m. class with mere seconds to spare parallel the labours of a triathlon athlete?)

Vocabulary

incur (13)   gassing (17)
exuberant (15)   hack (27)
exhilarating (16)

■ A REVISION WORKSHEET

As you write your rough drafts, consult Chapter 5 for guidance through the revision process. In addition, here are a few questions to ask yourself as you revise your process essay:

1. Is the essay's purpose clear to the reader?

2. Has the need for any special equipment been noted and explained adequately? Are all terms unfamiliar to the reader defined clearly?

3. Does the essay include all the steps (and warnings, if appropriate) necessary to understanding the process?

4. Is each step described in enough detail to make it understandable to all readers? Where could more detail be effectively added?

5. Are all the steps in the process presented in an easy-to-follow chronological order, with smooth transitions between steps or stages?

6. Are there any steps that should be combined in a paragraph describing a logical stage in the process?

7. Does the essay have a pleasing conclusion?

After you've revised your essay extensively, you might exchange rough drafts with a classmate and answer these questions for each other, making specific suggestions for improvement wherever appropriate. (For advice on productive participation in classroom workshops, see pages 102–104.)

Reviewing Your Progress

After you have completed your process essay, take a moment to measure your progress as a writer by responding to the following questions. Such analysis will help you recognize growth in your writing skills and may enable you to identify areas that are still problematic.

1. Which part of your essay is most successful? Why?

2. Select two details that contribute significantly to the clarity of your explanation. Why are these details effective?

3. What part of your essay gave you the most trouble? How did you overcome the problem?

4. If you had more time to work on this essay, what would receive additional attention? Why?

5. What did you learn about your topic from writing this essay? About yourself as a writer?

■ Strategy Three: Development by Comparison and Contrast

Every day you exercise the mental process of comparison and contrast. When you get up in the morning, for instance, you may contrast two choices of clothing—a short-sleeved shirt versus a long-sleeved one—and then make your decision after hearing the weather forecast. Or you may contrast and choose between Sugar-Coated Plastic Pops and Organic Mullet Kernels for breakfast, between the health advantages of walking to campus and the speed afforded by your car or bicycle. Once on campus, preparing to register, you may first compare both professors and courses; similarly, you probably compared the school you attend now to others before you made your choice. In short, you frequently use the process of comparison and contrast to come to a decision or make a judgment about two or more objects, persons, ideas, or feelings.

When you write a comparison or contrast essay, your opinion about the two elements* in question becomes your thesis statement; the body of the paper then shows why you arrived at that opinion. For example, if your thesis states that Mom's Hamburger Haven is preferable to McPhony's Mystery Burger Stand, your body paragraphs might contrast the two restaurants in terms of food, service, and atmosphere, revealing the superiority of Mom's on all three counts.

Developing Your Essay

There are two principal patterns of organization for comparison or contrast essays. For most short papers you should choose one of the patterns and stick with it throughout the essay. Later, if you are assigned a longer essay, you may want to mix the patterns for variety as some professional writers do, but do so only if you can maintain clarity and logical organization.

---

* It is possible to compare or contrast more than two elements. But until you feel confident about the organizational patterns for this kind of essay, you should probably stay with the simpler format.

Pattern One: Point by Point

This method of organization calls for body paragraphs that compare or contrast the two subjects first on point one, then on point two, then point three, and so on. Study the following example:

Thesis: Mom's Hamburger Haven is a better family restaurant than McPhony's because of its superior food, service, and atmosphere.

Point 1: Food
A. Mom's
B. McPhony's

Point 2: Service
A. Mom's
B. McPhony's

Point 3: Atmosphere
A. Mom's
B. McPhony's

Conclusion

If you select this pattern of organization, you must make a smooth transition from subject "A" to subject "B" in each discussion to avoid a choppy seesaw effect. Be consistent: present the same subject first in each discussion of a major point. In the essay outlined above, for instance, Mom's is always introduced before McPhony's.

Pattern Two: The Block

This method of organization presents body paragraphs in which the writer first discusses subject "A" on points one, two, three, and so on, and then discusses subject "B" on the same points. The following model illustrates this Block Pattern:

Thesis: Mom's Hamburger Haven is a better family restaurant than McPhony's because of its superior food, service, and atmosphere.

A. Mom's
1. Food
2. Service
3. Atmosphere

B. McPhony's
1. Food
2. Service
3. Atmosphere

Conclusion

If you use the Block Pattern, you should discuss the three points—food, service, atmosphere—in the same order for each subject. In addition, you must include in your discussion of subject "B" specific references to the points you made earlier about subject "A" (see outline). In other words, because your statements about Mom's superior food may be several pages away by the time your comments on McPhony's food appear, the readers may not remember precisely what you said. Gently, unobtrusively, remind them with a specific reference to the earlier discussion. For instance, you might begin your paragraph on McPhony's service like this: "Unlike the friendly, attentive help at Mom's, service at McPhony's features grouchy persons who wait on you as if they consider your presence an intrusion on their privacy." The discussion of atmosphere might begin, "McPhony's atmosphere is as cold, sterile, and plastic as its decor, in contrast to the warm, homey feeling that pervades Mom's." Without such connecting phrases, what should be one unified essay will look more like two distinct mini-essays, forcing readers to do the job of comparing or contrasting for you.

Which Pattern Should You Use?

As you prepare to compose your first draft, you might ask yourself, "Which pattern of organization should I choose—Point by Point or Block?" Indeed, this is not your simple "paper or plastic" supermarket choice. It's an important question—to which there is no single, easy answer.

For most writers, choosing the appropriate pattern of organization involves thinking time in the prewriting stage, before beginning a draft. Many times, your essay's subject matter itself will suggest the most effective method of development. The Block Method might be the better choice when a complete, overall picture of each subject is desirable. For example, you might decide that your "then-and-now" essay (your disastrous first day at a new job contrasted with your success at that job today) would be easier for your readers to understand if your description of "then" (your first day) was presented in its entirety, followed by the contrasting discussion of "now" (current success). Later in this section, you will see that Mark Twain chose this method in his essay "Two Ways of Viewing the River" to contrast his early and later impressions of the Mississippi.

On the other hand, your essay topic might best be discussed by presenting a number of distinct points for the reader to consider one by one. Essays that evaluate, that argue the superiority or advantage of one thing over another ("A cat is a better pet for students than a dog because of X, Y, and Z"), often lend themselves to Point-by-Point Method because each of the writer's claims may be clearly supported by the side-by-side details. "Bringing Back the Joy of Market Day," a student essay in this section, employs this method to emphasize three ways in which a small food cooperative is preferable to a chain grocery store.

However, none of the above advice always holds true. There are no hard-and-fast rules governing this rhetorical choice. Each writer must decide which method of organization works best in any particular comparison and/or contrast essay. Before drafting begins, therefore, writers are wise to sketch out an informal outline or rough plan using one method and then the other to see which is more effective for their topic, their purpose, and their audience. By spending time in the prewriting stage "auditioning" each method of development, you may spare yourself the frustration of writing an entire draft whose organization doesn't work well for your topic.

Problems to Avoid

The single most serious error is the "so-what" thesis. Writers of comparison and contrast essays often wish to convince their readers that something—a restaurant, a movie, a product—is better (or worse) than something else: "Mom's Hamburger Haven is a better place to eat than McPhony's." But not all comparison or contrast essays assert the absolute superiority or inferiority of their subjects. Sometimes writers simply want to point out the similarities or differences in two or more people, places, or objects, and that's fine, too—*as long as the writer avoids the "so-what" thesis problem.*

Too often novice writers will present thesis statements such as "My sister and I are very different" or "Having a blended family with two stepbrothers and stepsisters has advantages and disadvantages for me." To such theses, readers can only respond, "So what? Who cares?" There are many similarities and differences (or advantages and disadvantages) between countless numbers of things—but why should your readers care about those described in your essay? Comparing or contrasting for no apparent reason is a waste of the readers' valuable time; instead, find a purpose that will draw in your audience. You may indeed wish to write an essay contrasting the pros and cons of your blended family, but do it in a way that has a universal appeal or application. For instance, you might revise your thesis to say something like "Although a blended family often does experience petty jealousies and juvenile bickering, the benefits of having stepsiblings as live-in friends far outweigh the problems," and then use your family to show the advantages and disadvantages. In this way, your readers realize they will learn something about the blended family, a common phenomenon today, as well as learning some information about you and your particular family.

Another way to avoid the "so-what" problem is to direct your thesis to a particular audience. For instance, you might say that "Although Stella's Sweatateria and the Fitness Fanatics Gym are similar in their low student-membership prices and excellent instructors, Stella's is the place to go for those seeking a variety of exercise classes rather than hard-core body-building machines." Or your thesis may wish to show a particular relationship between two subjects. Instead of writing, "There are many similarities between the movie *Riot of the Killer Snails* and Mary Sheeley's novel *Salt on the Sidewalk*," write, "The many similarities in character and plot (the monster, the scientist, and vegetable garden scene) clearly suggest that the movie director was greatly influenced by—if not actually guilty of stealing—parts of Mary Sheeley's novel."

In other words, tell your readers your point and then use comparison or contrast to support that idea; don't just compare or contrast items in a vacuum. Ask yourself, "What is the significant point I want my readers to learn or understand from reading this comparison or contrast essay? Is my point specific and clear? Why do they need to know this?"

Describe your subjects clearly and distinctly. To comprehend a difference or a similarity between two things, the reader must first be able to "see" them as you do. Consequently, you should use many vivid examples and details as possible to describe both your subjects. Beware a tendency to over-elaborate on one subject and then grossly skimp on the other, an especially easy trap to fall into in an essay that asserts "X" is preferable to "Y." By giving each side a reasonable treatment, you will do a better job of convincing your reader that you know both sides and have made a valid judgment.

Avoid a choppy essay. Whether you organize your essay by the Point-by-Point Pattern or the Block Pattern, you need to use enough transitional devices to ensure a smooth flow from one subject to another and from one point to the next. Without transitions, your essay may assume the distracting movement of a Ping-Pong game, as you switch back and forth between discussions of your two subjects. Listed below are some appropriate words to link your points:

Comparison	**Contrast**
also	however
similarly	on the contrary
too	on the other hand
both	in contrast
like	although
not only . . . but also	unlike
have in common	though
share the same	instead of
in the same manner	but

(For a review of other transitional devices, see pages 69–72.)

▪ ESSAY TOPICS

Here are some topics that may be compared or contrasted. Remember to narrow your subject, formulate a thesis that presents a clear point, and follow one of the two organizational patterns discussed on pages 205–206. For additional ideas, turn to the "Suggestions for Writing" sections following the professional essays (pages 218–219 and page 221).

1. An expectation and its reality

2. A first impression and a later point of view

3. Two views on a current controversial issue (campus, local, national)

4. Two conflicting theories you are studying in another course

5. Your attitude toward a social custom or political belief and your parents' (or grandparents') attitude toward that belief or custom

6. Coverage of the same story by two newspapers or magazines (the *National Post* and *The Globe and Mail*, for example, or *Maclean's* and *Chatelaine*)

7. A hero today and yesterday

8. Two essays or pieces of literature with similar themes but different styles

9. Two pieces of technology or two pieces of sports equipment

10. Two paintings/photographs/posters/advertisements (You might select any two of the many images in this text. For example, consider the contrast in mood in *The Letter* [page 26] and *The Scream* [page 108]; the representation of women in *Zunoqua of the Cat Village* [page 310] and *Women's Hockey Game, Banff, Alberta* [page 73]; the relationship between the animal and human world in *Algonquin Park—Fox and Christmas Tree* [page 323] and *Horse and Train* [page 229]; the appeals of various advertisements [pages 294–301] to sway readers.)

11. Two solutions to a problem in your professional field
12. One of today's popular forms of entertainment and one from an earlier era
13. Two instructors or coaches whose teaching styles are effective but different
14. Two movies; a book and its movie; a movie and its sequel
15. An opinion you held before coming to university that has changed
16. Art or advertising developed by comparison and/or contrast (Consider, for example, *Breadline during the Louisville Flood, Kentucky 1937,* shown below. During the Great Depression in the United States, when floods were ravaging parts of the South previously gutted by drought, Margaret Bourke-White photographed people patiently standing in a breadline that stretched in front of a billboard advertising a new car. What comments on American society was Bourke-White's photo, with its powerful use of contrasts, making in 1937?)

Breadline during the Louisville Flood, Kentucky 1937, *by Margaret Bourke-White*

A Topic Proposal for Your Essay

Selecting the right subject matter is important to every writer. To help you clarify your ideas and strengthen your commitment to your topic, here is a proposal sheet that asks you to describe some of your preliminary ideas about your subject before you begin drafting. Although your ideas may change as you write (they will almost certainly become more refined), thinking through your choice of topic now may help you avoid several false starts.

1. What two subjects will your essay discuss? In what ways are these subjects similar? Different?

2. Do you plan to compare or contrast your two subjects?

3. Write one or two sentences describing your attitude toward these two subjects. Are you stating a preference for one or are you making some other significant point? In other words, what is the purpose of this essay?

4. Why would other people find this topic interesting and important? Would a particular group of people be more affected by your topic than others? Are you avoiding the "so-what" thesis problem?

5. List three or four points of comparison or contrast that you might include in this essay.

6. What difficulties might this topic present during your drafting? For example, would your topic be best explained using the Block or Point-by-Point pattern?

■ Sample Student Essays

Because there are two popular ways to develop comparison and contrast essays, this section offers two student essays so that each pattern is illustrated.

I. The Point-by-Point Pattern

Note that this writer takes a definite stand—that local food co-ops are superior to chain grocery stores—and then contrasts two local stores, Grocery Giant and the Island Co-op, to prove her thesis. She selected the Point-by-Point Pattern to organize her essay, contrasting prices, atmosphere, and benefits to local producers. See if you can identify her transitional devices, as well as some of her uses of detail that make the essay more interesting and convincing.

BRINGING BACK THE JOY OF MARKET DAY

1   Now that the old family-run corner grocery is almost extinct, many people are banding together to form their own neighbourhood stores as food cooperatives. Locally owned by their

Thesis   members, food co-ops such as the one here on Salt Spring Island

---

are welcome alternatives to the impersonal chain-store markets such as Grocery Giant. In exchange for volunteering a few hours each month, co-op members share savings and a friendly experience while they shop; local producers gain loyal local support from the members as well as better prices for their goods in return for providing the freshest, purest food possible.

Essay map

2   Perhaps the most crucial distinction between the two kinds of stores is that while supermarkets are set up to generate profit for their corporations, co-ops are nonprofit groups whose main purpose is to provide their members and the community with good, inexpensive food and basic household needs. At first glance, supermarkets such as Grocery Giant may appear to be cheaper because they offer so many specials, which they emphasize heavily through advertisements and in-store promotions. These special deals, known as "loss-leaders" in the retail industry, are more than compensated by the extremely high markups on other products. For example, around Thanksgiving Grocery Giant might have a sale on flour and shortening and then set up the displays with utmost care so that as customers reach for the flour they will be drawn to colourful bottles of pie spices, fancy jars of mincemeat, or maybe an inviting bin of fresh-roasted holiday nuts, all of which may be marked up 100 percent or more—way above what is being lost on the flour and shortening.

Point one: Prices

Examples of Grocery Giant's prices contrasted to examples of co-op prices

3   The Island Co-op rarely bothers with such pricing gimmicks; instead, it tries to have a consistent markup—just enough to meet overhead expenses. The flour at the co-op may cost an extra few cents, but that same fancy spice bottle that costs over a dollar from the supermarket display can be refilled at the co-op for less than 25 cents. The nuts, considered by regular groceries as a seasonal "gourmet" item, are sold at the co-op for about two-thirds the price. Great savings like these are achieved by buying in bulk and

having customers bag their own groceries. Recycled containers are used as much as possible, cutting down substantially on overhead. Buying in bulk may seem awkward at first, but the extra time spent bagging and weighing their own food results in welcome savings for co-op members.

Point two: Atmosphere

Description of Grocery Giant's atmosphere contrasted to description of the co-op's atmosphere

4   Once people have become accustomed to bringing their own containers and taking part in the work at the co-ops, they often find that it's actually more fun to shop in the friendly, relaxed atmosphere of the co-ops. At Grocery Giant, for example, I often find shopping a battle of tangled metal carts wielded by bored customers who are frequently trying to manage one or more cranky children. The long aisles harshly lit by rows of cold fluorescent lights and the bland commercial music don't make the chore of shopping any easier either. On the other hand, the Island Co-op may not be as expertly planned, but at least the chaos is carried on in a friendly way. Parents especially appreciate that they can safely let their children loose while they shop because in the small, open-spaced co-op even toddlers don't become lost as they do in the aisles of towering supermarket shelves. Moreover, most members are willing to look after the children of other members if necessary. And while they shop, members can choose to listen to the FM radio or simply to enjoy each other's company in relative quiet.

Point three: Benefits to local producers

5   As well as benefiting member consumers, co-ops also help small local producers by providing a direct market for their goods. Large chain stores may require minimum wholesale quantities far beyond the capacity of an individual producer, and mass markets like Grocery Giant often feel they are "too big" to negotiate with small local producers. But because of their small, independent nature, co-ops welcome the chance to buy direct from the grower or

producer. Direct selling offers two advantages for producers: they get a better price for their wares than by selling them through a middleman, and at the same time they establish an independent reputation for their business, which can be immensely valuable to their success later on. On Salt Spring Island, for example, Luna tofu (bean curd) stands out as an excellent illustration of this kind of mutual support. Several years ago my friend Gillie Campbell began making tofu in small batches to sell to the co-op as a way to earn a part-time income as well as to contribute to the co-op. Her enterprise has now grown so well that last year her husband quit his job to go into business with her full time. She currently sells to distributors and independent stores from here to St. John's; even Grocery Giant, who earlier would not consider selling her tofu even on a trial basis, is now thinking about changing its policy.

6　　Of course, not all co-ops are like the one here on Salt Spring, but that is one of their best features. Each one reflects the personalities of its members, unlike the supermarket chain stores that vary only slightly. Most important, though, while each has a distinctive character, co-ops share common goals of providing members with high-quality, low-cost food in a friendly, cooperative spirit.

Margin notes:

No benefits at Grocery Giant contrasted to two benefits at the co-op

Conclusion: Summarizing the advantages of co-ops over chain stores

II. The Block Pattern

After thinking through both methods of development, a second student writer chose the Block Pattern to contrast two kinds of backyards. He felt it was more effective to give his readers a complete sense of his first backyard, with its spirit of wildness, instead of addressing each point of the contrast separately, as did the first student writer in this section. Do you agree with his choice? Why or why not? Note, too, the ways in which this writer tries to avoid the "split essay" problem by making clear connections between the new yard and the older one.

BACKYARDS: OLD AND NEW

Thesis

1   Most of the time I like getting something new—new clothes, new CDs, new video games. I look forward to making new friends and visiting new places. But sometimes new isn't better than old. Five years ago, when my family moved to a house in a new area, I learned that a new, neat backyard can never be as wonderful as a rambling, untamed yard of an older house.

Block A: The older, "untamed" backyard

2   My first yard, behind our older house, was huge, the size of three normal backyards, but completely irregular in shape. Our property line zagged in and out around old, tall trees in a lot shaped like a large pie piece from which some giant had taken random bites. The left side was taken up by a lopsided garden that sometimes grew tomatoes but mainly wild raspberries, an odd assortment of overgrown bushes, and wildflowers of mismatched shapes and sizes. The middle part had grass and scattered shade trees, some that were good for climbing. The grassy part drifted off into an area with large old evergreen trees surrounded by a tall tangle of vines and bushes that my parents called "the Wild Spot," which they had carefully ignored for years. The whole yard sloped downhill, which, with the irregular shape and the trees, made my job of mowing the grass a creative challenge.

(Landscape variety: Irregular lot size and shape; trees, rambling mix of bushes, flowers, berries, and vines)

(Family activities)

3   Despite the mowing problem, there was something magical about that untamed yard. We kids made a path through the Wild Spot and had a secret hideout in the brush. Hidden from adult eyes, my friends and I sat around a pretend fire ring, made up adventures (lost in the jungle!), asked each other Important Questions (better to be a rock star or a baseball player?), and shared our secret fears (being asked to dance). The yard's grassy section was big enough for throwing a football with my brother (the here-and-there trees made catching long passes even more

spectacular), and my twin sisters invented gymnastic routines that rolled them downhill. Mom picked vegetables and flowers when she felt like it. It seemed like someone, family or friend, was always in our yard doing something fun.

4   When all the kids were teenagers, my parents finally decided we needed more space, so we moved into a house in a new development. Although the house itself was better (more bathrooms), the new backyard, in comparison to our older one, was a total disappointment. New Backyard was neat, tidy, tiny, flat, square, and completely fenced. There were not only no big old trees for shade or for climbing—there were no trees at all. My parents had to plant a few, which looked like big twigs stuck in the ground. No untamed tangles of bushes and flowers there—only identical fire hydrant–sized shrubs planted evenly every few feet in narrow, even beds along the fence. The rest of this totally flat yard was grass, easy to mow in mere minutes, but no challenge either. No wild berry bushes or rambling vegetable gardens were allowed in the new development. No wild anything at all, to be exact.

    Transition to Block B: The new backyard (contrasting bland landscape)

5   Nothing wild and no variety: that was the problem. To put it bluntly, the yard was neat but boring. Every inch of it was open to inspection; it held no secret spaces for the imagination to fill. There was no privacy either as our yard looked directly into the almost duplicate bland yards of the neighbours on all sides. The yard was too small to do any real physical activity in it; going out for a long pass would mean automatic collision with the chain fence in any direction. My sisters' dance routines soon dissolved under our neighbour's eyes, and our tomatoes came from the grocery store. With no hidden nooks, no interesting landscape, and no tumbling space, our family just didn't go into the backyard very often. Unlike the older, overgrown backyard that

    (Few activities)

was always inviting someone to play, the new backyard wasn't fun for anyone.

Conclusion: A future preference based on essay's thesis

6   Over the last five years, the trees have grown and the yard looks better, not so sterile and empty. I guess all new yards are on their way to becoming old yards eventually. But it takes decades and that is too slow for me. New houses have lots of modern conveniences, but I hope if I am lucky enough to own my own place someday, I will remember that when it comes to backyards, old is always better than new.

Professional Essays*

Because there are two common ways to develop comparison and contrast essays, this section offers two professional essays to illustrate each pattern.

I. The Point-by-Point Pattern

■ The 51-per-cent Minority

Doris Anderson

Doris Anderson, a teacher from rural Alberta, eventually became a journalist who was outspoken about women's rights during the mid-twentieth century. At a time when the discussion of issues like abortion, domestic violence, and workplace equity was often suppressed, Anderson, who had become the chief editor of *Chatelaine* magazine, published articles and successfully agitated for the existence of a Royal Commission on the Status of Women. Her dissatisfaction with the workings of this new Commission, which she chaired for years, eventually led to widespread activism by Canadian women, resulting in full and equal rights for women in the Canadian Constitution.

1   In any Canadian election the public will probably be hammered numb with talk of the economy, energy and other current issues. But there will always be some far more startling topics that no one will talk about at all.

2   No one is going to say to new Canadians: "Look, we're going through some tough times. Three out of four of you had better face the fact that you're always going to be poor. At 65 more than likely you'll be living below the poverty level."

---

* To help you read this essay analytically, review pages 160–162.

3   And no one is going to tell Quebeckers: "You will have to get along on less money than the rest of the country. For every $1 the rest of us earn, you, because you live in Quebec, will earn 72.5 cents."

4   I doubt very much that any political party is going to level with the Atlantic provinces and say: "We don't consider people living there serious prime workers. Forget about any special measures to make jobs for you. In fact in future federal-provincial talks we're not even going to discuss your particular employment problems."

5   And no politician is going to tell all the left-handed people in the country: "Look, we know it looks like discrimination, but we have to save some money somewhere. So, although you will pay into your company pension plan at the same rate as everyone else, you will collect less when you retire."

6   And no one is going to say to the Canadian doctors: "We know you do one of the most important jobs any citizen can perform, but from now on you're going to have to get along without any support systems. All hospital equipment and help will be drastically reduced. We believe a good doctor should instinctively know what to do—or you're in the wrong job. If you're really dedicated, you'll get along."

7   As for blacks: "Because of the colour of your skin, you're going to be paid less than the white person next to you who is doing exactly the same job. It's tough, but that's the way it is."

8   As for Catholics: "You're just going to have to understand that you will be beaten up by people with other religious beliefs quite regularly. Even if your assailant threatens to kill you, you can't do anything about it. After all, we all need some escape valves, don't we?"

9   Does all of the above sound like some nihilistic nightmare where Orwellian forces have taken over? Well, it's not. It's all happening right now, in Canada.

10   It's not happening to new Canadians, Quebeckers, residents of the Atlantic provinces, left-handed people, doctors, blacks or Indians. If it were, there would be riots in the streets. Civil libertarians would be howling for justice. But all of these discriminatory practices are being inflicted on women today in Canada as a matter of course.

11   Most women work at two jobs—one inside the home and one outside. Yet three out of four women who become widowed or divorced or have never married live out their old age in poverty.

12   Women workers earn, on an average, only 72.5 cents for every $1 a man gets—even though on average, women are better educated than men.

13   And when companies base pension plans on how long people live, women still pay the same rates as men but often collect less.

14   What politician could possibly tell doctors to train each other and get along without all their high technology and trained help? Yet a more important job than saving lives is surely creating lives. But mothers get no training, no help in the way of a family allowance, inadequate day-care centres, and almost non-existent after-school programmes.

15   No politician would dream of telling blacks they must automatically earn less than other people. But women sales clerks, waitresses and hospital orderlies often earn less than males doing the same jobs. It would be called discrimination if a member of a religious group was beaten up, and the assailant would be jailed. But hundreds of wives get beaten up by their husbands week in and week out, year after year. Some die, yet society still tolerates the fact that it's happening.

16   Women make up 51 per cent of the population of this country. Think of the kind of clout they could have if they used it at the polls. But to listen to the political parties, the woman voter just doesn't exist. When politicians talk to fishing folk they talk about improved processing plants and new docks. When they talk to wheat farmers they talk of better transportation and higher price supports. When they talk to people in the Atlantic provinces they talk about new federal money for buildings and more incentives for secondary industry. When they talk to ethnic groups they talk about better language training courses. But when they think of women—if they do at all—they assume women will vote exactly as their husbands – so why waste time offering them anything? It's mind-boggling to contemplate, though, how all those discriminatory practices would be swept aside if, instead of women, we were Italian, or black, or lived in Quebec, or the Atlantic provinces.

Questions on Content, Structure, and Style

1. What is Anderson's thesis?

2. According to Anderson, how does society treat women?

3. Why does Anderson choose the particular examples she does?

4. After carefully studying paragraphs 2 through 8, describe the pattern of organization Anderson uses to present her discussion.

5. Anderson uses a series of hypothetical audiences and statements to highlight the problems women face in society. What are the effects of this strategy? How does Anderson create symmetrical structures in her essay?

6. What is the advantage or disadvantage of developing the essay by using only one- or two-sentence paragraphs?

7. How does Anderson avoid the choppy seesaw effect as she compares and contrasts her subjects? Point out ways in which Anderson makes a smooth transition from point to point.

8. Evaluate Anderson's ability to engage the audience, looking carefully at her vocabulary and her examples.

9. What is Anderson's opinion of society's attitude toward women? Select words and passages to support your answer. How does Anderson's attitude affect the tone of this essay? Is her tone appropriate? Why or why not?

10. Many essays have concluding paragraphs that seem redundant, as they are merely repeating the ideas and material of the introduction and the body of the essay. How does Anderson use repetition to its advantage?

11. What kind of audience is Anderson addressing?

Suggestions for Writing

Try using Doris Anderson's "The 51-Per-Cent Minority" as a stepping stone to your writing. Comparing one kind of situation to another is a familiar activity. For example, people often discuss unjust situations by drawing analogies or comparing them with other injustices. Write your own essay about two comparable situations that interest you. You might be interested in comparing socio-historical situations (comparing, perhaps, the scapegoating of outsiders in the nineteenth century, using as your examples Canadian Louis Riel and Frenchman Alfred Dreyfuss; similar or different conditions that led to the rise of very different musical geniuses, such as Vivaldi and Beethoven); political situations (comparing two regimes); or economic situations (tax laws under different governing parties). The possibilities are endless and thought-provoking; use your essay to make an interesting specific point about the fascinating (and perhaps heretofore unrecognized) differences and/or similarities between the situations you choose.

Vocabulary

discrimination (5)	assailant (8)	Civil libertarian (10)
drastically (6)	nihilistic (9)	inflicted (10)
instinctively (6)	Orwellian (9)	clout (16)

II. The Block Pattern

■ Two Ways of Viewing the River

Samuel Clemens

Samuel Clemens, whose pen name was Mark Twain, is regarded as one of America's most outstanding writers. Well known for his humourous stories and books, Twain was also a pioneer of fictional realism and local colour. His most famous novel, *The Adventures of Huckleberry Finn* (1884), is often hailed as a masterpiece. This selection is from the autobiographical book *Life on the Mississippi* (1883), which recounts Clemens's job as a riverboat pilot.

1   Now when I had mastered the language of this water and had come to know every trifling feature that bordered the great river as familiarly as I knew the letters of the alphabet, I had made a valuable acquisition. But I had lost something, too. I had lost something which could never be restored to me while I lived. All the grace, the beauty, the poetry, had gone out of the majestic river! I still kept in mind a certain wonderful sunset which I witnessed when steamboating was new to me. A broad expanse of the river was turned to blood; in the middle distance the red hue brightened into gold, through which a solitary log came floating, black and conspicuous; in one place a long, slanting mark lay sparkling upon the water; in another the surface was broken by boiling, tumbling rings, that were as many-tinted as an opal; where the ruddy flush was faintest, was a smooth spot that was covered with graceful circles and radiating lines, ever so delicately traced; the shore on our left was densely wooded and the somber shadow that fell from this forest was broken in one place by a long, ruffled trail that shone like silver; and high above the forest wall a clean-stemmed dead tree waved a single leafy bough that glowed like a flame in the unobstructed splendor that was flowing from the sun. There were graceful curves, reflected images, woody heights, soft distances, and over the whole scene, far and near, the dissolving lights drifted steadily, enriching it every passing moment with new marvels of coloring.

2   I stood like one bewitched. I drank it in, in a speechless rapture. The world was new to me and I had never seen anything like this at home. But as I have said, a day came

when I began to cease from noting the glories and the charms which the moon and the sun and the twilight wrought upon the river's face; another day came when I ceased altogether to note them. Then, if that sunset scene had been repeated, I should have looked upon it without rapture, and should have commented upon it inwardly after this fashion: "This sun means that we are going to have wind tomorrow; that floating log means that the river is rising, small thanks to it; that slanting mark on the water refers to a bluff reef which is going to kill somebody's steamboat one of these nights, if it keeps on stretching out like that; those tumbling 'boils' show a dissolving bar and a changing channel there; the lines and circles in the slick water over yonder are a warning that that troublesome place is shoaling up dangerously; that silver streak in the shadow of the forest is the 'break' from a new snag and he has located himself in the very best place he could have found to fish for steamboats; that tall dead tree, with a single living branch, is not going to last long, and then how is a body ever going to get through this blind place at night without the friendly old landmark?"

3   No, the romance and beauty were all gone from the river. All the value any feature of it had for me now was the amount of usefulness it could furnish toward compassing the safe piloting of a steamboat. Since those days, I have pitied doctors from my heart. What does the lovely flush in a beauty's cheek mean to a doctor but a "break" that ripples above some deadly disease? Are not all her visible charms sown thick with what are to him the signs and symbols of hidden decay? Does he ever see her beauty at all, or doesn't he simply view her professionally and comment upon her unwholesome condition all to himself? And doesn't he sometimes wonder whether he has gained most or lost most by learning his trade?

Questions on Content, Structure, and Style

1. What is Clemens contrasting in this essay? Identify his thesis.
2. What organizational pattern does he choose? Why is this an appropriate choice for his purpose?
3. How does Clemens make a smooth transition to his later view of the river?
4. Why does Clemens refer to doctors in paragraph 3?
5. What is the purpose of the questions in paragraph 3? Why is the last question especially important?
6. Characterize the language Clemens uses in his description in paragraph 1. Is his diction appropriate?
7. Point out several examples of similes in paragraph 1. What do they add to the description of the sunset?
8. How does the language in the description in paragraph 2 differ from the diction in paragraph 1? What view of the river is emphasized there?
9. Identify an example of personification in paragraph 2. Why did Clemens add it to his description?
10. Describe the tone of this essay. Does it ever shift?
11. Who is the audience for this essay?

Suggestions for Writing

Try using Samuel Clemens' "Two Ways of Viewing the River" as a stepping stone to your own writing. Consider, as Clemens did, writing about a subject before and after you experienced it from a more technically informed point of view. Did your appreciation of your grandmother's quilt increase after you realized how much skill went into making it? Did a starry night have a different appeal after your astronomy course? Did your admiration of a story or poem diminish or increase after you studied its craft? Clemens felt a certain loss came with his expertise, but was this the case in your experience?

Vocabulary

trifling (1)	ruddy (1)
acquisition (1)	wrought (2)
conspicuous (1)	compassing (3)

▪ A REVISION WORKSHEET

As you write your rough drafts, consult Chapter 5 for guidance through the revision process. In addition, here are a few questions to ask yourself as you revise your comparison and/or contrast essay:

1. Does the essay contain a thesis that makes a significant point instead of a "so-what" thesis?

2. Is the material organized into the best pattern for the subject matter?

3. If the essay is developed by the Point-by-Point Pattern, are there enough transitional words used to avoid the seesaw effect?

4. If the essay is developed by the Block Pattern, are there enough transitional devices and references connecting the two subjects to avoid the split-essay problem?

5. Are the points of comparison and/or contrast presented in a logical, consistent order that the reader can follow easily?

6. Are both subjects given a reasonably balanced treatment?

7. Are both subjects developed in enough specific detail so that the reader clearly understands the comparison or contrast? Where might more detail be added?

After you've revised your essay extensively, you might exchange rough drafts with a classmate and answer these questions for each other, making specific suggestions for improvement wherever appropriate. (For advice on productive participation in classroom workshops, see pages 102–104.)

A Special Kind of Comparison: The Analogy

In the last few pages of this text, you've learned about essays developed by comparison and/or contrast, which generally point out similarities and differences between two things with enough common ground to merit meaningful discussion (two apartments, two computers, a book and its movie, etc.). In comparison and contrast essays, two subjects ("X" and "Y") are explained to make a point. An *analogy* is slightly different: it is a comparison that uses one thing ("X") only to clarify or argue a second thing ("Y"). In an analogy, one element is the main focus of attention.

You've probably heard several colourful analogies this week. Perhaps a friend who holds a hectic, dead-end job has tried to explain life at that moment by comparing herself to a crazed gerbil on a cage treadmill—always running, getting nowhere, feeling trapped in a never-changing environment. Or perhaps your science teacher explained the behaviour of cancer cells by comparing them in several ways to an invading army on a destructive mission. If you read the preface to this text, you were asked to view your writing instructor as a coach who helps you practise your skills, gives constructive criticism, and encourages your successes. Analogies are plentiful in our conversations and in both our reading and writing.

Writers often find analogies useful in three ways:

1. *To clarify and explain:* Most often writers use analogies to clarify an abstract, unfamiliar, or complex element by comparing it to something that is familiar to the reader, often something that is more concrete or easier to understand. For example, raising children has often been compared to nourishing baby birds, with parents feeding and nurturing but ultimately nudging offspring out of the nest. A relationship might be explained as having grown from a seed that eventually blossomed into a flower (or a weed!). Popular novelist Stephen King has used a roller coaster analogy to explain some people's enjoyment of horror movies.

Frequently, scientific and medical topics profit from analogies that a general audience of readers can more readily understand. A technical discussion of the human eye, for instance, might be explained using the analogy of a camera lens; photosynthesis might be compared to the process of baking bread. One biology teacher explains the semipermeability of a cell membrane with a football analogy: the offensive line wants to let out the running back with the ball but keep the defensive line in. In short, analogies can make new or difficult material easier to grasp.

2. *To argue and persuade:* Writers often use analogies to try to convince their audience that what is true about "X" would also be true about "Y" because the two elements have so many important similarities. For example, someone against new anti-drug laws might argue that they are similar to those passed under Prohibition, the banning of alcohol in the early twentieth century in the United States and Canada, and thus the drug laws are doomed to failure. Or perhaps a NASA official might argue for more money for space exploration by comparing trips into outer space with those expeditions to the New World by explorers such as Columbus. How convincing an analogy is depends to a large extent on how similar the two elements appear to be. Remember, however, that analogies by themselves cannot *prove* anything; they can merely suggest similarities between two cases or things.

3. *To dramatize or capture an image:* Writers (and speakers) often use analogies because they wish their audience to remember a particular point or to see something in a new way. Using a vivid analogy—sometimes referred to as an extended metaphor or simile—can effectively impress an image upon the reader's or listener's mind ("Using crack is like burning down your own house. And the insurance policy ran out a long time ago . . ."). Analogies can be enjoyable too for their sheer inventiveness and their colourful language. Perhaps one of the most well-known analogies in American literature is Thoreau's description, in *Walden,* of a battle between two ant colonies, with the tiny creatures drawn as rival warriors fighting to the death in classical epic style. Analogies may even be used for comic effect in appropriate situations (moving into your third-floor apartment in sweltering August heat as analogous to a trip to the Underworld, for instance). Fresh, creative analogies can delight your readers and hold their attention.

Although analogies can be helpful and memorable, they can also present problems if they are trite, unclear, or illogical. Analogies can be especially harmful to a writer's credibility in an argument if readers don't see enough logical similarities to make the comparison convincing. Some faulty analogies may seem acceptable at first glance but fall apart when the details of the comparison are considered closely. For example, consider a bumper sticker that reads "Giving money and power to the government is like giving whisky and car keys to teenage boys." Are the two situations really alike? Do government agencies and/or officials and adolescents share many similarities in maturity, experience, and goals? Does financial support have the same effect as alcohol? If too many points of comparison are weak, readers will not find the analogy persuasive. Or perhaps you have read that "Canada is like a lifeboat already full of people; letting in more immigrants will cause the boat to sink." If readers do not accept the major premise—that Canada, a country with many renewable resources, closely resembles a lifeboat, a confined space with unchanging dimensions—they are likely to reject the argument.

Also beware those writers who try to substitute an analogy in place of any other kind of evidence to support their points in an argument, and be especially suspicious of those using analogies as "scare tactics" ("This proposed legislation is just like laws passed in Nazi Germany"). As a writer, use only those analogies that will help your reader understand, remember, or accept your ideas; as a reader, always protect yourself by questioning the validity of the analogy offered to you. (For more on *faulty analogy* as a logical fallacy, see page 281.)

To illustrate the use of analogy, here are three examples from professional writers. In each case, what was the writer's purpose? How is "X" used to clarify or argue for "Y"? Which of these analogies do you find the most effective, and why?

> A good lab course is an exercise in *doing* science. As such it differs totally in mission from a good lecture course where the object is learning *about* science. In the same way that one can gain vastly greater insight into music by learning to play an instrument, one can experience the doing of science only by going into the lab and trying one's hand at measurement.
>
> —Miles Pickering, "Are Lab Courses a Waste of Time?"

> For a long time now, since the beginning, in fact, men and women have been sparring and dancing around with each other, each pair trying to get it together and boogie to the tune called Life. For some people, it was always a glide, filled with grace and ease. For most of us, it

is a stumble and a struggle, always trying to figure out the next step, until we find a partner whose inconsistencies seem to fit with ours, and the two of us fit into some kind of rhythm. Some couples wind up struggling and pulling at cross purposes; and of course, some people never get out on the floor, just stand alone in the corners, looking hard at the dancers.

—Jay Molishever, "Changing Expectations of Marriage"

One afternoon while we were there at that lake a thunderstorm came up. It was like the revival of an old melodrama that I had seen long ago with childish awe. The second-act climax of the drama of the electrical disturbance over a lake in America had not changed in any important respect. This was the big scene, still the big scene. The whole thing was so familiar, the first feeling of oppression and heat and a general air around camp of not wanting to go very far away. In midafternoon (it was all the same) a curious darkening of the sky, and a lull in everything that had made life tick; and then the way the boats suddenly swung the other way at their moorings with the coming of a breeze out of the new quarter, and the premonitory rumble. Then the kettle drum, then the snare, then the bass drum and cymbals, then crackling light against the dark. . . . Afterward the calm, the rain steadily rustling in the calm lake, the return of light and hope and spirits, and the campers running out in joy.

—E. B. White, "Once More to the Lake"

Analogies come in a variety of lengths, from several sentences to an entire essay, depending upon the writer's purpose. As you practise your writing in this composition class, you may find that incorporating an analogy into one of your essays is an effective way to explain, emphasize, or help support an idea.

Reviewing Your Progress

After you have completed your essay developed by comparison and/or contrast, take a moment to measure your progress as a writer by responding to the following questions. Such analysis will help you to recognize growth in your writing skills and may enable you to identify areas that are still problematic.

1. Which part of your essay do you like the best? Why?
2. Which point of comparison or contrast do you think is the most successful? Why is it effective?
3. What part of your essay gave you the most trouble? How did you overcome the problem?
4. If you had more time to work on this essay, what would receive additional attention? Why?
5. What did you learn about your topic from writing this essay? About yourself as a writer?

■ Strategy Four: Development by Definition

Frequently in conversation we must stop to ask, "What do you mean by that?" because in some cases our failure to comprehend just one particular term may lead to total misunderstanding. Suppose, for example, in a discussion with an American friend, your friend refers to a new law as a piece of "liberal legislation"; if you and your friend do not share the same definition of "liberal," your friend's remark may be completely misinterpreted. You are more likely, at least initially, to interpret the word to mean the Liberal Party of Canada, while your friend is probably saying the legislation is unconventional or too lenient toward some group he thinks is undeserving of consideration. Here's another example: if you ask your grandparents for some fins because you think you'll get bargoons today, will they know to open their wallets for your shopping trip? In other words, a clear understanding of terms or ideas is often essential to meaningful communication.

Sometimes a dictionary definition or a one- or two-sentence explanation is all a term needs (Hemingway, for example, once defined courage as "grace under pressure"). And sometimes a brief, humorous definition can cut right to the heart of the matter (comedian Robin Williams, for instance, once defined "cocaine" as "God's way of saying you're making too much money").*

Frequently, however, you will find it necessary to provide an *extended definition*—that is, a longer, more detailed explanation that thoroughly defines the subject. Essays of extended definitions are quite common; think, for instance, of the articles you've seen on "mercy killing," "assisted suicide," or abortion that define "life" in a variety of ways. Other recent essays have grappled with defining such complex concepts as free speech, animal rights, pornography, affirmative action, and gun control.

Many international discussions centre on controversial definitions. Following the events of September 11, 2001, the "War on Terror" has produced a host of terms whose meanings are frequently debated. For example, does legislation such as the USA Patriot Act ensure "homeland security" or legitimize unlawful invasions of privacy? Is "racial profiling" acceptable in the search for terrorists? Is it "patriotic" to oppose military actions of one's country? What is the difference between a "political prisoner," a "detainee," and a "prisoner of war"? What roles do official "spin doctors" play in distribution of public information? Today, perhaps more than ever, we need to clearly understand specific meanings of language before we can make intelligent choices or take appropriate actions.

Why Do We Define?

Essays of extended definition are usually written for one or more of the following reasons:

1. To clarify an abstract term or concept ("heroism," "success," "poststructuralism," "oppression")

2. To provide a personal interpretation of a term that the writer feels is vague, controversial, misused, or misunderstood ("feminist," "eco-terrorist," "senior citizen," "multiculturalism")

3. To explain a new or unusual term or phrase found in popular culture, slang, dialect, or within a particular geographic area or cultural group ("hip hop," "flash mob," "McJobs," "metrosexual," "lagniappe")

4. To make understandable the jargon or technical terms of a particular field of study, a profession, or an industry ("deconstruction," "blogs," "retinitis pigmentosa," "accelerated amortization")

---

* Even graffiti employ definition. One bathroom wall favourite: "Death is Nature's way of telling you to slow down." Another, obviously written by an English major: "A double negative is a no-no."

5. To offer information about a term or an idea to a particular interested audience (antique collectors learning about "Depression glass," movie buffs understanding "film noir")

6. To inform and entertain by presenting the colourful history, uses, effects, or examples of a word, expression, or concept ("soul food," "Zydeco music," "urban legends," "Kwanzaa")

Developing Your Essay

Here are four suggestions to help you prepare your essay of extended definition:

Know your purpose. Sometimes we need to define a term as clearly and objectively as possible. As a laboratory assistant, for instance, you might need to explain a technical measuring instrument to a group of new students. At other times, however, we may wish to persuade as well as inform our readers. People's interpretations of words, especially abstract or controversial terms, can, and often do, differ greatly depending on their point of view. After all, one person's protest march can be another person's street riot. Consequently, before you begin writing, decide on your purpose. If your readers need objective information only, make your definition as unbiased as you can; if your goal is to convince them that your point of view is the right or best one, you may adopt a variety of persuasive techniques as well as subjective language. For example, readers of a paper entitled "Corporate Care" should quickly realize that they are not getting an objective treatment of a proposal to privatize medical care in Canada.

Give your readers a reason to read. One way to introduce your subject is to explain the previous use, misuse, or misunderstanding of the term; then present your new or better interpretation of the term or concept. An introduction and thesis defining a new word in popular usage might state, "Although people who suffer from weak immune systems might suddenly fear breathing the same air as someone suffering from affluenza, they needn't worry. 'Affluenza' isn't germ-laden; it's simply a colourful term describing the out-of-control consumerism spreading like an epidemic through Canada today." Or consider this introduction and thesis aimed at a word the writer feels is unclear to many readers: "When the credits roll at the end of a movie, much of the audience may be perplexed to see the job of 'best boy' listed. No, the 'best boy' isn't the nicest kid on the set—he (or she) is, in fact, the key electrician's first assistant, who helps arrange the lights for the movie's director of photography."

Keep your audience in mind to anticipate and avoid problems of clarity. Because you are trying to present a new or improved definition, you must strive above all for clarity. Ask yourself, "Who is my intended audience? What terms or parts of my definition are strange to them?" You don't help your audience, for example, by defining one campus slang expression in terms of other bits of unfamiliar slang. If, in other words, you discuss "mouse potatoes" (people who spend all their time at their computers) as "Google bombers," you may be confusing some readers more than you are informing them. If your assignment doesn't specify a particular audience, you may find it useful to imagine one. You might pretend, for instance, that you're defining current campus slang for your parents, clarifying a local expression for a foreign visitor, or explaining a computer innovation to a technophobic friend. Remember that your definition is effective only if your explanation is clear, not just to you but to those unfamiliar with the term or concept under discussion.

Use as many strategies as necessary to clarify your definition. Depending on your subject, you may use any number of the following methods in your essay to define your term:

1. Describe the parts or distinguishing characteristics*
2. Offer some examples
3. Compare to or contrast with similar terms
4. Explain an operation or a process
5. State some familiar synonyms
6. Define by negation (that is, tell what the term doesn't mean)
7. Present the history or trace its development or changes from the original linguistic meaning
8. Discuss causes or effects
9. Identify times/places of use or appearance
10. Associate it with recognizable people, places, or ideas

To illustrate some of the methods suggested here, let's suppose you wanted to write an extended definition of "crossover" country music. You might choose one or more of these methods:

- Describe the parts: lyrics, musical sound, instruments, typical subject matter
- Compare to or contrast with other kinds of music, such as traditional country music, Western swing, or "pop"
- Give some examples of famous "crossover" country songs and artists
- Trace its historical development from traditional country music to its present state

In the paper on "crossover" country music or in any definition essay, you should, of course, use only those methods that will best define your term. Never include methods purely for the sake of exhibiting a variety of techniques. You, the writer, must decide which method or methods work best, which should receive the most emphasis, and in which order the chosen methods of definition should appear.

Problems to Avoid

Here is a list of "don'ts" for the writer of extended definition essays:

Don't present an incomplete definition. An inadequate definition is often the result of choosing a subject too broad or complex for your essay. You probably can't, for instance,

---

* With some topics, it may also be useful to describe the genus, class, or species to which the subject belongs.

do a good job of defining "twentieth-century modern art" in all its varieties in a short essay; you might, however, introduce your reader to some specific school of modern art, such as cubism or surrealism. Always narrow your subject to a manageable size and then define it as thoroughly as possible.

Don't begin every definition essay by quoting from a dictionary. If you must include a standard definition of your term, try to find a unique way of blending it into your discussion, perhaps as a point of contrast to your explanation of the word's meaning. Dictionary definitions are generally so overused as opening sentences that they often drive composition teachers to seek more interesting jobs, such as measuring spaghetti in a pasta factory. Don't bore your audience to death; it's a terrible way to go.

Don't define vaguely or by using generalities. As always, use specific, vivid details to explain your subject. If, for example, you define a shamrock as "a green plant with three leaves," you have also described hundreds of other plants, including poison ivy. Consequently, you must select details that will make your subject distinct from any other. Including concrete examples is frequently useful in any essay but especially so when you are defining an abstract term, such as "pride," "patriotism," or "prejudice." To make your definition both interesting and clear, always add as many precise details as possible. (For a review of using specific, colourful language, see pages 112–113, pages 124–127 and pages 144–147.)

Don't offer circular definitions. To define a poet as "one who writes poetry" or the Canadian Constitution as "a constitution for all Canadians" is about as helpful as a doctor telling a patient, "Your illness is primarily a lack of good health." Explain your subject; don't just re-name it.

■ ESSAY TOPICS

Here are several suggestions for terms whose meanings are often unclear. Narrow any topic that seems too broad for your assignment, and decide before writing whether your definition will be objective or subjective. (Student writers, by the way, often note that abstract concepts are harder to define than the more concrete subjects, so proceed at your own risk, and remember to use plenty of specific detail in your essay.) For additional ideas, turn to the "Suggestions for Writing" section following the professional essay (page 236).

1. A current slang, campus, local, or popular-culture expression
2. A term from your field of study
3. A medical term or condition
4. Success or failure
5. A good/bad teacher, clerk, coach, friend, parent, date, or spouse
6. Heroism or cowardice

7. A term from science or technology

8. A kind of music, painting, architecture, or dance

9. A social label ("Goth," "Prep," "Skater," etc.)

10. A current fad or style or one from the past

11. A rebel or conformist

12. Self-respect

13. Prejudice or discrimination

14. An important historical movement or group

15. A controversial political idea or term

16. Select a painting or photograph in which you think the artist offers a visual definition of the subject matter. Explain this definition by examining the artist's choice and arrangement of details in the picture. (For example, study Alex Colville's iconic painting, *Horse and Train.* What definition of nature's relationship to human technology is being presented here? What parts of the picture illustrate and clarify this point of view? Or consider two other pictures in this text, *Breadline during the Louisville Flood, Kentucky 1937* [page 209] or *The Scream* [page 108]. Other famous paintings that might work well for this assignment include Salvador Dali's surrealistic *Persistence of Memory* or any one of the many psychologically revealing self-portraits by Frida Kahlo.)

Gift of Dominion Foundries and Steel, Ltd. © Art Gallery of Hamilton.

Horse and Train, *by Alex Colville*

A Topic Proposal for Your Essay

Selecting the right subject matter is important to every writer. To help you clarify your ideas and strengthen your commitment to your topic, here is a proposal sheet that asks you to describe some of your ideas about your subject before you begin drafting. Although your ideas may change as you write (they will almost certainly become more refined), thinking through your topic now may help you avoid several false starts.

1. What subject will your essay define? Will you define this subject objectively or subjectively? Why?

2. Why are you interested in this topic? Do you have a personal or professional connection to the subject? State at least one reason for your choice of topic.

3. Is this a significant topic of interest to others? Why? Who specifically might find it interesting, informative, or entertaining?

4. Is your subject a controversial, ambiguous, or new term? What will readers gain by understanding this term as defined from your point of view?

5. Writers use a variety of techniques to define terms. At this point, list at least two techniques you think you might use to help readers understand your topic.

6. What difficulties, if any, can you foresee during the drafting of this essay? For example, do you need to do any additional reading or interviewing to collect information for your definition?

■ Sample Student Essay

A student with an interest in running wrote the following essay defining "runner's high." Note that he uses several methods to define his subject, one that is difficult to explain to those who have not experienced it firsthand.

BLIND PACES

Introduction: An example and a general definition of the term

1   After running the Mile-Hi ten-kilometre race in my hometown, I spoke with several of the leading runners about their experiences in the race. While most of them agreed that the course, which passed through a beautifully wooded yet overly hilly country area, was difficult, they also agreed that it was one of the best races of their running careers. They could not, however, explain why it was such a wonderful race but could rather only mumble something about the tall trees, cool air, and sandy path. When pressed, most

of them didn't even remember specific details about the course, except the start and finish, and ended their descriptions with a blank—but content—stare. This self-satisfied, yet almost indescribable, feeling is often the result of an experienced runner running, a feeling often called, because of its similarities to other euphoric experiences, "runner's high."

2   Because this experience is seemingly impossible to define, perhaps a description of what runner's high is not might, by contrast, lead to a better understanding of what it is. I clearly remember—about five years ago—when I first took up running. My first day, I donned my tennis shorts, ragged T-shirt, and white discount-store tennis shoes somewhat ashamedly, knowing that they were symbolic of my novice status. I plodded around my block—just over a half mile—in a little more than four minutes, feeling and regretting every painful step. My shins and thighs revolted at every jarring move, and my lungs wheezed uncontrollably, gasping for air, yet denied that basic necessity. Worst of all, I was conscious of every aspect of my existence—from the swinging of my arms to the slap of my feet on the road, and from the sweat dripping into my eyes and ears and mouth to the frantic inhaling and exhaling of my lungs. I kept my eyes carefully peeled on the horizon or the next turn in the road, judging how far away it was, how long it would take me to get there, and how much torture was left before I reached home. These first few runs were, of course, the worst—as far from any euphoria or "high" as possible. They did, however, slowly become easier as my body became accustomed to running.

Definition by negation, contrast

3   After a few months, in fact, I felt serious enough about this new pursuit to invest in a pair of real running shoes and shorts. Admittedly, these changes added to the comfort of my endeavour,

but it wasn't until two full years later that the biggest change occurred—and I experienced my first real "high." It was a fall day. The air was a cool sixty-five degrees, the sun was shining intently, the sky was a clear, crisp blue, and a few dead leaves were scattered across the browning lawn. I stepped out onto the road and headed north toward a nearby park for my routine jog. The

Personal example

next thing I remember, however, was not my run through the park, but rather my return, some forty-two minutes and six miles later, to my house. I woke, as if out of a dream, just as I slowed to a walk, cooling down from my run. The only memory I had of my run

Effects of the "high"

was a feeling of floating on air—as if my real self was somewhere above and detached from my body, looking down on my physical self as it went through its blind paces. At first, I felt scared—what if I had run out in front of a car? Would I have even known it? I felt as if I had been asleep or out of control, that my brain had, in some real sense, been turned off.

4   Now, after five years of running and hundreds of such mystical experiences, I realize that I had never lost control while in this euphoric state—and that my brain hadn't been turned off, or, at least, not completely. But what does happen is hard to prove. George Sheehan, in a column for *Runner's World,* suggests that "altered states," such as runner's high, result from the loss of

Possible causes of the feeling: Two authorities

conscious control, from the temporary cessation of left-brain messages and the dominance of right-brain activity (the left hemisphere being the seat of reason and rationality; the right, of emotions and inherited archetypal feelings) (14). Another explanation comes from Dr. Jerry Lynch, who argues, in his book *The Total Runner,* that the "high" results from the secretion of natural opiates, called beta endorphins, in the brain (213). My own explanation draws on both these medical explanations and is perhaps slightly more mystical. It's just possible that indeed natural opiates do go to work and consequently our brains lose track of the ins and outs of everyday activities—of jobs and classes and responsibilities. And because of this relaxed, drugged state, we are able to reach down into something more fundamental, something that ties us not only to each other but to all creation, here and gone. We rejoin nature, rediscovering the thread that links us to the universe.

The writer's explanation

5   My explanation is, of course, unscientific and therefore suspect. But I found myself, that day of the Mile-Hi Ten K run, eagerly trying to discuss my experience with the other runners: I wanted desperately to discover where I had been and what I had been doing during the race for which I received my first trophy. I didn't discover the answer from my fellow runners that day, but it didn't matter. I'm still running and still feeling the glow—whatever it is.

Conclusion: An incomplete understanding doesn't hamper enjoyment

WORKS CITED*

Lynch, Jerry. *The Total Runner: A Complete Mind-Body Guide to Optimal Performance.* Englewood Cliffs, NJ: Prentice Hall, 1987.

Sheehan, George. "Altered States." *Runner's World.* Aug. 1988: 14.

Professional Essay†

■ Being Canadian

Denise Chong

Before becoming a full-time writer, Vancouver-born Denise Chong worked as an economic advisor to Prime Minister Pierre Elliott Trudeau. Chong has often written on Chinese-Canadian identity. Her semiautobiographical book, *The Concubine's Children: Portrait of a Family Divided* (1994), expands some of the themes found in the following essay.

---

* Editor's note: In a formal research paper, the "Works Cited" list appears on a separate page.

† To help you read this essay analytically, review pages 160–162.

1   I ask myself what it means to be a Canadian. I was lucky enough to be born in Canada [, so] I look back at the price paid by those who made the choice that brought me such luck.

2   South China at the turn of the century became the spout of the teapot that was China. It poured out middle-class peasants like my grandfather, who couldn't earn a living at home. He left behind a wife and child. My grandfather was 36 when exclusion came. Lonely and living a penurious existence, he worked at a sawmill on the mud flats of the Fraser River, where the Chinese were third on the pay scale behind "Whites" and "Hindus." With the door to Chinese immigration slammed shut, men like him didn't dare even go home for a visit, for fear Canada might bar their re-entry. With neither savings enough to go home for good, nor the means once in China to put rice in the mouths of his wife and child there, my grandfather wondered when, if ever, he could return to the bosom of a family. He decided to purchase a concubine, a second wife, to join him in Canada.

3   The concubine, at age 17, got into Canada on a lie. She got around the exclusion law in the only way possible: she presented the authorities with a Canadian birth certificate. It belonged to a woman born in Ladner, British Columbia, and a middleman sold it to my grandfather at many times the price of the old head tax. Some years later, the concubine and my grandfather went back to China with their two Vancouver-born daughters. They lived for a time under the same roof as my grandfather's first wife. The concubine became pregnant. Eight months into her pregnancy, she decided to brave the long sea voyage back so that her third child could be born in Canada. [Her] false Canadian birth certificate would get her in. Accompanied by only my grandfather, she left China. Three days after the boat docked, on the second floor of a tenement on a back alley in Vancouver's Chinatown, she gave birth to my mother.

4   Canada remained inhospitable. Yet my grandparents *chose* to keep Canada in their future. Both gambled a heritage and family ties to take what they thought were better odds in the lottery of life. . . .

5   My own sense, four generations on, of being Canadian is one of belonging. I belong to a family. I belong to a community of values. I didn't get to choose my ancestors, but I can try to leave the world a better place for the generations that follow. The life I lead begins before and lingers after my time.

6   I am now the mother of two young children. I want to pass on a sense of what it means to be a Canadian. But what worries me as a parent, and as a Canadian, is whether we can fashion an enduring concept of citizenship that will be the glue that holds us together as a society. Curiously, Canadian citizenship elicits the most heartfelt response outside Canada. Any Canadian who has lived or travelled abroad quickly discovers that Canadian citizenship is a coveted possession. In the eyes of the rest of the world, it stands for an enlightened and gentle society.

7   Can we find a strong concept of citizenship that could be shared by all Canadians when we stand on our own soil? Some would say it is unrealistic to expect a symbol to rise out of a rather pragmatic past. We spilled no revolutionary blood, as did France— where the word *citoyen* was brought into popular usage—or America. Some lament the absence of a founding myth; we don't have the equivalent of a Boston Tea Party. Others long for versions of Canadian heroes to compete with the likes of American images that occupy our living rooms and our playgrounds. The one Canadian symbol with universal recognition is the flag. But where does the maple leaf strike a chord? Outside Canada. On the back packs of Canadian travellers. . . .

8   Some say Canadian citizenship is devalued because it is too easy to come here. But what sets Canadian society apart from others is that ours is an inclusive society. Canada's citizenship act remains more progressive than [the immigration laws of] many countries. Canadians by immigration have equal status with Canadians by birth. In contrast, in western Europe, guest workers, even if they descended from those who originally came, can be sent "home" any time. In Japan, Koreans and Filipinos have no claim to the citizenship of their birth. The plight of the Palestinians in Kuwait after the Gulf War gave the lie to a "free Kuwait."

9   Canadian citizenship recognizes differences. It praises diversity. It is what we as Canadians *choose* to have in common with each other. It is a bridge between those who left something to make a new home here and those born here. What keeps the bridge strong is tolerance, fairness, understanding, and compassion. Citizenship has rights and responsibilities. I believe one responsibility of citizenship is to use that tolerance, fairness, understanding, and compassion to leaf through the Canadian family album together. . . .

10   How we tell our stories is the work of citizenship. The motive of the storyteller should be to put the story first. To speak with authenticity and veracity is to choose narrative over commentary. It is not to glorify or sentimentalize the past. It is not to sanitize our differences. Nor [is it] to rail against or to seek compensation today for injustices of bygone times. In my opinion, to try to rewrite history leads to a sense of victimization. It marginalizes Canadians. It backs away from equality in our society, for which we have worked hard to find expression.

11   I believe our stories ultimately tell the story of Canada itself. In all our past is an immigrant beginning, a settler's accomplishments and setbacks, and the confidence of a common future. We all know the struggle for victory, the dreams and the lost hopes, the pride and the shame. When we tell our stories, we look in the mirror. I believe what we will see is that Canada is not lacking in heroes. Rather, the heroes are to be found within.

12   The work of citizenship is not something just for the week that we celebrate citizenship each year. It is part of every breath we take. It is the work of our lifetimes. . . .

13   If we do some of this work of citizenship, we will stand on firmer ground. Sharing experience will help build strength of character. It will explain our differences, yet make them less divisive. We will yell at each other less, and understand each other more. We will find a sense of identity and a common purpose. We will have something to hand down to the next generation.

14   My grandfather's act of immigration to the new world and the determination of my grandmother, the girl who first came here as a *kay toi neu*, to chance a journey from China back to Canada so that my mother could be born back here, will stand as a gift to all future generations of my family. Knowing they came hoping for a better life makes it easy to love both them and this country.

15   In the late 1980s, I [found] myself in China, on a two-year stint living in Peking, and working as a writer. In a letter to my mother in Prince George, I confessed that, despite the predictions of friends back in Canada, I was finding it difficult to feel any "Chineseness." My mother wrote back: "You're Canadian, not Chinese. Stop trying to feel anything." She was right. I stopped such contrivances. I was Canadian; it was that which embodied the values of my life.

Questions on Content, Structure, and Style

1. Why does Chong narrate the stories of her grandparents' immigration to Canada?
2. Why does she connect immigration with "being Canadian"?
3. How does Chong organize and develop her extended definition?
4. What is the main characteristic that defines Canadians?
5. How does the world define the Canadian character?
6. What examples does Chong use to support her definition?
7. What comparisons or analogies does she draw? What kinds of contrasts? What is the effect of these devices?
8. Evaluate the essay's conclusion. Is it an effective choice for this essay?
9. Who is the audience for this essay?
10. After reading Chong's descriptive details, examples, and analysis, do you feel you now have a general understanding of an abstract term? If the writer were to expand her definition, what might she add to make your understanding even more complete? More family stories? More stories about herself? The stories of other Canadians with a similar immigration history?

Suggestions for Writing

Try using Denise Chong's "Being Canadian" as a stepping stone to your essay. Select a broad, abstract term that seems to be used in many contrasting, even contradictory ways. Write an extended definition, as Chong did, that narrows down the term for your readers. As appropriate, include information about its characteristics, parts, history, possible causes, effects, solutions, benefits, or dangers. Or take a term about whose meaning most people seem to agree, such as "human rights," and offer an alternative, challenging definition. Remember that your essay should offer in-depth explanation, not just general description.

Vocabulary

penurious (2)	coveted (6)	veracity (10)
concubine (2)	enlightened (6)	marginalizes (10)
exclusion (3)	pragmatic (7)	stint (15)
elicits (6)	founding (7)	contrivances (15)

▪ A REVISION WORKSHEET

As you write your rough drafts, consult Chapter 5 for guidance through the revision process. In addition, here are a few questions to ask yourself as you revise your extended definition essay:

1. Is the subject narrowed to manageable size, and is the purpose of the definition clear to the readers?
2. If the definition is objective, is the language as neutral as possible?

3. If the definition is subjective, is the point of view obvious to the readers?

4. Are all the words and parts of the definition itself clear to the essay's particular audience?

5. Are there enough explanatory methods (examples, descriptions, history, causes, effects, etc.) used to make the definition clear and informative?

6. Have the various methods been organized and ordered in an effective way?

7. Does the essay contain enough specific details to make the definition clear and distinct rather than vague or circular? Where could additional details be added?

After you've revised your essay extensively, you might exchange rough drafts with a classmate and answer these questions for each other, making specific suggestions for improvement wherever appropriate. (For advice on productive participation in classroom workshops, see pages 102–104.)

Reviewing Your Progress

After you have completed your essay developed by definition, take a moment to measure your progress as a writer by responding to the following questions. Such analysis will help you recognize growth in your writing skills and may enable you to identify areas that are still problematic.

1. What do you like best about your essay? Why?

2. After considering the various methods of definition you used in your essay, which one do you think offered the clearest or most persuasive explanation of your topic? Why was that particular technique effective in this essay?

3. What part of your essay gave you the most trouble? How did you overcome the problem?

4. If you had more time to work on this essay, what would receive additional attention? Why?

5. What did you learn about your topic from writing this essay? About yourself as a writer?

■ Strategy Five: Development by Division and Classification

To make large or complex subjects easier to comprehend, we frequently apply the principles of *division* or *classification*.

Division

Division is the act of separating something into its component parts so that it may be better understood or used by the reader. For example, consider a complex subject such as the national budget. Perhaps you have seen a picture on television or in the newspaper of the budget represented by a circle or a pie that has been divided into parts and labelled: a certain percentage or "slice" of the budget designated for military spending, another slice for social services, another for education, and so on. By studying the budget after it has been divided into its parts, taxpayers may have a better sense of how their money is being spent.

As a student, you see division in action in many of your college or university courses. A literature teacher, for instance, might approach a particular drama by dividing its plot into stages such as exposition, rising action, climax, falling action, and dénouement. Or your chemistry lab instructor may ask you to break down a substance into its components to learn how the parts interact to form the chemical. Even this textbook is divided into chapters to make it easier for you to use. When you think of *division,* then, think of dividing, separating, or breaking apart one subject (often a large or complex or unfamiliar one) into its parts to help people understand it more easily.

Classification

While the principle of division calls for separating one thing into its parts, *classification* systematically groups a number of things into categories to make the information easier to grasp. Without some sort of imposed system of order, a body of information can be a jumble of facts and figures. For example, at some point you've probably turned to the classified advertisements in the newspaper; if the advertisements were not classified into categories such as "Houses for Rent," "Cars for Sale," and "Help Wanted," you would have to search through countless advertisements to find the service or item you needed.

Classification occurs everywhere around you. As a student, you may be classified as a first-year, graduate, or exchange student; you may also be classified by your major. If you vote, you may be categorized as a Liberal, Conservative, New Democrat, or something else; if you attend religious services, you may be classified as Baptist, Methodist, Catholic, Jewish, and so on. The books you buy may be grouped and shelved by the bookstore into "mysteries," "Westerns," "biographies," "adventure stories," and other categories; the movies you see have already been typed as "G," "PG," "PG-13," "R," or "NC-17." Professionals classify almost every kind of knowledge: ornithologists classify birds; etymologists classify words by origin; botanists classify plants; zoologists classify animals. Remember that *classification* differs from division in that it sorts and organizes *many* things into appropriate groups, types, kinds, or categories. *Division* begins with *one* thing and separates it into its parts.

Developing Your Essay

A classification or division paper is generally easy to develop. Each part or category is identified and described in a major part of the body of the essay. Frequently, one body paragraph will be devoted to each category. Here are three additional hints for writing your essay:

Select one principle of classification or division and stick to it. If you are classifying students by major, for instance, don't suddenly switch to classification by faculty: French, economics, psychology, *arts and sciences,* math, and chemistry. A similar error occurs in this classification of dogs by breeds because it includes a physical characteristic: spaniels, terriers, *long-haired,* hounds, and retrievers. Decide on what basis of division you will classify or divide your subject and then be consistent throughout your essay.

Make the purpose of your division or classification clear to your audience. Don't just announce that "There are four kinds of 'X'" or that "'Z' has three important parts." Why does your particular audience need this information? Consider these sample thesis statements:

> By recognizing the three kinds of poisonous snakes in this area, campers and backpackers may be able to take the proper medical steps if they are bitten.

> Knowing the four types of spinning reels will allow those new to ice fishing to purchase the equipment best suited to their needs.

> Although karate has become a popular form of exercise as well as of self-defence, few people know what the six levels of achievement—or "belts" as they are called—actually stand for.

Organize your material for a particular purpose and then explain to your readers what that purpose is.

Account for all the parts in your division or classification. Don't, for instance, claim to classify all the evergreen trees native to your province and then leave out one or more species. For a short essay, narrow your ruling principle rather than omit categories. You couldn't, for instance, classify all the architectural styles in Canada in a short paper, but you might discuss the major styles on your campus. In the same manner, the enormous task of classifying all types of mental illness could be narrowed to the most common forms of childhood schizophrenia. However you narrow your topic, remember that in a formal classification, all the parts must be accounted for.

Like most rules, the preceding one has an exception. If your instructor permits, you can also write a satirical or humorous classification. In this sort of essay, you make up your own categories as well as your thesis. One writer, for example, recently wrote about the kinds of moviegoers who spoil the show for everyone else, such as "the babbling idiot," "the laughing hyena," and "the wandering dawdler." Another female student described blind dates to avoid, including "Mr. Neanderthal," "Timothy Timid," "Red, the Raging Rebel," and "Frat-Rat Freddie," among others. In this kind of informal essay, the thesis rule still holds true: though you start by making a humorous or satirical point about your subject, your classification must be more than mere silliness. Effective humour should ultimately make good sense, not nonsense.

Problems to Avoid

Avoid underdeveloped categories. A classification or division essay is not a mechanical list; each category should contain enough specific details to make it clearly recognizable and interesting. To present each category or part, you may draw on the methods of development you already know, such as example, comparison and contrast, and definition. Try to use the same techniques in each category so that no one category or part of your essay seems underdeveloped or unclear.

Avoid indistinct categories. Each category should be a separate unit; there should be no overlap among categories. For example, in a classification of shirts by fabric, the inclusion of flannel with silk, nylon, and cotton is an overlap because flannel is a kind of cotton. Similarly, in a classification of soft drinks by flavour, to include sugar-free with cola, root beer, orange, grape, and so on, is misleading because sugar-free drinks come in many different flavours. In other words, make each category unique.

Avoid too few or too many categories. A classification essay should have at least three categories, avoiding the either–or dichotomy. On the other hand, too many categories give a short essay the appearance of a list rather than a discussion. Whatever the number, don't forget to use transitional devices for easy movement from category to category.

■ ESSAY TOPICS

Narrow and focus your subject by selecting an appropriate principle of division or classification. Some of the suggestions below may be appropriate for humourous essays ("The Three Best Breeds of Cats for Antisocial People"). For additional ideas, see the "Suggestions for Writing" section following the professional essays (pages 248 and 250).

1. Kinds of tools or equipment for a particular task in your field of study

2. First-year university students

3. Heroes in a particular field

4. Reasons people participate in some activity (or excuses for not participating)

5. Attitudes toward a current controversy

6. Kinds of popular tattoos

7. Specializations in your field of study

8. Approaches to studying a subject

9. Types of kinship groups in a particular culture

10. Dogs, cats, birds, or other pets

11. Popular kinds of movies, music, or video games (or types within a larger category: kinds of horror movie monsters or varieties of "heavy metal" music)

12. Diets, exercise, or stress-reduction programs (or their participants)

13. Types of medical training

14. Methods of accomplishing a task (ways to conduct an experiment, ways to raise funds for a cause)

15. Bosses or coworkers to avoid

16. Theories explaining "X" (the disappearance of the dinosaurs, for example)

Dr. Michael J. Ryan with the holotype skull of the Albertaceratops nesmoi, a horned dinosaur discovered in March 2007 in southern Alberta.

Photo Courtesy of Chad Kerychuck, Digital Dream Machine

A Topic Proposal for Your Essay

Selecting the right subject matter is important to every writer. To help you clarify your ideas and strengthen your commitment to your topic, here is a proposal sheet that asks you to describe some of your preliminary ideas about your subject before you begin drafting. Although your ideas may change as you write (they will almost certainly become more refined), thinking through your choice of topic now may help you avoid several false starts.

1. What is the subject of your essay? Will you write an essay of classification or division?

2. What principle of classification or division will you use? Why is this a useful or informative principle for your particular topic and readers?

3. Why are you interested in this topic? Do you have a personal or professional connection to the subject? State at least one reason for your choice of topic.

4. Is this a significant topic of interest to others? Why? Who specifically might find it interesting, informative, or entertaining?

5. List at least three categories you are considering for development in your essay.

6. What difficulties, if any, might arise from this topic during the drafting of your essay? For example, do you know enough about your topic to offer details that will make each of your categories clear and distinct to your readers?

■ Sample Student Essay

In the following essay, the student writer divided Canadian children's literature into three broad historical periods that correspond to the changes in attitudes toward childhood, gender, nationhood, and imagination.

THE HISTORY OF CHILDREN'S LITERATURE IN CANADA

1   Many Canadians know very little about Canadian children's books, other than the book which practically supports the economy of Prince Edward Island: Lucy Maud Montgomery's *Anne of Green Gables*. Literature written specifically for Canadian children developed in some of the same ways and at about the same times as in the rest of the Western world, but had to struggle with practical difficulties in publishing, and, for much of its history, against the prejudice that books published in England or France

Introduction: Establishing a reason for discussing the classification

---

were superior to local efforts. Canadian children's literature can be divided into three types, closely related to gender roles as well as historical periods. The eighteenth, nineteenth, and twentieth centuries show a growing variety, often based on a target audience of either boys or girls, in the treatment of common themes such as a child's relationship to the land, modelling of moral behaviour, and a child's place within the family, especially within an unorthodox family unit.

Principle of division for Canadian children's literature

2   Some of the earliest examples of what we would recognize as children's books were published in the late eighteenth century in Canada. These crude primers and other educational materials appear to have been aimed at young children, rather than adolescents, who presumably were reading adult books or adaptations of adult books, such as Defoe's adventure novel, *Robinson Crusoe* (if they even had access to such prized imports). Among the books written specifically for children, there was a preponderance of geographies. Some of the few books that were beginning to catch on to the new trend in England for delighting rather than instructing children, offered stories of famous Canadian explorers, in books such as *The Voyages and Distresses of Captain T. James, and Mr. Henry Ellis For the Discovery of a North-West Passage To the South Passages,* to spark the young Canadian's imagination and inspire him to further conquest of this new land. It was clear that most of these entertaining books were aimed at boys rather than girls, who were not expected to grow up to be active explorers, but domestic angels. Girls were thus given little domestic manuals along with their hornbooks and primers.

Era one: Late 18th-to-mid-19th-century books for children, initial focus on geography

3   The second period, which started roughly in the middle of the nineteenth century, saw more women authors, such as Catherine

Parr Traill, whose work focused not so much on the land, but on the maintenance of moral character. Although adventure books continued to be popular, tales that were directed toward girls proliferated in books and in new magazines published just for children. Tales for girls focused on domestic adventures and admonished naughty girls for disobedience, dishonesty, sloth and lack of interest, or even skill in domestic matters. When we look at her children's books today, Catherine Parr Traill's books seem primarily didactic, but to her contemporaries she was daring in that she softened up that didacticism in books of fairy tales, a choice that brought some disapproval from critics who were suspicious of any encouragement of "fancy" in children. Both boys and girls were supposed to grow up to be useful and highly moral, but these qualities were classified differently. Boys' usefulness was demonstrated in the great outdoors, girls' at home; boys' morality consisted of general integrity, bravery, and good citizenship, while girls' moral character had the added element of the unmentionable but vital womanly virtue. Canadian writers in the nineteenth century ensured their children had strong models of virtue to emulate, and clear models of unacceptable behaviour to reject.

Era two: 19th century and wider variety of narratives, especially moral instruction for girls

4   By the time they reached the twentieth century, some Canadian writers were acknowledging the reality that neither children nor their lives were necessarily ideal. The story of *Anne of Green Gables,* published at the beginning of the twentieth century in 1908, became a counter-model to the idealized girls in many girls' stories popular in the previous century. This absent-minded fantasizer who was hopeless at domestic tasks not only avoided a terrible end, but was rewarded by love and enthusiastic inclusion into her community. Her unorthodox family, consisting of a set of

Era three: 20th-21st centuries, unorthodox family units and child's place in them

elderly unmarried siblings, was also a departure, as it remained unorthodox till the end, while successfully and unexpectedly providing stability. Anne's story (which was continued in a series of books) anticipated a wider Western trend to examine the breakdown of earlier societal norms, particularly in the context of the family. This type of story, in which a child attempts to survive in and make sense of unusual family configurations, became particularly popular from the 1960s onward, sometimes in combination with some of the earlier literary themes, such as the connection with land. The books of Sarah Ellis and Susan Juby, for example, examine the lives of today's Canadian children, who must cope with divorced or absent parents, poverty and homelessness. This twin interest in unexpected family units that must survive a harsh environment is evident even in Monica Dickens' science fiction *Isis Trilogy*. In many of these stories, it is a young girl who is the focal point. Thanks to Anne Shirley of Green Gables, these girls are able to draw strength and respect from skills that are not limited to the domestic sphere.

5   Changing ideas about gender and national character in the adult world have had a profound effect on the literature written for Canadian children. Particular qualities, whether they include the courage to explore or the discipline to remain virtuous, may have increased or decreased in value over the years, and particular thematic concerns, whether they are a child's relationship to land or to family, may have changed in their approach, but some of the same qualities and same thematic concerns have been of interest from the eighteenth century to the present. The different types of children's literature also have something else in common: they have all tried to shape children's sense of self as well as their behaviour.

Conclusion: The importance of Canadian children's literature

WORKS CONSULTED

Demers, Patricia, ed. *From Instruction to Delight: An Anthology of Children's Literature to 1850*. Don Mills, Ont.: Oxford University Press, 2004.

Egoff, Sheila, comp. *Canadian Children's Books, 1799–1939: A Bibliographical Catalogue*. Vancouver: University of British Columbia Library, 1992.

Egoff, Sheila, and Judith Saltman. *The New Republic of Childhood: A Critical Guide to Canadian Children's Literature in English*. Toronto: Oxford University Press, 1990.

Montgomery, Lucy Maud. *Anne of Green Gables*. Ed. Mary Henley Rubio and Elizabeth Waterston. New York: Norton, 2007.

Reimer, Mavis, ed. *Home Words: Discourses of Children's Literature in Canada*. Waterloo, Ont.: Wilfred Laurier University Press, 2008.

Rowbotham, Judith. *Good Girls Make Good Wives: Guidance for Girls in Victorian Fiction*. Oxford: Blackwell, 1989.

Professional Essay: Classification*

■ In Defense of Graffiti

Alex Boyd

Canadian poet and essayist Alex Boyd has written for such publications as *The Globe and Mail* and *Quill & Quire*. Much of his work focuses on his varied experiences after leaving university. His essay "Warehouse" (1999) describes the reaction of an English graduate to the working-class community of warehouse workers, while "Paper Problems" (2001) compares his own experiences as a Chapters bookstore employee with George Orwell's encounters, sixty-three years before, with a philistine public. Boyd hosts the IV Lounge reading series in Toronto, and has recently published a book of poems entitled *Making Bones Walk* (2007).

1   There are two types of graffiti: one rambling, obscure, and sometimes offensive, the other more tangible, more political and accessible. Whatever negative associations people sometimes have of graffiti and whatever steps are taken against it are usually the result of a perception based on the first kind of graffiti. But I believe there are often enough examples of the second kind to demonstrate that graffiti deserves more consideration.

---

* To help you read this essay analytically, review pages 160–162.

If, after all, there is any value to it at all, then it deserves something more than automatic dismissal despite our comfortable and cherished notions of privacy and property.

2   Walking the streets of Toronto, I find it's simple enough to collect examples of fairly useless, or even damaging graffiti: stupid racist remarks, empty slogans, illegible signatures or comments like "Nick and Gloria sparkle." How excellent for Nick and Gloria. But the more overtly political and useful examples of graffiti are everywhere too. Here are some examples from the Toronto area:

> *Greed = Death*
>
> *Just because YOU said so?*
>
> *Fur is dead*
>
> *Creative survival*
>
> *The most common way people lose power is by thinking they don't have any*
>
> *Happiness can be yours forever! Order now!*
>
> *Peace, no religion*

3   In yet another category of Toronto graffiti are the cryptic yet interesting examples, like "Fix Signs," and in the category of trite but somehow warming comes "I Love You," placed at least a dozen times all over the downtown core this summer, as unconditional as they are blunt.

4   Anywhere attempts are made to smother freedom of speech, graffiti becomes an affordable, accessible method of communication. In El Salvador, graffiti takes the form of important and passionate social commentary:

> *We demand Freedom*
>
> *Today it's the turn of the victim*
>
> *The People first*
>
> *Respect for the rights of others is peace*

5   While living in Scotland, I noticed that a public debate had taken place entirely through graffiti. The first remark had been a confused, general statement about gay men (as opposed to pedophiles) sexually abusing children. Someone crossed out the remark and commented on the ignorance of the first person, and then the first person had returned to not only cross out the second person's comments but include a threatening remark as well. All the remarks were still legible, though, resulting in a permanent posted conversation that fairly obviously demonstrated that the first person was completely inflexible in his beliefs and would allow no dissent.

6   At Maeshowe, a Stone Age tomb in Scotland, there are examples of historical graffiti. In the twelfth century several groups of Norsemen broke into the tomb and left markings, some as simple as "Ingigerth is the most beautiful of all women," with the image of a slavering dog carved next to it. Another man stood on some shoulders or got a boost in order to write, "Tholfir Kolbeinsson carved these runes high up." Other runes explain the Viking's purpose, but the most startling thing is that the majority of examples, like the ones that I've provided, demonstrate how amazingly similar it is to modern graffiti. The simple fact that they've survived almost a thousand years gives them historical value and, therefore, legal protection, yet present attempts to make permanent statements are the acts of "vandals."

7   Some simply assume that everyone hates graffiti, and websites advertise cleaning services that fight those "vandals and their weapons of destruction—cans of spray paint and coloured markers." The use of the words "vandals," and "weapons" particularly struck me. My dictionary defines a vandal as someone who willfully damages or destroys things, especially beautiful or valuable ones (doesn't strike me as fair when applied to graffiti, which has the potential to be esthetically pleasing, and may cover a neutral or unused surface). The Vandals were a member of the Germanic peoples living south of the Baltic who plundered Gaul, Spain, and North Africa and even sacked Rome in AD 455, destroying many books and works of art. Again, not a very good fit with messages between citizens tucked away in alleys or emblazoned on corners.

8   As a culture we make little or no official effort to preserve or at least to photograph what these "vandals" have done with their "weapons" before whitewashing it. The obvious lessons being that something must survive in order to be called history, but also that we choose what survives, and are in the habit of being extremely shortsighted about it, or leaving it to luck, as demonstrated by Maeshowe.

9   Today graffiti isn't legal, so it becomes difficult to trace the whereabouts and details of all those who do it, but I suspect most graffiti is done by young people, whether they call themselves artists or not. I say this not just because it is rebellious but also because young people don't yet have the same kind of investment in society, and have a different perspective, a slightly distanced position. Not only are they still defining an identity and searching for a role, they may be more capable on some level of recognizing a basic unfairness: that a message with money behind it is called advertising while a public one is mere graffiti.

10   The message of most graffiti may not be about struggle, but its existence does involve an ongoing struggle between those who have and those who don't. It's not the wealthiest people who leave graffiti. It's more likely to be someone young, someone poor, or someone who is poor because they are young. Those of us who are most opposed to it are likely those of us who can afford to own at least a home if not other buildings, and take offence to anyone who would stain it with their own personal message. Yes, it can be an unwelcome intrusion on private property, but it's possibly the voice of someone who may never own his or her own house, business or anything else, which only leaves them the option of needling, in some small way, those who have money and power. This is perhaps the best reason for someone to call cans of spray paint weapons—they create the potential for a permanent, articulate voice for the disadvantaged. If it allows those who have less to be articulate, and critical of those who have more, naturally anyone in the better position will see it as a "weapon."

11   I don't believe I would want to live in a world where every inch of space cries out for my attention, (regardless of whether they were ads or private thoughts). But I also encourage everyone to be open to reading graffiti and to think of it as something that, like poetry, puts a finger on the real and honest pulse of the world. There is little financial profit in something like poetry, but there is even less in graffiti (in fact there is the risk of arrest, and it's fair to assume a belief in the importance of the statement to take such a risk. I have noticed that the more meaningful messages are concise, to conserve time in writing it, and the more useless ones are to be found all over alleys and in more hidden locations). This kind of logical assumption in the basic sincerity of graffiti has led corporations to try and co-opt it in advertising campaigns giving the impression, as long as you don't think about it too hard, that the word on the street

favours whatever corporation uses it. But ultimately, this has to be rejected. Graffiti is not a contrived or manufactured thing designed to make money. And for that reason alone, we should be willing to watch and read.

Questions on Content, Structure, and Style

1. Why does Boyd choose to develop his argument by using classification? What reaction do you think Boyd wants to evoke from his reading audience?

2. Where is Boyd's thesis statement? Can you trace how clearly it is followed in the rest of the essay?

3. Identify Boyd's categories and principle of classification. What do these categories have in common?

4. Why does Boyd give examples of items that belong to each category? Does this strengthen his essay? Why or why not?

5. Of the categories of graffiti discussed in the essay, which one is most effectively developed? List some examples of details.

6. Consider Boyd's use of historical examples as he talks about graffiti. What is his purpose in drawing these comparisons?

7. How does Boyd's word choice affect his tone? Would it be possible to make the same argument about this subject from a less serious or informative standpoint? From a more serious or informative standpoint? Why or why not?

8. What does Boyd's title contribute to his tone and his readers' understanding of his classifying principle?

9. Evaluate Boyd's conclusion. Is it effective? What commonly used concluding strategies can you see here?

10. What other categories of graffiti might you add to this essay? What items could you include under these new classifications?

Suggestions for Writing

Try using Alex Boyd's "In Defense of Graffiti" as a stepping stone to your writing. To parallel Boyd's criticisms of uncritical condemnation of graffiti, think about kinds of popular or even underground culture that you feel are unappreciated. Consider, for example, kinds of music that are only available on Internet sites. Or specialized fanzines. Or comedy routines too outrageous for regular television or stage shows. Or consider the kinds of art that challenge usual definitions of what "good" art is, for example, a cow's carcass divided into cross sections and separated by Plexiglas; a completely white canvas. Or even consider definitions of art itself. Your essay might have humorous examples or commentaries, like Boyd's, or be quite serious, as you defend your own classifications of art.

Vocabulary

rambling (1)	trite (3)	slavering (6)
tangible (1)	inflexible (5)	needling (10)
illegible (2)	dissent (5)	contrived (11)

Professional Essay: Division*

■ What I have Lived for

Bertrand Russell

Bertrand Russell was one of the twentieth century's foremost logicians, but was also known for his contributions to a great diversity of fields, such as philosophy, religious studies, and social criticism. The aristocratic but radical Russell led a controversial life, during which he was married several times, and was even imprisoned (once in 1918, for his protests against the First World War, and once in 1961, for his antinuclear protests). His antiwar stance also led to his dismissal from prestigious institutions such as Trinity College, Cambridge, as well as City College, New York. But Russell won an Order of Merit in 1949 and a Nobel Prize for literature in 1950. He died in 1970 at the age of 97, a revered public figure till the end.

1   Three passions, simple but overwhelmingly strong, have governed my life: the longing for love, the search for knowledge, and unbearable pity for the sufferings of mankind. These passions, like great winds, have blown me hither and thither, in a wayward course, over a deep ocean of anguish, reaching to the very verge of despair.

2   I have sought love, first, because it brings ecstasy—ecstasy so great that I would often have sacrificed the rest of life for a few hours of this joy. I have sought it, next, because it relieves loneliness—that terrible loneliness in which one shivering consciousness looks over the rim of the world into the cold unfathomable lifeless abyss. I have sought it, finally, because in the union of love I have seen, in a mystic miniature, the prefiguring vision of the heaven that saints and poets have imagined. This is what I sought, and though it might seem too good for human life, this is what—at last—I have found.

3   With equal passion I have sought knowledge. I have wished to understand the hearts of men. I have wished to know why the stars shine. And I have tried to apprehend the Pythagorean power by which number holds sway above the flux. A little of this, but not much, I have achieved.

4   Love and knowledge, so far as they were possible, led upward toward the heavens. But always pity brought me back to earth. Echoes of cries of pain reverberate in my heart. Children in famine, victims tortured by oppressors, helpless old people a hated burden to their sons, and the whole world of loneliness, poverty, and pain make a mockery of what human life should be. I long to alleviate the evil, but I cannot, and I too suffer.

5   This has been my life. I have found it worth living, and would gladly live it again if the chance were offered me.

Questions on Content, Structure, and Style

1. How does this essay illustrate division rather than classification?

2. What is Russell's purpose in writing this essay? What response to his subject matter is he trying to produce in his readers?

3. How does Russell organize the parts of his division?

4. For what audience is Russell writing? How did an awareness of his audience influence his explanations?

---

* To help you read this essay analytically, review pages 160–162.

5. As a reader, are you confident that Russell has accounted for all the parts in the subject of his division? If so, what gives you this sense of confidence? If not, what else could Russell have added?

6. In his explanation of each passion, Russell uses purely personal response. Why does he do so?

7. How does Russell employ comparison and cause-and-effect explanations to clarify his subject and inform his readers?

8. What does Russell's word choice reveal about his attitude toward his own life? Cite some examples of Russell's vivid language and strong imagery that transform this essay of division into a poetic statement.

9. What is one emotion that all his passions have in common?

10. Evaluate Russell's conclusion. Does it provide an ending that is consistent with Russell's tone and point of view throughout the essay? Is it adequately developed? Why or why not?

Suggestions for Writing

Use Bertrand Russell's essay "What I Have Lived For" as a stepping stone to your essay. How would you define and divide your own passions in life? Or, if you prefer, think about your goals in life. Who do you want to be? What do you want to achieve in your life? Do you focus mostly on professional goals or on personal ones? Or write an essay that analyzes how you have lived your life so far. Are your passions the same as Russell's? Can you divide your life into similar categories? Try to create a strong connection with your audience with vivid details and word choice.

Vocabulary

wayward (1)	abyss (2)	Pythagorean (3)
anguish (1)	mystic (2)	flux (3)
verge (1)	prefiguring (2)	reverberate (4)
ecstasy (2)	apprehend (3)	alleviate (4)
unfathomable (2)		

▪ A REVISION WORKSHEET

As you write your rough drafts, consult Chapter 5 for guidance through the revision process. In addition, here are a few questions to ask yourself as you revise your classification essay:

1. Is the purpose of the essay clear to the reader?

2. Is the principle of classification or division maintained consistently throughout the essay?

3. If the essay presents a formal division or classification, has the subject been narrowed so that all the parts of the subject are accounted for?

4. If the essay presents an informal or humorous division or classification, does the paper nevertheless make a significant or entertaining point?

5. Is each category developed with enough specific detail? Where might more details be effectively added?

6. Is each class distinct, with no overlap among categories?

7. Is the essay organized logically and coherently with smooth transitions between the discussions of the categories?

After you've revised your essay extensively, you might exchange rough drafts with a classmate and answer these questions for each other, making specific suggestions for improvement wherever appropriate. (For advice on productive participation in classroom workshops, see pages 102–104.)

Reviewing Your Progress

After you have completed your essay developed by classification or division, take a moment to measure your progress as a writer by responding to the following questions. Such analysis will help you recognize growth in your writing skills and may enable you to identify areas that are still problematic.

1. What is the best feature of your essay? Why?

2. Which category do you think is the clearest or most persuasive in your essay? Why does that one stand above the others?

3. What part of your essay gave you the most trouble? How did you overcome the problem?

4. If you had more time to work on this essay, what would receive additional attention? Why?

5. What did you learn about your topic from writing this essay? About yourself as a writer?

■ Strategy Six: Development by Causal Analysis

Causal analysis explains the cause-and-effect relationship between two (or more) elements. When you discuss the condition producing something, you are analyzing *cause;* when you discuss the result produced by something, you are analyzing *effect.* To find examples of causal analysis, you need only look around you. If your car stops running on the way to class, for example, you may discover the cause was an empty gas tank. On campus, in your political science class, you may study the causes of the Liberal Party's defeat in 2004; in your economics class, the effects of teenage spending on the cosmetics market; and in your biology class, both the causes and effects of heart disease. Over dinner you may discuss the effects of some crisis in the Middle East on Canadian foreign policy, and, as you drift to sleep, you may ponder the effects of your studying—or *not* studying—for your math test tomorrow.

To express it most simply, *cause* asks:

Why did "X" happen?

Or why does "X" happen?

Or why will "X" happen?

Effect, on the other hand, asks:

What did "Y" produce?

Or what does "Y" produce?

Or what will "Y" produce?

Some essays of causal analysis focus primarily on the cause(s) of something; others mainly analyze the effect(s); still others discuss both causes and effects. If, for example, you wanted to concentrate on the major causes of Canada's involvement in the First World War, you might begin by briefly describing the effects of the assassination of Archduke Franz Ferdinand on the political stability of Europe and explaining the connection between Canada and England, then devote your thesis and the rest of your essay to analyzing the major causes, perhaps allotting one major section (or one paragraph, depending on the complexity of the reasons) to each cause. Conversely, an effect paper might briefly note the causes of the war and then detail the most important effects. An essay covering both the causes and effects of something often demands a longer paper so that each part will be clear. (Your assignment will frequently indicate which kind of causal analysis to write. However, if the choice is yours, let your interest in the subject be your guide.)

Developing Your Essay

Whether you are writing an essay that primarily discusses either causes or effects, or one that focuses on both, you should follow these rules:

Present a reasonable thesis statement. If your thesis makes dogmatic, unsupportable claims ("The decreasing birth rate will result in a less powerful international presence for Canada") or overly broad assertions ("Peer pressure causes alcoholism among students"), you won't convince your reader. Limit or qualify your thesis whenever necessary by using such phrases as "may be," "a contributing factor," "one of the main reasons," "two important factors," and so on ("Peer pressure is *one of the major causes* of alcoholism among students").

Limit your essay to a discussion of recent major causes or effects. In a short paper you generally don't have space to discuss minor or remote causes or effects. If, for example, you analyzed your car accident, you might decide that the three major causes were defective brakes, a hidden yield sign, and bad weather. A minor, or remote, cause might include being slightly tired because of less-than-usual sleep, less sleep because of staying out late the night before, staying out late because of an out-of-town visitor, and so on—back to the womb. In some cases you may want to mention a few of the indirect causes or effects, but do be reasonable. Concentrate on the most immediate, most important factors. Often, a writer of a 500-to-800-word essay will discuss no more than two, three, or four major causes or effects of something; trying to cover more frequently results in an underdeveloped essay that is not convincing.

Organize your essay clearly. Organization of your causal analysis essay will vary, of course, depending on whether you are focusing on the causes of something or the effects, or both. To avoid becoming tangled in causes and effects, you might try sketching out a drawing of your thesis and essay map before you begin your first draft. Here, for instance, are a couple of sketches for essays you might write on your recent traffic accident:

Thesis Emphasizing the Causes:

Cause (defective brakes)
Cause (hidden yield sign)   produced   Effect (my car accident)
Cause (bad weather)

Thesis Emphasizing the Effects:

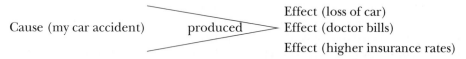

                                        Effect (loss of car)
Cause (my car accident)   produced   Effect (doctor bills)
                                        Effect (higher insurance rates)

Sometimes you may discover that you can't isolate "the three main causes/effects of 'X'"; some essays do, in fact, demand a narrative explaining a chain reaction of causes and effects. For example, a paper on the development of labour unions in Canada might show how one unjust labour practice or restriction after another led to solidarity and activism in workers. In this kind of causal analysis essay, be careful to limit your subject so that you'll have the space necessary to show your readers how each step in the chain led to the next. Here's a sketch of a slightly different car-accident paper presented in a narrative or chain-reaction format:

Cause ⎯⎯⎯→ 1st Effect ⎯*causes*→ 2nd Effect ⎯*causes*→ 3rd Effect
(bad weather)   (wet brakes)   (car accident)   (doctor bills)

Sometimes the plan for organizing your causal analysis paper will be suggested by your subject matter; often, however, you'll have to devote some of your prewriting time to deciding, first, whether you want to emphasize causes or effects and, then, in what arrangement you will present your analysis.

Convince your reader that a causal relationship exists by showing how the relationship works. Let's suppose you are writing an essay in which you want to discuss the three major changes you've undergone since coming to university. Don't just state the changes and describe them; your job is to show the reader how university has *brought about* these changes. If, for instance, your study habits have improved, you must show the reader how the academic demands of your university courses caused you to change your habits; a simple description of your new study techniques is not enough. Remember that a causal analysis essay should stress *how* (and sometimes *why*) "X" caused "Y," rather than merely describing "Y" as it now exists.

Problems to Avoid

Don't oversimplify by assigning one all-encompassing cause to some effect. Most complex subjects have more than one cause (or effect), so make your analysis as complete and objective as you can, especially when dealing with your own problems or beliefs. For example, was that car accident really caused only by the bad weather—or also because of your careless-ness? Did your friend do poorly in astronomy class only because the instructor didn't like her? Before judging a situation too quickly, investigate your own biases. Then provide a thoughtful, thorough analysis, effectively organized to convince your readers of the validity of your viewpoint.

Avoid the *post hoc* fallacy. This error in logic (from the Latin phrase *post hoc, ergo propter hoc,* meaning "after this, therefore because of this") results when we mistake a temporal con-nection for a causal relationship—or in other words, when we assume that because one event follows another in time, the first event caused the second. Most of our superstitions are *post hoc* fallacies; we now realize that bad luck after walking under a ladder is a matter of coincidence, not cause and effect. The *post hoc* fallacy provided the basis for a rather pop-ular joke in the debates of the 1960s over decriminalizing marijuana. Those against argued that marijuana led to heroin because most users of the hard drug had first smoked the weed. The proponents retorted that milk, then, was the real culprit, because both marijuana and heroin users had drunk milk as babies. The point is this: in any causal analysis, you must be able to offer proof or reasoned logic to show that one event *caused* another, not just that it preceded it in time.

Avoid circular logic. Often causal essays seem to chase their own tails when they include such circular statements as "There aren't enough parking spaces for students on campus because there are too many cars." Such a statement merely presents a second half that restates what is already implied in the first half. A revision might say, "There aren't enough parking spaces for students on campus because the parking permits are not distributed fairly." This kind of assertion can be argued specifically and effectively; the other is a dead end.

■ ESSAY TOPICS

The following subjects may be developed into essays emphasizing cause or effect, or both. "Suggestions for Writing" section following the pro-fessional essay (page 267).

1. A pet peeve or bad habit
2. A change of mind about some important issue or belief
3. An accident, illness, or misadventure
4. A political action (campus, local, state, national), historical event, or social movement (for inspiration, read Vaclav Havel's "The Divine Revolution")
5. A popular cultural trend (reality television programs)
6. An important idea, event, or discovery in your field of study
7. A radical change in your appearance
8. A superstition or irrational fear
9. The best (or worst) advice you ever gave, followed, or rejected
10. An important decision or choice

11. An act of heroism or sacrifice

12. Racism or sexism or some other kind of discrimination or prejudice

13. A disappointment or a success

14. A society's attitudes toward war

15. Educational trends

16. A piece of visual art promoting a particular cause or point of view (Consider, for example, the Second World War poster that follows. What does the text, a quote from Colonel John McCrae's poem "In Flanders Fields," indicate about the cultural background of the viewers? What effect would this text have on those viewers? What effects would the image of the male figure, holding a torch to the sky, have on both its male and female viewers? What specific elements in this picture produce these effects? What effect does this image have on viewers today? (If you prefer, select another visual image reproduced in this text, such as *The Letter* [page 26], or *Death of A Young Son by Drowning* [page 432], or *Algonquin Park—Fox and Christmas Tree* [page 323], and analyze its major effects on the viewer.)

The Torch, *Second World War poster*

A Topic Proposal for Your Essay

Selecting the right subject matter is important to every writer. To help you clarify your ideas and strengthen your commitment to your topic, here is a proposal sheet that asks you to describe some of your preliminary ideas about your subject before you begin drafting. Although your ideas may change as you write (they will almost certainly become more refined), thinking through your choice of topic now may help you avoid several false starts.

1. What is the subject and purpose of your causal analysis essay? Is this subject appropriately narrowed and focused for a discussion of major causes and/or effects?

2. Will you develop your essay to emphasize primarily the effects or the causes of your topic? Or is a causal chain the most appropriate method of development?

3. Why are you interested in this topic? Do you have a personal or professional connection to the subject? State at least one reason for your choice of topic.

4. Is this a significant topic of interest to others? Why? Who specifically might find it interesting, informative, or entertaining?

5. List at least two major causes and/or effects that you might develop in the discussion of your topic.

6. What difficulties, if any, might arise during your drafting on this topic? For example, how might you convince a skeptical reader that your causal relationship is not merely a temporal one?

■ Sample Student Essay

In the following essay, a student explains why working in a local motel damaged her self-esteem, despite her attempts to do a good job. Note that the writer uses many vivid examples and specific details to show the reader how she was treated and, consequently, how such treatment made her feel.

IT'S SIMPLY NOT WORTH IT

Introduction: Her job as a motel maid

Thesis: No appreciation, low pay, disgusting tasks (causes) produce damaged self-esteem and action (effects)

1　　It's hard to find a job these days, and with our country's unemployment rate reaching as high as 5 percent, most people feel obligated to "take what they can get." But after working as a maid at a local motel for almost a year and a half, I decided no job is worth keeping if it causes a person to doubt his or her worth. My hard work rarely received recognition or appreciation, I was underpaid, and I was required to perform some of the most

---

disgusting cleaning tasks imaginable. These factors caused me to devalue myself as a person and ultimately motivated me to return to school in hope of regaining my self-respect.

2   It may be obvious to say, but I believe that when a maid's hours of meticulous cleaning are met only with harsh words and complaints, she begins to lose her sense of self-esteem. I recall the care I took in making the motel's beds, imagining them as globs of clay and moulding them into impeccable pieces of art. I would teeter from one side of a bed to the other, over and over again, until I smoothed out every intruding wrinkle or tuck. And the mirrors—I would vigorously massage the glass, erasing any toothpaste splotches or oil smudges that might draw my customer's disapproval. I would scrutinize the mirror first from the left side, then I'd move to the right side, once more to the left until every possible angle ensured an unclouded reflection. And so my efforts went, room after room. But, without fail, each day more than one customer would approach me, not with praise for my tidy beds or spotless mirrors, but with nitpicking complaints that undermined my efforts: "Young lady, I just checked into room 143 and it only has one ashtray. Surely for $69.95 a night you people can afford more ashtrays in the rooms."

Cause one: Lack of appreciation

3   If it wasn't a guest complaining about ashtrays, it was an impatient customer demanding extra towels or a fussy stay-over insisting his room be cleaned by the time he returned from breakfast at 8:00 a.m. "Can't you come to work early to do it?" he would urge thoughtlessly. Day after day, my spotless rooms went unnoticed, with no spoken rewards for my efforts from either guests or management. Eventually, the ruthless complaints and thankless work began wearing me down. In my mind, I became a servant undeserving of gratitude.

Cause two: Low pay

4   The lack of spoken rewards was compounded by the lack of financial rewards. The $5.50 per hour appraisal of my worth was simply not enough to support my financial needs or my self-esteem. The measly $2.75 I earned for cleaning one room took a lot of rooms to add up, and by the end of the month I was barely able to pay my bills and buy some food. (My mainstay became generic sixty-two-cent macaroni and cheese dinners.) Because the flow of travellers kept the motel full for only a few months of the year, during some weeks I could only work half time, making a mere $440.00 a month. As a result, one month I was forced to request an extension on my rent payment. Unsympathetically, my landlord threatened to evict me if I didn't pay. Embarrassed, yet desperate, I went to a friend and borrowed money. I felt uneasy and awkward and regretted having to beg a friend for money. I felt like a mooch and a bum; I felt degraded. And the constant reminder from management that there were hundreds of people standing in line who would be more than willing to work for $5.50 an hour only aided in demeaning me further.

Cause three: Repulsive duties

5   In addition to the thankless work and the inadequate salary, I was required to clean some of the most sickening messes. Frequently, conventions for high-school clubs booked the motel. Once I opened the door of a conventioneer's room one morning and almost gagged at the odour. I immediately beheld a trail of vomit that began at the bedside and ended just short of the bathroom door. At that moment I cursed the inventor of shag carpet, for I knew it would take hours to comb this mess out of the fibres. On another day I spent thirty minutes dislodging the bed linen from the toilet where it had been stuffed. And I spent what seemed like hours removing from one of my spotless mirrors the lipstick-drawn message that read, " Maple Leafs are number one." But these inconsiderate acts were relaying another message, a message I took personally: "Lady, you're not worth the consideration—you're a maid and you're not worth respecting."

6   I've never been afraid to work hard or do jobs that weren't particularly "fun." But the line must be drawn when a person's view of herself becomes clouded with feelings of worthlessness. The thankless efforts, the inadequate wage, and the disgusting work were just parts of a total message that degraded my character and caused me to question my worth. Therefore, I felt compelled to leave this demeaning job in search of a way to rebuild my self-confidence. Returning to school has done just that for me. As my teachers and fellow students take time to listen to my ideas and compliment my responses, I feel once again like a vital, valued, and worthwhile person. I feel human once more.

Conclusion: Review of the problem and a brief explanation of the solution she chose

Professional Essay*

■ Wheels: The Car as a Cultural Driving Force

Pierre Berton

Well-known broadcaster and writer, Pierre Berton, was born in Dawson City, Yukon, in 1920. As a young man, he worked in the Klondike mines, but quickly found his métier as a journalist while working on the student newspaper, the *Ubyssey,* as a student at the University of British Columbia. Although he had early success as one of the youngest newspaper editors in Canada, the Second World War interrupted his career, and he trained in the military for several years. After the war, he was able to pick up his journalism career. Prominent posts as the managing editor of *Maclean's* from 1947, associate editor of *The Toronto Star* from 1958, and host of his own television program, *The Pierre Berton Show,* from 1962 to 1973 made him a household name in Canada. He wrote over 50 books and received numerous awards for his creative nonfiction on life in Canada.

1   The astonishing thing about the automobile is that there are people still living who can remember a time when there weren't any. I am not one; but I can remember a

---

* To help you read this essay analytically, review pages 160–162.

place where at one time there were scarcely any. The northern community in which I was raised boasted three livery stables and a blacksmith shop, but in the winter only one motor car was to be seen on the roads. It was the milkman's Model-T Ford and I remember him having to hand-crank it at every stop.

2   In the summer a few more cars took to the gravel streets. As befitted his station, Judge Macaulay had the poshest automobile in town, a black Studebaker with fabric top known then as a "tour car." That was a great word in the 1920s. Few of us owned a car but we all played the popular Parker card game, *Touring.*

3   Of course we lived in a backwater. For in 1926—that was the first year I can remember him squatting in Billy Bigg's blacksmith shop watching him hammer horseshoes into shape—the world beyond the Yukon had gone car crazy. We did not know it, but the greatest social transformation in history was under way.

4   We realize now that, more than any other invention, the automobile has changed our lives. It has affected the way we think, the way we act, the way we talk. It has up-ended the class system, sounded the death knell of Main Street, and played hell with the Lord's Day. As a precursor of the sexual revolution, it has been as important as the Pill. It has telescoped time and squeezed geography. It is both our slave and our master. For even as it has liberated us, it has made us its prisoner.

5   There was a time when transportation was the prerogative of the rich. Before the automobile arrived, the carriage, the coach-and-four, the private railway car, and the hansom cab were accepted modes of travel, but only for the well-to-do. We are reminded of that era today when the Governor General rides to Parliament in an open landau.

6   The motor car changed that. It has been the great leveller in terms of social distance as well as physical grace. The factory worker, sensing the surge of power under the gas pedal of his truck, feels himself the equal of the businessman in his Dodge convertible. As Marshall McLuhan pointed out, it is the pedestrian who has become a second-class citizen.

7   The car gave the masses geographical mobility; and that meant social mobility, for the ability to choose is a concomitant of class. With the invention of the automobile, the poor could escape the confines of city tenements and narrow villages. In fact, the development of new mass-production techniques—the technique of Henry Ford— blurred caste distinctions, creating in North America a vast middle class, most of whom owned cars.

8   The car brought to a settled world a glorious spontaneity that was not possible in the age of the horse and the railroad. Horses required long rest periods; they could not manage steep inclines without assistance. Railroads ran on schedule to predetermined destinations. But with the coming of the automobile, car owners could leap into their vehicles on impulse and take off in any direction. This ability to control time and the direction of travel marked for millions the beginning of a new freedom. It is also the reason why most wage earners today get a paid vacation.

9   With this independence came privacy. Alone in their cars people can sing, shout, talk to themselves, or quietly plan their day, free from importuning associates or carping relatives. This human desire to be alone is, I believe, the chief reason why the idea of the car pool has never really taken hold in Canada. The highways are crowded with five- and six-passenger automobiles, most carrying only a driver.

10   As examples of the way the motor car has affected our lives, one need only look at such basics as health care, religion, and education. The ambulance has brought swift

medical aid to everyone; the bus has done away with the little red schoolhouse; and rural Canada is littered with boarded-up churches because the car, which made it possible to travel longer distances to worship, also may have made it too attractive to skip worship in favour of a Sunday drive.

11   Since the early days of the Tin Lizzie we have talked the language of cars. Just as words and phrases such as *free wheeling, green light, fast lane, going like sixty* and *step on it* indicate the swifter pace of the automobile era, so words like *car hop, motel, passion pit* and *drive-in* suggest a totally different lifestyle.

12   Urban sprawl, urban rot, and urban renewal all spring out of the motor car era and hint at the problems created by the suburban explosion, perhaps the single most important demographic change wrought by the automobile. The car made possible the escape of Shelley's "smoky populous cities"; and from the very outset this was seen as its greatest liberating force.

13   As a 1908 advertisement for the Sears motor car put it: "The Sears is the car for the businessman who has tired of home life in a congested neighbourhood and yearns for a cottage in the suburb for his family." Such blandishments were remarkably prescient, even though reality does not quite mesh with the fantasy. The countryside [of the 1990s] is no facsimile of that of the century's first decade. One problem was that the people who escaped from the city were determined to bring the city with them.

14   It has been determined that, apart from vacations, the trip to work is the longest regular journey most car owners are prepared to make. With the growth of superhighways and faster cars, that trip lengthened in distance but not in time. Business followed the commuters with such amenities as shops, theatres, and department stores. The result was the suburban shopping centre.

15   It was the shopping centre that helped squeeze out that great Canadian institution, Eaton's catalogue. It sucked the life blood from the main streets of thousands of small towns. It turned the cores of such cities as Edmonton into virtual population deserts after work hours. It changed shopping habits and shopping hours. It encouraged the growth of retail chains, dooming individual merchant enterprise and contributing to the depersonalization and the conformity of the nation.

16   None of this, of course, could have been envisaged in 1900 when the automotive age can be said to have begun. That was the year when the early self-propelled vehicles began to look less like motorized buggies and more like motor cars, with a proper steering wheel instead of a tiller, a hood and a side door, and a speed that could reach a terrifying 40 miles an hour.

17   The universal phrase "get a horse!" suggests the derision in which early automobiles were held. In 1900, the horse was the pivot around which a vast industry revolved, an industry doomed to oblivion within 20 years. There were at least 16 million horses in the United States, perhaps two million in Canada. Harness shops and carriage factories ran full blast. Thousands of wheelwrights and blacksmiths depended on the horse for their livelihood. An entire industry thrived on nails manufactured for their horseshoes. Hay was one of the biggest cash crops. Every town had its livery stable, hitching post, and horse trough.

18   Today we think of pollution in terms of automobile exhaust. We forget that in the city of Toronto, in 1890, tons of manure had to be swept off the streets every day. The stench of urine and the clouds of flies rising from the roadway plagued pedestrians and drivers alike. Women crossing the stinking wooden cobbles at Yonge and College

streets were forced to raise their skirts and expose their ankles to prevent lumps of dung from sticking to their hems.

19   Nor is the traffic jam unique to our era. Photographs of Manhattan in the last century show traffic brought to a standstill by trams, cars, drays, carriages, and buggies.

20   As was the carriage, the early motor car was a toy for the wealthy, nothing more. After the turn of the century, John Craig Eaton of the Toronto department store family acquired a Wilton. Billy Cochrane, the famous Alberta rancher, bought a Locomobile. Automobile owners were considered eccentric and their cars examples of what many considered "conspicuous waste" (Thorstein Veblen had just coined the phrase). In 1906, Woodrow Wilson, then president of Princeton University, termed the motor car "a picture of arrogant wealth" and announced that "nothing has spread a socialist feeling more than the use of the automobile." Only a minority saw the automobile as a boon. Generally, it was reviled.

21   Like many later 20th-century institutions—movies, radio, television—the motor car was seen initially as a symbol of the sickness of contemporary society. In his book *The Condition of England,* published in 1909, C.P.C. Masterman wrote that "wandering machines, travelling at an incredible rate of speed, scramble and smash along all the rural ways. You can see evidence of their activity in the dust-laden hedges of the south country road, a gray, mud colour, with no evidence of green; in the ruined cottage gardens of the south country villages." The motor car, in short, was destroying the very countryside it also made available to the urbanites.

22   To the Canadian farmer, the car was also an anathema. It scared livestock and killed poultry. "Is it not time something was done to stop the automobile business?" the Newcastle, Ont., *Independent* asked in 1904. "They are becoming such a curse to the country that we cannot stand it. . . ."

23   If some saw the car as the wrecker of rural life, others saw it as a means of bringing the joys of the countryside to city dwellers. But it was one thing to extol those joys and quite another to enjoy them in the early automobile. The roads were almost impassable—a tangle of ruts and mudholes that sucked cars down to their axles. Signposts did not exist. Even towns could not be identified: the villagers knew where *they* lived. Local post offices bore the sign Post Office with no other identification. The treadless tires blew easily and often (they were rarely good for more than 3,000 miles), while changing one was a nightmare. A rear end projecting from beneath a hood on a country lane was a typical spectacle in pre-World War I days. Engines failed so often that one popular song of the era was "Get Out and Get Under."

24   The early motor car was also a repair shop on wheels. One store sold an automobile repair kit weighing 18 pounds. Driving was an experience akin to mountain climbing. The Damascus Hatchet, a patented device, was advertised, with enormous optimism, as follows: "When the wheel drops out of sight in the mud, get out the Damascus, cut a pole for a lever, right things up, and then on your way again."

25   Touring even required special clothing—linen duster, cap, and goggles for men; and for women, long skirts, sleeves fastened at the wrist with elastic bands, motor coats, and turbans or wide-brimmed hats tied under the chin.

26   Of course women were expected to be mere passengers. It was believed that they could never act with speed in an emergency or muster the strength to push in a clutch or struggle with a gear shift. These myths were shattered in 1909 when Alice Huyler Ramsay drove across the continent in a green Maxwell, without male help.

27   Such ocean-to-ocean trips marked the beginning of the end of the era of the motor car as a toy. Soon it was to become as essential as the telephone. Its change in stature was rapid and complete by the 1920s, thanks to a succession of ingenious devices that transformed what was essentially a motor-driven buggy into the family car of the mid-century. In 1911 the Dunlop company developed the anti-skid tire; within three years the electric self-starter was an option, signalling the ultimate demise of the hand crank. The all-steel body also arrived in 1911, a forerunner to the closed car of the early 1920s, "a power-driven room on wheels—storm proof, lockable . . . its windows (closed) against dust or rain." And in 1914, the introduction of the spare wheel eliminated the ghastly business of tire repairing.

28   But the greatest revolution was Henry Ford's introduction, in 1908, of the cheap car—the famous Model-T—followed by the company's development in 1914 of the assembly line. The affordable car had arrived. In 1908, a Model-T runabout cost about $825. By 1916, the Ford assembly line was turning out the same vehicle for $345.

29   The assembly line dealt a lethal blow to the old concept of craftsmanship based on long apprenticeship. Young, unskilled men with no previous training could master the simple techniques in a few weeks. To quote a pair of contemporary social observers: "As to machinists, old-time, all-round men, perish the thought. The Ford Motor Company has no use for experience, in the working ranks, anyway. It desires and prefers machine tool operators who have nothing to unlearn, who have no theories of perfect surface speeds for metal finishing, and who will simply do what they are told to do, over and over again, from bell-time to bell-time."

30   Individuality gave way to conformity with results that none could have foreseen. Since experience was not a precondition, immigrants and other unemployables soon found work on the assembly line—and that changed the demographic make-up of the continent. But the deadly monotony of the line (more easily endured by some than others) also required a much better wage rate and a shorter working day. Ford's $5, eight-hour day brought about the dominance of the middle class.

31   Again, because work was now seen to be boring and unfulfilling, mass production techniques—lampooned in Chaplin's movie, *Modern Times*—brought the Protestant work ethic into disrepute. Since work was no longer satisfying, leisure took on a new importance, aided and abetted by the shorter work week. People began to live for their off-hours.

32   Mass production was also responsible for the youth cult that has been a feature of North American life in our era. Unskilled 19-year-olds were quicker on the assembly line than their fathers and therefore more valued. As the craftsmen of one generation lost status to the blue-collar workers of the next, respect for age and parental authority began to decline. As the sociologist James J. Fink has pointed out, "maleness" was also to suffer with the slow realization that women could fill any job on the line as easily as a man. Mere strength was no longer a criterion.

33   As the 1920s dawned, it became clear that the horse had become the toy and the automobile the necessity. Robert and Helen Lynd, two sociologists who wrote a study on an American community they called Middletown, came up with some interesting revelations about the motor car. Families, they found, were mortgaging their homes to buy one—and most were buying on time payments. The automobile industry had helped launch the revolution in credit that marks this century.

34   "We'd rather do without clothes than give up the car," a mother of nine told the Lynds. "I'll go without food before I'll give up the car," said another. Pursuing their research, the Lynds asked people in rundown homes: "Do you have a bathtub? Do you own a car?" Of 26 persons questioned, who had no bathtubs, 21 owned a car. As one woman is said to have remarked, "you can't go to town in a bathtub."

35   The car, the Lynds concluded, had revolutionized the concept of leisure. The Sunday stroll, once a feature of the Lord's Day, was abandoned, replaced by the Sunday drive. And the car was the main device holding the family together. One mother declared, "I never feel as close to my family as when we are all together in the car."

36   The idea of a summer vacation was beginning to take hold because of the automobile. In the 1890s people worked the year round, "never took a holiday," as some boasted. But, by the 1920s, a two-week vacation had become a standard among the business class. The blue-collar workers had yet to receive that status but the rise of unionism in the automobile plants made it simply a matter of time.

37   The car was a perfect symbol for a restless decade, the quintessential artifact of the Roaring Twenties whose hallmarks were speed, sleekness, and glamour. The music was fast and the girls, it was claimed, were faster. So were the cars. The Tin Lizzie had become a joke—a chariot for rubes. The Stutz Bearcat in flaming red and yellow symbolized the era. The Canadian Good Roads Association, founded in 1919 in Montreal to lobby for better highways, was by 1927 also lobbying to cure the "speed mania."

38   No woman, dressed in the cumbersome styles of 1919, could feel comfortable in one of the new, closed automobiles. Overnight, to the horror of their elders, the bright young flappers chopped off their tresses, flung away their stays, hiked their skirts above the knee and piled into the rumble seat. "The auto," one American judge groaned, "has become a house of prostitution on wheels."

39   It had also become a symbol of sudden success. Each new model was awaited with national anticipation. No celebrity had arrived until he or she was pictured beside a custom-built car or at the wheel of a straight 12: Clara Bow, wheeling down Sunset Boulevard in an open Kissel; Gary Cooper dominated by his gigantic red and yellow Duesenberg. The gangsters too, were motorized and glamourized: Capone with his bulletproof Cadillac; Dillinger in his Ford (the Number One Public Enemy even wrote a personal testimonial to Henry). The car chase became a cinema staple; "taken for a ride" was the catch phrase of the era.

40   But for most of the continent, the motor car was something more than a glamorous status symbol. It could now be used to drive to work, to go shopping, to visit friends, to drive the kids to school or the dentist, to take the family picnicking. "I do not know of any other invention," Thomas Edison declared, "that has added to the happiness of most people more than the automobile."

41   When the new million-dollar Automotive Building opened at the Canadian National Exhibition in Toronto in the fall of 1929, it set the seal on a car-oriented decade. This was the largest and finest structure anywhere devoted exclusively to the display of automobiles and accessories. Here one would glimpse the tip of the industrial iceberg being created by the invention of the motor car. For behind the shiny new models, with their running boards and big headlamps, stood dozens of other industries, businesses, and services: oil refining, rubber manufacturing, retail sales, used-car lots, gas stations, auto-supply stores, car washes, metal and paint and glass industries, taxi companies; and, in the future, car radios, drive-in theatres, motels, driving schools, car

rental firms, and a vast array of roadside fast-food franchises that would turn the entrance to almost every city and town on the map into a true "Gasoline Alley."

42   Within a matter of weeks, Wall Street crashed and the Depression had arrived. Ironically, its greatest symbol of both hope and despair was a car—in the United States, the decrepit Hudson in which the Joad family in the movie *The Grapes of Wrath* moved from the dust bowl of Oklahoma to the fruit orchards of California; in Canada, the "Bennett buggy" (after Prime Minister R.B. Bennett) of the drought era, a car without an engine, drawn by a horse. For, as the Lynds found when they returned to their Middletown in the midst of the Depression, people refused to give up their cars.

43   The Joads' western pilgrimage symbolized the gypsy aspects of North American society, a restlessness that goes back to the days of the immigrant ships, the covered wagon, and the Red River cart. The automobile arrived just after the frontier had been tamed. It fulfilled the ancestral urge to move on. And its symbol became the motel, the lineal descendant of the wayside inn.

44   The "auto tourist camp" of the early 1920s—not much more than a park with washroom facilities, and handy to a garage—became, in 1925, the tourist cabin and the auto court. The tiny, spartan cabins grew more luxurious as the years went by but the lure was always the same: you could park your car at the front door of the motel room. Today, the small-town railway hotel, with its gloomy beer parlour, is all but obsolete; and in the cities, the major hostelries have had to change their entrances to accommodate the car. Who uses the front door of the Hotel Vancouver or Toronto's Royal York nowadays?

45   The auto court also flourished in the 1930s because people could not afford hotels, any more than they could afford a biannual model change. For 15 years of depression and war, the auto industry was stalled. Cars were sleeker, certainly. "Streamlining" was a word on everyone's lips. The traffic light arrived. People talked of "knee action" and "free wheeling." The roadster, the runabout and the rumble seat became obsolete. But when war came and people could again afford new models, they found there were none. Then, with the introduction of the flamboyant new Studebaker after 1945, the dam burst. The car became more than a workhorse. To quote a Buick ad in the mid-1950s: "It makes you feel like the man you are."

46   People went car crazy. They cared not a hoot for performance, efficiency, or safety. What they wanted was power, glamour, and status. The car was seen by psychologists as an extension of the owner's personality. Cadillac drivers were proud, flashy salesmen. DeSoto drivers were conservative, responsible members of the upper middle class. Studebaker owners were neat, sophisticated young intellectuals.

47   "One of the most costly blunders in the history of merchandising," Vance Packard wrote in *The Hidden Persuaders,* "was the Chrysler Corporation's assumption that people buy automobiles on a rational basis." The company decided, in the early 1950s, that the public wanted a car in tune with the times: sturdy, easy to park, no frills—a compact with a shorter wheelbase. That decision almost wrecked Chrysler, but in hindsight we can see that the company was almost 20 years ahead of its time. The car it thought the public of the 1950s wanted became the status symbol of the late 1970s. The idea of the car as a reverse status symbol—compact, gas-efficient, devoid of tail fins or chrome, and not obviously expensive—derives from a massive about-face of attitudes toward the automobile and what it signifies. The change was spurred, of course, by government decree after the oil shortage, by traffic snarls, by a rising toll of highway deaths, by inner city rot and

untrammelled suburban growth, and a consumer attitude that, for the want of a better word, we could call Naderism.

48   As the chairman of General Motors, James Roche, said in 1971, "the American love affair with the car is over." After half a century, the car was again seen as a villain, polluting the air, destroying the countryside, causing death and mutilation, wasting money, time, and gasoline, and fomenting a casual attitude to planned obsolescence.

49   Critics pointed to the car as the least-efficient means of transportation. In 1965, Elinor Guggenheimer, a New York City planning commissioner, pointed out that in 1911 a horse-drawn lorry could travel across Manhattan at an average speed of 11 miles per hour, while a modern taxi then could only achieve six.

50   Streets and parking lots, it was discovered, gobbled up between 35 and 50 per cent of the available space in a large city. Nine miles of freeway could destroy 24 acres of farmland; the average interchange took up 80 acres. Radio stations began to report daily pollution index in major cities, with the car as a leading culprit. And car manufacturers ceased boasting about "big car comfort." Foreign compacts became chic. Businessmen and housewives began to boast about how many miles their new car got to the gallon. North America's "Big Three" reeled under these blows and retooled. A new era had begun.

51   The new era has seen a return to the cities. People want to live downtown. Toronto has virtually no apartment space left in the inner city, but there are For Sale signs blossoming in the suburbs. There is even talk of closing the city centres to all cars except taxis, an experiment that has been tried in some European communities. Does this mean that Marshall McLuhan was right when he predicted that the car is finished? The guru of the 1960s insisted that the home computer would so diversify the work force that commuting would be unnecessary, that the car culture would die.

52   What he failed to realize, as all critics of the car have failed to realize, is that the automobile's greatest attraction is not as commuter vehicle or as an aid to shopping. The former suburbanites who got rid of their cars when they moved to the inner city still line up on weekends to rent them. For when all is said and done, the major appeal of the motor car, with all its faults and weaknesses, is still what it was at the turn of the century: a liberating force. People want the freedom to move off at will without waiting for the horse to recover or a taxi to arrive; without standing in line for a streetcar or looking up rail or air schedules. In that sense the car remains the genie in the bottle. Release it carelessly and it becomes our master. Guard it vigilantly and it remains what it was always meant to be, a slave ready to serve us at our whim.

Questions on Content, Structure, and Style

1. What, according to Berton, are the main effects of the automobile on North American society? What are some of the most significant of these effects?

2. Into what kinds of categories can the range of effects be classified?

3. Why is it necessary for him to start his cause and effect essay from the beginning of the car's invention? Why does his essay focus mostly on the car's effects in the first three decades of the 20th century?

4. What sort of analogies does Berton draw? What sorts of contrasts does he provide between past and present? How did the past affect the present?

5. How effective is the arrangement of the information in this essay?

6. What examples does Berton offer to back up his claims? How logical are the connections he draws between the invention of the car and social changes that occurred over the 20th century? What are his underlying assumptions about people's responses to the new working conditions brought about by the assembly line?

7. Describe the tone of this essay. Who is the intended audience for this essay?

8. Point out some examples of the car's effect on popular expressions (in paragraphs 11, 39, and 45, for example). Can you think of other such expressions?

9. Why does Berton choose to quote Thomas Edison in paragraph 40? Do you agree with Edison's statement?

Suggestions for Writing

Use Pierre Berton's essay "Wheels: The Car as a Cultural Driving Force" as a stepping stone to your essay. Imagine the social consequences of decreasing our dependence on cars today. Would society revert to the conditions that existed before the automobile's invention? Would the middle classes shrink, would families be torn apart, would our sense of self change? You might also write an essay in which you offer different causes for the same social changes Berton discusses, or write about some other effects cars have had (for instance, on the environment).

Vocabulary

prerogative (5)	prescient (13)	extol (23)
landau (5)	blandishments (13)	akin to (24)
caste (7)	derision (17)	demise (27)
importuning (9)	reviled (20)	criterion (32)
carping (9)	anathema (22)	lineal (43)

■ A REVISION WORKSHEET

As you write your rough drafts, consult Chapter 5 for guidance through the revision process. In addition, here are a few questions to ask yourself as you revise your causal analysis essay:

1. Is the thesis limited to a reasonable claim that can be supported in the essay?

2. Is the organization clear and consistent so that the reader can understand the purpose of the analysis?

3. Does the essay focus on the most important causes or effects, or both?

4. If the essay has a narrative form, is each step in the chain reaction clearly connected to the next?

5. Does the essay convincingly show the reader *how* or *why* relationships between the causes and effects exist, instead of merely naming and describing them?

6. Does the essay provide enough evidence to show the connections between causes and effects? Where could additional details be added to make the relationships clearer?

7. Has the essay avoided the problems of oversimplification, circular logic, and the post hoc fallacy?

After you've revised your essay extensively, you might exchange rough drafts with a classmate and answer these questions for each other, making specific suggestions for improvement wherever appropriate. (For advice on productive participation in classroom workshops, see pages 102–104.)

Reviewing Your Progress

After you have completed your essay developed by causal analysis, take a moment to measure your progress as a writer by responding to the following questions. Such analysis will help you recognize growth in your writing skills and may enable you to identify areas that are still problematic.

1. What do you like best about your essay? Why?

2. After considering your essay's presentation of the major causes or effects, which part of your analysis do you think readers will find the most convincing? Why?

3. What part of your essay gave you the most trouble? How did you overcome the problem?

4. If you had more time to work on this essay, what would receive additional attention? Why?

5. What did you learn about your topic from writing this essay? About yourself as a writer?

Chapter 10

Argumentation

Almost without exception, each of us, every day, argues for or against something with somebody. The discussions may be short and friendly ("Let's go to this restaurant rather than that one") or long and complex ("Mandatory motorcycle helmets are an intrusion on civil rights"). Because we do argue our viewpoints so often, most of us realized long ago that shifting into high whine did not always get us what we wanted. On the contrary, we've learned that we usually have a much better chance at winning a dispute or having our plan adopted or changing someone's mind if we present our side of an issue in a calm, logical fashion, giving sound reasons for our position. This approach is just what a good argumentative essay does: it presents logical reasoning and solid evidence that will persuade your readers to accept your point of view.

Some argumentative essays declare the best solution to a problem ("Raising the drinking age will decrease traffic accidents"); others argue a certain way of looking at an issue ("Beauty pageants degrade women"); still others may urge adoption of a specific plan of action ("Voters should pass ordinance 10 to fund the new ice rink"). Whatever your exact purpose, your argumentative essay should be composed of a clear thesis and body paragraphs that offer enough sensible reasons and persuasive evidence to convince your readers to agree with you.

Developing Your Essay

Here are some suggestions for developing and organizing an effective argumentative essay:

Choose an appropriate topic. Selecting a good topic for any essay is important. Choosing a focused, appropriate topic for your argument essay will save you enormous time and energy even before you begin prewriting. Some subjects are simply too large and complex to be adequately treated in a three-to-five-page argumentative essay; selecting such a subject might produce a rough draft of generalities that will not be persuasive. If you have an interest in a subject that is too general or complex for the length of your assignment, try to find a more focused, specific issue within it to argue. For example, the large, controversial subject "plastic surgery" might be narrowed and focused to a paper advocating ongoing professional counselling and support for patients or more stringent checks on plastic surgeons. A general opinion on "unfair college or university grading" might become a more interesting persuasive essay in which the writer takes a stand on the use of bell curve grading. Your general annoyance with smokers might move from "All smoking should be outlawed forever" to an essay focused on smoking bans in open-air sports stadiums. In other words, while we certainly do debate large issues in our lives, in a short piece of writing it may be more effective, and often more interesting, to choose a focused topic that will allow for more depth in the arguments. You must ultimately decide whether your choice of subject is appropriate for your assignment, but taking a close, second look at your choice now may save you frustration later.

Explore the possibilities ... and your opinions. Perhaps you have an interesting subject in mind for your argumentative essay, but you don't, as yet, have a definite opinion on the controversy. Use this opportunity to explore the subject! Do some research, talk to appropriate people, investigate the issues. By discovering your own position, you can address others who may be similarly uncertain about the subject.

Many times, however, you may want to argue for a belief or position you already hold. But before you proceed, take some time to consider the basis of your strong feelings. Not surprisingly, we humans have been known, on various occasions, to spout out opinions we can't always effectively support when challenged to do so. Sometimes we hold an opinion simply because on the surface it seems to make good sense to us or because it fits comfortably with our other social, ethical, or political beliefs. Or we may have inherited some of our beliefs from our families or friends, or perhaps we borrowed ideas from well-known people we admire. In some cases, we may have held an opinion for so long that we can't remember why we adopted it in the first place. We may also have a purely sentimental or emotional attachment to some idea or position. Whatever the original causes of our beliefs, we need to examine the real reasons for thinking what we do before we can effectively convince others.

If you have a strong opinion you want to write about, try jotting down a list of the reasons or points that support your position. Then study the list—are your points logical and persuasive? Which aren't? Why not? After this bit of prewriting, you may discover that although you believe something strongly, you really don't have the kind of factual evidence or reasoned arguments you need to support your opinion. In some cases, depending on your topic, you may wish to talk to others who share your position or to research your subject (for help with research or interviewing, see Chapter 14); in other cases, you may just need to think longer and harder about your topic and your reasons for maintaining your attitude toward it. Keep an open mind; your exploration may lead you to a surprising new position. But with or without formal research, the better you know your subject, the more confident you will be about writing your argumentative essay.

Anticipate opposing views. An argument assumes that there is more than one side to an issue. To be convincing, you must be aware of your opposition's views on the subject and then organize your essay to answer or counter those views. If you don't have a good sense of the opposition's arguments, you can't effectively persuade your readers to dismiss their objections and see matters your way. Therefore, before you begin your first rough draft, write down all the opposing views you can think of and an answer to each of them so that you will know your subject thoroughly. If you are unfamiliar with the major objections to your position, now is the time to investigate your subject further. (For the sake of clarity throughout this chapter, your act of responding to those arguments against your position will be called *refuting the opposition;* "to refute" means "to prove false or wrong," and that's what you will try to do to some of the arguments of those who disagree with you.)

Now you might be thinking, "What if my position on a topic as yet has no opposition?" Remember that almost all issues have more than one side, so try to anticipate objections and then answer them. For example, you might first present a thesis that calls for a new traffic signal at a dangerous intersection in your town and then address hypothetical counterarguments, such as "The City Council may say that a stop light at Lemay and Columbia will cost too much, but the cost in lives will be much greater" or "Commuters may complain that a traffic light there will slow the continuous flow of north–south traffic, but it is precisely the uninterrupted nature of this road that encourages motorists to speed." By answering hypothetical objections, you impress your readers by showing them you've thought through your position thoroughly before you asked them to consider your point of view.

You might also be thinking, "What if my opposition actually has a valid objection, a legitimate point of criticism? Should I ignore it?" Hoping that an obviously strong opposing point will just go away is like hoping the government will cancel income taxes this year—a nice thought but hardly likely. Don't ignore your opposition's good point; instead, acknowledge it, but then go on quickly to show your readers why that reason, though valid, isn't compelling enough by itself to motivate people to adopt your opposition's entire position. Or you might concede that one point while simultaneously showing why your position isn't really in conflict with that criticism, but rather with other, more important parts of your opponent's viewpoint. By admitting that you see some validity in your opposition's argument, you can again show your readers that you are both fair-minded and informed about all aspects of the controversy.

Know and remember your audience. Although it's important to think about your readers' needs and expectations whenever you write, it is essential to consider carefully the audience of your argumentative essay both before and as you write your rough drafts. Because you are trying to persuade people to adopt some new point of view or perhaps to take some action, you need to decide what kinds of supporting evidence will be most convincing to your particular readers. Try to analyze your audience by asking yourself a series of questions: "What do they already know about my topic? What information or terms do they need to know to understand my point of view? What biases might they already have for or against my position? What special concerns might my readers have that influence their receptiveness?" To be convincing, you should consider these questions and others by carefully reviewing the discussion of audience on pages 18–21 *before* you begin your drafts.

Decide which points of argument to include. Once you have a good sense of your audience, your own position, and your opposition's strongest arguments, try making a Pro-and-Con Sheet to help you sort out which points you will discuss in your essay.

Let's suppose you want to write an editorial on the poor voter turnout at student elections at your campus. Is it even important that more students should vote in student elections?

After reviewing the evidence on both sides, you have decided to argue that your fellow students should participate more fully in student issues by voting in student elections. To help yourself begin planning your essay, you list all the pro-and-con arguments you can think of concerning your position:

My Side: For Encouraging Student Voters

1. Most election issues are important for the majority of students.

2. Voting in student elections prepares students for participating in other elections.

3. Student candidates are working for other students.

4. Students get a say in issues that affect them if they vote.

5. Most successful candidates have experience and good platforms.

6. Information about election issues and candidates is readily available.

7. It takes only a few minutes to vote.

8. Becoming a responsible citizen is part of our education; a responsible citizen votes in elections.

9. Students need to take responsibility for the issues that affect them.

My Opposition's Side: Against Encouraging Student Voters

1. Voting is pointless, because election issues have no effect on most students.

2. Voting in student elections has no effect on preparing for participating in other elections.

3. Student candidates are only working for themselves.

4. Students get no say in issues, even if they vote.

5. Most successful candidates only win because they're popular, not because they know anything.

6. Most students don't know the candidates or issues.

7. It takes too much time away from studies to vote.

8. Students should concentrate on their studies, not on politics.

After making your Pro-and-Con Sheet, look over the list and decide which of your strongest points you want to argue in your paper and also which of your opposition's claims you want to refute. At this point you may also see some arguments on your list that might be combined and some that might be deleted because they're irrelevant or unconvincing. (Be careful not to select more arguments or counterarguments to discuss than the length of your writing assignment will allow. It's far better to present a persuasive analysis of a few points than it is to give an underdeveloped, shallow treatment of a host of reasons.)

Let's say you want to cover the following points in your essay:

- Students have the responsibility to participate in student elections because most elections deal with issues that affect them directly, and because it makes them more productive citizens (combination of 1, 2, 4, 8, and 9).

- Successful student candidates are knowledgeable and experienced, and are working for everyone's good (combination of 3 and 5).

- It's very easy to find out about election issues and candidates, and the voting process itself is very quick (combination of 6 and 7).

Your assignment calls for an essay of 750 to 1,000 words, so you figure you'll only have space to refute your opposition's strongest claim. You decide to refute this claim:

- Voting is pointless because election issues have no effect on most students (1).

The next step is to formulate a working thesis. At this stage, you may find it helpful to put your working thesis in an "although–because" statement so you can clearly see both your opposition's arguments and your own. An "although–because" thesis for the note-taking essay might look something like this:

> *Although* some students maintain that voting in student elections has no effect on student issues, they should vote *because* their votes elect knowledgeable and efficient students who work on behalf of all their peers, because voting is a necessary responsibility for all students, whether they are citizens or not, and because the voting process is so easy.

Frequently your "although–because" thesis will be too long and awkward to use in the later drafts of your essay. But for now, it can serve as a guide, allowing you to see your overall position before the writing of the first draft begins. (To practise compiling a Pro-and-Con List and writing an "although–because" thesis, turn to the exercise on page 282.)

Organize your essay clearly. Although there is no set model of organization for argumentative essays, here are some common patterns that you might use or that you might combine in some effective way.

Important note: For the sake of simplicity, the first two outlines present two of the writer's points and two opposing ideas. Naturally, your essay may contain any number of points and refuted points, depending on the complexity of your subject and the assigned length of your essay.

In Pattern A, you devote the first few body paragraphs to arguing points on your side and then turn to refuting or answering the opposition's claims.

Pattern A: Thesis

Body paragraph 1: you present your first point and its supporting evidence

Body paragraph 2: you present your second point and its supporting evidence

Body paragraph 3: you refute your opposition's first point

Body paragraph 4: you refute your opposition's second point

Conclusion

Sometimes you may wish to clear away the opposition's claims before you present the arguments for your side. To do so, you might select Pattern B:

Pattern B: Thesis

Body paragraph 1: you refute your opposition's first point

Body paragraph 2: you refute your opposition's second point

Body paragraph 3: you present your first point and its supporting evidence

Body paragraph 4: you present your second point and its supporting evidence

Conclusion

In some cases, you may find that the main arguments you want to present are the very same ones that will refute or answer your opposition's primary claims. If so, try Pattern C, which allows each of your argumentative points to refute one of your opposition's claims in the same paragraph:

Pattern C: Thesis

Body paragraph 1: you present your first point and its supporting evidence, which also refutes one of your opposition's claims

Body paragraph 2: you present a second point and its supporting evidence, which also refutes a second opposition claim

Body paragraph 3: you present a third point and its supporting evidence, which also refutes a third opposition claim

Conclusion

If you are feeling confident about your ability to organize an argumentative essay, you might try some combination of patterns if your material allows such a treatment. For example, you might have a strong point to argue, another point that simultaneously answers one of your opposition's strongest claims, and another opposition point you want to refute. Your essay organization might look like this:

Combination: Thesis

Body paragraph 1: A point for your side

Body paragraph 2: One of your points, which also refutes an opposition claim

Body paragraph 3: Your refutation of another opposition claim

Conclusion

In other words, you can organize your essay in a variety of ways as long as your paper is logical and clear. Study your Pro-and-Con Sheet and then decide which organization best presents the arguments and counterarguments you want to include. Try sketching out your essay following each of the patterns; look carefully to see which pattern (or variation of one of the patterns) seems to put forward your particular material most persuasively, with the least repetition or confusion. Sometimes your essay's material will clearly fall into a particular pattern of organization, so your choice will be easy. More often, however, you will have to arrange and rearrange your ideas and counterarguments until you see the best approach. Don't be discouraged if you decide to change patterns after you've begun a rough draft; what matters is finding the most effective way to persuade the reader to your side.

If no organizational pattern seems to fit at first, ask yourself which of your points or counterarguments is the strongest or most important. Try putting that point in one of the two most emphatic places: either first or last. Sometimes your most important discussion will lead the way to your other points and, consequently, should be introduced first; perhaps more often, effective writers and speakers build up to their strongest point, presenting it last as the climax of their argument. Again, the choice depends on your material itself, though it's rare that you would want to bury your strongest point in the middle of your essay.

Now let's return to the essay on student voting first discussed on page 271. After selecting the most important arguments and counterarguments (pages 272–273), let's say that you decide that your main point concerns the importance of voting in student elections. Since your opposition claims the contrary, that voting is pointless, you see that you can make your main point as you refute theirs. But you also wish to include a couple of other points for your side. After trying several patterns, you decide to put the "relevance" rebuttal last for emphasis and present your other points first. Consequently, Pattern A best fits your plan. A sketchy outline might look like this:

- *Revised working thesis and essay map:* More students should vote in student elections. Not only will this ensure they will have a say in important decisions made on their behalf and make them more responsible citizens in the long term, but it will help them recognize the important issues that affect them.

- *Body paragraph 1 (a first point for the writer's side):* Only voting in student elections can give students a say in important decisions that are being made on their behalf by student politicians and university administrators.

- *Body paragraph 2 (another point for the writer's side):* Students need to take responsibility for their own lives and the issues that affect them so they can become better citizens both on campus and beyond.

- *Body paragraph 3 (rebuttal of the opposition's strongest claim):* Many nonvoters believe election issues are either irrelevant or too difficult to be informed about, but these issues, whether related to tuition fees or transit programs, are easy to find out about and are directly relevant to students' lives.

Once you have a general notion of where your essay is going, plan to spend some more time thinking about ways to make each of your points clear, logical, and persuasive to your particular audience. (If you wish to see how one student actually developed an essay based on the preceding outline, turn to the sample student paper on pages 286–288.)

Argue your ideas logically. To convince your readers, you must provide sufficient reasons for your position. You must give more than mere opinion or emotional responses—you must offer logical arguments, based on solid evidence and connected reasons to back up your assertions. Some of the possible ways of supporting your ideas should already be familiar to you from writing expository essays; listed here are several methods and illustrations:

1. Give examples (real or hypothetical): "Finding out about election issues is easy; for instance, you can see summaries of election issues in the student paper, on posters all around campus, and on the student society website."

2. Present a comparison or contrast: "In contrast to letting others make all the decisions about student issues, you can take part in some of those decisions, simply by voting."

3. Show a cause-and-effect relationship: "Voting in student elections will give each student a direct say in decisions on issues that affect them."

4. Argue by definition: "A nonvoter is someone who gives up his or her constitutional rights because the responsibility is too much."

The Argumentative Appeals: Logos, Pathos, Ethos

As you put together your argument, you will be paying attention to your main thesis, your methods of reasoning (classical/Aristotelian, Rogerian, and so on), your organization, and your methods of development. You will also need to consider what in classical rhetoric are recognized as the three types of argumentative "appeals." The word "appeals" implies an active engagement with the audience you are trying to persuade. The well-thought-out arguments you choose to support your case may be called *logical appeals* (or appeals to *logos*) because they appeal to, and depend on, your readers' ability to reason and to recognize good sense when they see it. But there are two other kinds of appeals often used: the *emotional appeal* (or appeal to *pathos*) and the *ethical appeal* (or appeal to *ethos*).

Emotional appeals are designed to persuade people by playing on their feelings rather than appealing to their intellect. Rather than using thoughtful, logical reasoning to support their claims, writers and speakers using *only* emotional appeals often try to accomplish their goals by distracting or misleading their audiences. Frequently, emotional appeals are characterized by language that plays on people's fears, material desires, prejudices, or sympathies; such language often triggers highly favourable or unfavourable responses to a subject. For instance, emotional appeals are used constantly in advertising, where feel-good images, music, and slogans ("Always Fresh. Always Tim Hortons"; "I Am Canadian") are designed to sway potential customers to a product without them thinking about it too much. Some politicians also rely heavily on emotional appeals, often using scare tactics to disguise a situation or to lead people away from questioning the logic of a particular issue. Heavy or exclusive reliance on emotional appeals is also inappropriate in many rhetorical situations, such as your university work. To professional audiences such as professors or corporate boards, emotional appeals lessen the argument and the writer's credibility. Careless use of emotional appeal can sometimes lead to logical fallacies such as the bandwagon or ad hominem fallacies. For a discussion of fallacies, see pages 279–281.

But in some cases, emotional appeals can be used for legitimate purposes. Good writers should always be aware of their audience's needs, values, and states of mind, and they may be more persuasive on occasion if they can frame their arguments in ways that appeal to both their readers' logic and their emotions. For example, when Martin Luther King, Jr., delivered his famous "I Have a Dream" speech to the crowds gathered in Washington in 1963 and described his vision of little children of different races walking hand-in-hand, being judged not "by the color of their skin but by the content of their character," he certainly spoke with passion that was aimed at the hearts of his listeners. But King was not using an emotional appeal to keep his audience from thinking about his message; on the contrary, he presented powerful emotional images that he hoped would inspire people to act on what they already thought and felt, on their deepest convictions about equality and justice.

Appeals to emotions are tricky: you can use them effectively in conjunction with appeals to logic and with solid evidence, but only if you use them ethically. Too many appeals to the emotions are also overwhelming; readers tire quickly from excessive tugs on the heartstrings. To prevent your readers from suspecting deception, or feeling manipulated, support your assertions with as many logical arguments as you can muster, and use emotional appeals only when they legitimately advance your cause.

Ethical appeals generally establish your credibility as a writer and answer your audience's questions: Why should I listen to this person? Why should I take this person seriously? Why should I believe this person? This establishment of your credibility can take various forms. You can, as some authors do, indicate your expertise right from the beginning, citing relevant titles of books or articles you have written, or referring to degrees and other qualifications you have earned. You can also establish your credibility by talking about relevant experience, such as your role as a camp counsellor, or your time as a regular transit user. But establishing your credibility goes beyond credentials and experience. You also need to appear respectful of your opponent's claims and to be honest with your evidence. So a biased tone in which you tell your opponent that "all drivers are killers," or a use of evidence that deliberately leaves out or misinterprets key facts will diminish the respect your audience has for you and your arguments. Your credibility can be affected negatively both by too much humility ("I don't really know very much about this topic") and by too much arrogance (starting your essay with a long list of your credentials and interspersing the whole essay with references to them). Your credibility is also affected by the quality of work you are doing: how much research you have done, what kinds of sources you have used, and even how carefully you have documented those sources. Your choice of sources is important, as you need to use relevant and respected authorities to gain credibility. See Chapter 14 for a discussion on using sources and doing research. As with the case of emotional appeal, too much reliance on some ethical appeals, especially those that are about you as an individual, can cause you to commit logical fallacies and sideline the solid logical reasoning and evidence that should be the foundation and major part of your argument. The use of inappropriate sources can also lead to fallacies, such as the fallacy of false authority.

Offer evidence that effectively supports your claims. In addition to presenting thoughtful, logical reasoning, you may wish to incorporate a variety of convincing evidence to persuade your readers to your side. Your essay might profit from including, where appropriate, some of the following kinds of supporting evidence:

- Factual information you've gathered from research
- Statistics from current, reliable sources
- Charts, graphs, or diagrams
- Testimony from authorities and experts
- The experiences or testimony of others whose opinions are pertinent to the topic
- Hypothetical examples (but only if your instructor accepts them)
- Personal experiences

You'll need to spend quite a bit of your prewriting time thinking about the best kinds of evidence to support your case. Remember that not all personal experiences or research materials are persuasive. For instance, the experiences we've had (or that our friends have had) may not be representative of a universal experience and consequently may lead to unconvincing generalizations. Even testimony from an authority may not be convincing if the person is not speaking on a topic from his or her field of expertise; famous hockey players, for instance, don't necessarily know any more about pantyhose or soft drinks than anyone else. Always put yourself in the skeptical reader's place and ask, "Does this point convince me? If not, why not?" (For more information on incorporating research material into your essays, see Chapter 14. For more advice on the selection of evidence, see the section on critical thinking in Chapter 1.)

Find the appropriate tone. Sometimes when we argue, it's easy to get carried away. Remember that your goal is to persuade and perhaps change your readers, not alienate them. Instead of laying on insults or sarcasm, present your ideas in a moderate let-us-reason-together spirit. Such a tone will persuade your readers that you are sincere in your attempts to argue as truthfully and fairly as possible. If your readers do not respect you as a reasonable person, they certainly won't be swayed to your side of an issue. Don't preach or pontificate either; no one likes—or respects—a writer with a superior attitude. Write in your natural "voice"; don't adopt a pseudo-intellectual tone. In short, to argue effectively you should sound logical, sincere, and informed. (For additional comments on tone, review pages 139–141.)

Consider using Rogerian techniques, if they are appropriate. In some cases, especially those involving tense situations or highly sensitive issues, you may wish to incorporate some techniques of the noted psychologist Carl Rogers, who developed a procedure for presenting what he called the non-threatening argument. Rogers believed that people involved in a debate should strive for clear, honest communication so that the problem under discussion could be resolved. Instead of going on the defensive and trying to "win" the argument, each side should try to recognize common ground and then develop a solution that will address the needs of both parties.

A Rogerian argument uses these techniques:

1. A clear, objective statement of the problem or issue
2. A clear, objective summary of the opposition's position that shows you understand its point of view and goals
3. A clear, objective summary of your point of view, stated in non-threatening language
4. A discussion that emphasizes the beliefs, values, and goals that you and your opposition have in common
5. A description of any of your points that you are willing to concede or compromise
6. An explanation of a plan or proposed solution that meets the needs of both sides

By showing your opposition that you thoroughly understand its position and that you are sincerely trying to effect a solution that is in everyone's—not just your—best interests, you may succeed in some situations that might otherwise be hopeless because of their highly emotional nature. Remember, too, that you can use some of these Rogerian techniques in any kind of argument paper you are writing if you think they would be effective.

Problems to Avoid

Writers of argumentative essays must appear logical or their readers will reject their point of view. Here is a short list of some of the most common *logical fallacies*—that is, errors in reasoning. Check your rough drafts carefully to avoid these problems.

Students sometimes ask, "If a logical fallacy works, why not use it? Isn't all fair in love, war, and argumentative essays?" The honest answer is maybe. It's quite true that speakers and writers do use faulty logic and irrational emotional appeals to persuade people every day (one needs only to look at television or a newspaper to see example after example). Uncritical or inattentive audiences seem to accept arguments based on logical fallacies. But the cost of the risk is high: if you do try to slide one by your readers and they see through your trick, you will lose your credibility instantly. Your college and university audiences will be experienced readers who will not be impressed by fallacious reasoning. Deliberate use of faulty reasoning is also unethical. On the whole, it's far more effective to use logical reasoning and strong evidence to convince your readers to accept your point of view.

■ Common Logical Fallacies

Hasty generalization: The writer bases the argument on insufficient or unrepresentative evidence. Suppose, for example, you have owned two poodles and they have both attacked you. If you declare that all poodles are vicious dogs, you are making a hasty generalization. There are, of course, thousands of poodles who have not attacked anyone. Similarly, you're in error if you interview only campus athletes and then declare, "Students favour a new stadium." What about the opinions of the students who aren't athletes? In other words, when the generalization is drawn from a sample that is too small or select, your conclusion isn't valid.

Non sequitur ("it doesn't follow"): The writer's conclusion is not necessarily a logical result of the facts. An example of a *non sequitur* occurs when you conclude, "Professor Smith is a famous chemist, so he will be a brilliant chemistry teacher." As you may have realized by now, the fact that someone knows a subject well does not automatically mean that he or she can communicate the information clearly in a classroom; hence, the conclusion is not necessarily valid.

Begging the question: The writer presents as truth what is not proven by the argument. For example, in the statement "All useless laws such as Reform Bill 13 should be repealed," the writer has already pronounced the bill useless without assuming responsibility for proving that accusation. Similarly, the statement "Professors on our campus who are using their classroom solely for preaching their political ideas should be banned" begs the question (that is, tries like a beggar to get something for nothing from the reader), because the writer gives no evidence for what must first be argued, not merely asserted—that there are in fact professors on that particular campus using class time solely for spreading their political beliefs.

Red herring: The writer introduces an irrelevant point to divert the readers' attention from the main issue. This term originates from the old tactic used by escaped prisoners, of dragging a smoked herring, a strong-smelling fish, across their trail to confuse tracking dogs by making them follow the wrong scent. For example, roommate A might be criticizing roommate B for his repeated failure to do the dishes when it was his turn. To escape facing the charges, roommate B brings up times in the past when the other roommate failed to repay some money he borrowed. Although roommate A may indeed have a problem with remembering his debts, that discussion isn't relevant to the original argument about sharing the responsibility for the dishes. (By the way, you might have run across a well-known newspaper photograph of a California environmentalist group demonstrating for more protection of dolphins, whales, and other marine life; look closely to see, over in the left corner, almost hidden by the host of placards and banners, a fellow slyly holding up a sign that reads "Save the Red Herring!" Now, who says rhetoricians don't have a good sense of humour?)

Post hoc, ergo propter hoc. See page 254.

Argument *ad hominem* ("to the man"): The writer attacks the opponent's character rather than the opponent's argument. The statement "Dr. Bloom can't be a competent marriage counsellor because she's been divorced" may not be valid. Bloom's advice to her clients may be excellent regardless of her own marital status.

Faulty use of authority: The writer relies on "authorities" who are not convincing sources. Although someone may be well known in a particular field, he or she may not be qualified to testify in a different area. A baseball player in an advertisement for laser surgery may stress his need for correct vision, but he may be no more knowledgeable about eye care than anyone else on the street. In other words, name recognition is not enough. For their testimony to count with readers, authorities must have expertise, credentials, or relevant experience in the area under discussion. (See also pages 372–373, and "transfer of virtue" in the discussion of "bandwagon appeal" on this page.)

Argument *ad populum* ("to the people"): The writer evades the issues by appealing to readers' emotional reactions to certain subjects. For example, instead of arguing the facts of an issue, a writer might play on the readers' negative response to such words as "communism," "fascism," or "radicalism," and their positive response to words like "God," "country," "liberty," or "patriotism." In the statement "If you are a true Canadian, you will vote against the referendum on a two-tiered health care system," the writer avoids any discussion of the merits or weaknesses of the bill and merely substitutes an emotional appeal. Other popular "virtue words" include "duty," "common sense," "courage," and "healthy." (Advertisers, of course, also play on consumers' emotions by filling their advertisements with pictures of babies, animals, status objects, and sexually attractive men and women.)

Circular thinking. See page 254.

Either/or: The writer tries to convince the readers that there are only two sides to an issue—one right, one wrong. The statement "If you don't go to war against Iceland, you don't love your country" is irrational because it doesn't consider the other possibilities, such as patriotic people's right to oppose war as an expression of love for their country. A classic example of this sort of oversimplification was illustrated in the bumper sticker that was popular in America in the 1960s during the debate over the Vietnam War: "America: Love It or Leave It." Obviously, there are other choices ("Change It or Lose It," for instance, to quote another either/or bumper sticker of that era).

Hypostatization: The writer uses an abstract concept as if it were a concrete reality. Always be suspicious of a writer who frequently relies on statements beginning "History has always taught us . . ." or "Science has proven . . ." or "Research shows. . . ." The implication in each case is that history or science (or any other discipline) has only one voice, one opinion. On the contrary, "history" is written by a multitude of historians who hold a variety of opinions; doctors and scientists also frequently disagree. Instead of generalizing about a particular field, it is best to quote a specific, respected authority or to at least qualify your initial general statement by referring to "many" or "some" scientists, historians, or other professionals. You should be prepared to back up your general assertions and qualifications with specific evidence.

Bandwagon appeal: The writer tries to validate a point by intimating that "everyone else believes in this." Such a tactic evades discussion of the issue itself. Advertising often uses this technique: "Everyone who demands real taste smokes Phooey cigarettes"; "Discriminating women use Candy-Gloss lipstick." (The ultimate in "bandwagon" humour may have appeared on a recent Colorado bumper sticker: "Eat lamb—could 1000s of coyotes be wrong?") A variation of the "bandwagon" fallacy is sometimes referred to as "transfer of virtue," the sharing of light from someone else's sparkle. Advertisers often use this technique by paying attractive models or media stars to endorse their product. The underlying premise is this:

> Popular/beautiful/"cool"/rich people use/buy/wear "X"; if you use "X," you too will be popular/beautiful/and so on.

Intelligent readers and consumers know, of course, to suspect such doubtful causal relationships.

Straw man: The writer selects the opposition's weakest or most insignificant point to argue against, to divert the readers' attention from the real issues. Instead of addressing the opposition's best arguments and defeating them, the writer "sets up a straw man"—that is, the writer picks out a trivial (or irrelevant) argument against his or her own position and easily knocks it down, just as one might easily push over a figure made of straw. Perhaps the most famous example of the "straw man" occurred in 1952 when, during the American vice-presidential campaign, Richard Nixon was accused of misappropriating campaign funds for his personal use. Addressing the nation on television, Nixon described how his six-year-old daughter, Tricia, had received a little cocker spaniel named Checkers from a Texas supporter. Nixon went on about how much his children loved the dog and how, regardless of what anyone thought, by gosh, he was going to keep that cute dog for little Tricia. Of course, no one was asking Nixon to return the dog; they were asking about the $18,000 in missing campaign funds. But Nixon's canine gift was much easier for him to defend, and the "Checkers" speech is now famous as one of the most notorious "straw man" diversions.

Faulty analogy: The writer uses an extended comparison as proof of a point. Look closely at all extended comparisons and metaphors to see if the two things being compared are really similar. For example, in a recent editorial a woman protested the new laws requiring parents to use car seats for small children, arguing that if the province could require the seats, they could just as easily require mothers to breastfeed instead of using formula. Are the two situations alike? Car accidents are the leading cause of death of children under four; is formula deadly? Or perhaps you've read that putting teenagers in sex education classes is like taking an alcoholic to a bar. Is it? If readers don't see the similarity, the analogy may not be persuasive. Moreover, remember that even though a compelling analogy might suggest similarities, it alone cannot *prove* anything. (For more discussion of analogy, see pages 222–224.)

Quick fix: The writer leans too heavily on catchy phrases or empty slogans. A clever turn-of-phrase may grab one's attention, but it may lose its persuasiveness when scrutinized closely. For instance, a banner at a rally to protest gun registration read, "When guns are outlawed, only outlaws will have guns." Although the sentence had nice balance, it oversimplified the issue. The legislation in question was not trying to outlaw all guns, just to make the acquisition of guns more difficult for those with criminal records. Other slogans sound good but are simply irrelevant: a particular soft drink, for example, may be "the real thing," but what drink isn't? Look closely at clever lines substituted for reasoned argument; always demand clear terms and logical explanations.*

---

* Sometimes advertisers get more for their slogans than they bargained for. According to one news source, a popular soft-drink company had to spend millions to revise its slogan after introducing its product into parts of China. Apparently the slogan "Come alive! Join the Blah-Blah-Cola Generation!" translated into some dialects as "Blah-Blah Cola Brings Your Ancestors Back from the Dead"!

▪ PRACTISING WHAT YOU'VE LEARNED

A. Imagine that you are writing an argumentative essay addressing the controversial question "Should home-schooled students be allowed to play on public school athletic teams?" You have investigated the topic and have noted the variety of opinions listed here. Arrange the statements into two lists: A "Pro" list (those statements that argue for allowing home schoolers to play) and a "Con" list (those statements that are against allowing home schoolers to play). Cross off any inappropriate or illogical statements you find; combine any opinions that overlap.

1. Parents of home schoolers pay the same taxes as public school parents.

2. Public school kids must meet grade requirements to be eligible.

3. School rules prohibit non-enrolled youth on school property.

4. Home schoolers shouldn't get the benefits of a school they've rejected.

5. Public school kids are bad influences on home schoolers.

6. Home schoolers need the social interaction.

7. Public school teams can always use more good athletes.

8. More students will overburden athletic facilities.

9. Home schoolers miss their public school friends, and vice versa.

10. Home schoolers will displace public school students on teams.

11. Public school students have to meet attendance rules to be eligible.

12. Athletic competition is good for everybody.

13. Home schoolers often have controversial political beliefs that will cause fights.

14. Team members need to share the same community on a daily basis.

15. Home schoolers aren't as invested in school pride.

Once you have your two lists, decide your own position on this topic. Then select two points you might use to argue your position and one opposing criticism you might refute. Put your working thesis into an "although–because" format, as explained on page 273. Compare your choices to those of your classmates.

B. Errors in reasoning can cause your reader to doubt your credibility. In the following mock essay, for example, the writer includes a variety of fallacies that undermine his argument; see if you can identify all his errors.

Ban Those Books!

1   A serious problem faces Canada today, a problem of such grave importance that our very existence as a nation is threatened. We must either cleanse our schools of evil-minded books, or we must reconcile ourselves to seeing our children become welfare moochers and homeless bums.

2   History has shown time and time again that placement of immoral books in our schools is part of an insidious plot designed to weaken the moral fibre of our youth from coast to coast. In Fredericton, New Brunswick, for example, the year after books by Margaret Atwood, such as *The Handmaid's Tale,* were introduced into the school library by free-thinkers and radicals, the number of students cutting classes rose by 6 percent. And in that same year, the number of high-school seniors going on to college dropped from thirty to twenty-two.

3   The reason for this could either be a natural decline in intelligence and morals or the influence of those dirty books that teach our beloved children disrespect and irresponsibility. Since there is no evidence to suggest a natural decline, the conclusion is inescapable: once our children read about Atwood's characters breaking the rules set by their leaders and betters, they had to do likewise. If they hadn't read about such undesirable characters, our innocent children would never have behaved in those ways.

4   Now, I am a simple man, a plain old farm boy—the pseudo-intellectuals call me redneck just like they call you folks. But I can assure you that, redneck or not, I've got the guts to fight moral decay everywhere I find it, and I urge you to do the same. For this reason I want all you good folks to come to the ban-the-books rally this Friday so we can talk it over. I promise you all your right-thinking neighbours will be there.

■ ASSIGNMENT

Search for the following:

1. An example of an advertisement that illustrates one or more of the fallacies or appeals discussed on pages 279–281;

2. An example of illogical or fallacious reasoning in a piece of writing (you might try looking at the editorial page or letters-to-the-editor section of your local or campus newspaper);

3. An example of a logical, persuasive point in a piece of writing.

Be prepared to explain your analyses of your samples, but do not write any sort of identifying label or evaluation on the samples themselves. Bring your advertisements and pieces of writing to class and exchange them with those of a classmate. After ten minutes, compare notes. Do you and your classmate agree on the evaluation of each sample? Why or why not?

▪ ESSAY TOPICS

Write a convincing argument attacking or defending one of the following statements, or use them to help you think of your own topic. Remember to narrow and focus the topic as necessary. (Note that essays on some of the topics presented here might profit from research material; see Chapter 14 for help.) For additional ideas, see the "Suggestions for Writing" section following the professional essays (page 293).

1. Students should/should not work throughout the academic year.

2. To prepare students for a highly technical world, colleges and universities should make courses in advanced computer literacy a requirement for every student.

3. Drunk drivers should have their licences revoked permanently if they have caused any accidents.

4. The movie rating system should/should not be revised.

5. All adoption records should/should not be open to adopted people over 18.

6. Drivers should/should not be allowed to use cell phones while they are driving.

7. Students who do poorly in their academic courses should/should not be allowed to participate in athletic programs.

8. Online communities need/do not need stricter enforcement of rules of conduct.

9. Allowing animal and plant species to become extinct is/is not a necessary condition for human survival today.

10. Multicultural policies reduce/do not reduce people to stereotypes.

11. The math requirement (or some other requirement, rule, or policy) at this school should/should not be changed.

12. Off-road recreational vehicles should/should not be banned from our national parks.

13. Telephone solicitation bans do/do not infringe on freedom of speech.

14. By themselves, both sciences and the humanities lead/do not lead to a limited understanding of the world.

15. The current Prime Minister should/should not be required to step down.

16. Canada's role in the international arena should/should not be reconsidered.

17. More flexibility in prerequisites should/should not be given to First Nations students entering the university system.

18. Persons over age fourteen charged with crimes should/should not be tried as adults.

19. Men and women in the military should/should not serve in separate units.

20. Advertising for "Product X" rarely/often relies on use of emotional appeals and faulty logic. (Focus on one kind of product—cars, cosmetics, computers, soft drinks, cell phones, etc.—or on one especially popular brand, and collect a number of its advertisements to analyze. What does your analysis tell you about the major ways in which your particular product is advertised to its target audience? Do the advertisements appeal to consumers' reason or do they employ logical fallacies? Some combination? Which advertisements are more effective, and why? If it's helpful, start by considering the major appeals of the watch advertisement on page 301 or the Harry Potter advertisement on page 300.)

A Topic Proposal for Your Essay

Selecting the right subject matter is important to every writer. To help you clarify your ideas and strengthen your commitment to your topic, here is a proposal sheet that asks you to describe some of your preliminary ideas about your subject before you begin drafting. Although your ideas may change as you write (they will almost certainly become more refined), thinking through your choice of topic now may help you avoid several false starts.

1. What is the subject of your argumentative essay? Write a rough statement of your position on this subject.

2. Why are you interested in this topic? Is it important to your personal, civic, or professional life? State at least one reason for your choice of topic.

3. Is this a significant topic of interest to others? Why? Is there a particular audience you would like to address?

4. At this point, can you list at least two reasons that support your position on your topic?

5. Who opposes your position? Can you state clearly at least one of your opposition's major criticisms of your position?

6. What difficulties, if any, might arise during drafting? For example, might you need to collect any additional evidence through reading, research, or interviewing to support your points or to refute your opposition?

■ Sample Student Essay

The student who wrote this essay followed the steps for writing an argumentative paper discussed in this chapter. His intended audience was the readers of his school newspaper, primarily students but instructors as well. To argue his case, he chose Pattern A, presenting two of his own points and then concluding with a rebuttal of an important opposing view. Notice that this writer uses a variety of methods to convince his readers, including hypothetical examples, causal analysis, analogy, and testimony. Does the writer persuade you to his point of view? Which are his strongest and weakest arguments? What might you change to make his essay even more persuasive?

STUDENTS, PLEASE VOTE!

Introduction: Presenting the controversy

1   A walk across campus this week will reveal students going about their own lives, complaining about their problems to each other, exchanging gossip, and even discussing course material. But as they walk, few seem to notice the posters screaming at them from every notice board, doorway, and bus stop: "Student Elections: Please Vote!" They walk by the student candidates who try to tell them about election issues or their own platforms, and delete any e-mails the student society sends them about the election. When asked if they are going to vote in student elections

Essay map

this year, they say they are too busy, they don't know what the issues or who the candidates are, their votes don't really count and that student elections are fought over irrelevant issues anyway. But

Thesis

these students must vote in elections whenever they can, not only because this will ensure they will have a say in important decisions made on their behalf and make them more responsible citizens in the long term, but because it will help them recognize the important issues that affect them.

A point for the writer's position: Only voting in student elections can give students a say in important decisions that are being made on their behalf by student politicians and university administrators

2   Many students complain about various campus policies they encounter every day, yet seem to feel there is nothing they can do about them. Students need to understand the real cause-and-effect relationship between their votes and their lives as students. For example, perhaps the university administration wants to fund a new administration building, when most students polled on campus would prefer more subsidized student housing. If only 12 percent of students vote on the issue of subsidized housing, the administration would feel justified in going ahead with funding the new administration building, since they would get the message that students didn't care. The higher the percentage of student voters, the more likely student issues will be taken seriously. While

it is true that one individual student is unlikely to be able to make a significant change in campus policies, a student politician who represents a large group of students is more likely to be listened to, and her ideas more likely to be considered when decisions are going to be made.

3   Students need to take responsibility for their own lives and for the well-being of their greater community. Instead of complaining, students need to take action and make their voices heard when given the opportunity to do so! As students become informed about election issues and candidates, they will practise thinking critically as well. As they become increasingly aware of issues that affect them, they will also realize how politics and rhetoric function together. Their informed voting can help to make decisions that benefit the greater student community. In turn, the comprehensive skills they learn from voting in student elections can help them make informed choices for the rest of their lives as they begin to vote in municipal, provincial, and federal elections.

Another point for the writer's position: Students need to take responsibility for their own lives and the issues that affect them so they can become better citizens both on campus and beyond

4   Many students say they don't have access to information about election issues or about the platforms of various candidates. Since information is available to them through posters, student publications in print, the student society website, public debates, and candidate meetings, the accusation of limited information access seems illogical and even irresponsible. More importantly, non-voters say that election issues are irrelevant to their lives. It is true that there are tens of candidates for each election, and that some of these candidates focus on minor, sometimes even frivolous, issues. For example, one year, a student candidate promised to ensure there was more funding for student parties. However, university students are expected to be able to differentiate between serious and frivolous claims, and between

Presentation and rebuttal of the opposition's claim that election issues are either irrelevant or too difficult to be informed about

experienced and inexperienced candidates. All the serious candidates in student elections provide enough relevant background information on their own expertise, and focus on issues significant to their fellow students, such as tuition fee levels, campus safety, subsidized transit programs, class size, access to courses, and so forth.

Conclusion: Statement indicating significance of thesis, ending on a paradox to emphasize the main idea

5   The low voter turnout on this campus is due to student misconceptions about their relationship to campus issues, misconceptions this essay has attempted to address. Students need to recognize that student elections deal with issues that affect them directly, that their voices have real power in their community, whether on campus or beyond, and that they have the responsibility to use that power responsibly. Don't give up your rights because the responsibility is too much!

Professional Essays: Pro and Con*

The following essays on the issue of global warming are both written by groups of respected scientists. The first essay represents the official position taken by an international group of scientific academies (or main professional scientific communities), including the academies of Canada, Russia, China, and the United States. These scientific bodies wish to make the world aware of the seriousness of global warming; the second essay is a response by an opposing group of international scientists who aim to persuade Canada's prime minister that global warming doesn't exist. The first essay is signed by the Chair of each academy, who thus represents hundreds of scientists, while the second is signed by sixty respected individual scientists.

Although you may already hold a position on this controversy, try to remain objective as you analyze the strengths and weaknesses of both essays. Which points are most and least persuasive, and why?

---

* For help reading these essays analytically, review pages 160–162.

■ Joint Science Academies' Statement: Global Response to Climate Change

1 *Climate change is real*

There will always be uncertainty in understanding a system as complex as the world's climate. However there is now strong evidence that significant global warming is occurring.[1] The evidence comes from direct measurements of rising surface air temperatures and subsurface ocean temperatures and from phenomena such as increases in average global sea levels, retreating glaciers, and changes to many physical and biological systems. It is likely that most of the warming in recent decades can be attributed to human activities (IPCC 2001).[2] This warming has already led to changes in the Earth's climate.

2 The existence of greenhouse gases in the atmosphere is vital to life on Earth—in their absence average temperatures would be about 30 centigrade degrees lower than they are today. But human activities are now causing atmospheric concentrations of greenhouse gases—including carbon dioxide, methane, tropospheric ozone, and nitrous oxide—to rise well above pre-industrial levels. Carbon dioxide levels have increased from 280 ppm in 1750 to over 375 ppm today—higher than any previous levels that can be reliably measured (i.e., in the last 420,000 years). Increasing greenhouse gases are causing temperatures to rise; the Earth's surface warmed by approximately 0.6 centigrade degrees over the twentieth century. The Intergovernmental Panel on Climate Change (IPCC) projected that the average global surface temperatures will continue to increase to between 1.4 centigrade degrees and 5.8 centigrade degrees above 1990 levels, by 2100.

3 *Reduce the causes of climate change*

The scientific understanding of climate change is now sufficiently clear to justify nations taking prompt action. It is vital that all nations identify cost-effective steps that they can take now, to contribute to substantial and long-term reduction in net global greenhouse gas emissions.

4 Action taken now to reduce significantly the build-up of greenhouse gases in the atmosphere will lessen the magnitude and rate of climate change. As the United Nations Framework Convention on Climate Change (UNFCCC) recognizes, a lack of full scientific certainty about some aspects of climate change is not a reason for delaying an immediate response that will, at a reasonable cost, prevent dangerous anthropogenic interference with the climate system.

5 As nations and economies develop over the next 25 years, world primary energy demand is estimated to increase by almost 60%. Fossil fuels, which are responsible for the majority of carbon dioxide emissions produced by human activities, provide valuable resources for many nations and are projected to provide 85% of this demand (IEA 2004).[3] Minimising the amount of this carbon dioxide reaching the atmosphere presents a huge challenge. There are many potentially cost-effective technological options that could contribute to stabilising greenhouse gas concentrations. These are at various stages of research and development. However, barriers to their broad deployment still need to be overcome.

6   Carbon dioxide can remain in the atmosphere for many decades. Even with possible lowered emission rates we will be experiencing the impacts of climate change throughout the 21st century and beyond. Failure to implement significant reductions in net greenhouse gas emissions now, will make the job much harder in the future.

7   *Prepare for the consequences of climate change*

Major parts of the climate system respond slowly to changes in greenhouse gas concentrations. Even if greenhouse gas emissions were stabilised instantly at today's levels, the climate would still continue to change as it adapts to the increased emission of recent decades. Further changes in climate are therefore unavoidable. Nations must prepare for them.

8   The projected changes in climate will have both beneficial and adverse effects at the regional level, for example on water resources, agriculture, natural ecosystems and human health. The larger and faster the changes in climate, the more likely it is that adverse effects will dominate. Increasing temperatures are likely to increase the frequency and severity of weather events such as heat waves and heavy rainfall. Increasing temperatures could lead to large-scale effects such as the melting of large ice sheets (with major impacts on low-lying regions throughout the world). The IPCC estimates that the combined effects of ice melting and sea water expansion from ocean warming are projected to cause the global mean sea-level to rise by between 0.1-0.9 metres between 1990-2100. In Bangladesh alone, a 0.5 metre sea level rise would place about 6 million people at risk from flooding.

9   Developing nations that lack the infrastructure or resources to respond to the effects of climate change will be particularly affected. It is clear that many of the world's poorest people are likely to suffer the most from climate change. Long-term global efforts to create a more healthy, prosperous and sustainable world may be severely hindered by changes in the climate.

10   The task of devising and implementing strategies to adapt to the consequences of climate change will require worldwide collaborative inputs from a wide range of experts, including physical and natural scientists, engineers, social scientists, medical scientists, those in the humanities, business leaders and economists.

Conclusion

11   We urge all nations, in line with the UNFCCC principles,[4] to take prompt action to reduce the causes of climate change, adapt to its impacts and ensure that the issue is included in all relevant national and international strategies. As national science academies, we commit to working with governments to help develop and implement the national and international response to the challenge of climate change.

12   G8 nations have been responsible for much of the past greenhouse gas emissions. As parties to the UNFCCC, G8 nations are committed to showing leadership in addressing climate change and assisting developing nations to meet the challenges of adaptation and mitigation.

13   We call on world leaders, including those meeting at the Gleneagles G8 summit in July 2005, to:

- Acknowledge that the threat of climate change is clear and increasing.
- Launch an international study[5] to explore scientifically-informed targets for atmospheric greenhouse gas concentrations, and their associated emissions scenarios, that will enable nations to avoid impacts deemed unacceptable.

- Identify cost-effective steps that can be taken now to contribute to substantial and long-term reduction in net global greenhouse gas emissions. Recognize that delayed action will increase the risk of adverse environmental effects and will likely incur a greater cost.
- Work with developing nations to build a scientific and technological capacity best suited to their circumstances, enabling them to develop innovative solutions to mitigate and adapt to the adverse effects of climate change, while explicitly recognizing their legitimate development rights.
- Show leadership in developing and deploying clean energy technologies and approaches to energy efficiency, and share this knowledge with all other nations.
- Mobilise the science and technology community to enhance research and development efforts, which can better inform climate change decisions.

Notes and References

1. This statement concentrates on climate change associated with global warming. We use the UNFCCC definition of climate change, which is 'a change of climate which is attributed directly or indirectly to human activity that alters the composition of the global atmosphere and which is in addition to natural climate variability observed over comparable time periods'.
2. IPCC (2001). Third Assessment Report. We recognise the international scientific consensus of the Intergovernmental Panel on Climate Change (IPCC).
3. IEA (2004). World Energy Outlook 4. Although long-term projections of future world energy demand and supply are highly uncertain, the World Energy Outlook produced by the International Energy Agency (IEA) is a useful source of information about possible future energy scenarios.
4. With special emphasis on the first principle of the UNFCCC, which states: 'The Parties should protect the climate system for the benefit of present and future generations of humankind, on the basis of equity and in accordance with their common but differentiated responsibilities and respective capabilities. Accordingly, the developed country Parties should take the lead in combating climate change and the adverse effects thereof'.
5. Recognising and building on the IPCC's ongoing work on emission scenarios.

■ The Opposing View of Sixty Scientists: An Open Letter to Prime Minister Stephen Harper, Thursday, April 6, 2006

1 Dear Prime Minister,

As accredited experts in climate and related scientific disciplines, we are writing to propose that balanced, comprehensive, public-consultation sessions be held so as to examine the scientific foundation of the federal government's climate-change plans. This would be entirely consistent with your recent commitment to conduct a review of the Kyoto Protocol. Although many of us made the same suggestion to then-prime ministers Martin and Chrétien, neither responded, and to date, no formal, independent climate-science review has been conducted in Canada. Much of the billions of dollars earmarked for implementation of the protocol in Canada will be squandered without a proper assessment of recent developments in climate science.

2 Observational evidence does not support today's computer climate models, so there is little reason to trust model predictions of the future. Yet this is precisely what the United Nations did in creating and promoting Kyoto and still does in the alarmist

forecasts on which Canada's climate policies are based. Even if the climate models were realistic, the environmental impact of Canada delaying implementation of Kyoto or other greenhouse-gas reduction schemes, pending completion of consultations, would be insignificant. Directing your government to convene balanced, open hearings as soon as possible would be a most prudent and responsible course of action.

3   While the confident pronouncements of scientifically unqualified environmental groups may provide for sensational headlines, they are no basis for mature policy formulation. The study of global climate change is, as you have said, an "emerging science," one that is perhaps the most complex ever tackled. It may be many years yet before we properly understand the Earth's climate system. Nevertheless, significant advances have been made since the protocol was created, many of which are taking us away from a concern about increasing greenhouse gases. If, back in the mid-1990s, we knew what we know today about climate, Kyoto would almost certainly not exist, because we would have concluded it was not necessary.

4   We appreciate the difficulty any government has formulating sensible science-based policy when the loudest voices always seem to be pushing in the opposite direction. However, by convening open, unbiased consultations, Canadians will be permitted to hear from experts on both sides of the debate in the climate-science community. When the public comes to understand that there is no "consensus" among climate scientists about the relative importance of the various causes of global climate change, the government will be in a far better position to develop plans that reflect reality and so benefit both the environment and the economy.

5   "Climate change is real" is a meaningless phrase used repeatedly by activists to convince the public that a climate catastrophe is looming and humanity is the cause. Neither of these fears is justified. Global climate changes all the time due to natural causes and the human impact still remains impossible to distinguish from this natural "noise." The new Canadian government's commitment to reducing air, land and water pollution is commendable, but allocating funds to "stopping climate change" would be irrational. We need to continue intensive research into the real causes of climate change and help our most vulnerable citizens adapt to whatever nature throws at us next.

6   We believe the Canadian public and government decision-makers need and deserve to hear the whole story concerning this very complex issue. It was only 30 years ago that many of today's global-warming alarmists were telling us that the world was in the midst of a global-cooling catastrophe. But the science continued to evolve, and still does, even though so many choose to ignore it when it does not fit with predetermined political agendas.

7   We hope that you will examine our proposal carefully and we stand willing and able to furnish you with more information on this crucially important topic.

Questions on Content, Structure, and Style

1. What specific issue do these two documents debate and what are their respective positions on this subject?

2. Why does the group of sixty scientists in the second essay oppose adherence to the Kyoto protocol and to general climate control policies in Canada? What evidence does this essay offer to support its growing concern about "formulating

sensible science-based policy"? Is the evidence of one group more convincing than another's?

3. Who is the intended audience of each essay? What does vocabulary choice tell you about the audience?

4. Is either group's credibility stronger than the other's? Why or why not? Can you detect any biases in either essay?

5. What are the Academies' main arguments for implementing strict climate control policies? What are the sixty scientists' main arguments for reconsidering such policies?

8. Does either essay acknowledge agreement with the opposing point of view? If so, where and why? How are opponents characterized? How are opposing arguments represented?

9. What techniques are used in the conclusions of each essay? How appropriate and effective are these techniques for the purpose of each essay?

10. Overall, what are the major strengths and weaknesses of these two essays? What advice might you offer to improve their arguments?

Suggestions for Writing

Use the official statement of the Science Academies and the challenge by the sixty scientists as a stepping stone to your essay. Do you agree or disagree with one of the views on global warming? If you're not sure, start with some role-playing. Imagine yourself as a policymaker setting rules based on the Sciences Academies' recommendations for different groups of people, such as commuters, doctors, and construction workers in developed countries, or factory workers, small business owners, and architects in poorer countries. What kinds of arguments will you make to convince them the rules are necessary if they challenge you by citing the types of arguments the sixty scientists make? Will you make the same rules for members of countries with different economic levels? Write a brief argument in which you announce and defend your policy. Or, if you prefer, you can take the side of groups who refuse to accept the recommendations of the Science Academies, and defend your choice. One useful preliminary exercise would be to conduct a debate. Organize the claims on each side of the argument, and discuss the persuasive strength of each one, using the sections in this chapter (pages 275–281) on reasoning, proofs, and logical fallacies to guide you. Once you've tried some exploratory arguments like this, aim to write some more serious arguments by doing research. Read some scientific articles so you can argue from a more knowledgeable perspective. This would be a good opportunity to research the environmental investigations that are constantly reported on in the news and in journals today.

Vocabulary

The Science Academies' essay:

vital (2)	adverse (8)	mitigation (12)
tropospheric (2)	infrastructure (9)	incur (13)
deployment (5)	devising (10)	mobilise (13)

The 60 Scientists' essay:

comprehensive (1)   protocol (1)

convene (2)   prudent (2)

■ Analyzing Advertisements

Because they are designed to be persuasive, advertisements use a variety of logical and emotional appeals. Advertisements might be considered arguments in brief form, as they frequently try to convince the public to buy a product, take an action, vote for or against something, join a group, or change an attitude or a behaviour. By analyzing the advertisements that follow, you can practise identifying a variety of persuasive appeals and evaluating their effectiveness. After discussing these advertisements, apply what you've learned about logical appeals, target audiences, and choice of language to your argumentative essay.

Conflicting Positions: Smoking

The advertisements that follow address the controversial subject of smoking, and all feature strong, independent-looking people. The first advertisement ("2nd Hand Smoke Can Kill You") is one of a series published, and made into television spots, by Health Canada, a division of the Government of Canada. This advertisement warns against the dangers of secondhand smoke, and features a stark portrait of a woman who, in 2003, was dying of lung cancer developed from her exposure to secondhand smoke. Even after her death in 2006, her name continued to be used in antismoking campaigns. The second advertisement is a billboard for Marlboro, an American brand of cigarettes, which shows a man in a cowboy hat, with a cigarette dangling from his mouth. He is a strong, athletic man, as we can see from the casual way in which he carries a heavy saddle, the implication being that cigarette smokers can be vigorous and healthy. The billboard is framed by an intensely blue sky, as the Marlboro Man towers over the landscape. While this image emphasizes a certain lifestyle of relaxed, rugged wholesomeness, which is presumably achievable by an ordinary man, its overall relationship to the landscape around it implies a heroic dimension. Note that the Canadian government had outlawed cigarette advertising by 2003, but these advertisements continue to be available to Canadians through American and other foreign magazines, the Internet, and television channels. The third advertisement ("Children See, Children Do") is also a product of Health Canada's antismoking campaign, but here it is placed directly on cigarette packages. A mother who is smoking in front of her child is being watched all too closely by that child. The object is to make the potential cigarette consumer think twice about his or her parenting skills, because the focus is not so much on secondhand smoke as on parental influence. Analyze the appeals used in each advertisement. Which methods of persuasion do you think are the most effective, and why? Do you find any of the logical fallacies previously described in this chapter?

Health Canada—secondhand smoke—Heather Crowe

Marlboro cigarette advertisement

Health Canada Cigarette Warning Label: Children See, Children Do

Competing Products: The Environment

The advertisement by Scotiabank presented below promotes its commitment to environmental concerns, while the WonderCafe advertisement on the folllowing page uses a stained glass image to provoke a discussion in which environmental and faith issues are compared. In this second advertisement, are abstract ideas being converted into products? What emotional appeals do you see in these advertisements? Can you see any errors in reasoning? Are these appeals directed at the same readers? Overall, which advertisement do you find more persuasive, and why?

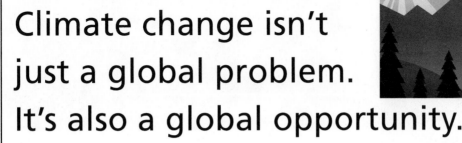

Scotiabank

WonderCafe

Popular Appeals: Spending Our Money

Although the products and target audiences are not at all similar, how might both of the advertisements that follow be said to employ variations of the "bandwagon" appeal? In the Harry Potter advertisement, look at the expressions on the faces of the two men who are presumably watching a Harry Potter movie. What sort of audience identity is represented with the picture of the two men watching—and enjoying—what might be considered a children's film? How does the advertiser indicate that the men are watching a Harry Potter movie? What aspects of this advertisement would persuade adults to buy a children's movie for themselves?

The Omega watch advertisement appeals to a different audience in its use of movie star Nicole Kidman, a respected actress also known for her impeccable style. What effect is "Nicole Kidman's choice" intended to have on the reader?

Harry Potter

Omega Watches with Nicole Kidman

■ A REVISION WORKSHEET

As you write your rough drafts, consult Chapter 5 for guidance through the revision process. In addition, here are a few questions to ask yourself as you revise your argumentative essay:

1. Does this essay present a clear thesis limited to fit the assigned length of this paper?

2. Does this essay contain a number of strong, persuasive points in support of its thesis?

3. Is the essay organized in an easy-to-follow pattern that avoids repetition or confusion?

4. Does the essay present enough supporting evidence to make each of its points convincing? Where could additional examples, factual information, testimony, or other kinds of supporting material be added to make the arguments even more effective?

5. Will all the supporting evidence be clear to the essay's particular audience? Do any terms or examples need additional explanation or special definition?

6. Has at least one major opposing argument been addressed?

7. Does the essay avoid any logical fallacies or problems in tone?

After you've revised your essay extensively, you might exchange rough drafts with a classmate and answer these questions for each other, making specific suggestions for improvement wherever appropriate. (For advice on productive participation in classroom workshops, see pages 102–104.)

Reviewing Your Progress

After you have completed your argument essay, take a moment to measure your progress as a writer by responding to the following questions. Such analysis will help you recognize growth in your writing skills and may enable you to identify areas that are still problematic.

1. Which part of your essay do you like best? Why?

2. After analyzing your essay's reasoning and evidence, which particular argument or point do you consider the strongest? What makes it so convincing?

3. What part of your essay gave you the most trouble? How did you overcome the problem?

4. If you had more time to work on this essay, what would receive additional attention? Why?

5. What did you learn about your topic from writing this essay? About yourself as a writer?

Chapter 11

Description

The writer of description creates a word-picture of persons, places, objects, and emotions, using a careful selection of details to make an impression on the reader. If you have already written expository or argumentative essays in your composition course, you almost certainly have written some descriptive prose. Nearly every essay, after all, calls for some kind of description; for example, in the student comparison and contrast essay (pages 210–213), the writer describes two kinds of stores; in the professional process essay (pages 195–198), the writer describes the embalming procedure in great detail. To help you write better description in your other essays, however, you may want to practise writing descriptive paragraphs or a short descriptive essay.

■ How to Write Effective Description

When descriptive prose is called for in your writing, consider these four basic suggestions:

Recognize your purpose. Description is not free-floating; it appears in your writing for a particular reason—to help you inform, clarify, persuade, or create a mood. In some essays you will want your description as *objective*—without personal impressions—as you can make it; for example, you might describe a scientific experiment or a business transaction in straight factual detail. Other times, however, you will want to convey a particular attitude toward your subject; this approach to description is called *subjective* or *impressionistic*. Note the differences between the following two descriptions of a tall, thin boy: the objective writer sticks to the facts by saying, "The eighteen-year-old boy was 6'1" and weighed 155 pounds," whereas the subjective writer gives an impressionistic description: "The young boy was as tall and scrawny as a birch tree in winter." Before you begin describing anything, you must first decide your purpose and whether it calls for objective or subjective reporting.

Describe clearly, using specific details.   To make any description clear to your reader, you must include a sufficient number of details that are specific rather than fuzzy or vague. If, for example, your family dog were missing, you wouldn't call the animal shelter to ask if they'd seen a "big brown dog with a short tail"—naturally, you'd mention every distinguishing detail about your pet you could think of: size, colour, breed, cut of ears, and special markings. Similarly, if your car were stolen, you'd give the police as clear and as complete a description of your vehicle as possible. Look at the following sentence. Does it clearly identify a vaulting horse?

> A vaulting horse is a thing usually found in gyms that has four legs and a beam and is used by gymnasts making jumps.

If you didn't already know what a vaulting horse was, you might have trouble picking it out in a gymnasium crowded with equipment. A description with additional details would help you locate it:

> A vaulting horse is a piece of equipment used by gymnasts during competition to help propel them into the air when they perform any of a variety of leaps known as vaults. The gymnasts usually approach the vaulting horse from a running start and then place their hands on the horse for support or for a push-off as they perform their vaults. The horse itself resembles a carpenter's sawhorse, but the main beam is made of padded leather rather than wood. The rectangular beam is approximately 160 cm (5 feet, 3 inches) long and 34 cm (13½ inches) wide. Supported by four legs usually made of steel, the padded leather beam is approximately 123 cm (4 feet, ½ inch) above the floor in men's competitions and 109 cm (3 feet, 7 inches) in women's competitions. The padded leather beam has two white lines marking off three sections on top: the croup, the saddle, and the neck. The two end sections—the croup and the neck—are each 39 cm (15½ inches) long. Gymnasts place their hands on the neck or croup, depending on the type of vault they are attempting.

Moreover, the reader cannot imagine your subject clearly if your description is couched in vague generalities. The following sentence, for example, presents only a hazy picture:

> Larry is a sloppy dresser.

Revised, the picture is now sharply in focus:

> Larry wears dirty, baggy pants, shirts too small to stay tucked in, socks that fail to match his pants or each other, and a stained coat the Salvation Army rejected as a donation.

Specific details can turn cloudy prose into crisp, clear images that can be reproduced in the mind like photographs.

Select only appropriate details.   In any description the choice of details depends largely on the writer's purpose and audience. However, many descriptions—especially the more subjective ones—will present a *dominant impression;* that is, the writer selects primarily those details that communicate a particular mood or feeling to the reader. The dominant impression is the controlling focus of a description; for example, if you wrote a description of your grandmother to show her thoughtfulness, you would select only those details that convey an impression of a sweet, kindly old lady. Here are two brief descriptions illustrating the concept of dominant impression. The first writer tries to create a mood of mystery:

Down a black winding road stands the abandoned old mansion, silhouetted against the cloud-shrouded moon, creaking and moaning in the wet, chill wind.

The second writer tries to present a feeling of joy and innocence:

A dozen kites filled the spring air, and around the bright picnic tables spread with hot dogs, hamburgers, and slices of watermelon, Tom and Annie played away the warm July day.

In the description of the deserted mansion, the writer would have violated the impression of mystery had the sentence read,

Down the black winding road stands the abandoned old mansion, surrounded by bright, multicoloured tulips in early bloom.

Including the cheerful flowers as a detail in the description destroys the dominant mood of bleakness and mystery. Similarly, the second example would be spoiled had the writer ended it this way:

Tom and Annie played away the warm July day until Tom got so sunburned he became ill and had to go home.

Therefore, remember to select only those details that advance your descriptive purpose. Omit any details you consider unimportant or distracting.

See if you can determine the dominant impression of each of the following descriptions:

The wind had curled up to sleep in the distant mountains. Leaves hung limp and motionless from the silent trees, while birds perched on the branches like little statues. As I sat on the edge of the clearing, holding my breath, I could hear a squirrel scampering through the underbrush. Somewhere far away a dog barked twice, and then the woods were hushed once more.

This poor thing has seen better days, but one should expect the sofa in a fraternity house den to be well worn. The large, plump, brown corduroy pillows strewn lazily on the floor and propped comfortably against the threadbare arms bear the pencil-point scars of frustrated students and foam-bleeding cuts of multiple pillow wars. No less than four pairs of rotting Nikes stand twenty-four-hour guard at the corners of its carefully mended frame. Obviously the relaxed, inviting appearance masks the permanent odours of cheap cigars from Thursday night poker parties; at least two or three guests each weekend sift through the popcorn kernels and Doritos crumbs, sprawl face down, and pass out for a nap. However, frequent inhabitants have learned to avoid the dark stains courtesy of the house pup and the red-punch designs of the chapter klutz. Habitually, they strategically lunge over the back of the sofa to an unsoiled area easily identifiable in flight by the large depression left by previous regulars. The quiet *hmmph* of the cushions and harmonious squeal of the exhausted springs signal a perfect landing and utter a warm greeting from an old and faithful friend.

Make your descriptions vivid. By using clear, precise words, you can improve any kind of writing. Chapters 7 (on words) and 6 (on sentences) offer a variety of tips on clarifying your prose style. In addition to the advice given there, here are two other ways to enliven your descriptions, particularly those that call for a subjective approach:

Use sensory details. If it's appropriate, try using images that appeal to your readers' five senses. If, for example, you are describing your broken leg and the ensuing stay in a hospital, tell your readers how the place smelled, how it looked, what your cast felt like, how your pills tasted, and what noises you heard. Here are some specific examples using sensory details:

Sight	The clean white corridors of the hospital resembled the set of a sci-fi movie, with everyone scurrying around in identical starched uniforms.
Hearing	At night, the only sounds I heard were the quiet squeaks of sensible white shoes as the nurses made their rounds.
Smell	The green beans on the hospital cafeteria tray smelled stale and waxy, like crayons.
Touch	The hospital bed sheet felt as rough and heavy as a feed sack.
Taste	Every four hours they gave me an enormous grey pill whose after-taste reminded me of the stale licorice my great-aunt kept in candy dishes around her house.

By appealing to the readers' senses, you better enable them to imagine the subject you are describing. Joseph Conrad, the famous nineteenth-century novelist, agreed, believing that all art "appeals primarily to the senses, and the artistic aim when expressing itself in written words must also make its appeal through the senses, if its highest desire is to reach the secret spring of responsive emotions." In other words, to make your readers feel, first make them "see."

Use figurative language when appropriate. As you may recall from Chapter 7, figurative language produces images or pictures in the readers' minds, helping them to understand unfamiliar or abstract subjects. Here are some devices you might use to clarify or spice up your prose:

1. Simile: a comparison between two things using the words "like" or "as" (see also pages 152–153)

   Example   Seeing exactly the video game he wanted, he moved as quickly as a starving teenager spotting pie in a refrigerator full of leftover vegetables.

2. Metaphor: a direct comparison between two things that does not use "like" or "as" (see also pages 152–153)

   Example   I was a puppet, with my father controlling all the financial strings.

3. Personification: the attribution of human characteristics and emotions to inanimate objects, animals, or abstract ideas

   Example   The old teddy bear sat in a corner, dozing serenely before the fireplace.

4. Hyperbole: intentional exaggeration or overstatement for emphasis or humour

Example   The cockroaches in my kitchen had now grown to the size of carry-on luggage.

5. Understatement: intentional representation of a subject as less important than the facts would warrant (see also irony, page 140)

Example   "The reports of my death are greatly exaggerated."—Mark Twain

6. Synecdoche: a part of something used to represent the whole

Example   A hundred tired feet hit the dance floor for one last jitterbug. [Here "feet" stand for the dancing couples themselves.]

Using figures of speech in appropriate places can make your descriptions clear, lively, and memorable. (For additional examples, see pages 152–153.)

Problems to Avoid

Keep in mind these three pieces of advice to solve problems that frequently arise in description:

Remember your audience. Sometimes the object of our description is so clear in our minds we forget that our readers haven't seen it too. Consequently, the description we write turns out to be vague, bland, or skimpy ("The big tree was beautiful"). Ask yourself about your audience: what do they need to know to see this sight as clearly as I do? Then fill in your description with ample, precise details that reveal the best picture possible. Don't forget to define or explain any terms you use that may be puzzling to your audience. (For more advice on clear, vivid language, see Chapter 7.)

Avoid an erratic organization of details. Too often descriptions are a hodgepodge of details, jotted down randomly. When you write a lengthy description, you should select a plan that will arrange your details in an orderly fashion. Depending on your subject matter and your purpose, you might adopt a plan calling for a description of something from top to bottom, left to right, front to back, and so on. For example, a description of a woman might begin at the head and move to the feet; furniture in a room might be described as your eyes move from one side of the room to another. A second plan for arranging details presents the subject's outstanding characteristics first and then fills in the lesser information; a child's red hair, for example, might be his most striking feature and therefore would be described first. A third plan presents details in the order you see them approaching: dust, then a car, then details about the car, its occupants, and so on. Or you might describe a subject as it unfolds chronologically, as in some kind of process or operation. Regardless of which plan of organization you choose, the reader should feel a sense of order in your description.

Avoid any sudden change in perspective. If, for example, you are describing the CN Tower from the outside, don't suddenly include details that could be seen only from the inside. Similarly, if you are describing a car from a distance, you might be able to tell the car's model, year, and colour, but you could hardly describe the upholstery or reveal the odometer's reading. It is, of course, possible for you—or your observer—to approach or move around the subject of your description, but the reader must be aware of this movement. Any shift in point of view must be presented clearly and logically, with no sudden, confusing leaps from a front to a back view, from outside to inside, and so on.

■ **PRACTISING WHAT YOU'VE LEARNED**

William Gibson is the author of the influential science fiction novel *Neuromancer*. This article was commissioned by *The Globe and Mail* in 2007. Analyze the effectiveness of this description: Does the writer succeed in making you "see" these places? What sort of world is this "gone world"? Identify several uses of sensory details and figurative language and explain how they help readers "see" the places of Gibson's memory.

■ Pining for Toronto's "Gone World"

1   A friend of mine in New York has been pointing out surviving bits of what he calls his city's "gone world" to me for the past 20 years or so. When I first started getting to know New York, in the early 1980s, it consisted of that gone world, or so it seemed to me. People who lived there didn't seem to believe it possible that this would change. My friend was the first New Yorker I knew who noticed that things were changing, becoming gone.

2   The sewing machine spare parts quarter, for instance (gone), or the tenement that once housed McGurk's Suicide Hall (gone). Bits and pieces of SoHo and TriBeCa and Chelsea, all gone. Had I not had so observant a guide, I certainly would have missed them, these glimpses of vanishing things, but my friend had treasured them all, and was pained by their going, and took care to show them to me. It was his conviction that they were invariably replaced by much less interesting things (to put it mildly), and I generally agreed.

3   But I had, in this, a secret, if only half-recognized. There was an element of déjà-vu for me about this "regooding" (my friend's term) of the gone world. I felt as though I knew where it was going. I felt as though I'd seen it before, and knew where it led, though I wasn't quite aware why.

4   Now, in retrospect, I know that I knew it from Toronto, which had been my first city (if one didn't count Roanoke, VA., or Tucson, ARIZ., or Los Angeles, none of which, for their various reasons, were quite the ticket).

5   Toronto was a city I discovered directly, stumbling upon it with almost no previous knowledge. Montreal I at least had heard of. Toronto. A city. In Canada. Quite a big one, it seemed, riding the bus in from Washington, one afternoon in 1967.

6   It consisted largely, I found, of the most amiable sort of re-purposed semi-ruins. A vast Victorian colonial seashell of blackened brick, shot through with big, grim grey bones of earnest civic Modernism. I marvelled that such an odd place could have existed without my having heard of it. North of New England, all this baroque, mad brick; sandstone gargoyles, red trams, the Queen's portrait everywhere.

7   New-found friends, often as not, rented high-ceilinged rooms in crumbling town-houses, their slate rooflines fenced with rusting traceries of cast-iron, curlicues I'd only seen in Charles Addams cartoons. Everything painted a uniform dead green, like the face of a corpse in those same Addams cartoons. If you took a penknife and scraped a little of the green away, you discovered marvels: brown marble shot with paler veins, ornate bronze fixtures, carved oak. In the more stygian reaches of the cellar, in such places, there were still to be found fully connected gaslight fixtures,

forgotten, protruding from dank plaster like fairy pipes, each with a little flowered twist-key to stop the gas.

8   This was mid-town, walking distance in various directions from Yonge and Bloor. And by the time my friend started citing the regooding of Manhattan, it was a gone world, massively regooded. When friends from New York returned from Toronto, and I told them that Yorkville had been my bohemia, they were baffled. I explained that it was as though the Trump Tower had been built on St. Mark's Place, but still they didn't get it, so thorough had that regooding been.

9   Toronto got there first, in my experience, and in getting there, lost me. Too much money, too much ambition. To remake oneself architecturally, too thoroughly, in the seventies, was to don a very wide tie indeed. And to then have to live with it. Toronto became my gone world, a source of some frustration, of early loss. Too much erased, too quickly, around the footprint of my early 20s. Too many tiny landmarks vanished beneath wide ties. The Uptown Nuthouse. The sepulchral dining room above the original Pilot Tavern, where I drank my first legal glass of beer. I married a girl from Vancouver, who took me there, where lots of things were still made of wood, and the regooding was still several decades away.

10   The experience taught me something about the past, how it moves into and inhabits the future. Or rather, about how it should, ideally. Because it doesn't. Always. When I first saw London, and Paris, I understood that (though they too would find their own regoodings, further along).

11   Wide tie development and big footprints belong particularly to China now. I recently wrote an introduction to Greg Girard's *Phantom Shanghai*. Girard's photographs of old Chinese houses standing forlornly amid fields scraped bare of rubble, awaiting the New Buildings, remind me of my Gone World Toronto.

12   When I return, there is no returning. Some crucial few square blocks are simply gone. Altered beyond recognition. Only the febrile tackiness of Yonge below Bloor preserves something of my past, and I invariably find myself walking there, considering how the cheap, flashy goods of the 21st century resemble the cheap flashy goods of the 20th. An immortality of battery-operated plastic crap, the business of its retail sheltering the actual texture of the gone world, these queer old buildings unnoticed above the lights and bright laminates and shining tat: weird Masonic dreams, blackened finials carved like chess pieces. Under a fresh fall of snow their former gaslight solidity can loom, breathtakingly peculiar, like Castle Gormenghast held overhead at bay, by sex shops and knockoff sneakers. To the extent that I ever find the place my memory tries to take me to, in Toronto, I find it there.

13   Having had this experience quite some time ago, I've long imagined my friend in New York headed for something similar, though without quite having had the heart to tell him. Times Square. Who would have dreamed? Not the science fiction writer, certainly.

14   I suppose this could all be put down to any generation's sense of nostalgia, but I find it rather more complicated. Nostalgia for a life lived among ruins, in cities that were transitional, semi-empty shells of what they once had been. The past as unmediated playground, raw material, cheap rent, absent landlords.

15   But I find I forgive Toronto. Now, as the regooding spreads ever further abroad.

16   Really it wasn't her fault.

■ ASSIGNMENT

Use this powerful painting, *Koskimo*, by Canadian artist Emily Carr, to practise your descriptive writing skills. What is the dominant impression or "mood" of this painting? What details in the picture support your interpretation? Consider, for example, the painting's setting (place, year, time); choice of colours and use of light and shadow; the focus of the scene. In a short descriptive essay, recreate this painting as you see it for someone who is unfamiliar with the work. After writing this essay, read Carr's own essay about the subject of this painting, on pages 317–321.

Emily Carr, *Koskimo*, 1930, charcoal on paper, 78.5 x 57.3 cm, Collection of the Vancouver Art Gallery, Emily Carr Trust, VAG 42.3.119, Photo: Vancouver Art Gallery.

Koskimo, 1930, by Emily Carr

■ ESSAY TOPICS

Here are some suggestions for a descriptive paragraph or essay; focus your topic to fit your assignment. Don't forget that every description, whether objective or subjective, has a purpose and that your details should support that purpose. For additional ideas, see "Suggestions for Writing" on page 322.

1. A favourite photograph or work of art (or choose a picture from this textbook)

2. Your best/worst job

3. A piece of equipment important to your field of study

4. Your favourite/least favourite fictional character

5. One dish or foodstuff that should be forever banned

6. Yourself (how you looked at a certain age or on a memorable occasion)

7. Your most precious material possession

8. The ugliest/most beautiful place on your campus or in town

9. A common social behavioural pattern

10. Your first or worst car or apartment

11. A piece of clothing that represents a historical period

12. A product that needs to be invented

13. An act of heroism

14. An emotion

15. An unforgettable moment

16. An unusual animal

17. A shopping mall, museum, or other crowded public place

18. An aspect of the weather

19. A special collection or hobby display

20. Your Special Place (Perhaps your place offers you solitude, beauty, or renewed energy. The scene below was painted ten times by nineteenth-century artist Claude Monet, who loved this tranquil lily pond near his farmhouse in France. Recreate your special place for your readers by choosing the right descriptive words, just as Monet did with each brush stroke of colour.)

© Superstock, Inc.

The Water-Lily Pond, *1899, by Claude Monet*

A Topic Proposal for Your Essay

Selecting the right subject matter is important to every writer. To help you clarify your ideas and strengthen your commitment to your topic, here is a proposal sheet that asks you to describe some of your preliminary ideas about your subject before you begin drafting. Although your ideas may change as you write (they will almost certainly become more refined), thinking through your choice of topic now may help you avoid several false starts.

1. What subject will your essay describe? Will you describe this subject objectively or subjectively? Why?

2. Why are you interested in this topic? Do you have a personal or professional connection to the subject? State at least one reason for your choice of topic.

3. Is this a significant topic of interest to others? Why? Who specifically might find it interesting, informative, or entertaining?

4. What is the main purpose of your description? In one or two sentences describe the major effect you'd like your descriptive essay to have on your readers. What would you like for them to understand or "see" about your subject?

5. List at least three details that you think will help clarify your subject for your readers.

6. What difficulties, if any, might arise during drafting? For example, what organizational strategy might you think about now that would allow you to guide your readers through your description in a coherent way?

■ Sample Student Essay

In her descriptive essay, this student writer recalls her childhood days at the home of her grandparents to make a point about growing up. Notice that the writer uses both figurative language and contrasting images to help her readers understand her point of view.

TREE CLIMBING

1   It was Mike's eighteenth birthday and he was having a little bit of a breakdown. "When was the last time you made cloud pictures?" he asked me absently as he stared up at the ceiling before class started. Before I could answer, he continued, "Did you know that by the time you're an adult, you've lost 85 percent of your imagination?" He paused. "I don't want to grow up." Although I doubted the authenticity of his facts, I understood that Mike—the hopeless romantic with his long ponytail, sullen black clothes, and glinting dark eyes—was caught in a Peter Pan complex. He drew those eyes from the ceiling and focused on me: "There are two types of children. Tree children and dirt children. Kids playing will either climb trees or play in the dirt. Tree children are the dreamers—the hopeful, creative dreamers. Dirt children, they just stay on the ground. Stick to the rules." He trailed off, and then picked up again: "I'm a tree child. I want to make cloud pictures and climb trees. And I don't ever want to come down." Mike's story reminded me of my own days as a tree child, and of the inevitable fall from the tree to the ground.

2   My childhood was a playground for imagination. Summers were spent surrounded by family at my grandparents' house in

*Introduction: The conversation that triggers her memory

Saskatoon, Saskatchewan. The rambling Lannonstone bungalow was located on 622 8th Avenue North, a few blocks away from Saskatoon's downtown centre, and only a fifteen-minute walk from the university campus. In the winter, all the houses looked alike, rigid and militant, like white-bearded old generals with icicles hanging from their moustaches. One European-styled house after the other lined the streets in strict parallel formation, block after block.

The grandparents' neighbourhood remembered in military images and sensory details

3   But in the summer it was different . . . softer. No subzero winds blew lonely down the back alley. Instead, kids played stickball in it. I had elegant, grass-stained tea parties with a neighbourhood girl named Maya, while my grandfather worked in his thriving vegetable garden among the honeybees, and watched sprouts grow. An ever-present warming smell of yeast filtered down every street as the nearby breweries pumped a constant flow of fresh beer. Above, the summer sky looked like an Easter egg God had dipped in blue dye.

4   Those summer trips to Saskatoon were greatly anticipated events back then. My brother and I itched with repressed energy throughout the long plane ride from the West Coast. We couldn't wait to see Grandma and Papa. We couldn't wait to see what presents Papa had for us. We couldn't wait to slide down the steep, blue-carpeted staircase on our bottoms, and then on our stomachs. Most of all, we couldn't wait to go down to the basement.

Use of parallel sentences to emphasize anticipation

5   The basement was better than a toy store. Yes, the old-fashioned milk cabinet in the kitchen wall was enchanting, and the laundry chute was fun because it was big enough to throw down Ernie, my stuffed dog companion, so my brother could catch him below in the laundry room, as our voices echoed up and down the

chute. But the basement was better than all of these, better even than sliding down those stairs on rug-burned bottoms.

6   It was always deliciously cool down in the basement. Since the house was built in the 1930s, there was no air conditioning. Upstairs, we slept in hot, heavy rooms. My nightgown stuck to the sheets, and I would lie awake, listening to crickets, inhaling the beer-sweet smell of the summer night, hoping for a cool breeze. Nights were forgotten, however, as my brother and I spent hours every day in the basement. There were seven rooms in the basement; some darker rooms I had waited years to explore. There was always a jumbled heap of toys in the middle room, most of which were leftovers from my father's own basement days. It was a child's safe haven; it was a sacred place.

The basement in contrast to other parts of the house

7   The hours spent in the basement were times of a gloriously secure childhood. Empires were created in a day with faded coloured building blocks. New territories were annexed when either my brother or I got the courage to venture into one of those Other Rooms—the dark, musty ones without windows—and then scamper back to report of any sightings of monsters or other horrific childhood creatures. In those basement days everything seemed safe and wholesome and secure, with my family surrounding me, protecting me. Like childhood itself, entering the basement was like entering another dimension.

Adventures in the basement

8   Last summer I returned to Saskatoon to help my grandparents pack to move into an apartment. I went back at seventeen to find the house—my kingdom—up for sale. I found another cycle coming to a close, and I found myself separated from what I had once known. I looked at the house. It was old; it was crumbling; it needed paint. I looked down the back alley and saw nothing but trash and weeds. I walked to the corner and saw smoke-choked,

The house and neighbourhood years later

dirty streets and thick bars in shop windows, nothing more than another worn-out prairie town. I went back to the house and down to the basement, alone.

9   It was grey and dark. Dust filtered through a single feeble sunbeam from a cracked window pane. It was empty, except for the overwhelming musty smell. The toys were gone, either packed or thrown away. As I walked in and out of rooms, the quietness filled my ears, but in the back of my head the sounds of childhood laughter and chatter played like an old recording.

The basement years later

10   The dark rooms were filled not with monsters but with remnants of my grandfather's business. A neon sign was propped against the wall in a corner: Ben Strauss Plumbing. Piles of heavy pipes and metal machine parts lay scattered about on shelves. A dusty purple ribbon was thumbtacked to a door. It said SHOOT THE WORKS in white letters. I gently took it down. The ribbon hangs on my door at home now, and out of context it somehow is not quite so awe-inspiring and mystifying as it once was. However, it does serve its purpose, permanently connecting me to my memories.

11   All children are tree children, I believe. The basement used to be my tree, the place I could dream in. That last summer I found myself, much to Mike's disappointment, quite mature, quite adult. Maybe Mike fell from his tree and was bruised. Climbing down from that tree doesn't have to be something to be afraid of. One needn't hide in the tree for fear of touching the ground and forgetting how to climb back up when necessary. I think there is a way to balance the two extremes. Climb down gracefully as you grow up, and if you fall, don't land in quicksand. I like to think I'm more of a shrubbery child: not so low as to get stuck in the mud and just high enough to look at the sky and make cloud pictures.

Conclusion: A return to the introduction's images and some advice

Professional Essay*

■ D'Sonoqua†

Emily Carr

Emily Carr (1871–1945) is probably the best-known artist in British Columbia. Trained in San Francisco, London, and Paris, Carr returned to her native Victoria when her money ran out, and spent many years working as a potter, dog trainer, and so on until Lauren Harris of the Group of Seven invited her to join this new artistic movement. Carr became an established member of this group and, according to her fellow modern artists, the mother of modern art in Canada. With these artists, she shared a fascination for the Canadian landscape. She divided her attention between painting trees and forests, and sketching the art she discovered in remote First Nations villages in British Columbia. Carr also wrote several memoirs. This essay was published in her book *Klee Wick* (1941), a name ("the laughing one") given to her by one of the many West Coast First Nations tribes she encountered.

1   I was sketching in a remote Indian village when I first saw her. The village was one of those that the Indians use only for a few months in each year; the rest of the time it stands empty and desolate. I went there in one of its empty times, in a drizzling dusk.

2   When the Indian agent dumped me on the beach in front of the village, he said "There is not a soul here. I will come back for you in two days." Then he went away.

3   I had a small Griffon dog with me, and also a little Indian girl, who, when she saw the boat go away, clung to my sleeve and wailed, "I'm 'fraid."

4   We went up to the old deserted Mission House. At the sound of the key in the rusty lock, rats scuttled away. The stove was broken, the wood wet. I had forgotten to bring candles. We spread our blankets on the floor, and spent a poor night. Perhaps my lack of sleep played its part in the shock that I got, when I saw her for the first time.

5   Water was in the air, half mist, half rain. The stinging nettles, higher than my head, left their nervy smart on my ears and forehead, as I beat my way through them, trying

---

* To help you read this essay analytically, review pages 160–162. For two other professional essays in Part Two that make extensive use of description, see "To Bid the World Farewell" (pages 195–198) and "Two Ways of Viewing the River" (pages 219–220).

† *Note on Context: Some of the language in this essay, such as "Indian Tom" (paragraph 18) or "dirty Indian vermin" (paragraph 43), seems shocking to us today. We are used to a level of linguistic sensitivity that has been built up over time, through much effort and public education. In Carr's time, it was common to use ethnic identifiers—such as "Indian Tom"—which would not be used today. This does not mean we have stopped classifying people, but that we perhaps classify people in different ways, and that we use language somewhat differently. In the same way, when we see an expression like "dirty Indian vermin," our first reaction is to say this is offensive, and, if we are uncritical readers, that, therefore, we cannot read anything that has such language in it. But any reader who reads thoughtfully, and considers not just historical context but the context within the essay itself, can see that there is a reason for the inclusion of such an expression. First, it represents a common attitude toward First Nations people at a certain period. But much more important is the response to that attitude in this essay. The narrator responds curtly (paragraph 44) and by refusing the help of the racist and mean-spirited boatman, she rejects his prejudices. Her rejection of those prejudices guides the reader into accepting her own more inclusive and respectful point of view toward First Nations peoples and cultures.*

all the while to keep my feet on the plank walk which they hid. Big yellow slugs crawled on the walk and slimed it. My feet slipped, and I shot headlong to her very base, for she had no feet. The nettles that were above my head reached only to her knee.

6   It was not the fall alone that jerked the "Oh's" out of me, for the great wooden image towering above me was indeed terrifying.

7   The nettle-bed ended a few yards beyond her, and then a rocky bluff jutted out, with waves battering it below. I scrambled up and went out on the bluff, so that I could see the creature above the nettles. The forest was behind her, the sea in front.

8   Her head and trunk were carved out of, or rather into, the bole of a great red cedar. She seemed to be part of the tree itself, as if she had grown there at its heart, and the carver had only chipped away the outer wood so that you could see her. Her arms were spliced and socketed to the trunk, and were flung wide in a circling, compelling movement. Her breasts were two eagle heads, fiercely carved. That much, and the column of her great neck, and her strong chin, I had seen when I slithered to the ground beneath her. Now I saw her face.

9   The eyes were two rounds of black, set in wider rounds of white, and placed in deep sockets under wide, black eyebrows. Their fixed stare bored into me as if the very life of the old cedar looked out, and it seemed that the voice of the tree itself might have burst from that round cavity, with projecting lips, that was her mouth. Her ears were round, and stuck out to catch all sounds. The salt air had not dimmed the heavy red of her trunk and rams and thighs. Her hands were black, with blunt finger-tips painted a dazzling white. I stood looking at her for a long, long time.

10   The rain stopped, and white mist came up from the sea, gradually paling her back into the forest. It was as if she belonged there, and the mist were carrying her home. Presently the mist took the forest too, and, wrapping them both together, hid them away.

11   "Who is that image?" I asked the little Indian girl, when I got back to the house.

12   She knew which one I meant, but to gain time, she said, "What image?"

13   "The terrible one, out there on the bluff." The girl had been to Mission School, and fear of the old, fear of the new, struggled in her eyes. "I dunno," she lied.

14   I never went to that village again, but the fierce wooden image often came to me, both in my waking and in my sleeping.

15   Several years passed, and I was once more sketching in an Indian village. There were Indians in this village, and in a mild backward way it was "going modern". That is, the Indians had pushed the forest back a little to let the sun touch the new buildings that were replacing the old community houses. Small houses, primitive enough to a white man's thinking, pushed here and there between the old. Where some of the big community houses had been torn down, for the sake of the lumber, the great corner posts and massive roof-beams of the old structure were often left, standing naked against the sky, and the new little house was built inside, on the spot where the old one had been.

16   It was in one of these empty skeletons that I found her again. She had once been a supporting post for the great centre beam. Her pole-mate, representing the Raven, stood opposite her, but the beam that had rested on their heads was gone. The two poles faced in, and one judged the great size of the house by the distance between them. The corner posts were still in place, and the earth floor, once beaten to the hardness of rock by naked feet, was carpeted now with rich lush grass.

17   I knew her by the stuck out ears, shouting mouth, and deep eye-sockets. These sockets had no eye-balls, but were empty holes, filled with stare. The stare, though not so fierce as that of the former image, was more intense. The whole figure expressed power, weight, domination, rather than ferocity. Her feet were planted heavily on the head of a squatting bear, carved beneath them. A man could have sat on either huge shoulder. She was unpainted, weather-worn, sun-cracked, and the arms and hands seemed to hang loosely. The fingers were thrust into the carven mouths of two human heads, held crowns down. From behind, the sun made unfathomable shadows in eye, cheek and mouth. Horror tumbled out of them.

18   I saw Indian Tom on the beach and went to him.

19   "Who is she?"

20   The Indian's eyes, coming slowly from across the sea, followed my pointing finger. Resentment showed in his face, greeny-brown and wrinkled like a baked apple,—resentment that white folks should pry into matters wholly Indian.

21   "Who is that carved woman?" I repeated.

22   "D'Sonoqua." No white tongue could have fondled the name as he did.

23   "Who is D'Sonoqua?"

24   "She is the wild woman of the woods."

25   "What does she do?"

26   "She steals children."

27   "To eat them?"

28   "No, she carries them to her caves; that," pointing to a purple scar on the mountain across the bay, "is one of her caves. When she cries 'OO-oo-oo-oeo', Indian mothers are too frightened to move. They stand like trees, and the children go with D'Sonoqua."

29   "Then she is bad?"

30   "Sometimes bad . . . sometimes good," Tom replied, glancing furtively at those stuck-out ears. Then he got up and walked away.

31   I went back, and, sitting in front of the image, gave stare for stare. But her stare so over-powered mine, that I could scarcely wrench my eyes away from the clutch of those empty sockets. The power that I felt was not in the thing itself, but in some tremendous force behind it, that the carver had believed in.

32   A shadow passed across her hands and their gruesome holdings. A little bird, with its beak full of nesting material, flew into the cavity of her mouth, right in the pathway of that terrible OO-oo-oo-oeo. Then my eye caught something that I had missed—a tabby cat asleep between her feet.

33   This was D'Sonoqua, and she was a supernatural being, who belonged to these Indians.

34   "Of course," I said to myself, "I do not believe in supernatural beings. Still—who understands the mysteries behind the forest? What would one do if one did meet a supernatural being?" Half of me wished that I could meet her, and half of me hoped I would not.

35   Chug—chug—the little boat had come into the bay to take me to another village, more lonely and deserted than this. Who knew what I should see there? But soon supernatural beings went clean out of my mind, because I was wholly absorbed in being naturally seasick.

36   When you have been tossed and wracked and chilled, any wharf looks good, even a rickety one, with its crooked legs stockinged in barnacles. Our boat nosed under its

clammy darkness, and I crawled up the straight slimy ladder, wondering which was worse, natural seasickness, or supernatural "creeps". The trees crowded to the very edge of the water, and the outer ones, hanging over it, shadowed the shoreline into a velvet smudge. D'Sonoqua might walk in places like this. I sat for a long time on the damp, dusky beach, waiting for the stage. One by one dots of light popped from the scattered cabins, and made the dark seem darker. Finally the stage came.

37   We drove through the forest over a long straight road, with black pine trees marching on both sides. When we came to the wharf the little gas mail-boat was waiting for us. Smell and blurred light oozed thickly out of the engine room, and except for one lantern on the wharf everything else was dark. Clutching my little dog, I sat on the mail sacks which had been tossed on to the deck.

38   The ropes were loosed, and we slid out into the oily black water. The moon that had gone with us through the forest was away now. Black pine-covered mountains jagged up on both sides of the inlet like teeth. Every gasp of the engine shook us like a great sob. There was no rail round the deck, and the edge of the boat lay level with the black slithering horror below. It was like being swallowed again and again by some terrible monster, but never going down. As we slid through the water, hour after hour, I found myself listening for the OO-oo-oo-oeo.

39   Midnight brought us to a knob of land, lapped by the water on three sides, with the forest threatening to gobble it up on the fourth. There was a rude landing, a rooming-house, an eating-place, and a store, all for the convenience of fishermen and loggers. I was given a room, but after I had blown out my candle, the stillness and the darkness would not let me sleep.

40   In the brilliant sparkle of the morning when everything that was not superlatively blue was superlatively green, I dickered with a man who was taking a party up the inlet that he should drop me off at the village I was headed for.

41   "But," he protested, "there is nobody there."

42   To myself I said, "There is D'Sonoqua."

43   From the shore, as we rowed to it, came a thin feminine cry—the mewing of a cat. The keel of the boat had barely grated in the pebbles, when the cat sprang aboard, passed the man shipping his oars, and crouched for a spring into my lap. Leaning forward, the man seized the creature roughly, and with a cry of "Dirty Indian vermin!" flung her out into the sea.

44   I jumped ashore, refusing his help, and with a curt "Call for me at sundown," strode up the beach; the cat followed me.

45   When we had crossed the beach and come to a steep bank, the cat ran ahead. Then I saw that she was no lean, ill-favoured Indian cat, but a sleek aristocratic Persian. My snobbish little Griffon dog, who usually refused to let an Indian cat come near me, surprised me by trudging beside her in comradely fashion.

46   The village was typical of the villages of these Indians. It had only one street, and that had only one side, because all the houses faced the beach. The two community houses were very old, dilapidated and bleached, and the handful of other shanties seemed never to have been young; they had grown so old before they were finished, that it was then not worthwhile finishing them.

47   Rusty padlocks carefully protected the gaping walls. There was the usual broad plank in front of the houses, the general sitting and sunning place for Indians. Little streams

ran under it, and weeds poked up through every crack, half hiding the companies of tins, kettles and rags, which patiently waited for the next gale and their next move.

48   In front of the Chief's house was a high, carved totem pole, surmounted by a large wooden eagle. Storms had robbed him of both wings, and his head had a resentful twist, as if he blamed somebody. The heavy wooden heads of two squatting bears peered over the nettle-tops. The windows were too high for peeping in or out. "But save D'Sonoqua, who is there to peep?" I said aloud, just to break the silence. A fierce sun burned down as if it wanted to expose every ugliness and forlornness. It drew the noxious smell out of the skunk cabbages, growing in the rich black ooze of the stream, scummed the water-barrels with green slime, and branded the desolation into my very soul.

49   The cat kept very close, rubbing and bumping itself and purring ecstatically; and although I had not seen them come, two more cats had joined us. When I sat down they curled into my lap, and then the strangeness of the place did not bite into me so deeply. I got up, determined to look behind the houses.

50   Nettles grew in the narrow spaces between the houses. I beat them down, and made my way over the bruised dank-smelling mass into a space of low jungle.

51   Long ago the trees had been felled and left lying. Young forest had burst through the slash, making an impregnable barrier, and sealing up the secrets which lay behind it. An eagle flew out of the forest, circled the village, and flew back again.

52   Once again I broke the silence, calling after him, "Tell D'Sonoqua—" and turning, saw her close, towering above the jungle.

53   Like the D'Sonoqua of the other villages she was carved into the bole of a red cedar tree. Sun and storm had bleached the wood, moss here and there softened the crudeness of the modelling; sincerity underlay every stroke.

54   She appeared to be neither wooden nor stationary, but a singing spirit, young and fresh, passing through the jungle. No violence coarsened her; no power domineered to wither her. She was graciously feminine. Across her forehead her creator had fashioned the Sistheutl, or mythical two-headed sea-serpent. One of its heads fell to either shoulder, hiding the stuck-out ears, and framing her face from a central parting on her forehead which seemed to increase its womanliness.

55   She caught your breath, this D'Sonoqua, alive in the dead bole of the cedar. She summed up the depth and charm of the whole forest, driving away its menace.

56   I sat down to sketch. What was this noise of purring and rubbing going on about my feet? Cats. I rubbed my eyes to make sure I was seeing right, and counted a dozen of them. They jumped into my lap and sprang to my shoulders. They were real—and very feminine.

57   There we were—D'Sonoqua, the cats and I—the woman who only a few moments ago had forced herself to come behind the houses in trembling fear of the "wild woman of the woods"—wild in the sense that forest-creatures are wild—shy, untouchable.

Questions on Content, Structure, and Style

1. Is Carr's description of D'Sonoqua primarily objective or subjective? Cite an example of her language to support your answer.

2. What aspects of this essay make it clear that the writer was an artist?

3. What "dominant impression" of D'Sonoqua does Carr present in this essay? What are some of the details Carr provides to help us understand this creature's power?

4. How does Carr physically describe the changing impressions D'Sonoqua makes on her as she encounters different artistic representations of this mythical creature? How does she create contrasting images?

5. Examine some of Carr's word choices. What, for example, is the effect of writing, "Across her forehead her creator had fashioned the Sistheutl, or mythical two-headed sea-serpent"? (paragraph 54) instead of "There was a two-headed snake on her forehead"?

6. What senses does Carr engage in her descriptions of walking in the forests? What does this reveal about the author's relationship with the wilderness?

7. What does Carr's occasional use of dialogue add to this essay? Why, for example, does she quote Indian Tom or the ferryman at times? Why does she occasionally convert her own musings into soliloquy?

8. Why does Carr organize her essay by starting with a recollection of her first encounter with D'Sonoqua? How does this organization contribute to our understanding of Carr's fascination with this mythical creature, who was the subject of many of her paintings and sketches?

9. Look at Carr's painting, *Zunoqua of the Cat Village*, on page 310. How does this essay represent the mood and subject of that painting?

10. Did Carr successfully create a picture of D'Sonoqua? Could you suggest some ways she might improve her description? What language might have been more specific or vivid?

Suggestions for Writing

Try using Emily Carr's "D'Sonoqua" as a stepping stone to your essay. Describe an unforgettable experience you had, or the effect that an unusual encounter had on you. Consider including ample physical details, dialogue, and actions illustrating your reactions, as Carr did, to make your description of this experience or encounter vivid for your reader. Or write a description of an ancestor whose photograph has always intrigued you. What is the dominant impression of this picture? What does this person's face (or posture or choice of clothing) say to you about his or her character or style?

Perhaps you would like to write about a place that was important to you, but has disappeared, as William Gibson found. What senses will you use to guide you in choosing your descriptive details? Look at the photograph that follows. How would you describe it to someone who hasn't seen it? Is this picture of the fox and Christmas tree intriguing or amusing? Perhaps you could start writing your description by imagining the motivation and attitude of the photographer toward his subject.

Vocabulary

desolate (1)	bole (8)	socketed (8)
unfathomable (17)	superlatively (40)	keel (43)
dilapidated (46)	noxious (48)	impregnable (51)

Algonquin Park—Fox and Christmas Tree, *1956,*
anonymous

Canada Science and Technology Museum

▪ A REVISION WORKSHEET

As you write your rough drafts, consult Chapter 5 for guidance through
the revision process. In addition, here are a few questions to ask yourself
as you revise your description:

1. Is the descriptive essay's purpose clear to the reader?

2. Are there enough specific details in the description to make the subject
   matter distinct to readers who are unfamiliar with the scene, person, or
   object? Where might more detail be added?

3. Are the details arranged in an order that's easy to follow?

4. If the assignment called for an objective description, are the details as
   "neutral" as possible?

5. If the assignment called for a subjective description, does your particular attitude
   come through clearly with a consistent use of well-chosen details or imagery?

6. Could any sensory details or figurative language be added to help the reader
   "see" the subject matter?

7. Does this essay end with an appropriate conclusion or does description
   merely stop?

After you've revised your essay extensively, you might exchange rough drafts with a
classmate and answer these questions for each other, making specific suggestions for
improvement wherever appropriate. (For advice on productive participation in classroom workshops, see pages 102–104.)

Reviewing Your Progress

After you have completed your descriptive essay, take a moment to measure your progress as a writer by responding to the following questions. Such analysis will help you recognize growth in your writing skills and may enable you to identify areas that are still problematic.

1. What is the best part of your essay? Why?

2. Which one descriptive detail or image do you think is the clearest or most vivid in your essay? Why does that one stand above the others?

3. What part of your essay gave you the most trouble? How did you overcome the problem?

4. If you had more time to work on this essay, what would receive additional attention? Why?

5. What did you learn about your topic from writing this essay? About yourself as a writer?

Chapter 12

Narration

When many people hear the word "narrative," they think of a made-up story. But not all stories are fiction. In this chapter we are not concerned with writing literary short stories—that's a skill to develop in a creative writing class—but rather with nonfiction *expository narratives,* stories that are used to explain or prove a point. We most often use two kinds of these stories:

1. the *extended narrative*—a long episode that by itself illustrates or supports an essay's thesis;

2. the *brief narrative*—a shorter incident that is often used in a body paragraph to support or illustrate a particular point in an essay.

Let's suppose, for example, you wanted to write an essay showing how confusing the registration system is at your school. To illustrate the problems vividly, you might devote your entire essay to the retelling of a friend's seven-hour experience signing up for classes last fall, thus making use of extended narration. Or take another example: in an argumentative essay advocating mandatory use of side-door air bags in automobiles, you might include a brief narrative about a car accident to support a paragraph's point about air bags' ability to save lives. Regardless of which type of narrative best fits your purpose, the telling of a story or an incident can be an interesting, persuasive means of informing your readers.

■ Writing the Effective Narrative Essay

Know your purpose. What are you trying to accomplish by writing this narrative essay? Are you, for example, offering an *objective* retelling of a historical event (the dropping of the atomic bomb) to inform your readers who may not be acquainted with the facts? Are you trying to explain how the event took place? Or are you presenting a *subjective* narrative, which persuasively tells a story (the struggles faced by Chinese railroad workers during the building of CN Railways) from a clearly defined point of view, perhaps comparing this situation to others? Perhaps your narrative is a personal story, whose lesson you wish to share with readers. Perhaps you are telling your story from the point of view of different characters, different historical periods, and so on. This can help you anticipate opposing arguments, understand alternate perspectives, and become alert to biases in writing, all of which can help you to construct a strong argument. Whatever your choice—an objective, factual retelling or a subjective interpretation—your narrative's purpose should be clear to your readers, who should never reach the end of the story wondering "What was that all about?" Knowing your purpose will help you select the information and language best suited to meet your audience's needs.

Present your main point clearly. To ensure that readers understand their purpose, many writers first state a thesis followed by a narrative that supports it. Sometimes writers begin with their narrative and use their concluding paragraph to state or sum up the point or "lesson" of their story. Still others choose to imply a main point or attitude through the unfolding action and choice of descriptive details. An implied thesis is always riskier than a stated one, so unless you are absolutely convinced that your readers could not possibly fail to see your point, work on finding a smooth way to incorporate a statement of your main idea into your essay.

Follow a logical time sequence. Many narrative essays—and virtually all brief stories used in other kinds of essays—follow a chronological order, presenting actions as they naturally occur in the story. Occasionally, however, a writer will use the flashback technique, which takes the readers back in time to reveal an event that occurred before the present scene of the essay. If you decide to use shifts in time, use transitional phrases or other signals to ensure that your readers don't become confused or lost.

Use sensory details to hold your readers' interest. For example, if the setting plays an important role in your story, describe it in vivid terms so that your readers can imagine the scene easily. Suppose you are pointing out the necessity of life preservers on sailboats by telling the story of how you spent a stormy night in the lake, clinging to a capsized boat. To convince your readers, let them "feel" the stinging rain and the icy current trying to drag you under; let them "see" the black waves and the dark menacing sky; let them "hear" the howling wind and the gradual splitting apart of the boat. Effective narration often depends on effective description, and effective description depends on vivid, specific detail. (For more help on writing description, see Chapter 11; review Chapter 7 for advice on word choice.)

Create authentic characters. Again, the use of detail is crucial. Your readers should be able to visualize the people (or animals) in your narrative clearly; if your important characters are drawn too thinly or if they seem phony or stereotyped, your readers will not fully grasp the meaning of your story. Show your readers the major characters as you see them by commenting unobtrusively on their appearance, speech, and actions. In addition, a successful narrative may depend on the reader's understanding of people's motives—why they act the way they do in certain situations. A narrative about your hometown's grouchiest miser who suddenly donated a large sum of money to a poor family isn't very believable unless we know the motive behind the action. In other words, let your readers know what is happening to whom by explaining or showing why.

Use dialogue realistically. Writers often use dialogue, their characters' spoken words, to reveal action or personality traits of the speakers. By presenting conversations, writers show rather than tell, often creating emphasis or a more dramatic effect. Dialogue may also help readers identify with or feel closer to the characters or action by creating a sense of "you-are-there." If your narrative would profit from dialogue, be certain the word choice and the manner of speaking are in keeping with each character's education, background, age, location, and so forth. Don't, for example, put a sophisticated philosophical treatise into the mouth of a ten-year-old boy or the latest campus slang into the speech of a fifty-year-old auto mechanic from Red Deer, Alberta. Also, make sure that your dialogue doesn't sound "wooden" or phony. The right dialogue can help make your story more realistic and interesting, provided that the conversations are essential to the narrative and are not merely padding the plot. (To see dialogue in narratives, read Margaret Atwood's "Under the Thumb: How I Became a Poet," pages 334–340. For help in punctuating dialogue, see page 500 in Part Four.)

Problems to Avoid

Weak, boring narratives are often the result of problems with subject matter or poor pacing; therefore, you should keep in mind the following advice:

Choose your subject carefully. Most of the best narrative essays come from personal experience or study, and the reason is fairly obvious: it's difficult to write convincingly about something you've never seen or done or read about. You probably couldn't, for instance, write a realistic account of a bullfight unless you'd seen one or at least had studied the subject in great detail. The simplest, easiest, most interesting nonfiction narrative you can write is likely to be about an event with which you are personally familiar. This doesn't mean that you can't improvise many details or create a hypothetical story to illustrate a point. Even so, you will probably still have more success basing your narrative—real or hypothetical—on something or someone you know well.

Limit your scope. When you wish to use an extended narrative to illustrate a thesis, don't select an event or series of actions whose retelling will be too long or complex for your assignment. In general, it's better to select one episode and flesh it out with many specific details so that your readers may clearly see your point. For instance, you may have had many rewarding experiences during the summer you worked as a lifeguard, but you can't tell about them all. Instead, you might focus on one experience that captures the essence of your attitude toward your job—say, the time you saved a child from drowning—and present the story so vividly that the readers can easily understand your point of view.

Don't let your story lag or wander. At some time you've probably listened to a storyteller who became stuck on some insignificant detail ("Was it Friday or Saturday the letter came? Let's see now . . ."; "Then Joe said to me—no, it was Sally—no, wait, it was . . ."). And you've probably also heard bores who insist on making a short story long by including too many unimportant details or digressions. These mistakes ruin the *pacing* of their stories; in other words, the story's tempo or movement becomes bogged down until the readers are bored witless. To avoid creating a sleeping tonic in word form, dismiss all inessential information and focus your attention—and use of detail—on the important events, people, and places. Skip uneventful periods of time by using such phrases as "A week went by before Mr. Smith called . . ." or "Later that evening, around nine o'clock. . . ." In short, keep the story moving quickly enough to hold the readers' interest. Moreover, use a variety of transitional devices to move the readers from one action to another; don't rely continuously on the "and then . . . and then . . ." method.

■ PRACTISING WHAT YOU'VE LEARNED

To practise collecting details that will strengthen your narrative, try this activity. First, study the painting below, *Night Target, Germany*, by Miller Brittain, and then list as many specific, descriptive details about the scene as you can see or imagine. For example, what is the effect of the intersecting lines in the painting? What kind of atmosphere does the contrast between light and dark create? What kinds of contradictory responses are created by the combination of romantic images of a moon, clouds, and points of light, and the underlying violence represented by the sky crowded with bomber planes, gunfire, and smoke? Is this a romantic or sinister picture? Consider your own response to the artist's description of this scene in a

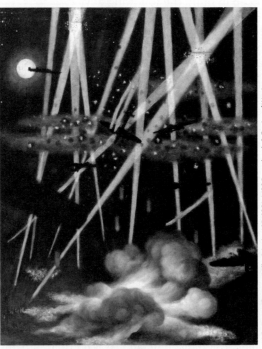

Night Target, Germany, Miller Brittain. 19710261-1436 Beaverbrook Collection of War Art.
© Canadian War Museum

Night Target, Germany, *1946, by Miller Brittain*

letter to his parents in 1944: "The night attacks although they are deadly are very beautiful from our point of view. The target is like an enormous lighted Christmas tree twenty miles away but straight beneath one looks like pictures I have seen of the mouth of hell."

What unusual noises and colours might be present and how might they be vividly described? What kind of atmosphere is evoked by the environment around the painting's focal points?

Now think of a time in which you experienced a narrow escape or conquered a fearful moment, some event in your life that might be retold in an exciting narrative essay. Using the impressions recorded from the painting as a guide to prompt your memory, compile a similar list of vivid sensory details describing the people, setting, dialogue, and action at the most dramatic point of your experience. You can also look at news stories, and put yourself in the shoes of the people involved to write a narrative essay from their perspective.

■ Essay Topics

Use one of the following topics to begin an essay that is developed by narration. Remember that each essay must have a clear purpose. For additional ideas, see the "Suggestions for Writing" section following the professional essay (page 340).

1. An act of courage or devotion
2. An event of historical, medical, or scientific importance
3. An interaction that changed your thinking on a particular subject
4. An account of a conflict from opposing perspectives
5. A family story passed down through the generations
6. Your worst accident or brush with danger
7. An unforgettable childhood experience
8. A memorable event governed by nature
9. A time you gained self-confidence or changed your self-image
10. A meaningful event experienced in another culture or country
11. The day everything went wrong (or right)
12. An event that led to an important decision
13. Your experience with prejudice or with an act of charity or friendship
14. Giving in to or resisting peer pressure
15. A gain or loss of something or someone important
16. A risk that paid off (or a triumph against the odds)
17. A non-academic lesson learned at school or on a job
18. An episode marking your passage from one stage of your life to another

19. An account of a pilot's experience in the Second World War, based on the painting and the letter by Miller Brittain, earlier in this chapter

20. Your day on September 11, 2001, showing how some specific aspect of the events informed or changed your thinking

The destruction of the World Trade Center Towers, September 11, 2001.

A Topic Proposal for Your Essay

Selecting the right subject matter is important to every writer. To help you clarify your ideas and strengthen your commitment to your topic, here is a proposal sheet that asks you to describe some of your preliminary ideas about your subject before you begin drafting. Although your ideas may change as you write (they will almost certainly become more refined), thinking through your choice of topic now may help you avoid several false starts.

1. In a sentence or two, briefly state the subject of your narrative. Did you or someone you know participate in this story?

2. Why did you select this narrative? Does it have importance for you personally, academically, or professionally? In some other way? Explain your reason, or purpose, for telling this story.

3. Will others be informed or entertained by this story? Who might be especially interested in hearing your narrative? Why?

4. What is the primary effect you would like your narrative to have on your readers? What would you like them to feel or think about after they read your story? Why?

5. What is the critical moment in your story? At what point, in other words, does the action reach its peak? Summarize this moment in a few descriptive words.

6. What difficulties, if any, might this narrative present as you are drafting? For example, if the story you want to tell is long or complex, how might you focus on the main action and pace it appropriately?

■ Sample Student Essay

In this narrative a student uses a story about a sick but fierce dog to show how she learned a valuable lesson in her job as a veterinarian's assistant. Notice the student's good use of vivid details that make this well-paced story both clear and interesting.

NEVER UNDERESTIMATE THE LITTLE THINGS

1   When I went to work as a veterinarian's assistant for Dr. Sam Holt and Dr. Jack Gunn last summer, I was under the false impression that the hardest part of veterinary surgery would be the actual performance of an operation. The small chores demanded before this feat didn't occur to me as being of any importance. As it happened, I had been in the veterinary clinic only for a total of four hours before I met a little animal who convinced me that the operation itself was probably the easiest part of treatment. This animal, to whom I owe thanks for so enlightening me, was a chocolate-coloured Chihuahua of tiny size and immense perversity named Smokey.

Introduction: A misconception

Thesis: Small preliminary details can be as important as the major action

2   Smokey could have very easily passed for some creature from another planet. It wasn't so much his gaunt little frame and overly large head, or his bony paws with nearly sabre-like claws, as it was his grossly infected eyes. Those once-shining eyes were now distorted and swollen into grotesque balls of septic, sightless flesh. The only vague similarity they had to what we'd normally think of as the organs of vision was a slightly upraised dot, all that was left of the pupil, in the centre of a pink and purply marble. As if that

Description of the main character: His appearance

His personality

were not enough, Smokey had a temper to match his ugly sight. He also had surprisingly good aim, considering his largely diminished vision, toward any moving object that happened to place itself unwisely before his ever-inquisitive nose; with sudden and wholly vicious intent, he would snap and snarl at whatever blocked the little light that could filter through his swollen and ruptured blood vessels. Truly, in many respects, Smokey was a fearful dog to behold.

The difficulty of moving the dog to the surgery room

3   Such an appearance and personality did nothing to encourage my already flagging confidence in my capabilities as a vet's assistant. How was I supposed to get that little demon out of his cage? Jack had casually requested that I bring Smokey to the surgery room, but did he really expect me to put my hands into the cage of that devil dog? I suppose it must have been my anxious expression that saved me, for as I turned uncertainly toward the kennel, Jack chuckled nonchalantly and accompanied me to demonstrate how professionals in his line of work dealt with professionals in Smokey's. He took a small rope about four feet long with a no-choke noose at one end and unlatched Smokey's cage. Then cautiously he reached in and dangled the noose before the dog's snarling jaws. Since Smokey could only barely see what he was biting at, his attacks were directed haphazardly in a semicircle around his body. The tiny area of his cage led to his capture, for during one of Smokey's forward lunges, Jack dropped the noose over his head and moved the struggling creature out onto the floor. The fight had only just begun for Smokey, however, and he braced his feet against the slippery linoleum tiling and forced us to drag him, like a little pull toy on a string, to the surgery.

4   Once Smokey was in the surgery, however, the question that hung before our eyes like a veritable presence was how to get the

dog from the floor to the table. Simply picking him up and plopping him down was out of the question. One glance at the quivering little figure emitting ominous and throaty warnings was enough to assure us of that. Realizing that the game was over, Jack grimly handed me the rope and reached for a muzzle. It was a doomed attempt from the start: the closer Jack dangled the tiny leather cup to the dog's nose, the more violent did Smokey's contortions and rage-filled cries become and the more frantic our efforts became to try to keep our feet and fingers clear of the angry jaws. Deciding that a firmer method had to be used, Jack instructed me to raise the rope up high enough so that Smokey would have to stand on his hind legs. This greatly reduced his manoeuvrability but served to increase his tenacity, for at this, the little dog nearly went into paroxysms of frustration and rage. In his struggles, however, Smokey caught his forepaw on his swollen eye, and the blood that had been building up pressure behind the fragile cornea burst out and dripped to the floor. In the midst of our surprise and the twinge of panic startling the three of us, Jack saw his chance and swiftly muzzled the animal and lifted him to the operating table.

The difficulty of moving the dog to the table

5   Even at that point it wasn't easy to put the now terrified dog under anesthetics for the operation. He fought the local anesthesia and caused Jack to curse as he was forced to give Smokey more of the drug than should have been necessary for such a small beast. After what seemed an eternity, Smokey lay prone on the table, breathing deeply and emitting soft snores and gentle whines. We also breathed deeply in relief, and I relaxed to watch, fascinated, while Jack performed a very delicate operation quite smoothly and without mishap.

The difficulty of anesthetizing the dog before the surgery

<table>
<tr><td>Conclusion: The lesson she learned</td><td>6</td><td>Such was my harrowing induction into the life of a veterinary surgeon. But Smokey did teach me a valuable lesson that has proven its importance to me many times since: wherever animals are concerned, even the smallest detail is important and should never be taken for granted.</td></tr>
</table>

Professional Essay*

■ Under the Thumb: How I Became a Poet

Margaret Atwood

Margaret Atwood is a prolific novelist who was a key player in the increasing respect and legitimacy Canadian literature gained from the 1960s onward. Her 1971 work, *Survival,* passionately argued for independence and recognition for Canadian writers, and her novels, short stories, and poetry are seen as essential cornerstones of Canadian literature. Some of her most famous novels, such as *The Handmaid's Tale,* have been made into films. She took a new direction in 2007 in writing *The Penelopiad,* a play written from the perspective of the women left behind during the Trojan War.

1   I recently read an account of a study that intends to show how writers of a certain age—my age, roughly—attempt to "seize control" of the stories of their own lives by deviously concocting their own biographies. However, it's a feature of our times that if you write a work of fiction, everyone assumes that the people and events in it are disguised biography—but if you write your biography, it's assumed you're lying your head off.

2   The latter may be true, at any rate of poets: Plato said that poets should be excluded from the ideal republic because they are such liars. I am a poet, and I affirm that that is true. About no subject are poets tempted to lie so much as about their own lives; I know one of them who has floated at least five versions of his autobiography, none of them real. I, of course, am a much more truthful person than that. But since poets lie, how can you believe me?

3   Here, then, is the official version:

4   I was once a snub-nosed blonde. My name was Betty. I had a perky personality and was a cheerleader for the college football team. My favourite colour was pink. Then I became a poet. My hair darkened overnight, my nose lengthened, I gave up football for the cello, my real name disappeared and was replaced by one that had a chance of being taken seriously, and my clothes changed colour in the closet, all by themselves, from pink to black. I stopped humming the songs from *Oklahoma!* and began quoting

---

* To help you read this essay analytically, review pages 160–162.

Kierkegaard. And not only that—all of my high-heeled shoes lost their heels, and were magically transformed into sandals. Needless to say, my many boyfriends took one look at this and ran screaming from the scene as if their toenails were on fire. New ones replaced them: they all had beards.

5   Believe it or not, there is an element of truth in this story. It's the bit about the name, which was not Betty but something equally nonpoetic, and with the same number of letters. It's also the bit about the boyfriends. But meanwhile, here is the real truth:

6   I became a poet at the age of 16. I did not intend to do it. It was not my fault.

7   Allow me to set the scene for you. The year was 1956. Elvis Presley had just appeared on the *Ed Sullivan Show,* from the waist up. At school dances, which were held in the gymnasium and smelled like armpits, the dance with the most charisma was rock 'n' roll. The approved shoes were saddle shoes and white bucks, and the evening gowns were strapless, if you could manage it; they had crinolined skirts that made you look like half a cabbage with a little radish head. Girls were forbidden to wear jeans to school, except on football days, when they sat on the hill to watch and it was feared that the boys would be able to see up their dresses unless they wore pants. TV dinners had just been invented.

8   None of this—you might think, and rightly so—was conducive to the production of poetry. If someone had told me a year previously that I would suddenly turn into a poet, I would have giggled. (I had a passable giggle, then.) Yet this is what did happen.

9   I was in my fourth year of high school. The high school was in Toronto, which in the year 1956 was still known as Toronto the Good because of its puritanical liquor laws. It had a population of 650,509 people at the time, and was a synonym for bland propriety, and although it has produced a steady stream of chartered accountants and one cabinet minister, no other poets have ever emerged from it, before or since—or none that I know of.

10   The day I became a poet was a sunny day of no particular ominousness. I was walking across the football field, not because I was sports-minded or had plans to smoke a cigarette behind the field house—the only other reason for going there—but because this was my normal way home from school. I was scuttling along in my usual furtive way, suspecting no ill, when a large invisible thumb descended from the sky and pressed down on the top of my head. A poem formed. It was quite a gloomy poem; the poems of the young usually are. It was a gift, this poem—a gift from an anonymous donor, and, as such, both exciting and sinister at the same time.

11   I suspect this is why all poets begin writing poetry, only they don't want to admit it, so they make up explanations that are either more rational or more romantic. But this is the true explanation, and I defy anyone to disprove it.

12   The poem that I composed on that eventful day, although entirely without merit or even promise, did have some features. It rhymed and scanned, because we had been taught rhyming and scansion at school. It resembled the poetry of Lord Byron and Edgar Allan Poe, with a little Shelley and Keats thrown in. The fact is that at the time I became a poet, I had read very few poems written after the year 1900. I knew nothing of modernism or free verse. These were not the only things I knew nothing of. I had no idea, for instance, that I was about to step into a whole set of preconceptions and social roles that had to do with what poets were like, how they should behave, and what they ought to wear; moreover, I did not know that the rules about these things were different if you were female. I did not know that "poetess" was an insult, and that I myself

would someday be called one. I did not know that to be told I had transcended my gender would be considered a compliment. I didn't know yet that black was compulsory. All of that was in the future. When I was 16, it was simple. Poetry existed; therefore it could be written. And nobody had told me—yet—the many, many reasons why it could not be written by me.

13   At first glance, there was little in my background to account for the descent of the large thumb of poetry onto the top of my head. But let me try to account for my own poetic genesis.

14   I was born on November 18, 1939, in the Ottawa General Hospital, two and a half months after the beginning of the Second World War. Being born at the beginning of the war gave me a substratum of anxiety and dread to draw on, which is very useful to a poet. It also meant that I was malnourished. This is why I am short. If it hadn't been for food rationing, I would have been six feet tall.

15   I saw my first balloon in 1946, one that had been saved from before the war. It was inflated for me as a treat when I had the mumps on my sixth birthday, and it broke immediately. This was a major influence on my later work.

16   As for my birth month, a detail of much interest to poets, obsessed as they are with symbolic systems of all kinds: I was not pleased, during my childhood, to have been born in November, as there wasn't much inspiration for birthday-party motifs. February children got hearts, May ones flowers, but what was there for me? A cake surrounded by withered leaves? November was a drab, dark, and wet month, lacking even snow; its only noteworthy festival was Remembrance Day, the Canadian holiday honouring the war dead. But in adult life I discovered that November was, astrologically speaking, the month of sex, death, and regeneration, and that November 1 was the Day of the Dead. It still wouldn't have been much good for birthday parties, but it was just fine for poetry, which tends to revolve a good deal around sex and death, with regeneration optional.

17   Six months after I was born, I was taken in a wooden box to a remote cabin in northwestern Quebec, where my father was doing research as a forest entomologist. I should add here that my parents were unusual for their time. Both of them liked being as far away from civilization as possible, my mother because she hated housework and tea parties, my father because he liked chopping wood. They also weren't much interested in what the sociologists would call rigid sex-role stereotyping. This was beneficial to me in later life, as it helped me to get a job at summer camp teaching small boys to start fires.

18   My childhood was divided between the forest, in the warmer parts of the year, and various cities, in the colder parts. I was thus able to develop the rudiments of the double personality so necessary for a poet. I also had lots of time for meditation. In the bush, there were no theaters, movies, parades, or very functional radios; there were also not many other people. The result was that I learned to read early—I was lucky enough to have a mother who read out loud, but she couldn't be doing it all the time, and you had to amuse yourself with something or other when it rained. I became a reading addict, and have remained so ever since. "You'll ruin your eyes," I was told when caught at my secret vice under the covers with a flashlight. I did so, and would do it again. Like cigarette addicts who will smoke mattress stuffing if all else fails, I will read anything. As a child I read a good many things I shouldn't have, but this also is useful for poetry.

19   As the critic Northrop Frye has said, we learn poetry through the seat of our pants, by being bounced up and down to nursery rhymes as children. Poetry is essentially oral, and is close to song; rhythm precedes meaning. My first experiences with poetry were Mother Goose, which contains some of the most surrealistic poems in the English language, and whatever singing commercials could be picked up on the radio, such as *You'll wonder where the yellow went/When you brush your teeth with Pepsodent!*

20   Also surreal. *What yellow?* I wondered. Thus began my tooth fetish.

21   I created my first book of poetry at the age of five. To begin with, I made the book itself, cutting the pages out of scribbler paper and sewing them together in what I did not know was the traditional signature fashion. Then I copied into the book all the poems I could remember, and when there were some blank pages left at the end, I added a few of my own to complete it. This book was an entirely satisfying art object for me, so satisfying that I felt I had nothing more to say in that direction, and gave up writing poetry altogether for another 11 years.

22   My English teacher from 1955, run to ground by some documentary crew trying to explain my life, said that in her class I had showed no particular promise. This was true. Until the descent of the giant thumb, I showed no particular promise. I also showed no particular promise for some time afterwards, but I did not know this. A lot of being a poet consists of willed ignorance. If you woke up from your trance and realized the nature of the life-threatening and dignity-destroying precipice you were walking along, you would switch into actuarial sciences immediately.

23   If I had not been ignorant in this particular way, I would not have announced to an assortment of my high school female friends, in the cafeteria one brown-bag lunchtime, that I was going to be a writer. I said "writer," not "poet"; I did have some common sense. But my announcement was certainly a conversation stopper. Sticks of celery were suspended in mid-crunch, peanut butter sandwiches paused halfway between table and mouth; nobody said a word. One of those present reminded me of this incident recently—I had repressed it—and said she had been simply astounded. "Why?" I said. "Because I wanted to be a writer?"

24   "No," she said. "Because you had the guts to say it out loud."

25   But I was not conscious of having guts, or even of needing them. We obsessed folks, in our youth, are oblivious to the effects of our obsessions; only later do we develop enough cunning to conceal them, or at least to avoid mentioning them at parties. The one good thing to be said about announcing myself as a writer in the colonial Canadian fifties was that nobody told me I couldn't do it because I was a girl. They simply found the entire proposition ridiculous. Writers were dead and English, or else extremely elderly and American; they were not 16 years old and Canadian. It would have been worse if I'd been a boy, though. Never mind the fact that all the really stirring poems I'd read at that time had been about slaughter, battles, mayhem, sex, and death— poetry was thought of as existing in the pastel female realm, along with embroidery and flower arranging. If I'd been male I would probably have had to roll around in the mud, in some boring skirmish over whether or not I was a sissy.

26   I'll skip over the embarrassingly bad poems I published in the high school year-book (had I no shame? Well, actually, no), mentioning only briefly the word of encouragement I received from my wonderful grade 12 English teacher, Miss Bessie Billings: "I can't understand a word of this, dear, so it must be good." I will not go into the dismay of my parents, who worried—with good reason—over how I would support

myself. I will pass over my flirtation with journalism as a way of making a living, an idea I dropped when I discovered that in the fifties, unlike now, female journalists always ended up writing the obituaries and the ladies' page, and nothing but.

27   But how was I to make a living? There was not then a roaring market in poetry. I thought of running away and being a waitress, which I later tried but got very tired and thin; there's nothing like clearing away other people's mushed-up dinners to make you lose your appetite. Finally, I went into English literature at university, having decided in a cynical manner that I could always teach to support my writing habit. Once I got past the Anglo-Saxon it was fun, although I did suffer a simulated cardiac arrest the first time I encountered T.S. Eliot and realized that not all poems rhymed anymore. "I don't understand a word of this," I thought, "so it must be good."

28   After a year or two of keeping my head down and trying to pass myself off as a normal person, I made contact with the five other people at my university who were interested in writing, and through them, and some of my teachers, I discovered that there was a whole subterranean wonderland of Canadian writing that was going on just out of general earshot and sight. It was not large: In 1960, you were doing well to sell 200 copies of a book of poems by a Canadian, and a thousand novels was a best-seller; there were only five literary magazines, which ran on the lifeblood of their editors. But while the literary scene wasn't big, it was very integrated. Once in—that is, once published in a magazine—it was as if you'd been given a Masonic handshake or a key to the Underground Railroad. All of a sudden you were part of a conspiracy. People writing about Canadian poetry at that time spoke a lot about the necessity of creating a Canadian literature. There was a good deal of excitement, and the feeling that you were in on the ground floor, so to speak.

29   So poetry was a vital form, and it quickly acquired a public dimension. Above ground, the bourgeoisie reigned supreme, in their two-piece suits and ties and camel-hair coats and pearl earrings (not all of this worn by the same sex). But at night, the bohemian world came alive, in various nooks and crannies of Toronto, sporting black turtlenecks, drinking coffee at little tables with red-checked tablecloths and candles stuck in Chianti bottles, in coffeehouses—well, in the one coffeehouse in town—listening to jazz and folk singing, reading their poems out loud as if they'd never heard it was stupid, and putting swear words into them. For a 20-year-old, this was intoxicating stuff.

30   By this time, I had my black wardrobe more or less together, and had learned not to say "Well, hi there!" in sprightly tones. I was publishing in little magazines, and shortly thereafter I started to write reviews for them too. I didn't know what I was talking about, but I soon began to find out. Every year for four years, I put together a collection of my poems and submitted it to a publishing house; every year it was—to my dismay then, to my relief now—rejected. Why was I so eager to be published right away? Like all 21-year-old poets, I thought I would be dead by 30, and Sylvia Plath had not set a helpful example. For a while there, you were made to feel that, if you were a poet and female, you could not really be serious about it unless you'd made at least one suicide attempt. So I felt I was running out of time.

31   My poems were still not very good, but by now they showed—how shall I put it?—a sort of twisted and febrile glimmer. In my graduating year, a group of them won the main poetry prize at the university. Madness took hold of me, and with the aid of a friend, and another friend's flatbed press, we printed them. A lot of poets published their own work then; unlike novels, poetry was short, and therefore cheap to do. We had to print

each poem separately, and then disassemble the type, as there were not enough a's for the whole book; the cover was done with a lino block. We printed 250 copies and sold them through bookstores for 50 cents each. They now go in the rare-book trade for $1,800 a pop. Wish I'd kept some.

32   Three years or so later—after two years at graduate school at the dreaded Harvard University, a year of living in a tiny rooming-house room and working at a market-research company, and the massive rejection of my first novel, as well as several other poetry collections—I ended up in British Columbia, teaching grammar to engineering students at eight-thirty in the morning in a Quonset hut. It was all right, as none of us were awake. I made them write imitations of Kafka, which I thought might help them in their chosen profession.

33   In comparison with the few years I had just gone through, this was sort of like going to heaven. I lived in an apartment built on top of somebody's house, and had scant furniture; but not only did I have a 180-degree view of Vancouver harbour, I also had all night to write. I taught in the daytime, ate canned food, did not wash my dishes until all of them were dirty—the biologist in me became very interested in the different varieties of molds that could be grown on leftover Kraft dinner—and stayed up until four in the morning. I completed, in that one year, my first officially published book of poems and my first published novel, which I wrote on blank exam booklets, as well as a number of short stories and the beginnings of two other novels, later completed. It was an astonishingly productive year for me. I looked like *The Night of the Living Dead*. Art has its price.

34   This first book of poems was called *The Circle Game*. I designed the cover myself, using stick-on dots—we were very cost-effective in those days—and to everyone's surprise, especially mine, it won the Governor General's Award, which in Canada then was the big one to win. Literary prizes are a crapshoot, and I was lucky that year. I was back at Harvard by then, mopping up the uncompleted work for my doctorate—I never did finish it—and living with three roommates named Judy, Sue, and Karen. To collect the prize, I had to attend a ceremony at Government House in Ottawa, which meant dressups—and it was obvious to all of us, as we went through the two items in my wardrobe, that I had nothing to wear. Sue lent me her dress and earrings, Judy her shoes, and while I was away they all incinerated my clunky, rubber-soled Hush Puppies shoes, having decided that these did not go with my new, poetic image.

35   This was an act of treachery, but they were right. I was now a recognized poet and had a thing or two to live up to. It took me a while to get the hair right, but I have finally settled down with a sort of modified Celtic look, which is about the only thing available to me short of baldness. I no longer feel I'll be dead by 30; now it's 60. I suppose these deadlines we set for ourselves are really a way of saying we appreciate time, and want to use all of it. I'm still writing, I'm still writing poetry, I still can't explain why, and I'm still running out of time.

36   Wordsworth was partly right when he said, "Poets in their youth begin in gladness / But thereof comes in the end despondency and madness." Except that sometimes poets skip the gladness and go straight to the despondency. Why is that? Part of it is the conditions under which poets work—giving all, receiving little in return from an age that by and large ignores them. Part of it is cultural expectation: "The lunatic, the lover, and the poet," says Shakespeare, and notice which comes first. My own theory is that poetry is composed with the melancholy side of the brain, and that if you do

nothing but, you may find yourself going slowly down a long dark tunnel with no exit. I have avoided this by being ambidextrous: I write novels too.

37   I go for long periods of time without writing any poems. I don't know why this is: as the Canadian writer Margaret Laurence indicates in *The Diviners*, you don't know why you start, and you also don't know why you stop. But when I do find myself writing poetry again, it always has the surprise of that first unexpected and anonymous gift.

Questions on Content, Structure, and Style

1. What is Atwood's main purpose in this narrative? What does she want to show about being given the "gift" of poetry?

2. Why does Atwood begin her essay with a short anecdote about a girl called Betty?

3. Where can you see examples of Atwood's characteristic ironic tone? For example, what is the effect of repeating her English teacher's words, "I can't understand a word of this, dear, so it must be good" (paragraph 26) in paragraph 27?

4. What kind of audience is Atwood addressing? How do her literary allusions indicate this? How do her descriptions of her early life indicate this?

5. What sorts of contrasts does Atwood draw between poets and "ordinary people"?

6. What methods of development does Atwood use to characterize Canadian literature? To help you determine this, review Chapter 9.

7. What sorts of contrasts does Atwood draw between past and present?

8. Throughout the essay, Atwood mentions the poetry she has written over her life, but she doesn't quote it or discuss the subjects of her poetry. Would such a discussion have added to your understanding of Atwood's development as a poet/writer? Why or why not?

9. Does Atwood use enough vivid details to make her narrative seem believable and her experiences realistic? Cite two or three examples of descriptive language that you think are particularly effective.

10. Is this how you would choose to write about the most significant experiences in your own life? What might you do differently?

Suggestions for Writing

Try using Margaret Atwood's "Under the Thumb: How I Became a Poet" as a stepping stone to your writing. Think of a moment in your life when you came to an important realization about yourself. How did you deal with this realization? Was it necessary to make difficult decisions in response to this realization? Or, was there a book that made a difference to your life? What kind of difference did it make? How about a person? Is there anyone who has inspired you to take a new direction in your life? This person might be a relative, a teacher, a neighbour, a coach, a friend's parent, a famous person. Tell a story that captures an important moment in your relationship with this person: your first meeting, a crucial event, or an incident that crystallized your awareness of this person's influence on you.

Vocabulary

deviously (1)	concocting (1)	Plato (2)
Kierkegaard (4)	charisma (7)	crinolined (7)
conducive (8)	puritanical (9)	propriety (9)
ominousness (10)	scuttling (10)	furtive (10)
scansion (12)	preconceptions (12)	transcended (12)
genesis (13)	substratum (14)	malnourished (14)
rudiments (18)	surrealistic (19)	precipice (22)
astounded (23)	oblivious (25)	proposition (25)
mayhem (25)	realm (25)	skirmish (25)
T.S. Eliot (27)	simulated (27)	subterranean (28)
Masonic (28)	bourgeoisie (29)	Sylvia Plath (30)
febrile (31)	glimmer (31)	disassemble (31)
Kafka (32)	ambidextrous (36)	

■ A REVISION WORKSHEET

As you write your rough drafts, consult Chapter 5 for guidance through the revision process. In addition, here are a few questions to ask yourself as you revise your narrative:

1. Is the narrative essay's purpose clear to the reader?

2. Is the thesis plainly stated or at least clearly implied?

3. Does the narrative convincingly support or illustrate its intended point? If not, how might the story be changed?

4. Does the story maintain a logical point of view and an understandable order of action? Are there enough transitional devices used to give the story a smooth flow?

5. Are the characters, actions, and settings presented in enough vivid detail to make them clear and believable? Where could more detail be effectively added? Would use of dialogue be appropriate?

6. Is the story coherent and well paced or does it wander or bog down in places because of irrelevant or repetitious details? What might be condensed or cut? Could bland or wordy description be replaced?

7. Does the essay end in a satisfying way or does the action stop too abruptly?

After you've revised your essay extensively, you might exchange rough drafts with a classmate and answer these questions for each other, making specific suggestions for improvement wherever appropriate. (For advice on productive participation in classroom workshops, see pages 102–104.)

Reviewing Your Progress

After you have completed your narrative essay, take a moment to measure your progress as a writer by responding to the following questions. Such analysis will help you recognize growth in your writing skills and may enable you to identify areas that are still problematic.

1. What do you like best about your narrative essay? Why?

2. After reading through your essay, select the description, detail, or piece of dialogue that you think best characterizes a major figure or most effectively advances the action in your story. Explain the reason for your choice in one or two sentences.

3. What part of your essay gave you the most trouble? How did you overcome the problem?

4. If you had more time to work on this essay, what would receive additional attention? Why?

5. What did you learn about your topic from writing this essay? About yourself as a writer?

Chapter 13

Writing Essays Using Multiple Strategies

In Part Two of this text, you have been studying essays developed primarily by a single mode or expository strategy. You may have, for example, written essays primarily developed by multiple examples, process analysis, or comparison and contrast. Concentrating on a single strategy in your essays has allowed you to practise, in a focused way, each of the patterns of development most often used in writing tasks. Although practising each strategy in isolation this way is somewhat artificial, it is the easiest, simplest way to master the common organizational patterns. Consider the parallels to learning almost any skill: before you attempt a complex dive with spins and flips, you first practise each manoeuvre separately. Having understood and mastered the individual strategies of development, you should feel confident about facing any writing situation, including those that would most profit from incorporating multiple strategies to accomplish their goal.

Most essays *do* call upon multiple strategies of development to achieve their purpose, a reality you have probably discovered for yourself as you wrote and studied various essays in this text. In fact, you may have found it difficult—or impossible—to avoid combining modes and strategies in your own essays. As noted in the introduction to Part Two, writers virtually always blend strategies, using examples in their comparisons, description in their definitions, causal analysis in their arguments, and so on. Therein is the heart of the matter: the single patterns of development you have been practising are *thinking* strategies—ways of considering a subject and generating ideas—as well as organizing tools. In most writing situations, writers study their tasks and choose the strategies that will *most effectively* accomplish their purpose.

In addition, some writing tasks, often the longer ones, will clearly profit from combining multiple strategies in distinct ways to thoroughly address the essay's subject, purpose, and audience. Suppose, for example, you are given a problem-solving assignment in a business class: selling the City Council on a plan to build a low-income housing project in a particular neighbourhood. You might call upon your writing resources and use multiple strategies to

- Describe the project
- Explain the causes (the need for such a project)
- Argue its strengths; deflect opposing arguments
- Contrast it to other housing options
- Cite similar successful examples in other cities
- Explain its long-term beneficial effects on tenants, neighbours, businesses, and so on.

Or perhaps you are investigating recent disciplinary action taken against local high-school students for decorating their graduation gowns with political messages. Your essay might combine strategies by first presenting examples of the controversy, explaining its causes and effects, and then contrasting the opinions of administrators, students, and parents. You might even conclude with a suggested process for avoiding future problems. In other words, many essay assignments—including the widely assigned summary-response paper*—might call for a multi-strategy response.

As a writer who now knows how to use a variety of thinking and organizational methods, you can assess any writing situation and select the strategy—or strategies—that will work best for your topic, purpose, and audience.

Choosing the Best Strategies

To help you choose the best means of development for your essay, here is a brief review of the modes and strategies, accompanied by some pertinent questions:

1. Example: Would real or hypothetical illustrations make my subject more easily understood?
2. Process: Would a step-by-step procedural analysis clarify my subject?
3. Comparison and Contrast: Would aligning or juxtaposing my subject to something else be helpful?
4. Definition: Would my subject profit from an extended explanation of its meaning?
5. Division and Classification: Would separating my subject into its component parts or grouping its parts into categories be useful?
6. Causal Analysis: Would explaining causes or effects add important information?

---

* For an in-depth look at this popular assignment, see pages 417–418.

7. Argument: Would my position be advanced by offering logical reasons and/or addressing objections?

8. Description: Would vivid details, sensory images, or figurative language help readers visualize my subject?

9. Narrative: Would a story best illustrate some idea or aspect of my subject?

Try using these questions as prompts to help you generate ideas and select those strategies that best accomplish your purpose.

Problems to Avoid

Avoid overkill. Being prepared to use any of the writing strategies is akin to carrying many tools in your carpenter's bag. But just because you own many tools doesn't mean you must use all of them in one project—rather, you select only the ones you need for the specific job at hand. If you do decide to use multiple strategies in a particular essay, avoid a hodgepodge of information that runs in too many directions. Sometimes your essay's prescribed length means you cannot present all you know; again, let your main purpose guide you to including the best or most important ideas.

Organize logically. If you decide that multiple strategies will work best, you must find an appropriate order and coherent flow for your essay. In the hypothetical problem-solving essay on the housing project mentioned earlier, for instance, the writer must decide whether the long-term effects of the project should be discussed earlier or later in the paper. In the student essay that follows, the writer struggled with the question of putting kinds of vegetarians before or after the discussion of reasons for adopting vegetarianism. There are no easy answers to such questions—each writer must experiment with outlines and rough drafts to find the most successful arrangement, one that will offer the most effective response to the particular material, the essay's purpose, and the audience's needs. Be patient as you try various ways of combining strategies into a coherent rather than choppy paper.

■ Sample Student Essay

In the essay that follows, the student writer responds to an assignment that asked her to write about an important belief or distinguishing aspect of her life. The purpose, audience, and development of her essay were left to her; the length was designated at 750 to 1,000 words. As a confirmed vegetarian for well over a decade, she often found herself questioned about her beliefs. After deciding to clarify (and encourage) vegetarianism for an audience of interested but often puzzled fellow students, she developed her essay by drawing on many strategies, including causal analysis, example, classification, contrast, argument, and process analysis. Because she found her early draft too long, the writer edited out an extended narrative telling the story of her own "conversion" to vegetarianism, viewing that section as less central to her essay's main purpose than the other parts.

Pass the Broccoli—Please!

Introduction: Famous examples

1   What do Benjamin Franklin, Charles Darwin, Leonardo da Vinci, Percy Bysshe Shelley, Mohandas K. Gandhi, Albert Einstein, and I have in common? In addition to being great thinkers, of course, we are all vegetarians, people who have rejected the practice of eating animals. Vegetarianism is growing rapidly in Canada today, but some people continue to see it as a strange choice. If you are thinking of making this decision yourself or are merely curious, taking time to learn about vegetarianism is worthwhile.

Thesis, purpose, audience

Contrast to other parts of the world

2   In a land where hamburgers, pepperoni pizza, and fried chicken are among our favourite foods, just why do Canadians become vegetarians anyway? Worldwide, vegetarianism is often part of religious faith, especially to Buddhists, Hindus, and others whose spiritual beliefs emphasize nonviolence, karma, and reincarnation. But in this country the reasons for becoming vegetarian are more diverse. Some people cite ecological reasons, arguing that vegetarianism is best for our planet because it takes less land and food to grow vegetables and grain than raise livestock. Others choose vegetarianism because of health reasons. Repeated studies by groups such as the Heart and Stroke Foundation of Canada show that diets lower in animal fats and higher in fibre decrease the risk of heart disease, cancer, diabetes, hypertension, and osteoporosis.

Causal analysis: Three reasons

3   Still other people's ethical beliefs bring them to vegetarianism. These people object to the ways that some animals, such as cows and chickens, are confined and are often fed various chemicals, such as growth hormones, antibiotics, and tranquillizers. They object to the procedures of slaughterhouses. They object to killing animals for consumption or for their decorative body parts (hides, fur, skins, tusks, feathers, etc.) and to their use in science or cosmetic experiments. These vegetarians believe that animals feel

fear and pain and that it is morally wrong for one species to inflict unnecessary suffering on another. I count myself among this group; consequently, my vegetarian choices extend to wearing no leather or fur and I do not use household or cosmetic products tested on animals.

Personal example

4   Regardless of the reasons for our choice, all vegetarians reject eating meat. However, there are actually several kinds of vegetarians, with the majority falling into three categories:

1. Ovo-lacto vegetarians eat milk, cheese, eggs, and honey;
2. Lacto vegetarians do not eat eggs but may keep other dairy products in their diet;
3. Vegans do not eat dairy products or any animal byproducts whatsoever.

Classification: Three types

Many people, including myself, begin as ovo-lacto vegetarians but eventually become vegans, considered the most complete or pure type.

5   Perhaps the most common objection to any type of vegetarianism comes from a misconception about deficiencies in the diet, particularly protein. But it is a mistake to think only meat offers us protein. Vegetarians who eat dairy products, grains, vegetables, beans, and nuts receive more than enough nutrients, including protein. In fact, according to the cookbook *The Higher Taste,* cheese, peanuts, and lentils contain more protein per ounce than hamburger, pork, or a porterhouse steak. Many medical experts think that Canadians actually eat too much protein, as seen in the revised food pyramid that now calls for an increase in vegetables, fruits, and grains over meat and dairy products. A vegetarian diet will not make someone a limp weakling. Kevin Eubanks, *The Tonight Show* band leader, is, for example, not only a busy musician but also a weightlifter. Some members of the Ottawa Rough Riders football team, according to their manager, no longer eat red meat at their training table.

Argument: Refutation, evidence, examples

6   For those who would like to give vegetarianism a try, here are a few suggestions for getting started.

Process: Four steps to begin

- Explore your motives. If you are only becoming a vegetarian to please a friend, for example, you won't stick with it. Be honest with yourself: the reasons behind your choice have a lot to do with your commitment.

- Read more. The library can provide you with answers to your questions and concerns. There are hundreds of books full of ecological, medical, and ethical arguments for vegetarianism.

(More argument and examples)

- Eat! Another popular misconception is that vegetarianism means a life of eating tasteless grass; nothing could be less true. Visit a vegetarian restaurant several times to see how many delicious dishes are available. Even grocery stores now carry a variety of vegetarian entrees. Try one of the many vegetarian cookbooks on the market today. You may be surprised to discover that tofu enchiladas, soy burgers, and stuffed eggplant taste better than you could ever imagine.

- Start slowly. You don't have to become a vegan overnight if it doesn't feel right. Some people begin by excluding just red meat from their diets. Feeling good as time goes by can direct your choices. Books, such as *The Beginning Vegetarian,* and magazines, such as *Vegetarian Times,* can offer encouragement.

7   It's never too late to change your lifestyle. Nobel Prize–winning author Isaac Bashevis Singer became a vegetarian at age fifty-eight. Making this choice now may allow you to live longer and feel better. In fifty years you may be like playwright George Bernard Shaw, who at twenty-five was warned against a vegetarian diet. As a vigorous old man, Shaw wanted to tell all those people they were wrong, but noted he couldn't: "They all passed away years ago"!

Conclusion: Additional famous examples, witty quotation

Professional Essay*

■ Why Ordinary People Torture Enemy Prisoners

Susan T. Fiske, Lasana T. Harris, and Amy J. Cuddy

Susan T. Fiske, the primary author of this article, is an eminent social psychologist who teaches at Princeton University. She has published several books and articles on the link between social relationships and stereotypes and prejudice, and is a co-editor of the scholarly journal *The Annual Review of Psychology*. Fiske and fellow social psychologists Lasana T. Harris and Amy J. Cuddy published this article in the journal *Science* (November 2004) in response to the heated discussions that followed reports of the use of torture by American soldiers on Islamic prisoners in Iraq's Abu Ghraib prison.

1   As official investigations and courts-martial continue, we are all taking stock of the events at Abu Ghraib last year. Initial reactions were shock and disgust. How could Americans be doing this to anyone, even Iraqi prisoners of war? Some observers immediately blamed "the few bad apples" presumably responsible for the abuse. However, many social psychologists knew that it was not that simple. Society holds individuals responsible for their actions, as the military court-martial recognizes, but social psychology suggests we should also hold responsible peers and superiors who control the social context.

2   Social psychological evidence emphasizes the power of social context: in other words, the power of the interpersonal situation. Social psychology has accumulated a century of knowledge about how people influence each other for good or ill (1). Meta-analysis, the quantitative summary of findings across a variety of studies, reveals the size and consistency of such empirical results. Recent meta-analyses document reliable experimental evidence of social context effects across 25,000 studies of eight million participant (2). Abu Ghraib resulted in part from ordinary social processes, not just extraordinary individual evil. This Policy Forum cites meta-analyses to describe how the right (or wrong) social context can make almost anyone agress, oppress, conform, and obey.

3   Virtually anyone can be aggressive if sufficiently provoked, stressed, disgruntled, or hot (3–6). The situation of the 800th Military Police Brigade guarding Abu Ghraib prisoners fit all the social conditions known to cause aggression. The soldiers were certainly provoked and stressed: at war, in constant danger, taunted and harassed by some of the very citizens they were sent to save, and their comrades were dying daily and unpredictably. Their morale suffered, they were untrained for the job, their command climate was lax, their return home was a year overdue, their identity as disciplined soldiers was gone, and their own amenities were scant (7). Heat and discomfort doubtless contributed.

4   The fact that the prisoners were part of a group encountered as enemies would only exaggerate the tendency to feel spontaneous prejudice against outgroups. In this context, oppression and discrimination are synonymous. One of the basic principles of social psychology is that people prefer their own group (8) and attribute bad behaviour to outgroups (9). Prejudice especially festers if people see the outgroup as threatening

---

*For help reading this essay analytically, review pages 160–162.

cherished values (10–12). This would have certainly applied to the guards viewing their prisoners at Abu Ghraib, but it also applies in more "normal" situations. A recent sample of U.S. citizens on average viewed Muslims and Arabs as not sharing their interests and stereotyping them as not especially sincere, honest, friendly, or warm (13–15).

5   Even more potent predictors of discrimination are the emotional prejudices ("hot" affective feelings such as disgust or contempt) that operate in parallel with cognitive processes (16–18). Such emotional reactions appear rapidly, even in neuroimaging of brain activations to outgroups (19,20). But even they can be affected by social context. Categorization of people as interchangeable members of an outgroup promotes an amygdala response characteristic of vigilance and alarm and an insular response characteristic of disgust or arousal, depending on social context; these effects dissipate when the same people are encountered as unique individuals (21,22).

6   According to our survey data (13,14), the contemptible, disgusting kind of outgroup—low-status opponents—elicits a mix of active and passive harm: attacking and fighting, as well as excluding and demeaning. This certainly describes the Abu Ghraib abuse of captured enemies. It also fits our national sample of Americans (14) who reported that allegedly contemptible outgroups such as homeless people, welfare recipients, Turks, and Arabs often are attacked or excluded (14).

7   Given an environment conducive to aggression and prisoners deemed disgusting and subhuman (23), well-established principles of conformity to peers (24,25) and obedience to authority (26) may account for the widespread nature of the abuse. In combat, conformity to one's unit means survival, and ostracism is death. The social context apparently reflected the phenomenon of people trying to make sense of a complex, confusing, ambiguous situation by relying on their immediate social group (27). People rioted in St. Paul's Church, Bristol, UK, in 1980, for example, in conformity to events they saw occurring in their immediate proximity (28). Guards abuse prisoners in conformity with what other guards do in order to fulfil a potent role; this is illustrated by the Stanford Prison Study, in which ordinary college students, randomly assigned to be full-time guards and prisoners in a temporary prison, nevertheless behaved respectively as abusers and victims (29). Social psychology shows that, whatever their own good and bad choices, most people believe that others would do whatever they personally chose to do, a phenomenon termed false consensus (30,31). Conformity to the perceived reactions of one's peers can be defined as good or bad, depending on how well the local norms fit those of larger society.

8   As every graduate of undergraduate psychology should know from the Milgram studies (32), ordinary people can engage in incredibly destructive behaviour if so ordered by legitimate authority. In those studies, participants acting as teachers frequently followed an experimenter's orders to punish a supposed learner (actually a confederate) with electric shock, all the way to administering lethal levels. Obedience to authority sustains every culture (33). Firefighters heroically rushing into the flaming World Trade Center were partly obeying their superiors, partly conforming to extraordinary group loyalty, and partly showing incredibly brave self-sacrifice. But obedience and conformity also motivated the terrorist hijackers and the Abu Ghraib guards, however much one might abhor their (vastly different) actions. Social conformity and obedience themselves are neutral, but their consequences can be heroic or evil. Torture is partly a crime of socialized obedience (34). Subordinates not only do what they are ordered to do but what they think their superiors would order them to do, given their

understanding of the authority's over-all goals. For example, lynching represented ordinary people going beyond the law to enact their view of the community's will.

9   Social influence starts with small, apparently trivial actions (in this case, insulting epithets), followed by more serious actions (humiliation and abuse) (35–37), as novices overcome their hesitancy and learn by doing (38). The actions are always intentional, although the perpetrator may not be aware that those actions constitute evil. In fact, perpetrators may see themselves as doing a great service by punishing and/or eliminating a group that they perceive as deserving ill-treatment (39).

10   In short, ordinary individuals under the influence of complex forces may commit evil acts (40). Such actions are human behaviours that can and should be studied scientifically (41,42). We need to understand more about the contexts that will promote aggression. We also need to understand the basis for exceptions—why, in the face of these social contexts, not all individuals succumb (43). Thus, although lay-observers may believe that explaining evil amounts to excusing it and absolving people of responsibility for their actions (44), in fact, explaining evils such as Abu Ghraib demonstrates scientific principles that could help to avert them.

11   Even one dissenting peer can undermine conformity (24). For example, whistle-blowers not only alert authorities but also prevent their peers from continuing in unethical behaviour. Authorities can restructure situations to allow communications. For example, CEOs can either welcome or discourage a diversity of opinions. Contexts can undermine prejudice (1). Individual, extended, equal-status, constructive, cooperative contact between mutual outgroups (whether American blacks and whites in the military or American soldiers and Iraqi civilians) can improve mutual respect and even liking. It would be harder to dehumanize and abuse imprisoned Iraqis if one had friends among ordinary Iraqis. A difficult objective in wartime, but as some Iraqis work alongside their American counterparts, future abuse is less likely. The slippery slope to abuse can be avoided. The same social contexts that provoke and permit abuse can be harnessed to prevent it. To quote another report [(45), p. 94]: "All personnel who may be engaged in detention operations, from point of capture to final disposition, should participate in a professional ethics program that would equip them with a sharp moral compass for guidance in situations often riven with conflicting moral obligations."

References and Notes

[1]S.T. Fiske, *Social Beings* (Wiley, New York, 2004).

[2]F.D. Richard, C.F. Bond. J.J. Stokes-Zoota, *Rev. Gen. Psychol.* 7, 331 (2003).

[3]B.A. Bettencourt, N. Miller, *Psychol. Bull.* 119, 422 (1996).

[4]M. Carlson, N. Miller, *Sociol. Soc. Res.* 72, 155, (1988).

[5]M. Carlson, A. Marcus-Newhall, N. Miller, *Pers. Soc. Psychol. Bull.* 15, 377 (1989).

[6]C.A. Anderson, B.J. Bushman, *Rev. Gen. Psychol.* 1, 19 (1997).

[7]A. Taguba, "Article 15-6. Investigation of the 800th Military Police Brigade," accessed 30 June 2004 from www.npr.org/iraq/2004/prison_abuse_report.pdf.

[8]B. Mullen, R. Brown, C. Smith, *Eur. J. Soc. Psychol.* 22, 103 (1992).

[9]B. Mullen, C. Johnson, *Br. J. Soc. Psychol.* 29, 11 (1990).

[10]J. Duckitt, in *Advances in Experimental Social Psychology,* M.P. Zanna, Ed. (Academic Press, New York, 2001).

[11]When their own mortality is salient, as in wartime, people particularly punish those outgroups seen to threaten basic values (12).

[12]S. Solomon, J. Greenberg, T. Pyszczynski, *Curr. Dir. Psychol. Sci.* 9, 200 (2000).

[13]S.T. Fiske, A.J. Cuddy, P. Glick, J. Xu. *J. Person. Soc. Psychol.* 82, 878 (2002).

[14]A.J. Cuddy, S.T. Fiske, P. Glick, "The BIAS map: Behaviors from intergroup affect and stereotypes," unpublished manuscript (Princeton University, Princeton, N.J., 2004).

[15]L.J. Heller, thesis, Princeton University, 2002.

[16]A.J. Har *et al., Neuroreport* 11, 2351 (2000).

[17]H. Schutz, B. Six, *Int. J. Intercult. Relat.* 20, 441 (1996).

[18]J.F. Dovidio *et al.,* in *Stereotypes and Stereotyping,* C.N. Macrae, C. Stangor, M. Hewstone, Ed. (Guilford, New York, 1996).

[19]C.A. Talaska, S.T. Fiske, S. Chaiken, "Predicting discrimination: A meta-analysis of the racial attitudes-behavior literature," unpublished manuscript (Princeton University, Princeton, N.J., 2004).

[20]E.A. Phelps *et al., J. Cogn. Neurosci.* 12, 729 (2000).

[21]Neuroimaging data represent college student reactions to photographs of outgroup members. These data should not be interpreted to mean that such reactions are innate or "wired in"; they result from long-term social context (46).

[22]M.E. Wheeler, S.T. Fiske, *Psychol. Sci.* in press.

[23]J.P. Leyens *et al., Eur. J. Soc. Psychol.* 33, 703 (2003).

[24]R. Bond, P.B. Smith, *Psychol. Bull.,* 119, 111 (1996).

[25]S. Tanford, S. Penrod, *Psychol. Bull.,* 95, 189 (1984).

[26]J. Tata *et al., J. Soc. Behav. Pers.* 11, 739 (1996).

[27]J.C. Turner, *Social Influence* (Brooks/Cole, Pacific Grove, CA, 1991).

[28]S.D. Reicher, *Eur. J. Soc. Psychol.* 14, 1 (1984).

[29]C. Haney, C. Banks, P. Zimbardo, *Int. J. Criminol. Penol.* 1, 69 (1973).

[30]B. Mullen *et al., J. Exp. Soc. Psychol.* 21, 262 (1985).

[31]B. Mullen, L. Hu, *Br. J. Soc. Psychol.* 27, 333 (1988).

[32]S. Milgram, *Obedience to Authority* (Harper and Row, New York, 1974).

[33]T. Blass, *J. Appl. Soc. Psychol.* 29, 955 (1999).

[34]H.C. Kelman, in *The Politics of Pain: Torturers and Their Masters,* R.D. Crelinsten. A.P. Schmidt, Eds. (Univ. of Leiden, Leiden, NL, 1991).

[35]A.L. Beaman *et al.*, *Pers. Soc. Psychol. Bull.* 9, 181 (1983).

[36]A.L. Dillard, J. E. Hunter, M. Burgoon, *Hum. Commun. Res.* 10, 461 (1984).

[37]E.F. Fern, K.B. Monroe, R.A. Avila, *J. Mark. Res.* 23, 144 (1986).

[38]E. Staub, *Pers. Soc. Psychol. Rev.* 3, 179 (1999).

[39]A. Bandura, *Pers. Soc. Psychol. Rev.* 3, 193 (1999).

[40]L. Berkowitz, *Pers. Soc. Psychol. Rev.* 3, 246 (1999).

[41]J.M. Darley, *Pers. Soc. Psychol. Rev.* 3, 269 (1999).

[42]A.G. Miller, Ed., *The Social Psychology of Good and Evil* (Guilford, New York, 2004).

[43]Although social context matters more than most people think, individual personality also matters, in accord with most people's intuitions: Social Dominance Orientation (SDO) describes a tough-minded view that it is a zero-sum, dog-eat-dog world, where some groups justifiably dominate other groups. People who score low on SDO tend to join helping professions, be more tolerant, and endorse less aggression; they might be less inclined to abuse. People choosing to join hierarchical institutions such as the military tend to score high on SDO, in contrast (47).

[44]A.G. Miller, A.K. Gordon, A.M. Buddie, *Pers. Soc. Psychol. Rev.* 3, 254 (1999).

[45]J.R. Schlesinger, H. Brown, T.K. Fowler, C.A. Homer, J.A. Blackwell, Jr., *Final Report of the Independent Panel to Review DoD Detention Operations,* accessed 8 November 2004, from www.informationclearinghouse.info/article6785.htm.

[46]L.T. Harris, S.T. Fiske, unpublished data.

[47]J. Sidanius, F. Pratto, *Social Dominance: An Intergroup Theory of Social Hierarchy and Oppression* (Cambridge Univ. Press, New York, 1999).

[48]B. Altemeyer, *Enemies of Freedom: Understanding Right-Wing Authoritarianism* (Jossey-Bass, San Francisco, 1988).

Note: The bibliographic format used in the notes for this essay is adapted for a specific publication, and does not follow the standard APA or MLA format explained in Chapter 14.

Questions on Content, Structure, and Style

1. What elements of this essay immediately indicate that this is an academic essay?

2. The authors use some specialist terminology that is common in their academic field. Using a dictionary or thesaurus, find the words in the "Vocabulary" section that follows, and then try to rewrite some of the essay's sentences with any synonyms for the specialist words. Do your synonyms represent the authors' ideas as precisely as the original words? Do they have the same connotations?

3. How do the authors define the essay's central terms? Are they clearly defined and explained? If not, could you define them more effectively?

4. Can you see the use of ethos in this essay? How do the authors set up and try to maintain their credibility on this subject? Can you see the use of any of the other argumentative appeals (pathos, logos) in this essay (see pages 275–277)?

5. The topic of this essay is challenging and potentially emotionally uncomfortable for many readers. How do you think this essay's tone affects readers who might be uncomfortable about this topic?

6. What is the central thesis of this essay? How is it supported? Is it convincing?

7. What are this essay's underlying assumptions about human nature and human behaviour?

8. The authors develop much of this essay by using examples. Can you distinguish between different categories of examples? How does each type of example function to support the essay's thesis?

9. This essay develops its thesis by using multiple strategies of development. List the main strategies, other than examples, that the authors use to develop their essay. Are there any that you find more effective than others?

10. Compare the multiple strategies used in this essay with those used in the essays by Martin Luther King and Barack Obama (Chapter 30). In different ways, all three essays address the issues of cultural difference and prejudice. How does the specific combination of strategies in each essay function to support the specific argument in each essay?

Suggestions for Writing

Try using Fiske, Harris, and Cuddy's "Why Ordinary People Torture Enemy Prisoners" as a stepping stone to an essay of your own. Social psychologists have studied the effects of group mentality and obedience to authority in a number of contexts and cultures. What examples of these above factors and their effects can you find within a Canadian context? After reading this essay, what conclusions could you draw about the ways in which our social relationships and our attitude toward authority affect our understanding of different cultures? What other arguments have you heard or read about why people engage in unethical actions? Write an essay in which you examine people's attitudes toward difference and identity. You might, for example, describe an incident, explain causes or effects, argue for ways to solve the problem, or outline steps you once took to make changes to unethical and/or prejudiced behaviour you experienced or observed. Read the essays by

Martin Luther King and Barack Obama in Chapter 30, and with the information gained from Fiske, Harris, and Cuddy's research, write an essay about stereotypes, prejudice, and identity. Or, use the information Fiske, Harris, and Cuddy provide in their endnotes to research the issues of stereotypes and prejudice, and then write an essay based on a question you have about the issues raised by the authors. Try using multiple strategies to develop your essay.

Vocabulary

social psychology (1)	scant (3)	conducive (7)
interpersonal (2)	potent (5)	ostracism (7)
accumulated (2)	cognitive (5)	lethal (8)
meta-analysis (2)	neuroimaging (5)	abhor (8)
quantitative (2)	amygdala (5)	epithets (9)
empirical (2)	insular (5)	succumb (10)
taunted (3)	comtemptible (6)	dissenting (11)

■ A REVISION WORKSHEET

As you write your rough drafts, consult Chapter 5 for guidance through the revision process. In addition, here are a few questions to ask yourself before and during the early stages of your writing:

1. What is my main purpose in writing this particular essay? Who is my audience?

2. Does my assignment or the subject itself suggest a primary method of development or would combining several strategies be more effective?

3. Have I considered my subject from multiple directions, as suggested by the questions on pages 344–345?

4. Have I selected the best strategies to meet the needs of my particular audience?

5. Would blending strategies help my readers understand my topic and my essay's purpose? Or am I trying to include too many approaches, move in too many directions, resulting in an essay that seems too scattered?

6. Have I considered an effective order for the strategies I've chosen? Do the parts of my essay flow together smoothly?

7. Have I avoided common weaknesses such as vague examples, fuzzy directions, circular definitions, overlapping categories, or logical fallacies, as discussed in the "Problems to Avoid" sections of Chapters 9–12?

After you've revised your essay extensively, you might exchange rough drafts with a classmate and answer these questions for each other, making specific suggestions for improvement wherever appropriate. (For advice on productive participation in classroom workshops, see pages 102–104.)

Reviewing Your Progress

After you have completed your essay, take a moment to measure your progress as a writer by responding to the following questions. Such analysis will help you recognize growth in your writing skills and may enable you to identify areas that are still problematic.

1. What do you like best about your essay? Why?

2. After considering the multiple strategies of development used in your essay, which one do you find most effective and why?

3. What part of your essay gave you the most trouble? How did you overcome the problem?

4. If you had more time to work on this essay, what would receive additional attention? Why?

5. What did you learn about your topic from writing this essay? About yourself as a writer?

Part 3

Special Assignments

The third section of this text addresses several kinds of assignments frequently included in many—but not all—composition classes. Chapter 14 will first explain ways to conduct formal research on a topic and then show you how to best incorporate your research into your essay. "Writing in Class: Exams and 'Response' Essays," Chapter 15, confronts the anxiety that writing under pressure may bring by helping you respond quickly but effectively to a variety of timed essays and exams. This chapter also addresses one of the most widely used in-class assignments, the summary-and-response (or reaction) essay. Chapter 16, "Writing about Literature," illustrates several uses of poetry and short stories in the composition classroom and provides some guidelines for both close reading and analytical thinking. The last chapter in Part Three, "Writing in the World of Work," presents advice for creating effective business letters, memos, electronic-mail messages, and résumés.

If you have worked through Parts One and Two of this book, you have already practised many of the skills demanded by these special assignments. Information in the next four chapters will build on what you already know about good writing. ■

Chapter 14

Writing a Paper Using Research

Although the words *research paper* have been known to produce anxiety worse than that caused by the sound of a dentist's drill, you should try to relax. A research paper is similar to the kinds of expository and argumentative essays described in the earlier parts of this book, the difference being the use of documented source material to support, illustrate, or explain your ideas. Research papers still call for thesis statements, logical sequences of paragraphs, well-developed evidence, smooth conclusions—or in other words, all the skills you've been practising throughout this book. By citing sources in your essays or reports, you merely show your readers that you have investigated your ideas and found support for them. In addition, using sources affords your readers the opportunity to look into your subject further if they so desire, consulting your references for additional information.

The process described in the next few pages should help you write a paper using research that is carefully and effectively documented. This chapter also contains sample documentation forms for a variety of research sources and a sample student essay using MLA style.

■ Focusing Your Topic

In some cases, you will be assigned your topic, and you will be able to begin your research right away. In other cases, however, you may be encouraged to select your own subject, or you may be given a general subject ("health-care reform," "recycling," "Canadian immigration policies") that you must narrow and then focus into a specific, manageable topic. If the topic is your choice, you need to do some preliminary thinking about what interests you; as in any assignment, you should make the essay a learning experience from which both you and your readers will profit. Therefore, you may want to brainstorm for a while on your general subject before you go to the library, asking yourself questions about what you already know and don't know. Some of the most interesting papers are argumentative essays in which writers set out to find an answer to a controversy or to find support for a solution they suspected might work. Other papers, sometimes called "research reports," expose, explain, or summarize a situation or a problem for their audience.

Throughout this chapter, we will track the research and writing process of Amy Lawrence, a composition student whose writing assignment called for an essay presenting her view of a controversy in her major field of study. As a History major, Amy is particularly interested in the Russian Revolution of 1918, when the Romanov family, the last ruling family of Russia, was assassinated by the Bolsheviks, the Communist revolutionaries led by Lenin. The long-standing controversy surrounding the assassination of Czar Nicholas II and his family focused on the question of whether the two youngest Romanov children, the beautiful Anastasia and the sickly Alexei, escaped execution. A series of forensic and historical discoveries concerning the controversy had made news in the 1990s, so Amy decided to investigate the Romanov assassination for her topic. Because she already had some general knowledge of the controversy, Amy was able to think about her topic in terms of some specific *research questions:* What would research tell her about the possibility of the Romanov children's escape? Would the new forensic evidence support the theory of an escape—or would it put such a claim to rest forever? (Amy's completed essay appears on pages 402–409.)

■ Beginning Your Library Research

Once you have a general topic (and perhaps have some research questions in mind), your next step is familiarizing yourself with the school or public library where you may do all or part of your research. Most university libraries today have both print and electronic resources to offer researchers, as well as access to the Internet. Your library's online central information system is likely to include a catalogue of its holdings, a number of selected databases, gateways to other libraries, and other kinds of resources. With appropriate computer connections, this system may be accessed from other places on or off campus, which is handy for those times when you cannot be in the library.

Most libraries also have information (printed or online) that will indicate the location of important areas, and almost all have reference librarians who can explain the various kinds of programs and resources available to you. Librarians are trained in advanced searching, so the smartest step you may take is asking a librarian for help before you begin searching. Library staff members may be able to save you enormous amounts of research time by pointing you in exactly the right direction. Do not be shy about asking the library staff for help at any point during your research!

Once you are familiar with your library, you may find it useful to consult one or more of the following research tools.

General Reference Works

If you need a general overview of your subject, or perhaps some background or historical information, you might begin your library research by consulting an encyclopedia, a collection of biographical entries, or even a statistical or demographic yearbook. You might use a comprehensive or specialized dictionary if your search turns up terms that are unfamiliar to you. These and many other library reference guides (in print and online) might also help you find a specific focus for your essay if you feel your topic is still too large or undefined at this point.

Online Catalogues

Today the online catalogue has replaced the print catalogue system as the primary guide to a library's holdings. You can access a library's catalogue through on-site computer terminals or, in many cases, connect from off-site locations through the Internet to the library's Web page.

Most computer catalogues allow you to look for information by subject, author, and title as well as by keyword(s), by the ISBN (publisher's book number), by the call number, or by a series title (Oxford World's Classics, for example). On-screen prompts will guide you through the process of searching. Because no two library catalogue systems are exactly alike, never hesitate to ask a librarian for help if you need it.

Unless you are already familiar with authorities or their works on your topic, you might begin your search by typing in keywords or your general subject. For example, Amy Lawrence began her research on the Romanov assassination by looking under the subject heading for Nicholas II, the Russian czar. After typing in her subject, she discovered that the library had several books on the czar; one book looked especially promising, so she pulled up the following screen to see more information.

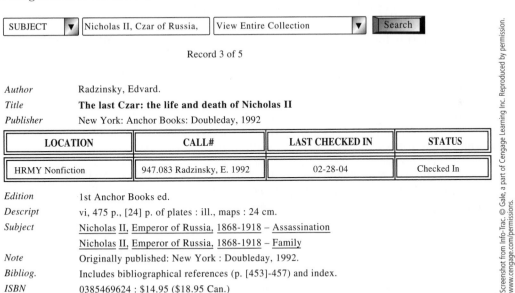

If you cannot find your topic in the subject catalogue, you may have to look under several headings to find the specific one your library uses. (For example, Amy's library might have used "Romanov" instead of "Nicholas II" in its subject catalogue.) If you can't find your subject under the headings that first come to mind, consult the *Library of Congress Subject Headings,* a common reference book that will suggest other names for your topic. Once you have a call number, a library map will help you find the book's location on the shelves.

Indexes

Indexes list magazines, journals, newspapers, audio and video sources, books, and collections that contain material you may wish to consult. Most of these indexes are now available as online databases; you will probably find the most current information there because databases are frequently updated. Some printed indexes, in contrast, may be revised and published only once a year.

Using the most appropriate index may save you valuable time as you research your subject. For example, if you think your topic has been the subject of general-interest magazines, you might consult the *Periodicals Index*, the *Reader's Guide to Periodical Literature*, for newspaper articles, you might check *The New York Times Index* or the *National Newspaper Index*. Most specialized disciplines have their own indexes: the *Humanities and Social Sciences Index*, the *Art Index*, the *Music Index*, the *Social Science Index*, the *Business Periodicals Index*, the *Canadian Business and Current Affairs Index*, the *Applied Science and Technology Index*, and so on.

Databases

Most libraries across the country subscribe to different information services that will lead researchers to appropriate databases for their subjects. A *database* allows users to scan electronic indexes that list thousands of bibliographic sources, abstracts, summaries, and texts.

After you access your library's database information screen, you will find some general-interest indexes and others that are more specialized. Page 363 shows a database screen from the University of British Columbia's Library, which has several library branches, both in the Vancouver and the Kelowna campuses.

Perhaps most helpful will be *full-text databases* that offer access to numerous academic and professional journals as well as magazines and newspapers. The full-text articles are the same as the articles that would be available in print, but are simply accessible to more people, since it's not necessary to get to a library in order to read them. When you look for full-text articles, under "Arts and Humanities," you might find this useful database:

> *ProQuest*—Magazine and newspaper articles from over 1,500 indexed publications, many of which are available in full-text and full-image format.

Other useful databases include the MLA database, JSTOR, Periodicals Archive Online, Project Muse, EBSCO, PsychARTICLES, and so on. The number of online full-text databases is growing daily, which gives researchers access to millions of articles published in different fields and in international journals.

InfoTrac is another highly useful database that offers full-text articles from nearly 5,000 newspapers, general-interest magazines, trade publications, and scholarly journals. You can now conveniently access *InfoTrac College Edition* from your own Web browser by registering with the passcode packaged with all new copies of this textbook; this free four-month subscription is offered by Nelson Education Ltd. (for more information, visit www.infotrac-college.com).

Online databases are updated frequently and may therefore provide you with the most current sources for your research. Do note, however, that because libraries contract and pay a fee for database services, they must restrict some database access to on-site use or use by particular patrons (for example, enrolled students only at a campus library). Know, too, that each database may have its own search method. Always ask a librarian for help if you are struggling with a database search.

As you search your electronic sources, remember that you may have to try a variety of keywords (and their synonyms) to find what you need. Sometimes your keyword search may turn up too few leads—and sometimes you may be overwhelmed with too many matches! (For example, when Amy Lawrence typed in the keyword "Anastasia," she discovered too many irrelevant entries focusing on Hollywood movies about the princess.) To save time and effort, you may be able to broaden or narrow your search by typing in words called *Boolean operators,** as illustrated below:

AND (Nicholas II AND Anastasia)—narrows your search to those references containing both terms

OR (Nicholas II OR Anastasia)—broadens search to find items containing either term

NOT (Anastasia NOT movie)—excludes items irrelevant to your search

NEAR (Nicholas II NEAR assassination)—finds references in which the terms occur within a set number of words (This option is not always available.)

Not all databases respond to Boolean operators, however, so it's always best to consult the searching advice offered by your particular information system.

Here is the *InfoTrac* "keyword" search screen Amy used to look for more information on the important Romanov DNA tests:

---

* Named for the nineteenth-century British mathematician and logician George Boole.

Keyword search

Click in the entry box and enter search term(s)

Romanov AND DNA   [Search] [Clear Form]

Search for words ⦿ in title, citation, abstract ○ in entire article content
Type words to search for. You can use AND, OR, NOT. Results are sorted by date.

The *InfoTrac* search for "Romanov and DNA" produced these two titles, whose full-text articles Amy found useful.

INFOTRAC· COLLEGE EDITION
From Gale Group and Thomson Learning

Keyword search (in title, citation, abstract): Romanov AND DNA

──────── **Citations 1 to 2** ────────

☐   Mark all items on this page
☐ 🗎 **DNA test confirms dead czar's identity.** (former Russian Czar Nicholas Romanov II)
Mark   (Biology)(Brief Article)
        Science News April 20, 1996 v149 n16 p255(1) (385 words)

☐ 🗎 **Royal D-loops.** (remains of Russian Czar Nicholas II and family proved authentic with
Mark   DNA) (1993 - The Year in Science) Josie Glausiusz.
        Discover Jan 1994 v15 n1 p90(1) (474 words)

Once you have found useful information, remember that libraries have printers available to print out the on-screen data you wish to keep; you may have to pay a small fee for this printing, so it's a good idea to take some cash along, preferably in correct change. (Sometimes library users with personal computers at home can avoid this expense by e-mailing data to themselves.)

And once again, the very best advice bears repeating: never hesitate to ask your library staff for help.

The Internet

You may have access to the Internet through your library, through your school network, or through a personal account with a service provider of your choice. The Internet can offer great research opportunities, but in many cases, it may only supplement—not replace—the information you will need to collect through library sources.

The most effective approach to discovering useful material on the Internet may be through the use of "search engines" that produce a list of potential electronic documents or websites in response to your search. Some search engines (such as Yahoo!) offer a "subject directory," which organizes an enormous amount of information into broad categories, such as arts, education, health, humanities, or science. To research a topic, you move through general categories to more specific subcategories until you find the information you need (arts → literature → classics → Greek classics → *The Iliad*). You might wish to consult a subject directory early in your search when you are looking for general information on your topic.

Perhaps more useful in an advanced search are those search engines that operate in a more focused way: you type in your keyword(s); the search engine explores its database for word or phrase matches; it then presents you with a list of potential sources, which include the Internet addresses (called URLs—"uniform resource locators"). You may access the sources that seem most promising (often those that appear first on the list), and you may also connect to other material by clicking on any highlighted words (hypertext links) appearing within the text of a particular document. At this time, the most popular search engine is Google, but there are many, many more worldwide, including AltaVista, Yahoo!, AlltheWeb, Wisenut, and Teoma; some systems, such as Metalib, Academic Search Premier, Metacrawler, and Kartoo, search multiple engines at once. Because each search engine pulls its results from a different (but often overlapping) pool of Web pages, and because each one offers distinct "extra features," it pays to try more than one. (If you aren't satisfied with your results, try another set of keywords before moving on.)

Most search engines have their own searching tips; to improve your chances for success, it's well worth the time to read the advice on advanced searches. For example, many search engines allow use of some or all of the Boolean operators (see page 363) to narrow or broaden your search. Some allow the use of plus and minus signs to show connected terms or unwanted matches:

Anastasia + Nicholas II (find sources containing both terms)

Anastasia – movie (find sources about Anastasia but exclude those that include the word "movie")

Some programs request quotation marks around a key term of multiple words ("Anne Frank"); some are case sensitive (capitalize proper nouns or not?); some use truncation to find various forms of a word (myth* will return *mythology* and *mythical*). Other search engines, such as Ask.com, allow users to ask questions in natural language ("Who was Marie Romanov?"). You'll see that some search engines evolve, even in changing their names (such as Ask Jeeves, which became Ask.com), and others seem to disappear, so be prepared to try different search engines in your research. As technology continues to improve, searching will no doubt become easier, so always take a moment to look at each search engine's current directions.

Here is one more hint for searching the Web: sometimes you can guess the URL you need. Simply fill in the name of a specific company, college, agency, or organization. Do not skip spaces between words (usnews.com).

Businesses: www.name of company.com

Canadian Universities: www.name of university.ca

Government agencies: www.name of agency.gov

Organizations: www.name of organization.org

You may also consult specialized directories to discover the addresses you need. One note: there may be some deregulation of domain names in the future, so companies such as Amazon might be able to have addresses that leave out ".ca" or ".com" in their addresses.

Once you find a useful document, you may print it, add the reference to your "bookmark" or "favourites" list, or copy it to a file if you are using your own computer. Whether at the library or at home, always keep a list of your important sites, their addresses, and the date you accessed them. You may need this information for an easy return to a particular document and also for your working bibliography. Sites such as Google Notebook (www.google.com/notebook) and Zotero (www.zotero.org) are useful, free tools for keeping track of your bibliographic citations. Some universities and colleges also offer access to other information management sites such as RefWorks (www.refworks.com) or Endnote (www.endnote.com) for help with preparing your working bibliography.

There are many other ways to use the Internet for research and for trading ideas with others. To explore the possibilities in more detail than may be presented here, invest in a current book on the Internet or go to one of the many sites offering research advice.

Words of Caution for Internet Users: Be Afraid, Be Very Afraid. . . .

The Internet offers researchers fast access to a wealth of information. However, the Internet poses problems too. It may offer a great deal of information on your essay topic—but it may not offer the *best* information, which might be found in a classic text on your library shelf. Background information or historical perspective may not be available; website information may be out of date. Moreover, simply finding the specific information you need can be frustrating and time-consuming, especially if your keywords and links don't lead in useful directions. The information superhighway is congested with scores of irrelevant distractions, so beware the wild Web chase.

There is, however, another much more serious problem: not all material found on the Internet is accurate or reliable. You do need to choose your databases carefully. Certain databases, such as Wikipedia and Sparksnotes are very convenient to access, and seem to provide readers with exactly the information they need, summarized and neatly organized. But the information in these websites is not peer-reviewed by specialist scholars, and there is no guarantee the information will be accurate. For example, in a recent search for information on Atwood's "Marrying the Hangman" (Chapter 16), a Wikipedia entry spelled the name of the hangman as "Cololère," citing an entry in the *Dictionary of Canadian Biography, Volume III: 1741–1777*. This name was found in a brief comment in the entry, which claimed to have summarized the entry on this individual in the *DCB*. This same summary was present, word for word, including the spelling of the hangman's name, in another website, www.poetryfoundation.org., which looks quite credible. However, the original entry in the *DCB* spelled the hangman's name slightly differently, as "Corolère." It was clear that both these websites had not only made careless errors, but had repeated them without verification. If you choose websites for convenience rather than accuracy and credibility, your own work will be built on inaccuracies and will lose its credibility.

How do you know you are using a credible source? When an article is printed in a respected journal or by an academic publisher, for example, readers can feel more confident in its credibility. Any academic article or book goes through a rigorous process of reviews by peers or experts in the field, editors, and fact-finding departments, so readers have assurances that editors have reviewed the information, writers have checked their facts, and authorities have been quoted correctly. The academic databases mentioned on page 362 will only list peer-reviewed articles. Remember that e-journals (accessed through links on academic databases and subscribed to by libraries) are different from Internet websites, even though both e-journals and websites are accessed online. Websites, on the other hand, may be created by anyone on any subject, from gene splicing to Elvis sightings, without any sort of editorial review. Opinions—wise or crackpot—may be presented as facts; rumours may be presented as reality. Because there is no "quality control" of websites, writers of research papers must evaluate their sources extremely carefully to avoid gathering unreliable information.

Always ask these questions of each source:

- What is the purpose of this website? (To inform, persuade, market a product or service, share an interest, entertain?) To whom is this site primarily directed, and why?

- Who is the sponsor, author, or creator of the site? (A business, an educational institution, a nonprofit organization, a government agency, a news bureau, an individual?) Is the sponsor or author known and respected in the particular content area?

- Does the sponsor or author reveal a clear bias or strong opinion? Does such a slant undercut the usefulness of the information?

- When was this site produced? When was it last updated or revised? If links exist, are they still viable? Up-to-date?

- Is the information accurate? How might the material be cross-checked and verified?

If you have doubts about the accuracy of any material you discover on the Internet, find another authoritative source to validate the information or omit it from your essay. It's also useful to consult a librarian about the legitimacy of any website. Following the guidelines on these pages will help you evaluate *all* your potential research sources.

Special Collections

Your library may contain special collections that will help you research your subject. Some libraries, for example, have extensive collections of government documents or educational materials or newspapers from foreign cities. Other libraries may have invested in manuscripts from famous authors or in a series of works on a particular subject, such as your province's history. Remember, too, that some libraries contain collections of early films, rare recordings, or unique photographs. Consult your librarian or the information sources describing your library's special holdings.

■ Conducting the Personal Interview

Depending on your choice of topic, you may find all the information you need for your essay by exploring sources through library and online research. However, sometimes you may discover that an authority on your subject lives in your town or works on your campus. In this case, you may wish to conduct a *personal interview* to gather valuable information for your essay. But before you prepare to interview anyone, you must check to see if your educational institution has any legal regulations and guidelines about interviewing. At some Canadian universities, for example, students who wish to conduct research that includes fieldwork and personal interviews must go through several stages of applications to their university's Research Office before they are given official permission to conduct any interviews.

Preparation is the key word governing a good interview. Here are some suggestions that may help you collect useful data in the most effective way possible.

Before You Interview:

1. *Know your purpose.* If you have only a vague notion of why you are talking to the interviewee, you will waste everyone's time as the conversation roams like a lost hiker wandering from one clearing to the next. A close look at your essay's outline or your early drafts should tell you why and how this person might contribute to your research. Be certain that the person you have selected for an interview is, in fact, the best source for the kind of information you are seeking.

2. *Make an appointment.* Calling to arrange an interview may make you a bit nervous, but remember that most people like to be asked for their opinions and are usually willing to help students with their research if their schedules permit. Be sure the interviewee understands who you are, why you are asking for an interview, and approximately how much time you are requesting. Whenever possible, allow the interviewee to select the hour and place most convenient for him or her. Do adjust your schedule to give yourself time after the meeting in case the interview runs long and to allow yourself a few minutes to review and fill in your notes.

3. *Educate yourself.* Before the interview, read about your topic and your interviewee. You want to appear knowledgeable about your subject; you can also save time by skipping questions that have already been answered in print. Busy experts appreciate not having to explain basic information that you could have—and should have—already looked up.

4. *Plan some questions.* Unless you have an excellent memory, it is best to jot down some specific questions to which you can refer during the interview. Some interviewers write each question at the top of an index card, and then use the rest of the card for their notes on the answer. Others use a notebook in which they write a question (or key words) at the top of each page. Try to create questions that are specific, clear, and logically ordered. Avoid "yes/no" questions that don't lead to discussion or that have the potential to lead to misleading results. If you don't leave room for more than two opposing possibilities, you can create an either–or fallacy. Look at the connotations of the words in your questions: are you asking leading questions that will only lead to the result you want or expect? Ask yourself what your own assumptions and expectations are about the subject. Being honest about your own biases can help you to avoid logical fallacies and to achieve more objective and accurate results. If you have a complicated or convoluted issue you want to discuss, try breaking it into a series of simpler questions that can be tackled by the interviewee one at a time.

During the Interview:

5. *Make a good first impression.* Always arrive on time, prepared with pens, paper, or other documents you need. Some interviewers like to use a small tape recorder, but you must first secure your interviewee's permission to use this equipment. (A recorder makes some people uncomfortably self-conscious and hesitant to speak freely, so consider whether the accuracy it may provide is more important than the spontaneity it may kill.) Always begin by thanking your interviewee for his or her time and briefly say again why you think he or she can provide helpful information to you.

6. *Ask, listen, ask.* Begin asking your prepared questions, but don't rush through them. Listen attentively to your interviewee's answers, and although it takes practise, try to maintain eye contact as you jot down abbreviated notes on the answers. Allow the interviewee to do almost all the talking; after all, you are there to collect information, not participate in a debate. Do politely ask for clarification (unfamiliar terms, spelling of names, unclear references, and so on) when you need it.

7. *Be flexible.* Sometimes your interviewee will talk about something fascinating that never occurred to you when you prepared your original list of questions. Be ready to adapt your plan and ask new questions that follow up on unexpected commentary.

8. *Silence is golden but. . . .* If an interviewee is quiet or hesitates to give the kind of detailed responses you are seeking, you may need to use phrases of this kind to draw out longer answers:

   Can you elaborate on that?
   Tell me more about X.
   Why did you think that?
   How did you react to that?
   When did you realize. . . ?
   Why do you believe that?
   What's your reading of that situation?
   Would you explain that for me?

   As you ask for more details, try to use a friendly, conversational tone that will put your interviewee at ease.

   On the other hand, sometimes interviewees talk too much! They become stuck on one aspect of a topic, going into unnecessary depth, or perhaps they begin to drift off the subject completely. Be courteous but firm in your resolve to redirect the flow of conversation. To get back to your topic, you may need to re-ask the original question, using slightly different words.

9. *Conclude thoughtfully.* At the end of the interview, ask for any additional comments the interviewee would like to offer and for any information (or other sources) he or she thinks you might find useful. Ask the interviewee if you may contact him or her again if you should have another brief question; if such permission is granted, ask for the best means of contact (a telephone number or e-mail address). Give the interviewee your most sincere thanks for his or her time and assistance.

After the Interview:

10. *Review your notes immediately.* Fill in gaps in your notes while your memory is fresh, and write out acronyms or abbreviations whose meanings you might forget in a few days. Make some notes to yourself about using the information in your essay.

Later, if the interview figures prominently in your essay, consider sending your interviewee a copy of your work. Within days of the interview, however, it is ALWAYS polite to send your interviewee a short thank-you note, acknowledging his or her help with your research project.

■ Preparing a Working Bibliography

As you search for information about your essay topic, keep a list of sources that you may want to use in your essay. This list, called a *working bibliography,* will grow as you discover potential sources, and it may shrink if you delete references that aren't useful. Ultimately, this working bibliography will become the list of references presented at the end of your essay.

There are several ways to record your sources. Some students prefer to make an index card for each title; others compile a list in a research notebook; still others prefer to create a computer file or a folder of printouts. As you add sources to your working bibliography, note the following information as appropriate:

Book

1. Author's or editor's full name (and name of translator if given)
2. Complete title, including subtitle if one exists
3. Edition number
4. Volume number and the total number of volumes if the book is part of a series
5. Publisher
6. City of publication
7. Date of publication
8. Library call number or location of source
9. Chapter title or page numbers of the information you need

Article in a Journal, Magazine, or Newspaper

1. Author's full name (if given)
2. Title of the article
3. Title of the journal, magazine, or newspaper
4. Volume and issue number of the journal or magazine
5. Date of publication
6. Page numbers of the article (section and page numbers for newspaper)

Electronic Sources

1. Author's full name or name of sponsoring organization
2. Title of document

3. Information about print publication (book: place, publisher, date; periodical: title, volume and issue if given, date, pages)

4. Information about electronic publication (source, such as database, website, CD-ROM, etc.; name of service; date of publication or most recent update)

5. Access information (date of access and URL)

Interview

1. Interviewee's name and title

2. Interviewee's organization or company, job description, or other information regarding his or her expertise, including pertinent publications, studies, presentations, and so on.

3. Subject of interview

4. Date, place, and method of interview (e.g., in person, by telephone, by e-mail)

Here are four sample index cards that might appear in Amy Lawrence's working bibliography:

Book

> *Radzinsky, Edvard*
>
> *The Last Czar: The Life and Death of Nicholas II*
>
> *Doubleday Publishers, 1992*
>
> *New York, New York*
>
> *pp. 8–10, 315–434*   *Translated by*
>
> *call number: AN947.083*   *Marian Schwartz*
>
> *(CSU Library, East Wing)*

Article in Magazine

> *Elliott, Dorinda*
>
> *"The Legacy of the Last Czar"*
>
> *Newsweek, pp. 60–61*
>
> *Sept. 21, 1992*

Electronic Source

> *Varoli, John*
>
> *"Nemtsov: Bury Czar in St. Petersburg July 17"*
>
> <u>*St. Petersburg Times*</u>
>
> *St. Petersburg, Russia*
>
> *Feb. 9–15, 1998*
>
> *<http://www.spb.ru/times/336–337/nemtsov.html>*
>
> *Internet*   *(date of access: 2/26/04)*

Interview

> *Wheeler, Anne (Dr.)*
>
> *Professor of History*
> *Department of History*
> *Colorado State University*
>
> *Teaches H456, Russian History and Culture*
>
> *Interview subject: Romanov assassination*
> *In-person interview: Feb. 15, 2004*
> *Office of Dr. Wheeler, Clark 305, campus, Ft. Collins, CO*

■ Choosing and Evaluating Your Sources

After you have found a number of promising sources, take a closer look at them. The strength and credibility of your research paper will depend directly on the strength and credibility of your sources. In short, a research paper built on shaky, unreliable sources will not convince a thoughtful reader. Even one suspect piece of evidence may lead your reader to wonder about the validity of other parts of your essay.

To help you choose your print and online sources, ask yourself the following questions as you try to decide which facts, figures, and testimonies will best support or illustrate your ideas.

What do I know about the author? Does this person have any expertise or particular knowledge about the subject matter? If the author of an article about nuclear fusion is a physics professor at a respected university, her views may be more informed than those of a writer of popular science. Although books and scholarly journals generally cite their author's qualifications, the credentials of journalists and magazine writers may be harder to evaluate. Internet sources, as mentioned earlier, may be highly suspect. In cases in which the background of a writer is unknown, you might examine the writer's use of his or her own sources. Can sources for specific data or opinions be checked or verified? In addition, the objectivity of the author must be considered: some authors are clearly biased and may even stand to gain economically or politically from taking a particular point of view. The president of a tobacco company, for instance, might insist that secondary smoke from the cigarettes of others will not harm nonsmokers, but does he or she have an objective opinion? Try to present evidence only from those authors whose views will sway your intelligent readers.

What do I know about the publisher? Who published your sources? Major, well-known publishing houses can be one indication of a book's credibility. (If you are unfamiliar with a particular publisher, consult a librarian or professor in that field.) Be aware that there are many publishers who only publish books supporting a specific viewpoint; similarly, many organizations support websites to further their causes. The bias in such sources may limit their usefulness to your research.

When you're looking for periodicals, consider the nature of the journal, magazine, or newspaper. Who is its intended audience? A highly technical paper on sickle cell anemia, for example, might be weakened by citing a very general discussion of the disease from *Health Digest*; an article from the *Canadian Medical Association Journal,* however, might be valuable. Is it a publication known to be fairly objective (*The Globe and Mail*) or does it have a particular cause to support (*Central Alberta Farmer*)? Looking at the masthead of a journal or other publication will often tell you whether articles are subjected to stringent review before acceptance for publication. In general, articles published in "open" or non-selective publications should be examined closely for credibility. For example, the newsletter for MENSA—a well-known international society for individuals who have documented IQs in the top 2 percent of the population—once created a furor when an article appeared recommending the euthanasia of the mentally and physically disabled, the homeless, and other so-called "non-productive" members of society. The newsletter editor's explanation was that all articles submitted for publication were generally accepted.

Is my research reasonably balanced? Your treatment of your subject—especially if it is a controversial one—should show your readers that you investigated all sides of the issue before reaching a conclusion. If your sources are drawn only from authorities well known for voicing one position, your readers may be skeptical about the quality of your research. For instance, if in a paper arguing against seal hunting, you cite only the opinions voiced by members of Greenpeace, you may antagonize the reader who wants a thorough analysis of all sides of the question. Do use sources that support your position, but don't overload your argument with obviously biased sources.

Are my sources reporting valid research? Is your source the original researcher or is he or she reporting someone else's study?* If the information is being reported secondhand, has your source been accurate and clear? Is the original source named or referenced in some way so that the information could be checked?

A thorough researcher might note the names of authorities frequently cited by other writers or researchers and try to obtain the original works by those authorities. This tip was useful for Amy Lawrence as she found the researcher Robert K. Massie mentioned in a number of magazine articles. Once she obtained a copy of his often-quoted book, she had additional information to consider for her paper.

Look too at the way information in your source was obtained in the first place. Did the original researchers themselves draw logical conclusions from their evidence? Did they run their study or project in a fair, impartial way? For example, a survey of people whose names were obtained from the rolls of the Liberal Party will hardly constitute a representative sampling of voters' opinions on an upcoming election.

Moreover, be especially careful with statistics, because they can be manipulated quite easily to give a distorted picture. A recent survey, for instance, asked a large sample of people to rate a number of Canadian cities based on questions dealing with quality of life. Vancouver—a lovely city to be sure—came out the winner, but only if one agrees that all the questions should be weighted equally; that is, the figures gave Vancouver the highest score only if one rates "outdoor living" to be as equally important as "educational opportunities," "number of crimes," "cultural opportunities," and other factors. In short, always evaluate the quality of your sources' research and the validity of their conclusions before you decide to incorporate their findings into your own paper. (And don't forget Mark Twain's reference to "lies, damned lies, and statistics.")

Are my sources still current? Although some famous experiments or studies have withstood the years, many topics demand the most current research. What was written two years or even two weeks ago may have been disproved or surpassed since, especially in our rapidly changing political world and ever-expanding fields of technology. A paper on the status of the U.S. space program, for example, demands recent sources, and research on personal computer use in Canada would be severely weakened by the use of a text published as recently as 2001 for "current" statistics.

If they're appropriate, journals and other periodicals may contain more up-to-date reports than books printed several years ago; library database searches can often provide the most current information. On the other hand, you certainly shouldn't ignore a "classic" study on your subject, especially if it is the one against which all the other studies are measured. A student researching the life of Abraham Lincoln, for instance, might find Carl Sandburg's multi-volume biography of over sixty years ago as valuable as more recent works. (Remember, too, that even though websites can be continually revised, they are sometimes neglected; always check to see if a "last updated" date has been posted or if the material contains current dates or references.)

 REMEMBER: For more advice to help you think critically about your sources, see Chapter 5.

---

* Interviews, surveys, studies, and experiments conducted firsthand are referred to as *primary sources;* reports and studies written by someone other than the original researcher are called *secondary sources.*

■ Preparing an Annotated Bibliography

While you are gathering and assessing your sources, you may be asked to compile an annotated bibliography—a description of each important source that includes the basic bibliographic facts as well as a brief summary of each entry's content. After reading multiple articles or books on your subject over a period of days or even weeks, you may discover that the information you've found has begun to blur together in your head. Annotating each of your sources will help you remember the specific data in each one so that you can locate the material later in the planning and drafting stages of your writing process. Although there are several bibliographic styles, such as the APA and AMA styles for psychology and medicine, and the Chicago style and the Turabian style for the humanities, in this chapter, we are using the MLA style for our annotations, as it is the most commonly used citation style in the humanities.

Here is a sample taken from Amy Lawrence's annotated bibliography:

Elliott, Dorinda. "The Legacy of the Last Czar." *Newsweek* 21 Sept. 1992: 60–61. Print.

Elliot offers the results of early forensic analysis of the Romanov gravesite and a brief description of the events surrounding the executions. The article quotes forensic experts and historians, and includes the views of Russian citizens on the significance of finding and identifying the remains of the Romanov family.

Compiling an annotated bibliography will also give you a clear sense of how complete and balanced your sources are in support of your ideas, perhaps revealing gaps in your evidence that need to be filled with additional research data. Later, when your essay is finished, your annotated bibliography might provide a useful reference for any of your readers who are interested in exploring your subject in more depth.

■ Taking Notes

As you evaluate and select those sources that are both reliable and useful, you will begin taking notes on their information. Most researchers use one or more of the following three methods of note-taking:

1. Some students prefer to make their notes on index cards rather than on notebook paper because a stack of cards may be added to, subtracted from, or shuffled around more easily when it's time to plan the essay. You may find it useful to label each card with a short topic heading that corresponds to a major idea in your essay. Then, as you read, put pertinent information on its appropriate card. Be sure to identify the source of all your notes. (Hint 1: If you have used bibliography cards, take your notes on cards of different sizes or colours to avoid any confusion; write on only one side of each card so that all your information will be in sight when you draft your essay.)

2. Other students rely on photocopies or printouts of sources, highlighting or underlining important details. (Hint 2: Copy a source's title page and other front matter so that you can clip complete bibliographic information to your pages.)

3. Students may prefer to store their notes as computer files because of the easy transfer of quoted material from file to essay draft. (Hint 3: Always make a hard copy of your notes and back up your files frequently in case of a crash!) If you are not

using a laptop, you will probably find yourself taking notes by hand on some occasions (library, classroom, interview, public speech, etc.), so carry index cards with you and transcribe your notes into your files later.

Whichever note-taking method you choose, always remember to record bibliographic information and the specific page numbers (in printed sources) or paragraph numbers (in some electronic sources) from which your material is taken. Your notes may be one of the following kinds:

1. *Direct quotations.* When you use material word for word, you must always enclose it in quotation marks and note the precise page number of the quotation, if given.* If the quoted material runs from one printed page onto another, use some sort of signal to yourself, such as a slash bar (child/abuse) or arrow ($\rightarrow$ p. 162) at the break, so if you use only part of the quoted material in your paper, you will know on which page it appeared. If the quoted material contains odd, archaic, or incorrect spelling, punctuation marks, or grammar, insert the word *sic* in brackets next to the item in question; [*sic*] means "this is the way I found it in the original text," and such a symbol will remind you later that you did not miscopy the quotation. Otherwise, always double-check to make sure you did copy the material accurately and completely to avoid having to come back to the source as you prepare your essay. If the material you want to quote is lengthy or complex, you will find it easier—though not cheaper—to photocopy (or print out) the text rather than transcribe it.

2. *Paraphrase.* You paraphrase when you put into your own words what someone else has written or said. Please note: *paraphrased ideas are borrowed ideas, not your original thoughts, and, consequently, they must be attributed to their owner just as direct quotations are.*

To remind yourself that certain information in your notes is paraphrased, always introduce it with some sort of notation, such as a handwritten $\circledP$ or a typed P//. Quotation marks will always tell you what you borrowed directly, but sometimes when writers take notes one week and write their first draft a week or two later, they cannot remember if a note was paraphrased or if it was an original thought. Writers occasionally plagiarize unintentionally because they believe only direct quotations and statistics must be attributed to their proper sources, so make your notes as clear as possible. (For more information on avoiding plagiarism, see pages 380–383.)

3. *Summary.* You may wish to condense a piece of writing so you can offer it as support for your own ideas. Using your own words, you should present in shorter form the writer's thesis and supporting ideas. You may find it helpful to include a few direct quotations in your summary to retain the flavour of the original work. Of course, you will tell your readers what you are summarizing and by whom it was written. Remember to make a note (sum:) to yourself to indicate summarized, rather than original, material. (For more information on writing a summary, see also pages 377–378.)

4. *Your own ideas.* Your notes may also contain your personal comments (judgments, flashes of brilliance, questions, notions of how to use something you've

---

* All tables, graphs, and charts that you copy must also be directly attributed to their sources, though you do not enclose graphics in quotation marks.

just read, notes to yourself about connections between sources, and so forth) that will aid you in the writing of your paper. In handwritten notes, you might jot these down in a different-coloured pen or put them in brackets that you've initialled so that you will recognize them later as your own responses.

Distinguishing Paraphrase from Summary

Because novice writers sometimes have a hard time understanding the difference between paraphrase and summary, here is an explanation and a sample of each. The original paragraph that appears here was taken from a scholarly article explaining historical context in a discussion about Canadian sports' connection to Canadian identity:

> The political motivations behind the modernization of sport cannot be separated from the actual changes that occurred in expressions of physical activity. In Canada, these motivations stemmed from a British Victorian sensibility. By the turn of the eighteenth century, sport in Britain was being realized as an excellent means of social control and conditioning (Jarvie and Maguire 1994:109). The successes that church and school officials had enjoyed by providing the ever-increasing urban working class with productive non-threatening activities, such as cricket and (a "refined" version of) football, were soon being implemented in the colonies as a means of "correcting" the rougher, more vulgar vernacular pastimes. Perhaps even more importantly, there was symbolic value in having newly colonized peoples engaging in these uniquely British activities: thus, regulated sport quickly became a vehicle for cultural imperialism.

> —from "Imagining a Canadian Identity Through Sport: A Historical
> Interpretation of Lacrosse and Hockey,"
> Michael A. Robidoux, *Journal of American Folklore*,
> 115.456 (2002), p. 211. Print.

Paraphrase

A *paraphrase* puts the information in the researcher's own words, but it does follow the order of the original text, and it does include the important details:

> The modernization of sport is closely linked to politics. Canada was influenced by Victorian Britain's recognition that organized sports controlled the urban masses by supplying safe and civilized outlets for physical activity (Jarvie and Maguire 1994:109). The methods that worked in schools and churches were extended to the colonies. Cricket and football, for example, were used to replace rougher sports and thus refine the more vulgar colonists. Organized sports thus functioned to impose a British cultural norm and solidify Britain's cultural dominance (Robidoux 211).

Summary

A *summary* is generally much shorter than the original; the researcher picks out the key ideas but often omits many of the supporting details:

> A 2002 study on Canadian sports and identity suggests that Canadian modernization of sports was influenced by British Victorian attitudes toward class and the necessity for social control. In Britain, organized sports provided safe, controlled physical outlets for the working classes; in the colonies, these replaced threatening physical activities and established British culture's dominance (Robidoux 211).

REMEMBER: Both paraphrased and summarized ideas must be attributed to their sources, even if you do not reproduce exact words or figures.

■ Incorporating Your Source Material

Be aware that a research paper is not a massive collection of quotations and paraphrased or summarized ideas glued together with a few transitional phrases. It is, instead, an essay in which you offer *your* thesis and ideas based on and supported by your research. Consequently, you will need to incorporate and blend in your reference material in a variety of smooth, persuasive ways. Here are some suggestions:

Use your sources in a clear, logical way. Make certain that you understand your source material well enough to use it in support of your own thoughts. Once you have selected the best references to use, be as convincing as possible. Ask yourself if you're using enough evidence and if the information you're offering really does clearly support your point. As in any essay, you need to avoid oversimplification, hasty generalizations, non sequiturs, and other problems in logic (for a review of common logical fallacies, see pages 279–281). Resist the temptation to add quotations, facts, or statistics that are interesting but not really relevant to your paper.

Don't overuse direct quotations. It's best to use a direct quotation *only* when it expresses a point in a far more impressive, emphatic, or concise way than you could say it yourself. Suppose, for instance, you were analyzing the films of a particular director and wanted to include a sample of critical reviews:

> As one movie critic wrote, "this film is really terrible, and people should ignore it" (Dennison 14).

The direct quotation above isn't remarkable and could be easily paraphrased. However, you might be tempted to quote the following line to show your readers an emphatically negative review of this movie:

> As one movie critic wrote, "this film's plot is so idiotic it's clearly intended for people who move their lips not only when they read but also when they watch TV" (Dennison 14).

When you do decide to use direct quotations, don't merely drop them in your prose as if they had fallen from a tall building onto your page. Instead, lead into them smoothly so that they obviously support or clarify what you are saying.

Dropped in	Scientists have been studying the ill effects of nitrites on test animals since 1961. "Nitrites produced malignant tumors in 62 percent of the test animals within six months" (Smith 109).
Better	Scientists have been studying the ill effects of nitrites on test animals since 1961. According to Dr. William Smith, head of the Farrell Institute of Research, who conducted the largest experiment thus far, "nitrites produced malignant tumors in 62 percent of the test animals within six months" (109).

Vary your sentence pattern when you present your quotations. Here are some sample phrases for quotations:

In her introduction to *The Great Gatsby,* Professor Wilma Smith points out that Fitzgerald "wrote about himself and produced a narcissistic masterpiece" (5).

Wilma Smith, author of *Impact,* summarized the situation this way: "Eighty-eight percent of the sales force threaten a walkout" (21).

"Only the Prime Minister can make the final decision," according to the Minister for Foreign Affairs, Wilma Smith.

As drama critic Wilma Smith observed last year in *The Globe and Mail,* the play was "a rousing failure" (212).

Perhaps the well-known poet Wilma Smith expressed the idea best when she wrote, "Love is a spider waiting to entangle its victims" (14).

"Employment figures are down 3 percent from last year," claimed Senator Wilma Smith, who leads opposition to the tax cut (32).

In other words, don't simply repeat "Wilma Smith said," "John Jones said," "Mary Brown said."

Punctuate your quotations correctly. The proper punctuation will help your reader understand who said what. For information on the appropriate uses of quotation marks surrounding direct quotations, see pages 507–508 in Part Four. If you are incorporating a long quoted passage into your essay, one that appears as more than four typed lines in your manuscript, you should present it in block form without quotation marks, as described on page 386. To omit words in a quoted passage, use ellipsis points, explained on pages 514–515.

Make certain your support is in the paper, not still in your head or back in the original source. Sometimes when you've read a number of persuasive facts in an article or a book, it's easy to forget that your reader doesn't know them as you now do. For instance, the writer of the following paragraph isn't as persuasive as she might be because she hides the support for her controversial point in the reference to the article, forgetting that the reader needs to know what the article actually said:

An organ transplant from one human to another is becoming an everyday occurrence, an operation that is generally applauded by everyone as a life-saving effort. But people are overlooking many of the serious problems that come with the increase in transplant surgery. A study shows that in Asia there may be a risk of traffic in organs on the black market. Figures recorded recently are very disturbing (Wood 35).

For the reader to be persuaded, he or she needs to know what the writer learned from the article: What study? What figures and what exactly do they show? Who has recorded these? Is the source reliable? Instead of offering the necessary support in the essay, the writer merely points to the article as proof. Few readers will take the time to look up the article to find the information they need to understand or believe your point. Therefore, when you use source material, always be sure that you have remembered to put your support on the page, *in the essay itself,* for the reader to see. Don't let the essence of your point remain hidden, especially when the claim is controversial.

Don't let reference material dominate your essay.   Remember that your reader is interested in *your* thesis and *your* conclusions, not just in a string of references. Use your researched material wisely whenever your statements need clarification, support, or amplification. But aim for a balance: don't use quotations, paraphrases, or summarized material at every turn just to show that you've done your homework.

■ Avoiding Plagiarism

Unfortunately, most discussions of research must include a brief word about plagiarism. Novice writers often unintentionally plagiarize, as noted before, because they fail to recognize the necessity of attributing paraphrased, summarized, and borrowed ideas to their original owners. And indeed it is sometimes difficult after days of research to know exactly what you have read repeatedly and what you originally thought. As long as you keep careful notes, you should be able to avoid unintentional plagiarism. You will not be tempted to plagiarize intentionally either if you think about the use of secondary sources (articles, books, etc.). First, research is a basic strategy you will be expected to use more and more in your work at the university and college level. So a paper with several cited sources will demonstrate you have done research. Second, if you are stuck, one of the easiest ways to move forward is to respond to specific ideas in the articles you want to use. You can ask questions, you can challenge an article's premise or thesis, you can add more points to the article's points and so on. You can make two different source materials "speak" with each other as you compare or contrast their arguments or evidence. Your response to the specific ideas in your research materials should be based on the techniques of logic (Chapter 10) and development (Parts One and Two) presented in this book. Two primary reasons for committing plagiarism are that students write their papers at the last minute or that they lack confidence in their own ideas. If you make yourself a schedule and plan your time carefully, you will not be tempted to plagiarize. If you remember that your reader is interested in your unique response to the materials you present, you will begin to gain confidence in your own voice. See the above guidelines on working with source materials to help you develop your critical research skills; this will help you avoid plagiarism. There are more suggestions on avoiding plagiarism on page 381–383.

General or Common Knowledge

There's frequently a thin line between general or common knowledge ("Tommy Douglas was the father of Medicare in Canada") that does not have to be documented and those ideas and statements that do ("TSX reported an operating loss of $4 million in its last quarter"). As a rule of thumb, ask yourself whether the majority of your readers would recognize the fact or opinion you're expressing or if it's repeatedly found in commonly used sources; if so, you may not need to document it. For example, most people would acknowledge that the Wall Street crash of 1929 ushered in the Great Depression of the 1930s, but the exact number of bank foreclosures in 1933 is not common knowledge and, therefore, needs documenting.

Well-Known Quotations and Allusions

Similarly, a well-known quotation from the Bible or Mother Goose or even *Hamlet* might pass without documentation, but a line from the Prime Minister's latest speech needs a reference to its source. You also need to give references for significant words and phrases, not just for complete sentences or paragraphs. Of course, you don't have to cite "the," but you do need to use quotation marks and cite a word like "spontaneous," since that is much more specific to the original author's style and intent.

Internet Material

Remember, too, that much of the material on the Internet is copyrighted, so the conventions about quoting and paraphrasing also apply here. But whether material is copyrighted or not, the honest and responsible researcher always gives credit to the original source of material she uses in her essay.

When in doubt, the best choice is to document anything that you feel may be in question. Careful and accurate documentation is not just a matter of avoiding penalties—and universities, colleges, and copyright holders take plagiarism very seriously—but of practising academic integrity.

Plagiarism and Proper Documentation

To help you understand the difference between plagiarism and proper documentation, here is an original passage and both incorrect and correct ways to use it in a paper of your own:

Original   It is a familiar nightmare: a person suffers a heart attack, and as the ambulance fights heavy traffic, the patient dies. In fact, 350,000 American heart-attack victims each year die without ever reaching a hospital. The killer in many cases is ventricular fibrillation, uncoordinated contraction of the heart muscle. Last week a team of Dutch physicians reported in *The New England Journal of Medicine* that these early deaths can often be prevented by administration of a common heart drug called lidocaine, injected into the patient's shoulder muscle by ambulance paramedics as soon as they arrive on the scene.

—from "First Aid for Heart Attacks,"
Newsweek, November 11, 1985, page 88

Plagiarized   It is a common nightmare: as the ambulance sits in heavy traffic, a person with a heart attack dies, often a victim of ventricular fibrillation, uncoordinated contraction of the heart muscle. Today, however, these early deaths can often be prevented by an injection into the patient's shoulder of a common heart drug called lidocaine, which may be administered by paramedics on the scene.

This writer has changed some of the words and sentences, but the passage has obviously been borrowed and must be attributed to its source.

Also plagiarized   According to *Newsweek*, 350,000 American heart attack victims die before reaching help in hospitals ("First Aid for Heart Attacks" 88). However, a common heart drug called lidocaine, which may be injected into the patient by paramedics on the scene of the attack, may save many victims who die en route to doctors and sophisticated life-saving equipment.

This writer did attribute the statistic to its source, but the remainder of the paragraph is still borrowed and must be documented.

Properly documented   Ambulance paramedics can, and often do, play a vital life-saving role today. They are frequently the first medical assistance available, especially to those patients or accident victims far away from hospitals. Moreover, according to a *Newsweek* report, paramedics are now being trained to administer powerful drugs to help the sick survive until they reach doctors and medical equipment. For instance, paramedics can inject the common heart drug lidocaine into heart attack victims on the scene, an act that may save many of the 350,000 Americans who die of heart attacks before ever reaching a hospital ("First Aid for Heart Attacks" 88).

This writer used the properly documented information to support her own point about paramedics and has not tried to pass off any of the article as her own.

Although plagiarism is often unintentional, it's your job to be as honest and careful as possible. If you're in doubt about your use of a particular idea, consult your instructor for a second opinion.

Here's a suggestion that might help you avoid plagiarizing by accident. When you are drafting your essay and come to a spot in which you want to incorporate the ideas of someone else, think of the borrowed material as if it were in a window.* Always frame the window at the top with some sort of introduction that identifies the author (or source) and frame the window on the bottom with a reference to the location of the material, as illustrated below.

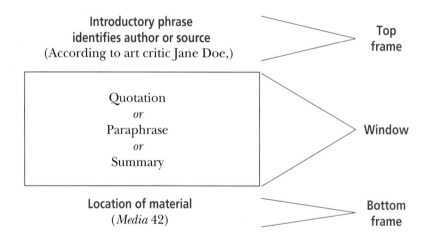

Introductory phrase
identifies author or source
(According to art critic Jane Doe,)   →   Top frame

Quotation
or
Paraphrase
or
Summary   →   Window

Location of material
(*Media* 42)   →   Bottom frame

---

* We are indebted to Professor John Clark Pratt of Colorado State University for this useful suggestion. Professor Pratt is the author of *Writing from Scratch: The Essay* (1987) published by Hamilton Press, and the editor of the *Writing from Scratch* series.

A sample might look like this:

Introductory phrase identifies author

As humorist Mike McGrady once said about housekeeping, "Any job that requires six hours to do and can be undone in six minutes by one small child carrying a plate of crackers and a Monopoly set—this is not a job that will long capture my interest" (13).

Window

Location

In a later draft, you'll probably want to vary your style so that all your borrowed material doesn't appear in exactly the same "window" format (see pages 378–379 for instructions). But until you acquire the habit of *always* documenting your sources, you might try using the "window" technique in your early drafts.

■ Practising What You've Learned

As Amy Lawrence researched the Romanov execution, she found the following information about one of the earlier Romanov czars. To practise some of the skills you've learned so far, read the following passage on Alexander II of Russia (1855–1881) and do the tasks that are listed after it.

Alexander's greatest single achievement was his emancipation of some forty million Russian serfs, a deed which won him the title of "Tsar Liberator." To visit a rural Russian community in the earlier nineteenth century was like stepping back into the Middle Ages. Nine-tenths of the land was held by something less than one hundred thousand noble families. The serfs, attached to the soil, could be sold with the estates to new landlords, conscripted into the nobleman's household to work as domestic servants, or even sent to the factories in the towns for their master's profit. Though some nobles exercised their authority in a kindly and paternal fashion, others overworked their serfs, flogged them cruelly for slight faults, and interfered insolently in their private affairs and family relations. A serf could not marry without his master's consent, could not leave the estate without permission, and might be pursued, brought back, and punished if he sought to escape. He lived at the mercy of his master's caprice.

1. The book from which the preceding passage was taken contains the following information. Select the appropriate information and prepare a working bibliography card.

   A Survey of European Civilization Part Two, Since 1660
   Third Edition
   Houghton Mifflin Company, Publishers
   Boston
   First edition, 1936
   853.21
   1,012 pages

Authors:
  Wallace K. Ferguson, The University of Western Ontario
  Geoffrey Brun, Formerly Visiting Professor of History, Cornell University
Indexes: general, list of maps
Picture Acknowledgments, xxvii
copyright 1962
page 716
44 chapters

2. Paraphrase the first four sentences of the passage.

3. Summarize the passage, but do not quote from it.

4. Select an important idea from the passage to quote directly and lead into
   the quotation with a smooth acknowledgment of its source.

5. Select an idea or a quotation from the passage and use it as support for a
   point of your own, being careful not to plagiarize the borrowed material.

■ ASSIGNMENT

1. In your library, look up a newspaper* from any city or
   province and find the issue published on the day of your birth
   or on some other significant date. Prepare a bibliography card and then summarize an important article from the front page. (Don't forget to acknowledge the source of your summary.)

2. To practise searching for and choosing source material, find three recent
   works on your essay topic available in your library. If you don't have an essay
   topic yet, pick a subject that interests you, one that is likely to appear in both
   print and electronic sources (the origin of table manners in France, the
   Halifax Explosion, reasons for Middle East tensions today, online communities and bullying, etc.). If possible, try to find three different kinds of sources,
   such as a book, a journal or magazine article, and a website. After you have
   recorded bibliographic information for each source, locate and evaluate the
   works. Does each of these sources provide relevant, reliable information?
   Use the steps on pages 372–374 to answer these questions in detail and
   explain why you believe each one would or would not be an appropriate
   source for your research essay.

---

* If the newspaper is not accessible, you might substitute a weekly news magazine, such as *Time* or *Maclean's*.

■ Choosing the Documentation Style for Your Essay

Once you begin to write your paper incorporating your source material, you need to know how to show your readers where your material came from. You may have already learned a documentation system in a previous writing class, but because today's researchers and scholars use a number of different documentation styles, it's important that you know which style is appropriate for your current essay. In some cases, your instructors (or the audience for whom you are writing) will designate a particular style; at other times, the choice will be yours.

In this chapter, we will look at two widely used systems—the MLA style and the APA style—and also briefly review the use of the traditional footnote and bibliography format.

MLA Style

Most instructors in the humanities assign the documentation form prescribed by the Modern Language Association of America (MLA). Since 1984, the MLA has recommended a form of documentation that no longer uses traditional footnotes or endnotes to show references.* The current form calls for *parenthetical documentation,* most often consisting of the author's last name and the appropriate page number(s) in parentheses immediately following the source material in your paper. At the end of your discussion, readers may find complete bibliographic information for each source on a "Works Cited" page, a list of all the sources in your essay.

MLA Citations in Your Essay

Here are some guidelines for using the MLA parenthetical reference form within your paper.

1. If you use a source by one author, place the author's name and page number after the quoted, paraphrased, or summarized material. Note that the parentheses go *before* the end punctuation, and there is no punctuation between the author's name and the page number. (Use the author's name and omit the page reference when citing a complete work or a one-page work.)

Example   Although pop art often resembles the comic strip, it owes a debt to such painters as Magritte, Matisse, and de Kooning (Rose 184).

2. If you use a source by one author and give credit to that author by name in your paper, you need only give the page number in the parentheses.

Example   According to art critic Barbara Rose, pop art owes a large debt to such painters as Magritte, Matisse, and de Kooning (184).

---

* If you wish for a more detailed description of the current MLA format, ask your local bookstore or library for the *MLA Handbook for Writers of Research Papers,* 7th ed. (New York: MLA, 2009) and also the *MLA Style Manual and Guide to Scholarly Publishing,* 3rd ed. (New York: MLA, 2008). A commonly used student research site is maintained by Purdue University: <http://owl.english.purdue.edu>. This site provides information on both MLA and APA methods. The most up-to-date documentation information may be found on the MLA website at <www.MLA.org>.

3. If you are directly quoting material of more than four typed lines, indent the material one inch from the left margin, double-space, and do not use quotation marks. Do not change the right margin. Note that in this case, the parentheses appear *after* the punctuation that ends the quoted material.

   Example   In our own country of Canada, for instance, the free trade agreement between Canada and the United States means that books published in the United States are freely available in Canada. Because they have to compete with these books, Canadian publishers of English-language books have a hard time remaining profitable by publishing exclusively for the much smaller Canadian market. (Nodelman and Reimer 112)

4. If you are citing more than one work by the same author, include a short title in the parentheses.

   Example   Within 50 years, the Inca and Aztec civilizations were defeated and overthrown by outside invaders (Thomas, *Lost Cultures* 198).

5. If you are citing a work by two or three authors, use all last names and the page number.

   Examples   Prisons today are overcrowded to the point of emergency; conditions could not be worse, and the government budget for prison reforms is at an all-time low (Smith and Jones 72).

   Human infants grow quickly, with most babies doubling their birth weight in the first six months of life and tripling their weight by their first birthday (Pantell, Fries, and Vickery 52).

6. For more than three authors, use all the last names or use the last name of the first author plus *et al.* (Latin for "and others") and the page number. There is no comma after the author's name.

   Examples   The mobility of young Canadians contributes to their difficulty in becoming part of the permanent voters list (Gidengil et al. 283).

   Fewer young Canadians have been voting since the late 1980s (Gidengil, Blais, Nadeau, and Nevitte 283).

7. If you are citing an author who is being quoted by someone else, indicate this clearly in the parenthesis:

   Example   Stuart Hall suggests that marginality is "the result of the cultural politics of difference, of the struggles around difference, of the production of new identities, of the appearance of new subjects on the political and cultural stage" (qtd. in Beckford 261).

Compiling a "Works Cited" List: MLA Style

If you are using the MLA format, at the end of your essay you should include a *Works Cited* page—a formal listing of the sources you used in your essay. (If you wish to show all the sources you consulted, but did not cite, add a *Works Consulted* page.) Arrange the entries alphabetically by the authors' last name; if no name is given, arrange your sources by the first important word of the title. Double-space each entry, and double-space after each one. If an entry takes more than one line, indent the subsequent lines one-half inch. Current MLA guidelines indicate one space following punctuation marks. (Some instructors still prefer two spaces, however, so you might check with your teacher on this issue.) See the sample entries that follow.

Sample Entries: MLA Style

Here are some sample entries to help you prepare a Works Cited page according to the MLA guidelines. Please note that MLA style recommends shortened forms of publishers' names: Holt for Holt, Rinehart & Winston; Harcourt for Harcourt Brace College Publishers; UP for University Press; and so forth. Also, omit business descriptions, such as Inc., Co., Press, or House.

MLA style now recommends italicizing (rather than underlining) the titles of books and journals. The titles of articles, essays, and chapters should be enclosed in quotation marks. All important words in titles are capitalized.

Books

- Book with one author

    Badami, Anita Rau. *Can You Hear the Nightbird Call?* Toronto: Random House, 2006. Print.

- Two books by the same author

    List books alphabetically by title. After the first entry, use three hyphens in place of the author's name.

    Badami, Anita Rau. *Can You Hear the Nightbird Call?* Toronto: Random House, 2006.

    ---. *Tamarind Mem.* Toronto: Penguin, 1996. Print.

- Book with two or three authors

    Shepherd, Simon, and Mick Wallis. *Drama/Theatre/Performance.* New York: Routledge, 2004. Print.

- Book with more than three authors

    You may use *et al.* for the other names or you may give all names in full in the order they appear on the book's title page.

    Barnet, Sylvan, et al. *A Short Guide to Writing About Literature.* Toronto: Pearson/ Longman, 2004. Print.

- Book with author and editor

    Chaucer, Geoffrey. *The Tales of Canterbury.* Ed. Robert Pratt. Boston: Houghton, 1974. Print.

- Book with corporate authorship

  National Fire Safety Council. *Stopping Arson before It Starts.* Washington: Edmondson, 1992. Print.

- Book with an editor

  Kroller, Eva-Marie, ed. *The Cambridge Companion to Canadian Literature.* Cambridge: CUP, 2004. Print.

- Selection or chapter from an anthology or a collection with an editor

  Munro, Alice. "Open Secrets." *Canadian Short Stories.* Eds. Russell Brown and Donna Bennett. Toronto: Pearson/Longman, 2005. 193–217. Print.

- One volume of a multi-volume work

  Delaney, John J., ed. *Encyclopedia of Saints.* Vol. 4. New York: Doubleday, 1998. Print.

- Work in more than one volume

  If the volumes were published over a period of years, give the inclusive dates at the end of the citation.

  Piepkorn, Arthur C. *Profiles in Belief: The Religious Bodies of the United States and Canada.* 2 vols. New York: Harper, 1976–78. Print.

- Work in a series

  Groening, Laura. *Listening to Old Woman Speak: Natives and Alternatives in Canadian Literature.* McGill-Queen's Native and Northern Ser. 44. Montreal: McGill-Queen's UP, 2004. Print.

- Translation

  Radzinsky, Edvard. *The Last Czar: The Life and Death of Nicholas II.* Trans. Marian Schwartz. New York: Doubleday, 1992. Print.

- Reprint

  Note that this citation presents two dates: the date of original publication (1873) and the date of the reprinted work (1978).

  Thaxter, Celia. *Among the Isles of Shoals.* 1873. Ed. Leslie Dunn. Hampton, NH: Heritage, 1978. Print.

- An introduction, preface, foreword, or afterword

  Begin the citation with the name of the writer of the section you are citing; then identify the section but do not underline or use quotation marks around the word. Next, give the name of the book and the name of its author, preceded by the word "By" as shown below.

  Soloman, Barbara H. Introduction. *Herland.* By Charlotte Perkins Gilman. New York: Penguin, 1992. xi–xxxi. Print.

Periodicals (Magazines, Journals, Newspapers)

If an article is not printed on consecutive pages, use the first page number and a plus sign.

- Signed article in a monthly magazine

   Dennis, Wendy. "Thinking Inside the Box." *Canadian House and Home* Sept. 2007: 78–82. Print.

- Unsigned article in a weekly magazine

   "The Wedding." *New Yorker* 11 Sept. 1989: 34–35. Print.

- Signed article in a journal

   Lockwood, Thomas. "Divided Attention in *Persuasion." Nineteenth-Century Fiction* 33 (1978): 309–23. Print.

- A review

   Spudis, Paul. Rev. of *To a Rocky Moon: A Geologist's History of Lunar Exploration,* by Don E. Wilhelms. *Natural History* Jan. 1994: 66–69. Print.

- Signed article in newspaper

   Picard, André. "Accept the Reality of Private Health Care: CMA Chief." *The Globe and Mail* 20 Aug. 2008: A1+. Print.

- Unsigned article in newspaper

   "Blackhawks Shut Down Gretzky, Kings, 4–0." *Washington Post* 11 Mar. 1994: C4. Print.

- Unsigned editorial in newspaper

   If the newspaper's city of publication is not clear from the title, put the location in brackets following the paper's name, as shown in the entry below.

   "Speech Therapy." Editorial. *The Vancouver Courier* [Vancouver, B.C.] 30 Jan. 2008: W29. Print.

- A letter to the newspaper

   Puil, George. Letter. *Vancouver Sun* 2 Feb. 2004: C2. Print.

Encyclopedias, Pamphlets, Dissertations

Use full publication information for reference works, such as encyclopedias and dictionaries, unless they are familiar and often revised. Delete volume and page numbers if the information is in alphabetical order.

- Signed article in an encyclopedia (full reference)

   Collins, Dean R. "Light Amplifier." *McGraw-Hill Encyclopedia of Science and Technology.* Ed. Justin Thyme. 3 vols. Boston: McGraw, 1997. Print.

- Unsigned article in a well-known encyclopedia

    "Sailfish." *Encyclopedia Britannica.* 18th ed. 1998. Print.

- A pamphlet

    Young, Leslie. *Baby Care Essentials for the New Mother.* Austin: Hall, 2004. Print.

- A government document

    Canada. Health Canada. *The Abuse and Diversion of Controlled Substances: A Guide for Health Professionals.* Ottawa: Health Canada, 2006. Print.

- Unpublished dissertations and theses

    Zheng, Qixing. "Structured Annotations to Support Collaborative Writing Workflow." Diss. U of British Columbia, 2006. Print.

Films, Television, Radio, Performances, Recordings

- A film

    Begin with the title (italicized) followed by the director, the distributor, the year of release, and the medium consulted. You may also include other data, such as the star performers, writer, or producer.

    Schindler's List. Dir. Steven Spielberg. Perf. Liam Neeson and Ben Kingsley. Universal, 1993. Film.

    If you are referring to the contribution of a particular individual, such as the director, writer, actor, or composer, begin with that person's name. Cite a video-cassette, DVD, or laser disc as a film but also include the medium, its distributor, and its distribution date.

    Spielberg, Steven, dir. *Schindler's List.* Perf. Liam Neeson and Ben Kingsley. Universal, 1993. Universal. 2004. DVD.

- A television or radio show

    Chef at Home. Food Network, Toronto. 12 Oct. 2007. Television.

    If your reference is to a particular episode or person associated with the show, cite that name first, before the show's name.

    "A Year in the Life of J.K. Rowling." *The Passionate Eye.* CBC. 10 Feb. 2008. Television.

    Moyers, Bill, writ. and narr. *Bill Moyers' Journal.* PBS. WABC, Denver. 30 Sept. 1980. Radio.

- Performances (plays, concerts, ballets, operas)

    Julius Caesar. By William Shakespeare. Dir. Andrew St. John. Perf. Patrick Stewart. Booth Theater, New York. 13 Oct. 1982. Performance.

If you are referring to the contribution of a particular person associated with the performance, put that person's name first.

Tovey, Bramwell, cond. *Dream of Gerontius.* By Edward Elgar. Perf. Ben Heppner. Vancouver Symphony Orch. Orpheum, Vancouver. 20 Oct. 2007. Performance.

- A recording

Indicate the type of medium after the date of publication.

Marsalis, Wynton. "Oh, But on the Third Day." Rec. 27–28 Oct. 1988. *The Majesty of the Blues.* Columbia, 1989. Audiocassette.

Letters, Lectures, and Speeches

- An unpublished letter, archived

Steinbeck, John. Letter to Elizabeth R. Otis. 11 Nov. 1944. Steinbeck Collection. Stanford U Lib., Stanford, CA. MS.

- A letter received by the author

Hall, Katherine. Letter to the author. 10 May 2004. Print.

- A lecture or speech

Give the speaker's name and the title of the talk first, before the sponsoring organization (or occasion) and location. Use an appropriate descriptive label, such as "lecture" or "speech" to indicate the form of delivery.

Dippity, Sarah N. "The Importance of Prewriting." CLAS Convention. President Hotel, Colorado Springs. 15 Feb. 2004. Speech.

Interviews

- A published interview

(Cite the person interviewed first and the title of the interview, if any. Use the word "Interview" if the interview has no title. The interviewer's name may be added if known and relevant. Conclude with publication information and medium of publication.)

Mailer, Norman. "Dialogue with Mailer." Interview. With Andrew Gordon. *Berkeley Times* 15 Jan. 1969: A12. Print.

- A personal interview

Give the name of the person interviewed, the kind of interview, and the date.

Adkins, Camille. Personal interview. 11 Jan. 2004.

Payne, Linda. Telephone interview. 13 April 2004.

Electronic Sources: MLA Style

The purpose of a citation for an electronic source is the same as that for printed matter: identification of the source and the best way to locate it. All citations basically name the author and the work and identify publication information. Citations for various types of electronic sources, however, may also include different kinds of additional information—such as network addresses—to help researchers locate the sources in the easiest way.

It's important to remember, too, that forms of electronic sources continue to change rapidly. As technology expands, new ways of documenting electronic sources must also be created. The problem is further complicated by the fact that some sources will not supply all the information you might like to include in your citation. In these cases, you simply have to do the best you can by citing what is available.

The guidelines and sample entries that follow are designed merely as an introduction to citing electronic sources according to the MLA style. If you need additional help citing other kinds of electronic sources, consult the most up-to-the-minute documentation guide available, such as the current *MLA Handbook for Writers of Research Papers* or the MLA website.

Before looking at the sample citations given here, you should be familiar with the following information regarding dates, addresses, and reference markers in online sources.

Use of multiple dates. Because online sources may change or be revised, a citation may contain more than one date. Your citation may present, for example, the original date of a document if it appeared previously in print form, the date of its electronic publication, or the date of its "latest update." Your entry should also include a "date of access," indicating the day you found the particular source.

Use of network addresses. The *MLA Handbook* now recommends inclusion of network addresses (URLs) in citations of online works as supplementary information only when the reader probably cannot locate the source without it or when your instructor requires it. If you present a URL, place it immediately following the date of access, followed by a period and a space. Enclose URLs in angle brackets, and, if you must divide an address at the end of a line, break it only after a slash mark. Do not use a hyphen at the break as this will distort the address. URLs are often long and easy to misread, so take extra time to ensure that you are copying them correctly.

Use of reference markers. Unfortunately, many online sources do not use markers such as page or paragraph numbers. If such information is available to you, include it in your citations by all means; if it does not exist, readers must fend for themselves when accessing your sources. If you want to be particularly considerate toward your readers, you might count the paragraphs yourself, and include the paragraph number in your citation. (Some readers might locate particular information in a document by using the "Find" tool in their computer program, but this option is not always available or useful.)

Scholarly Projects or Information Databases

An entry for an entire online scholarly project or information database may include the following information, *if available*: title of the project or database, editor's name, electronic publication information (including version number, publication date or latest update, name and place of sponsoring organization), date of access, and network address.

Early Canadiana Online. 2 Feb. 2008. Library and Archives Canada, Ottawa. 30 Jan. 2008
    <http://www.canadiana.org>.

Granger's World of Poetry. 1999. Columbia UP. 10 Dec. 2003 <http://www.grangers.org>.

Documents within a Library or Subscription Database

To cite a source that you have found through one of your library's databases, begin with the
author's name, if given. Follow the author's name with the name of the document, its
publication information, the name of the database (italicized), the name of the subscription service, the name of the library you used (with its city, provincial abbreviation, or both
if useful), and the date of access. If possible, conclude with the URL of the document;
however, if the URL is impracticably long, you may use the URL of the site's search page,
as shown below. If no service URL is available, you may simply end with the date of access.

Smith, Lucinda. "Was She Anastasia or a World-Class Imposter?" *Denver Post* 18
    July 1993: 5D. *ProQuest News & Magazines.* ProQuest. Banff Public Lib.,
    Banff, AB. 28 Feb. 2004 <http://0-proquest.umi.com.dalva.fcgov.com/>.

If you are using a source from a personal subscription service (e.g., Canada.com) that allows
you to search by keyword, end the citation by writing "Keyword:" followed by the word itself.

"Pneumonia." *Compton's Encyclopedia Online.* Vers. 3.0. 2003. Canada.com. 2 May
    2007. Keyword: Compton's.

Articles in Online Periodicals (Magazines, Journals, Newspapers)

In citing online periodicals, begin with the author's name; if no author is given, begin
with the title of the article. Continue with the name of the periodical (italicized), volume
and issue number (if given), date of publication, the number range or total number of
pages or paragraphs (if available), medium of publication consulted (Web), date of access,
and network address (if helpful for reader).

- Signed article in a magazine

    Bethune, Brian. "Did Bell Steal the Idea for the Phone?" *Macleans.ca* 23 Jan. 2008.
        Web. 4 Feb. 2008.

- Unsigned article in a magazine

    "School Violence." *U.S. News Online* 6 July 2000. Web. 21 Nov. 2003.

- Article in a journal

    Cummings, Robert. "Liberty and History in Jonson's 'Invitation to Supper.'" *Studies
        in English Literature* 40.1 (2000). Web. 29 Dec. 2003.

- Article in a newspaper or on a newswire

    Blatchford, Christie. "Canada's Native Reserves Deserve Foreign Correspondent
        Treatment." *The Globe and Mail* 2 Feb. 2008. Web. 4 Feb. 2008.
        <http://www.theglobeandmail.com/opinions/columnists/Christie+
        Blatchford.html>.

- An editorial

> "Success at Last." Editorial. *Front Range Times: Electronic Edition* 18 Jan. 2001.
> Web. 12 Feb. 2004 <http://www.frtimes.com/ed/2001/01/18/p04.html>.

- A review

> Anderson, Jason. Rev. of *Over Her Dead Body,* dir. Jeff Lowell. *Globe and Mail.com*
> 1 Feb. 2008. Web. 5 Feb. 2008.

Personal or Professional Websites

In citing websites, begin with the name of the person who created the site, if appropriate. If no name is given, begin with the title of the site (italicized) or a description, such as "home page" (but do not italicize or enclose a description in quotation marks). Continue with date of publication, or latest update, if given; the name of any organization associated with the site; date of access; and the network address.

> Czepiel, Brad. Home page. 11 Mar. 2003. 22 Apr. 2004 <http://www.chass.
> ucolorado.co:7070/~BC/>.

> *Department of English Home Page.* December 2007. University of British Columbia.
> 9 Jan. 2008 <http://www.english.ubc.ca/>.

Note that in the first example, the phrase "home page" is used as a description of a personal website and is therefore *not* italicized; in the second example, "Home Page" is part of the site's title and *is* italicized.

To cite a home page for an academic course, begin the entry with the instructor's name, followed by the name of the course (do not italicize or place in quotation marks). Continue with a description such as "Course home page" (again, do not italicize or place in quotation marks), the dates of the course, the names of the department and the institution, the date of access, and the network address.

> Baxter, Gisele. Studies in Prose Fiction. Course home page. Jan.–April 2008. Dept. of
> English, University of British Columbia. 10 Mar. 2008 <http://faculty.arts.
> ubc.ca/gmbaxter/406001.htm>.

Online Books

The texts of some books are now available online. Begin the citation with the author's name, the book's name, and any publication information given in the source (city of publication, publisher, date). Then list the title of the site (italicized), the name of the editor (if given), and the electronic publication information. Conclude with the medium of publication consulted (Web), date of access, and the network address of the book itself, if possible.

> Baum, Frank L. *Glinda of Oz.* 1920. *Project Gutenberg.* Ed. Frances Stewart. June
> 1997. Web. 6 May 2004 .

Non-periodical Publications on CD-ROM, Diskette, or Magnetic Tape

Non-periodical electronic citations are similar to those for a print book, but also include the medium of publication (CD-ROM, diskette, magnetic tape). If you are citing a specific entry, article, essay, poem, or short story, enclose the title in quotation marks.

"Acupuncture." *The Oxford English Dictionary.* 2nd ed. Oxford UP, 1992. CD-ROM.

E-Mail Communications

Begin with the name of the writer of the message, followed by the title taken from the subject line (if given), type of communication and its recipient, date of the message, and the medium of delivery.

Clinton, Hillary. "Election News." E-mail to Jean Wyrick. 31 Oct. 2003. E-mail.

APA Style

The American Psychological Association (APA) recommends a documentation style for research papers in the social sciences.* Your instructors in psychology and sociology classes, for example, may prefer that you use the APA form when you write essays for them.

The APA style is similar to the MLA style in that it calls for parenthetical documentation within the essay itself, although the information cited in the parentheses differs slightly from that presented according to the MLA format. For example, you will note that in the APA style the date of publication follows the author's last name and precedes the page number in the parentheses. Instead of a Works Cited page, the APA style uses a *References* page at the end of the essay to list those sources cited in the text. A *Bibliography* page lists all works that were consulted. Another important difference concerns capitalization of book and article titles in the reference list: in the MLA style, all important words are capitalized, but in the APA style, only proper names, the first word of titles, and the first word appearing after a colon are capitalized.

APA Citations in Your Essay

Here are some guidelines for using the APA parenthetical form within your paper.

1. APA style typically calls for an "author–publication year" method of citation, with the name and date inserted in the text at an appropriate place in the reference.

   Examples   A recent study (Jones, 2004) found no discernible differences in the absentee rate of men and women students on the main campus.

   Jones (2004) contrasted the absentee rates of men and women students on the main campus but found no discernible differences.

---

* If you wish a more detailed description of the APA style, you might order a copy of the *Publication Manual of the American Psychological Association,* 5th ed. (Washington, DC: American Psychological Association, 2001). The most up-to-date documentation forms may be found on the APA website at <www.apa.style.org>.

2. When you are quoting directly, place the author's name, the publication year, and the page number in parentheses following the quoted material. Note that in APA style, you place commas between the items in the parentheses, and you do include the "p." abbreviation for "page" (these are omitted in MLA style).

Example One crucial step in developing an antisocial personality may, in fact, be "the experience of being caught in some act and consequently being publicly labelled as a deviant" (Becker, 1983, p. 31).

3. If you use a print source by one author and give credit to that author by name within your paper, you need give only the date and the page number in parentheses. Note that the publication date follows directly after the name of the author.

Example According to Green (1994), gang members from upper-class families are rarely convicted for their crimes and are "almost never labelled as delinquent" (p. 101).

4. If you are citing a work with more than two authors, but fewer than six, list all names in the first reference; in subsequent references, use only the first author's last name and *et al.* (which means "and others"). For six or more authors, use only the last name of the first author followed by *et al.* for all citations, including the first. Note the use of "&" instead of "and" within parentheses.

Example *First reference:* In part the outrage often associated with forced displacement and resettlement comes from the contrast between the needs of "distant strangers," who are also weak, and the further gains of already more privileged urban groups and richer peasants (Rew, Fisher, & Pandey, 2006, p. 41).

Subsequent references: Even if there were enough of them, rehabilitation officers usually lack the skills needed to help people suffering the stresses and disorders of displacement and rehabilitation (Rew et al., 2006, p. 52).

5. If you cite a work that has a corporate author, cite the group responsible for producing the work.

Example In contrast, Statistics Canada (2008) concludes, "Consequently, there are no national life expectancy estimates for the Inuit component of the Canadian population" (p. 3).

6. Private interviews, e-mail messages, and other personal communications should be referred to in your text but *not* in your reference list. Provide the initials and last name of the communicator, the words "personal communication," and the date in your paper.

Example   A. E. Wheeler acknowledged that until the most recent DNA work, most historians rejected belief in the Romanov children's escape (personal communication, February 23, 2004).

7. When you provide an indirect quote, using a quote used by someone else, indicate this clearly. Note that the words used in the parenthesis are different from those in the MLA system.

Example   Marshall Berman's perspective on modernity is that it allows us to "find ourselves in an environment that promises adventure, power, growth, joy, transformation of ourselves and the world—and at the same time, that threatens to destroy everything we have, everything we know, everything we are" (as cited in Thompson, 1993, p. 261).

Compiling a "Reference" List: APA Style

If you are using the APA style, at the end of your essay you should include a page labelled "References"—a formal listing of the sources you cited in your essay. Arrange the entries alphabetically by the authors' last names; use initials for the authors' first and middle names. If there are two or more works by one author, list them chronologically, beginning with the earliest publication date. If an author published two or more works in the same year, the first reference is designated *a*, the second *b*, and so on (Feinstein 1999a; Feinstein 1999b).

Remember that in APA style, you italicize books and journal titles, volume numbers, and their associated punctuation, but you do not put the names of articles in quotation marks. Although you do capitalize the major words in the titles of magazines, newspapers, and journals, you do not capitalize any words in the titles of books or articles except the first word in each title, the first word following a colon, and all proper names.

Sample Entries: APA Style

Books

- Book with one author

  Laurence, M. (1964). <u>The stone angel</u>. Toronto: McLelland & Stewart.

- Book with two or more authors

  Forst, M. L., & Blomquist, M. (1991). <u>Missing children: Rhetoric and reality</u>. New York: Lexington Books.

- Books by one author published in the same year

    Hall, S. L. (1980a). <u>Attention deficit disorder</u>. Denver: Bald Mountain Press.

    Hall, S. L. (1980b). <u>Taming your adolescent</u>. Detroit: Morrison Books.

- Book with an editor

    Banks, A. S. (Ed.). (1988). <u>Political handbook of the world</u>. Binghamton, NY: CSA Publications.

- Selection or chapter from collection with an editor

    Newcomb, T. M. (1958). Attitude development as a function of reference groups: The Bennington study. In E. Maccoby, T. M. Newcomb, & E. L. Hartley (Eds.), <u>Readings in social psychology</u> (pp. 10–12). New York: Holt, Rinehart and Winston.

- A book with a corporate author

    Mentoring Group. (1997). <u>The new mentors and protégés: How to succeed with the new mentoring partnerships</u>. Grass Valley, CA: Author.

Articles (In Print)

Note that when a volume number appears, it is italicized, as is all associated punctuation. Use *p.* or *pp.* with page numbers in newspapers but not in magazines or journals.

- An article in a magazine

    Langer, E. T. (1989, May). The mindset of health. <u>Psychology Today</u>, *48,* 1138–1241.

- An article in a journal

    Escobar, A. (2001). Culture sits in places: Reflections on globalism and subaltern strategies of localization. <u>Political Geography</u>, *20,* 139–74.

- An article in a newspaper

    Milroy, Sarah. (2007, May 31). Beating hearts will light up the night sky. <u>The Globe and Mail</u>, p. R4.

Electronic Sources: APA Style

The most current guidelines for electronic citations appear on the APA website at <www.apastyle.org/elecsource.html>. Note that unlike MLA style, APA does not put a period at the end of the URLs nor enclose them in angle brackets. Only break a URL at a slash mark or at a period.

Internet Article Based on a Print Source

Most articles currently retrieved from online publications in psychology and the behavioural sciences are duplicates of those in print. However, if you have viewed the article only in its electronic form, add "Electronic version" in brackets after the article's title.

> Merrill, A. (2004). Use of group activities in first-year seminars [Electronic version]. Journal of Nursing Instruction, *2*, 31–33.

If you are citing an online article that does differ from the print version (e.g., different format, additional information), add the date you retrieved the document from the URL.

> Merrill, A. (2004). Use of group activities in first-year seminars. Journal of Nursing Instruction, *2*, 31–33. Retrieved April 10, 2004, from http://jni.org/articles.html

Article in an Internet-Only Journal

> Keen, M. L. (2003, April 5). Yoga for migraine headache relief. Prevention & Treatment, *2*, Article 0001a. Retrieved December 29, 2003, from http://journalsapa.org/prevention/volume2/pre00030001a.html

Article Retrieved from a Database

> Hall, K. E., Lind, S., & Michael, A. (2004). Sibling rivalry in adolescents. Journal of American Psychology, *22*, 121–124. Retrieved February 26, 2004, from PsycARTICLES database.

Footnote and Bibliography Format

Most research papers today use a parenthetical documentation style, as illustrated in the MLA and APA sections of this chapter. The APA, in particular, discourages footnotes and endnotes. However, in the event you face a writing situation that calls for use of traditional footnotes and bibliography page, here is a brief description of that format. This section will also help you understand the citation system of older documents you may be reading, especially those using Latin abbreviations.

If you are writing a paper using this format, each idea you borrow and each quotation you include must be attributed to its author(s) in a footnote that appears at the bottom of the appropriate page.* Number your footnotes consecutively throughout the essay (do not start over with "1" on each new page), and place the number in the text to the right of and slightly above the end of the passage, whether it is a direct quotation, a paraphrase, or a summary. Place the corresponding number, indented (one-half inch or five spaces) and slightly raised, before the footnote at the bottom of the page. Single-space each entry, and double-space after each footnote if more than one appears on the same page. Once you have provided a first full reference, subsequent footnotes for that source may include only the author's last name and page number. (See examples on the next page.)

---

* Some documents use endnotes that appear in a list on a page immediately following the end of the essay, before the Bibliography page.

You may notice the use of Latin abbreviations in the notes of some documents, such as *ibid.* ("in the same place") and *op. cit.* ("in the work cited"). In such documents, ibid. follows a footnote as a substitute for the author's name, title, and publication information; there will be a new page number only if the reference differs from the one in the previous footnote. Writers use *op. cit.* with the author's name to substitute for the title in later references.

Sources are listed by author in alphabetical order (or by title if no author exists) in the Bibliography at the end of the document.

First footnote reference	[5]Yann Martel, Life of Pi (New York: Harcourt, 2001), 23.
Next footnote	[6]Martel 79.
Later reference	[12]Martel 135.
Bibliographic entry	Martel, Yann. Life of Pi. New York: Harcourt, 2001.

■ Using Supplementary Notes

Sometimes when writers of research papers wish to give their readers additional information about their topic or about a particular piece of source material, they include *supplementary notes*. If you are using the MLA or APA format, these notes should be indicated by using a raised number in your text (The study seemed incomplete at the time of its publication.[2]); the explanations appear on a page called "Notes" (MLA) or "Footnotes" (APA) that immediately follows the end of your essay. If you are using traditional footnote form, simply include the supplementary notes in your list of footnotes at the bottom of the page or in the list of endnotes following your essay's conclusion.

Supplementary notes can offer a wide variety of additional information.

Examples

[1]For a different interpretation of this imagery, see Spiller 1021–1023.

[2]Greenslade and Paddock have also contributed to this area of investigation. For an analysis of causes, see The Working Conditions of Nurses: Confronting the Challenges 3.

[3]It is important to note here that Brown's study followed Smith's by at least six months.

[4]Later in his report Carducci himself contradicts his earlier evaluation by saying, "Our experiment was contaminated from the beginning" (319).

Use supplementary notes only when you think the additional information would be truly valuable to your readers. Obviously, information critical to your essay's points should go in the appropriate body paragraphs. (See page 407 for additional examples.)

■ Sample Student Paper Using MLA Style

Here is the result of Amy Lawrence's research into the latest forensic and historical discoveries concerning the 1918 Romanov assassination. As you read her essay, ask yourself how effectively she uses research material to explain and support her view of the controversy surrounding the assassination and possible escape. Do you find her essay informative? Interesting? Convincing? Point out major strengths and weaknesses that you see. Does her method of structuring her essay—the step-by-step revelation of the new "clues"—add to her argument?

Remember that the paragraphs in Amy's essay have been numbered for easy reference during class discussion. Do *not* number the paragraphs in your own essay.

The Romanovs: Olga, Marie, Czar Nicholas II, Czarina Alexandra, Anastasia, Alexei, and Tatiana

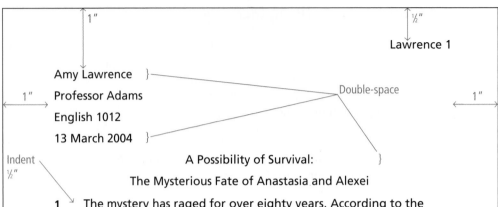

1"

½"

Lawrence 1

Amy Lawrence   }

1"   Professor Adams   Double-space   1"

English 1012

13 March 2004   }

Indent
½"

A Possibility of Survival: }

The Mysterious Fate of Anastasia and Alexei

1   The mystery has raged for over eighty years. According to the

history books, in 1918 Bolshevik revolutionaries brutally executed

Introduction:
History of the
controversy and
the research
questions

all seven members of the Russian royal family, the Romanovs.

Immediately following the murders, however, rumours appeared

claiming that one, or perhaps two, of the Romanov children had

escaped the assassination. Is there any evidence to support even the

possibility that seventeen-year-old Anastasia and/or thirteen-year-old

Alexei were somehow secreted away from the murder scene? Or is

this merely a romantic story that has been repeated generation after

generation?

2   Over the years, many people have come forth to claim their

identities as either Anastasia or Alexei. Movies, plays, and even a

ballet have repeatedly captured the public's fascination with this

story that just won't die.[1] Until recently, many dismissed the story

entirely as pure fiction. However, political changes in the Soviet

Union during the 1990s produced a government that is more open

to research into the haunting Romanov mystery. Today, historical

information and improved forensic research have provided exciting

evidence that points to a new conclusion based on facts, not

Thesis   rumours. It is indeed possible that Anastasia and Alexei survived the

execution designed to end the Romanov dynasty forever.

3   The first break in solving the mystery came in 1989 when the

Russian government released important information about the

1"

Lawrence 2

Romanovs' mass grave. Although the rumours had always insisted that discovery of the secret grave would confirm that two Romanovs had escaped, the location of the grave had never been revealed. In 1976 a Soviet writer claimed that he had uncovered the common grave in woods near the murder site, but its location was kept secret by the Communist government (Kurth 100). The 1989 revelation of this gravesite was important to Romanov scholars because it did support the often-retold escape stories: although <u>eleven</u> people were reported executed (seven Romanov family members and four attendants), only <u>nine</u> bodies were found in the grave (Massie 43). But was this really the Romanov grave?

Release of evidence: The gravesite

4   The next important historical information came in 1992 from Edvard Radzinsky, a Russian playwright whose research on the Romanovs could now be published. Radzinsky had spent two decades studying the Central State Archives in Moscow, discovering the unread diaries of the murdered Czar Nicholas II and Czarina Alexandra and, even more important, the previously secret "Yurovsky note." Yakov Yurovsky was the leader of the execution squad, and his statement contained not only his description of the horrible night but also testimony from other guards at the scene (Radzinsky 373). The "Yurovsky note" clearly emphasized the chaos of the execution and contributed to the possible explanation surrounding the persistent rumours of two survivors.

More historical information uncovered: The "Yurovsky note"

5   According to Yurovsky, in the early hours of July 17, 1918, the Romanov family—the Czar, the Czarina, four daughters, and son— were taken with their personal physician and three servants into the cellar in the house where they had been held prisoners by the revolutionaries.[2] During the executions, the room filled with smoke and noise, and the bullets seemed to be oddly ricocheting, "jumping

around the room like hail" (qtd. in Radzinsky 389). Although many bullets were fired at close range, Yurovsky mentions that the deaths of all five children were strangely hard to accomplish. Finally, as the guards hurriedly prepared to load the bodies onto a waiting truck, one of the guards heard a daughter cry out and then it was discovered that, amazingly, all the daughters were still alive (391). The daughters were then supposedly murdered by a drunken guard with a bayonet, who again experienced difficulty: "the point would not go through [the] corset" (qtd. in Radzinsky 391).

6   What the guards did NOT know until much later (at the gravesite) was that at least three of the daughters, and possibly all the children, were wearing "corsets made of a solid mass of diamonds" (Radzinsky 373). The hidden Romanov jewels had acted like bulletproof vests and were the reason the bullets and bayonet were deflected (373). Radzinsky argues that the chaos of the dark night, the drunken state of nervous, hurried guards, and the protective corsets cast serious doubt on the success of all the murder attempts (392).

7   The trip to the gravesite was not smooth either. The truck broke down twice, and it was hard to move the bodies from the truck through the woods to the actual grave site. Yurovsky wrote that to lighten the load two bodies were cremated, supposedly the Czarina and her son, but he also claims that by mistake the family maid was confused with Czarina Alexandra (Radzinsky 410). Although the cremation story would account for the two bodies missing in the common grave, no remains or signs of a cremation site have ever been found. Consequently, many Romanov researchers have another explanation. They argue that the two youngest Romanovs, wounded but still alive thanks to their protective corsets of jewels, were secretly removed from the truck during a breakdown by guards who

Lawrence 4

regretted their part in the killing of the Romanov children (Smith).
After all, why stop to burn only two bodies? Why just two and not
all? Wouldn't such a cremation have taken valuable time and
attracted attention? Why choose the boy and not Nicholas, the hated
Czar? Could Yurovsky have been covering up the fact that by the
time they reached the gravesite two bodies were missing—the boy
and a female (Radzinsky 416)?

8   Although the newly recovered historical evidence added
important pieces, it did not solve the puzzle. However, forensic
research, using techniques not available until 1993, began to shed
light on the decades-old controversy. An international team of
geneticists conducted DNA analysis on the nine recovered skeletons.
Through mitochondrial-DNA sequencing, a process that analyzes
DNA strains, and comparison to DNA samples donated by living
relatives of the Romanovs, the team concluded in July 1993 that the
skeletons were indeed the remains of five members of the Romanov
family and four members of their household staff (Dricks). Yurovsky's
story about the cremation of the maid was therefore not true—two
Romanovs were missing!

New forensic
research:
1. DNA analysis

9   Taking the next step, scientists used computer modelling to
superimpose facial photographs onto the skulls to determine
structural matches that would tell which family members the
skeletons actually were. The computer technology and dental work
positively identified the Czar and Czarina as two of the bodies. Then
more news: all of the remaining Romanov skeletons were of young
females (Elliott 61). Alexei, the heir to the throne, was one of the
missing—just as the rumours have always claimed.

2. Computer
modelling

10   To discover if the missing daughter was in fact Anastasia, the
scientists compared the size and age of the girls to the skeletons.

Lawrence 5

3. Skeletal
measurements

More controversy erupted. Although some Russian scientists argued that the missing skeleton was that of daughter Marie, Dr. William Maples, head of the American forensics team, strongly disagreed. According to Dr. Maples, all the skeletons were too tall and too developed to be Anastasia: "The bones we have show completed growth, which indicates more mature individuals" (qtd. in Toufexis 65). Dr. Peter Gill, head of the British Forensic Science Service that also studied the bones, agreed (O'Sullivan 6). According to these respected scientists, Anastasia was definitely not in the grave.

More tests lead
to official
announcement

11   Six more years of sophisticated scientific experiments followed these initial studies; DNA tests were replicated and results confirmed (Glausiusz). Finally, in February 1998, a special federal commission chaired by First Deputy Prime Minister Boris Nemtsov officially announced its findings to Russian President Boris Yeltsin and the world: the bones were, beyond a shadow of scientific doubt, those of the Romanovs—but the bodies of Alexei and one sister (Anastasia?) remained unaccounted for (Varoli).[3]

12   Throughout the years, stories speculating on the Romanov assassination have always focused on the survival of the beautiful Anastasia and her sickly brother, Alexei, often describing a devoted guard smuggling them out through dark woods or secret passages. Doubters have always said that the stories were folktales not worth serious investigation. American and British forensic research, however, argues this much: the real fate of Anastasia and Alexei is still unknown. Therefore, their survival of the execution is still a

Conclusion: the
search should
continue

possibility. Finally, after the decades of rumours, there is a scientific basis for continuing the search for the missing Romanovs. Someday, the mystery of their fate will be solved and the controversy will rest in peace.

Lawrence 6

Notes

[1] The most well-known story was told by Anna Anderson, a woman found in Berlin in 1920, who convinced many people throughout the world that she was indeed Anastasia. In 1956 her story was made into a popular movie starring Ingrid Bergman (Smith). The most recent treatment is the 1997 animated Fox film *Anastasia,* in which the young girl is saved by a servant boy, loses her memory, but is ultimately restored to her true identity (Rhodes).

[2] The Russian revolutionaries wanted to be rid of Czar Nicholas II and the entire Romanov family, which had ruled Russia since 1613. The Bolsheviks had held the family captive, charging Nicholas II with responsibility for Russia's poverty and social problems during the First World War ("Romanov").

[3] The bones were officially buried on July 17, 1998, in the Peter and Paul Cathedral in St. Petersburg, resting place of all the Romanov czars since Peter the Great. The date marked the eightieth anniversary of the Romanov execution (Caryl).

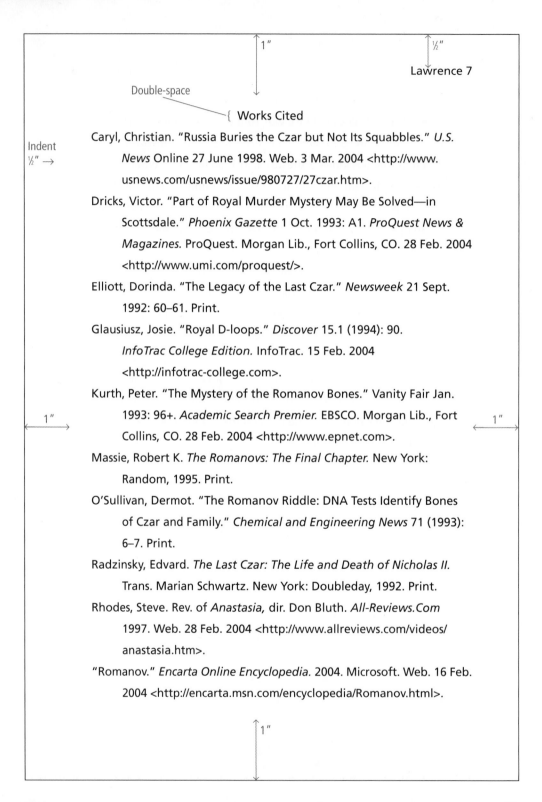

Works Cited

Caryl, Christian. "Russia Buries the Czar but Not Its Squabbles." *U.S. News* Online 27 June 1998. Web. 3 Mar. 2004 <http://www.usnews.com/usnews/issue/980727/27czar.htm>.

Dricks, Victor. "Part of Royal Murder Mystery May Be Solved—in Scottsdale." *Phoenix Gazette* 1 Oct. 1993: A1. *ProQuest News & Magazines.* ProQuest. Morgan Lib., Fort Collins, CO. 28 Feb. 2004 <http://www.umi.com/proquest/>.

Elliott, Dorinda. "The Legacy of the Last Czar." *Newsweek* 21 Sept. 1992: 60–61. Print.

Glausiusz, Josie. "Royal D-loops." *Discover* 15.1 (1994): 90. *InfoTrac College Edition.* InfoTrac. 15 Feb. 2004 <http://infotrac-college.com>.

Kurth, Peter. "The Mystery of the Romanov Bones." Vanity Fair Jan. 1993: 96+. *Academic Search Premier.* EBSCO. Morgan Lib., Fort Collins, CO. 28 Feb. 2004 <http://www.epnet.com>.

Massie, Robert K. *The Romanovs: The Final Chapter.* New York: Random, 1995. Print.

O'Sullivan, Dermot. "The Romanov Riddle: DNA Tests Identify Bones of Czar and Family." *Chemical and Engineering News* 71 (1993): 6–7. Print.

Radzinsky, Edvard. *The Last Czar: The Life and Death of Nicholas II.* Trans. Marian Schwartz. New York: Doubleday, 1992. Print.

Rhodes, Steve. Rev. of *Anastasia,* dir. Don Bluth. *All-Reviews.Com* 1997. Web. 28 Feb. 2004 <http://www.allreviews.com/videos/anastasia.htm>.

"Romanov." *Encarta Online Encyclopedia.* 2004. Microsoft. Web. 16 Feb. 2004 <http://encarta.msn.com/encyclopedia/Romanov.html>.

Lawrence 7

Lawrence 8

Smith, Lucinda. "Was She Anastasia or a World-Class Imposter?"
    Denver Post 18 July 1993: 5D. *ProQuest News & Magazines.*
    ProQuest. Fort Collins Public Lib., Fort Collins, CO. 28 Feb. 2004
    <http://0-proquest.umi.com.dalva.fcgov.com/>.

Toufexis, Anastasia. "It's the Czar All Right, but Where's Anastasia?"
    Time 14 Sept. 1992: 65. Print.

Varoli, John. "Bury Tsar in St. Petersburg July 17." *St. Petersburg
    Times* 9–16 Feb. 1998. Web. 26 Feb. 2004 <http://www.spb.ru/
    times/336-337/nemtsov.html>.

Chapter 15

Writing in Class: Exams and "Response" Essays

In-class writing assignments call for good writing skills, analytical reading skills, and confidence. When you write essays out of class, you have the luxury of time: you can mull over your ideas, talk about them with friends or classmates, prewrite, plan, revise, or even start over if you wish. Because essay assignments written in class must be planned and composed on the spot under the pressure of a time limit, they may induce anxiety in some students. (One composition-class student characterized his feelings of terror this way: "I felt like a slug caught in a sudden salt storm!")

Never fear! Hope reigns! By remembering what you already know about writing the short essay and by learning to analyze quickly the demands of the task you face, you can substantially reduce your anxiety level. With practice, you may discover that in-class writing assignments are not nearly as threatening as you once thought.

■ Steps to Writing Well under Pressure

1. After you are assigned in-class writing, your first step is to **clarify for yourself the kind of task you face.** Sometimes your instructor will tell you about the assignment's format or general design in advance. Other times, however, figuring out the demands of the assignment on the spot and following the instructions carefully will be part of the task itself. Understanding the kind of exam or essay question you face will help you prepare your response and boost your confidence. Here are some

common formats for in-class assignments that call for your writing skills:

- **Short-answer exam questions**

  Your instructor might give an exam that asks you to write a well-developed paragraph or two to identify, define, or explain a term or idea. For example, a political science instructor might ask for paragraphs explaining the importance of certain treaties or laws; a literature instructor might ask for paragraphs that explain the significance of certain lines, characters, or symbols in a particular work; a science instructor might ask for extended definitions of important biological terms, and so on. The paragraph skills you learned in Chapter 3—focus, development, unity, and coherence—are all relevant here.

- **Essay exam questions**

  Frequently, questions appear on exams that call for more detailed discussion of specific material studied in a course. An essay question on a history exam might ask you to "Explain the major causes of the Quebec Separatists' movement in the 1970s." In biology you might be asked to "Trace a drop of blood on its circulatory journey from the human heart throughout the body." You would be expected to shape your answer into a multi-paragraphed essay developed clearly in an easy-to-follow organizational pattern.

- **"Prompted" essays**

  Perhaps the most common in-class assignment in composition classes asks students to respond thoughtfully to some *prompt*—that is, students are asked to give their own opinion about a specific topic presented in a written passage or question, such as "Do you think teenage consumers are too influenced by the Internet?" At other times, students will be asked to read a quotation or proverb ("All that glitters is not gold") and then respond in a personal essay. Other prompts include a statement of a current controversy (students should/should not be assessed a special fee for athletics on this campus) or the description of a hypothetical problem (the developer of a discount superstore has applied for a building permit on the edge of a wildlife preserve). Each student is responsible for explaining and supporting his or her position on the topic presented by the prompt.

- **Summary-and-response essays**

  Some in-class essays ask students to do more than voice their opinions in response to a short prompt. One common assignment is known as the *summary-and-response* essay or the *summary-reaction* essay. Students first read an essay by a professional writer (the reading may be done either in or out of class, depending on the instructor's preference). Once in class, students write an essay that begins with a clear summary of the essay they have just read (an activity that demonstrates analytical reading abilities), and then they present a reasoned argument that agrees or disagrees with the professional essay's ideas. Summary-and-response essays are often used as entrance or exit exams for composition classes at many schools throughout the country because they allow students to display both reading and writing skills. Because the summary-and-response essay is so frequently assigned today, additional discussion, illustrated by a student paper, is provided on pages 420–423 of this chapter.

There are numerous kinds and combinations of essay exams and in-class writing assignments. You can best prepare yourself mentally if you know in advance the purpose and format of the writing task you will face. If possible, ask your instructor to clarify the nature of your assignment before you come to class to write. (Also, some teachers allow students to bring dictionaries, outlines, or notes to class, but others don't. Consult your instructor.)

2. Arrive prepared. Before class, determine what items you need to take to respond to your writing assignment. For example, do you need loose paper or will an exam book or paper be provided? (If you are writing on your own notebook paper, always bring a paper clip or, better, one of those mini-staplers to fasten your pages together.) Were you asked to bring a copy of a reading or essay questions that were handed out in advance? Are dictionaries permitted? Note cards? The two essential items for every in-class assignment, regardless of type, are a watch, to help you gauge your writing time, and extra pens, to rescue you when yours inevitably runs dry. Having adequate supplies on hand keeps you from rustling around to borrow from your neighbours, which not only costs you valuable minutes but also disturbs the other writers around you. In addition, speaking to your classmates, especially during an examination, may be erroneously perceived as scholastic dishonesty. To avoid all such problems, bring the right tools to class.

Perhaps this is also a good place to say a little more about classroom atmosphere. Students often complain about their classmates' annoying behaviours during in-class writing assignments or examinations. Repeated pen-clicking, gum snapping, or chair kicking can make life miserable for other writers in the room. Empty pop cans noisily clanking down aisles, musical cell phones, beeping watches, and even crinkling candy wrappers can distract and derail someone else's complex thought. Please be *courteous:* leave the snack bar at home, spit out that gum, and turn off electronic equipment.

One more piece of advice: many in-class writing situations are "closed door." That is, at the appointed time for the class or exam to begin, the door is closed and no one is permitted to enter late. Consequently, try to arrive at least five minutes early, in case your instructor's watch is faster than yours, but also to have the extra minutes to settle yourself mentally as well as physically. ("Closed door" may also mean that no one is permitted to leave and return to the room during the writing session, even for restroom trips, so think carefully about that extra cup of coffee or can of pop just before your class.)

3. Once you are in class ready to write, **read the entire assignment with great care.** First, underline *key words* that are important to the subject matter of your essay; then circle the *directional words* that give you clues to the method of development you might use to organize your response.

Example	Explain the effects of Louis Riel's trial and execution on Canadian politics in the nineteenth century.
Example	In *The Stone Angel*, Margaret Laurence examines the tensions created in the main character, Hagar Shipley, as she tries to suppress her natural independent and life-embracing self under a cold, "stony," and puritanical shell. Illustrate these tensions with three examples from the novel.

To help you identify some of the frequently used directional words and understand the approaches they suggest, study the following chart.

Directional Word or Phrase	**Suggested Method of Development**
Illustrate . . . Provide examples of . . . Show a number of . . . Support with references to . . .	Example
Explain the steps . . . Explain the procedure . . . Outline the sequence of . . . Trace the events . . . Review the series of . . . Give the history of . . .	Process or Narration
Discuss the effects of . . . Show the consequences of . . . Give the reasons for . . . Explain why . . . Discuss the causes of . . . Show the influence of . . .	Causal Analysis
Compare the following . . .* Contrast the positions of . . .* Show the differences between . . . Discuss the advantages and disadvantages . . . Show the similarities among . . . Relate X to Y . . .	Comparison/Contrast
Describe the following . . . Recreate the scene . . . Discuss in detail . . . Explain the features of . . .	Description
Agree or disagree . . . Defend or attack . . . Offer proof . . . Present evidence . . . Criticize . . . Evaluate . . . State reasons for . . . Justify your answer . . . What if . . .	Argument
Discuss the types of . . . Show the kinds of . . . Analyze the parts of . . . Classify the following . . .	Classification/Division
Define . . . Explain the meaning of . . . Identify the following . . . Give the origins of the term . . .	Definition

* Remember that the directional word "compare" may indicate a discussion of both similarities and differences; the directional word "contrast" focuses only on the differences.

Note that essay questions may demand more than one pattern of development in your response:

(Explain the meaning) of the term "hospice" and (show the differences) between the Hospice Movement in Great Britain and Canada. [definition and contrast]

(Discuss) Weber's three (types) of authority, giving (examples) of societies that illustrate each type. [classification and example]

(Explain) Prime Minister Trudeau's (reasons) for invoking the War Measures Act in October 1970 and then (defend or attack) Trudeau's decision. [causal analysis and argument]

Learning to quickly recognize key directional words will help you organize as you begin to focus your essay. Always read the assignment at least twice and ask your instructor for clarification if some part of the assignment seems confusing to you.

4. Once you have read and fully understood the purpose and direction of your assignment, **prepare to write.** The following advice may be helpful:

- Think positively: remind yourself that the task you face is not unknown to you. You are being asked to write—yes, quickly—the same kind of essay that you have been practising in your composition class. You *CAN* do this!

- If you are writing an in-class essay, take the first few minutes to think and plan. Many times it's helpful to formulate a thesis in a direct rephrasing of the exam question or "prompt" you have been assigned. For example:

  Assignment: After reading "How to Make People Smaller Than They Are" by Norman Cousins, write an essay agreeing or disagreeing with Cousins's suggestions for improving higher education today.

  Thesis: In his essay "How to Make People Smaller Than They Are," author Norman Cousins convincingly argues for requiring additional liberal arts courses for all students in college today. His suggestions for improving higher education are uniformly excellent and should be implemented immediately.

  Assignment: Discuss Weber's three types of authority, giving examples to clarify your answer.

  Thesis: Weber's three types of authority are traditional authority, charismatic authority, and legal authority. The three types may be exemplified, respectively, by the 19th-century absolute monarchs of Europe, by a variety of religious groups, and by the constitutional government of the United States.

- After deciding on your thesis, jot down on scratch paper a brief plan or outline that sketches out the main points that will appear in the body of your essay. You might scribble a few key words to remind yourself of the supporting evidence or important details you will use. Don't get too bogged down in detailed outlining—use just enough words to help you stay on track.

- You might also budget your time now—thinking "by 2:30 I should be done with two points in my discussion." Although such figuring is approximate at best, having a general schedule in mind might keep you from drifting or spending too much time on the first parts of your essay. In most cases, you should assume you will not be able to write a rough draft of your essay and then have the time to massively reorganize as you re-copy it.

5. As you **begin writing,** remember what you have learned about paragraphing, topic sentences, and supporting evidence. If you have been given multiple tasks, be sure that you are responding to all parts of the assignment. If the assignment asks you to present your own opinion, focus your answer accordingly. In timed-writing situations, you can't take on the world, but you can offer intelligent commentary on selected ideas. If you only have an hour or less to complete your essay, consider aiming for three well-developed points of discussion. You may be writing a rather conventional five-paragraph essay, but frequently such a clear pattern of organization works best when nervous writers are under pressure and time is short.

© Stockbyte/SuperStock

Two more suggestions:

- It may be a good idea to write on one side of your paper only, leaving wide margins on both sides; consider, too, leaving extra lines between paragraphs. If you discover that you have time after finishing your essay, you might wish to add additional information to your exam answer or perhaps another persuasive example to a body paragraph. Leaving plenty of blank spaces will allow you to insert information neatly, instead of jamming in handwriting too small for your instructor to decipher.

- If you are writing an essay (rather than a short answer), do try to conclude in a satisfactory way. Your conclusion may be brief, but even a few sentences are better than an abrupt mid-sentence halt when time runs out.

6. In the time remaining after writing the complete draft of your essay, **read what you have written.** Aim for sufficient, appropriate content and clear organization. Insert, delete, or make changes neatly. Once you are reasonably satisfied with the essay's content and flow, take a few minutes to proofread and edit. Although most instructors do not expect an in-class essay to be as polished as one written out of class, you are responsible for the best spelling, grammar, and punctuation you can muster under the circumstances. Take care to apply what you know to sentence problems, especially the run-ons, comma splices, and twisted predicates that tend to surface when writers are composing in a hurry. After all, information too deeply hidden in a contorted sentence is information that may not be counted in your favour.

7. Tips. Before you turn in your work, be sure your name is on every page of your essay or exam so your instructor will know whom to praise for a job well done. If appropriate, include other pertinent information, such as your class section number or your student number. Number and clip or staple the loose pages of your essay or exam (do *not* rely on folded corners to hold your pages together!).

Problems to Avoid

Misreading the assignment. Always read the directions and the assignment completely and carefully before you start prewriting. Mark key and directional words. Do you have multiple tasks? Consider numbering the tasks to avoid overlooking any parts. Important choices to make? Neatly put a line through the options you don't want. Grossly misreading your assignment may give you as much chance at success as a pig at a barbecue.

Incomplete essay. Don't begin writing an in-class essay without a plan, even if you are excited about the topic and want to dive right in. Having a plan and budgeting your time accordingly will avoid the common problem of not finishing, which, in the end, may cost you dearly. Don't allow yourself to ramble off on a tangent in one part of the assignment. Stay focused on your plan and complete the entire essay or exam. If you have left blank space as described previously, you can return to a part of the essay to add more information if time permits. Wear a watch and consult it regularly! Don't depend on a classmate or your instructor to advise you of the time remaining.

Composition amnesia. Writing essays under time pressure causes some students suddenly to forget everything they ever knew about essay organization. This memory loss often wreaks havoc on paragraphing skills, resulting in a half-dozen one- and two-sentence string-bean paragraphs without adequate development; at other times, it results in one long super-paragraph that stretches for pages before the eye like the Arctic tundra, no relief or rest stop in sight. Emphasize your good ideas by presenting them in a recognizable organizational structure, just as you would do in an out-of-class assignment.

Gorilla generalizations. Perhaps the biggest problem instructors find is the lack of adequate, specific evidence to explain or support shaggy, gorilla-sized generalities roaming aimlessly through students' essays. If, for example, you argue, "Team sports are good for kids because they build character," *why* do you believe this? What particular character traits do you mean? Can you offer a personal example or a hypothetical case to clarify and support your claim? Remember what you learned in Chapter 3 about using evidence—examples, personal experience, testimony—to illustrate or back up any general claims you are making. Your goal is to be as clear and persuasive as you can be—*show* what you know!

▪ PRACTISING WHAT YOU'VE LEARNED

Underline the key words and circle the directional words or phrases in the following assignments. What pattern(s) of development are suggested in each assignment?

1. Discuss three examples of animal imagery as they clarify the major themes of Timothy Findley's novel *The Wars*.
2. Trace the history of the founding of the Hudson's Bay Company in 1670.
3. Discuss the influence of the Battle of Vimy Ridge on Canadian national identity.

4. Agree or disagree with the following statement: "The CBC is successful at representing the highest standards in Canadian culture."

5. How would the word "egalitarian" be defined in a Canadian context?

6. Consider the similarities and differences between the impressionistic techniques of Claude Monet and Tom Thomson. Illustrate your answer with references to important works of both artists.

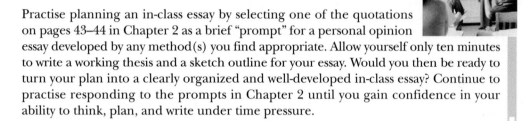

■ ASSIGNMENT

Practise planning an in-class essay by selecting one of the quotations on pages 43–44 in Chapter 2 as a brief "prompt" for a personal opinion essay developed by any method(s) you find appropriate. Allow yourself only ten minutes to write a working thesis and a sketch outline for your essay. Would you then be ready to turn your plan into a clearly organized and well-developed in-class essay? Continue to practise responding to the prompts in Chapter 2 until you gain confidence in your ability to think, plan, and write under time pressure.

■ Writing the Summary-and-Response Essay

The "summary-and-response essay" is such a common assignment today that it merits additional discussion and illustration. As noted earlier in this chapter, this kind of assignment frequently asks students to read a professional article, summarize its thesis and main points, and write a response expressing agreement or disagreement with the article's ideas.

You may have had experience with some form of this assignment before now. Many postsecondary entrance examinations have adopted this kind of essay to evaluate both reading comprehension and writing skills. Many postsecondary institutions also use this format as their composition placement exam to direct students into the appropriate writing class. Still other schools employ this kind of essay as a final exam or exit test for their composition requirement. And although this format is often assigned as in-class writing, it certainly is not limited to this use. Many composition classes and other academic courses include this type of essay as an out-of-class paper.

Though the format of this assignment may vary slightly depending on its purpose and occasion, throughout your college or university and professional life you will almost certainly be asked on more than one occasion to read information, summarize it for others, and then present your reaction to its ideas. To help you prepare for this kind of thinking and writing activity, here are a few suggestions, divided into three sections for clarity:

Reading the Assignment and the Article

1. Read your assignment's directions carefully to discover exactly what you are being asked to do. For example, are you being asked to present a one-paragraph

summary of a professional article* first and then write a personal response? Or are you being asked to respond to the professional article's major points one at a time? Perhaps you are being asked to critique the author's style as well as ideas. Because formats vary, be sure you understand your complete assignment—all its required parts—before you begin writing.

2. Before you can intelligently respond to any reading you need to thoroughly understand its ideas. To review suggestions for close reading, take the time now to review Chapter 8, "The Reading–Writing Connection," in this text. This chapter will help you identify and evaluate an article's thesis, main points, supporting evidence, and other rhetorical techniques.

3. If you are given an article to read out of class, study it carefully, annotating it as outlined in Chapter 8. If reading the article is part of the in-class activity, you may have only enough time to read it carefully once, underlining and annotating as you move through each paragraph. Minimally, you should mark the thesis and the main ideas of the body paragraphs. Underline or star important claims or supporting evidence. Are the claims logical and well supported, or does the author rely on generalizations or other faulty reasoning? Overall, do you agree or disagree with the article? Would you call it a weak or strong piece of writing? Why? (For help evaluating claims and supporting evidence, review the discussion of logical fallacies in Chapter 10, pages 279–281.)

Writing the Summary Section

If you are to begin with a brief summary of the article, follow the guidelines listed under "Writing a Summary" on pages 164–166 of Chapter 8. Remember that a good summary presents the author's name and full title of the article in the first sentence, which also frequently presents the article's thesis (In his article "Free Speech on Campus," author Clarence Page argues that . . .). The next sentences of your summary should present the article's main ideas, found in the article's body paragraphs. Unless you need to quote a word or phrase for clarity or emphasis, use your own words to present a concise version of the article. Normally, your summary will be an objective treatment of the article's ideas, so save your opinions for the "response" section.

Writing the Response Section

1. Before you begin writing the "response" part of your essay, look at the underlining and any marginal notes you made on the article. What was your general assessment of the article? Do you agree or disagree with the author? Perhaps you only agree with some points and disagree with others. Or perhaps you agree with the main ideas but think that this particular essay is a weak defence of those ideas. After looking over the article and your notes, decide on your overall reaction to this article. This assessment will become your thesis in the "response" portion of your essay.

---

* To avoid confusion in this discussion between the professional essay used as a "prompt" and the student's response essay, the word "article" will be used to refer to the professional reading.

2. Once you have a working thesis in mind, plan the rest of your essay. For example, if you disagree with the article, you might want to note two or three reasons you reject the author's position; these reasons may become the basis for your own body paragraphs. Important: Be sure you have evidence of your own to support your positions. Responding with personal examples is perhaps the most common kind of support for essays written in class, but if you have done any research on the subject and know facts, statistics, testimony, or other information that would support your position, these would be preferable.

3. If you have begun your essay with a summary, start the next paragraph with a sentence that clearly indicates the "response" section is now beginning. Present a smooth transition to your thesis and consider using an "essay map" to indicate to your readers the points you will discuss.

Example   Although in his article "Test!" Paul Perez correctly identifies a growing drug problem in our public schools, his plan to drug-test all students involved in school activities should be rejected. Such a test could not be implemented fairly and is an unreasonable invasion of students' privacy.

4. In each of your own body paragraphs make clear which of the author's claims or ideas you are refuting or supporting by using "tag lines" to remind the reader.

Example   Although Foxcroft argues that the proposed tuition increase will not discourage prospective students, she fails to understand the economic situation of most mature students, who are sacrificing income to return to school. In a recent survey. . . .

5. Once you have signalled the point in question and stated your position, develop each body paragraph with enough specific supporting evidence to make your claim convincing. If you disagree with a point, you must show why and present your position logically (you may wish to review Chapter 10 on argument). If you agree with the article, beware a tendency to simply restate the positions with which you are in agreement ("I think Brower is right when she says housing is too expensive on campus. She is also right about the lack of housing choices . . ."). Find other examples, reasons, or information that lend support to the points that you and the author think are valid.

6. Many assignments call for a straightforward personal opinion or "agree–disagree" response. In other assignments, you may be given the option of criticizing or praising an author's logic, style, or even tone. You might, for example, show that a particular argument is ineffective because it is based on a mass of overstated generalities, or you might show why the author's sarcastic tone alienates the reader. On the other hand, an author might deserve credit for a particularly effective supporting example or a brilliantly clever turn of phrase that captures the essence of an idea. Always check your assignment to see if this sort of critique is welcome or even required in your response.

7. Don't forget to write a brief concluding paragraph. If appropriate, you might emphasize the value of the article in question, or call for action for or against its ideas, or project its effects into the future (other suggestions for conclusions appear in Chapter 4). However you end your essay, your conclusion should always be consistent with your overall assessment of the article and its ideas.

■ Sample Student Essay

The essay that follows was written by a student who was assigned the article "Don't You Think It's Time to Start Thinking?" by Northrop Frye (pages 162–164 in Chapter 8) and then asked to write a one-paragraph summary and a response essay expressing her opinion of the article's proposal. Although the student thought the article itself could have been stronger, she agreed with Frye's assessment that literacy meant more than just reading and writing. Her approval of his assessment and of its implications became her essay's thesis, which she then developed through use of her own experience.

After you read Frye's article and the student's summary-and-response essay, what suggestions for revision might you offer her?

EDUCATION AND THE WELL-LIVED LIFE

1   In "Don't You Think It's Time to Start Thinking?" the influential Canadian academic Northrop Frye declares that a declining ability in hard analysis and clear communication not only indicates

Summary

laziness and anti-intellectualism in our society today, but actually poses a danger to society. When people can only think and communicate at a basic and practical level—to sign forms and read signs, for example—then they can be manipulated and victimized by those who hold power. He suggests that advanced thinking and mastery of language are inextricably tied together, and that these skills should be aggressively promoted in classrooms.

Response begins   2   Although Frye's article might have been more persuasive with some specific examples supporting its claims, his assessment of the situation is fair. Frye was writing this article in the late 1980s, before the Internet and instant messaging systems had exploded onto the world. His assessment is even truer in a world in which text messages, e-mails, and blogs have become the primary written forms for young people. People read and write short bytes of information; often, words are replaced by photographs. Who reads long, boring books anymore, in which difficult ideas might be worked out over 400 pages? "Correct" grammar, not to mention complex sentences and the complex ideas represented by those sentences, has almost become obsolete. Frye's argument has two aims: first, to suggest that intellectual skills have declined and, second, to point out that, as Orwell also noted earlier, that intellectual and linguistic weaknesses make people vulnerable to tyranny. Frye's urgent plea to teachers to teach advanced language and intellectual skills makes sense, especially to students who wish to have a say in their own lives and societies. Like many in my generation, I was a high-school graduate who found out how costly it was not to know how to think critically.

Thesis

3   After I graduated from high school, I didn't go to university because I didn't have any money saved and I couldn't see what I could learn in university that I hadn't learned in school. I decided to work for a while, but I didn't have any training for anything so I took a minimum-wage sales job in a mall clothing store. I had to look good for work, but since my wardrobe consisted of jeans and T-shirts, I had to buy new clothes. With clothes to buy, and transportation to work and other bills to pay, I was barely breaking even. On top of that, my employer cheated me, as well as his other employees, by constantly fining me for supposed carelessness with the merchandise, supposed lateness, and so forth. If I had known how to read the fine print in my contract—or even known there was fine print to read—I might have looked for another job much sooner, and if I had been trained to think critically about the world, I might have felt more confident about challenging my employer's actions. Instead, I just took the injustice for granted, and assumed I was doomed to be powerless.

Response to not valuing education beyond the basics

4   I was also frustrated because I was so tired after working that I had no energy to read, either for pleasure or for information. My job at the store wasn't meaningful or challenging; it was, in fact,

Response to the being inadequately trained intellectually

repetitive and boring. For example, a typical day during the summer months consisted of cleaning out dressing rooms and hanging up two-piece swimsuits from all over the floor. It took forever to match up the right sized tops and bottoms and then hang them back up on these crazy little double hangers so that everything was facing the right way with all the straps untwisted. In the winter it was pants and sweaters. Unlike Frye's intellectually trained students who could advance in society so they could have meaningful jobs or make their mark like Prime Minister Trudeau, I wasn't doing anything meaningful, I wasn't learning any skills for a better future, and I sure wasn't learning to think for myself. All I was doing was resigning myself to being yet another young woman exploited by the system.

5   About seven months into the job, I got a call from my aunt, who taught political science at Queen's. She had heard about my frustrations, and she had a suggestion. First, she told me to go to my local law society, which offered free legal advice to people who couldn't afford it, so I'd have some ideas about how to challenge my employer. She also told me to start reading some of the classic essays and books written by philosophers such as Montaigne and Paine. At first, I didn't see any point to this, and couldn't see how it could possibly affect my life. But my aunt kept insisting, and finally I took some books out of the library. They were very hard going, but my aunt and I started exchanging a few e-mails about what I was reading, and soon, we were on e-mail all the time, as she explained their ideas and answered my questions. I found, to my surprise, that these philosophers' ideas began to make sense, and that I was becoming more aware of the ways in which people with more knowledge than me—politicians, employers, and so on— were so easily taking advantage of people like me.

Response to challenging oneself intellectually

and increasing ability to think critically

6   I did go to the law society and discovered I had more rights than I'd realized. I successfully made my employer pay back all the money he had fined me unfairly. More important for the future, however, was the curiosity and critical thinking my aunt and those ancient philosophers had awakened in me. I finally had real goals. I applied to and got into university, where I finally started my real education. Armed with the skills and ability to analyze and communicate ideas clearly, I am neither a victim nor, I hope, intellectually lazy. My journey toward active critical thinking has given me hope for achieving a meaningful, well-lived life.

Conclusion emphasizes the results of critical thinking: Increased individual power

■ PRACTISING WHAT YOU'VE LEARNED

1. After reading Northrop Frye's "Don't You Think It's Time to Start Thinking?" (pages 162–164), write your own summary-and-response essay, drawing on your own knowledge and experience to support or reject his assessment of the intellectual quality of modern society and its implications. Is this a reasonable assessment and argument? Why or why not? Exchange your paper with a classmate and discuss each other's ideas and essay strategies.

2. Write a response to "Don't You Think It's Time to Start Thinking?" that presents at least one paragraph critiquing Frye's reasoning, use of supporting evidence, or other methods of persuasion. How might Frye have improved the arguments that support his assessment? Did he overlook any major problems or disadvantages that you see? How might his tone be modified? (In other words, if Frye asked you for help during a revision workshop, what major suggestion for change or addition would you offer to assist him in writing a stronger draft?)

■ ASSIGNMENT

Read and annotate the selection "The 51-Per-Cent Minority" (on pages 216–218 in Chapter 9) and then write your own summary-and-response essay, agreeing or disagreeing (wholly or in part) with the writer's view of minority rights and discrimination. Compare the situations and problems Anderson describes to the conditions of minority rights and discrimination today. What changes (or lack of changes) can you see? What kind of evidence can you find, both to support Anderson's claims and your own? Remember to support your position with logical reasons, persuasive examples, or relevant facts that you have found in your research. (If you prefer, you may select some other professional essay from this textbook or from another source, such as a newspaper or magazine, but be sure to obtain your instructor's approval of your selection in advance.)

Chapter 16

Writing about Literature

People read literature for many, many reasons, including amusement, comfort, escape, new ideas, exploration of values, intellectual challenge, and so on. Similarly, people write about literature to accomplish a variety of purposes. Literary essays may inform readers about the ideas in a work, analyze its craft, or focus on the work's relationship to the time or culture in which it was written. Other essays might explore biographical, psychological, archetypal, or personal readings of a work.

Although approaches to literature are diverse and may be studied in depth in other English courses, writing essays about literature is worthwhile in the composition classroom as well. Writing about literature offers an opportunity to practise the important skills of close reading, critical thinking, and effective expression of ideas.

■ Using Literature in the Composition Classroom

Teachers of writing most often use literature in their courses in three ways: as "prompts" to inspire personal essay topics, as subjects of interpretative essays based on what students have been taught about the elements of literature (theme, figurative language, etc.), and as subjects of interpretive essays based on research into literary criticism as well as on a student's own analytical skills.

1. *Prompts:* You might be asked to read a poem, short story, play, or novel and then use some aspect of it—its ideas or characters, for example—as a springboard to discover an essay topic of your own. For instance, after reading Madeleine

Thien's "Simple Recipes," a story about families, cooking and generational cultural differences, you might want to write about the ways in which your own family's cooking and eating habits represent your relationships to each other or maintain ties with ancestral cultures. Or your instructor might assign Timothy Findley's novel *The Wars,* and ask you to compare the protagonist's war experience during the First World War with what you can discover about the war experiences of young Canadian soldiers today.

2. *Literary Analysis:* Rather than responding to a piece of literature in a personal essay, you might be assigned a literary analysis, asking you to study a piece of literature and then offer your interpretation—that is, your insight into the work (or some important part of it). Your insight becomes your thesis; the body of your essay explains this reading, supported by textual evidence (material from the work) to help your reader understand your view and perhaps gain greater pleasure in, and appreciation of, the work itself.

3. *Analytical Research Paper:* In such an assignment, you are asked to combine your own analysis of a piece of literature with professional writing on that literary text. Here, it is best if you begin your essay using the guidelines above for literary analysis, and then read what other people have to say. In this type of essay, you will need to do some research to find the most relevant and credible sources of scholarly literary criticism on your subject. Use the published literary criticism to guide you in new directions, to give you new insights and information, and, sometimes, to present an opposing view against which you can argue. When you write a literary analysis in which you respond to professional literary criticism, you are joining in what Canadian academic Janet Giltrow calls the "scholarly conversation." If you think of yourself as interacting with other people's interpretations and analyses of literature, you will find yourself expanding your own ideas and writing more dynamic essays.

Literary analysis assignments may be focused in different ways, as well. Some common examples include essays whose main purpose is to show

- how the various parts or elements of a piece of literature work together to present the main ideas (for example, how the choices of narrator, stanza form, and figurative language in a poem effectively complement each other);

- how one element fits into the complex whole (for example, how setting contributes to a story);

- how two works or two elements may be profitably read together (two poems with similar ideas but different forms; two characters from one story);

- how one interpretation is more insightful than another reading;

- how a work's value has been overlooked or misunderstood.

There are as many possibilities for essay topics as there are readers!

Regardless of the exact assignment, you should feel confident about writing an essay of literary analysis. Working through Part Two of this text, you have already practised many of the strategies required. For example, to present a particular reading of a poem, you may organize your discussion by *dividing* it into its major literary elements: point of view, setting, structure, language, and so on. Your essay may offer specific lines or images from the work as *examples* illustrating your reading. Working with more than one piece of literature or literary element calls for *comparison and contrast* techniques. And every paper—whether it is a personal response or literary analysis—uses the skills you learned in Part One of this text: a clear thesis, adequate development of ideas, coherent organization, and effective use of language.

■ Suggestions for Close Reading of Literature

Writing about literature begins with careful reading—and, yes, rereading. The steps suggested here are certainly not exhaustive; one can ask literally hundreds of questions about a complex piece of literature. Rather, these questions are intended to give you a start. Practising close reading and annotation should help you generate ideas and lead you to additional questions of your own.

Our discussion in this chapter is limited to poems and short stories because composition courses frequently do not have the time to include novels and plays (or long narrative poems, for that matter). However, many of the suggestions for reading short stories and poems may be applied to the reading of longer fiction and drama.

Before you begin reading the suggestions that follow, let's dispel the myth about "hidden meanings." A work of literature is not a trick or puzzle box wherein the author has hidden a message for readers to discover if they can just uncover the right clues. Literary works are open to discussion and interpretation; that's part of their appeal. They contain ideas and images that the author thought important, and some ideas or elements the writer may not have consciously been aware of. You, as the reader, will have insights into a poem or story that your classmates don't. It's your job as the writer of your literary analysis to explain not only *WHAT* you see but also *WHY* and *HOW*, supporting your interpretation in ways that seem reasonable, persuasive, and satisfying to your readers.

Analysis is not plot summary. Sometimes you may want to offer your readers a brief overview of the work before you begin your in-depth analysis. And certainly there will be times in the body of your essay, especially if you are writing about fiction, that you will need to paraphrase actions or descriptions rather than quote long passages directly. Paraphrasing can indeed provide effective support, but do beware a tendency to fall into unproductive plot-telling. Remember that the purpose of your paper is to provide insight into the work's ideas and craft—not merely to present a rehash of the story line. Keep your eye on each of your claims and quote or paraphrase only those particular lines or important passages that illustrate and support your points. Use your editing pen as a sharp stick to beat back plot summary if it begins taking over your paragraphs.

■ Steps to Reading a Story

If possible, make your own copy of the story and read with pen in hand. Prepare to make notes, underline important lines, circle revealing words or images, and put stars, question marks, or your own symbols in the margins.

1. Before you begin the piece, read any *biographical, cultural, and historical information* that may accompany the story. Knowing information about the author and when the story was written or published may offer some insight. Also, note the *title*. Does it offer intriguing hints about the story's content?

2. Read through the story at least once to clearly acquaint yourself with its *plot,* the series of actions and events that make up the narrative. In other words, what happened and to whom? Is there a conflict of some sort? Is it resolved or is the story left open-ended?

3. Many times you'll see words in a story you don't know. Sometimes you can figure them out from their context, but if you find unknown words that might indeed have a critical bearing on your understanding of a character, for example, look these up now.

4. Jot a few notes describing your initial reactions to the story's main idea(s) or major *theme(s).* (If it's helpful, think of the story in terms of what it's about. What do you as reader think this story is about? Loss of innocence? The bitterness of revenge? The power of sympathy? Tragic lack of communication? The wonder of first love?) In other words, what comments or observations does this story make about the human condition?

5. As you review the story, begin to think about its parts, always asking yourself "why?": Why did the author choose to do it this way? What is gained (or lost) by writing it this way? What does "X" contribute to my understanding of the story? You might begin noting *point of view*—that is, who is narrating this story? Is a character telling this story or is it told by an all-knowing (omniscient) narrator? A narrator who is partially omniscient, seeing into the thoughts of only some characters? What is gained through the story's choice of narration?

6. Is the story's *structure* in chronological order or does the writer shift time sequences through flashbacks or multiple points of view? Does the story contain foreshadowing, early indications in the plot that signal later developments? Again, think about the author's choices in terms of communicating the story's ideas.

7. Think about the *characters,* their personalities, beliefs, motivations. How do they interact? Do any of them change—refuse or fail to change? Look closely at their descriptions, thoughts, and dialogue. Sometimes names are revealing too.

8. What is the relationship between the *setting* of the story and its action or characters? Remember that setting can include place, time of year, hour of day or night, weather or climate, terrain, culture, and so on. Settings can create mood and even function symbolically to reveal character or foreshadow a coming event.

9. Look closely at the *language* of the story, paying attention to revealing images, metaphors, and similes (for help identifying these, see pages 306–307). Note any use of *symbols*—persons, places, or things that bear a significant meaning beyond their usual meaning. (For example, in a particular story, a dreary rain might be associated with a loss of hope; a soaring bird might emphasize new possibilities.) Overall, would you characterize the story's *style* as realistic or something else? What is the *tone* of the story? Serious? Humorous? Does irony, the discrepancy between appearance and reality, play a part?

10. After you've looked at these and any other important elements of the reading, review your initial reactions. How would you now describe the main ideas or

major themes of this story? How do the parts of the story work together to clarify those themes?

11. After all of these preliminary steps in your own analysis, you might find it useful to read a few articles or books written by literary critics on your subject, so you can be exposed to ideas you may not have considered. Don't do this before you start reading, however, because you may become too influenced by someone else's ideas, and have no room for your own.

Remember to add your own questions to this list, ones that address your specific story in a meaningful way. (For help writing essays of literary analysis, turn to pages 443–445.)

■ Annotated Story

Using the preceding guidelines, a composition student annotated the story that follows. Some of the notes she made on imagery became the basis for her short essay, which appears on pages 433–436. Before you read the story, however, cover the marginal notes with a sheet of paper. Then read the story, making your own notes. Next, uncover the student's notes and reread the story. Compare your reactions to those of the student writer. What new or different insights did you have?

■ Marrying the Hangman

Margaret Atwood

Margaret Atwood's long career in writing stories, poems and novels has made her one of the most influential voices in Canadian literature. She has often written about female oppression in novels such as *The Handmaid's Tale* (1985) and in short story collections such as *Bluebeard's Egg* (1983). The following piece of prose fiction was published as a prose poem in her collection *Two-Headed Poems* (1978), but has also been read and anthologized as a short story. This is a good example of prose fiction that straddles two genres.

Atwood's story is based on that of Jean Corolère, a French-Canadian military drummer, and Françoise Laurent, which can be found in the *Dictionary of Canadian Biography, Volume III: 1741–1770*. Corolère and Laurent met in 1751 while Corolère was imprisoned for duelling, and Laurent for stealing. These prisoners in adjoining cells were under a death sentence that could be avoided in one of three ways: if the prisoner received an official letter of pardon, if a male prisoner became a hangman himself, or if a female prisoner married the hangman. Through whispered words between walls, Laurent persuaded Corolère first to apply to become the hangman, which meant his death sentence was commuted, and then to marry her, which secured their release. The note at the end of the story was included by Atwood. It is clear that Atwood read the *DCB* entry closely, as she uses the word "ensnare" so prominently in her own version of the story; this word is specifically used by André Lachance, the writer of the *DCB* entry, and represents not just eighteenth century, but modern attitudes to Laurent's actions. In 1999, composer Ronald Caltabiano wrote a chamber opera based on Atwood's text.

1   She has been condemned to death by hanging. A man may escape this death by becoming the hangman, a woman by marrying the hangman. But at the present time there is no hangman; thus there is no escape. There is only a death, indefinitely postponed. This is not fantasy, it is history.

2   To live in prison is to live without mirrors. To live without mirrors is to live without the self. She is living selflessly, she finds a hole in the stone wall and on the other side of the wall, a voice. The voice comes through darkness and has no face. The voice becomes her mirror.

3   In order to avoid her death, her particular death, with wrung neck and swollen tongue, she must marry the hangman. But there is no hangman, first she must create him, she must persuade this man at the end of the voice, this voice she has never seen and which has never seen her, this darkness, she must persuade him to renounce his face, exchange it for the impersonal mask of official death which has eyes but no mouth, this mask of a dark leper. She must transform his hands so they will be willing to twist the rope around throats that have been singled out as hers was, throats other than hers. She must marry the hangman or no one, but that is not so bad. Who else is there to marry?

4   You wonder about her crime. She was condemned to death for stealing clothes from her employer, from the wife of her employer. She wished to make herself more beautiful. This desire in servants was not legal.

5   She uses her voice like a hand, her voice reaches through the wall, stroking and touching. What could she possibly have said that would convince him? He was not condemned to death, freedom awaited him. What was the temptation, the one that worked? Perhaps he wanted to live with a woman whose life he had saved, who had seen down into the earth but had nevertheless followed him back up to life. It was his only chance to be a hero, to one person at least, for the others would now despise him. He was in prison for wounding another man, on one finger of the right hand, with a sword. This too is history.

6   My friends, who are both women, tell me their stories, which cannot be believed and which are true. They are horror stories and they have not happened to me, they have not yet happened to me, they have happened to me but we are detached, we watch our unbelief with horror. Such things cannot happen to us, it is afternoon and these things do not happen in the afternoon. The trouble was, she said, I didn't have time to put my glasses on and without them I'm blind as a bat, I couldn't even see who it was. These things happen and we sit at a table and tell stories about them so we can finally believe. This is not fantasy, it is history, there is more than one hangman and because of this some of them are unemployed.

7   He said: the end of walls, the end of ropes, the opening of doors, a field, the wind, a house, the sun, a table, an apple.

8   She said: nipple, arms, lips, wine, belly, hair, bread, thighs, eyes, eyes.

9   They both kept their promises.

Why is she unnamed?
Images of violent death and imprisonment

isolation
Female invisibility, images of being erased
Violence and marriage—disturbing combination
Atmosphere of desperation, vulnerability
Death, violence, erasure of individuality
Comment on class-based injustice

Reflects her society's judgement: She is manipulative and self-serving.
Mystery of their relationship

Continuity between past and present injustices in women's lives

Lists represent each person's actions, perspectives on life, experiences

10 The hangman is not such a bad fellow. Afterwards he goes to the refrigerator and cleans up the leftovers, though he does not wipe up what he accidentally spills. He wants only the simple things: a chair, someone to pull off his shoes, someone to watch him while he talks, with admiration and fear, gratitude if possible, someone in whom to plunge himself for rest and renewal. These things can be best had by marrying a woman who has been condemned to death by other men for wishing to be beautiful. There is a wide choice.

Ordinary man is not necessarily evil, but doesn't understand women

11 Everyone said he was a Fool.

12 Everyone said she was a clever woman.

13 They used the word *ensnare.*

Again, society judges women more harshly than men

14 What did they say the first time they were alone together in the same room? What did he say when she had removed her veil and he could see that she was not a voice but a body and therefore finite? What did she say when she discovered that she had left one locked room for another? They talked of love, naturally, though that did not keep them busy forever.

15 The fact is there are no stories I can tell my friends that will make them feel better. History cannot be erased, although we can soothe ourselves by speculating about it. At that time there were no female hangmen. Perhaps there would never have been any, and thus no man could save his life by marriage. Though a woman could, according to the law.

16 He said: foot, boot, order, city, fist, roads, time, knife.

17 She said: water, night, willow, rope, hair, earth, belly, cave, meat, shroud, open, blood.

Lists represent couple's future— bleak, violent, deadly imagery

18 They both kept their promises.

19 "After 9 April 1752, all trace of him and his wife is lost." ("Corolère, Jean." *The Dictionary of Canadian Biography, Vol. 3*).

Irony: She may have saved herself from the violent death of execution, but seems to have condemned herself to a life of violence from her hangman husband.

Initial Reactions: The condemned woman saves herself from hanging by seducing another prisoner into agreeing to be a hangman as well as agreeing to marrying her. The author speculates about their courtship and suggests that though the hangman isn't all bad, he becomes violent towards his wife—the list of words near the story's end, and footnote which says the couple can't be traced after their marriage make me think this.

After Re-Reading: I think Atwood wanted to highlight how poor women were victimized by their society, and how few choices they had in the 18th century. I felt sorry for the woman—who isn't even named—because she goes from one kind of prison to another.

All the throat, voice, and rope references, as well as the prison images, make me think not only of hanging, but of the reality that women's voices are figuratively choked shut and suppressed by a patriarchal society. Also, the lists of words spoken by the man and the woman represent the differences in the ideas associated with men and women.

Question: Why does Atwood bring in the paragraphs about talking to her friends?

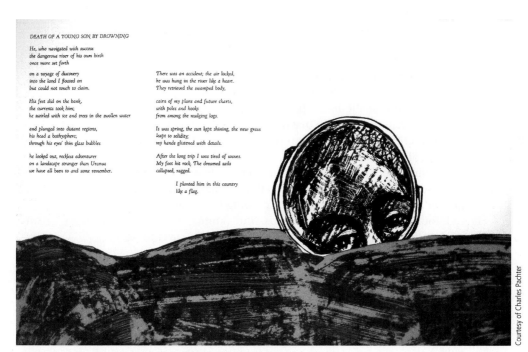

DEATH OF A YOUNG SON BY DROWNING

*He, who navigated with success
the dangerous river of his own birth
once more set forth*

*on a voyage of discovery
into the land I floated on
but could not touch to claim.*

*His feet slid on the bank,
the currents took him;
he swirled with ice and trees in the swollen water*

*and plunged into distant regions,
his head a bathysphere;
through his eyes' thin glass bubbles*

*he looked out, reckless adventurer
on a landscape stranger than Uranus
we have all been to and some remember.*

*There was an accident; the air locked,
he was hung in the river like a heart.
They retrieved the swamped body,*

*cairn of my plans and future charts,
with poles and hooks
from among the nudging logs.*

*It was spring, the sun kept shining, the new grass
leapt to solidity;
my hands glistened with details.*

*After the long trip I was tired of waves.
My foot hit rock. The dreamed sails
collapsed, ragged.*

*I planted him in this country
like a flag.*

Death of a Young Son by Drowning, 1970, *by Charles Pachter*

■ Sample Student Essay

After studying Atwood's story, this student writer jotted down marginal notes summarizing her response to various elements of the story. Although she was interested in the ironies implied in the piece, and about the references to blindness and darkness, she was particularly struck by the references to throats and voices, and by the lists of nouns in paragraphs 7, 8, 16 and 17. She decided to focus her essay on an important element in the work, the imagery of fragmentation, and to develop her discussion by responding to those lists of words and references to throats and eyes. Her essay's aim was to show how these images reveal Atwood's thesis about the oppression of women. She summarized the contextual information at the beginning of this section in the introductory paragraph to lead to her thesis. Numbers in parentheses following direct quotations refer to the paragraphs in the story.

Cutting Off Air

1   In Margaret Atwood's short story "Marrying the Hangman," a woman saves herself from execution by effecting a double transformation in another prisoner: she seduces him by her skillful use of language, into changing careers—from being a respectable soldier to being an executioner—and into being a husband to her. In the 18th century, which Atwood simply calls "history," a condemned female prisoner had the ironic option of saving her life by marrying the man employed to end it. Atwood suggests that such an option was no option, because women were merely moving from one kind of injustice and oppression to another. To help readers understand how limiting and life-destroying options were for women in the past, as well as in the present, the author uses images of fragmentation.

2   From the second paragraph of the story we see several references to disembodied voices, voices that come "through darkness" and have "no face[s]" (2). Even though the initial reference is to the voice of the man, and Atwood does acknowledge at times that men were also victimized by social realities, her focus is on the ways in which women are victimized. The author represents this victimization by showing the woman to be reduced to vulnerable parts of the body. These don't just include the "nipple . . . belly . . . thighs, eyes, eyes" (8) but even more importantly, a "wrung neck and swollen tongue" (3), the result of being strangled, of having her voice and her life choked off because she "wished to make herself more beautiful" (4). The fact that desire for self-improvement is categorized as criminal because of her class and sex demonstrates the injustices of this society.

3   Atwood further erases her characters' individuality by refusing to name either character, and reduces each to body parts and

Introduction: title and author identified: brief summary of plot and theme

Thesis

Images of fragmentation and vulnerability, illustrated by quotes from the story

Expanding
discussion of
vulnerability, loss
of self, contrast
between men
and women's
situations,
supported by
examples

disconnected actions. However, this strategy of reduction has contrasting effects. When the woman is associated with body parts, her vulnerability is emphasized. When she is reduced to having only her voice as a tool of survival, where her voice has to become her eyes (2) and hands (5), her powerlessness becomes clear. The images of the mirrorless room (2) and the "blind as a bat" (6) narrator create anxiety and fear of the unknown and of dangers lurking just outside our vision. The narrator even says that in this reduced state, the woman's identity itself is erased: "To live without mirrors is to live without the self" (2). But when the man is represented as a disembodied voice, he is seen as an unknown and unknowable creature, a terrifying and "impersonal mask of death, of official death which has eyes but no mouth, this mask of a dark leper" (3). We realize that the woman is being seen partially through the man's eyes, and the man, through the woman's, and that each expects something very different from the other.

4   Because the immediate freedom of each seems dependent on the other, each is ready to accept the other's promises. But the stakes are higher for the woman. She doesn't just need freedom, she needs to avoid execution. In order to survive, the woman must compromise and offer herself physically to the man. Her promises, starkly summarized into words like "nipple, arms, lips, wine, belly, hair, bread, thighs, eyes, eyes" (8) suggest this society only values women for their sexual, maternal, and domestic functions. The man's promises go beyond the private and physical to the material: "a house . . . a table, an apple" (7), but also suggest the dreams that would sway the woman: "the end of walls, the end of ropes, the opening of doors" (7). He has more to offer than the woman does, and his own seductive arts are effective. Atwood's use of a

Images of male
and female
desires,
supported by
examples and
comparison

series of disconnected words further underlines the fragmentation of these characters' identities.

5   The injustice faced by the couple continues after their marriage as their society continues to devalue the woman and blame her for the marriage. The assumption is that the woman gets the best end of the bargain because marriage and freedom are the best a woman can and should expect. She is condemned for ensnaring the man (13) and for being a "clever woman" (12), while the man is ridiculed for being a "Fool" (11). In other words, the woman is criticized for using the man, and the man is criticized for letting himself be used. As the footnote at the end suggests, once they marry, the couple drops out of the history books, perhaps because the most dramatic and interesting aspects of this otherwise ordinary couple's story are over.

Importance of historical context

6   But this is not a story with a happy ending. The author interrupts the narrative twice, in the sixth and the fifteenth paragraphs, instructing readers on how to read this as part of a whole history of past and continuing "horror stories" (6) of the lives of women. As the story continues, the narrator shows the sinister direction taken in this relationship. The best that can be said about the hangman is that he "is not such a bad fellow" (10). As a product of his society, he knows an ordinary man's best chance at being a "hero" (5) and of having both comfort and power is to marry a wholly dependent woman (10). The expectations he has from a wife, "someone to pull off his shoes, someone to watch him while he talks, with admiration and fear, gratitude if possible, someone in whom to plunge himself for rest and renewal" (10) are common for a man of his class and time and perhaps common even in contemporary male–female relationships. Such expectations continue to reduce women into objects and machines who are

Moving towards conclusion— victimization of both men and women by society's expectations

there to perform particular functions. They suggest women exist only to serve men. These expectations are in direct contrast to the expectations of freedom suggested in the man's initial promises to the woman (7) and suggest, instead, that the woman has exchanged one type of imprisonment and oppression for another.

7   The list at the end of the story confirms the fears anticipated by the images of death in the third paragraph. The narrator contrasts the generally positive and life-giving images of "the wind . . . the sun" and "an apple" (7) that were promised by the man with images of violence and oppression after the marriage and escape from prison. Now the images associated with the man are "boot . . . order . . . fist . . . knife" (16). The woman's list shows the effects of those nouns: "rope hair, earth . . . cave, meat, shroud . . . blood" (17). In combination with these lists, the historical footnote from the *Dictionary of Canadian Biography* implies an end to the story that challenges an assumption that this couple's lives just became too ordinary to record. The violence of the final images in the two lists suggests a tragic conclusion to the condemned woman's desperate plan to escape death from the hands of the hangman. In this short story, Atwood draws a grim picture of women's lives in the past, and shows that as long as men continue to reduce women to objects, oppression and tragedy will continue to be women's fate.

Conclusion: Restatement of thesis showing purpose of the imagery

■ Steps to Reading a Poem

Close reading of a poem is similar to reading a story in many ways. Again, try to read with pen in hand so you can take notes, circle important words, and make comments in the margins.

1. Pay attention to any biographical or wider contextual information on the author and the date of publication, which may give you insight into the poem. Also note the title, as it may introduce the poem's main idea or tone.

2. Read through the poem at least twice. Poetry does differ from prose in that poets often compress or turn sentence structure in unusual ways to create new images and fit rhyme and rhythm patterns. You might find it helpful to try to paraphrase (put into your own words) the lines of shorter poems (or summarize distinct parts) so that you have a clear understanding of the basic content. If you're lost in several lines, try to locate the subject, the verb, and objects of the action or description. And, always, before you begin to analyze a poem, be sure you know the meaning of *all* the words. Looking up unfamiliar words is critical here—short poems are compact, so every word counts.

3. Some poems are *narratives* and contain a plot; others, often referred to as *lyrics,* capture a scene, a series of images, an emotion, or a thought that has universal appeal. At this point, what action, situation, or ideas do you see presented in this poem? Is there a dominant tone or point of view expressed? Make some notes about your initial reactions to the poem's issues, themes, or ideas. As in fiction, poets often offer comments on the human condition or social values.

4. Now begin to analyze the elements of the poem. Identifying the *speaker* (or narrator) of the poem is a good place to start. Is it someone with recognizable characteristics or personality traits? Someone involved in the action of the poem? Young or old? Male or female? Mother, father, lover, friend? Tone of voice (angry, pleading, sad, joyful, etc.)? Remember that a speaker using "I" is not necessarily the poet but rather a persona or role the poet has assumed. Or is the speaker unidentified as she or he unfolds the poem for the reader? And to whom is the poem addressed? A specific person, a group of people, any readers?

5. What is the *setting* or *occasion* of the poem? Is the place, time, season, climate, or historical context important to understanding the poem? Why or why not?

6. What *characters,* if any, appear in the poem? What is the relationship between the speaker and others in the poem? What values, opinions, and motivations do these characters present? What conflicts or changes occur?

7. Look carefully at the poem's *diction* (choice of words). Most poems contain description and figurative language to create imagery, the vivid pictures that create meaning in the reader's mind. Look for similes and metaphors, as defined on page 306, that make abstract or unfamiliar images clear through comparisons, as well as personification and synecdoche (pages 306–307). Poets often use patterns or groups of *images* to present a dominant impression and concrete objects as *symbols* to represent abstract ideas within the poem (cold rain as death, a spring flower as rebirth). They also use *allusions,* brief references to other well-known persons, places, things, and literary works that shed light on their subject by comparison (for example, a reference to Romeo and Juliet might suggest ill-fated lovers). Underline or circle those words and images that you find most effective in communicating ideas or emotions.

8. How is the poem *structured?* There are too many poetic forms to define each one here (ballads, sonnets, odes, villanelles, etc.) so you might consult a more detailed handbook to help you identify the characteristics of each one. However, to help you begin, here is a brief introduction. Some poems are written in patterns called "fixed" or "closed" form. They often appear in stanzas, recognizable units often containing the same number of lines and the same rhyme and

rhythm pattern in those lines. They often present one main idea per unit and have a space between each one. Some poems are not divided into stanzas but nevertheless have well-known fixed forms, such as the Shakespearean sonnet, which traditionally challenges the poet to write within fourteen lines in a predictable line rhythm and rhyme scheme. Other poems are written in free verse (or "open" form), with no set line length or regular rhyme pattern; these poems may rely on imagery, line lengths, repetition, or sound devices to maintain unity and show progression of ideas.

Study your poem and try to identify its form. How does its structure help communicate its ideas? Why might have the poet chosen this particular structure?

9. *Sound devices* may help unify a poem, establish tone, emphasize a description, and communicate theme. There are many kinds of rhyme (end, internal, slant, etc.), which often help unify or link ideas and parts of poems. For example, stanzas often have set patterns of end rhyme that pull a unit together; a quatrain (four-line stanza), for example, might rhyme *abab*, as shown here:

   . . . free,   a
   . . . sky,   b
   . . . sea,   a
   . . . fly,   b

Four other common sound devices include:

- *Alliteration:* repetition of consonant sounds at the beginning of words ("The <u>S</u>oul <u>s</u>elects her own <u>S</u>ociety"), often used to link and emphasize a relationship among the words;
- *Assonance:* repetition of vowel sounds ("ch<u>i</u>ld br<u>i</u>de of t<u>i</u>me") to link and underscore a relationship among the words;
- *Onomatopoeia:* a word whose sound echoes, and thus emphasizes, its meaning (buzz, rustle, hiss, boom, sigh);
- *Repetition:* repetition of the same words, phrases, or lines for unity, emphasis, or musical effect ("Sing on, spring! Sing on, lovers!").

Sound devices not only unify poems but also add to their communication of images and meaning. Harsh-sounding, monosyllabic words ("the cold stone tomb") may slow lines and create a tone vastly different from one produced by multi-syllabic words with soft, flowing sounds. Poets pick their words carefully for their sounds as well as their connotations and denotations. Ask yourself: What sound devices appear in the poem I'm reading, and why?

10. *Rhythm,* the repetition of stresses and pauses, may also play an important part in the creation of tone and meaning. A poem about a square dance, for example, might echo the content by having a number of quick stresses to imitate the music and the caller's voice. You can discover patterns of rhythm in lines of poetry by marking the accented (ˊ) and unaccented (˘) syllables:

   My mistress' eyes are nothing like the sun

Many poems demand a prescribed rhythm as part of their fixed form; lines from a Shakespearean sonnet, as noted above, contain an often-used pattern called *iambic pentameter*: five units (called *feet*) of an unaccented syllable followed by an accented syllable.

Another device that contributes to the rhythm of a line is the *caesura,* a heavy pause in a line of poetry. Caesuras (indicated by a ‖ mark) may be used to isolate and thus emphasize words or slow the pace. Sometimes they are used to show strong contrasts, as in the following line: "Before, a joy proposed; ‖ behind, a dream." Caesuras may follow punctuation marks such as commas, semicolons, or periods, marks that say "slow down" to the reader.

After you have looked at the various elements of a poem (and there are many others in addition to the ones mentioned here), reassess your initial reaction. Do you understand the poem in a different or better way? Remember that the elements of an effective poem work together, so be sensitive to the poet's choices of point of view, language, structure, and so on. All these choices help communicate the tone and underscore the ideas of the poem. Ask yourself: What is gained through the poet's choice? What might be different—or lost—if the poet had chosen something else?

■ Annotated Poem

Using the suggestions of this chapter, a student responded to the Walt Whitman poem "When I Heard the Learn'd Astronomer" on the next page. The student essay on pages 441–443 presents an analysis developed from some of the notes shown there.

Starry Night, *1889, by Vincent Van Gogh*

Digital Image © The Museum of Modern Art/Licensed by Scala/Art Resource, NY

Educated

someone who studies the stars, sky

■ When I Heard the Learn'd Astronomer

Walt Whitman

used here too

Walt Whitman was a nineteenth-century American poet whose free-verse poems often broke with conventional style and subject matter. Some of his most famous poems, including "Song of Myself," "Crossing Brooklyn Ferry," and "Passage to India," extol the virtues of the common people and stress their unity with a universal spirit. This poem was published in 1865.

speaker: "I" in audience

settings: inside lecture hall

1   When I heard the learn'd astronomer;
2   When the proofs, the figures, were ranged in columns
        before me;
3   When I was shown the charts and diagrams, to
        add, divide, and measure them;
4   When I, sitting, heard the astronomer, where he
        lectured with much applause in the lecture-room.

scientific images, repetition, long lines, slow pace

outside at night

5   How soon, unaccountable, I became tired and sick;
6   Till rising and gliding out, I wander'd off by myself,
7   In the mystical moist night-air, and from time to time,
8   Look'd up in perfect silence at the stars.

Contrast to 4 lines above: quicker, smoother sounds; nature imagery; appeals to senses, not brain

assonance

multiple uses of alliteration

Initial Reaction: The speaker of the poem (a student?) is listening to an astronomer's lecture—lots of facts and figures. He gets tired (bored?) and goes outside and looks at the nice night himself.

After re-reading: I see two ways of looking at the sky here, two ways of understanding. You can learn academically and you can use your own senses. I think Whitman prefers the personal experience in this case because the language and images are much more positive in the last lines of the poem when the speaker is looking at nature for himself.

The poem shows the contrast between the two ways by using two stanzas with different styles and tones, Cold vs. warm. Passive vs. active. Facts vs. personal experience.

■ Sample Student Essay

After studying the Whitman poem, the student writer wrote this essay to show how many poetic elements work together to present the main idea. Do you agree with his analysis? Which of his claims seems the most or least persuasive, and why? What different interpretation(s) might you suggest?

TWO WAYS OF KNOWING

1   In the poem "When I Heard the Learn'd Astronomer," nineteenth-century American poet Walt Whitman contrasts two ways people may study the world around them. They can approach the world through lectures and facts, and they can experience nature firsthand through their own senses. Through the use of contrasting structures, imagery, diction, and sound devices in this poem, Whitman expresses a strong preference for personal experience.

Introduction: title, author, brief overview of content

Thesis

2   The poem's structure clearly presents the contrast between the two ways of experiencing the world, or in this specific case, two ways of studying the heavens. The eight-line, free-verse poem breaks into two stanzas, with the first four lines describing an indoor academic setting, followed by a one-line transition to three concluding lines describing an outdoor night scene. The two parts are unified by a first-person narrator who describes and reacts to both scenes.

Two-part structure

3   In the first four lines the narrator is described as sitting in "a lecture-room" (l. 4) as part of an audience listening to an astronomer's talk. The dominant imagery of lines 2–3 is scientific and mathematical: "proofs," "figures," "charts," and "diagrams" are presented so that the audience "may add, divide, and measure them" (l. 3). The words, mostly nouns, appear without any colourful modifiers; the facts and figures are carefully arranged "in columns" (l. 2) for objective analysis. This approach to learning is clearly logical and systematic.

Stanza 1: Inside lecture hall

4   The structure and word choice of the first four lines of the poem also subtly reveal the narrator's attitude toward the lecture, which he finds dry and boring. To emphasize the narrator's emotional uninvolvement with the material, Whitman presents

him passively "sitting" (l. 4), subject of the passive verb "was shown" (l. 3). Lines 2, 3, and 4, which describe the lecture, are much longer than the lines in the second stanza, with many caesuras, commas, and semicolons that slow the rhythm and pace (for example, l. 3: "When I was shown the charts and diagrams, to add, divide, and measure them;"). The slow, heavy pace of the lines, coupled with the four repetitions of the introductory "when" phrases, emphasizes the narrator's view of the lecture as long, drawn out, and repetitious. Even though the rest of the audience seems to appreciate the astronomer, giving him "much applause" (l. 4), the narrator becomes restless, "tired and sick" (l. 5), and leaves the lecture hall.

Slow pace to emphasize attitude

Stanza 2: Outside under stars

5   In the last three lines of the poem, the language and sound devices change dramatically, creating positive images of serenity, wonder, and beauty. The narrator leaves the hall by "rising and gliding out" (l. 6), a light, floating, almost spirit-like image that connects him with the "mystical" (l. 7) nature of the heavens. Whitman also uses assonance (repetition of the "i" sound) to strengthen the connection between the "r*i*sing and gl*i*ding" narrator and the "myst*i*cal . . . n*i*ght-air" (l. 7). In the lecture hall, the narrator was bored, passive, and removed from nature, but now he is spiritually part of the experience himself.

"mystical" imagery

contrasting diction, flowing lines, smooth sounds

6   Alone outside in the night, away from the noisy lecture hall, the narrator quietly contemplates the wonder of the sky, using his own senses of sight, touch, and hearing to observe the stars and feel the air. Positive words, such as "mystical" (l. 7) and "perfect" (l. 8), describe the scene, whose beauty is immediately accessible rather than filtered through the astronomer's cold "proofs" and "diagrams." Examples of alliteration tie together flowing images of natural beauty and serenity: "*m*ystical *m*oist night-air" (l. 7),

"from *time* *to* *time*" (l. 7), "silence at the *stars*" (l. 8). Whitman's choice of the soft "m" and "s" sounds here also adds to the pleasing fluid rhythm, which stands in direct, positive contrast to the harsher, choppier sounds ("charts," "add," "divide") and slow, heavy pauses found in the poem's first stanza.

7   Through careful selection and juxtaposition of language, sound, and structure in the two parts of this short poem, Whitman contrasts distinct ways of studying the natural world. One may learn as a student of facts and figures or choose instead to give oneself over to the wonders of the immediate experience itself. Within the context of this poem, it's no contest: firsthand natural experience wins easily over diagrams and lectures. Stars, 1; charts and graphs, 0.

Conclusion: Restatement of thesis and poem's main idea

■ Guidelines for Writing about Literature

Here are some suggestions that will improve any essay of literary analysis:

1. **Select a workable topic.** If the choice of subject matter is yours, you must decide if you will approach a work through discussion of several elements or if you will focus on some specific part of it as it relates to the whole work. You must also select a topic that is interesting and meaningful for your readers. If your topic is too obvious or insignificant, your readers will be bored. In other words, your essay should inform your readers and increase their appreciation of the work.

2. **Present a clear thesis.** Remember that your purpose is to provide new insight to your readers. Consequently, they need to know exactly what you see in the work. Don't just announce your topic ("This poem is about love"); rather, put forth your argumentative thesis clearly and specifically ("Through its repeated use of sewing imagery, the story emphasizes the tragedy of a tailor's wasted potential as an artist"). And don't waltz around vaguely talking about something readers may not have seen the first time through ("At first the warehouse scene doesn't look that important but after reading it a few times you see that it really does contain some of the meaningful ideas in the story"). "Get on with it!" cries your impatient reader. "Tell me what you see!"

3. **Follow literary conventions.** Essays of literary analysis have some customs you should follow, unless instructed otherwise. Always include the full name of the

author and the work in your introductory paragraph; the author's last name is fine after that. Do not use the author's first name ("Walt thinks the lecture is boring")! Titles of short poems and stories are enclosed in quotation marks. Most literary essays are written in present tense ("the poet presents an image of a withered tree"), from third-person point of view rather than the more informal first-person "I." So that your readers may easily follow your discussion, include a copy of the work or at least indicate publication information describing the location of the work (the name of volume, publisher, date, pages, and so forth).

Within your essay, it's also helpful to include a poem's line number following a direct quotation: "the silent schoolyard" (l. 10). Some instructors also request paragraph or page numbers in essays on fiction.

4. **Organize effectively.** Your method of organization may depend heavily on your subject matter. A poem, for example, might be best discussed by devoting a paragraph to each stanza; on the other hand, another work might profit from a paragraph on imagery, another on point of view, another on setting, and so on. You must decide what arrangement makes the best sense for your readers. Experiment by moving your ideas around in your prewriting outlines and drafts.

5. **Use ample evidence.** Remember that you are, in essence, arguing your interpretation—you are saying to your reader, "Understand this work the way I do." Therefore, it is absolutely essential that you offer your reader convincing evidence, based on reasonable readings of words in the work itself. The acceptance of your views depends on your making yourself clear and convincing. To do so, include plenty of references to the work through direct quotation and paraphrase. Don't assume that your reader sees what you see—or sees it in the way you do. You must *fight* for your interpretation by offering clearly explained readings substantiated with references to the work.

> *Unsupported claim:* Robert feels sorry for himself throughout the story.
>
> *Claim supported with text:* Robert's self-pity is evident throughout the story as he repeatedly thinks to himself, "No one on this earth cares about me" (4) and "There isn't a soul I can turn to" (5).

Ask yourself as you work through your drafts, am I offering enough clear, specific, convincing evidence here to persuade my reader to accept my reading?

6. **Find a pleasing conclusion.** At the end of your literary analysis, readers should feel they have gained new knowledge or understanding of a work or some important part of it. You might choose to wrap up your discussion with a creative restatement of your reading, its relation to the writer's craft, or even your assessment of the work's significance within the author's larger body of writing. However you conclude, the readers should feel intellectually and emotionally satisfied with your discussion.

Problems to Avoid

Don't assign meanings. By far the most common problem in essays of literary analysis involves interpretation without clear explanation of supporting evidence. Remember that your readers may not see what you see in a particular line or paragraph; in fact, they may see something quite different. The burden is on you to show cause—how you derived your reading and why it is a good one. Don't represent claims as truth even if they ever-so-conveniently fit your thesis: "It is clear that the moon is used here as a symbol of her family's loss." Clear to whom besides you? If it helps, each time you make an interpretative claim, imagine a classmate who immediately says, "Uh, sorry, but I don't get it. Show me how you see that." Or imagine a hostile reader with a completely different reading who sneers, "Oh yeah, says who? Convince me."

Use quoted material effectively. Many times your supporting evidence will come from quotations from the text you're analyzing. But don't just drop a quoted line onto your page, as if it had just tumbled off a high cliff somewhere. You run the risk of your readers reading the quoted material and still not seeing in it what you see. Blend the quoted material smoothly into your prose in a way that illustrates or supports your clearly stated point:

> *Dropped in:* Miranda is twenty-four years old. "After working for three years on a morning newspaper she had an illusion of maturity and experience" (280). [What exact point do you want your reader to understand?]

> *Point clarified:* Although Miranda is twenty-four and has worked on a newspaper for three years, she is not as worldly wise as she thinks she is, having acquired only the "illusion of maturity and experience" (280).

Review pages 378–380 for some ways to blend your quotations into your prose. Always double-check to ensure you are quoting accurately; refer to pages 385–386 and 507–508 for help with proper punctuation and block indention of longer quoted material.

■ Practising What You've Learned

A. Practise your skills of literary analysis on the short story that follows, "Weaver Spider's Web" by Peter Blue-Cloud (Aroniawenrate).

■ Weaver Spider's Web

Peter Blue-Cloud (Aroniawenrate)

Born into the Turtle Clan of the Mohawk Nation in Quebec, Peter Blue-Cloud has written poems and short stories that often feature Coyote, a trickster figure in much First Nations mythology. The fable style and structure of this story is characteristic of some genres of First Nations literature. Although there seem to be some clear moral lessons in this story, the fable structure is given a twist, rather than a conventional moral at the end. This story was published in a collection of short stories entitled *Elderberry Flute Song: Contemporary Coyote Tales* (1989).

1   Coyote was starving and freezing, and here it was only mid-winter. He'd forgotten to gather firewood and food. He'd planned on singing a very powerful song to make the winter a mild one, easy to live with, but he'd forgotten to sing the song.

2   The reason he'd forgotten was that he was fascinated by Weaver Spider, who'd moved into the entrance of Coyote's roundhouse and, there, had begun to weave the most intricate web imaginable.

3   Now Weaver Spider knew that Coyote was watching him, and he really showed off. He'd work on a tiny section of web, turning it into miniature landscapes with mountains and plants and creatures running all around. And Coyote just sat there on his butt watching the work in progress and making up little stories to go with each picture.

4   Yes, Coyote thought, this is very important to watch: I am learning many things in my head.

5   Weaver Spider was, of course, doing all this so that Coyote would starve and die. He wanted Coyote's house so he could get married and raise a family. And so he kept weaving to hypnotize Coyote, stopping only to eat an occasional bug. Whenever a bug got stuck in his web, he would sing, "Tee-vee-vee-vee," a song which put the bug to sleep and, so, ready to eat.

6   "Cousin, you're looking very skinny and sick. And it's sure cold in here!" said Grey Fox when he stopped by one day. Coyote agreed, but insisted that watching Weaver Spider was very important. "I am becoming much smarter," he said.

7   Grey Fox watched the weaving, but being a practical person, it didn't much move him. Instead he became suspicious of the spider, convinced he was up to no good.

8   Grey Fox felt pity for Coyote and went home to get food, and his axe for firewood.

9   Coyote ate the pine nuts and deer jerky while Grey Fox cut firewood. Then Grey Fox built a warming fire and suggested that maybe Coyote wanted to borrow the axe.

10   But Coyote just sat there, eating up all the food and saying, "Yes, I'm becoming much smarter."

11   Grey Fox became fed up with this nonsense. He sang a sleep song and a dream song, and soon Coyote was snoring away.

12   "Now," Grey Fox said to Weaver Spider, "I know you're up to no good. I want you to pack up and leave right now; if you don't, I'm going to have you for a snack." Weaver Spider got scared and quickly left.

13   Grey Fox tore away the spider's web and woke Coyote up. Coyote looked at the clear sky where the web had been and saw how beautiful it all was. This new clarity, he assured his cousin, had been brought about from watching the spider. And again he said, "Yes, I am much smarter now."

14   Grey Fox was angry with Coyote. "I'm going to make you twice as smart!" he said. "I'm going to give you a wife, then you can have children to pass your great wisdom on to." And Grey Fox picked up his axe and cut Coyote in half, from head to asshole. Then he sang a song and brought the halves alive. The better half turned out to be Coyote Woman.

15   "Now you are twice as smart," said Grey Fox. And Coyote Woman looked all around, then turned to Coyote, "Why don't you go catch some mice for dinner? And while you're out there, cut some firewood too."

16   And Coyote went out to do her bidding. After he'd gone, she turned to me and sort of looked me over before saying, "I suppose you think you'll be winning over women with your cute stories, huh? Well, let me tell you, you got a long way to go yet."

B.   Read the poem that follows several times and then use the suggestions in this chapter to help you analyze the work. Who is speaking in this poem and what do the poem's images say about Annie?

■ Now of Sleeping (Under Her Grandmother's Patchwork Quilt)

Leonard Cohen

Poet and singer-songwriter Leonard Cohen sets much of his poetry to melancholy music, which he composes and sings himself. Although his gravelly voice elicits much passionate debate about the quality of his musical performance, his poetry seems to speak to a widely ranging audience. Cohen has been publishing and recording since the 1960s. He has often been seen as a controversial figure, with his strong political views and recent ordination as a Buddhist monk, though he still considers himself Jewish as well. The following poem was published in *Spice-Box of Earth* (1961).

Under her grandmother's patchwork quilt
a calico bird's-eye view
of crops and boundaries
naming dimly the districts of her body
sleeps my Annie like a perfect lady

Like ages of weightless snow
on tiny oceans filled with light
her eyelids enclose deeply
a shade tree of birthday candles
one for every morning
until the now of sleeping

The small banner of blood
kept and flown by Brother Wind
long after the pierced bird fell down
is like her red mouth
among the squalls of pillow

Bearers of evil fantasy
of dark intention and corrupting fashion
who come to rend the quilt
plough the eye and ground the mouth
will contend with mighty Mother Goose

and Farmer Brown and all good stories
of invincible belief
which surround her sleep
like the golden weather of a halo

Well-wishers and her true lover
may stay to watch my Annie
sleeping like a perfect lady
under her grandmother's patchwork quilt
but they must promise to whisper
and to vanish by morning
all but her one true lover.

Suggestions for Writing

The two stories and two poems reprinted in this chapter may be used as stepping stones to your own essays. Some suggestions:

1. Write an essay that presents your interpretation of "Now of Sleeping (Under Her Grandmother's Quilt." Support your reading with specific references to the poem's images, structure, word choice, and other literary features.

2. Write an essay that discusses the major ways in which Peter Blue-Cloud's "Weaver Spider's Web" uses a folktale format to examine universal issues about self-delusion and victimization. Or perhaps you would like to write about the roles of Grey Fox and Coyote Woman in this story. Is there a lesson the author wants the reader to take away? You might want to look at the device of the spider's web, for example.

3. Use one of the works as a "prompt" for your own personal essay. For example, have you, like the woman in "Marrying the Hangman," found yourself in a situation that has made you feel trapped, with very limited choices? Or have you ever spent time observing other people and either imagining their inner lives or imaginatively interpreted their characters as in the Cohen poem? Perhaps the Whitman poem reminded you of a time when you learned something through hands-on experience rather than study. Or perhaps the opposite was true: you didn't fully appreciate an experience until you had studied it. As Grey Fox did, have you ever found yourself going out of your way to help out a friend? What did you learn from this experience?

4. Write an essay analyzing some other important element(s) in "Marrying the Hangman." For example, you could do some historical research on the eigh-teenth -century law that prompted the writing of this piece of prose fiction. Or consider the man in the story. How does he see himself, how does his society see him, how does the woman see him, and how does the narrator see him? What do all these interpretations of his character and role signify about gender relations, even today?

5. Read some literary criticism on any of the literary works in this chapter or in Chapter 31. Are most literary critics writing about similar aspects of the work, or are there diverse approaches to the critical analysis of the work? Write a process analysis essay in which you trace changes in approaches to a literary work over the last few decades (for example, how were critics responding to Atwood's work in 1978, and how have they responded more recently?). Or, write an essay in which you explain, classify, evaluate, or compare different critical arguments about a writer's work.

6. Write an essay in which you choose some aspect of the work (narrative or devel-opmental strategies, thematic elements, linguistic elements, etc.) and combine your own analysis with a response to the arguments and analysis you find in the works of professional scholars.

7. Find a poem or short story that you admire and, using this chapter as a guide, write your own essay of literary analysis. Be sure your readers have a copy of the work you choose.

Chapter 17

Writing in the World of Work

Imagine you are a manager of a business who receives the following memo from one of the sales representatives:

> Our biggest customer in Ottawa asked me to forward the shipment to the company warehouse and I said I could not realizing how serious a decision this was I changed my mind.
> This OK with you?

Did the salesperson mean to say that at first he thought he could send the shipment but then changed his mind? Or did he mean he thought he couldn't but then reconsidered? What would you do as the manager? Probably you would stop your current work and contact the salesperson to clarify the situation before you gave an okay. Because of the unclear communication, this extra effort will cost your business valuable time, energy, and perhaps even customer satisfaction.

The preceding scenario is not far-fetched; unclear writing hurts businesses and organizations in every country in the world. Consequently, here is a bold claim:

> Almost all workplaces today demand employees with good communication skills.

Although specific writing tasks vary from job to job, and profession to profession, successful businesses rely on the effective passage of information among managers, coworkers, and customers. No employer ever wants to see confusing reports or puzzling memos that result in lost production time, squandered resources, or aggravated clients. To maximize their organization's efficiency, employers look for and reward employees who can demonstrate the very writing skills you have been practising in this composition course. Without question, your ability to communicate clearly in precise, organized prose will give you a competitive edge in the world of work.

To help you address some of the most common on-the-job writing situations, this chapter offers general guidelines for business letters, office memos, and professional electronic-mail messages. A special section on the preparation of résumés at the end of the chapter will suggest ways to display your skills to any prospective employer.

■ Composing Business Letters

Letters in the workplace serve many purposes and audiences, so it isn't possible to illustrate each particular kind. However, it is important to note that all good business letters have some effective qualities in common. And although a business letter is clearly not a personal essay, they share many of the same features: consideration of audience, development of a main idea, organized paragraphs, appropriate tone and diction, and clear, concise expression of thoughts.

Before you begin any letter, prewrite by considering these important questions:

1. What is the main purpose of this letter? What do you want this letter to accomplish? Are you applying for a job, requesting material, offering thanks, lodging a complaint? Perhaps it is you who are answering a request for information about a product, procedure, service, or policy. The occasions for written correspondence are too many to list, but each letter should clearly state its purpose for the reader, just as a thesis in an essay presents your main idea.

2. Who is your "audience," the person to whom you are writing? As discussed in detail on pages 18–21 in Chapter 1, effective writers select the kinds of information, the level of complexity, and even the appropriate "voice" in response to their readers' needs, knowledge, and attitudes. Remember that no matter who your letter-reader happens to be, all readers want clarity, not confusion; order, not chaos; and useful information, not irrelevant chitchat. Put yourself in the reader's place: what should she or he know, understand, or decide to do after reading this letter?

3. What overall impression of yourself do you want your letter to present? All business correspondence should be courteous, with a tone that shows your appreciation for the reader's time and attention. Achieving this tone may be more difficult if you are writing a letter of complaint, but remember that to accomplish your purpose (a refund or an exchange of a purchase, for example), you must persuade, not antagonize, your reader. If you're too angry or frustrated to

maintain a reasonable tone, give yourself some time to cool off before writing. A respectful tone should not, on the other hand, sound phony or pretentious ("It is indeed regrettable but I must hereby inform you . . ."). Choose the same level of language you would use in one of your polished academic essays. In short, good business writing is clear, courteous, and direct.

Business Letter Format

Most traditional business letters are neatly typed on one side of 8½-by-11-inch white bond paper. Margins are usually set for a minimum of 1¼ inches at the top and at least one inch on the left and right sides and at the bottom. Almost all professional letters now use the "block form"—that is, lines of type are flush with the left margin and paragraphs are not indented. Envelopes should match the letter paper.

Business letters typically have six primary parts:

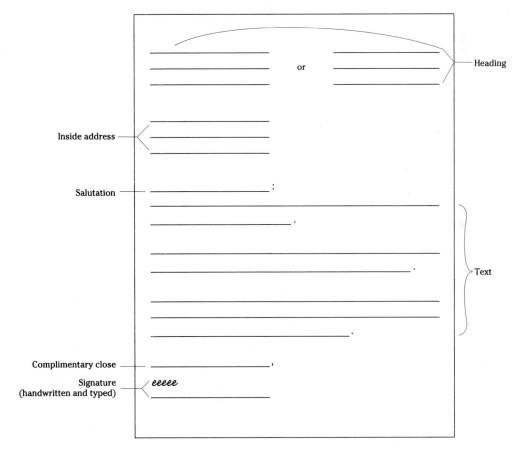

1. The **heading** of a letter is your address and the date, typed either above the inside address of the letter or in the upper right corner. If the heading is in the upper right position, the longest line should end at the one-inch margin on the right side of the page. All lines in your heading should begin evenly on the left. If you are using letterhead stationery (paper already imprinted with your business name, address, or logo), you need to add only the date.

2. The **inside address** contains the name of the person to whom you are writing, the person's title or position, the name of the company or organization, the full address (street or post office box, city, province, postal code). The first line of the inside address should appear at least two spaces below the last line of the heading. (The inside address information should be repeated exactly on your letter's envelope.)

Correct use of titles and positions can be tricky. Sometimes a person has a title and an additional position; other times, the title is lengthy. In general, if a person's title has more than two words, put it on a separate line:

Professor Cristina Amon

Dean, Faculty of Applied Science and Engineering

University of Toronto

Whenever possible, direct your letter to a specific person. If you do not know the name of the person and cannot discover it before your letter must be sent, you may address the correspondence to the position held by the appropriate person(s): General Manager, Graduate Advisor, Personnel Director, City Council, and so forth.

3. The **salutation** is your letter's greeting to your reader. Begin the salutation two lines down from the inside address, and greet the person formally using the word "Dear" plus title and name (Dear Mr. Smith, Dear Ms. Jones,* Dear Dr. Black). The salutation is traditionally followed by a colon rather than the more informal comma:

Dear Dr. Montoya:

Dear Personnel Director:

A caution: be careful to avoid sexist assumptions in your salutations. If you do not know the gender of the person to whom you are writing (initials and many first names—Chris, Pat, Jordan—are used by both men and women), do some research, if possible. When in doubt, use the title or position and last name (Dear Professor Chieu). Use of the full name (Dear Xin Chieu) or organization name (Dear Safety Council) may be preferable to the impersonal "Dear Sir or Madam," a phrase that seems stilted today.

4. The **text** of your letter refers to the message that appears in the paragraphs. As in essays, think of your text as having a beginning, a middle, and an ending.

---

*If you know that the woman you are writing to prefers to be addressed as Mrs. X, address her in this way. However, if you do not know her marital status or preferred title, Ms. may be the best choice. If possible, avoid the matter altogether by using her professional title: Dear Professor Smith, Dear Mayor Singh.

Although there is no rule about the number of paragraphs in any business letter, most letters contain:

- a first paragraph that clearly states the reason for writing (think about a thesis in an essay);

- one or more paragraphs that present the necessary details or explanation of the reason for writing (think body paragraphs in an essay);

- a last paragraph that sums up the message in a positive way, offers thanks if appropriate, and, on occasion, provides information to help reader and writer make contact (think conclusion in an essay).

Because professional people receive so much mail, business letters should be brief and to the point. *Above all, readers want clarity!* Scrutinize your prose for any words or phrases that might mislead or confuse your reader. Select precise words and create trim sentences that present your message in the clearest, most straightforward way possible. (For help writing clear, concise prose, review Chapters 6 and 7.)

If possible, without sacrificing clarity or necessary information, keep your letter to one page. Single-spaced paragraphs of eight lines or fewer are easiest to read. Leave a blank line between paragraphs. If you must go to a second page, type your name, the date, and the page number in an upper corner. If you discover that you have only one or two lines to carry over to the second page, try to condense your text or, if you must, squeeze or expand the margins just a bit. Try not to divide paragraphs between pages, and do not split a word between pages. Second and subsequent pages should be plain paper, without letterhead material.

5. The **complimentary closing** of a business letter is a conventional farewell to the reader, typed two lines below the last line of the text. The two most common phrases for closing formal business correspondence are "Sincerely" and "Yours truly." Stick with these unless you have a more informal relationship with the person you are writing. In those cases, you might use such closings as "Cordially" or "Warm regards." The first letter of the first closing word is capitalized, and the closing is followed by a comma.

6. The **signature** part of a business letter contains both your handwritten name and, beneath that, your typed name (plus your title, if appropriate). Leave approximately four blank lines for your handwritten name, which should be written in black ink:

Sincerely,

Jane Doe

Jane Doe
Professor of Philosophy

Do not forget to sign your letter! Such an oversight not only looks careless but may also suggest to the reader that this is merely a mass-produced form letter.

7. Some letters contain additional information below the signature. Typical notes include the word "enclosure" (or "encl.") to indicate inclusion of additional material (which may be named) or a distribution list to indicate other persons who are receiving a copy of this letter. Distribution is indicated by the word "copy" or by the letters *c, cc* (for "carbon copy"), or *xc* (for "Xeroxed copy"), followed by a colon and the name(s); if more than one person is listed, the names should appear in alphabetical order.

Copy: Mayor Sue Jones   Enclosure *or* Encl.
    or   *or*
cc: Mayor Sue Jones,   Enclosure: résumé
   Dr. Inga York

If someone else types your letter, put your initials in capital letters, a slash mark, and the typist's initials in lowercase:

JCW/ma

In formal business correspondence, avoid any sort of postscript (P.S.).

Some last advice: As in any piece of writing, always proofread for errors carefully—and repeatedly! Never trust your spell checker to catch all possible errors. Don't undercut the message you are sending by failing to revise misspelled words, inaccurate names, ungrammatical sentences, or sloppy punctuation. Also, be sure to select a clear, traditional type font (such as Times New Roman; no fancy script or gothic styles, please), set in a readable size (at least 12 point), and use only a printer that can produce dark, high-grade type.

▪ PRACTISING WHAT YOU'VE LEARNED

Find a recent business letter you or someone you know has received. This letter might be a request for a charitable donation, an announcement of some school policy, a letter of recommendation, or even a parking-violation summons. Assess the effectiveness of the letter: Is it clear? Informative? To the point? Write a one-paragraph critique of the letter that identifies both its strengths and any weaknesses you see.

▪ ASSIGNMENT

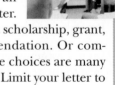

Writing business letters becomes easier with practise. Think of an upcoming occasion that will require you to write a professional letter. Perhaps you are asking for a job or accepting one. Or applying for a scholarship, grant, or school loan. Or requesting an interview or letter of recommendation. Or complaining to your landlord. Or ordering or returning a product. The choices are many but try to select a letter that you might indeed send sometime soon. Limit your letter to one page, and revise it as many times as necessary to illustrate your good understanding of purpose, audience, format, and style. Don't forget to proofread carefully!

■ Sample Business Letter

Art Tech Studio
802 Commercial Drive
Vancouver, BC V6J 3M7
May 10, 2008

Mr. Thomas Valdez
General Manager
Incredible Computers, Inc.
4255 Calgary Trail
Calgary, AB T5T 5R5

Dear Mr. Valdez:

Thank you for your May 5 order for twenty of my hand-designed covers for computer monitors and for your advance payment check of $250. I am delighted that your company wishes to stock my painted canvas dust covers in both your Calgary North and your Crossroads stores.

The computer covers are being packed in individual boxes this week and should arrive by Air Flight Mail at your main office no later than May 25. If you wish for me to express-mail the covers to you for quicker arrival, please let me know.

Many thanks again for your interest in my work and for your recent order. I am planning to attend a marketing seminar in Calgary, June 5–8; I will call you next week to see if we might arrange a brief meeting at your convenience on one of those days. Until then, should you need to contact me, please call my studio (970-555-6009).

Sincerely,

Rachel Zimmerman

Rachel Zimmerman

Enclosure: receipt

■ Creating Memos

A memo, short for "memorandum," is a common form of communication *within* a business or an organization. Memos are slightly more informal than business letters, and they may be addressed to more than one person (a committee, a sales staff, an advisory board, etc.). Memos may be sent up or down the chain of command at a particular workplace, or they may be distributed laterally, across a department or between offices. Although the format of the paper memo may vary slightly from organization to organization, it often appears arranged in this manner:

TO: name of recipient(s) and/or title(s)

FROM: name of sender and title; handwritten initials

DATE: day, month, year

SUBJECT: brief identification of the memo's subject matter

The message follows in one or more paragraphs.

Note that the name of the sender is usually accompanied by the sender's handwritten initials, rather than a full signature as in a business letter. Also, in some memos, the term "Re" ("in reference to") may be substituted for the word "Subject."

Many memos are brief, containing important bulletins, announcements, or reminders, as illustrated in this sample:

TO: Editorial Staff

FROM: Louise Presaria, Editor-in-Chief *LP*

DATE: April 22, 2004

RE: Silver Eagle Award Banquet

Because the current snowstorm is presenting problems with public transportation and also with heating outages in our building, the annual Silver Eagle Banquet originally scheduled for tomorrow night has been postponed for one week. It is now rescheduled for Thursday, April 29, beginning at 7:30 p.m., in the Whitaker Conference room.

I look forward to seeing you all there. Each of you has done a marvellous job this year and greatly deserves to share the benefits that come with our industry's most prestigious award.

Other in-house memos—those explaining policies or procedures, for example—may be long and complex. Lengthy memos may begin with a summary or statement of general purpose and may use headings (such as "Background Information," "Previous Action," or "Recommendations") to identify various parts of the discussion.

All business memos, regardless of length, share a common goal: the clear, concise communication of useful information from writer to reader.

■ Sending Professional E-Mail

Although the world of work will never be totally "paperless," more businesses today are relying on computer-based communications to send or request information, both inside and outside their organizations.

Electronic mail, or e-mail, has a number of advantages over the business letter, memo, and telephone. It's faster and easier than postal service (humorously known to some as "snail mail"), as you can compose or forward a message to one person or many people, across the building or across the country, and receive a reply almost instantly. Messages may be sent anytime, day or night, and are held until the recipient is able to open them. Unlike the telephone, most e-mail has an "attachments" feature that may contain documents, forms, graphics, or pictures.

Because e-mail is so useful in so many ways to many different kinds of businesses and organizations, there is no one-size-fits-all format. Consequently, it's always a good idea to acquaint yourself with the customary use of e-mail at your place of work. In addition, here are some suggestions for improving the quality of all electronic communications:

1. **Choose a professional e-mail address**. Make your name plain, so your recipient can identify you on their inbox right away, and so your business correspondents can remember your address intuitively. An address for Leeta Kosinsky can be easily remembered if the address is something like "lkosinsky@server.ca" or "leeta.kosinsky@server.ca," but if Leeta's address is based on some private joke or personal experience ("kitkat@server.ca"), then it's harder for her correspondent to remember her address easily. Private names or misspelled words ("ridikulus@server.ca; ludacris@server.ca") are unprofessional and they detract from your professional credibility. Avoid using hotmail and gmail addresses for business and formal needs, as messages from these servers often get automatically deleted by recipients' programs as spam, and themselves delete messages they interpret as mass mailings. Important messages you send might never get to your recipient, and important messages from a sender (for example, the company's head office is sending a time-sensitive message about health insurance to all 600 employees) might be lost.

2. **Use a helpful subject line.** Successful business leaders today may receive scores of e-mail messages every day, so many that they are tempted to delete any unrecognizable mail that might be "spam" (an unsolicited message or sales offer) or contain a "virus" that might destroy their files. To ensure that your message will be opened and read, always use specific words in the subject line to clearly delineate the central focus or key words of your correspondence ("Project Thunderbolt contracts"). Sometimes you may need to use an even more specific subject line. For example a subject line that reads "Subject: Class on Wednesday" could represent a variety of different messages, and a careless recipient who doesn't open the e-mail might not realize

there is a last-minute quiz that day and might just think it's a reminder that there is class that day. A subject line that reads "Subject: Bring Textbook to Class on Wednesday" would get the core message even to recipients who don't open the e-mail or put off opening the email. Using a specific subject line will also be helpful if your reader wants to reread your message later and needs to find it quickly in a long list of e-mails.

3. Begin appropriately. Unlike a business letter, e-mail needs no heading or inside address, but a new electronic communication should begin with an appropriate greeting, depending on the formality of the occasion. For example, if you are writing an officer of another company to ask for information, you might begin with a traditional salutation (Dear Mr. Hall:). An informal memo to a coworker might have a more casual greeting, depending on your relationship to that person (Hello, Bill; Good morning, Ms. Merrill). Some companies prefer the standard To-From-Date-Subject memo form discussed earlier in this chapter. In your university or college life you will need to send many formal e-mails, whether you are applying for a loan, asking about registration dates, or communicating about course materials. If you are e-mailing a person in the registrar's office, for example, or your college or university professor, it is inappropriate to address them with a colloquial greeting such as "Hey, Dr. Smith" or "Hi, Jasbinder," because your relationship with them is formal.

4. Keep your message brief. Long messages are difficult to read on screens; all that scrolling and flipping back and forth to check information can be tiresome. If possible, confine your message to one screen. Working people are busy, so try to follow the advice given previously in this chapter regarding business letters and memos: clearly state your purpose, explain in a concise manner, and conclude gracefully.

5. Make it easy to read. To avoid contributing to your reader's eyestrain, write messages that are visually pleasant. Keep your paragraphs short, and skip lines between each paragraph. If your message is long, break it up with headings, numbered lists, or "bullets" (use lowercase "o"). Use a readable, plain font. Some e-mails will not allow a change in type, so to indicate boldface or italics you may use asterisks (*) around a word or phrase for emphasis—but do so sparingly.

6. Check your tone. Your e-mail messages should sound professional and cordial. Unlike personal e-mail that may contain slang, fragments, asides, or funny graphics, business e-mails should be written in good standard English and be straight to the point. If you're angry, resist the temptation to fly to the computer and "flame"; cool off and compose a thoughtful, persuasive response instead. Be especially careful about the use of irony or humour: without nonverbal clues, readers may misinterpret your words and react in a manner opposite the one you intended. In general, strive for a polite, friendly tone, using the clearest, most precise words you can muster.

7. Sign off. If your e-mail is performing a task similar to that of a business letter, you may wish to close in a traditional way:

Yours truly,

Scott Muranjan

You may also want to create a standard sign-off that not only includes your name but also your title, telephone and fax number, mailing and e-mail address. Such information is helpful for readers who wish to contact you later.

However, if your e-mail is more akin to an informal memo between coworkers, you may find it appropriate to end with a friendly thought or word of thanks and your first name:

> I'm looking forward to working with you on the Blue file. See you at
> Tuesday's meeting.
> Scott

Allow your sense of occasion and audience to dictate the kind of closing each e-mail requires.

7. Revise, proofread, copy, send. The very ease of e-mail makes it tempting to send messages that may not be truly ready to go. All your professional correspondence should look just that: professional. Take some time to revise for clarity and tone; always proofread. Double-check figures and dates, and run the spell checker if you have one. If time permits, print out a paper or "hard copy" of important messages to look over before you hit the Send button. If you need to keep track of your correspondence, make a computer file or a print copy for your office. Think about the consequences of sending unfinished, factually inaccurate, ungrammatical, badly spelled messages.

Problems to Avoid

Electronic mail has revolutionized the workplace, but it is not without its disadvantages. Computers crash, files vaporize, printers freeze, and so on. Work on developing patience and give yourself time to use other methods of communication if necessary. Meanwhile, here are two other tips:

Business e-mail is not private. Perhaps because of individual passwords or because of experience with sealed postal mail, employees often believe that their e-mail is private correspondence. It is not! Employers have the legal right to read any e-mail sent from their organizations. Moreover, you never know when someone may be peering at a screen over the shoulder of the intended recipient. And there's always the danger of hitting the wrong button, sending your thoughts to an entire list of people when you meant to contact only one. To avoid embarrassing yourself—or even endangering your job—never send inappropriate comments, angry responses, petty remarks, or personal information through your business e-mail. Never send confidential or "top secret" business information through e-mail without proper authorization. Learn to use e-mail in a productive way that protects both you and your organization.

Mind your netiquette! Although no one requires that you don your white kid gloves to hit those computer keys, rules of etiquette for e-mail writers are taking form these days. Here are a few suggestions for well-behaved writers:

- Don't "shout" your messages in all capital letters. IT'S TOO HARD TO READ A SCREEN FULL OF SAME-SIZED LETTERS. Occasionally, you may type a word in capital letters for emphasis, but use this technique sparingly. (For more advice on proper tone, see page 458.)

- Be cautious about using Net and texting shorthand or in-house abbreviations ("the TR6 project"), especially in messages to other organizations. If certain shorthand signs or phrases, such as BTW (by the way), FWIW (for what it's worth), or G2G (got to go), are routinely used in casual e-mail at your place of work, feel free to adopt them. However, most business correspondence is more formal and not all abbreviations may be universally recognized. When in doubt, spell it out. Business messages depend on clarity and a mutual understanding of all terms.

- Don't ever, ever use "emoticons" in business writing. Emoticons are typed "smiley" faces read sideways that many people find more annoying than ground glass in a sandwich. Instead of relying on these gaggingly cute symbols to communicate emotions of happiness, sadness, surprise, or irony, find the right words instead.

- Never forward anyone else's e-mail message without permission, especially if that message contains controversial and/or hurtful statements or confidential material. (Because other people often break this rule, think twice before *you* write.)

■ Designing Résumés

A résumé is a document that presents a brief summary of your educational background, work experiences, professional skills, special qualifications, and honours; some résumés also contain a brief list of references. You may be asked to submit a résumé on a variety of occasions, most often to supplement your applications for jobs, interviews, promotions, scholarships, grants, fellowships, or other kinds of opportunities. Because prospective employers are the largest target audience for résumés, the following section offers advice to help job seekers design the most effective document possible.

Job seekers most frequently send their résumés with "cover letters" directed to particular employers. To prepare each cover letter, follow the basic steps for writing the traditional business letter, as outlined earlier in this chapter. In the first paragraph, clearly tell your reader why you are writing: the specific job you are applying for, and why. Devote one or more paragraphs in the "body" of your letter to noting your education or professional experience or both, explaining why you are a good match for the advertised position or how you might benefit the organization. Your concluding paragraph should express thanks for the employer's consideration and briefly re-emphasize your interest in the job; in this paragraph you may also mention contact information or, in some situations, indicate your availability for an interview. If the employer is interested, he or she will scan your résumé for more details and possibly distribute copies to others involved in the hiring process. The sample cover letter here would accompany Brent J. Monroe's résumé on page 466 in this chapter.

■ Sample Cover Letter

Brent J. Monroe
417 Kearney Lake Road
Halifax, NS B3M 4P6
(902) 555-4567
BJMonroe@server.ca
July 3, 2008

M. Choi, Human Resource Director
Windrush Exports
3290 Box Lane
Halifax, NS B8S 2G1

Dear Ms. Choi,

I would like to apply for the position of Assistant Payroll Manager, as advertised on your website. At a recruitment fair at Dalhousie University last fall, I was encouraged by Mr. Jorge Ramirez, the head of your payroll department, to apply for a position in Windrush Exports once I graduated with my business management degree. I am eager to become a part of a company with such a stellar level of integrity and high work standards.

My recent graduation with a B.S. in Business Administration from Dalhousie University and my experience as a manager at a restaurant qualify me for this position. A significant number of my degree courses were in accounting, with a special interest in payroll management and design. My coursework and practical experience with word processing combine to give me strong skills that are directly relevant to the requirements posted for the Assistant Payroll Manager position. As part of my degree requirement, I successfully completed several large projects in which I designed payrolls, spreadsheets, and verification programs for businesses with more than 200 employees. My abilities in my academic and business skills have been acknowledged at my university, with the honours I have received and the responsible positions I have held. The award for Outstanding Student Achievement (2008) and the President's Scholarship, which I received two years in a row, testify to my hard work and academic prowess. The elected position of Treasurer of the Business Students' Association represents the level of trust and responsibility conferred upon me by my peers. As the Treasurer, I was responsible for administering a budget of $100,000 over the fiscal year. I was able to save the Association 15 percent of its annual costs by negotiating new business contracts, which offered more cost-effective packages. In my position as Assistant Manager for Poppa's Pizza, I assisted in organizing schedules, training employees, and in maintaining positive customer relations. During my time there, I was able to design a more efficient, streamlined scheduling system, which resulted in fairer shift allotments and more reliable employee work attendance.

I believe that I can contribute well to your payroll department's needs. I have the necessary skills to do the tasks outlined in your advertisement, and the ability to learn new tasks quickly, and to work hard and efficiently. Please do not hesitate to contact me at BJMonroe@server.ca or at (902) 555-4567 with any questions. My references are listed at the end of my résumé. Thank you for your consideration of my application.

Sincerely,

Brent J. Monroe.
Brent J. Monroe

Because employers today may receive hundreds of applications for a single job, it is important to present yourself as positively as possible in your letter and résumé. If your campus has a career centre, seek it out as your first step. Career centres often have extraordinary resources: sample cover letters and résumés, hints for interviews, information on electronic job searching, and much more. Because there are multiple ways to arrange a résumé, you will find it useful to familiarize yourself with some representative samples before you begin working on your own.

Although there is no single blueprint for all résumés, there is one guiding principle: *select and arrange your information in the way that most effectively highlights your strengths to your prospective employer.* Think of your résumé as a one-page advertisement for yourself.

To find the best way to "sell" yourself to an employer, you might choose to adopt one of the two most popular arrangement styles:

- *Functional format:* This arrangement places the reader's focus more directly on the job seeker's education and skills than on limited work experience. It is better suited for job seekers who are new graduates or those just entering the work force. Most résumés of this type are one page.

- *Experiential format:* This style emphasizes professional experience by placing work history in the most prominent position, listing the current or most important employment first. This format might be best for non-traditional students who have a work history before school or for those students who have worked throughout their college careers. If the list of relevant professional experience is lengthy, this kind of résumé may extend to a second page, if necessary. You might want to leave out weak or unrelated work history if appropriate, as long as you do not lie by omission or mislead your potential employer.

Before you begin drafting your résumé, make a list of the information you want to include. Then think about the best ways to group your material, and select an appropriate title for each section. Some of the common content areas include the following:

1. **Heading.** Located at the top of your résumé, this section identifies you and presents your contact information: your full name, address, phone number, and

e-mail address if you have one. You may wish to put your name in slightly bigger type or in bold letters.

2. **Employment objective.** Some job seekers choose to include a statement describing the kind of employment or specific position they are seeking. Others omit this section, making this information clear in their cover letters. If you do include this section, always substitute a brief, specific objective for trite, overblown language any job seeker in the world might write:

> *Trite:* Seeking employment with a company offering intellectual challenges and opportunities for professional growth
>
> *Specific:* A microbiology research position in a laboratory or centre working on disease prevention and control

If you have the time and resources to customize a résumé for each job announcement you respond to, you can use this section to show that the position you most want matches the one advertised. However, if you plan to use one résumé for a variety of job applications, beware presenting an employment objective so narrowly focused that it excludes you from a particular application pool.

3. **Education.** If you have no extensive, relevant, or recent work experience, this section might best appear next on your résumé. Begin with the highest degree you have earned or, if you are about to graduate, you may present the anticipated graduation date. Include the name of the institution and its location and, if relevant, your major, minor, or special concentration. Some graduates with a high grade point average also include that information. This section might also contain any professional certificates or licenses (teaching, real estate, counselling, etc.) you have earned or other educational information you deem relevant to a particular job search (internships, research projects, study-abroad programs, honours classes, or other special training).

4. **Professional experience.** If you wish to emphasize your work history, place this section after your heading or employment objective, rather than your educational background. In this section, list the position title, name of employer, city and state, and employment dates, with the most current job or relevant work experience first. Some résumés include brief statements describing the responsibilities or accomplishments of each position. If you choose to include such descriptions, try to be specific (Prepared monthly payroll for 35 employees) rather than general (Performed important financial tasks monthly); use action verbs (supervised, developed, organized, trained, created, etc.) that present your efforts in a strong way. Use past tense verbs for work completed and present tense for current responsibilities.

   Note that résumés traditionally do not use the word "I"; beginning brief descriptive phrases with a strong verb, rather than repeating "I had responsibility for . . . ," saves precious space on a résumé.

5. **Skills.** Because you want to stress your value to a prospective employer, you may wish to note relevant professional skills or special abilities you have to offer. This section may be especially important if you do not have a work history; many recent graduates place this section immediately following the education section to underscore the skills they could bring to the workplace. For example, you

might list technical skills you possess or mention expertise in a foreign language if that might look useful to a company with overseas connections.

6. **Honours, awards, activities.** In this section, list those awards, scholarships, honours, and prizes that show others have selected you as an outstanding worker, student, writer, teacher, and so on. Here (or perhaps in a section for related skills or experiences) you might also add leadership roles in organizations, and even certain kinds of volunteer work, if mentioning these would further your case. Although you don't want to trivialize your résumé by listing irrelevant activities, think hard about your life from a "skills" angle. Coordinating a campus charity project, for example, may indicate just the kinds of managerial skills an employer is looking for. Don't pad your résumé—but don't undersell yourself either.

7. **References.** Some employers ask immediately for references, persons they may contact for more information about you and your work or academic experiences; other employers ask for references later in the hiring process. If references are requested with the initial application letter, the information may be listed at end of the résumé if it is a one-page résumé, or, preferably, on an attached page, especially if the résumé is several pages long. Reference information includes the person's full name and title or position, the name and address of the person's business or organization, telephone number, and e-mail address, if available. Do not list friends or neighbours as references; résumé references should be academics or professionals who are familiar with your work.

Critique Your Page Appeal

Once you have decided on your résumé's content, you also need to consider its visual appeal. Because employers often scan résumés quickly, your page should be not only informative but also professional looking and easy to read. Unless you have a compelling reason for another choice, always laser print your résumé on high-quality white or off-white paper. You may highlight your section titles (education, work experiences, skills, etc.) by using boldface or large print, but don't overuse such print. Balance your text and white space in a pleasing arrangement.

If you have problems arranging your material (too much information jammed on the page or so little that your text looks lonely, for example), go back to the career centre to look at ways others handled similar problems (some large copy shops also have sample books). A good page design, like a good haircut, can frame your best features in the most engaging way.

Most important: always proofread your résumé for errors in grammar, punctuation, spelling, spacing, or typing! Because you want your résumé to look as professional as possible, make a point of having several careful (human) readers proofread your final draft.

Problems to Avoid

Remain ethical. Never lie on a résumé! Never, ever! Although you want to present yourself in the best possible ways, never fib about your experience, forge credentials you don't have, take credit for someone else's work, or overstate your participation in a project. No matter what you have heard about "puffery" in résumés ("everyone exaggerates, so why shouldn't I?"), avoid embarrassment (or even legal action) by always telling the truth. Instead of misrepresenting yourself, find ways to identify and arrange your knowledge and skills in ways that best highlight your strengths.

Contact your references in advance. You *must* obtain permission from each person before you list him or her as a reference. Even if you know the person well, use your good manners here: in person or in a politely written note or letter, ask in advance of your job application if you may name him or her as a reference. Once permission is granted, it's smart to give your references your résumé and any other information that might help them help you if they are contacted by a prospective employer. Although a former boss or teacher may remember you well, they may be hazy about your exact dates of employment or the semester of your course work. Give them a helpful list of places, dates, skills, and—though you may have to overcome your sense of modesty—tactfully remind them of any outstanding work you did.

It's also good manners (and smart) to send your references a thank-you note, expressing your appreciation for their part in your job search (such notes are absolutely *required* if people wrote letters of recommendation for you). Thank-you notes should be written on stationery and sent through the mail; e-mail notes are not appropriate.

Add personal information thoughtfully. Federal law protects you: employers may not discriminate on the basis of ethnicity, race, religion, age, or gender. You should not include on your résumé any personal information (marital status, number of children, birth date, country of origin, etc.) that is not relevant to the job search. Although you may, if you wish, include information on your résumé about relevant personal interests (travel, theatrical experience, volunteer rescue work, etc.), you should be aware that employers may not consider such details useful. Don't squander your résumé space on inessential information! A better plan: if you've spent a great deal of your time in some after-work or extracurricular activity, identify the *skills* you have developed that will transfer to the workplace (customer relations, public speaking, editing, etc.). Instead of just describing yourself, show prospective employers what you can *do* for them.

Special Note: An increasing number of websites are helping employers and job seekers find each other through the posting of jobs and résumés. If you do post your résumé on such a site, choose your words carefully. Many prospective employers now use applicant tracking software to look for keywords in résumés to match their needs. For example, a business seeking an accountant to assist its offices in Paris and Rome might flag only those résumés containing the words "CGA," "French," and "Italian." So, if you are interested in a particular job advertised on the Web, study the language of the job description and consider repeating, where appropriate, its key words in your résumé. Do not, however, include links to personal websites that may include private or embarrassing information (photographs, etc.).

■ Sample Résumés

The first résumé that follows was designed by a recent university graduate. Because he did not have an extensive work record, he chose a functional format to emphasize his education, business skills, and scholastic honours. The second résumé briefly notes specific skills from previous academic and work experiences that might interest a prospective employer.

■ Sample Résumé #1

Brent J. Monroe

417 Kearney Lake Road   (902) 555-4567
Halifax, NS B3M 4P6   BJMonroe@server.ca

Education

B.S. in Business Administration, Dalhousie University, May 2008
A.S., Front Range Community College, May 2005

Professional Skills

Accounting

Spreadsheet programs
Amortization schedules
Payroll design and verification
Contracts and invoices

Computer

Word processing: Microsoft Word, WordPerfect
Spreadsheets: Excel, Select
Presentations: PowerPoint
Website design

Awards and Activities

Outstanding Student Achievement Award, School of Business Administration,
    Dalhousie University, 2008
President's Scholarship, Dalhousie University, 2006 and 2007
Treasurer, Business Students Association, Dalhousie University, 2006

Employment

Assistant Manager, Poppa's Pizza; Halifax, Nova Scotia, 6/02–12/03

References

Professor Gwen Lesser	Professor Ralph Berber	Mr. Randy Attree
Department of Accounting	Department of Finance	Manager, Poppa's Pizza
Dalhousie University	Dalhousie University	Halifax Shopping Centre
6100 University Ave.	6100 University Ave	Halifax, NS B3J CH6
Halifax, NS B3H BJ5	Halifax, NS B3H BJ5	(902) 555-1608
(902) 555-7890	(902) 555-2344	
Glesser@dal.ca	Rberber@dal.ca	

■ Sample Résumé #2

ROSEMARY SILVA

3000 Balliol Street   (416) 555-6428
Toronto, Ontario T3X 1M2   Rosesilva@netscape.net

Objective

To secure a full-time position as an admissions counsellor at a mental health or addiction recovery facility

Education

B.A., University of Toronto, May 2004. Major: Psychology. Minor: Spanish.

Internship and Research Experience

Intern Detoxification Counsellor, Angelwings Recovery Centre, Oshawa, Ontario; January–May 2004.

Provided one-on-one counselling for in-patient residents; conducted admission interviews and prepared mental and physical evaluation reports; monitored physical vitals of patients; responded to crisis phone calls from outpatients; performed basic paramedical techniques; referred patients to other community agencies; supplied substance abuse information to patients and families.

Psychology Research Lab Assistant, University of Toronto, under the direction of Professor Charlotte Turner; September–December 2003.

Helped conduct experiments on U of T student-volunteers to measure the relationship of memory and academic success: explained experiment procedures, set up computers, recorded student information, validated research credit slips.

Employment

Night Security Dispatcher, University of Toronto, Campus Police Department; May 2002–April 2004.

Accurately received and responded to emergency and non-emergency calls and radio transmissions; communicated emergency information to appropriate agencies, such as the Toronto Police Service and Rape Crisis Centre; dispatched security units to handle crisis situations; wrote detailed records of incoming calls, security patrols, and responses.

References Available Upon Request

▪ ASSIGNMENT

Prepare a one-page résumé for your professional use at this time or in the near future. While you are in school, you might use this résumé to apply for a scholarship, an internship, a summer job, or a part-time position. Arrange your information to emphasize your strengths, and don't forget to thoroughly proofread several times before you print your final draft. (If you keep a copy of this résumé handy and revise it regularly, you will be ready to respond quickly should a job or other opportunity unexpectedly present itself.)

▪ Writing Post-Interview Letters

After you interview for a job you want, consider writing a follow-up note to the prospective employer. This letter should be more than a polite thank you for the interview, however. Use the opportunity to again emphasize your skills. Begin by thanking the person for his or her time, but move on to show that you think, now more than ever, that you are the right person for the position and for the organization. Illustrate this claim by showing that during the interview you really listened and observed: "After hearing about your goals for new product X, I know I could contribute because. . . ." Or remind your interviewer of reasons to hire you: "You stressed your company's need for someone with XYZ skills. My internship training in that area. . . ." In other words, use this follow-up letter not only to offer your thanks but also to gently advertise yourself (and your good writing skills) one more time.

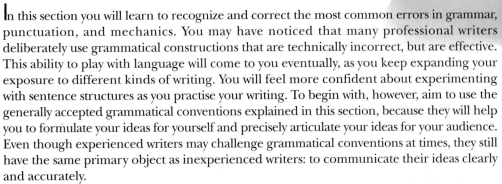

Part 4

A Concise Handbook

In this section you will learn to recognize and correct the most common errors in grammar, punctuation, and mechanics. You may have noticed that many professional writers deliberately use grammatical constructions that are technically incorrect, but are effective. This ability to play with language will come to you eventually, as you keep expanding your exposure to different kinds of writing. You will feel more confident about experimenting with sentence structures as you practise your writing. To begin with, however, aim to use the generally accepted grammatical conventions explained in this section, because they will help you to formulate your ideas for yourself and precisely articulate your ideas for your audience. Even though experienced writers may challenge grammatical conventions at times, they still have the same primary object as inexperienced writers: to communicate their ideas clearly and accurately.

To help you with the mechanics of your writing, the main parts of speech will be defined and explained with examples. Each error will then be explained as simply as possible, with a minimum of technical language. Beside each rule you will find the editing mark or abbreviation most often used to identify that error; each rule is also numbered for easy reference. Exercises throughout each chapter will help you practise your grammar and punctuation skills. ■

Chapter 18

Major Errors in Grammar

■ Parts of Speech

Before we begin our discussion of errors, here are some brief definitions and examples of the main parts of a sentence.

Noun: represents a person, place, thing or idea

Examples: Stephen Harper (person)

Lunenberg (place)

canoe (thing)

patriotism (idea)

Stephen Harper paddled his *canoe* in the *harbour* of historical *Lunenberg* to demonstrate his *patriotism*.

Note: a proper noun represents a person's name (Stephen Harper), while a common noun is more general, and can represent a variety of ideas such as relationships (brother) or professions (author). A group or collective noun, such as "community" or "family," functions as a single noun, even though it represents a group of people, places, or objects. Compound nouns, such as "work ethic," combine two different nouns to create new meaning.

Pronoun: refers to and represents the noun. The noun can be earlier in the sentence or in a directly related sentence within the paragraph.

Examples:	she, his
	Sarah could donate her bone marrow to Joel because *she* was *his* sister.
Singular:	represents one person, place, or thing
	Examples: dentist, town, rose, ideal
	The *dentist* in our small *town* has an awkward schedule.
Plural:	represents several people, places, or things
	Examples: magicians, beaches, towers, illusions
	The *magicians* were attempting some challenging *illusions.*
Verb:	represents an action. Verbs are affected by tense ("when") and singular or plural nouns.

Examples:

- reads, analyzes (simple present): He *reads* the articles and then *analyzes* them.

- have read, have analyzed (present perfect): I *have read* his report and *have analyzed* his findings.

- reading, analyzing (present progressive): Will *is reading* and *analyzing* the results of the experiment.

- read, analyzed (simple past): I *read* and *analyzed* the materials very carefully.

- had read, had analyzed (past perfect): Soledad *had analyzed* his treatise after Camille *had read* it.

- will read, will analyze (simple future): Clark will *read* and *analyze* Lois's report tomorrow.

- will have read, will have analyzed (future perfect): By Wednesday, I *will have read* and *analyzed* five conflicting studies on GM foods.

   Note that in some of the above examples, words such as "had" or "will have" are not repeated, but are assumed to be there in sentences that have used these terms already. In other words, in the sentence, "By Wednesday, I will have read and analyzed five conflicting studies on genetically modified foods," it is not necessary to write "will have" with the second verb, as it can create a wordy or awkward style.

Adjective:	describes a noun
	Example: tall, gracious, ideological
	The *tall, gracious* woman questioned the speaker's *ideological* position at the lecture.
Adverb:	describes an action
	Example: wildly, passionately, hopelessly
	"Cecily, I love you *wildly, passionately, hopelessly,*" cried Algernon as he held her hand *surreptitiously.* (here, the verbs being described are "love" and "held")

■ Sentences

The parts of speech defined above are used to construct entire thoughts in units or sentences. Here are some common terms used in referring to smaller units of those sentences.

Subject:	the focus of a sentence, usually a noun or pronoun
	Examples: *Tyler* cried.
	The dog ate my homework.
Compound Subject:	two or more connected subjects
	Example: Neither *pancakes and bacon* nor *blueberries and ice cream* make me dream, swoon, and faint.
Predicate:	usually includes a verb and represents what happens in the sentence, whether it is an action or a description. The predicate is connected to the subject.
	Examples: Tyler *cried.* (simple predicate consisting only of a verb)
	The dog *ate my homework.* (predicate consists of verb and direct object)
Compound Predicate:	two or more connected predicates
	Example: Pancakes and bacon make me *dream, swoon, and faint.*
Direct Object:	the sentence's action is directly linked to this; it is the verb's primary target
	Example: He loved *her.*
	The speaker's argument addresses *a serious social problem.*
Indirect Object:	the indirect object, usually a noun placed before the direct object and sometimes separated from it by a preposition, indicates what, to whom, or for whom the action is being done. It is the verb's secondary target.
	Examples: The carver showed his *assistant* a new design.
	Professor Higgins gave *Eliza, a cockney flower girl,* lessons in elocution.
	Eliza threw her *professor* a slipper.
Simple Sentence:	a group of words containing a subject and predicate that can stand on its own
	Example: Joy left her office.
	Jung disassociated himself from Freud's theories.
	Chantal's performance at the concert will not be televised.

Compound Sentence:	two simple sentences joined by a conjunction, or connecting word
	Example: *Joy left her office and walked to the market.*
	Jung disassociated himself from Freud's theories and wrote his own.
	Chantal will perform at the concert, but it will not be televised.
Complex Sentence:	usually contains at least an independent clause and a dependent clause
Independent Clause:	a group of words containing a subject and predicate, which is usually a part of a longer sentence but can stand on its own
	Example: *The dragon considered his options* before answering Bilbo.
Dependent or Subordinate Clause:	a group of words containing a subject and verb, but its connection to a subordinating word means it cannot stand on its own
	Example: *Although the broomstick was new,* no one could fly on it.

■ Errors with Verbs

18a Faulty Agreement   S–V Agr

Make your verb agree in number with its subject; a singular subject takes a singular verb, and a plural subject takes a plural verb.

Incorrect	*Lester Peabody,* principal of the Kung Fu School of Grammar, *don't* agree that gum chewing should be banned in the classroom.
Correct	*Lester Peabody,* principal of the Kung Fu School of Grammar, *doesn't* agree that gum chewing should be banned in the classroom.
Incorrect	The *actions* of the new premier *hasn't* been consistent with her campaign promises.
Correct	The *actions* of the new premier *haven't* been consistent with her campaign promises.

Compound subjects joined by "and" take a plural verb, unless the subject refers to a single person or a single unit.

Examples	*Bean sprouts* and *tofu are* dishes Fenfang won't consider eating. ["Bean sprouts" and "tofu" are a compound subject joined by "and"; therefore, use a plural verb.]
	The *winner* and new *champion refuses* to give up the microphone at the news conference. ["Winner" and "champion" refer to a single person; therefore, use a singular verb.]

Listed here are some of the most confusing subject–verb agreement problems:

1. With a collective noun: a singular noun referring to a collection of elements as a unit generally takes a singular verb.

Incorrect	During boring parts of the Transcendental Vegetation lecture, the *class* often *chant* to the music of Norman Bates and the Shower Heads.
Correct	During boring parts of the Transcendental Vegetation lecture, the *class* often *chants* to the music of Norman Bates and the Shower Heads.
Incorrect	The *army* of the new nation *want* shoes, bullets, and weekend passes.
Correct	The *army* of the new nation *wants* shoes, bullets, and weekend passes.

2. With a relative pronoun ("that," "which," and "who") used as a subject: the verb agrees with its antecedent, i.e., the word being described.

Incorrect	The manager rejected a shipment of *shirts, which was* torn.
Correct	The manager rejected a shipment of *shirts, which were* torn.

3. With "each," "everybody," "everyone," and "neither" as the subject: use a singular verb even when followed by a plural construction.

Incorrect	*Each* of the children *think* Mom and Dad are automatic teller machines.
Correct	*Each* of the children *thinks* Mom and Dad are automatic teller machines.
Incorrect	Although only a few of the students saw the teacher pull out his hair, *everybody know* why he did it.
Correct	Although only a few of the students saw the teacher pull out his hair, *everybody knows* why he did it.
Incorrect	*Neither have* a dime left by the second of the month.
Correct	*Neither has* a dime left by the second of the month.

4. With "either . . . or" and "neither . . . nor": the verb agrees with the nearer item.

Incorrect	Neither rain nor dogs nor *gloom of night keep* the mail carrier from delivering bills.
Correct	Neither rain nor dogs nor *gloom of night keeps* the mail carrier from delivering bills.
Incorrect	Either Setimkia or his *neighbours is* hosting a come-as-you-are breakfast.
Correct	Either Setimkia or his *neighbours are* hosting a come-as-you-are breakfast.

5. With "here is (are)" and "there is (are)": the verb agrees with the number indicated by the subject following the verb.

Incorrect	*There is* only two good *reasons* for missing this law class: death and jury duty.
Correct	*There are* only two good *reasons* for missing this law class: death and jury duty.

Incorrect	To help you do your shopping quickly, Mr. Scrooge, *here are* a *list* of gifts under a dollar.
Correct	To help you do your shopping quickly, Mr. Scrooge, *here is* a *list* of gifts under a dollar.

6. With plural nouns intervening between subject and verb: the verb still agrees with the subject.

Incorrect	The *jungle,* with its poisonous plants, wild animals, and biting insects, *make* Herman long for the sidewalks of Topeka.
Correct	The *jungle,* with its poisonous plants, wild animals, and biting insects, *makes* Herman long for the sidewalks of Topeka.

7. With nouns plural in form but singular in meaning: a singular verb is usually correct.

Examples	*News travels* slowly if it comes through the post office.
	Charades is the exhibitionist's game of choice.
	Politics is often the rich person's hobby.

18b Subjunctive   V Sub

When you make a wish or a statement that is contrary to fact, use the subjunctive verb form "were."

Incorrect	I wish I *was* queen so I could levy a tax on men who spit.
Correct	I wish I *were* queen so I could levy a tax on men who spit. [This expresses a wish.]
Incorrect	If "Fightin' Henry" *was* a foot taller and thirty pounds heavier, we would all be in trouble.
Correct	If "Fightin' Henry" *were* a foot taller and thirty pounds heavier, we would all be in trouble. [This proposes a statement contrary to fact.]

18c Tense Shift   T

In most cases, the first verb in a sentence establishes the tense of any later verb. Keep your verbs within the same time frame.

Incorrect	Tony *saw* the police car coming up behind, so he *turns* into the next alley.
Correct	Tony *saw* the police car coming up behind, so he *turned* into the next alley.
Incorrect	Horace *uses* an artificial sweetener in his coffee all day, so he *felt* a pizza and a hot-fudge sundae *were* fine for dinner.
Correct	Horace *uses* an artificial sweetener in his coffee all day, so he *feels* a pizza and a hot-fudge sundae *are* fine for dinner.

Incorrect	Rex the Wonder Horse *was* obviously very smart because he *taps* out the telephone numbers of the stars with his hoof.
Correct	Rex the Wonder Horse *was* obviously very smart because he *tapped* out the telephone numbers of the stars with his hoof.

18d Split Infinitive   Sp I

Many authorities insist that you never separate *to* from its verb; today, however, some grammarians allow the split infinitive except in the most formal kinds of writing. Nevertheless, because it offends some readers, it is probably best to avoid the construction unless clarity or emphasis is clearly served by its use.

Traditional	A swift kick is needed *to start* the machine properly.
Untraditional	A swift kick is needed *to* properly *start* the machine.
Traditional	The teacher wanted Lori *to communicate* her ideas clearly.
Untraditional	The teacher wanted Lori *to* clearly *communicate* her ideas.

18e Double Negatives   D Neg

Don't use a negative verb and a negative qualifier together.

Incorrect	I *can't hardly* wait until Jean-Claude gets his jaw out of traction, so I can challenge him to a bubble gum blowing contest.
Correct	I *can hardly* wait until Jean-Claude gets his jaw out of traction, so I can challenge him to a bubble gum blowing contest.
Incorrect	Even when he flew his helicopter upside down over her house, she *wouldn't scarcely* look at him.
Correct	Even when he flew his helicopter upside down over her house, she *would scarcely* look at him.

18f Passive Voice   Pass

"Active voice" refers to sentences in which the subject performs the action. "Passive voice" refers to sentences in which the subject is acted upon.

Active	The police *pulled* over the van full of stolen ski sweaters.
Passive	The van full of stolen ski sweaters *was pulled* over by the police.

Although conventions vary among disciplines, when passive constructions are chosen in professional writing, they are used to maintain objective distance. Practice is needed here to prevent unclear writing, however. Therefore, in general your prose style will improve if you choose strong, active-voice verbs over wordy or unclear passive constructions.

Wordy passive construction	For years Alberta schoolchildren *were taught* by their teachers that the fifth food group was gravy.
Active	For years teachers *taught* Alberta schoolchildren that gravy was the fifth food group.

Unclear passive construction	Much protest *is being voiced* over the new electric fireworks. [Who is protesting?]
Active verb	Members of the Fuse Lighters Association *are protesting* the new electric fireworks.

(For more examples of active- and passive-voice verbs, see page 121.)

■ PRACTISING WHAT YOU'VE LEARNED

Errors with Verbs

A. The following sentences contain subject–verb agreement errors. Correct the problems by changing the verbs. Some sentences contain more than one error.

1. A recent report on Cuban land crabs show they can run faster than horses.

2. Either the cocker spaniel or the poodle hold the honour of being the most popular breed of dogs in Canada, say the Canadian Kennel Club.

3. Neither of the students know that both mystery writer Agatha Christie and inventor Thomas Edison was dyslexic.

4. There is many children in this country who appreciate a big plate of poutine, but none of the Hall kids like this French-Canadian dish.

5. Clarity in speech and writing are absolutely essential in the business world today.

6. Some scholars believe that the world's first money, in the form of coins, were made in Lydia, a country that is now part of Turkey.

7. Bananas, rich in vitamins and low in fats, is rated the most popular fruit in Canada.

8. Each of the twins have read about Joseph Priestley's contribution to the understanding of oxygen, but neither were aware that he also invented the pencil eraser.

9. The team from Maple Leaf High School are considering switching from basketball to basket weaving because passing athletics are now required for graduation.

10. Many people considers the wizard Merlin a mythical figure, but now two historians, authors of a well-known book on the subject, argues he was a real person named Merlinus Ambrosius.

B. The following sentences contain incorrect verb forms, tense shifts, and double negatives. Correct any problems you see, and rewrite any sentences whose clarity or conciseness would be improved by using active rather than passive verbs.

1. He couldn't hardly wait to hear country star Sue Flay sing her version of "I've Been Flushed from the Bathroom of Your Heart."

2. "If you was in Wyoming and couldn't hear the wind blowing, what would people call you?" asked Jethro. "Dead," replies his buddy Herman.

3. It was believed by Aztec ruler Montezuma that chocolate had magical powers and can act as an aphrodisiac.

4. Tammy's favourite band is Opie Gone Bad so she always was buying their concert tickets, even though she can't hardly afford to.

5. Suspicions of arson are being raised by the Fire Department following the burning of the new Chip and Dale Furniture Factory.

■ Errors with Nouns   N

18g Possessive with "-ing" Nouns

When the emphasis is on the action, use the possessive pronoun plus the "-ing" noun.

Example	He hated *my* singing around the house, so I made him live in the garage. [The emphasis is on *singing*.]

When the emphasis is not on the action, you may use a noun or pronoun plus the "-ing" noun.

Example	He hated *me* singing around the house, so I made him live in the garage. [The emphasis is on the person singing—me—not the action; he might have liked someone else singing.]

18h Misuse of Nouns as Adjectives

Some nouns may be used as adjectives modifying other nouns: "horse show," "movie star," or "theatre seats." But some nouns used as adjectives sound awkward or like jargon. To avoid such awkwardness, you may need to change the noun to an appropriate adjective or reword the sentence.

Awkward	The group decided to work on local *environment* problems.
Better	The group decided to work on local *environmental* problems.
Jargon	The executive began a *cost estimation comparison study* of the two products.
Better	The executive began a *comparison study* of the two products' costs.

(For more information on ridding your prose of multiple nouns, see page 127.)

■ Errors with Pronouns

18i Faulty Agreement   Pro Agr

A pronoun should agree in number and gender with its antecedent (that is, the word the pronoun stands for).

Incorrect	To get Greta to sign a contract, the director would lock *them* in the dressing room.
Correct	To get Greta to sign a contract, the director would lock *her* in the dressing room.

Use the singular pronoun with "everyone," "anyone," and "each."

Incorrect	When the knife-thrower asked for a volunteer partner, *no one* in the men's gym class raised *their* hand.
Correct	When the knife-thrower asked for a volunteer partner, *no one* in the men's gym class raised *his* hand.
Incorrect	*Each* of the new wives decided to keep *their* own name.
Correct	*Each* of the new wives decided to keep *her* own name.

In the past, writers have traditionally used the masculine pronoun "he" when the gender of the antecedent is unknown, as in the following: "If a *spy* refuses to answer questions, *he* should be forced to watch James Bond movies until *he* cracks." Today, however, many authorities prefer the nonsexist "she/he," even though the construction can be awkward when maintained over a stretch of prose. Perhaps the best solution is to use the impersonal "one" when possible or simply rewrite the sentence in the plural: "If *spies* refuse to answer questions, *they* should be forced to watch James Bond movies until *they* crack." Do not use "they" as a singular pronoun in an attempt to be nonsexist: "If a student wishes to apply for a loan, they must submit three affidavits from their bank." (For more examples, see pages 149–151.)

18j Vague Reference   Ref

Your pronoun references should be clear.

Vague	If the trained seal won't eat its dinner, throw *it* into the lion's cage. [What goes into the lion's cage?]
Clear	If the trained seal won't eat its dinner, throw *the food* into the lion's cage.
Vague	After the dog bit Harry, *he* raised such a fuss at the police station that the sergeant finally had *him* impounded. [Who raised the fuss? Who was impounded?]
Clear	After being bitten, *Harry* raised such a fuss at the police station that the sergeant finally had the *dog* impounded.

Sometimes you must add a word or rewrite the sentence to make the pronoun reference clear:

Vague	I'm a lab instructor in the biology department and am also taking a statistics course. *This* has always been difficult for me. [What is difficult?]
Clear	I'm a lab instructor in the biology department and am also taking statistics, a *course* that has always been difficult for me.
Clear	I'm a lab instructor in the biology department and am also taking a statistics course. Being a teacher and a student at the same time has always been difficult for me.

18k Shift in Pronouns   P Sh

Be consistent in your use of pronouns; don't shift from one person to another.

Incorrect	*One* shouldn't eat pudding with *your* fingers.
Correct	*One* shouldn't eat pudding with *one's* fingers.
Correct	*You* shouldn't eat pudding with *your* fingers.
Incorrect	*We* left-handed people are at a disadvantage because most of the time *you* can't rent left-handed golf clubs or bowling balls.
Correct	*We* left-handed people are at a disadvantage because most of the time *we* can't rent left-handed golf clubs or bowling balls.

(For additional examples, see pages 127–128.)

18l Incorrect Case   Ca

1. The case of a pronoun is determined by its function in the particular sentence. If the pronoun is a subject, use the nominative case: "I," "he," "she," "we," and "they"; if the pronoun is an object, use the objective case: "me," "him," "her," "us," and "them." To check your usage, all you need to do in many instances is isolate the pronoun in the manner shown here and see if it sounds correct alone.

Incorrect	Give the treasure map to Jack and *I*.
Isolated	Give the treasure map to *I*. [awkward]
Correct	Give the treasure map to Jack and *me*.
Incorrect	Bertram and *her* suspect that the moon is hollow.
Isolated	*Her* suspects that the moon is hollow. [awkward]
Correct	Bertram and *she* suspect that the moon is hollow.
Incorrect	The gift is from Haley and *I*.
Isolated	The gift is from *I*. [awkward]
Correct	The gift is from Haley and *me*.

Sometimes the "isolation test" doesn't work and you just have to remember the rules. A common pronoun problem involves use of the preposition "between" and the choice of "me" or "I." Perhaps you can remember this rule by recalling there is no "I" in "between," only "e's" as in "me."

Incorrect	Just *between you and I,* the Russian housekeeper is a good cook but she won't iron curtains.
Correct	Just *between you and me,* the Russian housekeeper is a good cook but she won't iron curtains.

In other cases, to determine the correct pronoun, you will need to add implied but unstated sentence elements:

Examples	Mother always liked Jian more than *me.* [Mother liked Jian more than *she liked* me.]
	She is younger than *I* by three days. [She is younger than I *am* by three days.]
	Telephone exchange: May I speak to Kate? This is *she.* [This is she *speaking.*]

   2. To solve the confusing *who/whom* pronoun problem, first determine the case of the pronoun in its own clause in each sentence.

     A. If the pronoun is the subject of a clause, use "who" or "whoever."

Examples	I don't know *who* spread the peanut butter on my English paper. ["Who" is the subject of the verb "spread" in the clause "who spread the peanut butter on my English paper."]
	Anneliese is a librarian *who* only likes books with pictures. ["Who" is the subject of the verb "likes" in the clause "who only likes books with pictures."]
	He will sell secrets to *whoever* offers the largest sum of money. ["Whoever" is the subject of the verb "offers" in the clause "whoever offers the largest sum of money."]

     B. If the pronoun is the object of a verb, use "whom" or "whomever."

Examples	*Whom* am I kicking? ["Whom" is the direct object of the verb "kicking."]
	Sid is a man *whom* I distrust. ["Whom" is the direct object of the verb "distrust."]
	Whomever he kicked will probably be angry. ["Whomever" is the direct object of the verb "kicked."]

     C. If the pronoun occurs as the object of a preposition, use "whom," especially when the preposition immediately precedes the pronoun.

Examples	*With whom* am I speaking?
	To whom is the letter addressed?
	Do not ask *for whom* the bell tolls.

■ PRACTISING WHAT YOU'VE LEARNED

Errors with Nouns and Pronouns

A. In the sentences below, select the proper pronouns.

1. Please buy a copy of the book *The Celery Stalks at Midnight* for my sister and (I, me).

2. Between you and (I, me), some people define a Freudian slip as saying one thing but meaning your mother.

3. (Who, Whom) is the singer of the country song "You Can't Make a Heel Toe the Mark"?

4. Aunt May makes better cookies than (I, me).

5. (Him and me, He and I) are going to the movies to see *Attack of the Killer Crabgrass.*

6. I'm giving my accordion to (whoever, whomever) is carrying a grudge against our neighbours.

7. The Botox surprise party was given by Paige Turner, Justin Case, and (I, me).

8. She is the kind of person for (who, whom) housework meant sweeping the room with a glance.

9. (Her and him, She and he) are twins.

10. The judge of the ugly feet contest found choosing between (him and her, she and he) too difficult.

B. The sentences below contain a variety of errors with nouns and pronouns. Some sentences contain more than one error; skip any correct sentences you may find.

1. The executive knew she was in trouble when her salary underwent a modification reduction adjustment of 50 percent.

2. Of whom did Oscar Wilde once say, "He hasn't a single redeeming vice"?

3. It was a surprise to both Mary and I to learn that Switzerland didn't give women the right to vote until 1971.

4. Each of the young women in the Family Planning class decided not to marry after they read that couples today have 2.3 children.

5. Mabel explained to Frederic that the best way for him to avoid his recurring nosebleeds was to stay out of his employer's schemes .

6. Those of us who'd had the flu agreed that one can always get a doctor to return your call quicker if you get in the shower, but let's keep this tip confidential between you and I.

7. The stranger gave the free movie tickets to Indira and I after he saw people standing in line to leave the theatre.

8. The personnel director told each of the employees, most of who opposed him, to signify their "no" vote by saying, "I resign."

9. Clarence and me have an uncle who is so mean he writes the name of the murderer on the first page of mystery novels that are passed around the family.

10. One of the first movies to gross over $1 million was *Tarzan of the Apes* (1932), starring Johnny Weismuller, a former Olympic star who became an actor. This didn't happen often in the movie industry at that time.

■ Errors with Adverbs and Adjectives

18m Incorrect Usage   Adv   Adj

Incorrect use of adverbs and adjectives often occurs when you confuse the two modifiers. Adverbs qualify the meanings of verbs, adjectives, and other adverbs; they frequently end in "-ly," and they often answer the question "How?"

Incorrect	After Hana argued with the mechanic, her car began running *bad*.
Correct	After Hana argued with the mechanic, her car began running *badly*.

Adjectives, on the other hand, describe or qualify the meanings of nouns only.

Example   The *angry* mechanic neglected to put oil into Hana's car.

One of the most confusing pairs of modifiers is "well" and "good." We often use "good" as an adjective modifying a noun and "well" as an adverb modifying a verb.

Examples   *Aesop's Fables* is a *good* book for children, although it is not *well* organized.

Robin was such a *good* liar his wife had to call in the children at suppertime.

After eating Rocky Mountain oysters, Susie yodels exceptionally *well*.

Did you do *well* on your math test?

If you cannot determine whether a word is an adverb or an adjective, consult your dictionary and the definitions on page 472.

18n Faulty Comparison   Comp

When you compare two elements to a higher or lower degree (more, less), you often add "-er" or "-r" to the adjective.

Incorrect	Of the two sisters, Sarah is the *loudest*.
Correct	Of the two sisters, Sarah is the *louder*.

When you compare more than two elements, you often add "-est" to the adjective.

Example   Sarah is the *loudest* of the four children in the family.

Other adjectives use the words "more," "most," "less," and "least" to indicate comparison.

Examples   Bela Lugosi is *more* handsome than Lon Chaney but *less* handsome than Vincent Price.

Boris Karloff is the *most* handsome, and Christopher Lee is the *least* handsome, of all the horror film stars.

Beware using a double comparison when it is unnecessary:

Incorrect   It was the *most saddest* song I've ever heard.

Correct   It was the *saddest* song I've ever heard.

Note, too, that for most authorities, the word "unique" is a special adjective, one without a degree of comparison. Despite common usage to the contrary, an experience or thing may be unique—that is, one of a kind—but it may not be "very unique."

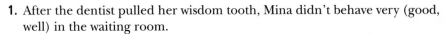

■ PRACTISING WHAT YOU'VE LEARNED

Errors with Adverbs and Adjectives

Choose the correct adverbs and adjectives in the sentences below.

1. After the dentist pulled her wisdom tooth, Mina didn't behave very (good, well) in the waiting room.

2. Which is the (worser, worse, worst) food, liver or buttermilk?

3. I didn't do (good, well) on my nature project because my bonsai sequoia tree grew (bad, badly) in its tiny container.

4. Don't forget to dress (warm, warmly) for the Arctic freestyle race.

5. Of the twins, Tweedledum is more (funner, fun) than Tweedledee.

6. Watching Justinian eat candied fruit flies made Theodora feel (real, really) ill, and his table manners did not make her feel (more better, better).

7. The Roman toothpick holder was (very unique, the uniquest, unique).

8. That was the (funniest, most funniest) flea circus I have ever seen.

9. Does the instructional guide *Bobbing for Doughnuts* still sell (good, well)?

10. The Fighting Mosquitoes were trained (well, good), but they just didn't take practices (serious, seriously).

■ Errors in Modifying Phrases

18o Dangling Modifiers   DM

A modifying—or descriptive—phrase must have a logical relationship to some specific words in the sentence. When those words are omitted, the phrase "dangles" without anything to modify. Dangling modifiers frequently occur at the beginnings of sentences and often may be corrected by adding the proper subjects to the main clauses.

Dangling	Not knowing how to swim, buying scuba gear was foolish. [Who didn't know how to swim? Who did the buying?]
Correct	Not knowing how to swim, *we* decided that buying scuba gear was foolish.
Dangling	Feeling too sick to ski, her vacation to the mountains was postponed. [Who was too sick to ski? This says her vacation was feeling too sick to ski.]
Correct	Feeling too sick to ski, *Laura* postponed her vacation to the mountains.

(For additional examples, see pages 115–116.)

18p Misplaced Modifiers   MM

When modifying words, phrases, or clauses are not placed near the word they describe, confusion or unintentional humour often results.

Misplaced	Teddy swatted the fly still dressed in his pyjamas.
Correct	Still dressed in his pyjamas, Teddy swatted the fly.
Misplaced	There are many things people won't eat, especially children.
Correct	There are many things people, especially children, won't eat.

(For additional examples, see pages 116–117.)

■ PRACTISING WHAT YOU'VE LEARNED

Errors in Modifying Phrases

Correct the errors in dangling and misplaced modifiers by rearranging or rewriting the sentences below.

1. After boarding Hard Luck Airlines, the meals convinced us to return by ship.

2. Here is the new telephone number for notifying the fire department of any fires that may be attached to your telephone.

3. The prize-winning ice sculptor celebrated her new open-air studio in Banff, where she lives with her infant daughter, purchased for $10,000.

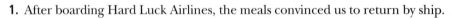

4. The movie star showed off letters from admirers that were lying all over his desk.

5. Running too fast during a game of "Kick the Can," my face collided with the flagpole.

6. Eloise bought a computer from her neighbour with faulty memory.

7. Baggy, wrinkled, and hopelessly out of style, Jean tossed the skirt from her closet.

8. Forgetting to pack underwear, the suitcase had to be reopened.

9. Hajo plans to teach a course next spring incorporating his research into the mating habits of the Sasquatch on the campus of Slippery Rock College.

10. After spending all night in the library, Kate's friends knew she'd need a trip to Special Coffee.

11. Squeezing the can, the tomatoes didn't seem ripe to the chef.

12. From birth to twelve months, parents don't have to worry about solid food.

13. He didn't think the bicycles would make it over the mountains, being so old.

14. I've read that a number of modern sailors, like Thor Heyerdahl, have sailed primitive vessels across the ocean in books from the public library.

15. Proofreading carefully, dangling modifiers may be spotted and corrected easily.

■ Errors in Sentences

18q Fragments   Frag

A complete sentence must contain a subject and a verb. A fragment is an incomplete sentence; it is often a participial ("-ing") phrase or dependent clause that belongs to the preceding sentence. To check for fragments, try reading your prose, one sentence at a time, starting at the *end* of your essay. If you find a "sentence" that makes no sense alone, it's probably a fragment that should either be rewritten or connected to another sentence.

Incorrect	Ludwig's parents refuse to send him to music camp. Although they both know he practises the piano day and night.
Correct	Ludwig's parents refuse to send him to music camp, although they both know he practises the piano day and night.
Incorrect	This recording of the symphony's latest concert is so clear you can hear every sound. Including the coughs and whispers of the audience.
Correct	This recording of the symphony's latest concert is so clear you can hear every sound, including the coughs and whispers of the audience.

Incorrect	At Liz's most recent wedding, the photographer used an instant camera. Because her marriages break up so fast.
Correct	At Liz's most recent wedding, the photographer used an instant camera because her marriages break up so fast.

You can also try this test to see if a group of words is a fragment: say the phrase "It is true that" in front of the words in question. In most cases, a complete sentence will still make sense, but a fragment won't.

Example	At Liz's most recent wedding, the photographer used an instant camera. Because her marriages break up so fast.
	Which is a fragment?
	It is true that *at Liz's most recent wedding, the photographer used an instant camera.* [This sentence makes sense, so it's not a fragment.]
	It is true that *because her marriages break up so fast.* [Yes, this is a fragment.]

■ PRACTISING WHAT YOU'VE LEARNED

Fragment Sentence Errors

A. Using the "it is true that" test, identify the fragments and the complete sentences in the samples below.

1. Canada's first air disaster occurred in the summer of 1957. Which killed seventy-nine people.

2. The cause was a violent thunderstorm over Quebec. Followed by a string of disasters in the 1960s. Including a TCA crash in 1963 and a CP explosion in 1965.

3. While these were terrible tragedies that took many lives. The air disaster that has most haunted Canadians is the Air India crash of 1985. Since 329 people had their lives taken from them.

4. The third-worst air disaster in history. Because it was not an accident. Attributed to militant activists fighting for a new homeland.

5. No one has yet paid for the crime of blowing up a plane full of innocent people. Although certain individuals have been prosecuted. And a full governmental investigation has taken place.

B. Rewrite the following sentences so that there are no fragments.

1. The idea of a credit card first appeared in 1887. According to Lawrence M. Ausbel, author of "Credit Cards," in the *McGraw-Hill Encyclopedia of Economics.*

2. Originally an imaginary concept in a futurist novel by Edward Bellamy. The card allowed characters to charge against future earnings.

3. Around the turn of the twentieth century some stores issued paper or metal "shoppers' plates." Although they were only used by retailers to identify their credit customers.

4. The first real credit card was issued in 1947 by a New York bank and was a success. Despite the fact that customers could only charge purchases in a two-block area in Brooklyn.

5. Travel and entertainment cards soon appeared that allowed customers to charge items and services across the country. For example, the American Express card in 1958 and Carte Blanche in 1959.

18r Run-On Sentence   R-O

Don't run two sentences together without any punctuation. Use a period, a semicolon, or a comma plus a coordinating conjunction (if appropriate), or subordinate one clause.

Incorrect	The indicted police chief submitted his resignation the mayor accepted it gratefully.
Correct	The indicted police chief submitted his resignation. The mayor accepted it gratefully.
Correct	The indicted police chief submitted his resignation; the mayor accepted it gratefully.
Correct	The indicted police chief submitted his resignation, and the mayor accepted it gratefully.
Correct	When the indicted police chief submitted his resignation, the mayor accepted it gratefully.

18s Comma Splice   CS

A comma splice occurs when two sentences are linked with a comma. To correct this error, you can (1) separate the two sentences with a period, (2) separate the two sentences with a semicolon, (3) insert a coordinating conjunction ("for," "but," "and," "or," "nor," "so," "yet") after the comma, or (4) subordinate one clause.

Incorrect	Grover won a stuffed Gila monster at the church raffle, his mother threw it away the next day while he was in school.
Correct	Grover won a stuffed Gila monster at the church raffle. His mother threw it away the next day while he was in school.
Correct	Grover won a stuffed Gila monster at the church raffle; his mother threw it away the next day while he was in school.
Correct	Grover won a stuffed Gila monster at the church raffle, but his mother threw it away the next day while he was in school.
Correct	Although Grover won a stuffed Gila monster at the church raffle, his mother threw it away the next day while he was in school.

(For more help on correcting comma splices, see pages 497–500; coordination and subordination are discussed in detail on pages 129–131.)

▪ PRACTISING WHAT YOU'VE LEARNED

Run-On Sentence and Comma Splice Errors

A. Correct the run-on sentences below. Try to use several different methods of correcting the errors, as illustrated in section 19r.

1. Workers in Canada take an average of thirteen days of vacation a year in Italy they take forty-two.

2. In 1901 a school teacher named Annie Edson Taylor became the first person to go over Niagara Falls in a wooden barrel she is the only woman known to survive this risky adventure.

3. The minister preached his farewell sermon the choir sang "Break Forth into Joy."

4. The first microwave oven marketed in 1959 was a built-in unit it cost a whopping $2,595.

5. Coffee was considered a food in the Middle Ages travellers who found it growing in Ethiopia mixed it with animal fat.

B. Correct the comma splices that appear in the sentences below. Use more than one method of correcting the errors.

1. Susanna Moodie's autobiographical writings about her life in Canada influenced future Canadian writers, both Robertson Davies and Margaret Atwood wrote works responding to *Roughing it in the Bush.*

2. However, they have interpreted her in a way that is at odds with the reality of the woman, as revealed through her letters, she was far more radical than in their portrayals.

3. She was extremely independent, in 1985, the publication of Moodie's letters revealed a more complex woman than people had thought.

4. In Robertson Davies' play *At My Heart's Core,* a somewhat prim and militant Moodie blames the radicalism of the Methodists for the Upper Canada Rebellion, he might have characterized her altogether differently had he known of her great sympathy with dissenting religious groups.

5. Margaret Atwood initially called Moodie's ambivalence toward the new country and her self-contradiction schizophrenic, this position has been echoed by other scholars as well, she changed her perspective after reading the letters.

C. Correct any run-on sentences or comma splice errors you see. Skip any correct sentences you find.

1. My mother is very politically conservative, she's written in Queen Elizabeth II for Prime Minister in the last two elections.

2. Elle decided not to eat the alphabet soup the letters spelled out "botulism."

3. A dried gourd containing seeds probably functioned as the first baby rattle, ancient Egyptian wall paintings show babies with such gourds clutched in their fingers.

4. *Nanook of the North* was praised as the first documentary film on the Inuit people, it was later discovered most of it had been staged.

5. A friend of mine offers a good definition of nasty theatre critics on opening night, according to him, they're the people who can't wait to stone the first cast.

6. When English scientist James Smithson died in 1829, he willed his entire fortune to the United States to establish a foundation for knowledge, that's how the Smithsonian Institution was started.

7. The word "jack-o'-lantern" may have come from the legend of Irish Jack, a mean old man in life, he was condemned after death to wander the earth carrying a hollow turnip with a lump of burning coal inside.

8. Canadians forget how large the blue whale is it has a heart as large as a Volkswagen Beetle and can hold an elephant on its tongue.

9. According to a study by the Fish and Wildlife Service, Canadians' favourite animals are dogs, horses, swans, robins, and butterflies; their least favourite are cockroaches, mosquitoes, rats, wasps, and rattlesnakes.

10. The famous Eiffel Tower, built for the 1889 Paris Exposition, has inspired many crazy stunts, for example, in 1891 Silvain Dornon climbed the 363 steps on stilts.

18t Faulty Parallelism   //

Parallel thoughts may be expressed in similar grammatical constructions. Repeated sentence elements, such as verbs, nouns, pronouns, and phrases, often appear in parallel form to emphasize meaning and to promote sentence fluency.

Examples

Parallel verbs: In his vaudeville act he *sang, danced,* and *juggled.*

Parallel prepositional phrases: She ran through the door, across the yard, and into the limo.

You may find it helpful to isolate the repeated elements in a sentence to see if they are parallel.

She ran

(1) through the door

(2) across the yard ⟶ parallel

(3) into the limo

Faulty Parallelism	Boa constrictors like *to lie* in the sun, *to hang* from limbs, and *swallowing* small animals.
Isolated	(1) to lie (2) to hang (3) swallowing [not parallel to #1 and #2]
Revised	Boa constrictors like *to lie* in the sun, *to hang* from limbs, and *to swallow* small animals.
Faulty Parallelism	Whether *roaming* the woods at night, *howling* at the moon, or *in his lair,* the werewolf always kept his hair combed.
Revised	Whether *roaming* the woods at night, *howling* at the moon, or *lounging* in his lair, the werewolf always kept his hair combed.

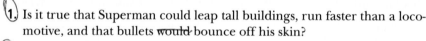

■ PRACTISING WHAT YOU'VE LEARNED

Errors in Parallelism

Revise the sentences that follow so that the parallel ideas are expressed in similar grammatical constructions.

1. Is it true that Superman could leap tall buildings, run faster than a locomotive, and that bullets ~~would~~ bounce off his skin?

2. To celebrate the canned meat product called Spam, we attended the Texas Spamarama Festival to participate in the Spambalaya cook-off, the Spam-can toss, the Spam-jam session, and were dancing to such favourites as "Twist and Snout."

3. My friend Lili swears she has seen Elvis snacking at the deli, browsing at the supermarket, munching at the pizza parlour, and in the cookbook section of a local bookstore.

4. According to my husband, summer air in Saskatoon is one part oxygen, nine parts water, and the rest is mosquitoes, about 90 percent.

5. Many instructors believe that the most important keys to success for students in college or university include attending class, keep up with reading assignments, and being brave enough to ask questions.

6. Yoga encourages its participants to work on their flexibility, strength, and how they can reduce their stress levels.

7. Drivers should hang up their cell phones, refrain from eating, and drinking too, leaving the radio buttons alone.

8. Smart people learn from their own mistakes; learning from the mistakes of others is what even smarter people do.

9. Theatre class helped me overcome my shyness, make new friends, and my confidence to do other activities was improved.

10. The writer Oscar Wilde, the dancer Isadora Duncan, the painter Max Ernst, and Jim Morrison, who was a rock star, are all buried in the same Paris cemetery.

18u False Predication   Pred

This error occurs when the predicate (that part of the sentence that says something about the subject) doesn't fit properly with the subject. Illogical constructions result.

Incorrect	The meaning of the sermon deals with love. [A "meaning" cannot deal with anything; the author, speaker, or work itself can, however.]
Correct	The sermon topic is love.
Incorrect	Energy is one of the world's biggest problems. ["Energy" itself is not a problem.]
Correct	The lack of fuel for energy is one of the world's biggest problems.
Incorrect	True failure is when you make an error and don't learn anything from it. [Avoid all "is when" and "is where" constructions. The subject does not denote a time, so the predicate is faulty.]
Correct	You have truly failed only when you make an error and don't learn anything from it.
Incorrect	My roommate is why I'm moving to a new apartment. [A roommate is not a reason.]
Correct	My roommate's habit of talking nonstop is driving me to find a new apartment.
Also Correct	Because of my annoying roommate, I'm moving to a new apartment.
Incorrect	Her first comment after winning the lottery was exciting. [Her comment wasn't exciting; she was excited.]
Correct	Her first comment after winning the lottery expressed her excitement.

(For other examples of faulty predication, see pages 117–118)

18v Mixed Structure   Mix S

"Mixed structure" is a catchall term that applies to a variety of sentence construction errors. Usually, the term refers to a sentence in which the writer begins with one kind of structure and then shifts to another in mid-sentence. Such a shift often occurs when writers are in a hurry, and their minds have already jumped ahead to the next thought.

Confused	By the time one litter of cats is given away seems to bring a new one.
Clear	Giving away one litter of cats seems to tell the mother cat that it's time to produce a new batch.

Confused	The bank robber realized that in his crime spree how very little fun he was having.
Clear	The bank robber realized that he was having very little fun in his crime spree.
Confused	The novel is too confusing for what the author meant.
Clear	The novel is too confused for me to understand what the author meant.
Confused	Children with messages from their parents will be stapled to the bulletin board.
Clear	To find messages from their parents, children should look at the bulletin board.

(For other examples of mixed structure, see pages 117–118.)

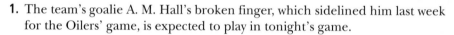

■ PRACTISING WHAT YOU'VE LEARNED

Errors of False Predication and Mixed Structure

Rewrite the following sentences so that each one is clear and coherent.

1. The team's goalie A. M. Hall's broken finger, which sidelined him last week for the Oilers' game, is expected to play in tonight's game.

2. The groom is a graduate of Centreville High School where he lived all his life.

3. On my way to the doctor's office, my universal joint went out, causing even more body damage after hitting the tree.

4. An example of his intelligence is when he brought home a twenty-pound block of ice after ice fishing all day.

5. For those new residents who have children and don't know about it, the town offers low-cost daycare services.

6. According to the nineteenth-century cynic Ambrose Bierce, marriage is where there is "a master, a mistress, and two slaves, making in all, two."

7. A successful diet is when the mind triumphs over platter.

8. My drama teacher is the reason why I am a big star today.

9. Some folks argue that sound travels slower than light such as when advice parents give their teenagers doesn't reach them until they're forty.

10. Hearing his cries for help is how he came to be found in a ditch by some stray cows.

Chapter 19

A Concise Guide to Punctuation

Punctuation marks do not exist, as one student recently complained, to make your life complicated. They are used to clarify your written thoughts so that the reader understands your meaning. Just as traffic signs and signals tell a driver to slow down, stop, or go, so punctuation is intended to guide the reader through your prose. Look, for example, at the confusion in the following sentences when the necessary punctuation marks are omitted:

Confusing	Has the tiger been fed Bill? [Bill was the tiger's dinner?]
Clear	Has the tiger been fed, Bill?
Confusing	After we had finished raking the dog jumped into the pile of leaves. [Raking the dog?]
Clear	After we had finished raking, the dog jumped into the pile of leaves.
Confusing	The coach called the swimmers names. [Was the coach fired for verbally abusing the swimmers?]
Clear	The coach called the swimmers' names.

Because punctuation helps you communicate clearly with your reader, you should familiarize yourself with the following rules.

19a The Period (.)   P

1. Use a period to end a sentence.

Examples   Employees at that company are not allowed to go on coffee breaks.

It takes too long to retrain them.

2. Use a period after initials and many abbreviations.

Examples   W. B. Yeats, 12 a.m., Dr., etc., M.A.

3. Only one period is necessary if the sentence ends with an abbreviation.

Examples   The elephant was delivered C.O.D.

To find a good job, you should obtain a B.Sc. or B.A.

19b The Question Mark (?)   P

1. Use a question mark after every direct question.

Examples   May I borrow your boots?

Is the sandstorm over now?

2. No question mark is necessary after an indirect question.

Examples   Jean asked why no one makes a paper milk carton that opens without tearing.

Dave wondered how the television detective always found a parking place next to the scene of the crime.

19c The Exclamation Point (!)   P

The exclamation point follows words, phrases, or sentences to show strong feelings.

Examples   Fire! Call the rescue squad!

The Canucks finally won the Stanley Cup!

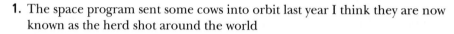

▪ PRACTISING WHAT YOU'VE LEARNED

Errors Using Periods, Question Marks, and Exclamation Points

Correct the following sentences by adding, deleting, or changing periods, question marks, or exclamation points, where appropriate.

1. The space program sent some cows into orbit last year I think they are now known as the herd shot around the world

2. Ms Anita Bath wants to know why erasers never outlast their pencils?

3. Her French class at St Claire's School on First Ave was taught by Madame Beau V Rhee, Ph.D.

4. Where do all the birds go when it's raining

5. I have wonderful news I won the lottery

19d The Comma (,)   P

1. Use a comma to separate two independent clauses* joined by a coordinating conjunction. To remember the coordinating conjunctions, think of the acronym FANBOYS: "for," "and," "nor," "but," "or," "yet," and "so." Always use one of the FANBOYS and a comma when you join two independent clauses.

Examples   You can bury your savings in the backyard, *but* don't expect Mother Nature to pay interest.

I'm going home tomorrow, *and* I'm never coming back.

After six weeks Louie's diet was making him feel lonely and depressed, *so* he had a bumper sticker printed that said, "Honk if you love groceries."

Do *not* join two sentences with a comma only; such an error is called a comma splice. Use a comma plus one of the coordinating conjunctions listed previously, a period, a semicolon, or subordination. See pages 502–505 for further information about semicolons and colons.

Comma splice	Beatrice washes and grooms the chickens, Samantha feeds the spiders.
Correct	Beatrice washes and grooms the chickens, and Samantha feeds the spiders.
Correct	Beatrice washes and grooms the chickens. Samantha feeds the spiders.
Correct	Beatrice washes and grooms the chickens; Samantha feeds the spiders.
Correct	When Beatrice washes and grooms the chickens, Samantha feeds the spiders.
Comma splice	Zack doesn't like singing groups, he won't go with us to hear Fed Up with People.
Correct	Zack doesn't like singing groups, so he won't go with us to hear Fed Up with People.
Correct	Jack doesn't like singing groups. He won't go with us to hear Fed Up with People.
Correct	Zack doesn't like singing groups; he won't go with us to hear Fed Up with People.
Correct	Because Zack doesn't like singing groups, he won't go with us to hear Fed Up with People.

(For additional help, see pages 489–491)

2. Conjunctive adverbs, such as "however," "moreover," "thus," "consequently," and "therefore," are used to show continuity and are frequently set off by commas when they appear in mid-sentence.

---

* An independent clause looks like a complete sentence; it contains a subject and a verb, and it makes sense by itself.

Examples   She soon discovered, *however,* that he had stolen her monogrammed towels in addition to her pet avocado plant.

She felt, *consequently,* that he was not trustworthy.

When a conjunctive adverb occurs at the beginning of a sentence, it may be followed by a comma, especially if a pause is intended. If no pause is intended, you may omit the comma, but inserting the comma is never wrong.

Examples   *Thus,* she resolved never to speak to him again.

Thus she resolved never to speak to him again.

Therefore, he resolved never to speak to her again.

Therefore he resolved never to speak to her again.

Please note that "however" can never be used as a coordinating conjunction joining two independent clauses. Incorrect use of "however" most often results in a comma splice.

Comma splice   The police arrested the thief, *however,* they had to release him because the plant wouldn't talk.

Correct   The police arrested the thief; *however,* they had to release him because the plant wouldn't talk.

Also correct   The police arrested the thief. *However,* they had to release him because the plant wouldn't talk.

   3. Set off with a comma an introductory phrase or clause.

Examples   After we had finished our laundry, we discovered one sock was missing.

According to the owner of the laundromat, customers have conflicting theories about missing laundry.

For example, one man claims his socks make a break for freedom when no one is watching the dryers.

   4. Set off nonessential phrases and clauses. If the information can be omitted without changing the meaning of the main clause, then the phrase or clause is nonessential. Do *not* set off clauses or phrases that are essential to the meaning of the main clause.

Essential   He looked worse than my friend *who gets his clothes from the "lost and found" at the bus station.* [The "who" clause is essential to explain which friend.]

The storm *that destroyed Mr. Peartree's outhouse* left him speechless with anger. [The "that" clause is essential to explain which storm angered Mr. Peartree.]

The movie *now showing at the Ritz* is very obscene and very popular. [The participial phrase is essential to identify the particular movie.]

Nonessential   Joe Medusa, *who won the jalapeño-eating contest last year,* is this year's champion cow-chip tosser. [The "who" clause is nonessential because it only supplies additional information to the main clause.]

Black widow spiders, *which eat their spouses after mating,* are easily identifiable by the orange hourglass design on their abdomens. [The "which" clause is nonessential because it only supplies additional information.]

The laptop computer, *now owned by 70 percent of Canadian university students,* first gained popularity during the 1990s. [The participial phrase is nonessential because it only supplies additional information.]

5. Use commas to separate items in a series of words, phrases, or clauses.

Examples   Julio collects coins, stamps, bottle caps, erasers, and pocket lint.

Mrs. Jones chased the burglar out the window, around the ledge, down the fire escape, and into the busy street.

Although journalists and some grammarians permit the omission of the last comma before the "and," many authorities believe the comma is necessary for clarity. For example, how many pints of ice cream are listed in the sentence below?

Please buy the following pints of ice cream: strawberry, peach, coffee, vanilla and chocolate swirl.

Four or five pints? Without a comma before the "and," the reader doesn't know if vanilla and chocolate swirl are (is?) one item or two. By inserting the last comma, you clarify the sentence:

Please buy the following pints of ice cream: strawberry, peach, coffee, vanilla, and chocolate swirl.

6. Use commas to separate adjectives of equal emphasis that modify the same noun. To determine if a comma should be used, see if you can insert the word "and" between the adjectives; if the phrase still makes proper sense with the substituted "and," use a comma.

Examples   She finally moved out of her cold, dark apartment.

She finally moved out of her cold and dark apartment.

I have a sweet, handsome husband.

I have a sweet and handsome husband.

He called from a convenient telephone booth.

But not: He called from a convenient and telephone booth. ["Convenient" modifies the unit "telephone booth," so there is no comma.]

Hand me some of that homemade pecan pie.

But not: Hand me some of that homemade, pecan pie. ["Homemade" modifies the unit "pecan pie," so there is no comma.]

7. Set off a direct address with commas.

Examples   Gentlemen, keep your seats.

Car fifty-four, where are you?

Not now, Eleanor, I'm busy.

8. Use commas to set off items in addresses and dates.

Examples   The sheriff followed me from Red Deer, Alberta, to question me about my uncle.

He found me on February 2, 1978, when I stopped in Moncton, New Brunswick, to buy sunscreen.

9. Use commas to set off a degree or title following a name.

Examples   John Dough, M.D., was audited when he reported only $5.68 in taxable income last year.

The Neanderthal Award went to Samuel Lyle, Ph.D.

10. Use commas to set off dialogue from the speaker.

Examples   Alexander announced, "I don't think I want a second helping of possum."

"Eat hearty," said Marie, "because this is the last of the food."

11. Use commas to set off "yes," "no," "well," and other weak exclamations.

Examples   Yes, I am in the cat condo business.

No, all the units with decks are sold.

Well, perhaps one with a pool will do.

12. Set off interrupters or parenthetical elements appearing in the middle of a sentence. A parenthetical element is additional information placed as explanation or comment within an already complete sentence. This element may be a word (such as "certainly" or "fortunately"), a phrase ("for example" or "in fact"), or a clause ("I believe" or "you know"). The word, phrase, or clause is parenthetical if the sentence parts before and after it fit together and make sense.

Examples   Jack is, *I think,* still a compulsive gambler.

Harvey, *my brother,* sometimes has breakfast with him.

Jack cannot, *for example,* resist shuffling the toast or dealing the pancakes.

▪ PRACTISING WHAT YOU'VE LEARNED

Comma Errors

A. Study the comma rules numbered 1–4 on pages 497–499. Correct any comma errors you see in the following sentences.

1. In 1870 inventor Alexander Graham Bell left England, he moved to Canada with his family.

2. From childhood he was interested in sound transmission, his mother's deafness was partially responsible, for his work on sound.

3. He created "Visible Speech" symbols to represent the unwritten Mohawk language, he was made a honorary Mohawk chief.

4. Bell was widely considered the inventor and thus the holder of the patent on the telephone, however, there is some dispute about whether Bell or his fellow inventor Elisha Gray really held the patent.

5. Ironically Bell didn't make as much money from his invention as the investors in the Bell Telephone Company, the president of Western Union who had turned down the opportunity to buy the patent for $100,000 because he didn't think it would catch on regretted it for the rest of his life.

B. Study the comma rules 5–12 on pages 499–500. Correct any comma errors you see in the following sentences.

1. Yes Hortense in the 1920s young women did indeed cut their hair raise their hemlines dab perfume behind their knees and dance the Charleston.

2. Former Prime Minister John Turner analyzed John A. Macdonald's leadership saying "The hero we add to our list of immortals John Alexander Macdonald had much of the force of an Oliver Cromwell some of the compacting and conciliating tact of a William Pitt the sagacity of a William Gladstone and some of the shrewdness of a Benjamin Disraeli."

3. Jane Marian Donna Ann and Cissy graduated from high school on June 5 1964 in Campbell River British Columbia in the old Walnut Street Auditorium.

4. "I may be a man of few opinions" said Henry "but I insist that I am neither for nor against apathy."

5. Did you know for instance that early North American settlers once thought the tomato was so poisonous they only used the plant for decoration?

C. The following sentences contain many kinds of comma errors, including the comma splice. Correct any errors you see by adding, deleting, or changing the commas as needed.

1. The father decided to recapture his youth, he took his son's car keys away.

2. Although ice cream didn't appear in Canada until the 1700s it now leads the world in ice-cream consumption, Australia is second I think.

3. Last summer the large friendly family that lives next door flew Discount Airlines and visited three cities on their vacation, however, their suitcases visited five.

4. Researchers in Balboa, Panama have discovered that the poisonous, yellow-belly, sea snake which descended from the cobra, is the most deadly serpent in the world.

5. Vashti, my cousin, spent the week of Sept. 1–7, 1986 in the woods near Flin Flon, Saskatchewan looking for additions to her extinct, butterfly collection, however she wasn't at all successful in her search.

For additional practice correcting comma splice errors, see pages 489–491 in Chapter 18.

19e The Semicolon (;)   P

1. Use a semicolon to link two closely related independent clauses.

Examples	Pierre has been cooking Cajun-style for years without realizing it; his specialty is blackened eggs.
	Claudette's mother does not have to begin a jogging program; she gets all the exercise she needs by worrying in place.

Avoid a "semicolon fragment" error by making sure there is an independent clause— a complete sentence, not a fragment—on either side of the semicolon.*

Semicolon fragment	Cutting your lawn with a push mower burns 420 calories; according to *Vitality* magazine. ["According to *Vitality* magazine" is a fragment. In this case, a comma, not a semicolon, is needed here.]
Correct	Cutting your lawn with a push mower burns 420 calories, according to *Vitality* magazine.

If you are unsure about recognizing a fragment, try using the "it is true that" test as described on page 488.

2. Use a semicolon to avoid a comma splice when connecting two independent clauses with words like "however," "moreover," "thus," "therefore," and "consequently."

Examples	Vincent Van Gogh sold only one painting in his entire life; however, in 1987 his *Sunflowers* sold for almost $40 million.
	All Esmeralda's plants die shortly after she gets them home from the store; consequently, she has the best compost heap in town.
	This town is not big enough for both of us; therefore, I suggest we expand the city limits.

3. Use a semicolon in a series between items that already contain internal punctuation.

Examples	Last year the Wildcats suffered enough injuries to keep them from winning the Chrysanthemum cup, as Jake Pritchett, goalie, broke his arm in a fight; Hugh Rosenbloom, defenceman, sprained his back on a trampoline; and Boris Baker, star forward, ate rotten clams and nearly died.
	Her children were born a year apart: Moe, 1936; Curley, 1937; and Larry, 1938.

---

* Some folks have noted that the semicolon might be better named the semi-period in that it functions like a weak period, joining two complete sentences together but with a weaker stop between thoughts than a period demands.

■ PRACTISING WHAT YOU'VE LEARNED

Semicolon Errors

Correct the sentences that follow by adding, deleting, or changing the semicolons.

1. The soloist sang the well-known hymn "I Will Not Pass This Way Again" at her concert last night the audience was delighted.

2. Apples have long been associated with romance for example, one legend says if you throw an apple peel over your shoulder, it will fall into the shape of your true love's initial.

3. According to an 1863 book of etiquette, the perfect hostess will see to it that the works of male and female authors are properly separated on her bookshelves, however, if the authors happen to be married, their proximity may be tolerated.

4. Today, there are some 60,000 North Americans older than 100 in 1960, there were only 3,222; according to *Health* magazine.

5. The sixth-grade drama club will present their interpretation of *Hamlet* tonight in the school cafeteria all parents are invited to see this tragedy.

6. Some inventors who named weapons after themselves include Samuel Colt, the Colt revolver, Henry Deringer, Jr., the derringer pistol, Dr. Richard J. Gatling, the crank machine gun, Col. John T. Thompson, the submachine or "tommy" gun, and Oliver F. Winchester, the repeating rifle.

7. My doctor failed in his career as a kidnapper, no one could read his ransom notes.

8. The highest point in Canada is Mount Logan at 5959 metres, in contrast, the lowest point is the Atlantic Ocean at 0 metres.

9. As we drove down the highway we saw a sign that said "See the World's Largest Prairie Dog Turn Right at This Exit," therefore we immediately stopped to look.

10. The next billboard read "See Live Jackalopes"; making us want to stop again.

19f The Colon (:)   P

1. Use a colon to introduce a long or formal list, but do not use one after "to be" verbs.

Correct	Please pick up these items at the store: garlic, wolfbane, mirrors, a prayer book, a hammer, and a wooden stake.
Incorrect	Jean is such a bad cook that she thinks the four basic food groups are: canned, frozen, ready-to-mix, and take-out.
Correct	Jean is such a bad cook that she thinks the four basic food groups are canned, frozen, ready-to-mix, and take-out.

Avoid needless colons.

Incorrect	At the store I couldn't find: wolfbane or a wooden stake.
Correct	At the store I couldn't find wolfbane or a wooden stake.

2. A colon may be used to introduce a quotation or definition.

Examples   Nineteenth-century writer Ambrose Bierce offers this definition of a bore: "A person who talks when you wish him to listen."

Critic Dorothy Parker was unambiguous in her review of the book:

"This is not a novel to be tossed aside lightly; it should be thrown with great force."

To novelist Robertson Davies, imagination was a crucial component of a fully realized life: "I get awfully tired of people who talk about real life as though it had no relation to the life of the imagination and the life of legends and myth."

3. Use a colon to introduce a word, phrase, or sentence that emphatically explains, summarizes, or amplifies the preceding sentence.

Examples   Harriet knew the one ingredient that would improve any diet dinner: chocolate.

Zsa Zsa Gabor's advice for becoming a marvellous housekeeper is simple: every time you leave a relationship, keep the house.

Fang made a big mistake at the office party: he kissed his boss's wife hello and his job goodbye.

■ **PRACTISING WHAT YOU'VE LEARNED**

Errors with Colons

Correct the following errors by adding, deleting, or substituting colons for faulty punctuation. Skip any correct sentences.

1. Experts have discovered over thirty different kinds of clouds but have separated them into three main types cirrus, cumulus, and stratus.

2. To those folks who may talk too much, Abraham Lincoln gives the following advice: "It is better to remain silent and be thought a fool than to speak out and remove all doubt."

3. A recent national poll found that Canadians only consider one activity more stressful than visiting the dentist hosting a dinner party.

4. Because Hindu custom forbids the eating of beef, McDonald's restaurants in India often feature: veggie-burgers and mutton-burgers.

5. Please remember to buy the following at the pet store, one pound of cat food, two flea collars, kitty fang floss, a bag of catnip, and thirty-six lint rollers.

6. A Director of Academic Services at Pennsylvania State University once nominated this sentence for Punctuation Error of the Year; "I had to leave my good friend's behind and find new ones."

7. Some of the significant Canadian inventions patented between 1874 and 1940 were: the telephone, the electron microscope, the modern television camera, and the anti-gravity flying suit.

8. There's only one thing that can make our lawn look as good as our neighbour's; snow.

9. In a Thurmont, Maryland, cemetery can be found this epitaph "Here lies an Atheist, all dressed up, and no place to go."

10. George Bernard Shaw, the famous playwright, claimed he wanted the following epitaph on his tombstone: "I knew if I stayed around long enough, something like this would happen."

19g The Apostrophe (')   AP

1. Use an apostrophe to indicate a contraction.

Examples   *It's* too bad your car burned.

Wouldn't the insurance company believe your story?

Many people today confuse "it's" (the contraction for "it is") and "its" (the possessive pronoun, which never takes an apostrophe).

Its = shows possession, functioning like "his" or "her"

It's = contraction for "it is"

Examples   The car is old, but *its* paint is new ["Its" shows the car's possession of paint.]

The car is old, but *it's* reliable. ["It's" is a contraction for "it is."]

If you are ever in doubt about your choice, read the sentence aloud, saying the words "it is" in place of the *its/it's* in question. If the sentence becomes nonsensical (The car is old but *it is* coat of paint is new), then the possessive form "its" is probably what you need. Many Canadians prefer not to see contractions in formal writing, so you can avoid any confusion by simply using "it is," "who is," and so on.

Special note: Its' = no such word exists in the English language! Forget you even thought about it!

2. Add an apostrophe plus "s" to a noun to show possession.

Examples   *Jack's* dog ate the *cat's* dinner.

The *veterinarian's* assistant later doctored the *puppy's* wounds.

3. Add only an apostrophe to a plural noun ending in "s" to show possession.

Examples   Goldilocks invaded the *bears'* house.

She ignored her *parents'* warning about breaking and entering.

Be careful to avoid adding an apostrophe when the occasion simply calls for the plural use of a word.

Incorrect	*Apple's* are on sale now.
Correct	*Apples* are on sale now.
Incorrect	We ordered *chip's* and dip.
Correct	We ordered *chips* and dip.

4. In some cases you may add an apostrophe plus "s" to a singular word ending in "s," especially when the word is a proper name or for ease of pronunciation.

Examples	*Doris's* name was popular in the 1950s.
	The silent screen *actress's* favourite flowers were mums.

5. To avoid confusion, you may use an apostrophe plus "s" to form the plurals of letters, figures, and words discussed as words, but Canadians prefer no apostrophe unless you have single letters, as in the first example here.

Examples	He made four *"C's"* last fall. [or *"Cs"*]
	The influx of draft dodgers into Canada was a major issue in the *1960s.* [or *1960's*]
	You use too many *"ands"* in your sentence. [or *"and's"*]

▪ PRACTISING WHAT YOU'VE LEARNED

Errors with Apostrophes

A. Correct the apostrophe errors you see in the following phrases.

1. A horses' pyjamas

2. The queens throne

3. A families' vacation

4. Ten students grades

5. The turmoil of the 1970s' was over.

6. That dress of hers'

7. The childrens' toys

8. Worm's for sale

9. Phil Jones car

10. All essay's are due today.

B. Show that you understand the difference between "it's" and "its" by correcting any errors in the sentences that follow. Skip any correct use you see.

1. Its unfortunate that the game ended in a tie.

2. The tree lost its leaves.

3. Its beginning to feel like fall now.

4. The library was closing its' doors.

5. I realize its none of my business.

19h Quotation Marks (" " and ' ')   P

1. Use quotation marks to enclose someone's spoken or written words.

Examples   The daughter wrote, "Remember, Daddy, when you pass on you can't take your money with you."

"But I've already bought a fireproof money belt," answered her father.

2. Use quotation marks around the titles of essays,* articles, chapter headings, short stories, short poems, and songs.

Examples   "How to Paint Ceramic Ashtrays"

"The Fall of the House of Usher"

"In Flanders Fields"

"Raven and Coyote"

3. You may either underline or place quotation marks around a word, phrase, or letter used as the subject of discussion.

Examples   Never use "however" as a coordinating conjunction.

The word "bigwig," meaning an important person, is derived from the large wigs worn by seventeenth-century British judges.

Is your middle initial "X" or "Y"?

Her use of such adjectives as "drab," "bleak," and "musty" gives the poem a sombre tone.

4. Place quotation marks around uncommon nicknames and words used ironically. Do not, however, try to apologize for slang or clichés by enclosing them in quotation marks; instead, substitute specific words.

Examples   "Scat-cat" Malone takes candy from babies.

Her "friend" was an old scarecrow in an abandoned barn.

Slang   After work Chuck liked to "simple out" in front of the television.

Specific   After work Chuck liked to relax by watching old movies on television.

---

* Do *not,* however, put quotation marks around your own essay's title on either the title page or the first page of your paper.

5. The period and the comma go inside quotation marks; the semicolon and the colon go outside. If the quoted material is a question, the question mark goes inside; if the quoted material is a part of a whole sentence that is a question, the mark goes outside. The same is true for exclamation points.

Examples   According to cartoonist Matt Groening, "Love is a snowmobile racing across the tundra; suddenly it flips over, pins you underneath, and at night the ice weasels come."

"Love is a snowmobile racing across the tundra; suddenly it flips over, pins you underneath, and at night the ice weasels come," says cartoonist Matt Groening.

According to cartoonist Matt Groening, "Love is a snowmobile . . . suddenly it flips over, pins you underneath, and at night the ice weasels come"; Groening also advises that bored friends are one of the first signs that you're in love.

Did he really say, "At night the ice weasels come"?

Sally asked, "Do you think you're in love or just in a snowmobile?"

6. Use single quotation marks to enclose a quotation (or words requiring quotation marks) within a quotation.

Examples   Professor Hall asked his class, "Do you agree with Samuel Johnson, who once said that a second marriage represents 'the triumph of hope over experience'?"

"One of my favourite songs is 'In My Life' by the Beatles," said Jane.

"I'm so proud of the 'A' on my grammar test," Sue told her parents.

▪ Practising What You've Learned

Errors with Apostrophes and Quotation Marks

Correct the following errors by adding, changing, or deleting apostrophes and quotation marks.

1. Its true that when famous wit Dorothy Parker was told that American President Coolidge, also known as Silent Cal, was dead, she exclaimed, How can they tell?

2. When a woman seated next to Coolidge at a dinner party once told him she had made a bet with a friend that she could get more than two words out of him, he replied You lose.

3. Twenty-one of Elvis Presleys albums have sold over a million copies; twenty of the Beatles albums have also done so.

4. Cinderellas stepmother wasn't pleased that her daughter received an F in her creative writing class on her poem Seven Guys and a Gal, which she had plagiarized from her two friend's Snow White and Dopey.

5. Wasn't it Mae West who said, When choosing between two evils, I always like to try the one I've never tried before? asked Olivia.

6. Gordon said Believe me, its to everybodies' advantage to sing the popular song You Stole My heart and Stomped That Sucker Flat, if thats what the holdup man wants.

7. A scholars research has revealed that the five most commonly used words in written English are the, of, and a, and to.

8. The triplets mother said that while its' hard for her to choose, Alice Munro's famous short story How I Met My Husband is probably her favourite.

9. Despite both her lawyers advice, she used the words terrifying, hideous, and unforgettable to describe her latest flight on Golden Fleece Airways, piloted by Jack One-Eye Marcus.

10. Its clear that Nick didnt know if the Christmas' tree thrown in the neighbours yard was ours, theirs', or your's.

19i Parentheses ( )   P

1. Use parentheses to set off words, dates, or statements that give additional information, explain, or qualify the main thought.

Examples   To encourage sales, some automobile manufacturers name their cars after fast or sleek animals (Impala, Mustang, and Thunderbird, for example).

Mohawk author Peter Blue-Cloud (Aroniawenrate) writes new fables based on old myths in *Elderberry Flute Song: Contemporary Coyote Tales* (1989).

The Ford Motor Company once rejected the name Utopian Turtletop for one of its new cars, choosing instead to call it the Edsel (that name obviously didn't help sales either).

2. The period comes inside the close parenthesis if a complete sentence is enclosed; it occurs after the close parenthesis when the enclosed matter comes at the end of the main sentence and is only a part of the main sentence.

Examples   The Quebec ice storm of 1998 broke records for low temperatures. (See pages 72–73 for temperature charts.)

Jean hates Edmonton winters and would prefer a warmer environment (such as the Yukon, the North Pole, or a meat locker in Hull).

3. If you are confused trying to distinguish whether information should be set off by commas, parentheses, or dashes, here are three guidelines:

a. Use commas to set off information closely related to the rest of the sentence.

Example   When Claudius married Gertrude, his brother's young widow, the
                     family was shocked. [The information identifies Gertrude and tells
                     why the family was shocked.]

    b. Use parentheses to set off information loosely related to the rest of the sentence
or material that would disturb the grammatical structure of the main sentence.

Examples   Claudius married Gertrude (his fourth marriage, her second) in
                     Las Vegas on Friday. [The information is merely an additional
                     comment not closely related to the meaning of the sentence.]

                     Claudius married Gertrude (she was previously married to his
                     brother) in Las Vegas on Friday. [The information is an additional
                     comment that would also disturb the grammatical structure of the
                     main sentence were it not enclosed in parentheses.]

    c. Use dashes to set off information dramatically or emphatically.

Example   Claudius eloped with Gertrude—only three days after her husband's
                     funeral—without saying a word to anyone in the family.

19j Brackets [ ]   P

  1. Use brackets to set off editorial explanations in the work of another writer.

Examples   According to the old letter, the treasure map could be found "in the
                     library, taped to the back of the portrait [of Catherine the Great]
                     that faces north."

                     The country singer ended the interview by saying, "My biggest hit so
                     far is 'You're the Reason Our Kids Are Ugly' [original version by
                     Sarah Bellham]."

  2. Use brackets to set off editorial corrections in quoted material. By placing the
bracketed word "*sic*" (meaning "thus") next to an error, you indicate that the mistake
appeared in the original text and that *you* are not misquoting or misspelling.

Examples   The student wrote, "I think it's unfair for teachers to count off for
                     speling [*sic*]." ["*Sic*" in brackets indicates that the student who is
                     quoted misspelled the word "spelling."]

                     The highway advertisement read as follows: "For great stakes [*sic*],
                     eat at Joe's, located right behind Daisy's Glue Factory." [Here, "*sic*"
                     in brackets indicates an error in word choice; the restaurant owner
                     incorrectly advertised "stakes" instead of "steaks."]

19k The Dash (—)*   P

  1. Use a dash to indicate a strong or sudden shift in thought.

Examples   Now, let's be reasonable—wait, put down that ice pick!

                     "It's not athlete's foot—it's deadly coreopsis!" cried Dr. Mitty.

---

* Please note that in some typed work, a dash is indicated by *two* bar marks ("—"); one bar mark ("-")
indicates a hyphen.

2. Use dashes to set off parenthetical matter that deserves more emphasis than parentheses denote.

Examples   Wanda's newest guru—the one who practised catatonic hedonism—taught her to rest and play at the same time.

He was amazed to learn his test score—a pitiful 43.

(To clear up any confusion over the uses of dashes, commas, and parentheses, see the guidelines on pages 509–510.)

3. Use a dash before a statement that summarizes or amplifies the preceding thought. (Dashes can also be used to introduce a humorous or ironic twist on the first idea in the sentence.)

Examples   Aged wine, delicious food, someone else picking up the check—the dinner was perfect.

Not everyone agrees with football coach Vince Lombardi, who said, "Winning isn't everything—it's the only thing."

According to Hollywood star Cher, "The trouble with some women is that they get all excited about nothing—and then marry him."

▪ PRACTISING WHAT YOU'VE LEARNED

Errors with Parentheses, Brackets, and Dashes

Show that you understand the difference between parentheses, brackets, and dashes by using the best choice in the sentences that follow. Skip any correct sentences you see. (For additional practice, see also the exercise that appears on pages 515–516.)

1. George Eliot (the pen name of Mary Ann Evans) wrote the novel *Middlemarch.*

2. The Apostrophe Protection Society, founded in London in 2001, fights against the gross misuse of this mark of punctuation. Editor's note: For help with apostrophes, see pages 505–507 in this text.

3. A Russian woman holds the record for the highest number of children born to one mother: sixty-nine babies in a total of twenty-seven pregnancies sixteen pairs of twins, seven sets of triplets, and four sets of quadruplets.

4. More men holding first-class tickets on the *Titanic* were saved than childrens (sic) in the third-class section of the ship

5. Martin could stay married to Michelle as long as he played his cards right [his Visa card, his Mastercard, his American Express card.]

19l The Hyphen (-)   P

1. Use a hyphen to join words into a single adjective before a noun.

Examples   a wind-blown wig

the mud-caked sneakers

a made-for-television movie

a well-written essay

a five-year-old boy

Do *not* use a hyphen when the modifier ends in "ly."

Examples   a highly regarded worker

a beautifully landscaped yard

2. Writers who create original compound adjectives often join the words with hyphens.

Examples   Compulsive shoppers suffer from stuff-lust syndrome.

She prefers novels with they-lived-wretchedly-ever-after endings.

3. Some compound words are always spelled with a hyphen; check your dictionary when you're in doubt.

Examples   mother-in-law

president-elect

runner-up

good-for-nothing

twenty-one

Compound words made from combining verb forms are frequently hyphenated: The psychiatrist insisted his birthday presents be *shrink-wrapped*.

4. Some words with prefixes use a hyphen; again, check your dictionary if necessary. (Hint: If the second word begins with a capital letter, a hyphen is almost always used.)

Examples   ex-wife

self-esteem

all-American

non-English

Indo-Canadian

5. Use a hyphen to mark the separation of syllables when you divide a word at the end of a line. Do not divide one-syllable words; do not leave one or two letters at the end of a line. (In most dictionaries, dots are used to indicate the division of syllables: va • ca • tion.)

Examples   In your essays you should avoid using fragment sentences.

Did your father try to help you with your homework?

■ PRACTISING WHAT YOU'VE LEARNED

Errors with Hyphens

Correct the errors in the phrases that follow by adding, deleting, or changing hyphens. Skip any correct uses you see. (For additional practice using hyphens, turn to the exercise on pages 515–516.)

1. A first class event

2. The well done steak

3. A self employed person

4. His completely fabricated story

5. Her one word answer

6. Pre-Columbian art

7. A once in a lifetime experience

8. A fifteen year-old girl

9. The overly-excited dog

10. His fifty sixth birthday

19m Underlining and Italicizing* (_____)   P

1. Underline, italicize, or place quotation marks around a word, phrase, or letter used as the subject of discussion. Whether you underline, italicize, or use quotation marks, always be consistent. (See also pages 507–509.)

Examples   No matter how I spell <u>offered</u>, it always looks wrong.

Is your middle initial <u>X</u> or <u>Y</u>?

Her use of such words as <u>drab</u>, <u>bleak</u>, and <u>musty</u> give the poem a sombre tone.

No matter how I spell *offered,* it always looks wrong.

Is your middle initial *X* or *Y*?

Her use of such words as *drab, bleak,* and *musty* give the poem a sombre tone.

---

* In most printed matter, including this textbook, words that might otherwise be underlined are presented in italics: She had just finished reading *The English Patient.* Italics are often preferred to underlines, especially when you are writing the title of a book. Check the MLA and APA guidelines for different guidelines on underlining and italicizing, and consult your instructor's preferences before you submit your assignments.

2. Italicize or underline the title of books, magazines, newspapers, movies, works of art, television programs (but use quotation marks for individual episodes), airplanes, trains, and ships.

Examples	*Moby Dick*/<u>Moby Dick</u>
	The Reader's Digest/<u>The Reader's Digest</u>
	The Toronto Star/<u>The Toronto Star</u>
	Who Has Seen the Wind?/<u>Who Has Seen the Wind?</u>
	Mona Lisa/<u>Mona Lisa</u>
	The Nature of Things/<u>The Nature of Things</u>
	Spirit of St. Louis/<u>Spirit of St. Louis</u>
	Arrow/<u>Arrow</u>
	Titanic/<u>Titanic</u>

Exceptions: Do not italicize or underline the Bible or the titles of legal documents, including the Canadian Constitution, or the name of your own essay when it appears on your title page. Do not italicize or underline the city in a newspaper title unless the city's name is actually part of the newspaper's title.

3. Italicize or underline foreign words that are not commonly regarded as part of the English language.

Examples	He shrugged and said, "<u>C'est la vie</u>."
	He shrugged and said, "*C'est la vie*."
	Under the "For Sale" sign on the old rusty truck, the farmer had written the words "<u>caveat emptor</u>," meaning "Let the buyer beware."
	Under the "For Sale" sign on the old rusty truck, the farmer had written the words "*caveat emptor*," meaning "Let the buyer beware."

4. Use underlining or italics sparingly to show emphasis.

Examples	Everyone was surprised to discover that the butler <u>didn't</u> do it.
	"Do you realize that <u>your</u> son just ate a piece of my priceless sculpture?" the artist screamed at the museum director.
	Everyone was surprised to discover that the butler *didn't* do it.
	"Do you realize that *your* son just ate a piece of my priceless sculpture?" the artist screamed at the museum director.

19n Ellipsis Points (. . . or . . . .)   P

1. To show an omission in quoted material within a sentence, use three periods set tight, with spaces preceding and following. Do not overuse this, however, or use it to suppress ideas or information that might mislead your reader or might hurt your own thesis.

Original	Every time my father told the children about his having to trudge barefooted to school in the snow, the walk got longer and the snow got deeper.
Quoted with omission	In her autobiography, she wrote, "Every time my father told the children about his having to trudge barefooted to school . . . the snow got deeper."

2. Three points may be used to show an incomplete or interrupted thought.

Example	This first novel is a witty, profound examination of the beauty of life in the prairies. On the other hand, F. Lame's novel on snowstorms . . . well, it is hard to explain.

3. If you omit any words at the end of a quotation and you are also ending your sentence, use three points plus a fourth to indicate the period. Do not add space before the first point.

Example	According to Ferdinand de Saussure, without language to shape it and give it form, thought is a "shapeless and indistinct mass. . . ."

4. If the omission of one or more sentences occurs at the end of a quoted sentence, use four points with no space before the first point.

Example	"The Lord is my shepherd; I shall not want. . . . he leadeth me in the paths of righteousness for his name's sake."

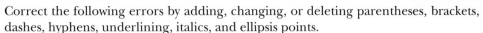

▪ PRACTISING WHAT YOU'VE LEARNED

Errors with Parentheses, Brackets, Dashes, Hyphens, Underlining, and Ellipses

Correct the following errors by adding, changing, or deleting parentheses, brackets, dashes, hyphens, underlining, italics, and ellipsis points.

1. Many moviegoers know that the ape in King Kong the original 1933 version, not the re-make was only an eighteen inch tall animated figure, but not everyone realizes that the Red Sea Moses parted in the 1923 movie of The Ten Commandments was a quivering slab of Jell O sliced down-the-middle.

2. We recall the last words of General John B. Sedwick at the Battle of Spotsylvania in 1864: "They couldn't hit an elephant at this dist   ."

3. In a person to person telephone call the twenty five year old starlet promised the hard working gossip columnist that she would "tell the truth . . . and nothing but the truth" about her highly-publicized feud with her exhusband, editor in chief of Meat Eaters Digest.

4. While sailing across the Atlantic on board the celebrity filled yacht Titanic II, Dottie Mae Haskell she's the author of the popular new self

help book Finding Wolves to Raise Your Children confided that until recently she thought chutzpah was an Italian side dish.

5. During their twenty four hour sit in at the melt down site, the anti-nuclear protestors began to sing, "with glowing hearts we see thee rise. . ."

6. Few people know that James Arness later Matt Dillon in the long running television series Gunsmoke got his start by playing the vegetable creature in the postwar monster movie The Thing 1951.

7. Not many people know the well known novelist Timothy Findley he died of cancer in 2002 was part of the original Stratford Festival Company in Niagara on the Lake playing a small role in Richard III.

8. A French chemist named Georges Claude invented the first neon sign in 1910. For additional information on his unsuccessful attempts to use seawater to generate electricity, see pages 200–205.

9. When Lucille Ball, star of I Love Lucy, became pregnant with her first child, the network executives decided that the word expecting could be used on the air to refer to her condition, but not the word pregnant.

10. In mystery stories the detective often advises the police to cherchez la femme. Editor's note: Cherchez la femme means "look for the woman."

Chapter 20

A Concise Guide to Mechanics

20a Capitalization   Cap

1. Capitalize the first word of every sentence. Do not capitalize random words within a sentence, but follow the rules in this chapter.

Example   The lazy horse leans against a tree all day.

2. Capitalize proper nouns—the specific names of people, places, and products—and also the adjectives formed from proper nouns.

Examples   John Doe
Ottawa, Ontario
Bank of Montreal
the Eiffel Tower
Chevrolets
Japanese cameras
Spanish class
an English major

3. Always capitalize the days of the week, the names of the months, and holidays.

Examples   Saturday, December 14
Tuesday's meeting
Halloween parties
Yom Kippur

Special events are often capitalized: Stanley Cup, World Series, Festival of Lights.

4. Capitalize titles when they are accompanied by proper names.

Examples   Prime Minister Harper, Major Smith, Lieutenant-Governor Brown, Judge Wheeler, Professor Plum, Queen Elizabeth

5. Capitalize all the principal words in titles of books, articles, stories, plays, movies, and poems. Prepositions, articles, and conjunctions are not capitalized unless they begin or end the title.

Examples   "The Face on the Barroom Floor"

The Rise and Fall of the Third Reich

Roughing It in the Bush

6. Capitalize the first word of a direct quotation.

Examples   Shocked at actor John Barrymore's use of profanity, the woman said, "Sir, I'll have you know I'm a lady!"

Barrymore replied, "Your secret is safe with me."

7. Capitalize "east," "west," "north," and "south" when they refer to particular sections of the country but not when they merely indicate direction.

Examples   The East has produced many excellent writers, including Timothy Findley and Margaret Atwood. ["East" here refers to a section of the country.]

If you travel east for ten miles, you'll see the papier-mâché replica of the world's largest hamburger. [In this case, "east" is a direction.]

8. Capitalize a title when referring to a particular person;* do not capitalize a title if a pronoun precedes it.

Examples   The Prime Minister announced a new national holiday honouring Frank H. Fleer, inventor of bubble gum.

The new car Dad bought is guaranteed for 15,000 kilometres or until something goes wrong.

My mother told us about a Hollywood party during which Zelda and F. Scott Fitzgerald collected and boiled all the women's purses.

■ PRACTISING WHAT YOU'VE LEARNED

Errors with Capitalization

A. Correct the errors in capitalization in the following phrases.

   1. delicious chinese food

   2. mother's day memories

---

* Some authorities disagree; others consider such capitalization optional.

3. fiery southwestern salsa

4. his latest novel, the story of a prince among thieves

5. my son's Wedding at the baptist church

6. count Dracula's castle in transylvania

7. japanese-canadian heritage

8. a dodge van driven across the lion's gate bridge

9. sunday morning newspapers

10. the british daughter-in-law of senator Snort

20b Abbreviations   Ab

1. Abbreviate the titles "Mr.," "Mrs.," "Ms.," "St.," and "Dr." when they precede names.

Examples   Dr. Dhillon, Ms. Steinham, Mrs. Kwok, St. Jude

2. Abbreviate titles and degrees when they follow names.

Examples   Charles Byrd, Jr.; Xue-Ying Chu, Ph.D.; Dudley Carpenter, D.D.S.

3. You may abbreviate the following in even the most formal writing: a.m. (*ante meridiem*, before noon), p.m. (*post meridiem*, after noon), A.D. (*anno Domini*, in the year of our Lord), B.C. (before Christ), C.E. (common era), etc. (*et cetera*, and others), i.e. (*id est*, that is), and e.g. (*exempli gratia*, for example).

4. In formal writing, do *not* abbreviate the names of days, months, centuries, provinces, countries, or units of measure. Do *not* use an ampersand (&) unless it is an official part of a title.

Incorrect in formal writing	Tues., Sept., 18th century, Ont., Mex., lbs.
Correct	Tuesday, September, eighteenth century, Ontario, Mexico, pounds
Incorrect	Bob & Doug went to the store to buy new toques.
Correct	Bob *and* Doug went to the A & N to buy new toques. [The "&" in "A & N" is correct because it is part of the store's official name.]

5. In formal writing, do *not* abbreviate the words for page, chapter, volume, and so forth, except in footnotes and bibliographies, which have prescribed rules of abbreviation.

(For additional information on proper abbreviation, consult your dictionary.)

20c Numbers   Num

1. Use figures for dates, street or room numbers, page numbers, telephone numbers, percentages, and hours with a.m. and p.m.*

Examples   April 22, 1946

710 West 14th Street

page 242

room 17

(905) 476-1423

40 percent

10:00 a.m.

2. Some authorities say spell out numbers that can be expressed in one or two words; others say spell out numbers under one hundred. When in doubt, choose the system that you think will be clearest to your audience and be consistent.

Examples   ten thousand dollars or $10,000

twenty-four hours

thirty-nine years

five partridges

$12.99 per pair

1,294 essays

3. When several numbers are used in a short passage, use figures.

Examples   In the anchovy-eating contest, Jennifer ate 22, Juan ate 21, Pete ate 16, and I ate 6.

According to a national poll, on an average day 11,000 babies are born, 6,000 people die, 7,000 couples marry, and 3,000 couples divorce.

4. Never begin a sentence with a figure.

Incorrect   50 spectators turned out to watch the surfing exhibition at Niagara Falls.

Correct   Fifty spectators turned out to watch the surfing exhibition at Niagara Falls.

5. When a date containing a day and a year appears within a sentence, always set off the year by placing commas on each side.

Examples   She married her first husband on February 2, 1978, in Nova Scotia.

The first birth on a commercial airliner occurred on October 28, 1929, as the plane cruised over Miami.

_____

* 8:00 a.m. or 8 a.m., but eight o'clock in the morning.

■ **PRACTISING WHAT YOU'VE LEARNED**

Errors in Capitalization, Abbreviations, and Numbers

Correct the following errors by adding, deleting, or changing capitals, abbreviations, and numbers. Skip any correct words, letters, or numbers you may find.

1. In a house of Commons speech in November 2007, the honourable Josée Verner, member of Parliament, reported that new grants have been made to support women's initiatives, including eighty-five thousand dollars to training programs for single mothers, $165,000 to art projects for the canadian women at risk, and $200,000 to the st john chapter of the Urban Core Support Network.

2. My sister, who lives in the east, was amazed to read studies by Thomas Radecki, MD, showing that 12-year-olds commit 300 percent more murders than did the same age group 30 years ago.

3. In A.D. 67 the roman emperor Nero entered the chariot race at the olympic games, and although he failed to finish the race, the judges unanimously declared him the Winner.

4. According to John Alcock, a Behavioral Ecologist at Arizona State University, in the U.S.A. the chance of being poisoned by a snake is 20 times less than that of being hit by lightning and 300 times less than the risk of being murdered by a fellow American.

5. The official chinese news agency, located in the city of xinhua, estimates that there are ten million guitar players in their country today, an amazing number considering that the instrument was banned during the cultural revolution, which lasted 10 years, from nineteen sixty-six to nineteen seventy-six.

6. In 1921 there were 235 elected seats, of which the liberal party won 116, but Mackenzie King only led his party to a minority government, while the conservatives, who had fewer votes than the Progressives, formed the official Opposition.

7. The british soldier T. E. Lawrence, better known as "lawrence of arabia," stood less than 5 ft. 6 in. tall.

8. Drinking a glass of french wine makes me giddy before my 10 a.m. english class, held in wrigley field every other friday except on New Year's day.

9. During the debates on language divisions in Canada in the 1970s, Prime Minister Diefenbaker declared, "we shall never build the nation which our potential resources make possible by dividing ourselves into Anglophones, Francophones, multiculturalphones, or whatever kind of phoneys you choose."

10. Alexander Graham Bell, inventor of the telephone, died in nova scotia on aug. 2, 1922; 2 days later, on the day of his burial, for 1 minute no telephone in north america was allowed to ring.

20d Spelling   Sp

For some folks, learning to spell correctly is harder than trying to herd cats. Entire books have been written to teach people to become better spellers, and some of these are available at your local bookstore (and, no, not listed under witchcraft!). Here, however, are a few suggestions that seem to work for many students:

1. Keep a list of the little beasties you misspell. After a few weeks, you may notice that you tend to misspell the same words again and again or that the words you misspell tend to fit a pattern—that is, you can't remember when the *i* goes before the *e* or when to change the *y* to *i* before *ed*. Try to memorize the words you repeatedly misspell, or at least keep the list somewhere handy so you can refer to it when you're editing your last draft (listing the words on the inside cover of your dictionary also makes sense).

2. Become aware of a few rules that govern some of our spelling in English. For example, many people know the rule in the jingle "*I* before *E* except after *C* or when sounded as *A* as in *neighbour* and *weigh*." Not everyone, however, knows the follow-up line, which contains most of the exceptions to that jingle: "Neither the weird financier nor the foreigner seizes leisure at its height."

3. Here are some other rules, without jingles, for adding suffixes (new endings to words), a common plague for poor spellers:

- Change final *y* to *i* if the *y* follows a consonant.

  bury → buried

  marry → marries

- But if the suffix is *-ing*, keep the *y*.

  marry + ing = marrying

  worry + ing = worrying

- If the word ends in a single consonant after a single vowel and the accent is on the last syllable, double the consonant before adding the suffix.

  occur → occurred

  cut → cutting

  swim → swimmer

- If a word ends in a silent *e*, drop the *e* before adding *-able* or *-ing*.

  love + able = lovable

  believe + able = believable

4. Here's an easy rule governing the doubling of letters with the addition of prefixes (new beginning syllables): most of the time, you simply add all the letters you've got when you mix the word and the prefix.

  mis + spell = misspell

  un + natural = unnatural

  re + entry = reentry

5. Teach yourself to spell the words that you miss often by making up your own silly rules or jingles. For instance:

dessert (one *s* or two?): I always want two helpings so I double the *s*.

apparently (apparantly?): Ap*parent*ly, my *parent* knows the whole story.

separate (seperate?): I'd be *a rat* to sep*arat*e from you.

a lot (or alot?): A cot (not *acot*) provides *a lot* of comfort in a tent.

questionnaire (one *n* or two?): Questio*nn*aires have *n*umerous *n*umbered questions (two *n*'s).

And so on.

6. Don't forget to proofread your papers carefully. Anything that looks misspelled probably is, and deserves to be looked up in your dictionary. Don't rely on your spell checker alone (see Chapter 5). Reading your paper one sentence at a time from the end helps, too, because you tend to start thinking about your ideas when you read from the beginning of your paper. (And if you are writing on a word processor that has a spell program, don't forget to run it.)

Although these few suggestions won't completely cure your spelling problems, they may make a dramatic improvement in the quality of your papers and give you the confidence to continue learning and practising other rules that govern the spelling of our language. Good luck!

Part 5

Additional Readings

Part Five offers twenty-four additional readings to help you improve your writing skills. In nine chapters, two selections illustrate each of the strategies previously explained in Part Two. In addition, Chapter 30 includes a speech and an essay illustrating multiple strategies for further analysis; Chapter 31 offers additional poetry and fiction to supplement literary assignments; Chapter 32 presents essays on writing and language. Overall, the readings in Part Five were selected not only to model methods of development but also to illustrate a variety of styles and tones, including humour and irony.

A close reading of these selections can help you become a better writer in several ways. Identifying the various methods by which these writers focused, organized, and developed their material may spark new ideas as you plan and shape your own essay. Familiarizing yourself with different styles and tones may encourage new uses of language. Analyzing the rhetorical choices of other writers will also help you revise your prose because it promotes the habit of asking questions from the reader's point of view. Moreover, reading the opinions or sharing the experience of these authors may suggest interesting topics for your own essays. In other words, to help yourself become a more effective writer, read as much and as often as you can. ∎

Chapter 21

Exposition: Development by Example

■ Our Essential Function

Alberto Manguel

Alberto Manguel is an Argentinean writer who has lived in many places, including Argentina, Italy, Tahiti, Israel, Canada, and England, and has written both in Spanish and in English. He was the Massey Lecturer at the University of Toronto in 2007, and the lectures in this series, entitled *The City of Words* (2007), continue his exploration of the power of words in constructing cultural identity and effecting social change. His works include *The Dictionary of Imaginary Places* (1980), *Reading Pictures: A History of Love and Hate* (2000), *A Reading Diary* (2004), and *A History of Reading* (1996), from which the following excerpt was taken.

1   I first discovered that I could read at the age of four. I had seen, over and over again, the letters that I knew (because I had been told) were the names of the pictures under which they sat. The boy drawn in thick black lines, dressed in red shorts and a green shirt (that same red and green cloth from which all the other images in the book were cut, dogs and cats and trees and thin tall mothers), was also somehow, I realized, the stern black shapes beneath him, as if the boy's body had been dismembered into three clean-cut figures; one arm and the torso, **b**; the severed head so perfectly round, **o**; and the limp, low-hanging legs, **y**. I drew eyes in the round face, and a smile, and filled in the hollow circle of the torso. But there was more: I knew that not only did these shapes mirror the boy above them, but they also could tell me precisely what the boy

was doing, arms stretched out and legs apart. **The boy runs**, said the shapes. He wasn't jumping, as I might have thought, or pretending to be frozen into place, or playing a game whose rules and purpose were unknown to me. **The boy runs**.

2   And yet these realizations were common acts of conjuring, less interesting because someone else had performed them for me. Another reader—my nurse, probably—had explained the shapes and now, every time the pages opened to the image of this exuberant boy, I knew what the shapes beneath him meant. There was pleasure in this, but it wore thin. There was no surprise.

3   Then one day, from the window of a car (the destination of that journey is now forgotten), I saw a billboard by the side of the road. The sight could not have lasted very long; perhaps the car stopped for a moment, perhaps it just slowed down long enough for me to see, large and looming, shapes similar to those in my book, but shapes I had never seen before. And yet, all of a sudden, I knew what they were; I heard them in my head, they metamorphosed from black lines and white spaces into a solid, sonorous, meaningful reality. I had done this all by myself. No one had performed the magic for me. I and the shapes were alone together, revealing ourselves in a silently respectful dialogue. Since I could turn bare lines into living reality, I was all-powerful. I could read.

4   What that word was on the long-past billboard I no longer know (vaguely I seem to remember a word with several As in it), but the impression of suddenly being able to comprehend what before I could only gaze at is as vivid today as it must have been then. It was like acquiring an entirely new sense, so that now certain things no longer consisted merely of what my eyes could see, my ears could hear, my tongue could taste, my nose could smell, my fingers could feel, but of what my whole body could decipher, translate, give voice to, read.

5   The readers of books, into whose family I was unknowingly entering (we always think that we are alone in each discovery, and that every experience, from birth to death, is terrifyingly unique), extend or concentrate a function common to us all. Reading letters on a page is only one of its many guises. The astronomer reading a map of stars that no longer exist, the Japanese architect reading the land on which a house is to be built so as to guard it from evil forces; the zoologist reading the spoor of animals in the forest; the card-player reading her partner's gestures before playing the winning card; the dancer reading the choreographer's notations, and the public reading the dancer's movements on the stage; the weaver reading the intricate design of a carpet being woven; the organ-player reading various simultaneous strands of music orchestrated on the page; the parent reading the baby's face for signs of joy or fright, or wonder; the Chinese fortune-teller reading the ancient marks on the shell of a tortoise; the lover blindly reading the loved one's body at night, under the sheets; the psychiatrist helping patients read their own bewildering dreams; the Hawaiian fisherman reading the ocean currents by plunging a hand into the water; the farmer reading the weather in the sky—all these share with book-readers the craft of deciphering and translating signs. Some of these readings are coloured by the knowledge that the thing read was created for this specific purpose by other human beings—music notation or road signs, for instance—or by the gods—the tortoise shell, the sky at night. Others belong to chance.

6   And yet, in every case, it is the reader who reads the sense; it is the reader who grants or recognizes in an object, place or event a certain possible readability; it is the

reader who must attribute meaning to a system of signs, and then decipher it. We all read ourselves and the world around us in order to glimpse what and where we are. We read to understand, or to begin to understand. We cannot do but read. Reading, almost as much as breathing, is our essential function.

■ A False Utopia

Mark Kingwell

Mark Kingwell, a philosophy professor at the University of Toronto, is also contributing editor of *Harper's Magazine* and *The Globe and Mail*. He has written several books, including *Dreams of Millennium: Report from a Culture on the Brink* (1997) and the best-selling work, *In Pursuit of Happiness: Better Living from Plato to Prozac* (2000), from which this excerpt was chosen. Kingwell writes commentary on popular culture, and conducts research on social and political theory, as well as the philosophy of art.

1   The ideological sleight of hand contained in the suggestion that money has nothing to do with happiness is insidious, because even as it seems to repudiate old-fashioned material fulfillment as somehow tawdry or sordid and therefore beneath the true seeker, it blithely takes for granted that basic material needs are met. Thus those who are unhappy not because they lack self-fulfilment but because they lack food are wrong-footed, summarily judged to be spiritually impaired—or, more simply, unable to see the silver lining in life's inevitable clouds. It is no longer "Pull yourself together and get a job"; now it's "Pull yourself together and be happy." Here Maslow's plain common sense about the hierarchy of needs is turned on its head. Instead of seeing the hierarchy as based on prepotence—fulfillment is not even an issue if I don't have enough to eat—it is shifted around to suggest that any failures in achieving happiness demonstrate an unfortunate attachment to the material things in life.

2   Notice, in another example of this inversion, the sort of twisted, quasi-Maslovian thinking that is buried in one of American culture's most endurable exports, Gene Roddenberry's "Star Trek" vision of the future. A gushing thirtieth anniversary celebration for "Star Trek" and its various spinoffs happened to coincide with certain lively manifestations of the happiness-therapy boom in Britain and North America during 1996, making the comparison illuminating and irresistible. (The same issue of the *Radio Times* with the happiness quiz features a "Star Trek" cover story and eighteen glossy pages of full-colour raving; the show is as popular in Britain as in North America, even if the goofy, geeks-only conventions are happily less common.) "Star Trek" offers the most powerful utopian vision in cultural play right now in the various updatings and spinoffs of the original, rather cheesy television series; note in particular the techno-spiritual liberalism and New Age corporate groupthink of Captain Picard's Enterprise D on "Star Trek: The Next Generation." Actually, there is little difference among the various mutations of the original concept once you get past the surface decoration and a few insignificant shifts in tone. Both vintages of "Star Trek" are actually apologies for American cultural imperialism, the gospel according to comfort and market-based happiness. As one critic has put it, Picard, in contrast to the overheated and boyish militarism of Captain James Kirk, "usually takes an anguished meeting with his senior officers before bagging the Prime Directive."

3   Of course people love the future offered by Gene Roddenberry and his conceptual heirs. With no poverty, no hunger, lots of virtual-reality diversions and little meaningful conflict—the wars and battles are often no more than special-effects window dressing, hardly challenging the overall social structure—the subtext of the various series and movies is clearly one of self-actualization: a celebration of the human factor against encroaching technology, an insistence on psycho-spiritual development, the embracing of paradoxes as a means to hike humankind into the next evolutionary bracket. With synthetic pleasures and food on tap twenty-four hours a day, there is no reason to suppose anyone lacks the basic conditions of happiness. In other words, "Star Trek" doesn't just use soma-like devices in its basic fantastic infrastructure—recreational holodecks, frankly sex-for-sale holosuites, a popular vacation planet full of cheerful prostitutes—*it is itself a form of soma.* Ingested as a television drug, it dulls our sense of its own unreality by playing on immature teenage visions of a future where nobody is poor, sex is always free, and drinks make you witty and playful but never drunk.

4   Not that this vision goes entirely unchallenged. In one memorable episode of the "Star Trek" spinoff series "Deep Space Nine," a group of renegades decrying the lack of moral fibre in the United Federation of Planets tries to sabotage the sex-driven resort planet called Raisa, offering a fine denunciation of the adolescent world-view that dominates the "Star Trek" empire. This is an astonishing piece of self-criticism—except that the moral revolutionaries, known as the New Essentialists, are eventually exposed in the episode as crazed right-wingers, Jesse Helms types with bright shining eyes and violent hearts. Thus the important kernel of truth in their message –that the Federation world is indeed one of greedy self-fulfilment that fails to confront the problems of economic inequality—falls to the ground, safely ignored. The tables are effectively turned so that our superficial political disapproval of the reactionary "solution" to dissipation is made to occlude the deeper, more insidious conservatism of the basic premise.

5   These critical interventions drive us to the conclusion that the future imagined by "Star Trek"—one that resonates powerfully with many people around the world—is dangerously misleading. It asks us to conceive a world in which all the hard problems of political life are swept under the carpet, and suggests, along the way, that anybody who resists that piece of self-delusion is in fact a psychological and political neanderthal. "Star Trek" seduces us with a shortcut to self-actualization by cynically disposing of our baser needs with a too-simple solution. Happiness or nothing! "Star Trek," like all cheap forms of self-fulfilment, is utopian in the worst possible sense.

Chapter 22

Exposition:
Process Analysis

■ And the Best Damn Stew-Maker Too

Peter Gzowski

Peter Gzowski was a well-loved Canadian broadcaster, whose radio program, *Morningside*, brought him much acclaim. He began his career as a journalist and was the youngest managing editor of *Maclean's* magazine when he joined the staff in 1958. Gzowski's interviews with prominent Canadians, from prime ministers to musicians, were famous for their combination of friendliness and directness.

1   One of the nicest things about growing up is the way you can enjoy all the foods you turned your nose up at as a kid.

2   Take liver. When I was young, liver was right up there with bullies and social studies on my list of things to be avoided. I still don't like bullies, and social studies, though I make a lot of my living talking about them on the radio, still gives me trouble. (I miss all the blue questions at Trivial Pursuit, too.) But on liver I've come all the way round. From a pet hate it's turned into a favoured food; I eat it now—I would never have believed this when I was six—by choice, and lick my lips when I'm finished.

3   The liver I ate as a child, of course, was cut in slabs as thick as beaverboard and cooked till you could fix your roof with it. Now, I buy my slices as thin as I can—a quarter inch is about right—and it is as rare as filet mignon. To cook it, I fry up some bacon first, and while it's sizzling I cut up a couple of onions. When the bacon's done, I set it aside on a paper towel, turn the heat down and sauté the onions in the drippings. When the onions are soft but not translucent, I set them aside, too, crank the heat

back up, splash some wine vinegar into the pan ("deglazing" is too fancy a word for the way I cook) and sear my liver each side for less time than it took Northern Dance to win the Kentucky Derby—two minutes flat. Smothered in the bacon and onions, and with a little watercress vinaigrette on the side, it's food for the gods—or a grown-up.

4   Or spinach. Spinach was *punishment* when I was a kid: a soggy, mossy blob that lay on your plate like a mud pie, leaking green effluvium.

5   The trick with spinach, I know, is to cook it as little as possible. Just grab a handful, chop off the heaviest stems, run cold water over what you have left and, without shaking it dry, pop it into a saucepan, jam the lid on and cook on high heat for *one minute*— Northern Dancer's time for five furlongs. Want to get fancy? Squeeze half a lemon over the spinach before you start to steam it. Want to get *really* fancy? Plop a dab of sour cream on top as you bring your spinach to the table. With either or neither or both, it's wonderful.

6   This side-dish, come to think of it, could go with your liver-and-bacon-and-onions, even though, if my mother found out I was recommending liver and spinach in one meal, she'd push her halo aside and scratch her head in wonderment.

7   The greatest treat of all among the foods I once disdained is stew.

8   Stew was my mother's admission she'd run out of either ideas or money, a kind of dinner-hour equivalent of—and about as tasty as—the Red River Cereal she tried to convince me to eat in the mornings.

9   For the grown-up me, stew has become a source of sheer pleasure. I like eating it, spearing the tenderest cubes of nut-brown meat, savouring the gay orange carrots and pale parsnips—*parsnips?* my mother's halo just clattered to heaven's floor—and sopping up the last rivulets of dark gravy with chunks of fresh bread. I *love* cooking it, and in the long cold winter there is no happier way for me to spend a late Friday afternoon than to follow the ritual I am pleased to share with you now. The quantities, I should tell you, are for two people, though there'll be enough extra if someone drops in or, failing that, for a reheated (and delicious) Saturday lunch.

10   At the liquor store, get a bottle of dark, fairly dry sherry. Make sure they put it in a brown paper bag. (This may not help your reputation in a strange town, but be brave.)

11   At the butcher's, get a pound and a quarter of lean stewing beef, cut into inch-and-a-half cubes.

12   At the grocer's, pick up some leeks, cooking onions, a few carrots and parsnips, a tin of beef stock, a nineteen-ounce tin of tomatoes and a tin of whole, peeled potatoes. From a guy who likes things simple and old-fashioned, I know this last suggestion will surprise you. But experience has taught me that even the best potatoes, cooked from scratch in a stew, get just a bit starchier than those little ones they put in the cans.

13   If you don't have butter, olive oil, flour, pepper (beef stews need no salt), garlic and other spices at home, pick those up too. Oh, what the heck, get another couple of heads of garlic anyway.

14   And from your favourite bakery, get a fresh baguette.

15   If you have a fireplace, begin by lighting a fire to take the chill from the fading day. Then open your sherry and pour yourself a small glass—the shopping was cold, after all. Put a sinfully thick slice of butter and about a quarter cup of your best olive oil into a generously sized saucepan or soup kettle, and turn the heat to medium high. While the butter melts and blends with the golden oil, take the paper bag from the

booze store, put a cup of flour into it and grind some pepper on top. Throw the cubes of meat in the bag and shake it vigorously. Pick the meat out by hand—the way the flour coats every piece evenly is surely one of the great miracles of the kitchen—and put it in the pan. As it browns, chop three or four peeled onions into eighths, and the white parts of the same number of leeks into inches. Chop a *lot* of garlic—I use about five cloves, but you can never have too much—and scrape everything in with the meat. Reduce the heat, have sip of sherry and take a moment to enjoy the seductive smell rising from the pan. Stir from time to time with a wooden spoon.

16   When the meat is brown, splash in about a cup—who measures?—of the sherry and the tin of beef stock. Add a sprinkle of oregano, if it pleases you, or a bit of sweet basil. Lower the heat a notch (you don't want to *boil* it), and savour the smell again as you open the tin of tomatoes.

17   This is a good time to cut up the carrots and parsnips, as well—I peel the parsnips but just scrape the roughest skin off the carrots. Try to get all your pieces roughly the size of Brazil nuts.

18   You can slow down now, while your stew simmers. In another twenty minutes or so, add the tomatoes, liquid and all, and root veggies, and, half an hour after that, the tinned potatoes. Give it another ten or fifteen minutes—there's no rush, you know—while you put out some bowls, forks and spoons. You can rip up the baguette by hand.

19   The result, like youth itself, would be wasted on kids anyway.

■ Dogs and Monsters

Stanley Coren

Stanley Coren, who is a professor of psychology at the University of British Columbia, has two careers. His extensive research on human cognitive processes has won him many academic honours, and his textbook, *Sensation and Perception,* is perhaps the most used undergraduate textbook on this subject. Coren is also recognized for his best-selling books on dog behaviour, and his efforts at creating public awareness about dog training and dog–human relationships have led to North American lecture tours and numerous television appearances. This essay originally appeared in the magazine *Saturday Night* (2000).

1   Today's headlines routinely raise fears about genetic engineering. The biggest concern is that "tampering with creation" to fashion new strains of plants and animals may result in the devastation of the world by upsetting the natural balance among species. Even Prince Charles has joined the debate, claiming that genetic engineering "takes us into areas that should be left to God. We should not be meddling with the building blocks of life in this way." But the genetic manipulation of species is far from new. In fact, it began at least 14,000 years ago, when human beings created the first deliberately engineered organism—the dog.

2   The bioengineered canine was not created in a high-level bio-containment lab; rather, its beginnings were accidental. Wolves and jackals (the domestic dog's predecessors) were attracted to human camps because primitive humans left bones, bits of skin, and other scraps of leftover food scattered near their dwellings. The wolves and jackals learned that they could grab an occasional bite to eat without the exertion involved in hunting. These primitive dogs were initially tolerated by humans because they functioned as *de facto* garbage disposal units.

3   The dogs near the campsite provided another key benefit: security. They barked whenever wild beasts or strangers approached, removing the need for human guards to be posted at night, and thus affording the villagers more rest and increased safety. The bark was critical—the most effective guard dogs, obviously, were those with loud, persistent barks. And so a selective breeding program was begun: those dogs that barked loudly were kept and bred with other loud barkers, while those that did not bark were simply killed or chased off. In fact, one of the major distinctions between wild canines and domestic dogs today is that domestic dogs bark, while wild dogs seldom do. The persistent racket that irritates so many people is actually a human innovation.

4   It wasn't until the end of the fifteenth century, though, that the dog as a genetic creation became truly unique—almost more an invention than a species. At this point people began cross-breeding dogs, not just to cater to their changing needs, but to suit an advancing technology. Typically, humans had tailored machines to suit organisms. With dogs, they began modifying an organism to fit a machine. The machine was the gun, and the organism was the gun dog.

5   The earliest gun dogs were the pointers, which appeared in Europe in the 1500s. The hunting weapon of choice at the time was a muzzle-loading musket, a primitive device that was notoriously laborious to use. On sighting his quarry, a hunter had to take out his powder horn, dump gunpowder down the barrel, followed by a lead ball wrapped with oiled paper or cloth, and tamp down the shot and powder with a tamping rod; then he had to fire the gun. The process took a minimum of thirty seconds, all in the service of a weapon with an effective range of twenty-five to fifty yards. To accommodate musket technology, the pointer was designed to be slow, silent, and patient. The pointer's job was to find a bird, then to hold its position while pointing at the bird's location for the agonizingly long time it took the hunter to load and shoot his weapon. If a lucky shot actually killed a bird the pointer was expected to go out and bring the game back as well. But the retrieval was window-dressing; the pointer's genetic value lay in its ability to stretch time out, to live in a slow-motion world.

6   As weapons technology improved, guns became easier to load, with better range and accuracy. To match this new equipment, dog breeders in the late 1700s created a new kind of dog—the setter. Setters moved much more quickly than pointers, and indicated their proximity to the prey not by the stillness of their point but by the beat of their tails. The faster a setter wagged its tail, the closer it was to the game.

7   As more land was cultivated and cities and towns sprang up, hunters were forced to turn to wilderness areas, particularly wetlands, where they hid behind blinds and waited for their quarry to come to them. These circumstances placed a premium on a dog that was not simply quiet, as the pointer had been, but that possessed an almost preternatural obedience and patience. Thus, the retriever became the bioengineered star of the next century. Retrievers were bred to wait—to do nothing: not to point, not to flush, not to run and bark—and retrieve. They were bred to be less, not more, which, given the physiognomy of the species, may have been the more remarkable biotechnological feat.

8   Canada is responsible for the newest and most intriguing genetic invention in the retriever group: the Nova Scotia duck tolling retriever, a handsome, auburn-hued dog that stands about twenty inches high and weighs about forty-five pounds. The need for the toller arose when duck hunters found that they could better attract their quarry by having wooden "lures," or decoys, carved to look like ducks, floating in the nearby

water. Ducks are also attracted to unusual movement and activities. This is where the toller comes in. Tolling simply means that the dog runs back and forth on the shore, spinning and making noise, or swims erratically near the shore to attract the birds. Curious ducks fly near to see what all the activity is about, and come within range of the hunter's gun. Tollers will do this for hours if needed. Of course, once the bird is shot the dog is then expected to swim out and bring it back to its lazy master.

9   Like any piece of technology—the 78 rpm record player, or the pedal-driven sewing machine—a bioengineered dog can become outmoded and obsolete. One of the most common breeds of the eighteenth and nineteenth centuries, the Spanish pointer, was so popular in its day that it can be seen in scores of early paintings of hunts. These dogs were perfect for the era of the muzzle-loading musket—slow, quiet, and the most meticulous of the pointers. Today the breed is effectively extinct. Spanish pointers were simply too slow for impatient modern hunters, with their new, superior equipment—both guns and dogs.

10   Walk into homes today, and what you'll find are dogs engineered for a wholly different piece of technology: the TV remote control. Perhaps our faith in biogenetic engineering would be improved if we recognized that for those of us who don't hunt, some dogs have also been designed specifically to be our companions—to fit the couch-potato mentality of our current, leisure-addicted era. It is a wonder to me that starting with the DNA of a wolf, we have spent 14,000 years of biotechnology and genetic manipulation in the creation of the little white beast who is right now gently snoring with his head resting against my foot.

Chapter 23

Exposition:
Comparison and Contrast

■ Ottawa vs. New York

Germaine Greer

Germaine Greer's feminist manifesto *The Female Eunuch* (1970) made her a household name in her native Australia, as well as in the rest of the English-speaking world. Her controversial views about gender roles and aboriginal rights in Australia have caused furious public debates, from her early years as a doctoral candidate at Cambridge, to her present life as a university professor and a cultural icon. Her early academic work on Romantic poetry and Elizabethan drama made way for art history and, later, women's studies. As a professor and Director of the Centre for the Study of Women's Literature at the University of Tulsa, Oklahoma, she founded the important academic journal *Tulsa Studies in Women's Literature*. Greer has written several newspaper and journal articles, and books, including *The Beautiful Boy* (2003). In her role as controversial feminist icon, she has appeared on many popular culture programs on British radio and television. She is currently a professor at the University of Warwick, England. The following article was written for the *Times Literary Supplement* in 1999.

1   Waking up in Ottawa is not something I expect to do more than two or three times in this lifetime, and two of those times have already happened. This is not solely because Ottawa coffee is perhaps the worst in Canada and Canadian coffee on the whole the bitterest and weakest you will ever encounter, though these truths have some bearing. The badness of the coffee could be directly related to the current weakness of the currency; there was certainly an air of poverty-strickenness about the once great hotel I woke up in. My room was huge; as long as it was lit only by the forty-watt bulbs in the four

lamps that cowered by the walls I could not see the dispiriting dun colour of the quarter-acre or so of carpet, but I could smell its depressing cocktail of sixty years of food, smoking, cosmetics and sex, overlaid by a choking amalgam of air-freshener, carpet-deodoriser, dry cleaner and shampoo. I slept with the window open as the first line of defence, and then leapt out of bed and into a shower that could not be regulated heat-wise or pressurewise, and scooted off to an equally dun, dispiriting and malodorous dining room for breakfast, to wit, one bran muffin and juice made from concentrate. It is sybaritism, rather than self-discipline, that has reduced me to the semi-sylph-like pro-portions that I at present display. Mind you, giving interviews and making speeches "over lunch" effectively prevents ingestion of anything solid. The Women of Influence lunches I spoke at in Canada featured cold noodle salad and polystyrene chicken thighs, suggesting more plainly than words could that Canadian businesswomen have at their command small influence and less money.

2   To escape from Ottawa . . . to New York and the Pierpoint Morgan Library, I took a plane to La Guardia. Air Canada, as desperate to penny-pinch as all other Canadian operations, was sneakily folding the Newark flight into mine, which made me forty-five minutes late, and all the good people who needed to travel to New Jersey a great deal later. In that forty-five minutes the best-run hotel on the planet, or on Fifth Avenue, which comes to the same thing, let some interloper have my room.

3   The yingling at reception was so very, very sorry. Would I endure a night in a suite at room rate instead of the statutory $3,000 a night, and let them move me to my own room tomorrow? I hummed and hawed and sighed for as long as I thought decent, then leapt at the chance. The yingling took me up himself, and threw open the door. I strode past him into forty-foot mirrored salon hung with yellow silk damask; through the French windows a terrace hedged with clipped yew offered a spectacular view of aerial New York, as well as serried ranks of terracotta planters in which green and rose parrot tulips exhibited themselves. The east end of my salon was crowded with sofas and armchairs, all paying homage to a state-of-the-art music centre which, if I'd come equipped, I could have programmed for the whole evening. The west end featured a baronial fireplace and a ten-seater dining table. The yingling showed me my kitchen, my two bathrooms, and my seven-foot-square bed in my twenty-foot bedroom, and swept out before I could decide whether he should be tipped or not.

4   The only way to bring such magnificence into perspective was to take off all my clothes and skip about as naked as a jaybird, opening and shutting my closets, cup-boards and drawers, turning all my appliances off and on, my phones, my faxes, my safe. If I had been anything more substantial than a nude scholar, I could have invited forty friends for cocktails, nine friends for dinner and a hundred for after-dinner drinks, and scribbled my signature on a room service check somewhere in the high six figures.

5   The salon soon felt less welcoming than vast, so I took a Roederer from the fridge and a salad into the bedroom, where, perched amid piles of pillows and bolsters stuffed with goosedown, I watched the fag-end of the Florida Marlins' batting order knock the Atlanta Braves' relief pitcher all over the park. The bed was meant for better things; under the television there was a VCR player. I could have ordered a selection of video-porn from room service, and had a cute somebody sent up to watch them with me.

6   Which is the great thing about New York. Anything, but anything, can be had for money, from huge diamonds of the finest water, furs of lynx and sable, wines of vintages

long said to have been exhausted, important works of art and rock cocaine, to toy-boys of the most spontaneous, entertaining and beautifully made, of any sexual orientation and all colours. Every day, planes land at JFK freighted with orchids from Malaysia, roses from Istanbul, mangoes gathered that morning from trees in Karnataka, passion-fruit from Townsville, limes from Barbados, truffles from Perigord, lobsters brought live from the coldest seas on the planet. Within twenty-four hours all will have been put on sale and consumed. The huge prices are no deterrent. The New York elite likes to be seen to pay them with nonchalance, on the J. P. Morgan principle that if you need to know how much something costs you can't afford it. Nobody looks at the tab; the platinum credit card is thrown down for the obsequious sales person to do his worst with.

7   That is what I don't like about New York. Below the thin upper crust of high rollers there is a dense layer of struggling aspirants to elite status, and below them dead-end poverty, which no longer aspires, if it ever did. The vast mass of urban New Yorkers are struggling to get by, in conditions that are truly unbearable, from the helots who open the hair salons at six in the morning and lock them up at eight at night to the dry-cleaners who have worked twelve hours a day in the steam and fumes ever since they stepped off a boat from Europe sixty or seventy years ago. It's great that I can get my hair washed at any hour of day or night and my clothes altered or invisibly mended within four hours of dropping them off, but it is also terrible. If I ask these people about their working lives they display no rancour; they tell me that they cannot afford to retire and are amused at my consternation. They would rather keep on working, they say. What else would they do? The pain in the hair-dresser's feet and back, the listlessness and pallor of the dry-cleaner, can't be complained of. Everybody has to be up.

8   The power of positive thinking is to persuade people that the narrative of their grim existence is a success story. Though New Yorkers have been telling themselves that story for so long that they have stopped believing it, they cannot permit themselves to stop telling it. Everywhere in New York, wizened ancients are drudging. The lift-driver who takes me up to my hotel room looks ninety if a day. Her bird-body balances on grossly distorted feet; the hands in her white gloves are knobby with arthritis; her skeletal face is gaily painted and her few remaining hairs coloured bright auburn and brushed up into a transparent crest. She opens and shuts the doors of her lift as if her only ambition had ever been to do just that. I want to howl with rage on her behalf. The covers of the bolsters I frolic on have all been laundered, lightly starched and pressed by hand; as I play at being a nabob, I imagine the terribleness of the hotel laundry-room, all day, every day.

9   Though I love New York, I disapprove of it. Dreary as Ottawa was, it was in the end a better place than New York. Canadians believe that happiness is living in a just society; they will not sing the Yankee song that capitalism is happiness, capitalism is freedom. Canadians have a lively sense of decency and human dignity. Though no Canadian can afford freshly squeezed orange juice, every Canadian can have juice made from concentrate. The lack of luxury is meant to coincide with the absence of misery. It doesn't work altogether, but the idea is worth defending.

■ Food Connections

David Suzuki

Canadian scientist David Suzuki is world-famous as a broadcaster with a mission to make both governments and ordinary individuals take responsibility for protecting the environment and recovering damage that has been done already. Suzuki was an early voice of warning about climate change, when the evidence for climate change was not widely accepted. Suzuki has written many books and articles on environmental issues, has hosted the program *The Nature of Things* for the CBC for many years, and has established an organization, The David Suzuki Foundation, that promotes environmental concerns and environmental literacy. The following is an essay from his book *Time to Change* (1994).

1   Food is what nourishes us, connects us with the Earth, and reminds us of the cycles of the seasons. But in the industrialized countries of the world, fresh fruit and vegetables are available throughout the year, and we often forget that food remains a gift of the soil, water, and air. A vivid reminder is a visit to a traditional market—especially those in Third World countries. Such markets assault our senses with an incredible collage of sounds—vendors hawking their products (and some of the live produce adding their own squawks); buyers haggling over price and old friends greeting and exchanging gossip; smells that range from the perfume of flowers and spices to nonrefrigerated meat and fish; and splashes of colours in clothing, fruits, and flowers.

2   Markets give us a sense of the people. That's not surprising, since food is what keeps us alive and every society has evolved elaborate rituals around the gathering of food. In poor countries, where only a few people own refrigerators, most have to shop for food daily. For them, the market is a focal point of their lives.

3   Markets at different times of the year reveal nature's rhythms in types of fruits, fish, and vegetables available. Variations in abundance, size, and variety of products may reflect the consequences of drought or a severe winter. In poor countries, the market products are invariably "indigenous" and grown locally. They give us an idea of the kind of agriculture practiced in a locale and the variety of products grown or collected in the area. Blemishes and the odd shapes of fruit and vegetables tell us they are still grown by traditional methods. And the sharp aroma and flavour of these fresh fruits and vegetables are often a delightful shock for those of us from cities in rich countries.

4   I have seen the floating markets in Thailand, street markets in Shanghai, a covered market on the Amazon, and village markets in Madagascar. On those visits, I feel not only the spirit of the local people, but a direct sense of connection to the land through the fruits and vegetables and the seasonal change. There is an immediate bond between people and the productive Earth.

5   It is the contrast with markets of the Third World countries that gives us a measure of our own society. Try looking at our markets as if you were a foreign visitor. In most urban centres in Canada, traditional markets have been superseded by "*super*markets." What a contrast to a village market. Our supermarkets are immense shopping opportunities under a single roof that offer everything from cosmetics to hardware and clothing. Oh, yes, and food, too. They are temperature-controlled and squeaky clean with little hint of the terrestrial origin of our nutrition. Not surprisingly, the word *dirt* in our society is a pejorative.

6   A television producer recounted a telling anecdote. While dating a woman who had a university education, he took her to the country to buy some fresh vegetables. At a "U-pick" farm, they went to the field for cucumbers. The woman tugged at the producer's sleeve and asked, "What are these cucumbers doing on the ground?" When told they grow that way, she exclaimed in disgust, "But they are covered in *dirt!*" We have become so used to clean food presented in plastic packages that we no longer think about where it comes from. It's small wonder that a BBC April Fool's Day broadcast showing how farmers grow and harvest spaghetti as a crop was taken seriously by many viewers.

7   Seasonal variation in industrial societies is minimized by importing many products that mature in specific seasons from different parts of the world—apples from New Zealand, asparagus from Peru, grapes from Argentina and, of course, everything from California. When I was a boy, the first fresh fruit or vegetables of the year that appeared on the table were a delight, a signal to celebrate the change of the seasons and a renewal of the productivity of the Earth. I regret the loss of that celebration today.

8   Food grown naturally *without* chemicals is marked "organic," as if it's special, while food that has been treated with pesticides, herbicides, hormones, preservatives, and antibiotics requires no special label. So naturally grown food is no longer considered normal while food raised under total human control and management is.

9   The overriding concern in our supermarkets is with appearance. We have become accustomed to near-perfect uniformity and the absence of blemishes. When I was a child, my mother would sit with a basket of apples and nick out the scabs and worms before cooking them or putting them in a bowl for us. We thought nothing of sharing those apples with other organisms. Today we aren't nearly as tolerant and demand bug-free products even if it means poisoning air, water, and soil to get it. By fostering the illusion of escape from the vagaries of pests, abnormality, and seasons, we are no longer of the land—we have removed ourselves from nature.

10   This isn't just the nostalgic yearning of an aging man for the good old days. We are paying a terrible price for our separation from the natural world. Traditional markets where those who consume can come into direct contact with produce and their producers are a strong reminder of our lost contract with Mother Earth.

Chapter 24

Exposition: Definition

■ I'm a Banana and Proud of It

Wayson Choy

Wayson Choy, a second-generation Chinese-Canadian author writes prolifically of the immigrant experience. His best-known works are *The Jade Peony* (1994) and *All That Matters* (2004). Choy earned a degree in creative writing at the University of British Columbia, and taught at Humber College in Toronto for many years. He became a member of the Order of Canada in 2005. The following well-known essay, published in *The Globe and Mail* in 1997, examines some of the complexities of labels and racism.

1   Because both my parents came from China, I look Chinese. But I cannot read or write Chinese and barely speak it. I love my North American citizenship. I don't mind being called a "banana," yellow on the outside and white inside; I'm proud I'm a banana.

2   After all, in Canada and the United States, native Indians are "apples" (red outside, white inside); blacks are "Oreo cookies" (black and white); and Chinese are "bananas." These metaphors assume, both rightly and wrongly, that the culture here has been primarily anglo-white. Cultural history made me a banana.

3   History: My father and mother arrived separately to the B.C. coast in the early part of the century. They came as unwanted "aliens." Better to be an alien here than to be dead of starvation in China. But after the Chinese Exclusion laws were passed in North America (late 1800s, early 1900s), no Chinese immigrants were granted citizenship in either Canada or the United States.

4   Like those Old China village men from the *Toi San* who, in the 1850s, laid down cliff-edge train tracks through the Rockies and the Sierras, or like those first women who came as mail-order wives or concubines and who as bond-slaves were turned into cheaper labourers or even prostitutes—like many of those men and women, my father and mother survived ugly, unjust times. In 1917, two hours after he got off the boat from Hong Kong, my father was called "chink" and told to go back to China. "Chink" is a hateful, racist term, stereotyping the shape of Asian eyes: "a chink in the armour," an undesirable slit. For the Elders, the past was humiliating. Eventually, the Second World War changed hostile attitudes against the Chinese.

5   During the war, Chinese men volunteered and lost their lives as members of the Canadian and American military. When hostilities ended, many more were proudly in uniform, waiting to go overseas. Record Chinatown dollars were raised to buy War Bonds. After 1945, challenged by such money and ultimate sacrifices, the Exclusion laws in both Canada and the United States were revoked. Chinatown residents claimed their citizenship and sent for their families.

6   By 1949, after the Communists took over China, those of us who arrived here as young children, or were born here, stayed. No longer "aliens," we became legal citizens of North America. Many of us also became "bananas."

7   Historically, "banana" is not a racist term. Although it clumsily stereotypes many of the children and grandchildren of the old Chinatowns, the term actually follows the old Chinese tendency to assign endearing nicknames to replace formal names, semicomic names to keep one humble. Thus, "banana" describes the generations who assimilated so well into North American life.

8   In fact, our families encouraged members of my generation in the 1950s and sixties to "get ahead," to get an English education, to get a job with good pay and prestige. "Don't work like me," Chinatown parents said. "Work in an office!" The *lao wah-kiu* (the Chinatown old-timers) also warned, "Never forget—you still be Chinese!"

9   None of us ever forgot. The mirror never lied.

10 Many Chinatown teenagers felt we didn't quite belong in any one world. We looked Chinese, but thought and behaved North American. Impatient Chinatown parents wanted the best of both worlds for us, but they bluntly labeled their children and grandchildren "*juk-sing*" or even "*mo no.*" Not that we were totally "shallow bamboo butt-ends" or entirely "no brain," but we had less and less understanding of Old China traditions, and less and less interest in their village histories. Father used to say we lacked Taoist ritual, Taoist manners. We were, he said, "*mo li.*"

11 This was true. Chinatown's younger brains, like everyone else's of whatever race, were being colonized by "white bread" U.S. family television programmes. We began to feel Chinese home life was inferior. We co-operated with English-language magazines that showed us how to act and what to buy. Seductive Hollywood movies made some of us secretly weep that we did not have movie-star faces. American music made Chinese music sound like noise.

12 By the 1970s and eighties, many of us had consciously or unconsciously distanced ourselves from our Chinatown histories. We became bananas.

13 Finally, for me, in my 40s or 50s, with the death first of my mother, then my father, I realized I did not belong anywhere unless I could understand the past. I needed to find the foundation of my Chinese-ness. I needed roots.

14   I spent my college holidays researching the past. I read Chinatown oral histories, located documents, searched out early articles. Those early citizens came back to life for me. Their long toil and blood sacrifices, the proud record of their patient, legal challenges, gave us all our present rights as citizens. Canadian and American Chinatowns set aside their family tongue differences and encouraged each other to fight injustice. There were no borders. "After all," they affirmed, "*Daaih ga tohng yahn . . . we are all Chinese!*"

15   In my book, *The Jade Peony,* I tried to recreate this past, to explore the beginnings of the conflicts trapped within myself, the struggle between being Chinese and being North American. I discovered a truth: these "between world" struggles are universal.

16   In every human being, there is "the Other"—something that makes each of us feel how different we are to everyone else, even to family members. Yet, ironically, we are all the same, wanting the same security and happiness. I know this now.

17   I think the early Chinese pioneers actually started "going bananas" from the moment they first settled upon the West Coast. They had no choice. They adapted. They initiated assimilation. If they had not, they and their family would have starved to death. I might even suggest that all surviving Chinatown citizens eventually became bananas. Only some, of course, were more ripe than others.

18   That's why I'm proudly a banana: I accept the paradox of being both Chinese and not Chinese.

19   Now, at last, whenever I look in the mirror or hear ghost voices shouting, "You still Chinese," I smile.

20   I know another truth: In immigrant North America, we are all Chinese.

■ Conservation Defined

Roderick Haig-Brown

Roderick Haig-Brown was a British-born writer and conservationist who lived in Campbell River, British Columbia, for the last forty years of his life, writing over twenty-five books (including children's books) and numerous articles on the Canadian landscape. His early upbringing in England brought him in contact with Thomas Hardy, a friend of his grandfather's. His rebellious behaviour as a young man eventually led to his travels to Canada, where he worked as a logger and fisherman on northern Vancouver Island during the early 1930s. In his varied career, he wrote for the CBC and, during the Second World War, was seconded from the Canadian Army to the Royal Canadian Mounted Police (which allowed him to travel all over Canada); he was a magistrate in Campbell River, Chancellor of the University of Victoria, and a Trustee of the Nature Conservancy of Canada. The following definition is excerpted from *The Living Land* (1961), in which he extols British Columbia's natural resources.

1   An easy definition of the word conservation is "Proper use of natural resources." But this still leaves a difficult and wide-open question: What is "proper use"?

2   This is as it should be because conservation is a dynamic, not a static, conception. It does not mean simply hanging on to things, like a miser to his gold. It means putting them to use, seeking a valuable return from them and at the same time ensuring future yields of at least equal value. It means having enough faith in the future to respect the future and the needs of future people; it means accepting moral and practical restraints that limit immediate self-interest; it means finding a measure of wisdom and understanding of natural things that few peoples have attained; ultimately, though we no

longer see it in this way, it is a religious concept—the most universal and fundamental of all such concepts, the worship of fertility to which man has dedicated himself in every civilization since his race began. We may well believe now that an intellectual and scientific approach is more likely to succeed than a mystical one. But without moral concepts and without a sense of responsibility for the future of the human race, the idea of conservation could have little meaning. Since it deals for the future as well as for the present, it must always be as much an act of faith as an intellectual exercise.

3   The basic resources of any country are soil and water and, largely depending on these, climate. All three can be damaged by misuse, utterly destroyed by persistent misuse—and when they are so destroyed the civilizations that grew upon them, however great and powerful, are utterly destroyed with them. The Sahara Desert, the arid lands of the eastern Mediterranean and the Euphrates valley all supported civilizations that were supreme in their time, wise in their time and secure in their time. But the wisdom of the time was not enough; the water failed, the soil eroded and blew away and desert sands blew in to bury the wonderful cities whose wealth the land once supported.

4   Soil and water and climate are the permanent resources; together they make habitat, the set of conditions that favours the growth of timber, wildlife, fish, cattle and farm crops. Used within proper limits they are renewable and perpetual resources. Used without regard for those limits they deteriorate steadily and may quickly pass beyond the stage where the knowledge and effort of man can restore them.

Chapter 25

Exposition:
Division and Classification

■ A World Not Neatly Divided

Amartya Sen

Economist and Harvard professor Amartya Sen has taught at many prestigious universities, including Delhi University, the London School of Economics, Oxford, Cambridge, and MIT. His work has been on developmental economics, inspired by his exposure to the famine and continuing poverty experienced by the rural poor in Bangladesh and India where he grew up, and where he continues to live for several months of the year. His groundbreaking work to challenge the economic assumption about self-interest as the prime motivator for human action earned him the Nobel Prize for Economics in 1998. Sen used some of his Nobel Prize money to establish the Pratichi Trust in Bangladesh and India, aimed at improving literacy, basic health care, and gender equality. This essay was first published in *The New York Times* in November 2001.

1   When people talk about clashing civilizations, as so many politicians and academics do now, they can sometimes miss the central issue. The inadequacy of this thesis begins well before we get to the question of whether civilizations must clash. The basic weakness of the theory lies in its programme of categorizing people of the world according to a unique, allegedly commanding system of classification. This is problematic because civilizational categories are crude and inconsistent and also because there are other ways of seeing people (linked to politics, language, literature, class, occupation or other affiliations).

2   The befuddling influence of a singular classification also traps those who dispute the thesis of a clash: To talk about "the Islamic world" or "the Western world" is already to adopt an impoverished vision of humanity as unalterably divided. In fact, civilizations are hard to partition in this way, given the diversities within each society as well as the

linkages among different countries and cultures. For example, describing India as a "Hindu civilization" misses the fact that India has more Muslims than any other country except Indonesia and possibly Pakistan. It is futile to try to understand Indian art, literature, music, food or politics without seeing the extensive interactions across barriers of religious communities. These include Hindus and Muslims, Buddhists, Jains, Sikhs, Parsees, Christians (who have been in India since at least the fourth century, well before England's conversion to Christianity), Jews (present since the fall of Jerusalem), and even atheists and agnostics. Sanskrit has a larger atheistic literature than exists in any other classical language. Speaking of India as a Hindu civilization may be comforting to the Hindu fundamentalist, but it is an odd reading of India.

3   A similar coarseness can be seen in the other categories invoked, like "the Islamic world." Consider Akbar and Aurangzeb, two Muslim emperors of the Mogul dynasty in India. Aurangzeb tried hard to convert Hindus into Muslims and instituted various policies in that direction, of which taxing the non-Muslims was only one example. In contrast, Akbar revelled in his multiethnic court and pluralist laws, and issued official proclamations insisting that no one "should be interfered with on account of religion" and that "anyone is to be allowed to go over to a religion that pleases him."

4   If a homogeneous view of Islam were to be taken, then only one of these emperors could count as a true Muslim. The Islamic fundamentalist would have no time for Akbar; Prime Minister Tony Blair, given his insistence that tolerance is a defining characteristic of Islam, would have to consider excommunicating Aurangzeb. I expect both Akbar and Aurangzeb would protest, and so would I. A similar crudity is present in the characterization of what is called "Western civilization." Tolerance and individual freedom have certainly been present in European history. But there is no dearth of diversity here, either. When Akbar was making his pronouncements on religious tolerance in Agra, in the 1590's, the Inquisitions were still going on; in 1600, Giordano Bruno was burned at the stake, for heresy, in Campo dei Fiori in Rome.

5   Dividing the world into discrete civilizations is not just crude. It propels us into the absurd belief that this partitioning is natural and necessary and must overwhelm all other ways of identifying people. That imperious view goes not only against the sentiment that "we human beings are all much the same," but also against the more plausible understanding that we are diversely different. For example, Bangladesh's split from Pakistan was not connected with religion, but with language and politics.

6   Each of us has many features in our self-conception. Our religion, important as it may be, cannot be an all-engulfing identity. Even a shared poverty can be a source of solidarity across the borders. The kind of division highlighted by, say, the so-called "anti-globalization" protesters—whose movement is, incidentally, one of the most globalized in the world—tries to unite the underdogs of the world economy and goes firmly against religious, national or "civilizational" lines of division.

7   The main hope of harmony lies not in any imagined uniformity, but in the plurality of our identities, which cut across each other and work against sharp divisions into impenetrable civilizational camps. Political leaders who think and act in terms of sectioning off humanity into various "worlds" stand to make the world more flammable—even when their intentions are very different. They also end up, in the case of civilizations defined by religion, lending authority to religious leaders seen as spokesmen for their "worlds." In the process, other voices are muffled and other concerns silenced. The robbing of our plural identities not only reduces us; it impoverishes the world.

■ Flagging Attention

Gwynne Dyer

Gwynne Dyer, who has served in the navies of Canada, the United States, and Britain, is a military historian, and freelance journalist and broadcaster, whose articles on international affairs are published in newspapers in over forty countries in the world. Dyer taught at Sandhurst, the elite British military academy, before he decided to concentrate on his writing career. Many of his television and radio documentary series, such as *War, The Human Race,* and *Millennium,* have won or been nominated for awards. Dyer is a Newfoundlander who now lives in London. The following article originally appeared in the magazine *enRoute* in 1999.

1   If you want to see my favourite flag in the whole world—more bizarre than the Nepalese flag, which looks like two scraps of red bikini fluttering in the wind; more literal-minded even than Cyprus's flag, which consists of an orange map of Cyprus on a white background—you don't have to go that far. Just go to Vancouver.

2   I spent some time in the Navy during the late Jurassic, and reservists I knew from Vancouver would actually boast about it. It was the flag of Her Majesty's Canadian Ship *Discovery* (which is actually a building, or "stone frigate"). How will you know which one that is? Easy. It's a neat circle nestled in the crotch of a large letter "Y." Or to put it another way: It is a "disc over" a "Y."

3   Visual puns are to ordinary puns as Ebola fever is to measles. A long time ago (back when I had pimples) I used to collect visual puns, but after HMCS *Discovery* I just gave up. You can search the front and back pages of any dictionary you like, and no flag in the world even begins to approach it for sheer awfulness. Though they do try.

4   All this stuff about flags came up after my six-year-old, Kate, saw *Mulan* and wanted to know what the Chinese flag looked like. So out with the trusty dictionary, and there it was in all its minimalist splendour: a plain red flag with some stars in the corner.

5   She seemed a bit disappointed by China's flag, so to cheer her up I started making fun of some of the more lurid flags that jostled alongside it on the page. Brazil's, for example, has the slogan of a dead political movement—*Ordem e Progresso* (Order and Progress)—written on a white band stretched like an equator across a blue globe with the southern night sky superimposed on it, and the whole mess being contained within a yellow diamond on a green background. Kate was riveted.

6   While there were about 50 flags at the back of the dictionary when I was a kid, there are now close to 200, and the style has changed.

7   Boring old horizontal or vertical stripes are out. Diagonal slashes, nested triangles and heraldic animals are in, and any flag with less than five colours just isn't in the running. I get around a lot, but I haven't seen even half of them in real life—expect maybe outside the United Nations building in New York, where the flagpoles are now crowded so closely together that you can't make anything out.

8   What struck both me and my daughter was that there are obviously three quite different kinds of flags. There are the traditional ones, with a few dignified stripes and maybe some stars or a crest. There are the designer ones, ranging from ad-agency flash to playschool messy. And there are the ones that are just trying too hard, like Mozambique's flag: crossed black hoe and AK-47 superimposed on a white book, all on a yellow star, which is, in turn, on a red triangle, with a broad green, thin white, broad black, thin white and broad yellow stripes off to the right. (Yes, I know it's all symbolic, but even so . . .)

9   Canada's flag falls into the designer category. Three vertical stripes, red-white-red, still look quite traditional, and if you were feeling bold you might even get away with having a discreet little shield or badge on the middle stripe—in fact, more than half the flags of Latin America follow exactly that pattern—but the maple leaf is just too big and in-your-face to qualify as traditional. This is a flag halfway to being a logo. Well, good. The whole idea of a new Canadian flag, back in the '60s, was to re-brand the country, and it has worked a treat: Everybody now understands that we're not British, we're Canadian. Québec went through a similar exercise 15 years before, adopting the old pre-revolutionary French flag in colour-reverse, with an equally satisfactory rise in the recognition factor.

10   If it works, don't knock it. But what you notice, looking across the pages and pages of flags, is that (a) most of the good ideas were taken some time ago; (b) the smaller the country, the more elaborate the flag; and (c) there are fashions in flags, as in everything else. The new South African flag, for example, looks like a collision between Jamaica's and Vanuatu's. After 200 other countries have dipped into the pot, there aren't any elegant designs left. While Japan (pop.125 million) has made do with a plain red circle on a white background for over 1,000 years, latecomer Grenada (pop. 101,000) wound up with a multi-coloured extravaganza involving stars, circles, triangles, rectangles and what appears to be a leaf shape.

11   As for fashion, it's not just Muslim countries putting crescent moons on their flags, or half the countries of Africa going in for stars. For some reason, it has become de rigueur among small island states—Trinidad and Tobago, St. Kitts-Nevis, the Marshall Islands, the Solomon Islands—to put bold diagonal slashes on their flags.

12   But no matter how gaudy or silly the flag, somewhere a bunch of school kids or army conscripts is being taught to love it, pledge alliance to it, maybe even kill or die for it. Now, I understand the need for a sense of unity and community, and I realize that people need symbols. In my time, I have served in various people's navies and saluted their flags without feeling abused or humiliated. It's just part of the package. Once, in the Canadian Navy, I was the guy out front with the sword and shiny boots when we did the Sunset Ceremony, and even felt a surge of emotion myself at the climax of the ceremony.

13   We are all tribesmen under the skin, and there's no point in beating ourselves up about it. But we don't have to fall for it either; we are not *only* tribesmen. I'll pledge allegiance to any flag you like if it will keep me out of jail. But frankly, I'd rather pledge allegiance to a bedspread.

Chapter 26

Exposition: Causal Analysis

■ The Ticking Bomb

Wade Davis

B.C. anthropologist and biologist Wade Davis has written several books on traditional cultures. His best-known book, *The Serpent and the Rainbow* (1986), which explored voodoo practices, was made into a film. The following essay was published in *The Globe and Mail* in 2002, only a few months after the events of September 11, 2001.

1   On Sept. 11, in the most successful act of asymmetrical warfare since the Trojan Horse, the world came home to America. "Why do they hate us?" asked George W. Bush. This was not a rhetorical question. Americans really wanted to know—and still do, for their innocence has been shattered. The President suggested that the reason was the very greatness of America, as if the liberal institutions of government had somehow provoked homicidal rage in fanatics incapable of embracing freedom. Other, dissenting voices claimed that, to the contrary, the problem lay in the tendency of the United States to support, notably in the Middle East, repressive regimes whose values are anti-thetical to the ideals of American democracy. Both sides were partly right, but both overlooked the deeper issue, in part because they persisted in examining the world through American eyes.

2   The United States has always looked inward. A nation born in isolation cannot be expected to be troubled by the election of a President who has rarely been abroad, or a Congress in which 25 per cent of members do not hold passports. Wealth too can be

blinding. Each year, Americans spend as much on lawn maintenance as the government of India collects in federal tax revenue. The 30 million African-Americans collectively control more wealth than the 30 million Canadians.

3   A country that effortlessly supports a defence budget larger than the entire economy of Australia does not easily grasp the reality of a world in which 1.3 billion people get by on less than $1 a day. A new and original culture that celebrates the individual at the expense of family and community—a stunning innovation in human affairs, the sociological equivalent of the splitting of the atom—has difficulty understanding that in most of the world the community still prevails, for the destiny of the individual remains inextricably linked to the fate of the collective.

4   Since 1945, even as the United States came to dominate the geopolitical scene, the American people resisted engagement with the world, maintaining an almost willful ignorance of what lay beyond their borders. Such cultural myopia, never flattering, was rendered obsolete in an instant on the morning of Sept. 11. In the immediate wake of the tragedy, I was often asked as an anthropologist for explanations.

5   Condemning the attacks in the strongest possible terms, I nevertheless encouraged people to consider the forces that gave rise to Osama bin Laden's movement. While it would be reassuring to view al-Qaeda as an isolated phenomenon, I feared that the organization was a manifestation of a deeper and broader conflict, a clash between those who have and those who have nothing. Mr. bin Laden himself may be wealthy, but the resentment upon which al-Qaeda feeds springs most certainly from the condition of the dispossessed.

6   I also encouraged my American friends to turn the anthropological lens upon our own culture, if only to catch a glimpse of how we might appear to people born in other lands. I shared a colleague's story from her time living among the Bedouin in Tunisia in the 1980s, just as television reached their remote villages. Entranced and shocked by episodes of the soap opera *Dallas,* the astonished farm women asked her, "Is everyone in your country as mean as J.R.?"

7   For much of the Middle East, in particular, the West is synonymous not only with questionable values and a flood of commercial products, but also with failure. Gamel Abdul Nasser's notion of a pan-Arabic state was based on a thoroughly Western and secular model of socialist development, an economic and political dream that collapsed in corruption and despotism. The Shah of Iran provoked the Iranian revolution by thrusting not the Koran but modernity (as he saw it) down the throats of his people.

8   The Western model of development has failed in the Middle East and elsewhere in good measure because it has been based on the false promise that people who follow its prescriptive dictates will in time achieve the material prosperity enjoyed by a handful of nations of the West. Even were this possible, it is not at all clear that it would be desirable. To raise consumption of energy and materials throughout the world to Western levels, given current population projections, would require the resources of four planet Earths by the year 2100. To do so with the one world we have would imply so severely compromising the biosphere that the Earth would be unrecognizable.

9   In reality, development for the vast majority of the peoples of the world has been a process in which the individual is torn from his past and propelled into an uncertain future only to secure a place on the bottom rung of an economic ladder that goes nowhere.

10   Consider the key indices of development. An increase in life expectancy suggests a drop in infant mortality, but reveals nothing of the quality of the lives led by those who survive childhood. Globalization is celebrated with iconic intensity. But what does it really mean? The *Washington Post* reports that in Lahore, one Muhammad Saeed earns $88 (U.S.) a month stitching shirts and jeans for a factory that supplies Gap and Eddie Bauer. He and five family members share a single bed in one room off a warren of alleys strewn with human waste and refuse. Yet, earning three times as much as at his last job, he is a poster child for globalization.

11   Even as fundamental a skill as literacy does not necessarily realize its promise. In northern Kenya, for example, tribal youths placed by their families into parochial schools do acquire a modicum of literacy, but in the process also learn to have contempt for their ancestral way of life. They enter school as nomads; they leave as clerks, only to join an economy with a 50-per-cent unemployment rate for high-school graduates. Unable to find work, incapable of going home, they drift to the slums of Nairobi to scratch a living from the edges of a cash economy.

12   Without doubt, images of comfort and wealth, of technological sophistication, have a magnetic allure. Any job in the city may seem better than backbreaking labour in sun-scorched fields. Entranced by the promise of the new, people throughout the world have in many instances voluntarily turned their backs on the old.

13   The consequences can be profoundly disappointing. The fate of the vast majority of those who sever ties with their traditions will not be to attain the prosperity of the West, but to join the legions of urban poor, trapped in squalor, struggling to survive. As cultures wither away, individuals remain, often shadows of their former selves, caught in time, unable to return to the past, yet denied any real possibility of securing a place in the world whose values they seek to emulate and whose wealth they long to acquire.

14   Anthropology suggests that when people and cultures are squeezed, extreme ideologies sometimes emerge, inspired by strange and unexpected beliefs. These revitalization movements may be benign, but more typically prove deadly both to their adherents and to those they engage. China's Boxer Rebellion of 1900 sought not only to end the opium trade and expel foreign legations. The Boxers arose in response to the humiliation of an ancient nation, long the centre of the known world, reduced within a generation to servitude by unknown barbarians. It was not enough to murder the missionaries. In a raw, atavistic gesture, the Boxers dismembered them and displayed their heads on pikes.

15   However unique its foundation, al-Qaeda is nevertheless reminiscent of such revitalization movements. Torn between worlds, Mr. bin Laden and his followers invoke a feudal past that never was in order to rationalize their own humiliation and hatred. They are a cancer within the culture of Islam, neither fully of the faith nor totally apart from it. Like any malignant growth they must be severed from the body and destroyed. We must also strive to understand the movement's roots, for the chaotic conditions of disintegration and disenfranchisement that led to al-Qaeda are found among disaffected populations throughout the world.

16   In Nepal, the rural farmers spout rhetoric not heard since the death of Stalin. In Peru, the Shining Path turned to Mao. Had they invoked instead Tupac Amaru, the 18th century indigenous rebel, scion of the Inca, and had they been able to curb their reflexive disdain for the very indigenous people they claimed to represent, they might

well have set the nation aflame, as was their intent. Lima, a city of 400,000 in 1940 is today home to 9 million, and for the majority it is a sea of misery in a sun-scorched desert.

17   We live in an age of disintegration. At the beginning of the 20th century there were 60 nation states. Today there are 190, many poor and unstable. The real story lies in the cities. Throughout the world, urbanization, with all its fickle and forlorn promises, has drawn people by the millions into squalor. The populations of Mexico City and Sao Paolo are unknown, probably immeasurable. In Asia there are cities of 10 million people that most of us in the West cannot name.

18   The nation state, as Harvard sociologist Daniel Bell wrote, has become too small for the big problems of the world and too big for the little problems of the world. Outside the major industrial nations, globalization has not brought integration and harmony, but rather a firestorm of change that has swept away languages and cultures, ancient skills and visionary wisdom. Of the 6,000 languages spoken today, fully half are not being taught to children. Within a single generation, we are witnessing the loss of half humanity's social, spiritual and intellectual legacy. This is the essential backdrop of our era.

19   In the immediate aftermath of 9/11, I was asked at a lecture in Los Angeles to name the seminal event of the 20th century. Without hesitation I suggested the assassination of Archduke Ferdinand in 1914. The bullets sparked a war that destroyed all faiths in progress and optimism, the hallmarks of the Victorian age, and left in its wake the nihilism and alienation of a century that birthed Hitler, Mao, Stalin and another devastating global conflict that did not fully end until the collapse of the Soviet empire in 1989.

20   The question then turned to 9/11, and its struck me that 100 years from now that fateful date may well loom as the defining moment of this century, the day when two worlds, long kept apart by geography and circumstance, came together in a violent conflict. If there is one lesson to be learned from 9/11, it is that power does not translate into security. With an investment of $500,000, far less than the price of one of the baggage scanners now deployed in airports across the United States, a small band of fanatics killed some 2,800 innocent people. The economic cost may well be incalculable. Generally, nations declare war on nations; Mr. Bush has declared war on a technique and there is no exit strategy.

21   Global media have woven the world into a single sphere. Evidence of the disproportionate affluence of the West is beamed into villages and urban slums in every nation, in every province, 24 hours a day. *Baywatch* is the most popular television show in New Guinea. Tribesmen from the mountainous heartland of an island that embraces 2,000 distinct languages walk for days to catch the latest episode.

22   The voices of the poor, who deal each moment with the consequences of environmental degradation, political corruption, overpopulation, the gross distortion in the distribution of wealth and the consumption of resources, who share few of the material benefits of modernity, will no longer be silent.

23   True peace and security for the 21st century will only come about when we find a way to address the underlying issues of disparity, dislocation and dispossession that have provoked the madness of our age. What we desperately need is a global acknowledgment of the fact that no people and no nation can truly prosper unless the bounty of our collective ingenuity and opportunities are available and accessible to all.

24   We must aspire to create a new international spirit of pluralism, a true global democracy in which unique cultures, large and small, are allowed the right to exist, even as we learn and live together, enriched by the deepest reaches of our imaginings. We need a global declaration of interdependence. In the wake of Sept. 11, this is not idle or naïve rhetoric, but rather a matter of survival.

■ The Divine Revolution

Vaclav Havel

Vaclav Havel was an activist and playwright before taking his place on the world stage in politics. His best-known plays include *The Garden Party* (1963), *The Memorandum* (1965), *The Increased Difficulty of Concentration* (1968), *The Beggar's Opera* (1976), and *Temptation* (1986). As a dissident writer and, later, leader of the opposition in the former Communist Czechoslovakia, Havel was regularly imprisoned until the Velvet Revolution of 1989, after which he was the tenth as well as the last president of Czechoslovakia, and the first of the new state of the Czech Republic from 1993–2003. He has won many international honours, including the Gandhi Peace Prize from India (2002) and the Presidential Medal of Freedom from the United States (2004). Havel's latest play is *Leaving* (2007), and his latest non-fiction work is his memoir, *To the Castle and Back* (2007). This essay appeared in the July/August 1998 edition of the *Utne Reader*.

1   Humankind today is well aware of the spectrum of threats looming over its head. We know that the number of people living on our planet is growing at a soaring rate and that within a relatively short time we can expect it to total in the tens of billions. We know that the already-deep abyss separating the planet's poor and rich could deepen further, and more and more dangerously, because of this population growth. We also know that we've been destroying the environment on which our existence depends and that we are headed for disaster by producing weapons of mass destruction and allowing them to proliferate.

2   And yet, even though we are aware of these dangers, *we do almost nothing to avert* them. It's fascinating to me how preoccupied people are today with catastrophic prognoses, how books containing evidence of impending crises become bestsellers, but how very little account we take of these threats in our everyday activities. Doesn't every schoolchild know that the resources of this planet are limited and that if they are expended faster than they are recovered, we are doomed? And still we continue in our wasteful ways and don't even seem perturbed. Quite the contrary: *Rising production is considered to be the main sign of national success,* not only in poor states where such a position could be justified, but also in wealthy ones, which are cutting the branch on which they sit with their ideology of indefinitely prolonged and senseless growth.

3   The most important thing we can do today is to study the reasons why humankind does little to address these threats and why it allows itself to be carried onward by some kind of perpetual motion, unaffected by self-awareness or a sense of future options. It would be unfair to ignore the existence of numerous projects for averting these dangers, or to deny that a lot already has been done. However, all attempts of this kind have one thing in common: *They do not touch the seed from which the threats I'm speaking of sprout,* but merely try to diminish their impact. (A typical example is the list of legal acts, ordinances, and international treaties stipulating how much toxic matter this or that plant may discharge into the environment.) I'm not criticizing these safeguards; I'm only saying that they are technical tricks that have no real effect on the substance of the matter.

4   What, then, is the substance of the matter? What could change the direction of today's civilization?

5   It is my deep conviction that the only option is a change in the sphere of the spirit, in the sphere of human conscience. It's not enough to invent new machines, new regulations, new institutions. We must develop a new understanding of the true purpose of our existence on this earth. Only by making such a fundamental shift will we be able to create new models of behaviour and a new set of values for the planet. In short, it appears to me that it would be better to start from the head rather than the tail.

6   Whenever I've gotten involved in a major global problem—the logging of rainforests, ethnic or religious intolerance, the brutal destruction of indigenous cultures—I've always discovered somewhere in the long chain of events that gave rise to it a basic lack of responsibility for the planet.

7   There are countless types of responsibility—more or less pressing, depending on who's involved. We feel responsible for our personal welfare, our families, our companies, our communities, our nations. And somewhere in the background there is in every one of us, a small feeling of responsibility for the planet and its future. It seems to me that this last and deepest responsibility has become a very low priority—dangerously low, considering that the world today is more interlinked than ever before and that we are, for all intents and purposes, living one global destiny.

8   At the same time, our world is dominated by several great religious systems, whose differences seem to be coming to the fore with increasing sharpness and setting the stage for innumerable political and armed conflicts. In my opinion, this fact—which is attracting, understandably, a great deal of media attention—partly conceals a more important fact: that the civilization within which this religious tension is taking place is, in essence, a deeply atheistic one. Indeed, it is the first atheistic civilization in the history of humankind.

9   Perhaps the real issue is a crisis of respect for the moral order extended to us from above, or simply a crisis of respect for any kind of authority higher than our own earthly being, with its material and thoroughly ephemeral interests. Perhaps our lack of responsibility for the planet is only the logical consequence of the modern conception of the universe as a complex of phenomena controlled by certain scientifically identifiable laws, formulated for God-knows-what purpose. This is a conception that does not inquire into the meaning of existence and renounces any kind of metaphysics, including its own metaphysical roots.

10   In the process, we have lost our certainty that the universe, nature, existence, our own lives are works of creation that have a definite meaning and purpose. This loss is accompanied by loss of the feeling that whatever we do must be seen in the light of a higher order of which we are part and whose authority we must respect.

11   In recent years the great religions have been playing an increasingly important role in global politics. Since the fall of communism, the world has become multipolar instead of bipolar, and many countries outside the hitherto dominant Euro-American cultural sphere have grown in self-confidence and influence. But the more closely tied we are by the bonds of a single global civilization, the more the various religious groups emphasize all the ways in which they differ from each other. This is an epoch of accentuated spiritual, religious, and cultural "otherness."

12   How can we restore in the human mind a shared attitude to what is above if people everywhere feel the need to stress their otherness? Is there any sense in trying to turn the human mind to the heavens when such a turn would only aggravate the conflict among our various deities?

13   I'm not, of course, an expert on religion, but it seems to me that the major faiths have much more in common than they are willing to admit. They share a basic point of departure—that this world and our existence are not freaks of chance but rather part of a mysterious, yet integral, act whose sources, direction, and purpose are difficult for us to perceive in their entirety. And they share a large complex of moral imperatives that this mysterious act implies. In my view, whatever differences these religions might have are not as important as these fundamental similarities.

14   Perhaps the way out of our current bleak situation could be found by searching for what unites the various religions—a purposeful search for common principles. Then we could cultivate human coexistence while, at the same time, cultivating the planet on which we live, suffusing it with the spirit of this religious and ethical common ground—what I would call the common spiritual and moral minimum.

15   Could this be a way to stop the blind perpetual motion dragging us toward hell? Can the persuasive words of the wise be enough to achieve what must be done? Or will it take an unprecedented disaster to provoke this kind of existential revolution— a universal recovery of the human spirit and renewed responsibility for the world?

Chapter 27

Argumentation

■ The Implications of a Free Society

Lester B. Pearson

Lester B. Pearson, who served in both the First and Second World Wars, studied at Oxford and taught history at the University of Toronto. A key player in the founding of the United Nations and NATO, Pearson won the Nobel Peace Prize in 1957 for helping to avert possible disastrous hostilities between the Middle East and Western powers during the Suez Canal crisis. His peacekeeping solutions were established as a model for many UN countries' future roles in the world. Pearson led the Liberal Party to power in 1963, becoming Canada's fourteenth prime minister. He established many significant Canadian social programs, including universal health care (with Tommy Douglas), the Canada Pension Plan, and the Canada Student Loan system. Pearson's policies allowed for a move toward bilingualism and improving the status of women, and away from racially charged immigration policies. Under Pearson's government, the maple leaf became the symbol of Canada due to the newly designed Canadian flag. This essay was published in a collection titled *Words and Occasions* (1970).

1   The essential lubricant for a free society is tolerance. This, however, does not necessarily apply to *all* societies. There are obvious examples of states which are held together without the least regard for tolerance. It does apply, however, to all states where there is government by consent. Canada, where various groups live and work together within the boundaries of a national state, is a good example of this principle in operation. This country exists on the assumption that, as far as is humanly possible, the interests of no group—racial, geographic, economic, religious or political—will prevail at the expense of any other group. We have committed ourselves to the principle that by

compromise and adjustment we can work out some sort of balance of interests which will make it possible for the members of all groups to live side by side without any of them arbitrarily imposing its will on any other. It is my belief that this is the only basis upon which Canada can possibly exist as a nation, and that any attempt to govern the country on any other basis would destroy it. In these circumstances, the basic quality of tolerance in our national character is of the first importance.

2   Of almost equal importance for our national welfare, and indeed arising out of the practice of tolerance, is the avoidance of extreme policies. This is often called walking in the middle of road. This of course is not so easy as people usually think. It imposes both self-restraint and discipline, even when we assume that the traffic is all going in the one direction. Anyone who chooses to travel in the middle of the road must not deny the use of either side of it to persons who prefer to walk there. He condemns himself, therefore, to accept during the journey the constant jostling of companions on either side. This middle ground is, I think, becoming more and more difficult to maintain, and the temptation to abandon it is constantly increasing, especially in the face of the road blocks thrown up by unfriendly fellow travellers. I do not wish here to criticize those who choose other ground upon which to walk, or to question the basis of their choice. I wish only to make a strong plea for the preservation of this middle position in our national life. Paradoxically, it is only in this way that the existence of many of those on each side can also be preserved. If the middle group is eliminated, less tolerant elements fall under the irresistible temptation to try to capture the whole roadway. When the middle of the road is no longer occupied firmly by stable and progressive groups in the community, it is turned into a parade ground for those extremist forces who would substitute goose-stepping for walking. All others are driven to hide, disconsolate and powerless, in the hedges, ditches, and culverts.

3   How can the meaning of the middle way in our free society be described in a few words? What principle does it stand for? Where does it lead in practice? Is it merely the political line of least resistance along which drift those without the courage of their convictions, or simply without convictions? It is, or should be, far more than that. The central quality of this approach is the stress it always lays on human values, the integrity and worth of the individual in society. It stands for the emancipation of the mind as well as for personal freedom and well-being. It is irrevocably opposed to the shackling limitations of rigid political dogma, to political oppression of, and to economic exploitation by, any part of the community. It detests the abuse of power either by the state or by private individuals and groups. It respects first of all a person for what he is, not who he is. It stands for his right to manage his own affairs, when they *are* his own; to hold his own convictions and speak his own mind. It aims at equality of opportunity. It maintains that effort and reward should not be separated and it values high initiative and originality. It does not believe in lopping off the tallest ears of corn in the interests of comfortable conformity.

4   The middle way presents no panacea for the easy attainment of general welfare; but it accepts the responsibility of government to assist in protecting and raising the living standards of all, and, if necessary, to take bold and well-planned action to help maintain economic activity for that purpose.

5   The middle way, unlike extremism in political doctrine, has positive faith in the good will and common sense of most people in most circumstances. It relies on their intelligence, their will to co-operate, and their sense of justice. From its practitioners,

it requires determination and patience, tolerance and restraint, the discipline of the mind rather than the jackboot, and the underlying belief that human problems, vast and complicated though they may be, are capable of solution.

■ Capital Punishment

Tommy Douglas

Thomas Clement Douglas, a lifelong social activist, rejected his early support for eugenics or the sterilization and culling of "unfit" citizens—on which he wrote his master's thesis in Sociology at McMaster University—and went on to fight for the rights of the ordinary citizen. He became Premier of Saskatchewan as the leader of the first North American democratic socialist government in 1944, and is widely known as the father of Canada's universal health-care system, established in 1961. Douglas became the first leader of the New Democratic Party that same year. His tireless call for a bill of rights for all Canadians eventually led to the Canadian Charter of Rights and Freedoms, established in 1982.

1   There are times, Mr. Speaker, when the House of Commons rises to heights of grandeur and becomes deeply conscious of its great traditions. I think this debate has been one of those rare occasions. There has been a minimum of rancour and there has been no imputation of motives because I think the abolitionists and retentionists alike have been sincerely searching their consciences to see if we can honestly resolve a moral problem. This problem is, how can we abolish a brutal punishment without endangering the safety of society?

2   I am in favour of the motion to abolish capital punishment and I am also supporting the amendment to put it on a five-year trial basis. I doubt that there is much new that can be said in this debate. The entire field has been well covered but I should like to put very briefly four reasons for my opposition to capital punishment. The first is that capital punishment is contrary to the highest concepts of the Judaic-Christian ethic. I do not propose to go into theological arguments, but both in this debate and in the discussions which have taken place outside the House many people have been quoting Scripture in support of retaining the death penalty.

3   It is always a dangerous practice to quote isolated passages of Scripture. The Bible has been quoted in times past to support slavery, child labour, polygamy, the burning of witches, and subservience to dictators. The Scriptures have to be viewed as a whole. The Bible is not one book; it is many books. It does not have a static concept. It represents man's emerging moral concepts as they have grown through the centuries.

4   It is true that the Mosaic law provided the death penalty for murder. It is equally true, if one looks particularly at the 20th chapter of the book of Leviticus, that the Mosaic law provided the death penalty for 33 crimes including such things as adultery, bestiality, homosexuality, witchcraft and sacrificing to other gods than Jehovah. It seems to me that those who want to pick out isolated texts from the Bible in support of retaining the death penalty for murder have to be equally consistent and ask that the death penalty be retained for all the other crimes listed in the Mosaic law.

5   Of course, those who take this position overlook several facts. They overlook, first of all, the fact that the Mosaic law was an advanced law for the primitive times in which it was formulated. It was later succeeded by the Hebrew prophets who introduced the idea of justice superseded by mercy, the possible redemption and reestablishment of the individual. They overlook the fact that if any nation in the world ought to feel itself

bound by Mosaic law it should be the state of Israel. The state of Israel abolished the death penalty many years ago except for Nazi war criminals and for treason committed in times of war. The religious hierarchy of the state of Israel enthusiastically supported the Knesset in abolishing the death penalty in that country.

6   But for those of us who belong to the Christian religion it seems to me we have to remember also that the Christian religion went far beyond the Mosaic law. In the days of the founder of Christianity the Mosaic law still obtained. This law decreed that a woman taken in adultery could be stoned to death. We should remember the statement of Jesus of Nazareth when he came upon a group of people preparing to stone such a woman to death. He said, "Let him who is without sin among you cast the first stone."

7   When the crowd has dwindled away so that only the woman was left he said to the woman, "Go and sin no more." It seems to me that this is the ultimate culmination of the Christian concept of the application of mercy and the possible redemption of the individual.

8   My second reason for opposing capital punishment is that I believe capital punishment brutalizes the society that uses it without providing any effective deterrent that cannot be provided equally well by life imprisonment. I believe that any society that practices capital punishment brutalizes itself. It has an effect upon that society and I do not believe that society can rid itself of murderers by itself becoming a murderer. Surely if brutality would deter the committing of a crime Great Britain should have been a place of law-abiding citizens because a little over 150 years ago there were over 200 crimes for which an individual could be put to death. Instead of making Britain a nation of law-abiders it was a country where crime abounded, where human sensibilities were dulled by public execution of criminals. It is rather significant that in that day, as in this, it was often the juries who were more humane than the lawmakers. It was only because juries refused to convict, knowing the terrible punishment which would follow, that the lawmakers were forced 150 years ago to remove the death penalty from a great many of the crimes for which it had been prescribed.

9   All of the evidence which can be gathered seems to indicate that the death penalty is not a unique deterrent and that life imprisonment can be equally effective. . . .

10   I readily agree, Mr. Speaker, that quoting endless statistics is not going to prove either the case for abolition or the case for retention, but there certainly seems to be no convincing volume of evidence which would satisfy any unbiased individual that abolishing the death penalty has resulted in an upsurge of homicide or that those states which have retained the death penalty are any freer of capital crimes than those which have not.

11   After all, Mr. Speaker, who is it that the death penalty deters? It has certainly not deterred the man who commits murder. Will it deter him in the future? Surely he can be deterred in the future by being incarcerated for the remainder of his life. Who is deterred if this man is hanged? Is he to be hanged as an example to the rest of the community? I can conceive of nothing more immoral than to break a man's neck as an example to other people, but if that is the argument then surely, as the Leader of the Opposition [Mr. Diefenbaker] said yesterday, we ought to have public executions.

12   The hon. Member for Winnipeg South Centre [Mr. Churchill] said that the fear of death will deter men. The fear of death will deter normal men but when a man commits murder, is he normal? Can we understand the motivation that causes a man to take a human life? When a man commits homicide, does he sit down and assess whether

he is committing it in a state that has capital punishment or in a state that has abolished capital punishment? I think not. In the main the man who kills does not make the common, rational judgments that are made by the average individual.

13   An individual who has become so mentally sick that he will take another life or ravage a child is certainly not a mentally healthy or normal individual.

14   The third reason I am opposed to capital punishment, Mr. Speaker, is that I believe there are better ways to ensure the safety of society. I completely disagree with the hon. Member for Winnipeg South Centre who argued that we must be concerned about the safety of the public. When he asks which is the more important, the life of an innocent person who may be killed or the life of a murderer, there is no doubt that the life of the innocent person is the more important. But is the fact that we break a man's neck any guarantee that innocent people will not be hurt?

15   We are not suggesting removing the penalty. We are saying that the penalty which ought to be retained is one that will do the two things which are important. First of all, it must be a penalty which will remove the convicted person from human society as long as that person is likely to be a menace to the safety and well-being of his fellow-men. Second, that person should be given an opportunity to receive whatever psychiatric treatment and rehabilitation is possible in the light of his own particular circumstances.

16   What we have to decide is what we are trying to do, Mr. Speaker. Are we thinking purely of punishing somebody because they have done wrong? Are we thinking purely in punitive terms? Are we thinking purely in terms of vengeance or retribution? Or are we thinking of the two things I have mentioned, first, the safety of society by incarcerating the convicted murderer for life and, second, the possible rehabilitation and redemption of that individual? There is additionally the third great advantage that if society has made a mistake it is possible to rectify the mistake because justice is a human institution and like all human institutions it is liable to error.

17   I maintain that society has no right to take from a man something which it cannot restore to him. If society makes a mistake and confines a man to prison, depriving him of his freedom, when that mistake is found out society can at least restore to him his freedom and provide him with some compensation for the years he has been incarcerated. But if we hang a man and then find that a mistake has been made there is nothing at all which can be done to make amends.

18   My quarrel with the death penalty is that it is purely a negative attempt to promote the safety of society. We need to adopt positive measures to promote the safety of society. For instance, we need better law enforcement. In both Canada and the United States every year a great many unsolved crimes are committed. One of the best deterrents is for the criminal to know that if he does commit a crime he will be found out, that he will be incarcerated and put in a place where he can no longer be a menace to the community. We need quicker crime detection methods. For some types of crimes, particularly for those involving psychotics, there ought to be indeterminate sentences.

19   We all recall a case a few years ago in which a man sexually assaulted a child. He was sentenced to five years in jail. To my mind this was ridiculous because it was based purely on the punitive concept and not out of regard for the safety of the community. It was assumed that at five years less one day, when he was in jail, he was a menace but at five years plus one day he was no longer a menace. Such an individual ought to be sentenced to be kept out of circulation until such time as a panel of judges, psychiatrists and social workers are as certain as a human person can be that the individual is no

longer a menace to the safety of the community. I think that in many cases indeterminate sentences to keep out of circulation psychotics who are likely to commit crimes would be of great advantage. In the case I referred to the man got out of jail after five years. Within six months he had not only assaulted another child but had killed the child in the process. Had that individual been sentenced to an indeterminate sentence in the first instance he would not have committed this second heinous crime.

20   If we want genuine deterrents in this country we need a program of penal reform for the segregation of prisoners and for their rehabilitation so that young first offenders do not go to jail to take what is virtually a postgraduate course in crime.

21   Let us face the fact that when we talk about retaining capital punishment as a deterrent we are really trying to take the easy way out from solving our problems. In the long run society often gets the criminals it deserves.

22   Why do we have criminals? What is wrong with the society that produces criminals? Some years ago when I was attending Chicago University I remember that every newspaper in the United States had a heading, "Where is Crawley?" Crawley was a young gunman who was being hunted across the United States for a series of murders.

23   A very great columnist in the United States wrote a column which he headed, "Why is Crawley?" He said that the people of the United States, instead of asking "Where is Crawley?", ought to take a little time out to ask "Why is Crawley?" The columnist went over his history. He came from a broken home which the father had deserted and where the mother was out working all day. The boy lived on the streets. He was part of a gang of hoodlums. He was sent to a reformatory and then was back on the streets. He was without proper education and without any counselling. He was sent to jail and associated with hardened criminals. He came out of jail twice as tough as when he went in. By 19 he was a hardened criminal. By the time he was 21 he was a killer. He was finally shot down by the police who were trying to capture him.

24   I suppose one of the most lamentable murders in our time has been the killing of President John F. Kennedy. Yet, when one reads the story of the man who is believed to have been responsible for his death, we find that when Lee Oswald was a boy in school he was recommended to undergo psychiatric treatment because of the dangerous psychotic tendencies he often displayed. But there were not enough psychiatrists to look after all the children in that particular part of New York city and this boy was not treated. This boy grew up with his psychotic tendencies expanding, and he is believed to have been responsible for extinguishing one of the brightest lights of our generation.

25   If we really want to tackle the problem of eliminating crime, we must tackle the problem of the slums which breed crime and we must tackle the problem of the lack of psychiatric clinics to take care of psychotics and persons who may become criminally dangerous. We need the kind of penal reform that will make possible the rehabilitation of first offenders with proper probation and parole. We need to go the roots of the cause of crime and to ask ourselves what it is that produces the murderer in society. . . .

26   My final point is that I am opposed to capital punishment because I believe that the measure of a nation is the manner in which it treats its misfits and its offenders. Capital punishment has already been abolished in most of the advanced nations of the Western world. The abolition of capital punishment has come to be taken as the hallmark of a nation's conscience. I want to see Canada take this great forward step, and I want to make a special appeal to the members of the House to consider how important for Canada and for its future will be the vote we shall take tonight.

27   I should not want to be in the shoes of the Prime Minister and the members of his cabinet who have to face up to this very difficult problem. Nobody has hanged in Canada since 1962. If the motion tonight is defeated the government is going to be in an awkward position. Either it will have to commute those sentenced to death to life imprisonment, knowing that the House of Commons has just rejected a motion suggesting the abolition of the death penalty, or it will have to take the defeat of the motion as an expression of opinion and allow the death sentences to be carried out.

28   I urge the members of the House to consider the predicament which faces the Prime Minister and the cabinet. I want to urge the House to give a five-year trial to the abolition of the death penalty. If the fears that have been expressed prove to be warranted, if there is an upsurge in the rate of homicide, if we are faced with an increase in crime rate, then in five years the members of the House of Commons who are here then can allow the death penalty to become active again simply by taking no action. But I would urge that we give this a chance, that we step into line with the progressive countries of the world which have already abolished the death penalty.

29   What I plead for is that we pass this resolution tonight, with the amendment, which will declare in principle that the House is in favour of abolishing capital punishment and replacement with life imprisonment. If we do that then I believe the House of Commons will have won a great victory, not a victory that will be accompanied by the blaring of trumpets or the rolling of drums but a victory in that we will have taken a forward, moral step and left behind one of the last relics of barbarianism. We will be moving forward to a more humane approach is dealing with crime.

Chapter 28

Description

■ No Drama in Lortie's Dew-Kissed Mozart

Elissa Poole

Elissa Poole is a freelance journalist, based in Vancouver Island, who regularly writes classical music reviews for *The Globe and Mail*. She also teaches music appreciation at the University of Victoria, and is a classical musician. The following is a review that appeared in *The Globe and Mail* on March 18, 2008.

1   If Mozart thought of almost everything he wrote in operatic terms, what kind of operas was he imagining when he wrote the music we heard on Sunday, when Montreal-born pianist Louis Lortie led the CBC Radio Orchestra in an all Mozart program on the 10th anniversary of the Chan Centre for the Performing Arts Orchestra in Vancouver? I asked myself that question a lot, even in the opening piece, the overture to *Don Giovanni*, where the answer was self-explanatory. That both the *Piano Concerto No. 20 in D minor, K. 466* and the *Symphony No. 39 in E flat major, K. 543* conjured up elegant period pieces shows how sensitive (or vulnerable) Mozart's music is to changes in style and interpretation.

2   The piano concerto, which Lortie directed from the piano, was the ideal companion piece to the *Overture to Don Giovanni,* for they are in the same key, and they establish the same dark, tumultuous world (which is not to say that either piece is without moments of grace or comedy). The syncopated, pulsating violins, the gruff impetus of the bass line, the descending four-note pattern in the melody and the harsh accents in the trumpets all set the stage for something serious or tragic. Lortie's vision of the opening

is more neutral, however. The syncopations were dry and precise rather than tense, the attacks were rounded, the descent at the tail of the phrase was without emotional affect. It did not prepare us for tragedy, nor did we get it when the solo piano entered. Lortie gave us, instead, a lyrical, somewhat resigned melody, smooth, pearly, dew-kissed. This is the Mozart we inherited from the last century, aristocratic and courtly. Passage-work glitters, melodies are fluid, the orchestra transports us (like a tourist bus) from one theme to the next. It's beautiful, but it's hardly dramatic, and although Lortie delivered plenty of charm in the slow movement, he could not justify the anxiety at its core, a contrasting middle section where plaintive winds and restless arpeggios imply that the charm rests on precarious ground. He also denied the final movement its violence, the jagged opening gesture hardly registering as such in the piano. Lortie's poise and bounce is what we remember of this movement, as well as the brilliance of his playing.

3   The introduction to *Symphony No. 39* is similarly stern and formidable, with cascading scales, forceful timpani, dissonant harmonies and dense textures. Here, too, Mozart seems to suggest that the musical topic under discussion is weighty. Here, too, Lortie chose elegance over drama.

4   There's plenty of paradox in this symphony, and the tension (or interest) is often the result of the way Mozart subverts convention: The music is constantly trying to break free of something. The move into a faster triple rhythm after so imposing an introduction is awkward; the intervals of the slow-movement melody, with its obsessive dotted rhythms, progressively widen and wander; the apparently jaunty rondo theme of the last movement tries out different keys relentlessly, sometimes only a step away from the previous attempt; and there's so much reinforcement in the accompaniment that we sometimes lose the melody altogether.

5   For me the meaning of the piece lies in these contradictions. But Lortie's reading was so buoyant and fluid that he tended to normalize them, as indeed our ears, in a general sense, normalize so much of what in Mozart speaks beyond the balance and elegance we take for granted. If the music were poetry we might say this: The sounds of the words, chosen and ordered to maximize their sensuous compatibility, continue to give pleasure. We respond to the symmetry of phrases and their narrative logic, even if they are not granted a rhetorical delivery. But the metaphors have lost their sting, their capacity to shock and forge new, and sometimes painful, connections. The poem retains its beauty, but, like Lortie's Mozart, it has lost its dramatic range. Tragedy is out of the question.

■ SNOW

Isabel Huggan

Isabel Huggan writes short stories and nonfiction works. Her first book, *The Elizabeth Stories* (1984), on small-town life in Ontario, raised much controversy in her own small community, whose citizens were convinced she had written about them. Her other books of nonfiction prose, such as *You Never Know* (1993) and *Belonging* (2003), explore the everyday lives of women. The following selection is taken from *Belonging*, which was awarded the Governor-General's Award for nonfiction. Here, Huggan writes of her experience living in a small village in the Cévennes region of France.

1   Yesterday we had a snowstorm that lasted from early morning right on through the night, and now the world is clothed in white. Snowfall this heavy is rare, here on the

lower edge of the Cévennes, where the foothills begin rolling up out of the vineyards. Farther north and into the mountains, there's always enough to ensure winter skiing but in Latourne, if it comes at all, it's only a light teasing tickle, a mere frosting. Today's snow, however, is thick and deep and means to stay. *This* snow would do Ottawa proud.

2   Shortly before dawn this morning—the sky still dark—the telephone rings, and a gruff male voice informs me that he is the courier service and has a package to deliver, and where is my house. He is calling on his cellphone from the *mairie* on the main road, and he needs directions. I explain—I've memorized this patter in French—and when I get to the bit about his turning the corner around the monastery and continuing over the small bridge, he stops me.

3   He says he will not be able to come to my house, for not only are the narrow country roads leading to Mas Blanc blocked with snow, but he will not attempt to cross the bridge. He understands now where I am located, and he knows that little bridge: it has no railing. Under the snow, the roads are sheer ice, he says, he could slide off. He will not do it. Don't I know that overnight everything has been freezing? It's too dangerous, *madame*, he says.

4   My stars, I say to myself, what a wimpy courier. But I do know that he has reason to be fearful, as I was out in the blizzard yesterday and saw for myself that cars were slipping and sliding out of control, several in accidents and even more headfirst in ditches along the highway. Of course, given the unlikelihood of this kind of weather, no one has snow tires, and there are no plows or machines to scatter sand and salt: one simply manages as best as one can and waits for the snow to melt and disappear, which, ordinarily, it will do within hours.

5   Thus I am understanding and polite, and when he asks if I will come over to meet him, if he drives as far as the old church of St-Baudile across the way, I agree. It never occurs to me, I realize later, that I might ask *him* to walk to my house. No, and he wouldn't have done it, either.

6   I throw on clothes over my flannel pajamas and pull on a pair of old winter boots I smartly brought back last summer from the attic where they'd been stored in Ottawa since I left in 1987. As soon as I step out the door and smell the silvery fragrance of new snow, I realize this call has been a gift from the gods, for without it I would never have ventured out so early and would have missed this odd sensation of being enveloped in pastel light, as if I am dancing through a dream sequence in an old Hollywood musical. The rising sun, filtered through pearly clouds and reflected by the snow, shines everywhere. The eastern sky is rose grey streaked with lemony gold, and the vineyards are glowing blue and apricot. The world has turned, overnight, into an opal.

7   The birds are already at their feeder under the *micocoulier* tree, making busy little "dix-huit, dix-huit" noises, but as I walk farther down the lane I hear nothing and am struck by the solemn and ponderous nature of snow itself, the grave way it stifles sound. The silence feels like a secret I cannot tell.

8   As I walk across the narrow bridge and around the monastery, I see that the courier has been right, for the road is really quite icy under the snow, and he would easily have gone off into the stream that still runs merrily, not yet frozen over. I make my way through the vineyard instead of the road to reach the church, where I can see there's a small blue van parked and waiting. Inside sits the courier, a red-faced man about my age, who has been watching me scuff through the snow. I am wearing my old rabbit-fur hat held on by a plaid scarf, and he probably finds me pretty funny, for I see that he is laughing.

9   He gets out to give me the package—I have to sign for it—and we exchange a few pleasantries about the weather. I tell him I am Canadian and this is nothing, monsieur, really nothing, compared with what one encounters in Ottawa. If one has the correct tires, one can drive in snow like this with no problem, I say but of course here . . . I shrug meaningfully and let the sentence dangle, sharp criticism of France—and all things French—implied.

10   He laughs again and drives off, and I walk home with the sun, now fully up from behind the clouds, making everything ahead of me glitter and gleam. I feel a great ball of joy welling up in my throat, a balloon of laughter ready to float out into the bright air. White snow lies luminous everywhere and the package in my hands, I can see from the address, is from a Canadian publisher. Too curious to wait, I stop and tear open the end of the padded envelope and pull out a letter telling me that, at the author's request, I have been sent these galleys of her new novel, *A Student of Weather.** Might I consider providing a comment and if so, could I . . .

11   I spin around twice, kicking up the snow, and laughing out loud, and run then through the drifts onto the road, heading home happy but more than just happy, amazed—and as thrilled as a gambler by patterns of chance and probability. What else in the world but *this* book, so propitiously titled, might have called me out early to walk in the fresh snow? Am I not, this winter's morning, a true student of weather? Nevertheless, far stronger than the book's coincidental pull, is a new friendship that seems, suddenly, enormously powerful.

12   On the lane to the house, I stop for breath at the olive grove and think how strange the green oval leaves appear, so thickly covered with snow. I pull a branch toward me and stick out my tongue, licking the lovely stuff off in one sweeping mouthful. The instant prickle of melting snow explodes in my mouth—flakes disintegrate like stars— as it transforms itself to a swallow of water. A sweet, chalky taste, and then gone in a gulp. Another mouthful and another, and I stand there for a long time, thinking of you and eating snow . . . far away in another country but, in my heart, home.

---

* Elizabeth Hay is the author of *A Student of Weather*. She is also the author of *Crossing the Snowlines* and *The Only Snow in Havana* [author's note].

Chapter 29

Narration

■ A Secret Lost in Water

Roch Carrier

Quebec author Roch Carrier is known to many Canadian schoolchildren as the writer of "The Hockey Sweater" ("Le chandail de hockey"), the most famous of his "contes," or brief short stories. Carrier has had a long and distinguished career as a novelist, playwright, and short story writer. He first made his name with his novel (later play), *La Guerre! Yes Sir!* (1968). Carrier was educated in New Brunswick and Montreal, and received his doctorate from the Sorbonne in Paris. He has won numerous literary awards, including the 1992 Stephen Leacock Memorial Medal for Humour for his book *The Prayers of a Very Wise Child* (*Prières d'un enfant très très sage*). He has been the head of the Canada Council, the last National Librarian of Canada, and is an Officer of the Order of Canada. The following narrative comes from *The Hockey Sweater and Other Stories* (1979).

1   After I started going to school my father scarcely talked any more. I was very intox-
icated by the new game of spelling; my father had little skill for it (it was my mother who
wrote our letters) and was convinced I was no longer interested in hearing him tell of
his adventures during the long weeks when he was far away from the house.

2   One day, however, he said to me:

3   "The time's come to show you something."

4   He asked me to follow him. I walked behind him, not talking, as we had got in the
habit of doing. He stopped in the field before a clump of leafy bushes.

5   "Those are called alders," he said.

6   "I know."

7   "You have to learn how to choose," my father pointed out.

8   I didn't understand. He touched each branch of the bush, one at a time, with religious care.

9   "You have to choose one that's very fine, a perfect one, like this."

10   I looked; it seemed exactly like the others.

11   My father opened his pocket knife and cut the branch he'd selected with pious care. He stripped off the leaves and showed me the branch, which formed a perfect Y.

12   "You see," he said, "the branch has two arms. Now take one in each hand. And squeeze them."

13   I did as he asked and took in each hand one fork of the Y, which was thinner than a pencil.

14   "Close your eyes," my father ordered, "and squeeze a little harder . . . Don't open your eyes! Do you feel anything?"

15   "The branch is moving!" I exclaimed, astonished.

16   Beneath my clenched fingers the alder was wriggling like a small, frightened snake. My father saw that I was about to drop it.

17   "Hang on to it!"

18   "The branch is squirming," I repeated. "And I hear something that sounds like a river!"

19   "Open your eyes," my father ordered.

20   I was stunned, as though he'd awakened me while I was dreaming.

21   "What does it mean?" I asked my father.

22   "It means that underneath us, right here, there's a little freshwater spring. If we dig, we could drink from it. I've just taught you how to find a spring. It's something my own father taught me. It isn't something you learn in school. And it isn't useless: a man can get along without writing and arithmetic, but he can never get along without water."

23   Much later, I discovered that my father was famous in the region because of what the people called his "gift:" before digging a well they always consulted him; they could watch him prospecting the fields or the hills, eyes closed, hands clenched on the fork of an alder bough. Wherever my father stopped, they marked the ground; there they would dig; and from there water would gush forth.

24   Years passed; I went to other schools, saw other countries, I had children, I wrote some books and my poor father is lying in the earth where so many times he had found fresh water.

25   One day someone began to make a film about my village and its inhabitants, from whom I've stolen so many of the stories that I tell. With the film crew we went to see a farmer to capture the image of a sad man: his children didn't want to receive the inheritance he'd spent his whole life preparing for them—the finest farm in the area. While the technicians were getting cameras and microphones ready the farmer put his arm around my shoulders, saying:

26   "I knew your father well."

27   "Ah, I know. Everybody in the village knows each other . . . No one feels like an outsider."

28   "You know what's under your feet?"

29   "Hell?" I asked, laughing.

30   "Under your feet there's a well. Before I dug I called in specialists from the Department of Agriculture; they did research, they analyzed shovelfuls of dirt; and they made a report where they said there wasn't any water on my land. With the family, the animals, the crops, I need water. When I saw those specialists hadn't found any I thought of your father and I asked him to come over. He didn't want to; I think he was pretty fed up with me because I'd asked those specialists instead of him. But finally he came; he went and cut off a little branch, then he walked around for a while with his eyes shut; he stopped, he listened to something we couldn't hear and then he said to me: 'Dig right here, there's enough water to get your whole flock drunk and drown your specialists besides.' We dug and found water. Fine water that's never heard of pollution."

31   The film people were ready; they called to me to take my place.

32   "I'm gonna show you something," said the farmer, keeping me back. "You wait right here."

33   He disappeared into a shack which he must have used to store things, then came back with a branch which he held out to me.

34   "I never throw nothing away; I kept the alder branch your father cut to find my water. I don't understand, it hasn't dried out."

35   Moved as I touched the branch, kept out of I don't know what sense of piety—and which really wasn't dry—I had the feeling that my father was watching me over my shoulder; I closed my eyes and, standing above the spring my father had discovered, I waited for the branch to writhe, I hoped the sound of gushing water would rise to my ears.

36   The alder stayed motionless in my hands and the water beneath the earth refused to sing.

37   Somewhere along the roads I'd taken since the village of my childhood I had forgotten my father's knowledge.

38   "Don't feel sorry," said the man, thinking no doubt of his farm and his childhood: "nowadays fathers can't pass on anything to the next generation."

39   And he took the alder branch from my hands.

■ Where the World Began

Margaret Laurence

Margaret Laurence was one of Canada's finest writers of short stories, essays, and novels about Canadian women's lives, but she also wrote about her experience of life in Africa. She is best remembered for *The Stone Angel* (1964) and *The Diviners* (1974). Early in her career, she worked as a journalist, but started writing short stories soon after her marriage. She served as the Chancellor of Trent University (1981–1983) and was made a Companion of the Order of Canada. Laurence took her own life in 1987 when she was diagnosed with untreatable cancer. The following essay was published in a collection of travel essays entitled *The Heart of a Stranger* (1976).

1   A strange place it was, the place where the world began. A place of incredible happenings, splendours and revelations, despairs like multitudinous pits of isolated hells. A place of shadow-spookiness, inhabited by the unknowable dead. A place of jubilation and of mourning, horrible and beautiful.

2   It was, in fact, a small prairie town.

3   Because that settlement and that land were my first and for many years my only real knowledge of this planet, in some profound way they remain my world, my way of viewing. My eyes were formed there. Towns like ours, set in a sea of land, have been described thousands of times as dull, bleak, flat, uninteresting. I have had it said to me that the railway trip across Canada is spectacular, except for the prairies, when it would be desirable to go to sleep for several days, until the ordeal is over. I am always unable to argue this point effectively. All I can say is—well, you really have to live there to know that country. The town of my childhood could be called bizarre, agonizingly repressive or cruel at times, and the land in which it grew could be called harsh in the violence of its seasonal changes. But never merely flat or uninteresting. Never dull.

4   In winter, we used to hitch rides on the back of the milk sleigh, our moccasins squeaking and slithering on the hard rutted snow of the roads, our hands in ice-bub-bled mitts hanging onto the box edge of the sleigh for dear life, while Bert grinned at us through his great frosted moustache and shouted the horses into speed, daring us to stay put. Those mornings, rising, there would be the perpetual fascination of the frost feathers on windows, the ferns and flowers and eerie faces traced there during the night by unseen artists of the wind. Evenings, coming back from skating, the sky would be black but not dark, for you could see a cold glitter of stars from one side of the earth's rim to the other. And then the sometime astonishment when you saw the Northern Lights flaring across the sky, like the scrawled signature of God. After a bliz-zard, when the snowploughs hadn't yet got through, school would be closed for the day, the assumption being that the town's young could not possibly flounder through five feet of snow in the pursuit of education. We would then gaily don snowshoes and flounder for miles out into the white dazzling deserts, in pursuit of a different kind of knowing. If you came back too close to night, through the woods at the foot of the town hill, the thin black branches of poplar and chokecherry now meringued with frost, sometimes you heard coyotes. Or maybe the banshee wolf-voices were really only inside your head.

5   Summers were scorching, and when no rain came and the wheat became bleached and dried before it headed, the faces of farmers and townsfolk would not smile much, and you took for granted, because it never seemed to have been any different, the fre-quent knocking at the back door and the young men standing there, mumbling or thrusting defiantly their request for a drink of water and a sandwich if you could spare it. They were riding the freights, and you never knew where they had come from, or where they might end up, if anywhere. The Drought and Depression were like evil deities which had been there always. You understood and you did not understand.

6   Yet the outside had its continuing marvels. The poplar bluffs and the small river were filled and surrounded with a zillion different grasses, stones, and weed flowers. The meadowlarks sang undaunted from the twanging telephone wires along the gravel highway. Once we found an old flat-bottomed scow, and launched her, polling along the shallow brown waters, mending her with wodges of hastily chewed Spearmint, grounding her among the tangles of soft yellow marsh marigolds that grew succulently along the banks of the shrunken river, while the sun made our skins smell dusty-warm.

7   My best friend lived in an apartment above some stores on Main Street (its real name was Mountain Avenue, goodness knows why), an elegant apartment with

royal-blue velvet curtains. The back roof, scarcely sloping at all, was corrugated tin, of a furnace-like warmth on a July afternoon, and we would sit there drinking lemonade and looking across the back lane at the Fire Hall. Sometimes our vigil would be rewarded. Oh joy! Somebody's house burning down! We had almost-perfect callousness in some ways. Then the wooden tower's bronze bell would clonk and toll like a thousand speeded funerals in a time of plague, and in a few minutes the team of giant black horses would cannon forth, pulling the fire wagon like some scarlet chariot of the Goths, while the firemen clung with one hand, adjusting their helmets as they went.

8   The oddities of the place were endless. An elderly lady used to serve, as her afternoon tea offering to other ladies, soda biscuits spread with peanut butter and topped with a whole marshmallow. Some considered this slightly eccentric, when compared with chopped egg sandwiches, and admittedly talked about her behind her back, but no one ever refused these delicacies or indicated to her that they thought she had slipped a cog. Another lady dyed her hair a bright and cheery orange, by strangers mistaken at twenty paces for a feather hat. My own beloved stepmother wore a silver fox neckpiece, a whole pelt, *with the embalmed (?) head still on.* My Ontario Irish grandfather said, "sparrow grass," a more interesting term than asparagus. The town dump was known as "the nuisance grounds," a phrase fraught with weird connotation, as though the effluvia of our lives was beneath contempt but at the same time was subtly threatening to the determined and sometimes hysterical propriety of our ways.

9   Some oddities were, as idiom had it, "funny ha ha"; others were "funny peculiar." Some were not so funny at all. An old man lived, deranged, in a shack in the valley. Perhaps he wasn't even that old, but to us he seemed a wild Methuselah figure, shambling among the underbrush and the tall couchgrass, muttering indecipherable curses or blessings, a prophet who had forgotten his prophesies. Everyone in town knew him, but no one knew him. He lived among us as though only occasionally and momentarily visible. The kids called him Andy Gump, and feared him. Some sought to prove their bravery by tormenting him. They were the medieval bear baiters, and he the lumbering bewildered bear, half blind, only rarely turning to snarl. Everything is to be found in a town like mine. Belsen, writ small but with the same ink.

10   All of us cast stones in one shape or another. In grade school, among the vulnerable and violet girls we were, the feared and despised were those few older girls from what was charmingly termed "the wrong side of the tracks." Tough in talk and tougher in muscle, they were said to be whores already. And may have been, that being about the only profession readily available to them.

11   The dead lived in that place, too. Not only the grandparents who had, in local parlance, "passed on" and who had gloomed, bearded or bonneted, from the sepia photographs in old albums, but also the uncles, forever eighteen or nineteen, whose names were carved on the granite family stones in the cemetery, but whose bones lay in France. My own young mother lay in that graveyard, beside other dead of our kin, and when I was ten, my father too, only forty, left the living town for the dead dwelling on the hill.

12   When I was 18, I couldn't wait to get out of that town, away from the prairies. I did not know then that I would carry the land and town all my life within my skull, that they would form the mainspring and source of the writing I was to do, wherever and however far away I might live.

13   This was my territory in the time of my youth, and in a sense my life since then has been an attempt to look at it, to come to terms with it. Stultifying to the mind it certainly would be, and sometimes was, but not to the imagination. It was many things, but it was never dull.

14   The same, I now see, could be said for Canada in general. Why on earth did generations of Canadians pretend to believe this country dull? We knew perfectly well it wasn't. Yet for so long we did not proclaim what we knew. If our upsurge of so-called nationalism seems odd or irreverent to outsiders, and even some of our own people (*what's all the fuss about?*), they might try to understand that for many years we valued ourselves insufficiently, living as we did under the huge shadows of those two dominating figures, Uncle Sam and Britannia. We have only just begun to value ourselves, our land, our abilities. We have only just begun to recognize our legends and give shape to our myths.

15   There are, God knows, enough aspects to deplore about this country. When I see the killing of our lakes and rivers with industrial wastes, I feel rage and despair. When I see our industries and natural resources increasingly taken over by America, I feel an overwhelming discouragement, especially as I cannot simply say, "damn Yankees." It should never be forgotten that it is we ourselves who have sold such a large amount of our birthright for a mess of plastic Progress. When I saw the War Measures Act being invoked in 1970, I lost forever the vestigial remains of the naïve wish-belief that repression could not happen here, or would not. And yet, of course, I had known all along in the deepest and often hidden caves of the heart that anything can happen anywhere, for the seed of both man's freedom and his captivity are found everywhere, even in the microcosm of a prairie town. But in raging against our injustices, our stupidities, I do so as *family*, as I did, and still do, in writing about those aspects of my town which I hated and which are always in some ways aspects of myself.

16   The land still draws me more than other lands. I have lived in Africa and in England, but splendid as both can be, they do not have the power to move me in the same way as, for example, that part of southern Ontario where I spent four months last summer in a cedar cabin beside a river. "Scratch a Canadian and you find a phony pioneer," I used to say to myself in warning. But all the same it is true, I think, that we are not yet totally alienated from physical earth, and let us only pray that we do not become so. I once thought that my lifelong fear and mistrust of cities made me a kind of old-fashioned freak; now I see it differently.

17   The cabin has a long window across its front western wall, and sitting at the oak table there in the mornings, I used to look out at the river and at all the tall trees beyond, green-gold in the early light. The river was bronze; the sun caught it strangely, reflecting upon its surface the near-shore sand ripples underneath. Suddenly, the crescenting of a fish, gone before the eye could clearly give image to it. The old man next door said these leaping fish were carp. Himself, he preferred muskie, for he was a real fisherman and the muskie gave him a fight. The wind most often blew from the south, and the river flowed toward the south, so when the water was wind-riffled, the river seemed to be flowing both ways. I liked this, and interpreted it as an omen, a natural symbol.

18   A few years ago, when I was back in Winnipeg, I gave a talk at my old college. It was open to the public, and afterward a very old man came up to me and asked me if my maiden name had been Wemyss. I said yes, thinking he might have known my father or

my grandfather. But no. "When I was a young lad," he said, "I once worked for your great-grandfather, Robert Wemyss, when he had the sheep ranch at Raeburn." I think that was a moment when I realized all over again something of great importance to me. My long-ago families came from Scotland and Ireland, but in a sense that no longer mattered so much. My true roots were here.

19   I am not very patriotic, in the usual sense of the word. I cannot say, "My country right or wrong" in any political, social or literary context. But in one this is inalterable, for better or worse, for life.

20   This is where my world began. A world which includes ancestors—both my own and other people's ancestors who became mine. A world which formed me, and continues to do so even while I fought it some of its aspects, and continue to do so. A world which gave me my own lifework to do, because it was here that I learned the sight of my own particular eyes.

Chapter 30

Essays for Further Analysis: Multiple Strategies and Styles

■ I Have a Dream

Martin Luther King, Jr.

The Rev. Martin Luther King, Jr., president of the Southern Christian Leadership Conference, was the most well-known leader of the civil rights movement of the 1960s, and the recipient of the 1964 Nobel Peace Prize. He was assassinated in 1968. King delivered this speech in 1963 at a celebration of the Emancipation Proclamation, before a crowd of 250,000 who had marched to the Lincoln Memorial in Washington, D.C.

1   Five score years ago, a great American, in whose symbolic shadow we stand, signed the Emancipation Proclamation. This momentous decree came as a great beacon light of hope to millions of Negro slaves who had been seared in the flames of withering injustice. It came as a joyous daybreak to end the long night of captivity.

2   But one hundred years later, we must face the tragic fact that the Negro is still not free. One hundred years later, the life of the Negro is still sadly crippled by the manacles of segregation and the chains of discrimination. One hundred years later, the Negro lives on a lonely island of poverty in the midst of a vast ocean of material prosperity. One hundred years later, the Negro is still languishing in the corners of American society and finds himself an exile in his own land. So we have come here today to dramatize an appalling condition.

3   In a sense we have come to our nation's capital to cash a check. When the architects of our republic wrote the magnificent words of the Constitution and the Declaration of Independence, they were signing a promissory note to which every American

was to fall heir. This note was a promise that all men would be guaranteed the unalienable rights of life, liberty, and the pursuit of happiness.

4   It is obvious today that America has defaulted on this promissory note insofar as her citizens of color are concerned. Instead of honoring this sacred obligation, America has given the Negro people a bad check; a check which has come back marked "insufficient funds." But we refuse to believe that the bank of justice is bankrupt. We refuse to believe that there are insufficient funds in the great vaults of opportunity of this nation. So we have come to cash this check—a check that will give us upon demand the riches of freedom and the security of justice. We have also come to this hallowed spot to remind America of the fierce urgency of *now*. This is no time to engage in the luxury of cooling off or to take the tranquilizing drugs of gradualism. *Now* is the time to make real the promises of Democracy. *Now* is the time to rise from the dark and desolate valley of segregation to the sunlit path of racial justice. *Now* is the time to open the doors of opportunity to all of God's children. *Now* is the time to lift our nation from the quicksands of racial injustice to the solid rock of brotherhood.

5   It would be fatal for the nation to overlook the urgency of the moment and to underestimate the determination of the Negro. This sweltering summer of the Negro's legitimate discontent will not pass until there is an invigorating autumn of freedom and equality. Nineteen sixty-three is not an end, but a beginning. Those who hope that the Negro needed to blow off steam and will now be content will have a rude awakening if the nation returns to business as usual. There will be neither rest nor tranquillity in America until the Negro is granted his citizenship rights. The whirl-winds of revolt will continue to shake the foundations of our nation until the bright day of justice emerges.

6   But there is something that I must say to my people who stand on the warm threshold which leads into the palace of justice. In the process of gaining our rightful place we must not be guilty of wrongful deeds. Let us not seek to satisfy our thirst for freedom by drinking from the cup of bitterness and hatred. We must forever conduct our struggle on the high plane of dignity and discipline. We must not allow our creative protest to degenerate into physical violence. Again and again we must rise to the majestic heights of meeting physical force with soul force. The marvelous new militancy which has engulfed the Negro community must not lead us to distrust of all white people, for many of our white brothers, as evidenced by their presence here today, have come to realize that their destiny is tied up with our destiny and their freedom is inextricably bound to our freedom. We cannot walk alone.

7   And as we walk, we must make the pledge that we shall march ahead. We cannot turn back. There are those who are asking the devotees of civil rights, "When will you be satisfied?" We can never be satisfied as long as the Negro is the victim of the unspeakable horrors of police brutality. We can never be satisfied as long as our bodies, heavy with the fatigue of travel, cannot gain lodging in the motels of the highways and the hotels of the cities. We cannot be satisfied as long as the Negro's basic mobility is from a smaller ghetto to a larger one. We can never be satisfied as long as a Negro in Mississippi cannot vote and a Negro in New York believes he has nothing for which to vote. No, no, we are not satisfied, and we will not be satisfied until justice rolls down like waters and righteousness like a mighty stream.

8   I am not unmindful that some of you have come here out of great trials and tribulations. Some of you have come fresh from narrow jail cells. Some of you have come from areas where your quest for freedom left you battered by the storms of persecution

and staggered by the winds of police brutality. You have been the veterans of creative suffering. Continue to work with the faith that unearned suffering is redemptive.

9   Go back to Mississippi, go back to Alabama, go back to South Carolina, go back to Georgia, go back to Louisiana, go back to the slums and ghettos of our northern cities, knowing that somehow this situation can and will be changed. Let us not wallow in the valley of despair.

10   I say to you today, my friends, that in spite of the difficulties and frustrations of the moment I still have a dream. It is a dream deeply rooted in the American dream.

11   I have a dream that one day this nation will rise up and live out the true meaning of its creed: "We hold these truths to be self-evident; that all men are created equal."

12   I have a dream that one day on the red hills of Georgia the sons of former slaves and the sons of former slaveowners will be able to sit down together at the table of brotherhood.

13   I have a dream that one day even the state of Mississippi, a desert state sweltering with the heat of injustice and oppression, will be transformed into an oasis of freedom and justice.

14   I have a dream that my four little children will one day live in a nation where they will not be judged by the color of their skin but by the content of their character.

15   I have a dream today.

16   I have a dream that one day the state of Alabama, whose governor's lips are presently dripping with the words of interposition and nullification, will be transformed into a situation where little black boys and black girls will be able to join hands with little white boys and white girls and walk together as sisters and brothers.

17   I have a dream today.

18   I have a dream that one day every valley shall be exalted, every hill and mountain shall be made low, the rough places will be made plain, and the crooked places will be made straight, and the glory of the Lord shall be revealed, and all flesh shall see it together.

19   This is our hope. This is the faith with which I return to the South. With this faith we will be able to hew out of the mountain of despair a stone of hope. With this faith we will be able to transform the jangling discords of our nation into a beautiful symphony of brotherhood. With this faith we will be able to work together, to pray together, to struggle together, to go to jail together, to stand up for freedom together, knowing that we will be free one day.

20   This will be the day when all of God's children will be able to sing with new meaning

> My country, 'tis of thee,
> Sweet land of liberty,
>   Of thee I sing:
> Land where my fathers died,
> Land of the pilgrims' pride,
> From every mountain-side
>   Let freedom ring.

21   And if America is to be a great nation this must become true. So let freedom ring from the prodigious hilltops of New Hampshire. Let freedom ring from the mighty mountains of New York. Let freedom ring from the heightening Alleghenies of Pennsylvania!

22   Let freedom ring from the snowcapped Rockies of Colorado!

23   Let freedom ring from the curvaceous peaks of California!

24   But not only that; let freedom ring from Stone Mountain of Georgia!

25   Let freedom ring from Lookout Mountain of Tennessee!

26   Let freedom ring from every hill and molehill of Mississippi. From every mountain-side, let freedom ring.

27   When we let freedom ring, when we let it ring from every village and every hamlet, from every state and every city, we will be able to speed up that day when all of God's children, black men and white men, Jews and Gentiles, Protestants and Catholics, will be able to join hands and sing in the words of the old Negro spiritual, "Free at last! free at last! thank God almighty, we are free at last!"

■ Speech for the Democratic Convention of 2004

Barack Obama

In 2004, Senator John Kerry was the Democratic presidential candidate. Barack Obama, American senator and, later, himself a presidential candidate, was just beginning his rise to power. Obama studied at Columbia University and Harvard Law School, and worked as a civil rights lawyer as well as a community organizer before he entered politics. His rich cultural background includes his Kenyan heritage and childhood upbringing in Hawaii and Indonesia. Obama's best-selling account of his relationship with his Kenyan heritage, *Dreams from my Father: A Story of Race and Inheritance* (1995), and equally successful analysis of American politics, *The Audacity of Hope: Thoughts on Reclaiming the American Dream* (2006), have established him as a powerful rhetorician. The eloquence of the following keynote speech for the 2004 Democratic Convention made Americans take notice of this formerly obscure politician.

1   Thank you so much. Thank you. Thank you. Thank you so much. Thank you so much. Thank you. Thank you. Thank you, Dick Durbin. You make us all proud.

2   On behalf of the great state of Illinois, crossroads of a nation, Land of Lincoln, let me express my deepest gratitude for the privilege of addressing this convention.

3   Tonight is a particular honor for me because, let's face it, my presence on this stage is pretty unlikely. My father was a foreign student, born and raised in a small village in Kenya. He grew up herding goats, went to school in a tin-roof shack. His father—my grandfather—was a cook, a domestic servant to the British.

4   But my grandfather had larger dreams for his son. Through hard work and perseverance my father got a scholarship to study in a magical place, America, that shone as a beacon of freedom and opportunity to so many who had come before.

5   While studying here, my father met my mother. She was born in a town on the other side of the world, in Kansas. Her father worked on oil rigs and farms through most of the Depression. The day after Pearl Harbor my grandfather signed up for duty; joined Patton's army, marched across Europe. Back home, my grandmother raised a baby and went to work on a bomber assembly line. After the war, they studied on the G.I. Bill, bought a house through F.H.A., and later moved west all the way to Hawaii in search of opportunity.

6   And they, too, had big dreams for their daughter. A common dream, born of two continents.

7   My parents shared not only an improbable love, they shared an abiding faith in the possibilities of this nation. They would give me an African name, Barack, or "blessed," believing that in a tolerant America your name is no barrier to success. They imagined me going to the best schools in the land, even though they weren't rich, because in a generous America you don't have to be rich to achieve your potential.

8   They're both passed away now. And yet, I know that on this night they look down on me with great pride.

9   They stand here—And I stand here today, grateful for the diversity of my heritage, aware that my parents' dreams live on in my two precious daughters. I stand here knowing that my story is part of the larger American story, that I owe a debt to all of those who came before me, and that, in no other country on earth, is my story even possible.

10   Tonight, we gather to affirm the greatness of our Nation—not because of the height of our skyscrapers, or the power of our military, or the size of our economy. Our pride is based on a very simple premise, summed up in a declaration made over two hundred years ago:

11   *We hold these truths to be self-evident, that all men are created equal, that they are endowed by their Creator with certain inalienable rights, that among these are Life, Liberty and the pursuit of Happiness.*

12   That is the true genius of America, a faith—a faith in simple dreams, an insistence on small miracles; that we can tuck in our children at night and know that they are fed and clothed and safe from harm; that we can say what we think, write what we think, without hearing a sudden knock on the door; that we can have an idea and start our own business without paying a bribe; that we can participate in the political process without fear of retribution, and that our votes will be counted—at least most of the time.

13   This year, in this election we are called to reaffirm our values and our commitments, to hold them against a hard reality and see how we're measuring up to the legacy of our forbearers [*sic*] and the promise of future generations.

14   And fellow Americans, Democrats, Republicans, Independents, I say to you tonight: We have more work to do—more work to do for the workers I met in Galesburg, Illinois, who are losing their union jobs at the Maytag plant that's moving to Mexico, and now are having to compete with their own children for jobs that pay seven bucks an hour; more to do for the father that I met who was losing his job and choking back the tears, wondering how he would pay 4500 dollars a month for the drugs his son needs without the health benefits that he counted on; more to do for the young woman in East St. Louis, and thousands more like her, who has the grades, has the drive, has the will, but doesn't have the money to go to college.

15   Now, don't get me wrong. The people I meet—in small towns and big cities, in diners and office parks—they don't expect government to solve all their problems. They know they have to work hard to get ahead, and they want to. Go into the collar counties around Chicago, and people will tell you they don't want their tax money wasted, by a welfare agency or by the Pentagon. Go into any inner city neighborhood, and folks will tell you that government alone can't teach our kids to learn; they know that parents have to teach, that children can't achieve unless we raise their expectations and turn off the television sets and eradicate the slander that says a black youth with a book is acting white. They know those things.

16   People don't expect government to solve all their problems. But they sense, deep in their bones, that with just a slight change in priorities, we can make sure that every child in America has a decent shot at life, and that the doors of opportunity remain open to all.

17   They know we can do better. And they want that choice.

18   In this election, we offer that choice. Our Party has chosen a man to lead us who embodies the best this country has to offer. And that man is John Kerry.

19   John Kerry understands the ideals of community, faith, and service because they've defined his life. From his heroic service to Vietnam, to his years as a prosecutor and lieutenant governor, through two decades in the United States Senate, he's devoted himself to this country. Again and again, we've seen him make tough choices when easier ones were available.

20   His values and his record affirm what is best in us. John Kerry believes in an America where hard work is rewarded; so instead of offering tax breaks to companies shipping jobs overseas, he offers them to companies creating jobs here at home.

21   John Kerry believes in an America where all Americans can afford the same health coverage our politicians in Washington have for themselves.

22   John Kerry believes in energy independence, so we aren't held hostage to the profits of oil companies, or the sabotage of foreign oil fields.

23   John Kerry believes in the Constitutional freedoms that have made our country the envy of the world, and he will never sacrifice our basic liberties, nor use faith as a wedge to divide us.

24   And John Kerry believes that in a dangerous world war must be an option sometimes, but it should never be the first option.

25   You know, a while back I met a young man named Shamus in a V.F.W. Hall in East Moline, Illinois. He was a good-looking kid—six two, six three, clear eyed, with an easy smile. He told me he'd joined the Marines and was heading to Iraq the following week. And as I listened to him explain why he'd enlisted, the absolute faith he had in our country and its leaders, his devotion to duty and service, I thought this young man was all that any of us might ever hope for in a child.

26   But then I asked myself, "Are we serving Shamus as well as he is serving us?"

27   I thought of the 900 men and women—sons and daughters, husbands and wives, friends and neighbors, who won't be returning to their own hometowns. I thought of the families I've met who were struggling to get by without a loved one's full income, or whose loved ones had returned with a limb missing or nerves shattered, but still lacked long-term health benefits because they were Reservists.

28   When we send our young men and women into harm's way, we have a solemn obligation not to fudge the numbers or shade the truth about why they're going, to care for their families while they're gone, to tend to the soldiers upon their return, and to never ever go to war without enough troops to win the war, secure the peace, and earn the respect of the world.

29   Now let me be clear. Let me be clear. We have real enemies in the world. These enemies must be found. They must be pursued. And they must be defeated. John Kerry knows this. And just as Lieutenant Kerry did not hesitate to risk his life to protect the men who served with him in Vietnam, President Kerry will not hesitate one moment to use our military might to keep America safe and secure.

30   John Kerry believes in America. And he knows that it's not enough for just some of us to prosper—for alongside our famous individualism, there's another ingredient in the American saga, a belief that we're all connected as one people. If there is a child on the south side of Chicago who can't read, that matters to me, even if it's not my child. If there is a senior citizen somewhere who can't pay for their prescription drugs, and having to choose between medicine and the rent, that makes my life poorer, even if it's not my grandparent. If there's an Arab American family being rounded up without benefit of an attorney or due process, that threatens my civil liberties.

31   It is that fundamental belief—It is that fundamental belief: I am my brother's keeper. I am my sister's keeper that makes this country work. It's what allows us to pursue our individual dreams and yet still come together as one American family.

32   E pluribus unum: "Out of many, one."

33   Now even as we speak, there are those who are preparing to divide us—the spin masters, the negative ad peddlers who embrace the politics of "anything goes." Well, I say to them tonight, there is not a liberal America and a conservative America—there is the United States of America. There is not a Black America and a White America and Latino America and Asian America—there's the United States of America.

34   The pundits like to slice-and-dice our country into Red States and Blue States; Red States for Republicans, Blue States for Democrats. But I've got news for them, too. We worship an "awesome God" in the Blue States, and we don't like federal agents poking around in our libraries in the Red States. We coach Little League in the Blue States and yes, we've got some gay friends in the Red States. There are patriots who opposed the war in Iraq and there are patriots who supported the war in Iraq. We are one people, all of us pledging allegiance to the stars and stripes, all of us defending the United States of America.

35   In the end—In the end—In the end, that's what this election is about. Do we participate in a politics of cynicism or do we participate in a politics of hope?

36   John Kerry calls on us to hope. John Edwards calls on us to hope.

37   I'm not talking about blind optimism here—the almost willful ignorance that thinks unemployment will go away if we just don't think about it, or the health care crisis will solve itself if we just ignore it. That's not what I'm talking about. I'm talking about something more substantial. It's the hope of slaves sitting around a fire singing freedom songs; the hope of immigrants setting out for distant shores; the hope of a young naval lieutenant bravely patrolling the Mekong Delta; the hope of a millworker's son who dares to defy the odds; the hope of a skinny kid with a funny name who believes that America has a place for him, too.

38   Hope—Hope in the face of difficulty. Hope in the face of uncertainty. The audacity of hope!

39   In the end, that is God's greatest gift to us, the bedrock of this nation. A belief in things not seen. A belief that there are better days ahead.

40   I believe that we can give our middle class relief and provide working families with a road to opportunity.

41   I believe we can provide jobs to the jobless, homes to the homeless, and reclaim young people in cities across America from violence and despair.

42   I believe that we have a righteous wind at our backs and that as we stand on the crossroads of history, we can make the right choices, and meet the challenges that face us.

43   America! Tonight, if you feel the same energy that I do, if you feel the same urgency that I do, if you feel the same passion that I do, if you feel the same hopefulness that I do—if we do what we must do, then I have no doubt that all across the country, from Florida to Oregon, from Washington to Maine, the people will rise up in November, and John Kerry will be sworn in as President, and John Edwards will be sworn in as Vice President, and this country will reclaim its promise, and out of this long political darkness a brighter day will come.

44   Thank you very much everybody. God bless you. Thank you.

C h a p t e r 3 1

Literature

■ Ozymandias

Percy Bysshe Shelley

Percy Bysshe Shelley is considered one of the finest English poets and a major figure in the nineteenth-century Romantic movement. Born in 1792, Shelley was educated at Eton but was expelled from Oxford. He married Mary Wollstonecraft (later famous for her novel *Frankenstein*) and travelled in Europe, where he produced some of his best work, including "To a Skylark," "The Cloud," and "Ode to the West Wind." In 1822, at age twenty-nine, Shelley drowned in Italy. The sonnet presented here was written in 1818.

I met a traveller from an antique land
Who said: Two vast and trunkless legs of stone
Stand in the desert . . . Near them, on the sand,
Half sunk, a shattered visage lies, whose frown,
5   And wrinkled lip, and sneer of cold command,
Tell that its sculptor well those passions read
Which yet survive, stamped on these lifeless things,
The hand that mocked them, and the heart that fed:
And on the pedestal these words appear:
10   "My name is Ozymandias, king of kings:
Look on my works, ye Mighty, and despair!"
Nothing beside remains. Round the decay
Of that colossal wreck, boundless and bare
The lone and level sands stretch far away.

■ The Orange Fish

Carol Shields

Canadian writer Carol Shields (1935–2003) wrote novels, poems, plays, and short stories, including *Swann* (1987), *Larry's Party* (1997), and *The Stone Diaries* (1993), for which she won the Pulitzer Prize and the Governor-General's Award, among many others. Shields was a well-loved author who received many honours. She was a Companion of the Order of Canada and a Fellow of the Royal Society of Canada. Shields's writing explored the lives of women, and was particularly profound in its ability to represent everyday experiences of ordinary people. "The Orange Fish" is the title story in a short story collection published in 1989.

1   Like many others of my generation I am devoted to food, money and sex; but I have an ulcer and have been unhappily married to Lois-Ann, a lawyer, for twelve years. As you might guess, we are both fearful of aging. Recently, Lois-Ann showed me an article she had clipped from the newspaper, a profile of a well-known television actress who was described as being "deep in her thirties."

2   "That's what we are," Lois-Ann said sadly, "deep in our thirties." She looked at me from behind a lens of tears.

3   Despite our incompatibility, the two of us understand each other, and I knew more or less what it was she was thinking: that some years ago, when she was twenty-five, she made up her mind to go to Vancouver Island and raise dahlias, but on the very day she bought her air ticket, she got a letter in the mail saying she'd been accepted at law school. "None of us ever writes our own script," she said to me once, and of course she's right. I still toy—I confess this to you freely—with my old fantasy of running a dude ranch, with the thought of well-rubbed saddles and harnesses and the whole sweet leathery tip of possibility, even though I know the dude market's been depressed for a decade, dead in fact.

4   Not long ago, on a Saturday morning. Lois-Ann and I had one of our long talks about values, about goals. The mood as we sat over breakfast was sternly analytical.

5   "Maybe we've become trapped in the cult of consumerism and youth worship," I suggested.

6   "Trapped by our *zeitgeist*," said Lois-Ann, who has a way of capping a point, especially my point.

7   A long silence followed, twenty seconds, thirty seconds. I glanced up from an emptied coffee cup, remembered that my fortieth birthday was only weeks away, and felt a flare of panic in my upper colon. The pain was hideous and familiar. I took a deep breath as I'd been told to do. Breathe in, then out. Repeat. The trick is to visualize the pain, its substance and colour, and then transfer it to a point outside the body. I concentrated on a small spot above our breakfast table, a random patch on the white wall. Often this does the trick, but this morning the blank space, the smooth drywall expanse of it, seemed distinctly accusing.

8   At one time Lois-Ann and I had talked about wall-papering the kitchen or at least putting up an electric clock shaped like a sunflower. We also considered a ceramic bas-relief of cauliflowers and carrots, and after that a little heart-shaped mirror bordered with rattan, and, more recently, a primitive map of the world with a practical acrylic surface.

9   I felt Lois-Ann watching me, her eyes as neat and neutral as birds' eggs. "What we need," I said, gesturing at the void, "is a picture."

10   "Or possibly a print," said Lois-Ann, and immediately went to get a coat.

11   Three hours later we were the owners of a cheerful lithograph titled *The Orange Fish*. It was unframed, but enclosed in a sandwich of twinkling glass, its corners secured by a set of neat metal clips. The mat surrounding the picture was a generous three inches in width—we liked that—and the background was a shimmer of green; within this space the orange fish was suspended.

12   I wish somehow you could see this fish. He is boldly drawn, and just as boldly coloured. He occupies approximately eighty per cent of the surface and has about him a wet, dense look of health. To me, at least, he appears to have stopped moving, to be resting against the wall of green water. A stream of bubbles, each one separate and tear-shaped, floats above him, binding him to his element. Of course he is seen in side profile, as fish always are, and this classic posture underlines the tranquility of the whole. He possesses too, a Buddha-like sense of being in the *right* place, the only place. His centre, that is, where you might imagine his heart to be, is sweetly orange in colour, and this colour diminishes slightly as it flows towards the semi-transparency of fins and the round, ridged, non-appraising mouth. But it was his eye I most appreciated, the kind of wide, ungreedy eye I would like to be able to turn onto the world.

13   We made up our minds quickly; he would fit nicely over the breakfast table. Lois-Ann mentioned that the orange tones would pick up the colours of the seat covers. We were in a state of rare agreement. And the price was right.

14   Forgive me if I seem condescending, but you should know that, strictly speaking, a lithograph is not an original work of art, but rather a print from an original plate; the number of prints is limited to ten or twenty or fifty or more, and this number is always indicated on the piece itself. A tiny inked set of numbers in the corner, just beneath the artist's signature in the corner will tell you, for example, that our particular fish is number eight out of an existing ten copies, and I think it pleased me from start to think of those other copies, the nine brother fish scattered elsewhere, suspended in identical seas of green water, each pointed soberly in the same leftward direction. I found myself in a fanciful mood, humming, installing a hook on the kitchen wall and hanging our new acquisition. We stepped backward to admire it, and later Lois-Ann made a Spanish omelet with fresh fennel, which we ate beneath the austere eye of our beautiful fish.

15   As you well know, there are certain necessary tasks that coarsen the quality of everyday life, and while Lois-Ann and I went about ours, we felt calmed by the heft of our solemn, gleaming fish. My health improved from the first day, and before long Lois-Ann and I were on better terms, often sharing workaday anecdotes or pointing out curious items to each other in the newspaper. I rediscovered the girlish angularity of her arms and shoulders as she wriggled in and out of her little nylon nightgowns, smoothing down the skirts with a sly, sweet glance in my direction. For the first time in years she left the lamp burning on the bedside table and, as in our early days, she covered me with kisses, a long nibbling trail up and down the ridge of my vertebrae. In the morning, drinking our coffee at the breakfast table, we looked up, regarded our orange fish, smiled at each other, but were ritualistically careful to say nothing.

16   We didn't ask ourselves, for instance, what kind of fish this was, whether it was a carp or a flounder or a monstrously out-of-scale goldfish. Its biological classification, its authenticity, seemed splendidly irrelevant. Details, just details; we swept them aside. What mattered was the prismatic disjection of green light that surrounded it. What

mattered was that it existed. That it had no age, no history. It simply *was*. You can understand that to speculate, to analyze overmuch, interferes with that narrow gap between symbol and reality, and it was precisely in the folds of that little gap that Lois-Ann and I found our temporary refuge.

17   Soon an envelope arrived in the mail, an official notice. We were advised that the ten owners of *The Orange Fish* met on the third Thursday of each month. The announcement was photocopied, but on decent paper with an appropriate logo. Eight-thirty was the regular time, and there was a good-natured reminder at the bottom of the page about the importance of getting things going punctually.

18   Nevertheless we were late. At the last minute Lois-Ann discovered a run in her panty-hose and had to change. I had difficulty getting the car started, and of course traffic was heavy. Furthermore, the meeting was in a part of the city that was unfamiliar to us. Lois-Ann, although a clever lawyer, has a poor sense of spatial orientation and told me to turn left when I should have turned right. And then there was the usual problem with parking, for which she seemed to hold me responsible. We arrived at eight-forty-five, rather agitated and out of breath from climbing stairs.

19   Seeing that roomful of faces, I at first experienced a shriek in the region of my upper colon. Lois-Ann had a similar shock of alarm, what she afterwards described to me as a jolt to her imagination, as though an axle in her left brain had suddenly seized.

20   Someone was speaking as we entered the room. I recognized the monotone of the born chairman. "It is always a pleasure," the voice intoned, "to come together to express our concerns and compare experiences."

21   At that moment the only experience I cared about was the sinuous river of kisses down my shoulders and backbone, but I managed to sit straight on my folding chair and to look alert and responsible. Lois-Ann, in a lawyer-like fashion, inspected the agenda, running a little gold pencil down the list of items, her tongue tight between her teeth.

22   The voice rumbled on. Minutes from the previous meeting were read and approved. There was no old business. Nor any new business. "Well, then," the chairman said, "who would like to speak first?"

23   Someone at the front of the room rose and gave his name, a name that conveyed the double-pillared boom of money and power. I craned my neck, but could only see a bush of fine white hair. The voice was feeble yet dignified, a persisting quaver from a soft old silvery throat, and I realized after a minute or two that we were listening to a testimonial. A mystical experience was described. Something too, about the "search for definitions" and about "wandering in the wilderness" and about the historic symbol of the fish in the Western Tradition, a secret sign, an icon expressing providence. "My life has been altered," the voice concluded, "and given direction."

24   The next speaker was young, not more than twenty I would say. Lois-Ann and I took in the flare of dyed hair, curiously angled and distinctively punk in style. You can imagine our surprise: here of all places to find a spiked bracelet, black nails, cheeks outlined in blue paint, and a forehead tattooed with the world's most familiar expletive. *The Orange Fish* had been a graduation gift from his parents. The framing alone cost two hundred dollars. He had stared at it for weeks, or possibly months, trying to understand what it meant; then revelation rushed in. "Fishness" was a viable alternative. The orange fins and sneering mouth said no to "all that garbage that gets shovelled on your head by society. So keep swimming and don't take any junk," he wound up, then sat down to loud applause.

25   A woman in a neatly tailored mauve suit spoke for a quarter of an hour about her investment difficulties. She'd tried stocks. She'd tried the bond market. She'd tried treasury bills and mutual funds. In every instance she found herself buying at the peak and selling just as the market bottomed out. Until she found out about investing in art. Until she found *The Orange Fish.* She was sure, now, that she was on an upward curve. That success was ahead. Recently she had started to be happy, she said.

26   A man rose to his feet. He was in his mid-fifties, we guessed, with good teeth and an aura of culture lightly worn. He had been through a period of professional burnout, arriving every day at his office exhausted. "Try to find some way to brighten up the place," he told his secretary, handing her a blank check. *The Orange Fish* appeared the next day. Its effect had been instantaneous: on himself, his staff, and also on his clients. It was as though a bright banner had been raised. Orange, after all, was the colour of celebration, and it is the act of celebration that has been crowded out of contemporary life.

27   The next speaker was cheered the moment he stood. He had, we discovered, travelled all the way from Japan, from the city of Kobe—making our little journey across the city seem trivial. As you can imagine, his accent was somewhat harsh and halting, but I believe we understood something of what he said. In the small house where he lives, he has hung *The Orange Fish* in the traditional tokonoma alcove, just above the black lacquered slab of wood on which rests a bowl of white flowers. The contrast between the sharp orange of the fish's scales and the unearthly whiteness of the flowers' petals reminds him daily of the contradictions that abound in the industrialized world. At this no one clapped louder than myself.

28   A fish is devoid of irony, someone else contributed in a brisk, cozy voice, and is therefore a reminder of our lost innocence, of the era which predated double meanings and trial balloons. But, at the same time, a fish is more and also less than its bodily weight.

29   A slim, dark-haired woman, hardly more than a girl, spoke for several minutes about the universality of fish. How three-quarters of the earth's surface is covered with water, and in this water leap fish by the millions. There are people in this world, she said, who have never seen a sheep or a cow, but there is no one who is not acquainted with the organic shape of the fish.

30   "We begin our life in water," came a hoarse and boozy squawk from the back row, "and we yearn all our days to return to our natural element. In water we are free to move without effort, to be most truly ourselves."

31   "The interior life of the fish is unknowable," said the next speaker, who was Lois-Ann. "She swims continuously, and is as mute, as voiceless as a dahlia. She speaks at the level of gesture, in circling patterns revived and repeated. The purpose of her eye is to decode and rearrange the wordless word."

32   "The orange fish," said a voice which turned out to be my own, "will never grow old."

33   I sat down. Later my hand was most warmly shaken. During the refreshment hour I was greeted with feeling and asked to sign the membership book. Lois-Ann put her arms around me, publicly, her face shining, and I knew that when we got home she would offer me a cup of cocoa. She would leave the bedside lamp burning and bejewel me with a stream of kisses. You can understand my feeling. Enchantment. Ecstasy. But waking up in the morning we would not be the same people.

34   I believe we all felt it, standing in that brightly lit room with our coffee cups and cookies: the woman in the tailored mauve suit, the fiftyish man with the good teeth, even the young boy with his crown of purple hair. We were, each of us, speeding along a trajectory, away from each other, and away from that one fixed point in time, the orange fish.

35   But how helplessly distorted our perspective turned out to be. What none of us could have known that night was that *we* were the ones who were left behind, sheltered and reprieved by a rare congeniality and by pleasure that each of us feels when our deepest concerns have been given form.

36   That very evening, in another part of the city, ten thousand posters of the orange fish were rolling off a press. These posters—which would sell first for $10, then $8.49, and later $1.95—would decorate the rumpled bedrooms of teenagers and the public washrooms of filling stations and beer halls. Within a year a postage stamp would be issued, engraved with the image of the orange fish, but a fish whose eye, miniaturized, would hold a look of mild bewilderment. And sooner than any of us would believe possible, the orange fish would be slapped across the front of a Sears flyer, given a set of demeaning eyebrows, and cruelly bisected with an invitation to stock up early on back-to-school supplies.

37   There can be no turning back at this point, as you surely know. Winking off lapel buttons and earrings, stamped onto sweatshirts and neckties, doodled on notepads and in the margin of love letters, the orange fish, without a backward glance, will begin to die.

Chapter 32

Writing and Language

■ The Importance of Email Punctuation: A Cautionary Tale

J. Kelly Nestruck

J. Kelly Nestruck is a freelance writer and theatre critic for *The Globe and Mail*. He has also written for many other newspapers, including the *Boston Globe* and *The Guardian*, and for *Maclean's* magazine. A former arts reporter for the *National Post,* Nestruck also writes on politics and pop culture. This 1999 essay appeared in the student newspaper, *The McGill Daily,* when Nestruck was still an undergraduate majoring in English and History.

1 Never before in my life had I considered a colon so carefully.

2 I spent a full 20 minutes staring at it at the very top of the message. Kelly, colon. It was perhaps the first time I had thought about the affective meaning of punctuation, particularly in email. Linguists have become increasingly interested in communication through email. This abbreviated, instant form of discourse has revolutionized the world. Even though I have only been using email for six or seven years, I can no longer imagine life without it. Classes now have discussion listservs. I can email an article minutes before a deadline from across the city. The relationship with my father in Winnipeg has become more personal than it had been with the alternating Saturday father-son telephone call. Because of its brief nature every single character in an email takes on enormous significance. This includes the colon that I found preceded by my name at the top of the email.

3   Previous emails from this person had begun with Kelly followed by a resounding exclamation point. My, how I savoured those exclamation points, each one echoing throughout my entire body. This correspondent of mine, whose slender fingers I imagine now gently depressing the Shift key and then caressing the 1, is not one of those who overuses the exclamation point. She is not like others in my database who write valley girl messages littered with smilies like, "Kelly! I just got a new garbage can! It has a pedal you push to make the lid go up!:) I'm going to Peel Pub later! TTFN!"

4   Likewise, my slender-fingered email friend never adopted the punctuation of fakes, phoneys, and ostentatious schmucks: the semi-colon. The semi-colon, while popular outside of the cyberworld, should be relegated to formal modes of communication. A semi-colon in an email ("We should meet at Peel Pub; it is finally wet T-shirt night again.") is as out of place as an exclamation point in an essay ("The Miskitu Indians were subordinate to both the Nicaragua state and the institution of American neo-colonialism!").

5   Occasionally, when my delicately digited correspondent's heart was heavy with some crisis or another, the exclamation point would disappear after my name. Short messages sometimes had my name followed by a comma. None of this bothered me. The colon, however, shattered me. Colons are the punctuation of lawyers, bankers and junk emailers trying to get me to take out a $50,000 loan over the net. How cold and antiseptic that colon was. Two little bulletholes through my heart.

6   Then, later in the message, came the ellipsis. There is a world of difference between "We should get together to talk about stuff" period and "We need to get together to talk about stuff" period, period, period. I expected the period from the colon on down. The cautionary colon foreshadowed what was to come.

7   And now our relationship is in parentheses, as I await the anticipated appointment to talk about stuff, period, period, period. In person, the only commas will be drawn nervously in the air with her aforementioned slender fingers. The only dashes will be in her stilted, anxious speech. The only periods will be her small, black, intense pupils submerged in her beautiful green eyes, darting away from mine. And as she recedes into the distance, I will be left standing there like an ellipsis.

8   Two little bulletholes through my heart.

■ In Search of a Modest Proposal

Fred Stenson

Fred Stenson, who has been the director of the Wired Writing Studio at the Banff Centre, is an award-winning Albertan author of both fiction and nonfiction. A long-time faculty member in the writing programs at the Centre, Stenson has been nominated for the Giller prize for his book *The Trade* (2000) and has won awards from the Alberta Motion Picture Industry Association for his documentary film scripts. His latest book, *Brush and Pen* (2006), was written in collaboration with artist Brent Laycock, whose paintings of Albertan landscapes are accompanied by Stenson's essays. The following essay about the dangers of reductivism in modern perspectives on essay writing was published in *AlbertaViews* in 2004.

1   My gratitude to the education system for teaching my children to read lasted for many years. Whenever teachers were attacked in my earshot, I rose to defend them. Then my daughter hit Grade 9 and was taught to write the essay.

2   When she told me she had been assigned to write an essay, I felt a thrill. She was about to learn one of the great literary forms, used for hundreds of years to persuade

and argue. In the hands of a great writer, the essay could shape society. Part of the thrill was also that she had finally reached a topic about which I knew something. I was eager to help, and she allowed that I could.

3   The essay, as I recall (it's been a few years), was about "why it is good to converse with seniors." I was surprised in that I didn't know my daughter held that opinion, and here she was making it the thesis of a personal essay.

4   When I asked her about the choice, she said, oh no, it was just one of a list that the teacher had given them to choose from. "But yet you chose it?" I countered. "Well, my small group did. We did all the preparation in group."

5   Teacher? Group? The whole point of a personal essay is to be personal. Her personal opinion. Something she wanted to convince others of. She waved this away as immaterial. Time was wasting. The essay was due on Friday.

6   The thesis statement, that it was good to visit with old people, had to be in paragraph one. That was mandatory. Also, the first paragraph had to contain the three arguments, one per sentence. After that, she must devote one paragraph to each argument. Restate the argument; give five points to support that argument. And so on.

7   Her arguments were on a very messy piece of paper, covered in many people's handwriting, the result of a brain-storming session of the small group.

8   "Seniors know a lot."

9   "Seniors get lonely because their families neglect them."

10   "Seniors deserve respect."

11   "Seniors are nice."

12   "A lot of seniors are not neglected by their families," I said. "Some seniors are not even slightly nice. I might turn out to be one of them."

13   Again, I was waved silent. My daughter and her friends were much better qualified than I to determine how the subject should be approached, and what should be said about it.

14   My daughter had already started writing. I read what she had so far.

15   "It's fine," I said, "but you shouldn't use all those words like 'therefore' and 'consequently' at the start of every paragraph. I mean, really. 'Henceforth'?"

16   My daughter looked at me with pity. She pulled out a sheet, a class handout, and she read: "Each paragraph is to be connected to the next paragraph by a transitional word or phrase at the beginning of the new paragraph. Use transitional words within each paragraph as well for greater unity and cohesion." There was a list. "Henceforth" was on it.

17   "And you're repeating a lot," I said. "That's not good writing."

18   She pointed to a different place on the handout.

19   "Repeat important words and phrases."

20   "What's with all the adjectives and adverbs?"

21   "Says here: 'Use bright descriptive language.'"

22   "What else does it say?"

23   "Support each of your three arguments with five points, in three separate paragraphs. Then repeat the three arguments in the concluding paragraph, ending with a strong conclusion statement."

24   "That's not an essay!" I cried. "That's, that's . . ."

25   "A formula," she said. "A formula I have to stick to, or I will flunk. Now, let's get busy."

* * *

26   A couple of months later, it was parent/teacher day. I confronted my daughter's Language Arts teacher with my concerns about how the essay was being taught. I suspect I buttered it on a bit thick about the tradition of Rousseau and Swift, and the great modern practitioners like Richler and Fussell. The teacher was a pleasant, able-seeming woman, who instantly deflated me with agreement. No, theirs was not a creative approach to the essay. No, that approach probably would not endear the students to the essay form. Asked why it was so, she shrugged and said, "It's the curriculum, on which they will be tested. The results of the test will determine their future in high school. So we teach it that way."

27   I sought out the Grade 9 curriculum for Language Arts. Everything was there. "Bright descriptive language." The mathematical equation: this many arguments supported by this many points. Special emphasis on transitional words and phrases, the more the merrier. I said no more about it. My daughter passed her provincial Language Arts exam and moved on to high school.

28   *Nonetheless,* it is sad about the essay. I find myself thinking about Jonathan Swift's "A Modest Proposal," the essay he published in 1729 to address the problem of Irish poverty and starvation. He proposed that the higher classes eat Irish children while they were still young and succulent, thus reducing the number of poor to a more manageable level.

29   This "modest proposal" is the essay's thesis statement. When I examined the essay with the Alberta Language Arts curriculum in mind, I was disturbed to find that Swift does not actually state his thesis until he has expended over 1,000 words! His use of transitional devices is equally shoddy. Out of 28 paragraphs, he uses transitional words and phrases to begin only eight of them. Of the eight, six are an enumeration of his strongest points toward the essay's end. This enumeration is good and would get him some important marks. *But,* "finally," "similarly" and "in addition" are absent from the essay, leaving Swift's thoughts sadly unconnected.

30   *However,* let us remember that this essay was written almost 300 years ago. On that account, let us be kind to Mr. Swift and give him a "C." It would be a shame to keep him out of Grade 10.

Credits

This page constitutes an extension of the copyright page. We have made every effort to trace the ownership of all copyrighted material and to secure permission from copyright holders. In the event of any question arising as to the use of any material, we will be pleased to make the necessary corrections in future printings. Thanks are due to the following authors, publishers, and agents for permission to use the material indicated.

296: © Carl & Ann Purcell/Corbis

297: Licensed under Health Canada copyright. Reprinted by permission of Health Canada.

297: Courtesy of Scotiabank/ScotiaFunds.

298: Reprinted by permission of Emerging Spirit/The United Church of Canada.

300: AP Images.

301: Reprinted by permission of Omega SA.

Chapter 11

308–309: William Gibson, "Pining for Toronto's 'Gone World'." *Globe and Mail.* May 31, 2007. Reprinted by permission of the Martha Millard Literacy Agency.

310: Emily Carr, *Koskimo,* 1930, charcoal on paper, 78.5 × 57.3 cm, Collection of the Vancouver Art Gallery, Emily Carr Trust, VAG 42.3.119, Photo: Vancouver Art Gallery.

312: © SuperStock, Inc.

323: Canada Science and Technology Museum.

Chapter 12

328: *Night Target, Germany.* Miller Brittain. 19710261-1436 Beaverbrook Collection of War Art. © Canadian War Museum.

330: © Reuters/CORBIS.

334–340: Margaret Atwood, "Under the Thumb: How I Became a Poet." © O.W. Toad Ltd. Reprinted by permission of the author.

Chapter 13

349–353: From Susan T. Fiske, Lasana T. Harris, and Amy J.C. Cuddy. "Why Ordinary People Torture Enemy Prisoners," *Science, 306* (2004): 1482–3. Printed with permission from AAAS.

Chapter 14

361: Screenshot from Info-Trac. © Gale, a part of Cengage Learning, Inc. Reproduced by permission. www.cengage.com/permissions.

363: Reprinted by permission of UBC Library.

364: Screenshot from Info-Trac. © Gale, a part of Cengage Learning, Inc. Reproduced by permission. www.cengage.com/permissions.

401: © Bettmann/CORBIS.

Chapter 15

415: © Stockbyte/Superstock.

Chapter 16

430–431: From *Selected Poems 1966–1984* by Margaret Atwood. Copyright © Margaret Atwood 1990. Reprinted by permission of Oxford University Press Canada.

432: Courtesy of Charles Pachter.

439: Digital Image © The Museum of Modern Art/Licensed by Scala/Art Resource, NY.

445–446: Peter Blue–Cloud, "Weaver Spider's Web." Reprinted by permission of the author.

447: "Now of Sleeping" from *Spice-Box of the Earth* by Leonard Cohen © 1961. Published by McClelland & Stewart. Used with permission of the publisher.

Chapter 17

450: © Yang Liu/CORBIS.

Chapter 21

527–529: Alberto Manguel, an Extract from *A History of Reading.* © Alberto Manguel. c/o Guillermo Schavelzon & Asociados, Agencia Literaria. info@schavelzon.com.

529–530: From *In Pursuit of Happiness* by Mark Kingwell, copyright © 1998 by Mark Kingwell. Used by permission of Crown Publishers, a division of Random House, Inc.

Chapter 22

531–533: "And the Best Damn Stew–Maker Too" from *Friends, Moments, Countryside: Selected Columns from Canadian Living, 1993–98* by Peter Gzowski © 1998. Published by McClelland & Stewart. Used with permission of the publisher.

533–535: Stanley Coren, "Dogs and Monsters." Reprinted with permission by the author and St. Joseph Media (2008).

Chapter 23

536–538: Germaine Greer, "Ottawa vs. New York." Reprinted by permission of Aitken Alexander Associates.

539–540: David Suzuki, "Food Connections," from *Time to Change.* Reprinted with permission of the author.

Chapter 24

541–543: "I'm a Banana and Proud of It," copyright © 1997 by Wayson Choy. First published in Canada by *The Globe and Mail.* Reprinted by permission of the author.

543–544: Roderick Haig–Brown, "Conservation Defined," from *The Living Land* (1961). Reprinted by permission of Valerie Haig–Brown.

Chapter 25

545–546: Amartya Sen, "A World Not Neatly Divided." *New York Times.* November 23, 2001. Reprinted by permission of The New York Times.

547–548: Gwynne Dyer, "Flagging Attention." *enRoute* (July 1999). Reprinted by permission of the author.

Chapter 26

549–553: Wade Davis, "The Ticking Bomb." *Globe and Mail.* July 6, 2002. Reprinted by permission of the author.

Chapter 27

556–558: Lester B. Pearson, "The Implications of a Free Society." *Words and Occasions.* © University of Toronto Press, 1970. Reprinted by permission of the publisher.

558–562: Tommy Douglas, "Capital Punishment." *Debates, House of Commons, 1st Session, 27th Parliament, Volume IV,* pages 3867–3871. Reprinted by permission of the House of Commons.

Chapter 28

563–564: Elissa Poole, "No drama in Lortie's dew–kissed Mozart." *Globe and Mail.* March 18, 2008. Reprinted by permission of Elissa Poole.

564–566: Extracted from *Belonging: Home Away From Home* by Isabel Huggan. Copyright © 2003 Isabel Huggan. Reprinted by permission of Knopf Canada.

Chapter 29

567–569: "A Secret Lost in the Water" from *The Hockey Sweater and Other Stories* copyright © 1979 by House of Anansi Press. Reproduced with the permission of House of Anansi Press, Toronto.

569–573: "Where the World Began" from *Heart of a Stranger* by Margaret Laurence © 1976. Published by McClelland & Stewart. Used with permission of the publisher.

Chapter 30

574–577: Reprinted by arrangement with The Heirs to the Estate of Martin Luther King Jr., c/o Writers House as agent for the proprietor New York, NY. Copyright 1963 Dr. Martin Luther King Jr.; copyright renewed 1991 Coretta Scott King.

577–580: Barack Obama, "Speech for the Democratic Convention of 2004." Reprinted by permission of the Democratic National Committee.

Chapter 31

582–586: "The Orange Fish" extracted from *The Orange Fish* by Carol Shields. Copyright © 1989 Carol Shields Literary Trust. Reprinted by permission of Random House Canada.

Chapter 32

587–588: J. Kelly Nestruck, "The Importance of Email Punctuation: A Cautionary Tale." *McGill Daily.* November 15, 1999. Reprinted by permission of the author.

588–590: Fred Stenson, "In Search of a Modest Proposal." *Alberta Views* (Jan./Feb. 2004). Reprinted by permission of Alberta Views.

Index